INTERNATIONAL TRADE OPENING AND THE FORMATION OF THE GLOBAL ECONOMY

ECONOMISTS OF THE TWENTIETH CENTURY

General Editors: David Colander, *Christian A. Johnson Distinguished Professor of Economics, Middlebury College, Vermont, USA* and Mark Blaug, *Professor Emeritus, University of London, Professor Emeritus, University of Buckingham and Visiting Professor, University of Exeter, UK*

This innovative series comprises specially invited collections of articles and papers by economists whose work has made an important contribution to economics in the late twentieth century.

The proliferation of new journals and the ever-increasing number of new articles make it difficult for even the most assiduous economist to keep track of all the important recent advances. By focusing on those economists whose work is generally recognized to be at the forefront of the discipline, the series will be an essential reference point for the different specialisms included.Wherever possible, the articles in these volumes have been reproduced as originally published using facsimile reproduction, inclusive of footnotes and pagination to facilitate ease of reference.

A list of published and future titles in this series is printed at the end of this volume.

International Trade Opening and the Formation of the Global Economy

Selected Essays of P.J. Lloyd

P.J. Lloyd

Professor of Economics, University of Melbourne, Australia

ECONOMISTS OF THE TWENTIETH CENTURY

Edward Elgar

Cheltenham, UK • Northampton, MA, USA

Published by   call
Edward Elgar Publishing Limited
Glensanda House
Montpellier Parade
Cheltenham
Glos GL50 1UA
UK

Edward Elgar Publishing, Inc.
6 Market Street
Northampton
Massachusetts 01060
USA

A catalogue record for this book
is available from the British Library

Library of Congress Cataloguing in Publication Data

Lloyd, P. J. (Peter John)
    International trade opening and the formation of the global
economy : selected essays of P.J. Lloyd / P. J. Lloyd.
    (Economists of the twentieth century)
    Includes bibliographical references and index.
    1. International trade. 2. Free trade. 3. Protectionism.
4. International economic integration. 5. Regionalism. I. Title.
II. Series.
HF1379.L593   1999
382—dc21   98–46606
                                                             CIP

ISBN 1 85898 956 6

Printed and bound in Great Britain by MPG Books Ltd, Bodmin, Cornwall

Contents

Acknowledgements

The publishers wish to thank the following who have kindly given permission for the use of copyright material.

Asian-Pacific Economic Literature for article: 'East Asian Export Competitiveness: New Measures and Policy Implications', with Hisako Toguchi, *Asian-Pacific Economic Literature*, **10**(2), November 1996, 1–15.

Blackwell Publishers for articles and excerpt: 'Aggregation by Industry in High-Dimensional Models', *Review of International Economics*, **2**(2), 1994, 97–111; 'Offshore Production and the Base of Import Taxation', *The World Economy*, **17**(5), September 1994, 719–35; 'A Tariff Substitute for Rules of Origin in Free Trade Areas', *The World Economy*, **16**(6), November 1993, 699–712; 'Competition and Trade Policy: Identifying the Issues after the Uruguay Round', with Gary Sampson, *The World Economy*, **18**(5), September 1995, 681–705; 'Protection Policy and the Assignment Rule' in Henryk Kierzkowski (ed.), *Protection and Competition in International Trade: Essays in Honor of W.M. Corden*, Basil Blackwell, 1987, 4–21.

The Economic Record for articles: 'The Empirical Measurement of Intra-Industry Trade', with H.G. Grubel, *Economic Record*, **47**, December 1971, 494–517; 'Terms of Trade Indices in the Presence of Re-Export Trade', with R.J. Sandilands, *Economic Record*, **61**, September 1985, 667–73.

Elsevier Science for articles: 'A More General Theory of Price Distortions in Open Economies', *Journal of International Economics*, **4**, 1974, 365–86; '3x3 Theory of Customs Unions', *Journal of International Economics*, **12**, 1982, 41–63; 'Trade Expenditure Functions and the Gains from Trade', with A.G. Schweinberger, *Journal of International Economics*, **24**, 1988, 275–97; 'Conflict Generating Product Price Changes: The Imputed Output Approach', with A.G. Schweinberger, *European Economic Review*, **41**, 1997, 1569–87.

Harvester Wheatsheaf for excerpt: 'The Problem of Optimal Environmental Policy Choice' in Kym Anderson and Richard Blackhurst (eds), *The Greening of World Trade Issues*, 1992, 49–72.

Institute of Policy Studies for excerpt: 'The Future of the CER Agreement: A Single Market for Australia and New Zealand' in Ross Garraut and Peter Drysdale (eds), *Asia Pacific Regionalism: Readings in International Relations*, 1994, 341–61.

Institute of Southeast Asian Studies for excerpt: 'The Uruguay Round, World Trade Organization and Asia-Pacific Trade Liberalization', with Christian F. Bach and Will Martin in *Facilitating Interdependence in the Asia-Pacific Region*, 1995.

JAI Press for articles: 'The Role of Foreign Investment in the Success of Asian Industrialization', *Journal of Asian Economics*, **7**(3), 1996, 407–33; 'An APEC or Multilateral Investment Code?', *Journal of Asian Economics*, **6**(1), 1995, 53–70.

Macmillan for excerpts: 'Unilateral and Regional Trade Policies of the CER Countries' in J.J. Piggott and A.D. Woodland (eds), *International Trade Policy and the Pacific Rim*, 1998, 59–83; 'Reflections on Intra-Industry Trade Theory and Factor Proportions' in P.K.M. Tharakan and Jacob Kol (eds), *Intra-Industry Trade: Theory, Evidence and Extensions*, 1989, 15–30, references.

Melbourne Institute for articles: 'The Singapore Ministerial Conference: An Overview', *The Australian Economic Review*, **30**(1), 1997, 71–4; 'The Asian Economic and Financial Crisis: The Effects of Market Integration and Market Fragility', with Kim R. Sawyer, *Quarterly Bulletin of Economic Trends*, **4**, 1997, 40–60.

OECD for article: 'Regionalisation and World Trade', *OECD Economic Studies*, **18**, Spring 1992, 7–43.

Oxford University Press for article and excerpt: 'Uncertainty and the Choice of Protective Instrument', with R.E. Falvey, *Oxford Economic Papers*, **43**, 1991, 463–78; 'The Changing Nature of Regional Trading Arrangements' in Bijit Bora and Christopher Findlay (eds), *Regional Integration and the Asia-Pacific*, 1996, 25–48, references.

PAFTAD for excerpt: 'Competition Policy in APEC: Principles of Harmonisation' in Rong-I Wu and Yun-Peng Chu (eds), *Business, Markets and Government in the Asia Pacific*, Routledge, 1998, 157–77.

BR Title

Introduction   P. J. Lloyd

B31

I Biographical notes

A personal history

Perhaps the most salient feature of my upbringing is that I was born and raised in a country area of what is, from the point of view of international trading relations at least, one of the most remote countries in the world – New Zealand. I was what is called in the vernacular a 'boy from the bush'. My New Zealand origins have probably affected my work in more ways than I am conscious of. One way is that the subject of international economics has always been one of the most important in the curriculum of university courses in economics in New Zealand. When I was an undergraduate and later a Masters student at Victoria University of Wellington in the late 1950s, it was one of the few recognized fields, along with Public Finance and Monetary Economics. (There were no subjects in Industrial Organization, any area of Mathematical Economics and little Econometrics.) Consequently when I went to graduate school I already regarded International Economics as the primary area in which I wanted to specialize.

Another effect of this upbringing was the choice of the United States for my postgraduate education. At the time I graduated in New Zealand, the numbers of local graduates going overseas was roughly equally divided between those going to England, the 'home country' as many called it, and the traditional destination for New Zealand students, and those going to the United States which was becoming more popular. I was at that time, and have remained ever since, a fervent believer in republicanism and a staunch opponent of the monarchy and the class divisions which seem to me to be inevitably associated with monarchy. This attitude in turn is probably the product of two factors. One is the egalitarianism which has been such a dominant feature of the New Zealand history (though this has changed substantially since the introduction of the economic reforms from 1984). The second is that my own family were of Irish-Welsh-Scottish origin and had no reason to look back fondly on the 'home country'.

In going to the United States, I chose to go to Duke University. Or rather Duke University chose me. Duke University had at that time a Commonwealth Studies Center with a programme of studies on the British Commonwealth which was unique in the United States. A part of this programme was the offer of one scholarship to a student from New Zealand to study at Duke in the field of Economics, Political Science or History. (Similar scholarships were offered to students from the other Dominions, Canada and Australia.) These scholarships were, according to my recollection, the highest value available to any graduate students in the United States. Certainly they paid more than the Frank Knox Scholarship to Harvard University for example. I remember this well because that was the only other scholarship for which I applied, only to be ranked second – the student ranked first being my own identical twin brother who went to Harvard and followed a very distinguished academic career in the field of evolutionary botany.

Duke University provided a good, standard, North American professional education. It did not leave any profound impressions on me. Most of my teachers were uninspiring. The most notable exception was Charlie Ferguson, who had just graduated from the University of North Carolina and gave the basic PhD course on Microeconomics. He was methodical and completely dedicated to Neoclassical economics and the belief in rational individualistic actions. My own commitment to these beliefs dates from this time.

One anecdote concerning Charlie Ferguson is worth recording here. In class one day he was questioned by a fellow student about the lack of correspondence between some model of individual utility maximizing behaviour and the behaviour of consumers in the real world. He replied wittily that 'the real world is a very special case'. This remark actually raises deep methodological issues about the way we construct models and the way of testing hypotheses which were being vigorously debated at the time by Milton Friedman, with his belief that one should only test a theory by its predictions and not by its assumptions, and his opponents. These issues have troubled me during my career and I find myself siding more and more with those who opposed Friedman at that time. Sadly, the methods and methodology of economics are less subject to debate these days.

Another teacher was John Chipman who happened to be a visitor in the Department during the semester in which I took the graduate course in International Economics. In his idiosyncratic but ponderous way, he drove home to me the details and the logic of the Heckscher-Ohlin model of international trade. Since my first year of undergraduate studies in New Zealand I had been familiar with the Principle of Comparative Advantage, a result which Ronald Findlay (1987) in his survey in the *The New Palgrave Dictionary of Economics* lauded as '[the] deepest and most beautiful result in all economics'. Chipman also taught me to appreciate the general equilibrium of the whole economy which lies behind this principle. The Heckscher-Ohlin model is indeed the general equilibrium model which has been most thoroughly explored. Its explication has given rise to two of the few comparative static theorems which have been derived from general equilibrium models, namely the Stolper-Samuelson and the Rybczynski Theorems, although strictly speaking these theorems apply to any closed or open economy. My understanding of general equilibrium theory began with these multi-country models of what we now call 'the global economy', not with the closed economy world of Walras and Arrow-Debreu.

After completing my PhD in only two and a half years, I returned to my *alma mater*, Victoria University of Wellington, for a stint of teaching. After another three years, I received a lucky and totally unexpected break in the form of an invitation from the Chairman of the Department of Economics at Michigan State University, Bob Lanzillotti, to take up an Assistant Professorship at that university. In those days it was possible, though quite unusual, to receive a job offer without a visit to the campus or even an interview. The next three years at Michigan State University were among the most enjoyable of my career. They were also formative. It was in my days as a teacher there that I first studied mathematics, statistics and econometrics. I was not able to teach international economics at the graduate level because my senior colleague and good friend Max Kreinen guarded this prerogative.

In 1969 I went to the Australian National University, first as a very temporary

Research Fellow and after one year as a permanent Fellow. I stayed for 14 years in one of the best research environments for economists there has been anywhere in the world and at any time. We enjoyed the privileges of no compulsory teaching and, for all of those other than the Head of the Department, no administrative duties, abundant research assistance and numerous visitors and top quality colleagues. Neither before nor since have I enjoyed an environment so conducive to research.

Throughout my research-only appointments at ANU I always stated that I wanted eventually to return to a normal teaching-and-research position, as they are officially designated in Australia. In 1983, the University of Melbourne made me the offer of a Chair which I thought I could not resist. Little did I know at the time that the wave of budget reductions and other 'reforms' which has reduced the resources available to Australian universities, increased teaching loads and made working conditions less favourable was to begin a few years later. In this more difficult environment, the University of Melbourne has succeeded in maintaining standards better than perhaps any other Australian university. It has the avowed and unashamed goal of becoming the best university in Australia. Despite the distractions of teaching and a turbulent period of six years as the Dean of the Faculty of Economics and Commerce, the university has enabled me to continue a steady output of research.

Paradoxically it was during my time at the University of Melbourne, rather than my time in the Research School of Pacific Studies (or the Research School of Pacific and Asian Studies as it is now called) at ANU, that my interest in Asian economies developed. One catalyst for this was the period of one year I spent as a Visiting Professor at the National University of Singapore in 1982–83, immediately before taking up the position at the University of Melbourne. This visit accounts for my publications on Singapore and the subsequent association with NUS as an External Examiner which still continues. Again I was fortunate in working in a very congenial department, the Department of Economics and Statistics. This Asian interest has allowed me to research the region of the world economy which has been opening to the rest of the world and growing more rapidly than any other region. It is a good location to explore some of the new policy issues in the global economy.

All of my work as an economist after graduation has taken place in Australia and New Zealand, apart from three years in the United States and periodic sabbaticals in England (twice), Sweden, Singapore and the United States itself. The environment of Australia and New Zealand has affected my work in the field of international economics in many ways. There is a tradition in Australia and New Zealand of combining theory and policy. Academics are readily and frequently involved in the public debates and in government decision making. Conversely, there is less opportunity to participate in the development of economic theory which occurs in the major centres of learning in North America and Europe. However, this latter constraint has been relaxed greatly in my lifetime, first through the lower cost of international travel and later through the development of electronic communication (both of these being forms of international trade in services).

Australia and New Zealand were good environments for the study of international economic problems in other ways too. In the period after the Second World War in which I have worked, New Zealand had the invidious distinction of having the highest level of border barriers to international trade in goods of all the OECD countries and

Australia ranked second in these stakes. This was a legacy of the increase in tariffs in the Great Depression and the introduction of a comprehensive system of quantitative barriers in the form of import licensing by both countries just before the outbreak of the Second World War. It was aggravated by both Australia and New Zealand getting a free ride in the earlier GATT multilateral negotiations; Australia made few tariff reductions and New Zealand made none and neither bound a significant number of tariffs until the Uruguay Round. On top of this both Australia and New Zealand have been severely affected by the failure of the GATT to prevent an increase in barriers to trade in agricultural goods from the 1950s and to reduce these barriers in later rounds of negotiations. Indeed New Zealand has probably been more adversely affected by barriers to the exports of the goods in which it has a comparative advantage than any other member of the GATT, and Australia too has been badly affected by these restrictions and by the much less well-known but very high barriers to trade in mineral products in its case. In both countries these foreign barriers, coupled with their own trade restrictions and fixed exchange rates until the 1980s, produced abundant problems of inefficient resource allocation and chronic balance of payments deficits for an international economics specialist to work on.

Beginning in the mid-1980s, Australia and New Zealand reversed this bad record with a vengeance. Both countries have carried out rapid unilateral reforms of tariffs and other border barriers to trade in goods. Indeed, while it is difficult to make cross-comparisons of reforms because of the lack of comparable measures of these barriers over time and countries, it can safely be said that no other countries anywhere in the world have matched this speed of reform. For the subset of 16 countries in the APEC organization, this is confirmed by the series for tariffs and non-tariff barriers constructed over the period 1988 to 1993 in PECC (1995a and b).

Australia has in addition a unique institution which facilitates research in international economics. Since the 1920s, it has had a statutory body charged with enquiries on matters relating to changes in tariffs and bounties and other trade barriers. This is now the Industry Commission; its predecessors were the initial Tariff Board and then the Industries Assistance Commission. The constant enquiries of these bodies have stimulated enormous debate about trade policies and, since 1969, they have produced data on the pattern of nominal and effective assistance available to manufacturing and primary industries which is much more comprehensive and detailed than that available in any other country.

The convictions of an economist
Each economist carries a number of convictions which determine his or her view of the world and profoundly influence research output. A few remarks on this subject may help to explain my interest in certain subjects or my approach to these subjects.

As a discipline, differences in convictions among economists are certainly less marked now than they were at the time of my introduction to the discipline. When I was an undergraduate and graduate student there were huge differences in judgements about key issues relating to the size and role of governments and efficiency of markets. A specific example of direct relevance to the global economy is the debate which raged in the 1950s over flexible versus fixed exchange rates. When Milton Friedman (1953) and James Meade (1955) put forward proposals for replacing pegged exchange rates, which were the basis of the then new regime managed by the International Monetary Fund, by freely floating exchange rates, the proposal was regarded as radical and unworkable by many international economists who otherwise were market-oriented in the policies they advocated. Now floating exchange predominates, though many of the floats are not clean. There has been a sea change in attitudes to the role of prices in markets for foreign exchange.

In the grand panoply of economic policymaking, this example is merely one among very many. More generally, up to the 1960s and 1970s, there were many eminent and respected economists who argued that planned economies would outperform unplanned economies or, less radically in countries such as Great Britain and France as well as Australia and New Zealand, who argued that indicative planning in the form of industry target setting and other government guidelines would improve the performance of economies which relied on market prices as signals for producers and consumers. These arguments were supported by many of the leading economists of the time. However, in the 1970s and 1980s arguments in favour of a greater role for markets become dominant. This is a huge change in the profession which has affected our societies and polities as well as our economies. Indeed, so momentous is this change, that it has been dubbed by the American historian Francis Fukuyama (1989) as the 'End of History' meaning that one general liberal-democratic view has replaced a number of competing ideologies such as communism, socialism and fascism.

Of course the argument for free international goods trade is one of the oldest expressions of the liberal view. While challenged repeatedly, and most seriously in recent years by Strategic Trade Policy, it has never lost its dominant position among international economists since the English classical economists put forward the Principle of Comparative Advantage. I have believed unswervingly in the Principle and have remained sceptical of all arguments for selective assistance to industries on the grounds of infant industries, strategic trade policy or other grounds.

Another conviction which I have inherited from the Neoclassical tradition is the belief in the power of theory to explain the behaviour of human agents. This applies particularly to microeconomic theory. At the level of individual agents, this theory is extremely powerful in giving predictions about agent behaviour such as the response to changes in consumer or producer prices or incomes or other exogenous variables. I decided early in my career that I would combine teaching and research in two areas, international economics as my primary field and microeconomic theory as a secondary supporting field. This was a most fortunate choice. In its role as a support, micro-economic theory is the ideal complement to international economics.

As a specific example of cross-fertilization between these two fields, I cite duality theory. As a part of my teaching and research in microeconomics, I devoted con-siderable energy to the study of the seminal work on duality theory by Ronald Shephard (1953, 1970). I regard his 1970 book as the most difficult book I ever studied in economics. It is the combination of novel and subtle dual relationships and advanced mathematics with no concession made to the reader in terms of examples or explanations that make it so difficult. But I was well rewarded. I was prepared for the sudden rise of duality methods in economics which was spearheaded by the microeconomic textbook by Hal Varian (1978). And specialized duality concepts have proven to be enormously useful in international economics. They were introduced into international economics by the influential textbooks of Dixit and Norman (1980) and Woodland (1982) but they have been developed further. The concept of the 'trade expenditure function' in Chapter 6 of this volume (Lloyd and Schweinberger, 1988) is an example of the power of tailor-made duality concepts to cut through complex general equilibrium relationships among variables and make it possible to analyse problems which are intractable without these concepts.

A related conviction which I hold strongly is that economic theory is only useful insofar as it elucidates real world behaviour. This means that the construction of the models and the questions one puts to them are guided by policy issues. Personally, I have always sought to combine theorizing with policy advice. A good theory is one which leads directly to policy prescriptions.

I dare say almost all economic theorists would support the claim that the only ultimate justification of theory is the elucidation of real world behaviour but in reality, it seems to me, this claim is more honoured in the breach than the observance. With growing specialization among economists, more journals and an academic incentive system that rewards those who publish in the most highly-rated journals, an increasing proportion of academic writers devote their efforts to theory which is divorced from any policy advice or even any general interest in policies. There is more interest today in theory for its own sake. This is most notable in the United States but it is increasingly true in Australia. Specialization in the activities of economists has produced much higher levels of skills and much inventive theorizing but the profession of economics would in my view be more productive as a social instrument if closer links between theory and policy were re-established. This gripe is the one concession I feel I have to make to the usual retrospection of authors of selected papers. I remain convinced of the essentiality of theory to understanding the real world and to policy advice.

II The basis of selection

I have written in many and diverse areas. These include production theory, welfare economics and theory of price indices, public finance, history of economic thought, macroeconomics, mathematical economics, economic demography, finance theory and the economics of Aids (not the AIDS model of consumer behaviour!) as well as international economics.

The selection of papers in this volume has been confined to one area, namely, international economics. Moreover, this field is interpreted, with the exception of the paper on the recent Asian crises, more narrowly to mean the theory and policy of the so-called real models with no markets for money and foreign exchange. And within this restriction, I have confined the selection further to those papers which are likely to be of interest to readers around the world. Much of my output has been devoted to analyses of specific Australia and New Zealand trade policy problems. This work is omitted with the exception of one paper on unilateral reforms in Australia, New Zealand and Britain and one on the regional trading arrangement between Australia and New Zealand, both of which policies contain important precedents which are of interest to students and practitioners of trade policy in all countries. The papers within this narrowed field comprise a much more cohesive collection than papers which range more widely.

This selection actually produced a result which surprised me. In making the selection,

I realized there has been one theme in my writings of which I was at times only dimly aware. This theme is the gradual emergence over the last two or perhaps three decades of what has come to be known quite recently as the global economy. Preference has been given to recent papers on this theme though I have included a few of my older papers as appropriate.

III The book plan

The integration of national economies is commonly analysed by international economists in terms of actions which occur at three levels:

- unilateral actions
- regional actions
- multilateral actions

The first are the result of actions by the government of a single nation, the second involve joint decisions by the governments of two or more nations under the aegis of a regional trading arrangement and the third, in the sphere of international trade, involve the decisions of the GATT or WTO.

The selection of essays is organized around this three-way division of trade policy decisions. First, I thought it desirable to offer some current thoughts on the nature of the global economy. The next section contains papers dealing with protectionism and the national origins of protectionist pressures. Then there are papers dealing with the theory and practice of policies at the unilateral, regional and multilateral levels respectively. The last two sections deal with new global issues and intra-industry trade. These aspects of the global economy are effects of the integration of national economies.

Brief introductions are attached before each section. These put the papers in context and, in some cases, offer comments on origins of papers or developments since their publication.

Co-authors

I wish to acknowledge the invaluable assistance I have received from a large number of co-authors. Without their cooperation many of the papers reproduced here could not have been written as I did not possess the knowledge and technical skills which, in different ways, they have brought to me. This is itself proof of the gains from specialization within our profession as well as the increasing complexity of the issues in the global economy.

References

Dixit, A.K. and V. Norman (1980), *Theory of International Trade*, James Nisbet and Cambridge University Press, Digswell Place.

Findlay, R. (1987), 'Comparative Advantage', in J. Eatwell, M. Milgate and P. Newman (eds), *The New Palgrave Dictionary of Economics*, vol. 1, Macmillan, London, 514–17.

Friedman, M. (1953), 'The Case for Flexible Exchange Rates', in M. Friedman, *Essays in Positive Economics*, University of Chicago Press, Chicago.

Fukuyama, F. (1989), 'The End of History?', *The National Interest*, Summer, 3–18.

Meade, J.E. (1955), 'The Case for Variable Exchange Rates', *Three Banks Review*, September, 3–27.

Pacific Economic Cooperation Council (1995a), *Milestones in APEC Liberalisation: A Map of Market Opening Measures by APEC Economies*, PECC, Singapore.

Pacific Economic Cooperation Council (1995b), *Survey of Impediments to Trade and Investment in the APEC Region*, PECC, Singapore.
Shephard, R.W. (1953), *Cost and Production Functions*, Princeton University Press, Princeton.
Shephard, R.W. (1970), *Theory of Cost Functions*, Princeton University Press, Princeton.
Varian, H.R. (1978), *Microeconomic Analysis*, W.W. Norton and Company, New York.
Woodland, A.D. (1982), *International Trade and Resource Allocation*, North Holland, Amsterdam.

PART I

THE GLOBAL ECONOMY

BK Title

The global economy

author

For G1

What is the global economy?

Although many writers use the term 'global economy', the meaning of the concept is not clear. The term seems to have emerged in general usage around 1990, a little later than the term 'globalization' which became current in the mid-1980s (see, for example, Porter, 1986). The global economy is associated mostly with international trade in goods and services whereas 'globalization' seems usually to be associated with multinational companies and their global production strategies. For example, the United Nations Conference on Trade and Development (UNCTAD) produces the annual *World Investment Report* and they have defined globalization as 'integrated international production' (see UNCTAD, 1993). This definition encompasses most of the activities usually regarded as a part of globalization, including sourcing abroad, offshore production, multidomestic strategies and complex integration of production activities.

First, we can distinguish the global economy from the world economy. The latter is simply the set of all national economies. For example, the world economy can be modelled in computable general equilibrium models which include all countries. There are now a number of computable general equilibrium models of the world economy. The term 'global economy' means something more. It is a qualitative property of the world economy. By the term 'global economy', I mean that these national economies are integrated to such an extent that the interdependence among national economies is so large that one cannot consider events and policies in a national economy separate from those in other national economies.

The concept of the global economy puts the emphasis on the interdependencies among the economies and the way in which the world economy functions rather than on the consequences of opening for the individual economies which are more commonly analysed in the literature on trade liberalization and integration. The formation of the global economy has led to qualitative changes in the behaviour of national economies and in microeconomic and macroeconomic policy-making.

As a result of increased interdependence among national economies, economists now analyse a wide range of polices in an international context which used to be regarded as purely 'domestic'. In the microeconomic sphere, labour laws and environmental policies are now the subject of discussions at the World Trade Organization (WTO) and other international fora because of spillovers of national actions into international markets or environments. As a less familiar example, competition policy problems used to be regarded in all countries as a matter of competition among local competitors which could be addressed adequately by national competition laws but the international dimension of competition was recognized during the Uruguay Round negotiations and is now the subject of examinations by many governments and the WTO, the Organization for Economic Cooperation and Development (OECD), Asia-Pacific Economic Cooperation (APEC) and other international fora. At the macroeconomic level, the subject of open economy macro-economics has developed extensively in the last 20 years.

The opening of trade and the formation of the global economy

Growing interdependence among national economies is in turn due to the liberalization of international trade through reductions in border barriers to this trade, that is, the opening of these economies.

Sachs and Warner (1995) adopt the approach of dividing the world into 'open' and 'closed' economies. They construct a dataset for some 135 countries and then make a binary partition of these national economies into those which are sufficiently open to be classified as 'open' and those which are not. To make this partition, they use various criteria such as levels of tariffs and non-tariff barriers and currency convertibility. They regard an economy as closed if average tariff rates are 40 per cent or more, or if non-tariff barriers cover 40 per cent or more of trade, or if there is a premium in the foreign exchange black market of 20 per cent or more or if there is a state monopoly of major exports or a socialist economic system. Their data show that most of the developed countries had opened their economies after the Second World War by the early 1960s but most of the developed countries had not. More of the developing countries opened during the 1980s and 1990s, though 35 were still closed in 1994, according to their criteria. This dating of the year of opening is a crude but very useful way of documenting the liberalization of trade barriers.

We can use this classification to define the global economy. The global economy might be defined crudely as one in which most of world economy is open. Sachs and Warner (1995, Figure 1) plot the percentage of world GDP accounted for by the 'open' economies. Their figure is reproduced in Figure 1 below.

According to these estimates, the open economies accounted for less than 50 per cent of aggregate world gross domestic product (GDP) in 1960 but this share rose to almost 70 per cent by 1995. If we use population weights rather than GDP weights for countries, the share of the open economies is much lower, passing 50 per cent only in the 1990s. 'It was not until 1993 that more than 60 per cent of the world's GDP, and more than 50 per cent of the world's populations, was located in open economies' (Sachs and Warner, 1995, p. 12). By this time certainly one can regard the global economy as a reality, even though it still excludes some large economies such as China and Russia.

The openness of an economy (or its complement closedness) is really a continuous variable but the definition of openness is vague.

One common measure is the ratio of exports plus imports of goods and services to gross national product (GNP). Certainly many countries in the world have become more open according to this measure in the last four decades but some have not. One of the difficulties with this measure is that the figures in the numerator and denominator are in current prices. Over time the prices of goods and services traded internationally and those of goods and services produced may diverge. In its annual reports the WTO compares the rate of growth of real world merchandise exports and real world merchandise outputs. (They cannot do the comparison for services as there are no series of prices for services traded internationally.) These series show clearly that in every year since 1982 the growth in the volume of goods traded internationally has exceeded the growth in the volume of goods produced globally (see Figure 2).

Thus, more of the world's output of goods produced is traded internationally.

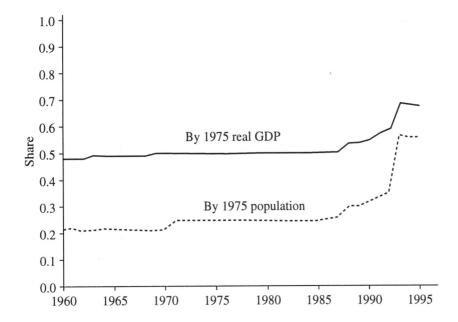

Note: [a] Let PO_t be the proportion of the world's economies that are open in year t. PO_t is constructed as $PO_t = \sum w_{175} D_{it-1}$, where D_{it-1} is a dummy variable set equal to one if the country is open as of year $t-1$, and zero otherwise. w_{175} is the weight of country i in the world in 1975.

Source: Sachs and Warner (1995, Figure 1).

Figure 1   Share of open economies in the world, 1960–95[a]

But this measure of openness depends on resource endowments, country size and many other determinants of trade as well as the levels of trade restrictions. A country may have a high trade ratio becauce it is small or has resources which are valuable to other countries rather than because it has low restrictions on trade with other countries.

There are statistical measures of the closeness or similarity between the prices in one country and world prices but these require observations of prices in all countries and their economic meaning is unclear. A closely related method is to test whether the law of one price holds in goods markets. Empirical studies confirm that the law does not hold (for a recent example, see Engel and Rogers, 1996).

The most promising approach is to construct a measure which is an average of the levels of trade restrictions on different commodities. It is the level of trade restrictions which is the concern of policy-makers and analysts. The difficulty here is that there are no measures of trade barriers which are comparable among countries. The General Agreement on Tariffs and Trade (GATT) has collected statistics of average tariff levels and UNCTAD and other organizations have constructed some measures of the incidence of non-tariff barriers. But these have not been combined into summary measures of the levels of trade restrictions for each country. For some periods the trends in these series are in opposite directions. During the early and mid-1980s, for

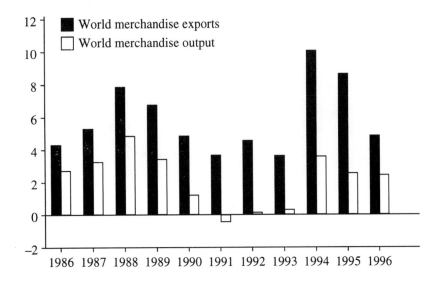

Figure 2   Growth in the volume of world merchandise exports and merchandise output, 1986–96 (annual percentage change)

example, the incidence of non-tariff barriers increased in many countries while average tariff levels decreased.

In the world economy at present, only two countries have achieved virtually total freedom of trade in goods. These are Hong Kong and Singapore, which are island states and have been duty-free ports since the last century. These countries have some significant restrictions on some areas of services trade; for example, restrictions on the establishment and operations of foreign banks and insurance companies in Singapore through a licensing system. New Zealand is probably next in the world currently in order of the freedom of its international trade economy; all of its tariff rates are *ad valorem*, it has no non-tariff barriers, few restrictions on services trade and it has committed itself under the Asia-Pacific Economic Cooperation Conference (APEC) action plans to free trade with all tariff rates bound at zero by the year 2010.

For some groups of countries collations of statistics are available. For the APEC countries, PECC (1995a, b) has collated numerous series of tariff rates, tariff bindings and the incidence of non-tariff barriers over the period 1988 to 1993. These show a substantial liberalization of trade in goods and services in this region.

For a few individual countries, there are detailed calculations of average nominal and effective rates of assistance. Australia has a series of nominal and effective rates of assistance to industries which are more detailed and longer than those of any other country. They go down to the 4-digit industries and back to 1968–69 for the manufacturing and agricultural sectors. They show a clear and substantial decline in average rates of assistance and in the standard deviations of these rates within industries since the mid-1980s. These are discussed below in Chapter 7. This pattern is typical of a number of countries which have been carrying out unilateral reforms of border restrictions on trade.

Looking ahead, for the first time in world economic history, the goal of global free trade is being discussed in APEC, the WTO and other international fora and is a real possibility sometime after the year 2000.

A true measure of openness
The concept of openness of a national economy can be made precise. It is desirable to measure openness on the continuum of the closed interval (0,1). The end-points are well identified. 0 is the point of no interdependence, that is, the national economy is closed. Hence, the markets in the country clear independently and there is for each commodity a set of distinct national prices. 1 is the point of 'complete' openness with no restrictions or distortions of international trade; there are no border restrictions or distortions of trade imposed by the country.

Any point on the open interval (0,1) away from the end situations represents some openness of its national economy but less than complete openness or complete integration with the rest of the world. We need a measure which includes these situations.

A measure of openness should have a solid welfare interpretation. The obvious measure of openness is the uniform tariff equivalent of the Trade Restrictiveness Index (TRI), the uniform trade tax rate which yields the same utility vector as the differentiated set of tariff rates which exist in reality. This was developed by Anderson and Neary in a series of papers (see in particular Anderson and Neary, 1994, 1996). They use the money metric provided by the trade expenditure function for some internationally trading economy. Suppose trade in goods between countries is possible but restricted but there is no trade in factors. The trade expenditure function measures the lump-sum money transfer to or from a country which is needed to achieve some arbitrary utility vector. This is the function $B(p^*, p, v, u)$ where p^* and p are the vectors of the international and domestic prices of tradables respectively, v is the endowment of primary factors and u is the utility vector. If all border restrictions are *ad valorem* tariffs or equivalents and there are n commodities, in the trade expenditure function, p can be replaced by the vector of these tariff rates, say $t = (t_1, \ldots, t_N)$. The TRI is then given by solving the equation $B(p^*, t, v, u) = B(p^*, T, v, u)$ where T is the vector of uniform tariff rates, $T = (t, \ldots, t)$.

This ingenious but very simple concept solves the index number problem in calculating an average measure of trade restrictions. It overcomes the problem of selecting arbitrary trade or production weights to average tariffs which had vexed international economists for decades. The Index can incorporate quantitative restrictions as well as tariffs (see Anderson and Neary, 1994, 1996). (There are technical choices in defining the measure when there are distortions of export trade as well as import trade and when the country is not small.) Furthermore, this index is a welfare-weighted average of the levels of restrictions. An increase in the TRI induces a Pareto reduction in welfare. Hence, the TRI is a true or constant-utility measure of the average level of trade restrictions. This welfare link is a very desirable property.

But this index decreases as trade becomes more free and it ranges from 0 to plus infinity. We want an index which increases as distortions in the economy are reduced and lies on the unit interval. The following measure has these properties

$$L = 1 - (T/\bar{T})$$

T is the *TRI* and $\bar{T}$ is the level of this index which would eliminate international trade with other countries in the world economy, the prohibitive tariff level. $\bar{T}$ is the maximum value of T. L is, therefore, a transformation of the TRI. By construction, $L\varepsilon(0,1)$. It is 0 when there is no international trade, increases as trade becomes more free and is 1 when there are no border tax distortions in any markets of the national economy. We might call it the 'index of openness' or possibly the 'index of trade freedom'.

Ideally, the measure of openness should apply to trade in services as well as trade in goods. In practice, at the present time, the index of openness would have to be restricted to trade in goods as there are no comprehensive measures of restrictions on trade in services. Moreover, trade in some services is linked to trade in factors. Some comments on trade in services are made in the next section.

One could also, if desired, compute an index of openness for a subset of traded goods, say manufactures, or for individual industries in the same manner.

One could also apply this scale to the world economy. The limit situation of no trade is one in which the value of the index of openness is 0 for all countries. The limit situation of free world trade is the situation in which the value of the index of openness is 1 for all countries. This is the 'borderless' world, to use the catchy phrase coined by Ohmae (1990). In between the limit situations of no and free trade, one could construct a measure of the level of trade restrictions averaged across countries by applying the transformed TRI to the world economy.

The concept of a completely open or borderless economy is closely related to the concept of a fully integrated economy. Cooper (1968, p. 10; 1976) defined a fully integrated economy in terms of equalization of goods prices across countries, that is, the law of one price holds in all goods markets. With this definition, the process of integration is the movement towards full integration, that is, price convergence.

A borderless global economy is not sufficient for the law of one price to hold generally. Commodity taxes-subsidies and other non-border regulations create differences in commodity prices between countries. The law therefore requires the harmonization of rates of taxes-subsidies and the absence of differences in treatment in regulations between goods of different national origin. Hence, the integration of national economies is a process which combines the lowering of cross-border restrictions on the movement of goods with the removal of differential treatment and differences in domestic taxes and laws. A fully integrated global economy is much more than a 'borderless' global economy.

Formation of global service markets
Traditionally, economists have regarded many services as not tradable across borders. International trade in services first received close attention in regional trading arrangements. The 1957 Treaty of Rome guaranteed freedom of movement of services as well as goods and factors but there was little attempt to enforce this freedom until the EC '92 measures which were concerned mostly with non-border distortions of trade in all markets. In the 1980s the North American Free Trade Agreement (NAFTA) and the Closer Economic Relations Agreement (CER) between Australia and New Zealand included measures to liberalize trade in services. At the multilateral level, the General Agreement on Trade in Services (GATT), which was a part of the Uruguay Round, was the first attempt to regulate world trade in services.

The integration of markets for services requires more than the removal of border and non-border distortions of trade in services, national treatment and the harmonization of rates of taxes-subsidies. For those services whose mode of delivery involves commercial presence or the movement of natural persons, it also involves free movement across borders and national treatment within borders of the factors.

The liberalization of trade in services is partly the result of reduction of border restrictions on trade and, for those service providers who require commercial presence or the movement of natural persons, partly the result of reduction of border controls on the movement of capital and labour. The liberalization of trade in services is, however, much less well documented than that of trade in goods. PECC (1995a) documents the liberalization of trade in services in the APEC countries. The liberalization of international trade in services has probably proceeded more rapidly than the liberalization of trade in goods because of rapid liberalization of trade in factors, including the granting of rights of establishment in many service industries as national monopolies were deregulated and privatized.

Trade in services has also been greatly facilitated in recent years by the development of new information. This has benefited some service trade in particular, for example, trade in financial services and telecommunications. The Director-general of the WTO believes that the spread of information technology is 'increasingly the critical resource and the main driver of the integration process' and refers to a new age of a 'borderless information-based [global] economy' (Ruggiero, 1997).

Formation of global factor markets

Integration of the national economies has proceeded from the liberalization of the movement of factors between nations as well as the liberalization of trade in goods and services. Yet, with a few exceptions, the theory of international trade has traditionally dealt with trade in goods only, usually assuming that there is no trade in factors. In recent years, however, much more attention has been paid to international trade in factors, especially foreign direct investment. I shall regard this process as the formation of global markets for mobile productive factors.

We seek a measure of the openness of world factor markets. Consider first cross-border movements of direct capital. A measure of openness for capital movements can be constructed which parallels the ratio of trade in goods and services to GNP. World flows of foreign direct investment have increased more rapidly than world commodity trade and therefore world output, though the flows are subject to much greater annual fluctuations than commodity trade. In the analysis of international flows of capital, it is customary to measure the inflows of capital relative to some domestic measure rather than the sum of inflows and outflows. This reflects the greater concern in this analysis with issues relating to capital inflows (though there are also some important issues relating to capital outflows).

UNCTAD has related the growing inflows of FDI to aspects of production. Between 1980 and 1994 the ratio of world FDI flows to world gross domestic investment doubled, from around 2 per cent to 4 per cent. Furthermore, 'The world gross product of foreign affiliates (a value added measure of their output produced abroad) accounted for 6 per cent of world GDP in 1991 (the latest year for which statistics are available) (UNCTAD, 1996, p. 16).

These ratios clearly show a great increase in FDI flows relative to production and capital formation in the world economy. But, as with goods trade, these measures are affected by many variables other than restrictions on cross-border movements. We should construct a measure of the restrictiveness of the border regulations of capital flows.

Unfortunately, the statistical measures available to construct an average measure of the level of restrictions on flows of capital across borders of factor markets are much worse than those for the goods markets. The basic explanation for this is that most government policies which restrict inflows of capital do not, unlike the most common restrictions on imports, take the form of a tax wedge. In the case of foreign direct investment inflows, the typical restriction is a prohibition on foreign investment in certain sectors or industries. This is comparable to a prohibitive quota on imports of a good. Other restrictions are a denial of national treatment. Similarly, in the case of inflows of labour, the controls are quantitative controls in almost all cases. (Switzerland is the only country which allows foreigners to buy residence, though a few other countries such as Australia and Canada have special programmes for business migrants who must put up a minimum amount of capital to qualify for immigration.)

Liberalization of capital movements has resulted principally from systematic but uncoordinated unilateral actions. Almost every country in the world has liberalized inflows (and in many cases outflows too) of foreign direct capital over the last 15 years, many of them very substantially by allowing rights of establishment and more national treatment. There has been no multilateral reduction in barriers to capital flows as there is no global body responsible for the regulation of government actions in the area of capital flows. However, the OECD has promoted the liberalization of these flows among its members. With the exception of the European Union (EU), there has been no significant regional liberalization of trade in capital.

There have been few attempts to measure or document the liberalization of capital flows. Dooley (1996) surveys the literature on controls on international capital transactions. PECC (1995a, Chapter 5) documents the liberalization of measures relating to foreign direct investment in the Asia-Pacific region. Petri (1997) makes a bold and provisional attempt to measure the restrictions on foreign direct investments. He represents these restrictions as a tax on FDI profits, that is, the profits tax equivalent of a complex set of measures. His calculations show that the rates of tax on foreign investors are about one half as high as the tariff equivalent on trade in goods.

The liberalization of movements of capital between nations has come about because there has been a huge change in attitudes of governments to these movements. In the 1960s and 1970s there was concern in many countries over foreign investors because of fears of foreign control and specific issues such as transfer pricing. The economics literature was replete with articles on immiserizing growth due to foreign investment. However, in the 1980s and 1990s these concerns diminished and the view that foreign investors were valuable and important agents of change who introduced new products and technologies became widespread.

International movements of labour can, in principle, be treated in the same way as the international movements in capital. There is the added complication that migration flows are divided between migration which is permanent and that which is temporary. The latter is comparable to foreign direct investment as the owners of foreign-invested capital reside in the foreign country. There is no parallel in capital markets to the permanent migration of labour. However, movements of labour have received less attention by those interested in the global economy than movements of capital. The statistics of international movement of labour are worse than those of capital.

The main contemporary flows of permanent migration are from the developing countries to the developed countries. There are only four countries in the world which have had a relatively free immigration policy in recent decades to the extent of having significant numbers of permanent settlers year after year and selecting these immigrants from a wide range of countries. These four countries are Australia, Canada, New Zealand and the United States. Between them these four traditional immigration countries have accepted a total of fewer than a million immigrants a year in recent years. A larger number of countries, though still a small subset of those in the world, have been significant countries of resettlement of refugees; this list includes European countries such as Denmark, France, Sweden and the United Kingdom. A few countries have accepted large numbers of settlers of particular ethnic groups; for example, Israel, Germany and India. Temporary migrants, mainly to Western Europe and the Middle East, outnumber on an annual basis the permanent immigration flows, but most of these return to their home countries after a few years. For example, one outcome of the increase in the relative price of petroleum products from the early 1970s was a massive influx of labour from India, Pakistan and other Asian countries into the oil-rich Middle East countries, reaching at its peak in the early 1980s over a million temporary workers a year.

In relation to the total world population and labour force, these flows are very small. Indeed, the world economy could rather roughly be characterized as one in which capital movements between countries are now close to being completely free and labour movements are close to being completely restricted.

There are no statistics of 'openness' with respect to migration or international labour movements. However, it is possible to make some rough calculations for some countries. As an example, Singapore relies heavily on migrants for the supply of some labour markets and in the aggregate almost 20 per cent of its labour force are foreign workers (Chew and Chew, 1995). Yet, this figure is less than the percentage of the FDI inflow as a percentage of gross capital formation; over the period 1985–90 the latter figure averaged 59.3 per cent but it was 24.6 per cent in 1995 (UNCTAD, 1996, Annex Table B.5). Moreover, the Singapore migrant share of total labour is the highest in Asia and one of the highest in the world.

The obvious explanation for the lower international mobility of labour is that every country in the world, with no exception, tightly regulates inflows of labour and people whereas a number of countries have no or little restriction on capital, at least into some sectors and industries.

Yet, there has been a notable intensification in the extent of international movements of labour in recent years. Rod and Williams (1996) and Quibria (1997) provide surveys of international migration in the Asia-Pacific region.

Despite this intensification of labour movements, world labour markets are very far from being integrated. Wages in high-income developed countries are many times those of labour doing comparable work in the poorest countries. This is a major source of inefficiency in world labour markets because large differences in the marginal productivity of labour across countries persist. Hamilton and Whalley (1984) show that the elimination of these differences from the international movement of labour could lead to very large gains, perhaps doubling world GNP. These potential gains are much larger than those from the elimination of barriers to trade in goods.

There is considerable doubt as to whether real wage levels are even converging. Williamson (1995) has tested the hypothesis of convergence among labour markets over the long-term period 1830 to 1988 using purchasing-power-parity-adjusted real wage rates for unskilled labour in some 15 countries. He finds convergence but it should be noted that all of the countries in his sample are now OECD countries and therefore relatively high income. Convergence among the high wage rate countries could be consistent with divergence between the low and the high wage rate countries. This possibility is supported by studies of trends in per capita real incomes which show long-run divergence of incomes between the poorer and the richer countries (Pritchett, 1997).

There are important links between the formation of global markets for goods and the formation of global markets for factors which arise from the relationship between these two types of trade. First, goods prices and factor prices are linked in general equilibrium. In a seminal paper, Mundell (1957) showed that, under certain conditions, goods price equalization resulting from free trade in goods lead to the equalization of the prices of factors, even if the factors were not traded, and vice versa. Falvey (1998) established less stringent conditions under which the prices of the factors converge without full equalization. Under other conditions the factor prices may diverge. Second, the quantities of goods and factors trade are related by input–output relations and other links. If an increase in trade leads to a decrease (increase) in the quantity of factors traded internationally, the goods and factors are said to be substitutes (complements).

There has been a debate in recent years as to whether trade in goods and trade in factors are substitutes or complements. This theory is well surveyed in Ethier (1996). Most international economists seem now to believe that trade in goods and factors are more frequently complementary than substitutable, and there is some empirical evidence to support this view in the positive statistical associations of exports and international production or FDI at the level of firms and nations (Cantwell, 1994, pp. 316–22; WTO, 1996, pp. 53–54).

The complementarity of trade in goods and services on the one hand and international flows of capital on the other has one consequence which has not received attention. The liberalization of commodity trade and the liberalization of international flows of FDI, which have occurred in the last decade or so, have been super-additive because of the complementarity of trade in goods and trade in capital. That is, the combined effect of the liberalization of commodity trade and of international flows of FDI on the levels of international commodity trade and FDI has been greater than the sum of the effects separately. There would have been less FDI if commodity trade had not been liberalized. Part of the explanation of the growth of acquisition of capital assets by foreign corporations is the liberalization of trade in goods and services and the new profit opportunities which this has created. Conversely, there would have been less trade in goods and services if FDI had not been liberalized. FDI has led to more opportunities for the profitable exporting of goods and services.

The situation in which the goods *and* factor markets are fully integrated has been used in trade analysis. Dixit and Norman (1980, p.109), call this situation a 'fully integrated world economy'. This concept has been used extensively by Krugman and Helpman (1985). The law of one price holds in all goods and factor markets. There is perfect arbitrage among national markets, differences in market prices reflecting only differences in transport costs and other real transfer costs which differentiate commodities.

For goods and factors alike, a fully integrated world economy requires the absence of differences in the treatment of goods and factors according to national origin. That is, it requires national treatment of foreign goods and factors. It also requires the removal of differences in commodity and factor taxes among nations. Departures from this state provide the most comprehensive measure of the freedom of movement between national economies.

The formation of global financial markets

Finally, one must consider globalization in financial markets, that is, in the markets for stocks, securities and other financial assets. Financial assets are omitted from most general equilibrium models, but as with foreign direct investments international trade in these assets has increased greatly and these markets interact with other markets.

The literature on financial markets is the oldest which deals with issues of market integration and globalization. In financial circles, the term 'globalization' refers to financial market integration. Thus, there is no distinction in this area between globalization and the formation of a global economy. A fully integrated market for a financial asset is again one in which the law of one price holds but this concept is more complex in markets with risk due to own market variations and to exchange risk. The law holds for a financial asset with a given risk profile when expected rates of return are equal across national markets. Financial market integration refers to the convergence towards a single risk-adjusted rate of return on capital. Financial markets were probably the first markets in which a single market was defined in terms of the law of one price. Irving Fisher (1930) established the condition required for interest parity across countries in an uncertain world. Early discussions of the concept of financial market integration are given by Kenen (1976) and Llewellyn (1980).

In this area of market integration, there has been much empirical work to measure the extent of integration of markets across borders, especially tests of interest rate parity for interest-bearing assets. These studies have found a steady convergence in the prices of assets in the major markets as asset markets have been deregulated and cross-border trade has been liberalized. Reidel (1997) provides a recent survey of financial capital market integration in the developing countries of Asia. However, other evidence based on savings investment patterns and the low level of portfolio diversification across borders indicates that capital immobility is still substantial (see Gordon and Bovenberg, 1990). There is a distinct 'home bias' in portfolio allocations (see Lewis, 1995).

Some consequences of the formation of the global economy

The formation of the global economy has many implications. This is why the subject is so important. I shall merely indicate the main areas of discussion and research.

There are the traditional issues of efficiency. Markets which are separated or imperfectly linked because of restrictions across national borders lead to inefficiency. This applies to markets for goods and services and factors.

A more recent development is the analysis of convergences of policies relating to non-border interventions. These include industrial standards, government procurement and the new issues of competition policies, the environment and labour standards.

The convergence of national policies may be hastened by international capital and labour mobility. Governments are effectively in competition with each other when they devise policies to promote industries or research and development (R&D) or develop infrastructure or when they impose taxes which reduce the profitability of particular activities. A high degree of capital and labour mobility may force a government to bring its tax and regulatory policies into line with those of other less punitive governments. This factor was recognized by Cooper (1968, Chapter 6). It applies to a wide range of markets now, including service markets such as the provision of education to overseas students, some professional services and the location of corporate headquarters.

Some authors regard the loss of national sovereignty involved in the harmonization of national policies and the growth of the multinational corporations as a negative feature of the formation of the global economy. Others, chiefly popular commentators, contend that deindustrialization, growing unemployment and widening income differentials have stemmed from 'globalization'. These views differ from those who view the formation of the global economy as one of integration and believe that integration brings efficiency gains to the world economy.

Another set of policy concerns relate to the macroeconomic behaviour of inter-dependent economies. There is now a huge literature on the transmission of shocks due to monetary or fiscal policies, oil shocks and other exogenous events from one country to others. Since the work of Mundell (1968) in particular there has been much analysis of the efficacy of monetary and fiscal policies under fixed and floating exchange rate regimes. There are more recent literatures on the transmission of the business cycle and international coordination of national government macroeconomic policies.

The formation of global financial markets has many consequences. These include issues of efficiency of portfolio selection, the transmission of financial market shocks across borders and the role of financial markets in macroeconomic stabilization or destabilization.

In the longer run, the formation of the global economy has led to much interest in the effects of opening of economies and the integration of goods and factor markets on rates of economic growth. In particular, there has been a vigorous debate as to whether openness leads to income convergence across countries. This is a system-wide effect of the global economy. It is a vital issue but too large to pursue here (for a recent survey, see Slaughter, 1997).

Finally, issues relating to the global economy and globalization are receiving increasing attention by political scientists, international relations specialists and other social scientists. As a group, they seem to have a less optimistic view of the formation of the global economy than economists with concerns over the loss of sovereignty because of the spread of multinational enterprises and the integration of national markets, other cross-border environmental spillovers and different labour standards.

References
Anderson, J. E. and J.P. Neary (1994), 'Measuring the Restrictiveness of Trade Policy', *World Bank Economic Review*, **8**, 151–69.
Anderson, J.E. and J.P. Neary (1996), 'A New Approach to Evaluating Trade Policy', *Review of Economic Studies*, **63**, 107–25.
Cantwell, J. (1994), 'The Relationship between International Trade and International Production', in D. Greenaway and A.L. Winters (eds), *Surveys in International Trade*, Blackwell, Oxford.
Chew Soon-Beng and R. Chew (1995), 'Immigration and Foreign Labour in Singapore', *ASEAN Economic Bulletin*, **122**, November, 191–200.
Cooper, R. (1968), *The Economics of Interdependence: Economic Policy in the American Community*, McGraw-Hill, New York.
Cooper, R. (1976), 'Worldwide Regional Integration: Is there an Optimal Size of the Integrated Area?', in Fritz Machlup (ed.), *Economic Integration Worldwide, Regional and Sectoral*, Macmillan, New York.
Dooley, M.P. (1996), 'A Survey of the Literature on International Capital Transactions', *International Monetary Fund Staff Papers*, **43**, 639–87.
Dixit, A.K. and V. Norman (1980), *Theory of International Trade*, James Nisbet and Cambridge University Press, Digswell Place.
Engel, C. and J.H. Rogers (1996), 'How Wide is the Border?', *American Economic Review*, **86**, December, 1112–25.
Ethier, W.J. (1996), 'Theories about Trade Liberalisation and Migration: Substitutes or Complements?', in P.J. Lloyd and Lynne Williams (eds), *International Trade and Migration in the APEC Region*, Oxford University Press, Melbourne.
Falvey, R. (1998), 'Factor Price Convergence', *Journal of International Economics* (forthcoming).
Fisher, I. (1930), *The Theory of Interest*, Macmillan, New York.
Fukuyama, F. (1989), 'The End of History?', *The National Interest*, Summer, 3–18.
Gordon, R.H. and A.L. Bovenberg (1996), 'Why is Capital so Immobile Internationally? Possible Explanations and Implications for Capital Income Taxation', *American Economic Review*, **86**, December.
Hamilton, B. and J. Whalley (1984), 'Efficiency and Distributional Implications of Global Restrictions on Labor Mobility', *Journal of Development Studies*, **14**, 61–75.
Helpman, E. and P.R. Krugman (1985), *Market Structure and Foreign Trade*, Wheatsheaf, Brighton.
Kenen, P.B. (1976), *Capital Mobility and Financial Integration: A Survey*, Princeton Studies in International Finance No. 39, Princeton University, Princeton.
Lewis, K.K. (1995), 'Puzzles in International Financial Markets', in G.M. Grossman and K. Rogoff (eds), *Handbook of International Economics*, vol.3, North-Holland, Amsterdam.
Llewellyn, D.T. (1980), *International Financial Integration*, Macmillan, London.
Mundell, R.A. (1957), 'International Trade and Factor Mobility, *American Economic Review*, **47**, 321–37.
Mundell, R.A. (1968), *International Economics*, Macmillan, New York.
Ohmae, K. (1990), *The Borderless World: Power and Strategy in the Interlinked Economy*, Harper Collins, Glasgow.
Pacific Economic Cooperation Council (1995a), *Milestones in APEC Liberalisation: A Map of Market Opening Measures by APEC Economies*, Pacific Economic Cooperation Council, Singapore.
Pacific Economic Cooperation Council (1995b), *Survey of Impediments to Trade and Investment in the APEC Region*, PECC, Singapore.
Petri, P. (1997), 'Foreign Direct Investment in a Computable General Equilibrium Framework', paper presented to the Conference on making APEC Work: Economic Challenges and Policy Alternatives, Keio University, Tokyo.
Porter, M.E. (1986), *Competition in Global Industries*, Harvard Business School Press, Boston.
Pritchett, L. (1997), 'Divergence, Big Time', *Journal of Economic Perspectives*, **11**, Summer, 3–18.
Quibria, M.G. (1997), 'Labour Migration and Labour Market Integration in Asia', *The World Economy*, **20**, January, 21–42.
Reidel, J. (1997), 'Capital Market Integration in Asia', *The World Economy*, **20**, 1–21.
Rod, T. and L. Williams (1996), 'Migration Intensification in the APEC Region' in P.J. Lloyd and Lynne Williams (eds), *International Trade and Migration in the APEC Region*, Oxford University Press, Melbourne.

Ruggiero, R. (1997), 'Charting the Trade Routes of the Future: Towards a Borderless Economy, WTO Press/77, 25 September 1997.

Sachs, J.D. and A. Warner (1995), 'Economic Reform and the Process of Global Integration', *Brookings Papers on Economic Activity*, **1**, 1–118.

Shephard, R.W. (1970), *Theory of Cost Functions*, Princeton University Press, Princeton.

Slaughter M.J. (1997), 'Per Capita Income Convergence and the Role of International Trade', *American Economic Review*, **87**, May, 194–99.

United Nations Conference on Trade and Development (UNCTAD) (1996), *World Investment Report 1996: Investment, Trade and International Policy Arrangements*, UNCTAD, New York.

Williamson, J.G. (1995), 'The Evolution of Global Labor Markets since 1830: Background Evidence and Hypotheses', *Explorations in Economic History*, **32**, 141–96.

Woodland, A.D. (1982), *International Trade and Resource Allocation*, North Holland, Amsterdam.

World Trade Organization (WTO) (1996), *Annual Report 1996*, Vols. I and II, WTO, Geneva.

PART II

PROTECTIONISM

Introduction

The first selection, 'Protection policy and the assignment rule' shows how market failures, if they exist, call for an intervention which is most clearly linked to the basis of the failure. This is the Assignment Rule. In the case of protection which is designed to increase the income of particular groups, the analysis has, since the publication of the famous article by Stolper and Samuelson (1941), begun with the Stolper–Samuelson theorem. This theorem states that the adjustment in the price of one of two or more commodities due, say, to the change in the rate of tariff on an import-competing commodity, has different effects on households which own different factors. The Stolper–Samuelson theorem has, however, proven very difficult to generalize to models with dimensions greater than 2×2 (that is, more than two goods and/or more than two factors). This paper shows how the Stolper–Samuelson theorem can be extended to a class of models to yield unambiguous results. In these models every household has an industry whose price increase will benefit the household. Thus there is universal incentive for rent-seeking. Moreover, when the price of the output of any industry increases, some households gain and some lose. Thus there is universal conflict among households.

Virtually all of the literature on the Stolper–Samuelson theorem is confined to models in which households are completely undiversified in their factor ownership. 'Conflict-generating product price changes: the imputed output approach' (Chapter 2), co-authored with Albert Schweinberger, extends this theory to models in which there any dimensions and households are diversified. This paper makes use of the concept of the imputed outputs of households, first developed in Lloyd and Schweinberger (1988) and reproduced in section III (Chapter 6).

The next selection on 'Uncertainty and the choice of instrument', written with Rod Falvey, focuses on the problem of defining and quantifying the non-equivalence between the tariff as a protective instrument and a quota. The explanation offered is that, under uncertainty relating to the price of imports, these two instruments give a very different distribution of the rates of protection. A quota offers more downside protection and is, therefore, preferred by producers (but not consumers) when there is substantial downside risk or risk aversion.

'Protectionism', written on the occasion of the sesquicentenary of the signing of the Treaty of Waitangi at the beginning of white settlement in New Zealand, uses the examples of New Zealand, Australia and the United Kingdom to discuss the economic phenomenon of protectionism. It is a local version of the masterly survey of protectionism globally by Bhagwati (1988). New Zealand, and to a lesser extent Australia, are especially interesting country cases as they have represented in an extreme form both high levels of protection to manufacturing producers and rapid reductions in these rates. The explanation for these events lies only partly in the standard political economy arguments. One must also take account of the force of academic argument, aided by modern computable general equilibrium analyses, and the influence of public discussion as in the activities of the statutory bodies in Australia, in changing public opinion and aiding anti-protectionism.

References

Bhagwati, J.N. (1988), *Protectionism*, MIT Press, Cambridge, Mass.

Stolper, W.F. and P.A. Samuelson (1941), 'Protection and real wages', *Review of Economic Studies*, **9**, 58–73.

[1]

Protection Policy
and the Assignment Rule

Peter J. Lloyd

The debate about protection policy is perennial in virtually all countries. For many years economists have been circumscribing more and more narrowly the set of conditions under which border protection is a policy which is optimal or even welfare-improving. Moreover, in recent years there has been a growing awareness of why legislators are prepared to supply protection in order to promote their selfish political interests. Yet, the profession of international economics has been conspicuously unsuccessful in persuading politicians and the public at large that industries should not generally be assisted by instruments of protection.

This paper reconsiders the issues of protection policy as an assignment problem, that is, as one of choosing the optimal instrument for a policy problem. This is, of course, an old perception, but some recent developments in the theory of international trade make it possible to extend earlier results. Section 1 outlines the model which is used to analyse the demand for protection and the design of optimal policy rules. This is an extension of the specific-factor model of Jones (1971, 1975) to incorporate inter-industry and international flows of intermediate inputs. Section 2 considers the optimal assignment rules for some problems and in particular for problems involving so-called 'non-economic objectives'. These are often used to justify protective policies, and they illustrate well the deficiencies of protection policies. Section 3 puts forward two very general propositions concerning the universal demand for protection. These are couched in terms of the concepts of 'true friends' and 'true enemies', which are alternatives to the Jones–Scheinkman (1977) concepts of 'natural friends' and 'natural enemies'. Finally, Section 4 indicates the ineffectiveness and sometimes the inefficacy of protective policies which are sub-optimal assignments.

1   THE MODEL

The model used throughout this paper is the extension of the Jones model

Protection policy and the assignment rule 5

developed by Burgess (1980) and Hosios (1982). In the Jones (1975) model there are n industries, each of which uses one specific input and one mobile or non-specific input, a total of $n+1$ inputs. These two types of inputs are arbitrarily called 'capital' and 'labour', respectively. Thus, the dimensions of the model are $n \times (n+1)$. For the minimum-dimension 2×3 version of this model, Burgess and Hosios independently added the complication that the outputs of each industry can be used for intermediate or final demand. This makes the model considerably richer for the purpose of policy analysis. In this paper I shall generalize the Burgess–Hosios extension to the $n \times (n+1)$ version. This will be called the Jones–Burgess–Hosios (JBH) model.[1]

The technology of each industry is described by a single-output production function:

$$g_i = f^i(v_i, q_i) \tag{1}$$

where $v_i = (K_i, L_i)$ is the vector of the two primary inputs used in the industry, one specific and one non-specific, and

$$q_i = (g_{1i}, \ldots, q_i = (g_{1i}, \ldots, g_{ni})$$

is the vector of intermediate inputs. Intermediate inputs may be produced locally or imported. Some of the elements of q_i may be zero. f^i satisfy regularity properties; in particular, they are linearly homogeneous and strictly quasiconcave for all i. This permits us to assume that the industries are all competitive. The supplies of both the mobile factor and the specific factors are assumed to be fixed and the factor markets to be competitive with flexible prices that clear the markets. The country is assumed to be small. With these assumptions, we can define the net output and the real value added of industry i:

$$y_i = f^i(v_i, q_i) - \sum_j g_{ij} \tag{2}$$

and

$$z_i = f^i(v_i, q_i) - \sum_j (p_j/p_i) g_{ji} \tag{3}$$

$$z_i = F^i(v_i, \bar{p}_i) \tag{4}$$

respectively, where $\bar{p}_i$ is the vector of relative prices of intermediate inputs whose jth elements is (p_j/p_i), z_i is the value added in industry i in units of output of this industry, and F^i is the multiple-input–commodity version of the real value added function introduced by Khang (1971).

For such a small open economy, the equilibrium conditions for the production sector are

Peter J. Lloyd

$$p - A(u)u = 0$$
$$a_L(u)g \quad = L \qquad\qquad (5)$$
$$a_{Ki}(u)g_i \quad = K_i$$

where p denotes the $n \times 1$ vector of commodity prices, u the $(2n+1) \times 1$ vector of prices for primary and intermediate inputs, A the $n \times (2n+1)$ transpose of the matrix of least-cost input–output coefficients, a_L the vector of labour coefficients, g the vector of gross outputs, a_{Ki} the specific capital coefficient and g_i the gross output of industry i. The equations relate to the n commodities which are produced in strictly positive quantities. (These may be regarded as the solution from a larger system of equations for $s \geq n$ commodities where some commodities which the economy is capable of producing may not be produced because the profits are strictly negative.) The first equation in (5) represents the zero profit conditions and the remaining equations the factor market conditions. This is the JBH model of dimension $n \times (n+1)$. It will be assumed that the set of produced commodities does not change when commodity prices change.

One variant of the model is obtained by assuming that the factor labour is also industry-specific. In this variant equation (5) separates into n sub-systems:

$$p_i - A_i(u_i)u_i = 0$$
$$a_{Li}(u_i)g_i \quad = L_i \qquad\qquad (6)$$
$$a_{Ki}(u_i)g_i \quad = K_i.$$

Here, $u_i = (w_i, r_i, p')'$ is the $(n+2) \times 1$ vector of prices of inputs for industry i and A_i is the ith row of A. This gives a $n \times 2n$ model of the economy.

A second variant is obtained by assuming instead that both factors are mobile. This is the $n \times 2$ version of the Heckscher–Ohlin model with intermediate input flows. However, it is well-known that the output vector is indeterminate with these dimensions. One way of overcoming indeterminary is to assume there are n primary inputs. These primary inputs can be considered as types of mobile labour and capital. In this variant the equilibrium conditions become:

$$p - A(u)u = 0$$
$$a_k(u)g \quad = v_k \qquad k = 1, \ldots, n. \qquad\qquad (7)$$

Here, u is $2n \times 1$ vector of input prices and A is an $n \times 2n$ matrix. a_k is the vector of inputs of the kth factor into all industries and v_k is the national endowment of factor k. This gives the $n \times n$ version of the Heckscher–Ohlin model with intermediate inputs.

The basic model and its two variants can be arrayed in terms of increasing factor mobility. Hosios (1982) identifies this array with periods of time. The variant with both factors specific is called the Very Short Run, the standard JBH model the Short Run and the third model the Long Run. I shall employ the Short Run and Long Run variants. These give a versatile set of models for analysing issues of movement of factors and real incomes and policies relating to these movements.

2   OPTIMAL ASSIGNMENT RULES

For an economy whose production structure is specified as in the JBH model of section 1, we can now determine optimal policy in any policy situation.

We seek to maximize the utility of one household, say household 1, $U_1(x_{11}, \ldots, x_{1n})$, given the utility levels of other households,

$$\{U_h(x_{h1}, \ldots, x_{hn}) - \mu_h\} = 0 \qquad h = 2, \ldots, H \qquad (8)$$

and subject to the constraints. The constraints are the technology (equation (1)) and net imports, defined as the differences between consumption and net output (equation (2)), which can be combined in the set of equations

$$\{\sum_h x_{hi} - f^i(v_i, q_i) - \sum_j g_{ij} - m_i\} = 0 \qquad i = 1, \ldots, n, \qquad (9)$$

the fixed supplies of primary factors,

$$(\sum_i v_{ki} - v_k) = 0 \qquad k = 1, \ldots, \ell, \qquad (10)$$

the balance of payments,

$$(\sum_i p_i^* m_i) = 0 \qquad (11)$$

and any other constraints which may be added. $h = 1, \ldots, H$ indexes the households of the economy. Thus, x_{hi} is the consumption by household h of the commodity i. In equation (10), ℓ is the number of mobile factors. This specification covers both the Short Run and Long Run variants where $\ell = 1$ and n, respectively. $(p_i^*, \ldots, p_n^*)$ is the vector of international prices and $m = (m_1, \ldots, m_n)$ is the vector of quantities of imports of these commodities. $\lambda_{1h} = (\lambda_{11}, \ldots, \lambda_{1H})$, $\lambda_2 = (\lambda_{21}, \ldots, \lambda_{2n})$, $\lambda_3 = (\lambda_{31}, \ldots, \lambda_{3\ell})$ and λ_4 are the Lagrange multipliers for these constraints in equations (8), (9), (10) and (11), respectively. This maximization gives the Pareto-efficient allocations for the economy. The choice variables are x_{hi}, v_{ki}, m_i and g_{ji}.

If there are no additional constraints on the economy and the utility functions of all households are strictly quasi-concave, the first-order conditions for Pareto-efficient allocations may be written as:

$$\begin{aligned}
\lambda_{1h} \partial U_h / \partial x_{hi} &= \lambda_4 p_i^* & h &= 1, \ldots, H, \ i = 1, \ldots, n \qquad (12) \\
\lambda_4 p_i^* \, \partial f^i / \partial v_{ki} &= \lambda_{3k} & k &= 1, \ldots, \ell. \\
p_i^* \, \partial f^i / \partial g_{ji} &= p_j^* & i &= 1, \ldots, n, \ j = 1, \ldots, n
\end{aligned}$$

These equations have a solution which is unique up to a factor of proportionality. $\lambda_4 p^*$ and λ_3 may be interpreted as the vectors of

Peter J. Lloyd

commodity and primary factor prices, respectively. The standard theorem that Pareto efficiency is achieved by a 'free trade' (zero price distortion) competitive economy applies.

If there are other additional constraints because of unremovable price distortions (tariffs, subsidies and so on) or non-economic objectives or other factors, the optimal policy can be determined. J. N. Bhagwati enunciated the following important general principle:

> i. Optimal policy intervention in the presence of distortions involves a tax-cum-subsidy policy addressed directly to offsetting the source of the distortions, when the causes are endogenous or autonomous, policy-imposed [and] ii. When distortions have to be introduced into the economy, because the values of certain variables (e.g. production or employment of a factor in an activity) have to be constrained, the optimal (or least-cost) method of doing this is to choose that policy intervention that creates the distortion affecting directly the constrained variable.
>
> (Bhagwati, 1971, p. 77)

I shall call this rule the Assignment Rule. It applies to price distortions and non-economic objectives. However, the same principle also applies to other justifications for government intervention in an open economy. For example, when applicable, the infant-industry and the terms-of-trade justification for intervention can be interpreted in the same way. Indeed, any standard market failure justifications for intervention can be interpreted in this way. The elementary but powerful idea is that each optimal policy instrument has to be tailored to the exact source of the problem and that this generally requires an instrument whose base is directly related to the source of the problem.

This rule can be illustrated by the theory of so-called 'non-economic objectives'. (This description is rather inapt, as the 'objectives' are usually treated as constraints and the 'non-economic' constraint is specified in terms of economic variables and derives from economic arguments.) The standard reference is to Bhagwati and Srinivasan (1969). However, the term seems to have been coined by Johnson (1960) and the central idea of ranking policies can be traced to the seminal paper by Corden (1957). This theory has received little attention in recent years except for special cases such as the revenue constraint under uncertainty (for example, Young, 1980), but it is still an accepted part of international economic theory and is commonly cited in the USA, UK and other countries as a justification of protection policies such as 're-industrialization', that is, the promotion of output and/or employment in the manufacturing sectors of these countries. Similar problems of optimal policy determination arise with price distortions and other second-best problems.

Consider first that the additional constraint relates to *production*. Corden (1957) introduced this case for a model with a much simpler structure and a single importable commodity. In the JBH model we may constrain the model by assuming that there is a set of importable commodities (α_1) for which the aggregate (real) value added cannot fall below some specified minimum, P. This gives the additional constraint

$$[\sum_{i\epsilon\alpha_1} \{p_i^* f(v_i, q_i) - \sum_j p_j^* g_{ji}\} - P] = 0 \qquad (13)$$

whose associated Lagrange multiplier is λ_5. Maximization of the objective function now yields the modified set of first-order conditions.

$$\left.\begin{array}{lll}
\lambda_{1h} \partial U_h/\partial x_{hi} & = \lambda_4 p_i^* & i\epsilon(\alpha_1 \cup \alpha_1^c) \\
\lambda_4 p_i^* \partial f^i/\partial v_{ki} & = \lambda_{3k} & k = 1, \ldots, \ell \\
\lambda_4 p_i^* (1 - \lambda_4/\lambda_5) \partial f^i/\partial v_{ki} & = \lambda_{3k} & i\epsilon\alpha_1, k = 1, \ldots, \ell \\
p_i^* \partial f^i/\partial g_{ji} & = p_j^* & i\epsilon\alpha_1^c, j\epsilon\alpha_1^c \\
p_i^* (1 - \lambda_5/\lambda_4) \partial f^i/\partial g_{ji} & = p_j^* & i\epsilon\alpha_1, j\epsilon\alpha_1^c \\
p_i^* \partial f^i/\partial g_{ji} & = p_j^* & i\epsilon\alpha_1, j\epsilon\alpha_1
\end{array}\right\} \qquad (14)$$

where α_1^c is the complement of α_1. This set of equations is satisfied if a uniform *ad valorem* subsidy at the rate $(-\lambda_5/\lambda_4)$ is granted on the gross outputs of the set, including those outputs which are used as inputs in the production of some other commodity or commodities in this set; that is, a subsidy on real value added by these industries. The subsidy rate is positive since $\lambda_5 < 0$ and $\lambda_4 > 0$. Equivalently, the system is satisfied by a uniform subsidy at the same rate on all domestic inputs used in the production of this set of commodities. One may note that this solution implies inefficient production since the price to producers of outputs of these α_1 industries which are used as inputs by another industry in this set will differ from the price to producers in industries outside this set. This generalized the results obtained by Corden (1957), Bhagwati and Srinivasan (1969), Tan (1971) and Vandendorpe (1974).

We may instead, following Bhagwati and Srinivasan (1969), add the constraint that the aggregate *employment* of some factor k in some specified set of industries (α_2) must not fall below a critical minimum, V. This gives the constraint:

$$(\sum_{i\epsilon\alpha_2} \lambda_{ki} - V) = 0 \qquad (15)$$

whose associated Lagrange multipler is λ_6. This case may be solved in the same way. The optimal policy is a uniform *ad valorem* rate of subsidy at the rate (λ_6/λ_{4k}) on units of this factor employed in the set of industries only. Like the previous case, this results in inefficient production because the policy distorts the relative factor prices across industries.

These two examples suffice to show how the base of the corrective tax subsidy instruments must be modified when the variable entering the additional constraint changes.

The Assignment Rule seems to give admirable guidance to the formulation of policies relating to non-economic objectives. Yet, there are a number of difficulties with this formulation. In the first instance, it is assumed implicitly that the net revenue required (or obtained) from the optimal set of taxes–subsidies can be raised (dispersed) by non-distortionary lump-sum taxes (payments). But the main difficulties relate to the formulation of the policy problems themselves. The constraint is of the fixed target type. (During the 1950s and 1960s fixed target models were frequently used for the assignment of multiple macroeconomic instruments.) Hence the choice of level at which the target variable is fixed is quite arbitrary. However, the basic question concerns the choice of target variable itself. Why should a government seek to constraint the level of output or employment in some set of industries? This state of theory is quite inadequate. We should seek to endogenize the target.[2]

An insight into the problem can be had by applying an equivalence relation from the theory of mathematical programming. Under certain conditions, which are satisfied here because of the concavity restrictions imposed on the technologies and the utility functions, one may interchange one of several constraints in an optimization problem with the objective function and still obtain the same solution. Consider, for example, the problem in which the added constraint is real value added in some industry. Call this problem A. Denote the solution values to this problem obtained from equation (14) as $(x_{hi}^*, v_{hi}^*, m_i^*, g_{ji}^*)$. Formulate a second problem by substituting the additional constraint of problem A as the objective function of the new problem and add the objective function of problem A as the added constraint of this problem. Call this problem B. It is

$$\max [\ \underset{i \in \beta}{\Sigma}\ \{p_i^* f^i(v_i, q_i) - \underset{j}{\Sigma}\ p_j^* g_{ji}\}] \tag{16}$$

subject to the constraints of problem A minus that of equation (13) plus $U_1(x_1) \geqq \mu_1^*$. μ_1^* is the solution value for U_1 in problem A. It is easy to verify that problem B has the same solution as problem A. Why should any government seek to maximize the value added (or employment) in these industries?

The answer to this question must be, it seems to me, that the choice of constraint (or 'objective') in these problems was ill-conceived. In some cases it may be possible to derive the constraint from a full model in which there is a market failure. Bhagwati and Srinivasan (1976) construct a two-period model in which the possibility of a market-disruption-induced quota on second-period exports is a function of the level of first-period trade. This may justify a restraint on first-period trade. This problem is really very different from an arbitrary initial assumption that trade should be restricted to some level. The level of restriction – and, indeed, whether there should be any restriction – will be a function of the probability of a quota and it should apply only to first-period trade. Furthermore, when the full problem is revealed it raises the possibility that there are other instruments which might rank above a restraint on trade. In particular, it may be that inter-government negotiation or the threat of retaliation will avoid the imposition of the second-period quota and therefore remove the problem. In all cases we must ask for the ultimate cause of any problem and a complete specification of it.

Earlier literature on non-economic objectives tended merely to cite 'ideology' or 'national pride' as a justification of sectoral output or employment targets. Currently, 're-industrialization' is also based on the premise that there is some unidentified additional merit in the production of the manufacturing sector. A more likely explanation is that these policies have been advocated as a form of income support by some factors employed in the industries who advance any supposed public benefit to support their private cause. The next section considers two basic propositions concerning universal rent-seeking.

3   TWO GENERAL PROPOSITIONS

Since the famous article by Stolper and Samuelson (1941), international economists have analysed the relationships between changes in (relative) commodity prices on the one hand and the real incomes of factor owners on the other in terms of the matrix of real income changes measured in terms of wage goods. For the Short Run version of the JBH model, in which only 'labour' is mobile, this $(n+1) \times n$ matrix is

$$U = \begin{bmatrix} \hat{u}_1/\hat{p}_1 & \cdots & \hat{u}_1/\hat{p}_n \\ \vdots & & \vdots \\ \hat{u}_{n+1}/\hat{p}_1 & \cdots & \hat{u}_{n+1}/\hat{p}_n \end{bmatrix}$$

where $u^* = (w, r_1, \ldots, r_n)$ is the vector of primary input prices, the wage rate and capital rentals. It is understood that each commodity price is varied one at a time and the circumflex denotes the corresponding proportionate rate of change of the variable. The rows of this matrix show the effects on one factor of changes in the price of each commodity while the columns show the effects on each factor of changes in the price of one commodity. For the Long Run variant in which all n primary inputs are mobile, u reduces to an $n \times n$ matrix.

In the context of the $n \times n$ model, Jones and Scheinkman (1977) introduced the useful terminology of 'natural friends' and 'natural enemies'. A commodity i is a natural friend of a factor k if and only if $(\hat{u}_k/\hat{p}_i) > 1$, and a commodity i is a natural enemy of factor k if and only if $(\hat{u}_k/\hat{p}_i) < 0$. Thus a natural friend is a commodity for which a price increases the real income of the factor in terms of all wage goods and, therefore, unambiguously increases the real income ($=$ utility) of the factor. Similarly, a natural enemy is a commodity for which a price increase lowers the real income of the factor in terms of all wage goods and, therefore, unambiguously lowers the real income of the factor.

It is these concepts which underlie the original Stolper–Samuelson theorem. While they have proven very productive in the context of the 2×2 version of the Heckscher–Ohlin model, they have not proven so useful for the $m \times n$ dimensional generalization of this model. The source of the problem is that elements of the U matrix may lie in the interval $[0, 1]$. If this occurs, and assuming the jth commodity and at least one other are consumed in strictly positive quantities, the change in real income of the factor is ambiguous on the basis of this information. Nevertheless, using these concepts, Jones and Scheinkman (1977) were able to show that every factor has at least one natural enemy, but concerning natural friends, which are the more interesting property, they were not able to show that every factor must have a natural friend unless further restrictions are imposed on the technology. If restrictions are imposed on the factor intensity pattern, the Stolper–Samuelson pattern generalizes to the $n \times n$ version but the restrictions required are very strict (see Ethier, 1984, section 6.2).

More progress may be made if we revert to the pre-Stolper–Samuelson method of considering real income in the sense of utility. This is best stated in terms of the indirect utility function. For the hth household, this function is $V^h(I^h, p)$ where I^h is the income of the household. Differentiating totally,

$$\hat{V}^h = \hat{I}^h - \sum_i \phi_{hi} \hat{p}_i$$

where ϕ_{hi} is the share of commodity i in the budget of household h[3]. This reduces to

$$\hat{V}^h = \hat{u}_k - \sum_i \phi_{ki} \hat{p}_i \qquad (18)$$

if the household earns its income solely from factor k. When each commodity price is varied singly, we obtain the vector of utility changes for the household:

$$\hat{V}^h = (\hat{V}^h / \hat{p}_1, \ldots, \hat{V}^h / \hat{p}_n). \qquad (19)$$

If there is another household which earns its income solely from each of the other factors, we can obtain the matrix of real income changes:

$$W = \begin{bmatrix} \hat{u}_1/\hat{p}_1 - \phi_{11} & \cdots & \hat{u}_1/\hat{p}_n - \phi_{1n} \\ \vdots & & \vdots \\ \hat{u}_{n+1}/\hat{p}_1 - \phi_{n+1,1} & \cdots & \hat{u}_{n+1}/\hat{p}_n - \phi_{n+1,n} \end{bmatrix} \qquad (20)$$

In this matrix the households $h = 1, \ldots, n+1$ have been numbered in accordance with the factors from which they earn their incomes. Evidently, $W = U - \phi$ where ϕ is the transpose of the matrix of household expenditure shares. For the Long Run variant the corresponding W matrix is $n \times n$.

The element W_{kj} represents the proportionate change in the indirect utility of a household which earns income from factor k with respect to the price of commodity j. The first term of the expression is the effect on the household as an income earner and the second term, the effect as a consumer. If $W_{kj} > 0$ we say that commodity j is a 'true' friend of the household owning factor k, and if $W_{kj} < 0$ we say that commodity j is a 'true' enemy of the household. This terminology is employed because W_{kj} are true quantity indices, that is, indices which index utility, in differential form. $W_{kj} > (<)0$ is the necessary and sufficient condition for commodity j to increase (decrease) utility. Ignoring the borderline case in which the two effects exactly cancel, for every household in the matrix every commodity must be either a true friend or a true enemy. Unlike the natural friend and natural enemy matrix, there can be no ambiguity. The matrix in this form is defined only for households which earn income from only one factor. This is a limitation, but it should be noted that the same limitation applies to the U matrix whose elements have meaning in terms of utility only for a single-factor household. It should also be noted that the element W_{kj} has been defined for a single household owning factor k. In general, preferences and therefore the expenditure shares ϕ_{kh} will differ across households owning a factor. Consequently, the magnitude of the one element and perhaps also the sign will differ among households which earn income solely from the same factor. Perhaps surprisingly, this does not turn out to be a difficulty in deriving the two qualitative propositions below. Finally, it can be noted that a commodity j, which is a natural friend (enemy) of household k, is by definition, a true friend (enemy) of household k, but the converse is not true.[4]

The following two basic propositions hold for the Short Run and Long Run variants of the JBH model.

Proposition 1   Every household which earns its income from the ownership of a single factor has at least one true friend and at least one true enemy.

Proposition 2   When the price of any single commodity chosen arbitrarily increases, it will increase the real income (= utility) of some set of households which derive their income from the ownership of a single factor and decrease the real income of some other set of households which derive their incomes from the ownership of some other factor–provided only that the commodity requires at least one primary input whose nominal income increases and which is used elsewhere in the economy. For the first household(s) the commodity is a true friend, and for the second household(s) it is a true enemy.

Propositions 1 and 2 are proven in the Appendix. The expressions contained in the W matrix were applied in Cassing (1981) for the case of the Hecksher–Ohlin model which is $n \times n$ but has no intermediate flows. He established, in the terminology adopted here, that in this model every factor must have at least one true friend and at least one true enemy. Proposition 2 extends a result obtained by Jones and Scheinkman (1977) for the $n \times n$ Heckscher–Ohlin model. The extensions cover intermediate flows and specific inputs. Thus, in the Jones (1975) model with specific inputs but no intermediate inputs, it is well-known that every specific factor gains from an increase in the price of the industry i in which it is employed and loses from an increase in any other commodity price. That is, its own industry is its true (and natural) friend and every other industry is its true (and natural) enemy. What proposition 2 adds for this model is that the mobile factor labour has a commodity which is a true (but not a natural) friend.

The first proposition states that every row of the W matrix must contain at least one positive and at least one negative element. The second proposition states that every column must have at least one positive and at least one negative element, subject to the proviso. These propositions hold for any number of commodities and any pattern of inter-industry input–output relations.

The first of these propositions implies that all such households have an incentive to seek to persuade the state to intervene in the economy to raise the price of their friendly commodity. There is a *universal incentive for rent-seeking*. For tradable commodities this leads to rent-seeking by means of border protection. The second of these propositions implies that, whenever any household or group of households seeks rents by means of changes in relative commodity prices, there exist other households whose real incomes will suffer and who will have, therefore, an incentive to oppose the change. In this sense there is *universal opposition* to the changes. Together, these propositions imply that there is a perpetual conflict between the claims being made on the government administering an economy. These two propositions are the foundations of the political economy of protection.

From proposition 1, if all households earning their incomes from one factor have identical expenditure shares, they will form a natural coalition to lobby for assistance to their friendly commodity. If they have distinct expenditure shares, a commodity which is a true friend to some households earning their incomes from a factor used in the industry may be a true enemy to other households earning their incomes solely from the same factor. In practice, however, we can ignore this aspect since the expenditure shares for the outputs of most other industries will be close to zero.

More importantly, there are many households which earn income from endowments of more than one factor. Diversification of income sources is important since it reduces the benefit to the household from an increase in the price of a particular commodity friend. For a household with more than one source of factor income, the proportionate change in its income when the output price for one industry which employs one of these factors changes is only $b_k \hat{u}_k$, where b_k is the fraction of income earned from this source. A true friend may cease to be a true friend as b_i decreases. Indeed, if all households owned an equal share of the national endowments of all factors, they would all lose from protection in a small open economy.

In the Very Short Run an increase in the price of a single commodity may lower the real income of households owning one specific factor in terms of both commodities, as Hosios (1982, p. 149) noted; that is, it may lower the utility of owners of one factor. If, as seems reasonable to assume, there is zero substitutability between intermediate inputs and primary inputs in the Very Short Run, the price of both primary inputs rises in proportion to the output price. Hence, both factors have their own commodity as their true friend. This result becomes important if factor-owners are myopic.

4 THE INEFFECTIVENESS OF PROTECTIVE POLICIES

Given the universality of incentives for rent-seeking, economists should be sceptical of arguments put forward, at times by other economists, for assistance to particular activities. In the last ten years or so these arguments have shifted away from the traditional grounds of infant industries, terms of trade and non-economic objectives. The arguments used nowadays in most countries to justify increases in industry assistance mostly relate to structural adjustment difficulties in the presence of alleged market failures. If there are distortions in domestic markets arising from, say, rigid or sticky factor prices, markets might fail to take account of the full social costs of adjustment. Or, if firms have less than perfect information, this might cause them in some instances to undervalue existing assets and to close plants and lay off workers prematurely and/or to underestimate the rates of return on prospective developments.

Such arguments too may be evaluated individually, but the Assignment Rule establishes a presumption that an intervention, if any is called for, will be based on variables directly related to the structural adjustment and not on imports. For example, Neary (1982) examined the adjustment process in a Jones-type specific factor model with the added complication of sticky real wages. Adjustments are in general desirable, but they may in some cases call for a temporary subsidy on labour employed in the adjusting activities which is reduced over time to zero. Similarly, Mussa (1982) examined a variant in which industry-specific capital can be converted into capital for the other industry instantaneously but only by the use of labour. If all prices are flexible and expectations are rational, the first-best policy is zero intervention. The government should intervene only to correct distortions which induce privately perceived costs or benefits of adjustment to diverge from the true social costs or benefits. Thus, to correct the distortion of the adjustment process created by the private discount rate exceeding the social discount rate, the appropriate optimal intervention is to subsidize capital at a rate equal to the difference between the social and private rates. To correct the distortion created by capital owners undervaluing the net benefits of capital movement, the appropriate optimal intervention is a subsidy on capital movements.

The Assignment Rule must be applied cautiously. The examples discussed so far assume, unrealistically, that the intervening government is omniscient and altruistic. Apart from the design of optimal policies for each problem, economists must be careful in the design of the problems themselves. Quite a large body of literature on the theory of the second best has, in my opinion, been based on assumptions as to the nature of the second-best situation that are inappropriate. I have commented above on the unacceptability of the constraints in the literature on 'non-economic objectives'. Similarly, the literature on price distortions and piecemeal policy-making is based on an unquestioning assumption that there are pre-existing taxes–subsidies on certain commodities which are unalterable, and the policy problem is to find

Peter J. Lloyd

the optimal (second-best) policies subject to these distortions acting as a constraint on the economy. All taxes and subsidies are alterable; if some are deemed unalterable it is because of the inability or unwillingness of legislators to offend income groups dependent upon these prior interventions.

Economists have sometimes played into the hands of such groups by accepting too readily that these difficulties should be treated as permanent restrictions on the instrument set. As a third example, many economists have constructed models of policy-making in economies with rigid or sticky prices. In some instances such inflexibility is due to convention or institutional restraints when wages are fixed by wage-fixing bodies. Such restraints should be subject to analysis and policy recommendations rather than treated as taboos.[5]

If an instrument that is not optimal is assigned to a problem, the theory of optimal interventions indicates that this choice imposes avoidable costs on some households in the economy. In this sense it is an ineffective assignment. It may also be an inefficacious assignment in the sense that it fails to achieve the stated objective (see Baldwin, 1982). Protection policy may be inefficacious because imports as the base of the explicit or implicit taxes are not closely related to the stated source of the problem. Thus, for example, in the context of the infant industry argument, Baldwin (1969) pointed out that border protection provides no incentive for a firm to acquire more knowledge than it otherwise would, even though the social gains from its doing so exceed the private gains. Similarly, a number of economists have recently emphasized that industry protection which was intended to protect jobs in declining industries such as textiles, clothing, footwear and steel has not prevented large declines in the aggregate employment levels of these industries (see for example Lawrence, 1985). Output protection does not ensure the protection of individual inputs.

Ultimately, the objection to distortionary trade policies is not that they impose costs on consumers and other income groups. Virtually any economic policy will adversely affect some group or groups in the economy. The objection is that they harm these groups unnecessarily because there are other policy options which achieve the objectives to a greater degree and reduce these costs. We need to emphasize that, aside from the terms-of-trade argument which is unimportant and/or infeasible for most countries, border protection is never the optimal instrument of government intervention.[5]

APPENDIX

Proof of Proposition 1

In the JBH model there are n zero-profit conditions for the n produced commodities:

$$A(u)u = p. \tag{A1}$$

Protection policy and the assignment rule   17

These equations are not sufficient to determine the $(n+1)$ factor prices. However, substitution among the remaining equations of equations (5) gives the additional equation

$$\frac{a_L}{a_{Ki}}\,(u)K = L \qquad K = (K_1, \ldots, K_n)'. \tag{A2}$$

Differentiating (A1) and (A2) and transferring the terms involving inputs of commodities to the right-hand side, we have

$$\gamma \hat{u}^* = \hat{p}^* \tag{A3}$$

or, in full,

$$
\begin{bmatrix}
\theta_{L1} & \theta_{K1} & 0 \\
\vdots & \vdots & \vdots \\
\theta_{Ln} & 0 & \theta_{kn} \\
-\sum_j \lambda_{Lj}\theta_{Lj}\,(\sigma_{LL}^j - \sigma_{LK}^j) & \lambda_{L1}\theta_{K1}(\sigma_{KK}^1 - \sigma_{KL}^1) & \lambda_{Ln}\theta_{Kn}(\sigma_{KK}^n - \sigma_{KL}^n)
\end{bmatrix}
$$

$$
\begin{bmatrix}
\hat{u}_1 \\ \vdots \\ \hat{u}_n \\ \hat{u}_{n+1}
\end{bmatrix}
=
\begin{bmatrix}
\hat{p}_1^* \\ \vdots \\ \hat{p}_n^* \\ S
\end{bmatrix}
$$

where

$$\hat{p}_i^* = (\hat{p}_i - \sum_{j \neq 1}\theta_{ji}\hat{p}_j)$$

and

$$S = - \sum_i \lambda_{Li} \sum_{j \neq 1}\theta_{ji}(\sigma_{jL}^i - \sigma_{jK}^i)\hat{p}_j$$

where γ is an $(n+1)\times(n+1)$ matrix; u^* is the vector of specific and non-specific primary input prices; $(\theta_{Li}, \theta_{ki})$ are the shares of capital and labour costs and θ_{ji} is the share of input commodity j in the total cost of producing commodity i; λ_{Li} is the proportion of the labour stock employed in industry i; and σ_{rs}^i is the partial Allen–Uzawa elasticity of substitution between two inputs, r and s, in industry i.

The output prices can be varied singly; that is, $\hat{p}_i \neq 0$ and $\hat{p}_j = 0$ for $j \neq i$. Equation (A3) can be solved for $U = (\hat{u}_k/\hat{p}_i)$. By summation and substitution, it can be shown that the sum of the elements of each row is unity.

However, this summation property follows directly from the observation that the kth equation in the solution to equations (A1) and (A2),

$$u_k = u_k(p, L, K), \tag{A4}$$

is homogeneous of degree $+1$ in p. That is,

Peter J. Lloyd

$$\sum_i \partial u_k / \partial p_i \, p_i = u_k$$

or

$$\sum_i (\hat{u}_k / \hat{p}_i) = 1. \tag{A5}$$

Similarly, in the Long Run version the solution of the n profit conditions yields n factor price equations, $u_k(p)$, which are homogeneous of degree $+1$ in p.

ϕ is also row-stochastic. Hence, for any household h earning its income from factor k,

$$\sum_j \hat{w}_k / \hat{p}_j - \sum_j \phi_{kj} = 1 - 1 = 0; \tag{A6}$$

that is, the rows of W sum to zero. Every row must have at least one negative and at least one positive element. Thus, the household earning its income from one factor must have at least one true friend. If any row of ϕ is replaced by the expenditure vector of any other household which also earns its income solely from this factor k but has different preferences and/or income, the same qualitative result applies.[6]

Proof of Proposition 2

For the ith commodity in equation (A3), we have

$$\sum_k \theta_{ki} \hat{w}_k = \hat{p}_i - \sum_{j \ne 1} \theta_{ji} \hat{p}_j \qquad j \ne i.$$

Setting $\hat{p}_i > 0$ and $p_j = 0$ for all $j \ne i$, this becomes

$$\sum_k \theta_{ki} \hat{w}_k = \hat{p}_i > 0. \tag{A7}$$

Since θ_{ki} are non-negative and less than unity, this implies that there exists at least one primary input g, for which $\hat{w}_g > \hat{p}_i$. The real income of this factor must increase in these circumstances. That is, for this factor commodity i is a true friend. Assume that the factor whose real income has increased is employed elsewhere in the economy, say, in the production of some commodity $h \ne i$. Then, from equation (A3), we have

$$\theta_{gh} \hat{w}_g + \sum_{k \ne g} \theta_{kh} \hat{w}_k = \hat{p}_h = 0. \tag{A8}$$

This implies that there is at least one other factor, f, for which $\hat{w}_f < 0$. The real income of this factor must decrease in these circumstances.

In the Jones (1975) model, all factors but one are specific to only one industry. However, in this model it turns out that all of the specific factors which are specific to industries other than industry i experience a decrease

Protection policy and the assignment rule   19

in nominal and real income. Inspection of equations (A7) and (A8) shows that the proof requires only that there be some factor in industry i whose nominal income increases ($\hat{w}_g > 0$) and which is employed elsewhere in the economy. In the Jones model this factor is labour, whose real income in the sense of the wage good commodity i need not increase ($0 < \hat{w}_L < \hat{p}_i$).

Q.E.D.

NOTES

1   Jones (1975, section III) actually considered a special case of the JBH model in which the intermediate inputs were pure intermediates that were traded but not produced locally.

2   These expressions ignore the redistribution of tariff proceeds to households. While some households in the economy must receive these revenues, it seems unreasonable to suppose that any group which coincides with a group of owners of one factor can claim them.

3   Bhagwati and Srinivasan (1969) endogenize the constraint by incorporating it into the objective function. This merely provides a maximization problem which validates the original solution: it does nothing to explain the underlying problem.

4   Ruffin and Jones (1977) use the terms W_{Li} to sign the change in utility for the mobile factor, labour, in the Jones model. Without the consumption effect, the change in real income of this factor in terms of a single wage good is ambiguous. They called this the 'Neoclassical ambiguity'. It is curious that Jones and Scheinkman (1977) did not use these terms to resolve the ambiguities of real income changes which remain when the analysis is conducted in terms of natural friends and enemies.

5   Johnson (1960) demonstrated that, if a maximum level of imports is added as a 'non-economic' constraint, the optimal policy is a tariff. Vandendorpe (1974) extended this to a uniform *ad valorem* tariff when the constraint is a maximum level of the value of imports for a set of commodities. In the JBH model this can be extended further to a uniform *ad valorem* tariff on all imports of final and intermediate goods when the constraint is a maximum for the net value of imports. However, this problem is subject to the objection of section 2 that this arbitrary constraint is not acceptable.

6   Two cases are of special interest. One is the $n \times n$ Heckscher–Ohlin model with no intermediate inputs. In this case equation (A3) reduces to $\theta\hat{u} = \hat{p}$ where θ is non-negative and row-stochastic (since the rows are the shares of the factors in the costs of producing commodities) but not column-stochastic. Hence, we have $\hat{u} = \theta^{-1}\hat{p}$. The elements of U can be identified as the corresponding elements of θ^{-1}. Since θ is row-stochastic, so its inverse, θ^{-1}. Consequently, $W = \theta^{-1} - \phi$ has rows with zero sums, as Cassing (1981) observed.

The second case is the Jones (1975) model, which is $n \times (n+1)$ but has no intermediate inputs. Again, the elements of U can be identified as elements of γ^{-1}.

However, if there are intermediate input flows, the elements of γ^{-1} are not elements of U, and γ is no longer a stochastic matrix. Since the proposition depends crucially on the homogeneity of the factor demand function, it applies more generally than the JBH model.

REFERENCES

Baldwin, R. E. (1969). 'The case against infant industry protection'. *Journal of Political Economy*, 77, 295–305.
Baldwin, R. E. (1982). *The Inefficacy of Trade Policy*. International Finance Section, 'Essays in International Finance', no. 150. Princeton: Princeton University Press.
Bhagwati, J. N. (1971). 'The generalized theory of distortions and welfare'. In J. N. Bhagwati et al. (eds), *Trade, Balance of Payments and Growth: Papers in Honor of Charles P. Kindleberger*. Amsterdam: North-Holland.
Bhagwati, J. N. and Srinivasan, T. N. (1969). 'Optimal intervention to achieve non-economic objectives'. *Review of Economic Studies*, 36, 27–38.
Bhagwati, J. N. and Srinivasan, T. N. (1976). 'Optimal trade policy and compensation under endogenous uncertainty: the phenomenon of market disruption'. *Journal of International Economics*, 6, 317–36.
Burgess, D. F. (1980). 'Protection, real wages, and the neoclassical ambiguity with interindustry flows'. *Journal of Political Economy*, 88, 783–802.
Cassing, J. (1981). 'On the relationship between commodity price changes and factor owners' real positions'. *Journal of Political Economy*, 89, 593–5.
Corden, W. M. (1957). 'Tariffs, Subsidies and the Terms of Trade'. *Economica*, n.s., 24, 235–42.
Ethier, W. J. (1984). 'Higher dimensional issues in trade theory'. In R. W. Jones and P. B. Kenen (eds), *Handbook of International Economics*, vol. 1. Amsterdam: North-Holland.
Hosios, A. J. (1982). 'Short-run and long-run equilibrium for a small open economy with intermediate goods'. *Journal of International Economics*, 13, 143–61.
Johnson, H. G. (1960). 'The costs of protection and the scientific tariff'. *Journal of Political Economy*, 68, 327–45.
Jones, R. W. (1971). 'A three-factor model in theory, trade and history'. In J. N. Bhagwati et al. (eds), *Trade, Balance of Payments and Growth: Papers in Honor of Charles P. Kindleberger*. Amsterdam: North-Holland.
Jones, R. W. (1975). 'Income distribution and effective protection in a multicommodity trade model'. *Journal of Economic Theory*, 11, 1–15.
Jones, R. W. and Scheinkman, J. A. (1977). 'The relevance of the two-sector production model in trade theory'. *Journal of Political Economy*, 85, 909–1035.
Khang, C. (1971). 'An isovalue locus involving intermediate goods and its application to the pure theory of international trade. *Journal of International Economics*, 1, 315–26.
Lawrence, R. Z. (1985). 'Industrial policy in the United States and Europe: economic principles and political practices'. Paper presented to the Fifteenth Pacific Trade and Development Conference, Tokyo, August 1985.
Mussa, M. (1982). 'Government policy and the adjustment process'. In J. N. Bhagwati (ed.), *Import Competition and Response*. Chicago: University of Chicago Press.
Neary, J. P. (1982). 'Intersectoral capital mobility, wage stickiness, and the case for adjustment assistance'. In J. N. Bhagwati (ed.), *Import Competition and Response*. Chicago: University of Chicago Press.
Ruffin, R. and Jones, R. W. (1977). 'Protection and real wages: the neoclassical ambiguity'. *Journal of Economic Theory*, 14, 337–48.
Stolper, W. and Samuelson, P. A. (1941). 'Protection and real wages'. *Review of Economic Studies*, 9, 58–73.

Tan, A. H. H. (1971). 'Optimal trade policies and non-economic objectives in models involving imported materials, inter-industry flows and non-traded goods'. *Review of Economic Studies*, 36, 105–11.

Vandendorpe, A. L. (1974). 'On the theory of non-economic objectives in open economies'. *Journal of International Economics*, 4, 15–24.

Young, L. (1980). 'Optimal revenue-rising trade restrictions under uncertainty'. *Journal of International Economics*, 10, 425–40.

EUROPEAN
ECONOMIC
REVIEW

ELSEVIER   European Economic Review 41 (1997) 1569–1587

Conflict generating product price changes: The imputed output approach

P.J. Lloyd [a], A.G. Schweinberger [b,*]

[a] *Department of Economics, The University of Melbourne, Melbourne, Australia*
[b] *Faculty of Economics and Statistics, The University of Konstanz, Postfach 5560, D-78434, Konstanz, Germany*

Received 15 November 1994; revised 15 April 1996

Abstract

A novel approach to the generalisation of the conflict generating effects of product price changes on household incomes and utilities is developed. It is based upon the concepts of household production of goods and complementarities in production between households. Economy outputs are imputed to households. The imputed household outputs may be positive or negative. Households have an incentive to supply factors to firms if and only if at least one imputed output is negative. It is shown that households which are complementary in production are competitive in distribution. The results are generalised to economies with increasing returns to scale industries.

JEL classification: F11; F12; F13

Keywords: Price changes; Conflict generation; Distribution; Increasing returns to scale

1. Introduction

The sense in which product price changes are conflict generating between households is undoubtedly one of the most important and fundamental issues in

---

* Corresponding author. Tel.: (+49) 7531-882632; Fax: (+49) 7531-883560.

1570   *P.J. Lloyd, A.G. Schweinberger / European Economic Review 41 (1997) 1569–1587*

the whole of economics. Yet to date sharp answers to this question are elusive unless very restrictive assumptions are made.

The standard result is the Stolper–Samuelson theorem (see Stolper and Samuelson, 1941). In a recent survey Jones (1992) appraised the theorem in the following extraordinary terms: "The word seminal fails to do justice to the prolonged effect this article was to have both, for the field of international economics and, more broadly, for the acceptance of simple general equilibrium models of analysis in trade, public finance and other realms of economics".

The popularity of the theorem derives from its key message: product price changes are necessarily conflict generating between factor owners. It is widely regarded as the foundation stone of political economy approaches.

However it is now generally recognised that the Stolper–Samuelson theorem has two major shortcomings:

(a) Generalisations to more than two dimensions generally have not yielded sharp results, unless very restrictive assumptions on the technology are made (see e.g. Kemp and Wegge (1969), Chipman (1969), Ethier (1984) and the more recent extensions by Mitra and Jones (1992) and Jones and Mitra (1995)).

(b) The theorem is concerned with the effect of product price changes on factor prices and household utilities, having assumed that each household only owns one factor (for a partial exception see Woodland (1974)). Given that households are endowed with more than one factor this is a serious limitation.

In the light of these shortcomings it is doubtful that the Stolper–Samuelson theorem can or should be regarded as the foundation stone of modern political economy approaches.

Another model which is popular in political economy approaches is the so called specific factor model. This model features some interesting conflict generating properties. However it is by no means clear that this model yields a better basis for political economy approaches. There are two reasons for this:

(a) the sharpness of its conclusions is lost even if only one additional mobile factor is introduced, and

(b) it too is restricted to households which are endowed with only one factor.

The imputed output approach has been developed to overcome these difficulties. Its key (and apparently novel) ideas are:

Given the product prices, production functions and household endowments with factors an imputed equilibrium is constructed. A key assumption in this construction is that all households know the production functions for all goods. In this imputed (household production) equilibrium economy outputs are imputed to the various households. These imputed outputs may be positive or negative.

According to the sign pattern of imputed outputs, households can be defined to have a comparative advantage or disadvantage in the *production* of various goods. The sign pattern of the imputed outputs of a household is directly related to the specialisation pattern of production if households engage in 'cottage production', i.e., do not supply factors to firms (at the given prices). If and only if the imputed

P.J. Lloyd, A.G. Schweinberger / European Economic Review 41 (1997) 1569-1587   1571

outputs of at least some goods are negative, there exists an incentive for a household to supply factors to firms.

To derive the pattern of outputs *imputed* to households and thus make our approach operational, we only need to know the input coefficient matrix of the economy and the factor endowments of households.

These concepts and results of the imputed output approach are developed in Section 2. The main message of Section 2 is simple and general: households which are complementary in production are competitive in distribution. Households are said to be complementary in production if they specialise in the imputed equilibrium in a different set of goods.

In Section 3 we show how the imputed output approach can be applied to a generalisation of the standard Stolper–Samuelson theorem to any finite and equal dimensions of goods and factors. By a generalisation of the Stolper–Samuelson theorem we mean a generalised relationship between changes in goods and factor prices. In this case a unique association between households and factors is assumed. What is of special interest in Section 3 is that the factor intensity conditions (which are generally associated with the factor share matrix approach) are shown to be a special case of household comparative advantage in production. On the various concepts of factor intensity conditions, see Chipman (1969), Kemp and Wegge (1969), Jones et al. (1993), Mitra and Jones (1992), and Jones and Mitra (1995).

In the concluding Section 4 we turn our attention to an economy with increasing returns to scale. The incentive to set up specialised production agents is, needless to say, much stronger in this case. As will be shown the conflict generating potential of product price changes increases accordingly. This kind of reasoning is also the driving force behind the achievement of what is often referred to as gains from trade in the new theory of trade but could also be termed gains from economic integration (see e.g. Krugman, 1979). [1]

By imputing economy outputs to households at given product prices we shall make use of a hypothetical decomposition of an equilibrium of a multihousehold small open economy. This decomposition is not directly related to the literature on factor price equalisation. In this literature one generally assumes identical, homothetic preferences and endogenous goods prices. Also, of course, this literature is not concerned with the derivation of conditions under which exogenous product price changes are conflict generating. [2]

---

[1] Krugman (1979) states that the effect of trade is the same as the effect of migration. This holds under restrictive assumptions.

[2] The multicountry analogue of a small open economy with many households is a set of small countries with multinational firms. In this case factor prices are equalised, between these countries even if there is no trade between them. In the literature on factor price equalisation on the other hand it is the free goods trade between the countries which brings about factor price equalisation.

1572   *P.J. Lloyd, A.G. Schweinberger / European Economic Review 41 (1997) 1569–1587*

2. The imputed output approach

We assume a small open multihousehold economy in which all goods are freely traded at fixed world market prices. It satisfies all the standard properties. [3] All factors are in fixed supply. Each household is endowed with the vector v^h of primary factors of production. Production functions of all goods are common knowledge. The number of goods is assumed equal to the number of factors in Sections 2 and 3. It will be explained in Section 4 how this assumption can be relaxed.

In standard trade theory it is generally assumed that households do not engage in production. They sell their factors to specialised production agents called firms. To date it seems that this assumption has not been examined. As we shall see, this assumption provides the key to a better understanding of the condition under which product price changes are conflict generating.

Every household has the choice of engaging in household (or cottage) production or supplying factors to firms. If it chooses the former it can trade its outputs in world markets without the mediation of firms. [4]

We now proceed to the definition of imputed outputs. To this end we make use of the following notation:

v = the vector of economy endowments,

v^h = the vector of the endowments of household h,

p = the vector of the exogenous product prices,

$w(p, v)$ = the vector of factor prices (rentals),

$A(w)$ = the input coefficient matrix of the economy (in the integrated equilibrium). $A(w)$ is square and nonsingular;

y = the output vector of the economy.

In a competitive equilibrium with profit maximising firms, y and w depend in general on p and v. $A(w)$ is the input coefficient matrix chosen by firms. We now make use of a hypothetical decomposition of the equilibrium outputs of the economy. In this context the following assumption is important.

Assumption 1.   Households supply factors of production to firms if and only if it improves their real income.

The output vector *imputed* to household h, $\tilde{y}^h$, is defined by

$$\tilde{y}^h = A^{-1}(w)v^h. \tag{1}$$

The vector $\tilde{y}^h$ may contain negative as well as positive elements. It will contain negative elements if and only if the vector v^h does not lie within the cone spanned

---

[3] Such as perfect competition in all goods and factor markets and constant returns to scale production functions (see e.g. Dixit and Norman, 1980).

[4] Below we shall derive conditions under which households have an incentive to supply factors to firms.

P.J. Lloyd, A.G. Schweinberger / European Economic Review 41 (1997) 1569–1587   1573

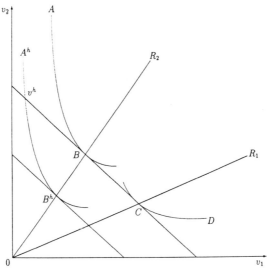

Fig. 1.

by the vectors of $A(w)$, the input coefficient matrix for the production sector of the economy. That is, $\bar{y}^h$ will contain negative elements if v^h does not lie within the diversification cone.

Clearly, the definition stated as expression (1), is consistent in the following sense:

$$y = \sum_h \bar{y}^h = A^{-1}(w)v.$$ (2)

From expressions (1) and (2) it follows that no knowledge of the rates of changes of factor prices with respect to commodity prices is required to calculate the outputs imputed to the households. As we shall show below a knowledge of the sign pattern of imputed outputs of different households is sufficient to make general predictions regarding the conflict generating effects of product price changes.

We now proceed to state and prove the following Lemma.

Lemma. A household supplies factors of production to firms if and only if at least one of the imputed outputs is negative.

Proof. To prove the Lemma we first make use of a diagrammatic approach and then present a formal mathematical proof. [5] In Fig. 1, R_2OR_1 represents the

---

[5] We are heavily indebted to a referee for suggesting this. Of course he is not responsible for any errors.

1574   *P.J. Lloyd, A.G. Schweinberger / European Economic Review 41 (1997) 1569–1587*

diversification cone of the economy, *ABCD* an isorevenue curve. The prices of the factors v_1 and v_2 are given by the slope of the straight line through B and C.

Assume that there exists a household h with factor endowments v^h. Clearly the endowments of this household lie outside the diversification cone. The imputed output of good 2 will be positive, the imputed output of good 1 negative. If this household chose to engage in cottage production, it could attain only a lower isorevenue curve, A^h. It would suffer a welfare loss. The reason for this is that the autarkic shadow prices, the slope of A^h at v^h, are different from the 'social opportunity costs' given by the slope of the line through BC. In cottage production the household foregoes the gains from implicit factor trade with other households. As shown in the diagram, the welfare gain of the household from supplying its factors to firms in terms of factor v_1 or v_2 at the social opportunity costs is readily measurable.

The choice problem of the household can be formalised as follows:

$$\max_{v_{1j},\ldots,v_{nj}} \sum_j f_j(v_{1j},\ldots,v_{nj})$$

s.t.

$$\sum_j \sum_i w_i v_{ij} = \sum_i w_i v_i^h \text{ and } v_{1j},\ldots,v_{nj} \geq 0$$

where: $f_j(\cdot)$ stand for the constant returns to scale, *value* production functions and i is the factor and j the goods index. v_i^h stands for the endowment of household h with factor i.

If the endowments of household h lie within the diversification cone the additional constraints

$$\sum_j v_{ij} = v_i^h \quad \forall_i,$$

are not binding. If v^h lies outside the diversification cone these additional constraints are binding and therefore reduce the value of the objective function. This completes the proof of the Lemma.   Q.E.D.

In the derivation and proof of the main results of the paper the following Definition will be useful.

Definition 1. A household is said to have a comparative advantage (disadvantage) in the *production* of a set of goods if the imputed outputs of these goods are positive (negative).

Our use of the term 'comparative advantage' differs from the standard use for the economy. A household's imputed output vector $\tilde{y}^h$ can be decomposed into $\tilde{y}_1^h$ and $\tilde{y}_2^h$ where all the elements of $\tilde{y}_1^h$ are positive and all the elements of $\tilde{y}_2^h$ negative. If this household chose not to supply factors to firms it would specialise in the production of the goods with positive imputed outputs. Conversely, if in an equilibrium with only household (cottage) production it specialises in the production of a subset of goods, the outputs of these goods in the *imputed* household production equilibrium are positive too. For a proof, see Appendix A. It is important to understand the relationship between the concept of household comparative advantage in production (see Definition 1) and household comparative advantage in imputed trade. From the preceding definitions we know that: $p_1(x_1^h - \tilde{y}_1^h) + p_2 (x_2^h - \tilde{y}_2^h) = 0$, where x_1^h and x_2^h stand for the consumption vector of household h of the sets of goods 1 and 2 respectively. It follows that if household h has a comparative advantage in the *production* of good 1 and a comparative disadvantage in the *production* of good 2, then $p_2(x_2^h - y_2^h) > 0$ and $p_1(x_1^h - y_1^h) < 0$, i.e.: this household has a comparative advantage in the imputed *trade* of good 1 and a comparative disadvantage in the imputed *trade* of good 2. However the converse does not hold. Generally no conclusions can be drawn about the household pattern of comparative advantage in production from the pattern of comparative advantage in imputed trade.

To focus on essentials Definition 1 contains what may be termed a definition of the physical comparative advantage in production of a household. A more general definition would be in terms of the *value* of the imputed outputs. None of the results of the paper are affected if the 'physical' definition is replaced by the 'value' definition.

Definition 2.   Any two households are said to be *complementary* in production if and only if the intersection of the goods in which they have a comparative advantage in production is empty.

In an advanced economy it appears that labour skills are highly differentiated. The same applies to nonhuman factors of production. Given this high degree of differentiation in the factors of production, many household types exist which are complementary in production as described in Definition 2.

The main ideas and concepts of the analysis so far may be explained conveniently by means of Fig. 2.

In Fig. 2 we show three goods, three factors and any finite number of households (identified by their endowments). The triangle is borrowed and adapted from Leamer (1987). In our case the triangle is applied to individual households rather than countries (see footnote 2 for the multicountry analogue). It is used to represent graphically in two-dimensional space the relative proportions of the three factors used in the production of goods and also the relative endowments of households with these factors. It is, of course, the unit simplex. The points 1, 2 and 3 stand for the appropriately normalised input coefficient vectors of goods 1, 2 and 3 respectively (the diversification cone of the economy). The vector k is the endowment vector of the economy.

All the endowment vectors of households lie outside the diversification cone. In addition to the diversification cone we have cones of complete or incomplete

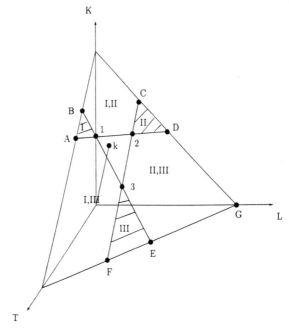

Fig. 2.

specialisation. The cones of complete specialisation are the shaded areas I, II and III. Cones of incomplete specialisation are denoted by I, II; I, III and II, III. If the endowment of a household lies strictly within I the household specialises in the production of good 1. In the imputed equilibrium its outputs of goods 2 and 3 are negative. All households whose endowments lie within I are complementary in production with all households whose endowments lie within II, III. The latter households have a comparative advantage in the production of goods 2 and 3, whilst the former households have a comparative advantage in the production of good 1.

It should be noted that according to Fig. 2 there is no one to one association between goods and factors or factors and households. In the standard generalisations of the Stolper–Samuelson theorem one is precisely looking for conditions under which one good can be uniquely associated with one factor (by some factor intensity condition). This approach appears far too narrow if one is interested in predicting the effect of product price changes on household incomes or utilities. Indeed Fig. 2 shows that the approach is even too narrow if the aim is to establish a unique relationship between goods and factors (for example, good 1, according to Fig. 2, is intensive neither in the usage of factor K nor factor T alone).

We are now in a position to state and prove our main theorem.

Theorem 1.   *Assume two households are complementary in production, according to Definition 2. Then ceteris paribus increases in the prices of goods in which either household has a comparative advantage in production are conflict generating in terms of nominal income changes.*

Proof.   Let $g^h = v^h w(p, v)$ stand for the income function of household h. To prove Theorem 1 we first prove that $g_p^h = \tilde{y}^h$. From expression (1) and the fact that $A^{-1}(w) = w_p$ we can write (making use of row vectors) [6]

$$\tilde{y}^{hT} = v^{hT} A^{-1}(w) = v^{hT} w_p(p,v) = g_p^{hT}. \tag{3}$$

Hence

$$dg^h = \tilde{y}^{hT} dp. \tag{4}$$

Assume households 1 and 2 are complementary in production and household 1 has a comparative advantage in the production of a set of goods S_1 and household 2 in a set of goods S_2 and $S_1 \cap S_2$ is empty. Then, if all the prices of the set of goods S_1 rise, $dg^1 > 0$ and $dg^2 < 0$. The converse holds if the prices of the set of goods S_2 rise.   Q.E.D.

Theorem 1 is concerned with conflict generation in terms of nominal income changes of households.

The imputed output approach can also be applied to characterising conflict generating product prices changes in terms of real income and utility changes. This is of considerable interest because of the relationship to the strong version of the Stolper–Samuelson theorem.

Theorem 2.   *Let any two households (say households 1 and 2) be complementary in production, see definition 2. Assume that the prices of all the goods in which household 1 has a comparative advantage in production rise. Then the increase in the nominal income of household 1 is more than proportionate to the smallest price increase. The real income of the household 2 falls.*

Proof.   From the linear homogeneity of the household income functions in prices:

$$g^h = \sum_j \frac{\partial g^h}{\partial p_j} p_j, \quad h = 1, 2, \tag{5}$$

---

[6] We could also define a national product or revenue function $g = g(p, v)$. this function is differentiable under standard assumptions if the number of factors does not fall short of the number of goods and the Jacobian determinant of the cost functions is nonvanishing. In this case we obtain from well known symmetry properties: $g_{pv} = y_v = g_{vp} = w_p = A^{-1}(w)$.

1578   *P.J. Lloyd, A.G. Schweinberger / European Economic Review 41 (1997) 1569–1587*

Rewriting expression (5) we have

$$1 = \sum_j \frac{\partial \log g^1}{\partial \log p_j} .$$
(6)

Assume that household 1 has a comparative advantage in the production of goods S_1 and household 2 in the production of goods S_2 and $S_1 \cap S_2$ is empty. Then from expressions (3) and (6):

$$\sum_{j \in S_1} \frac{\partial \log g^1}{\partial \log p_j} > 1 \quad \text{and} \quad \frac{\partial \log g^2}{\partial \log p_j} < 0, \quad j \in S_1.$$
(7)

Also,

$$d \log g^1 = \sum_{j \in S_1} \frac{\partial \log g^1}{\partial \log p_j} d \log p_j \quad \text{and} \quad d \log g^2 = \sum_{j \in S_1} \frac{\partial \log g^2}{\partial \log p_j} d \log p_j$$
(8)

Dividing $d \log g^1$ by the smallest $d \log p_j$, $j \in S_1$ and taking into account expression (7), Theorem 2 follows.   Q.E.D.

Theorem 2 has direct implications for the generalisation of the strong version of the Stolper–Samuelson theorem. They are stated in the following Corollary.

Corollary (to Theorem 2).   *Let the prices of all the goods in which household 1 has comparative advantage increase equiproportionately. Then the real income of household 1 rises and the real income of household 2 falls.*

Traditionally, the Stolper–Samuelson theorem focusses on an even more special case. Each household has a comparative advantage in the production of one and only one good. Then Theorem 2 and the Corollary may be interpreted as direct generalisations of the strong version of the Stolper–Samuelson theorem. This is taken up in following Section 3.

To conclude Section 2 note that there exists a large literature on the relationship between the terms of trade and welfare. Making use of the household trading pattern in the imputed equilibrium and induced preference theory (see Rader, 1978) it is easy to show that, for example, the welfare of a household increases if the value of imputed imports rises at the new prices and only if the value of imputed imports rises at the old prices. Postulating the relevant differences in the imputed trading pattern of households one could derive conditions for conflict generating product price changes. This alternative approach is certainly useful for

P.J. Lloyd, A.G. Schweinberger / European Economic Review 41 (1997) 1569–1587   1579

certain purposes but it has one major drawback: a detailed knowledge of demand patterns is necessary. [7]

Finally it should be stressed that though household income functions have been used in the proofs of Theorems 1 and 2, a knowledge of household income functions is not necessary to calculate imputed outputs and therefore make the imputed output approach operational. Just as indirect utility functions of households are useful in the efficient derivation of demand functions of households, household income functions are useful in the derivation of imputed output functions. As is well known, indirect utility functions are derived by substituting demand functions in the direct utility function, however in applications they have proved to be very useful in the derivation of demand functions. The same applies to the household income and imputed output functions. To test the theory one may start by assuming special forms of household income functions and then derive special forms of imputed output functions by differentiation.

3. Application to the generalisation of the Stolper–Samuelson theorem

For more than fifty years economists have tried to generalise the celebrated Stolper and Samuelson (1941) theorem by expanding the number of factors and goods in order to make it more applicable to the derivation of policy prescriptions. The difficulties encountered in this endeavour are probably best reflected in the work of Chipman (1969) and Kemp and Wegge (1969). Generalising the theorem from three factors and goods to four factors and goods they faced insurmountable problems.

The general wisdom now is that precise links between goods and factor price changes are obtainable in higher dimensions only if a strong structure is imposed upon technology (see Jones and Mitra, 1995). To date, the focus in all the recent work, see Jones et al. (1993), is on comparisons of factor intensities between sectors.

In Jones and Mitra (1995), for example, factor intensities between sectors are compared making use of a benchmark share rib of factor shares. Jones and Mitra obtain results, i.e. a generalisation of the strong version of the Stolper–Samuelson theorem, if declining share ribs are flatter than the benchmark case.

This approach and its results are undoubtedly of considerable interest. They should be regarded as a further development of the factor share matrix approach. The new economic insight of our approach is that the gains from the implicit

---

[7] By contrast in our approach household types are distinguished only by their factor endowments not by their preferences. In fact all the results hold independently of demand. Also note that in part of the received literature on conflict generating product prices the terminology of 'friends and enemies' between households is established; see e.g. Jones and Scheinkman (1977), Ethier (1984) or Lloyd and Schweinberger (1988). In stating our Theorems 1 and 2 we could have made use of this terminology.

factor trade, see the Lemma in Section 2, as reflected in negative imputed outputs, are directly related to the link between factor and product price changes. This insight should have real world relevance because in the modern world of highly specialised factors and goods it seems very plausible that the factor endowment vectors of many households lie outside the diversification cone of the economy.

Which general observations can be made regarding the relationship between the imputed output approach and the strong version of the Stolper–Samuelson results?

Firstly, the information (knowledge of the inverse of the input coefficient matrix) that makes the imputed output approach useful is strong enough also to make precise predictions of factor reward changes based on output price changes.

Secondly, a principal observation about generalized Stolper–Samuelson results (see e.g. Jones and Mitra, 1995) is that they do not need precise quantitative information about the inverse of the input coefficient matrix. The qualitative information that, for example, the inverse of the input coefficient matrix has positive diagonal and negative offdiagonal entries is sufficient to derive Stolper–Samuelson type results. However, this kind of qualitative information is in general not sufficient to make predictions about changes in the real incomes of households due to product price changes. To achieve that we have to make use of Theorem 2. This follows because households are assumed to be endowed with many factors. [8]

We now proceed to show how the imputed output approach can be used to shed light on the strong version of the Stolper–Samuelson theorem. By the strong version of the Stolper–Samuelson theorem we mean a relationship between goods and factor price changes such that a ceteris paribus increase in the price of any one good results in an increase in the real income accruing to the factor associated with that good by some factor intensity condition and a decrease in the real income of all other factors.

Turning to Fig. 3, a necessary and sufficient condition for the strong version of the Stolper–Samuelson theorem to hold with respect to all goods and factors is that the complete specialisation comes, I, II, and III (the shaded areas) contain the vertices of the unit simplex. As proven before, if the endowment vectors of households 1, 2 and 3 lie within the specialisation cones I, II and III respectively, all three households are complementary in production. The output of good 1 imputed to household 1 is positive and the imputed outputs of the other goods are negative. Good 1 is clearly the capital, good 2 land and good 3 labour intensive. In this case the solution of

$$A(w)\,\tilde{y}^h = v^h \quad \forall h$$

yields a pattern of imputed outputs which from Theorem 2 and the Corollary

---

[8] We are heavily indebted to an unknown referee for clarification in this context.

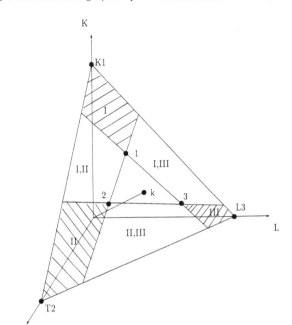

Fig. 3.

implies the strong version of the Stolper–Samuelson theorem. It is easy to see that this can be generalised to any finite dimensions.

Assume that households are endowed only with either capital or land or labour, i.e.: only one factor of production. Then the strong version of the Stolper–Samuelson theorem holds if and only if there exists an ordering of factors and goods such that all the signed cofactors associated with diagonal elements of $|A|$ are of the same sign as $|A|$ and all the other signed cofactors of a different sign.

These sign conditions are necessary and sufficient for the existence of a household pattern of comparative advantage in production such that each household whose endowments lie within the specialisation cone, has a comparative advantage in the production of one and only one good and a comparative disadvantage in the production of all the other goods.

This household pattern of comparative advantage in the production of goods is equivalent to the Kemp–Wegge condition, see Kemp and Wegge (1969). In fact, the Kemp–Wegge restrictions on technology imply that the vertices are within the complete specialisation cones as shown in Fig. 3. But this standard 3×3 result is clearly a very special case. Theorem 2 and the Corollary generalise this result to any finite (and equal) number of goods, factors and households (which are endowed with more than one factor of production). In fact, see Section 4, the imputed output approach can also be applied if the number of goods and factors is unequal as well as in the presence of increasing returns to scale in production.

1582   *P.J. Lloyd, A.G. Schweinberger / European Economic Review 41 (1997) 1569–1587*

4. Increasing returns to scale

The driving assumption of Section 2 was that households supply factors to firms if and only if this leads to income gains. Section 2, by postulating the existence of constant returns to scale production functions in all industries, neglects an important reason for the existence of production agents in the real world: increasing returns to scale. The existence of increasing returns to scale and the associated gains from integration of production structures of countries has been one of the main motivations for the new trade theory. However, rather surprisingly, the new trade theory has paid little attention to the issue of the personal distribution of income and the conditions under which product prices are conflict generating. [9] In what follows we assume a general equilibrium production model in which the increasing returns to scale are external to firms but internal to the industry, see e.g. Helpman (1984). In this case increasing returns to scale are consistent with average cost pricing and perfect competition.

An important feature of economies with increasing returns and/or imperfect competition, which in trade theory apparently only recently has been noted, see Kemp and Schweinberger (1991), is that in such economies agents are guided by price *and* quantity signals. [10] With average cost pricing, see e.g. Kemp and Negishi (1970), we obtain the following income function for household h:

$$g^h = v^h w(p, y, v) \tag{9}$$

where $w(p, y, v)$ the factor price (rental) functions are obtained from

$$\min_{w} wv \quad \text{s.t.} \quad f^j(w, y) \geq p_j \ \forall j, \quad w \geq 0,$$

where $f^j(\cdot)$ denotes the per unit cost function for good j.

Summing the expressions (9) over all the households:

$$vw(p, y, v) \equiv \sum_h v^h w(p, y, v). \tag{10}$$

As in Section 2 imputed outputs can be derived by solving $\tilde{y}^h A(w, y) = v^h$ for

---

[9] Another important policy problem which is generally bypassed is the existence of involuntary unemployment.

[10] A number of other well-known problems should be faced. The value of production is not maximised at given prices, the diversification cone depends also upon economy outputs and outputs are generally nonunique. However, due to lack of space and because these problems are not central to our key aim they are not considered.

each household or by partial differentiation of the household income function with respect to p:

$$vw_p(\cdot) \equiv \sum_h v^h w_p(\cdot) \tag{11}$$

or

$$y = \sum_h \tilde{y}^h. \tag{12}$$

The imputed output vectors again may contain positive as well as negative elements. However, in contrast to Section 2, there is no compelling reason that the imputed output vector of each household contains at least one negative element. This is because households may gain by supplying factors to firms because of increasing returns to scale. Does this then reduce the potential for conflict generation through price changes? If prices change, outputs change and hence quantity signals. The latter play an important part in the income generation of any household, see Eq. (9). It is therefore imperative to derive not only imputed outputs as in Section 2 but also *imputed externality effects* (*associated with quantity signals*). Differentiating Eq. (10) partially with respect to y we have

$$vw_y = \sum_h v^h w_y. \tag{13}$$

The LHS of expression (13) can readily be seen to be the vector of *economy marginal costs*. It is equal to the sum of the households or imputed marginal cost. From the assumption of perfect competition in factor market and cost minimisation we know (see e.g. Markusen and Schweinberger, 1990) that

$$vw_y \, dy = 0. \tag{14}$$

Hence

$$\sum_h \lambda^h dy = 0, \tag{15}$$

where dy denotes the vector of output changes associated with the given changes in product prices and λ^h the vector of economy marginal costs imputed to household h.

From the definition of the household income function it therefore follows that

$$dg^h = \tilde{y}^h dp + \lambda^h dy. \tag{16}$$

Expression (16) highlights that with increasing returns to scale which are external to firms but internal to the industry, changes in goods prices per se may not be conflict generating as between two households because the signs of their imputed outputs are the same; however by changing the outputs, the quantity signals, changes in goods prices may be conflict generating. Of course, the converse may also apply.

Eq. (15) captures the conflict generating potential of changes in outputs. It gives rise to the following Theorem 3.

Theorem 3.   The externality effects associated with increasing returns to scale per se are conflict generating, i.e., there exist at least two households such that $\lambda^h dy$ lie in different halfspaces.

Proof.   Theorem 3 follows directly from Eq. (15).   Q.E.D.

To understand the meaning of Theorem 3 it is useful to assume that all households are on the same side of the market for all goods and their endowments lie within the diversification cone (see Weymark, 1979). In this extreme case there are no incentives to set up firms within the framework of Section 2. However, with increasing returns to scale such incentives clearly exist. Product price changes per se are not conflict generating in this special case, however product price changes imply output changes and as can be seen from Theorem 3, the latter per se are conflict generating between at least two households. [11]

Throughout the paper we have assumed that the numbers of goods and factors are equal. This considerably facilitated the exposition. However, the imputed output approach can also be applied to economies with unequal numbers of factors and goods.

Clearly, the definition of imputed outputs given in expression (1) cannot be used if the number of factors is in excess of the number of goods. Households may be endowed with more factors than produced goods. If this is the case, the imputed output approach has to make use of the production equilibrium of each household in the disintegrated (cottage production) equilibrium to determine the pattern of specialisation of production. To generalise Theorem 1 to this case note that no knowledge of the actual imputed outputs but only their sign pattern is required.

If the number of factors owned by each household is not in excess of the number of produced goods, imputed outputs can be calculated from expression (1) with appropriate interpretation of the matrix $A(w)$. The assumption that each household is endowed at most with as many factors as there are produced goods in the integrated equilibrium seems a very reasonable one.

If the number of produced goods is in excess of the number of factors there is an indeterminacy with regard to imputed outputs and patterns of specialisation in household production. At given international prices the production pattern in terms of imputed outputs may be nonunique. However, this problem can be overcome. We know that the solution sets are convex. For any household the optimal patterns of specialisation in production are therefore connected. The term comparative

---

[11] The imputed output effects associated with changes in product prices per se may be reinforced or counteracted by the imputed externality effects (effects associated with changes in quantity signals).

advantage in production of a household is now redefined to include all possible connected patterns of specialisation in production which are consistent with the same value of household income. Therefore, subject to this small reinterpretation and the assumptions mentioned above, the imputed output approach can be applied to economies with *any* finite number of goods and factors.

In conclusion it should be stressed that many other extensions and applications of the imputed output approach are possible. The most obvious and direct extension is the modelling of multinational firms (see footnote 2). The same holds with regard to the extension to variable factor supplies. It is also relatively straightforward to generalise the imputed output approach to factor unemployment and/or imperfect competition provided that firms minimise costs and factor markets are perfectly competitive. Under imperfect competition there is, of course, the additional challenge of distinguishing between households which obtain income from the selling of factors and others which are entitled to residual income (pure profits). Last but not least a very interesting and promising area of application is the analysis of conflict generation through changes in the prices of private goods in economies with pure or impure public goods and/or in economies with environmental problems (production, consumption externalities).

Acknowledgements

We would like to thank Murray Kemp and Ron Jones for helpful comments on a previous draft. Special thanks are due to two anonymous referees and the Editor, Professor Honkapohja, for many detailed and substantial comments which resulted in considerable improvements. A preliminary version of this paper was presented by one of the authors at a workshop in International Economics at the University of Konstanz in June 1992. We would like to record our gratitude for all the comments received from participants. Of course, the usual caveat applies.

Appendix A

The household production decisions in the case of cottage production can be described by means of application of a so called optimisation theorem (see Woodland, 1982, p. 53). The following two constrained optimisation problems are equivalent:

$$\max_{y^h} py^h \quad \text{subject to} \quad A(w)\,y^h \le v^h; \quad y^h \ge 0, \tag{A.1}$$

and

$$\min_{w} wv^h \quad \text{subject to} \quad f(w) \ge p; \quad w \ge 0, \tag{A.2}$$

where $f(w)$ denote the per unit cost functions and all the other symbols are explained in the text.

Formulating the two problems as Lagrangean functions we have:

$$L^1\left(y^h, \gamma_1^T\right) = py^h - \gamma_1^T\left[A(w)y^h - v^h\right] \tag{A.3}$$

and

$$L^2\left(w, \gamma_2^T\right) = wv^h - \gamma_2^T\left[f(w) - p\right], \tag{A.4}$$

where γ_1 stands for the vector of Lagrangean multipliers associated with the constraints of the first problem and $\gamma_1 = w$, and γ_2 stands for the vector of Lagrangean multipliers associated with the constraints of the second problem and $\gamma_2 = y^h$.

Making use of Kuhn–Tucker theory we obtain

$$\frac{\partial L^1}{\partial y^h} = p - \gamma_1^T A(w) \leq 0, \tag{A.5}$$

$$\frac{\partial L^1}{\partial \gamma_1^T} = \left[A(w)y^h - v^h\right] \geq 0, \tag{A.6}$$

$$\frac{\partial L^2}{\partial w} = v^h - \gamma_2^T A(w) \geq 0, \tag{A.7}$$

$$\frac{\partial L^2}{\partial \gamma_2^T} = -\left[f(w) - p\right] \leq 0. \tag{A.8}$$

Noting that $\gamma_1 = w$ and $\gamma_2 = y^h$ it is obvious that the two constrained optimisation problems are equivalent.

In the imputed as well as in the equilibrium with cottage production factor prices are treated parametrically. There is only one difference: in the imputed equilibrium the outputs of some but not all goods may be negative. It follows from the inequalities (A.5) and (A.8) that the specialisation pattern of production is the same in the equilibrium with cottage production and in the imputed equilibrium. From expressions (A.5) and (A.8) the specialisation pattern of production is independent of the domain of definition of the maximising variables y^h. The specialisation pattern of production is determined by technology, the factor endowments and the given prices of goods. In the imputed equilibrium the factor prices, w, are, from the household point of view, exogenous. The per unit costs of production of the goods which are not produced in the equilibrium with cottage production are still higher than prices, however this is consistent with the maximisation of household income because the outputs of these goods are negative, releasing resources for the production of goods in which household h has a comparative advantage.

References

Chipman, John, 1969, Factor price equalization and the Stolper–Samuelson Theorem, International Economic Review 10, 399–406.

Dixit, Avinash and Victor Norman, 1980, Theory of international trade: A dual, general equilibrium approach (Cambridge University Press, Cambridge).

Ethier, Wilfred, 1984, Higher dimensional issues in trade theory, In: Ronald Jones and Peter Kenen, eds., Handbook of international economics, Vol. I (North-Holland, Amsterdam) 131–184.

Helpman, Elhanan, 1984, Increasing returns, imperfect markets and trade theory, In: Ronald Jones and Peter Kenen, eds., Handbook of international economics, Vol. I (North-Holland, Amsterdam) 325–365.

Jones, Ronald, 1992, Reflections on the Stolper–Samuelson Theorem, In: Current issues in international trade theory, Festschrift in honor of Murray C. Kemp.

Jones, Ronald and Tapan Mitra, 1995, Share ribs and income distribution, Review of International Economics 3, 36–52.

Jones, Ronald and José Scheinkman, 1977, The relevance of the two-sector production model in trade theory, Journal of Political Economy 85, 909–935.

Jones, Ronald, Sugata Marjit and Tapan Mitra, 1993, The Stolper–Samuelson theorem: links to dominant diagonals, In: General equilibrium, growth and trade II (Harwood, Academic Press, London).

Kemp, Murray and Takashi Negishi, 1970, Variable returns to scale, comodity taxes, factor market distortions and their implications for trade gains, Swedish Journal of Economics 72, 1–11.

Kemp, Murray and Albert Schweinberger, 1991, Variable returns to scale, non-uniqueness of equilibrium and the gains from international trade, Review of Economic Studies 58, 807–816.

Kemp, Murray and Leon Wegge, 1969, Generalization of the Stolper–Samuelson and Samuelson–Rybczynski theorems in terms of conditional input–output coefficients, International Economic Review 10, 414–425.

Krugman, Paul, 1979, Increasing returns, monopolistic competition and international trade, Journal of International Economics 9, 469–479.

Leamer, Edward, 1987, Paths of development in the three-factor, n-good general equilibrium model, Journal of Political Economy 95, 961–999.

Lloyd, Peter and Albert Schweinberger, 1988, Trade expenditure functions and the gains from trade, Journal of International Economics 24, 275–297.

Markusen, James and Albert Schweinberger, 1990, The positive theory of production externalities under perfect competition, Journal of International Economics 29, 69–91.

Mitra, Tapan and Ronald Jones, 1992, Factor shares and the Chipman condition, Unpublished.

Rader, Trout, 1978, Induced preferences on trades when preferences may be intransitive and incomplete, Econometrica 46, 137–146.

Stolper, Wolfgang and Paul Samuelson, 1941, Protection and real wages, Review of Economic Studies 9, 58–73.

Weymark, John, 1979, A reconciliation of recent results in optimal taxation theory, Journal of Public Economics 12, 171–189.

Woodland, Alan, 1974, Demand conditions in international trade theory, Australian Economic Papers 13, 209–224.

Woodland, Alan, 1982, International trade and resource allocation (North-Holland, Amsterdam).

[3]

Oxford Economic Papers 43 (1991), 463–478

UNCERTAINTY AND THE CHOICE OF PROTECTIVE INSTRUMENT

By R. E. FALVEY * *and* P. J. LLOYD **

1. Introduction

GOVERNMENTS have a wide range of tariff and non-tariff instruments available to assist domestic industries in competition with imports. If governments possessed certain knowledge of future events and markets were perfectly competitive and there were no foreign retaliation, a given level of protection could be assured with any of the alternative instruments. Under these conditions the allocation of instruments across protected industries would be arbitrary and immaterial.

Far from being arbitrary, however, there appear to be consistent patterns in the instruments actually applied (see Ray (1981) and Ray and Marvel (1984)). In particular, quantitative restrictions are much more prevalent than an arbitrary allocation of instruments would imply, and in recent years non-tariff instruments have generally become more important. This suggests the existence of some underlying basis for selecting instruments which has not so far been noted.

Three possibilities present themselves. First the actual choice of instrument may be constrained. Obvious examples are the binding of tariff rates and other obligations associated with GATT membership. These external constraints clearly account in part for the decline in the significance of tariff restrictions over the last two decades. Internal constraints may also exist which limit the ease with which some instruments can be applied and varied. These would include the degree to which legislative action is necessary and the 'transparency' of the policy (i.e. the degree to which those who bear the cost of the policy correctly perceive the source of their loss). However the significance of these transparency motives has declined over time as estimates of the 'cost of protection' have become more widely available.

A second possibility based on market structure has recently been explored by Cassing and Hillman (1985). They develop a model of a monopolized industry in which the specific instrument chosen emerges as a result of the government maximizing its political support by trading off the interests of producers, consumers and 'revenue seekers'. Without the revenue motive, they find monopolized industries will prefer tariffs to quotas.

An alternative basis for the choice of instrument is uncertainty about future events. Uncertainty is always present. Different instruments will yield different outcomes in different states of nature. This introduces the possibility that the selection may be based on the characteristics of the uncertainty in the industry seeking protection. This is the approach developed below. We examine the choice among protective instruments on the basis of their relative effects on households' expected welfare under uncertainty, in the absence of markets for trading claims to uncertain income streams.

Questions of appropriate trade policy instruments under uncertainty have received attention in the literature. Partial rankings of policy instruments have been established for some policy constraints and sources and magnitudes of uncertainty.[1] One early conclusion of this analysis was that the greater flexibility of tariffs over quotas in allowing the volume of imports, and hence the domestic price, to respond to changes in cost conditions in the rest of the world, did not necessarily imply that tariffs should be ranked higher. Fishelson and Flatters (1974) and Young (1980) have shown that tariffs may in fact induce excessive flexibility in some circumstances.

Yet, with few exceptions, this previous work has adopted only a 'national' (aggregate) welfare perspective and has considered only 'non-protective' motives for trade restrictions.[2] In reality, different income groups have opposing interests in protection policies. For this reason we expand the scope of the analysis to encompass differences among households and 'political economy' considerations. From this perspective, the protection received by an industry can be viewed as being determined in an implicit market, where domestic import-competing producers become demanders of protection, and domestic politicians become suppliers. The politician's willingness to provide protection will depend on the strength of the anticipated adverse reaction of other groups—consumers in particular. This approach has been used with some success in predicting the relative *levels* of protection granted to import-competing industries under certainty.[3] We believe it may also prove useful in explaining the *choice of instrument* under uncertainty, and we extend the analysis in this direction below.

Part 1 considers the general problem of how a government acting to maximize a political support function would determine the optimal choice of protective instrument and its level. Part 2 then looks at how this optimal protection varies according to the sources of disturbances, the weight attached in the objective function to various household groups, attitudes to risk and other factors. It also derives second best rankings of two popular instruments, *ad valorem* tariffs and quotas. Part 3 offers a summary and some concluding remarks.

1. Optimal protection

Consider a competitive import-competing industry that produces an homogeneous product. A single industry focus seems reasonable in this context

---

[1] Constraints on expected revenue (Young (1980)), expected imports or expected expenditure on imports (Young (1982)), Young and Anderson (1982)), and the expected quantity of (and expenditure on) imports above some critical level (Anderson and Young (1982)) have been examined.

[2] In general agents are also assumed to be risk-neutral. Exceptions which consider risk-averse agents are Young and Anderson (1982), Young (1984), de Meza (1987) and Cassing, Hillman and Long (1986). In combination the assumptions of risk aversion and imperfect insurance markets provides a role for commercial policy instruments that stabilize income. Lloyd and Falvey (1986) present a model with risk-averse consumers and producers with different preferences over instruments but they do not model the political determination of instrument choice.

[3] See Baldwin (1984) for a survey. For a recent theoretical development, see Mayer (1984).

as government decisions relating to industry assistance, and particularly decisions with respect to the introduction of new instruments of assistance, are typically made separately for each industry rather than simultaneously for all industries.

In general different 'states of nature' (θ) may involve different demand and supply functions for this product in both the domestic and foreign markets. To make the analysis more tractable we assume that the foreign relative price of the industry's output ($p*$) is determined exogeneously but may be state dependent. This small country assumption is realistic for many import-competing industries, and retains the essence of the protection issue. The domestic relation price (p) is then also a random variable whose distribution depends on both the distribution of $p*$ and the form and level of protective instrument chosen.

A fixed non-prohibitive *ad valorem* tariff simply raises the domestic price above the world price in each state by a constant percentage. However, any other instrument yields a nominal rate of protection, expressed as the percentage by which the domestic price exceeds the foreign price, which is state dependent. If one were to choose the level of each instrument so as to give equal increases in the expected value of the domestic price, different instruments would imply different distributions around this common mean. For example, the nominal protection implied by a specific tariff varies inversely with the corresponding world price.

The general political problem of selecting an optimal protective instrument can, therefore, be modelled as the implicit choice of a functional relationship between the domestic price and the state of nature—the 'pricing rule', $p(\theta)$. To ensure that only 'protective' instruments are applied this relationship is constrained to satisfy $p(\theta) \geqq p*(\theta)$ for all states.[4]

In any given state the effects of protection on the welfare of an individual household (i) can be obtained from its indirect utility function $U^i(p, I_i)$, where I_i is household income. Differentiating totally we have

$$\frac{dU^i}{dp} = U^i_p + U^i_I \frac{dI_i}{dp} \tag{1}$$

where U^i_p, U^i_I are the corresponding partial derivatives. From Roy's Identity

$$U^i_p = -x_i U^i_I \tag{2}$$

where x_i is household i's demand for the product. In general, household income may be derived from two sources—ownership of primary factors ($h_i = (h_{i1}, \ldots, h_{in})$) and a share of import rents/revenues, $T = (p - p*)m$, where m is total imports. We assume that government revenues are returned to

---

[4] The extension to allow domestic consumption subsidies when $p(\theta) < p*(\theta)$ is straightforward. Such a modification would seem to fit the European Community's Common Agricultural Policy for example.

households according to some predetermined allocation rule:[5] $T_i = \psi_i T$ where T_i is the revenue received by household i, $\sum_i \psi_i = 1, \psi_i \geq 0$. Hence, household income is $I_i(p) = \sum_j w_j h_{ij} + \psi_i T$ where w_j is the return to factor j. Differentiating with respect to p

$$\frac{dI_i}{dp} = \sum_j \frac{\delta w_j}{\delta p} h_{ij} + \psi_i \frac{dT}{dp} \equiv y_i + \psi_i T_p \qquad (3)$$

The term y_i can be regarded as that part of this industry's output which is imputed to household i as a factor supplier,[6] and $\psi_i T_p$ is the component of the change in income which derives from the household's claim on import rent generated in this commodity market. Substituting (3) into (1) gives

$$\frac{dU^i}{dp} = -V_i U_I^i \qquad (4)$$

where $V_i = m_i - \psi_i T_p$ and $m_i = x_i - y_i$ is household i's excess demand for this product. Since $U_I^i > 0$, this is a generalization of the familiar result that an economic unit, in this case a household, gains or loses from protection as it is a net 'producer' or 'consumer' of the product, to include the effects of changes in protection on import rents. The terms net producer ($V_i < 0$) and net consumer ($V_i > 0$) will be used in this more general sense below. The sign of the rent effect (T_p) is the same for all households, and depends on whether the existing tariff is at, above or below its revenue maximizing level.

The expected welfare of each household will depend on the distribution of domestic prices across all states of the world. In a certain environment, the welfare of each household depends only on the level of assistance provided. But in an uncertain environment households are not indifferent to the choice of instrument because their rankings of instruments will differ according to their ownership of factors, claims on rents and preferences as is demonstrated in Section 2 below.[7]

---

[5] This rule is fairly general and can, for example, encompass the distribution of rent from non-auctioned quotas to households with import quota entitlements etc. However it does not allow the distribution to be different for different instruments, so that all instruments are treated as equivalent from the perspective of rent distribution. While this assumption has the advantage that it allows us to focus on the implications of uncertainty for the choice of instrument, it does mean that we ignore the problems of discrimination, corruption and inefficiency often associated with the allocation of import licences under a non-auctioned quota regime.

[6] This can be shown as follows. Let $Y(P, H) = \sum_i \sum_j w_j h_{ij}$ where P is the vector of prices of final outputs and H is the vector of national endowments of primary factors. $Y(P, H)$ is then the national product function whose derivatives $\partial Y/\partial p = y(P, H)$ is the supply function for the industry concenred. Hence $\partial Y/\partial p = \sum_i \sum_j (\partial w_j/\partial p) h_{ij}$.

[7] This formulation takes the ownership of factors, claims on rents and preferences as given. All agents are able to make production decisions after the states are revealed. Modification to explicitly allow for household decision taking with respect to the allocation of factors prior to the resolution of uncertainty would not affect the basic results. See Eaton and Grossman (1985). For a criticism of their approach see Dixit (1987).

Suppose the government selects a protective instrument for this industry so as to maximize a political support function[8] $(R(p, \theta))$ which contains as its arguments the indirect utility functions of the households. For simplicity we adopt a linear form

$$R(p, \theta) = \sum_i \alpha_i U^i(p, I_i) \tag{5}$$

where α_i is the relative weight attached to household i, with $0 \leq \alpha_i \leq 1$ and $\sum_i \alpha_i = 1$. Changes in the state of nature may shift both the world price and incomes. Hence, we have $U^i[p(p*(\theta)), I_i(\theta)]$ and $R = R(p, \theta)$.

If there were no uncertainty, the domestic price would be chosen so as to maximize $R(p)$. The first order condition is

$$R_p = \sum_i \alpha_i \frac{dU^i}{dp} = 0 \tag{6}$$

This determines the optimum (unconstrained) price, provided R is concave in p (see below). A comparison of this price with $p*$ yields the appropriate protection level. This level can be attained by an arbitrary selection from the arsenal of instruments.

To interpret Equation (6) under uncertainty, we rewrite it, using Equation (4), as

$$R_p = - \sum_i \alpha_i U^i_I V_i \tag{7}$$

$\alpha_i U^i_I \geq 0$ for all i and the country is assumed to be a net importer in all states ($\sum_i m_i = m > 0$). $\alpha_i U^i_I$ is the marginal political support from an increase in the income of household i. If there is only one household in the economy, or all households are identical, $R_p = -U_I(m - T_p) = U_I(p - p*)(dm/dp) < 0$ for all p. That is, the optimum requires zero protection. However when there are multiple households with distinct endowments and preferences and no lump sum transfers among households, the optimum depends on the effects which varying the level of protection has on all individual households. For protection to be offered (i.e. $R_p > 0$ at $p = p*$) $\alpha_i U^i_I$ and V_i must be negatively correlated. That is, negative values of V_i (a net producer) must be associated with high values of $\alpha_i U^i_I$, and positive values of V_i (a net consumer) must be associated with low values of $\alpha_i U^i_I$. In effect this gives a higher weighting when p is varied to net producer interests. This in turn may come about because of either a relatively high weighting of net producer interests in the political support function (α_i) or relatively high marginal utilities of income for net producers.

In an uncertain environment the government's choice problem becomes one of selecting a 'pricing rule' to maximize expected political support. Essentially

---

[8] Hillman (1982) uses a political support function to explain the level of protection. $R(p, \theta)$ could, alternatively, be interpreted as a Social Welfare Function with the same outcomes.

this means that in each state the government chooses the level of protection to maximise $R(p, \theta)$. Formally the government selects the pricing rule, $p(\theta)$, to solve the following problem

$$\max \int_{\theta_0}^{\theta_1} R(p, \theta)f(\theta)d\theta = E[R(p, \theta)] \tag{8}$$

s.t. $p(\theta) \geq p*(\theta)$ for all θ,

where θ has the density function $f(\theta)$ defined over the interval $[\theta_0, \theta_1]$. To solve this problem one forms the Hamiltonian

$$H(p, \theta) = R(p, \theta)f(\theta)$$

and the Lagrangean

$$L(p, \theta) = H(p, \theta) + \mu(p(\theta) - p*(\theta))$$

If $H(p, \theta)$ is strictly concave in p, the first order conditions for this problem determine a maximum. Since $H_{pp} = R_{pp}f(\theta)$, strict concavity of $H(p, \theta)$ requires that

$$R_{pp} = -\sum_i \alpha_i \frac{d}{dp}(V_i U_I^i) < 0 \tag{9}$$

From the definition of V_i, we have

$$\frac{dV_i}{dp} = \frac{dm_i}{dp} - \psi_i T_{pp}$$

Using equation (3) and Roy's Identity, one obtains

$$\frac{dU_I^i}{dp} = -U_I^i \left[\frac{x_i}{I_i} \varepsilon_I^i - \frac{V_i}{I_i} r_i \right] \tag{10}$$

and

$$\frac{dm_i}{dp} = -\left(\frac{x_i}{p} e_D^i + \frac{y_i}{p} e_S^i \right) + \frac{x_i(x_i - V_i)}{I_i} \varepsilon_I^i \tag{11}$$

where r_i is the Arrow-Pratt measure of household i's relative risk aversion, ε_I^i is the household's income elasticity of demand for this product, e_D^i is its price elasticity of demand and e_S^i is its 'output' price elasticity. Substituting these terms in (9) gives

$$R_{pp} = \sum_i \alpha_i U_I^i \left\{ \frac{x_i}{p} e_D^i + \frac{y_i}{p} e_S^i + (2V_i - x_i) \frac{x_i}{I_i} \varepsilon_I^i - \frac{V_i^2}{I_i} r_i + \psi_i T_{pp} \right\} \tag{12}$$

Thus concavity ($R_{pp} \leq 0$) is more likely the greater is household risk aversion (since $V_i^2 \geq 0$), the smaller are the demand and output price elasticities, the larger is the income elasticity of a net producer ($V_i < 0$), the smaller the income elasticity of a net consumer ($V_i > 0$), and if import rents are concave in domestic prices $(T_{pp} \leq 0)$.[9] Risk aversion is clearly important in determining whether $R(p, \theta)$ is concave in prices, and from now on we assume there is sufficient risk aversion for $H(p, \theta)$ to be concave in p.[10]

From the Maximum Principle the necessary and sufficient conditions for $\hat{p}(\theta)$ to be an optimal control include

$$\frac{\partial L}{\partial p} | \hat{p} = R_p f(\theta) + \mu \leq 0 \qquad (13)$$

and

$$\mu \geq 0; \hat{p}(\theta) - p*(\theta) \geq 0 \text{ and } \mu[\hat{p}(\theta) - p*(\theta)] = 0$$

States can them be partitioned into two subsets.

(1)   Those in which protection is optimal—

i.e. $\hat{p}(\theta) > p*(\theta), \mu = 0$ and $R_p = 0$

(2)   Those in which free trade is preferred—

i.e. $\hat{p}(\theta) = p*(\theta), \mu > 0$ and $R_p < 0$

In states in which protection is applied, equation (5) implicitly determines the corresponding pricing rule. This rule will determine both the instrument and the level at which it is set. The average rate of protection will depend on the effect of protection in each state on households and their political weights (from equation (5)).

Some insight into the operation of this rule can be gained, for a given state of nature, by considering the effects of a price increase on three extreme households—a 'pure producer', a 'pure rent recipient' and a 'pure consumer'. The welfare effects of price changes for these groups are shown in Table 1. The utility of a pure producer is increasing and, assuming sufficient risk aversion (i.e. $(py_i/I_i)r_i > e^i_s$) concave in p. Hence, the marginal gain in utility from a given price increase is higher at lower prices, and therefore the marginal gain from a unit of protection increases as the price falls. The utility of a 'pure rent

---

[9] One can write $T_p = m(1 - t\varepsilon)$, where $\varepsilon = (-p/m)(dm/dp)$ and $t = (p - p*)/p$. Then $T_{pp} = (-m/p)\varepsilon[((1 + t)(1 - t\varepsilon) + 1/1 + t)]$ which is negative for a range of tariffs, including the revenue maximizing tariff ($t = 1/\varepsilon$).

[10] As noted above, risk aversion introduces an income stabilizing role for commercial policy, although, as will be shown below, even where $R(p, \theta)$ is concave in p income stabilization need not be the dominating motive in the choice of protective instrument. Concavity of the political support function implies that, for any state of nature, if protection is used it will be aimed at achieving some minimum domestic price. Convexity of the political support function in prices, however, implies that, for any state of nature, the chosen outcome will be extreme—either free trade or prohibitive protection—depending on which yields the higher level of political support. In particular to take one of the specific instances considered below, if the only source of uncertainty is in world markets, and the income effects of fluctuations in world prices are negligible, then convexity would imply free trade at low world prices and prohibitive restrictions at high world prices. Because concavity implies policy outcomes closer to those observed in practice, it is the assumption maintained here.

TABLE 1

Household Type

	pure producer	*pure rent recipient*	*pure consumer*
	$y_i > 0; x_i = \psi_i = 0$	$\psi_i > 0; x_i = y_i = 0$	$x_i > 0; y_i = \psi_i = 0$
$\dfrac{dU^i}{dp}$	$y_i U^i_I > 0$	$\psi_i T_p U^i_I$	$-x_i U^i_I < 0$
$\dfrac{d^2U^i}{dp^2}$	$\dfrac{y_i U^i_I}{p}\left(e^i_S - \dfrac{py_i}{I_i}r_i\right)$	$\psi_i U^i_I\left(T_{pp} - \dfrac{\psi_i T_p^2}{I_i}r_i\right)$	$\dfrac{x_i U^i_I}{p}\left[e^i_D + \dfrac{px_i}{I_i}(\varepsilon^i_I - r_i)\right]$

recipient' is increasing in price up to the revenue maximizing tariff and decreasing thereafter. If rents are concave in p, then risk aversion is not necessary for the utility of rent recipients to be concave in p. The utility of a consumer household is a decreasing, convex function of price under fairly weak conditions (Turnovsky, Shalit and Schmitz (1980)). The marginal loss to such a household from a unit of protection (price increase) itself increases as the price increases.

When the interests of all types of households are combined via the $R()$ function, the level of protection is set in each state where the marginal (net producer household) gains and (net consumer household) losses are equal. Clearly the level of protection will be higher in protective states in which the marginal loss of utility to net producers and the weights given to net producer interests overall are higher. The converse is true for net consumers.

Since R_p is state dependent in general, the nominal rate of protection implied by the pricing rule can vary across states in a fairly complex way. The response of the desired domestic price to changes in the state of nature under this pricing rule can be obtained implicitly by totally differentiating $R_p(p, \theta) = 0$. This yields

$$\frac{d\hat{p}(\theta)}{d\theta} = -\frac{R_{p\theta}}{R_{pp}} \tag{16}$$

The term $R_{p\theta}$ is then obtained by differentiating (7) with respect to θ, which implies that

$$\frac{d\hat{p}(\theta)}{d\theta} = \frac{\sum_i \alpha_i U^i_I\left\{\left(\dfrac{x_i}{I_i}\varepsilon^i_I - \dfrac{V_i}{I_i}r_i\right)\dfrac{dI_i}{d\theta} - \dfrac{d}{d\theta}\left(\dfrac{dI_i}{dp}\right)\right\}}{R_{pp}} \tag{17}$$

Since the denominator in (17) is negative from the assumption that $R(p, \theta)$ is concave, the key terms in determining the sign of (17) are $\gamma_i \equiv (x_i/I_i)\,\varepsilon^i_I - (V_i/I_i)\,r_i$, and the effects of the change in the state of nature on (a) household income $(dI_i/d\theta)$ and (b) the marginal income effect of protection $(d/d\theta(dI_i/dp))$. Considering (b), if the change in θ raises the marginal income effect of protection for household i, then *ceteris paribus*, the optimal level of protection for that household will rise. The implication of (a) for any household depends on the sign of γ_i. While this coefficient is positively related to the household's income elasticity of demand for this product, the influence of risk aversion depends on the household's net market position. For a 'net producer' ($V_i < 0$), γ_i is unambiguously positive. For a 'net consumer' ($V_i > 0$), the sign of γ_i is ambiguous.

This ambiguity reflects two opposing influences of price changes on a household's welfare in these circumstances. An increase in incomes increases the quantity demanded at any given price and hence raises the consumption cost of a given price increase. On this count households would prefer to have prices lower when incomes are higher ($\delta \hat{p}/\delta \theta < 0$). On the other hand, if households are risk averse variations in this domestic price could be used as a stabilizing device to (partially) offset the effects of (real) income fluctuations on welfare. This requires a reduction in price when income is high for a net producer, and an increase in price when income is high for a net consumer. Thus for a net producer both motivations work in the same direction ($\gamma_i > 0$), they prefer a decline in protection when income increases. But for a net consumer the direction of the desired price adjustment depends on which of the two motivations dominates.

In our instrument choice problem we assume that the level of the instrument must be fixed before the state of nature is revealed, that is, it cannot be state-dependent. This is the source of the difference between instruments. It also rules out the choice of a variable import levy which is by design a state-dependent instrument. In some cases there may not exist a corresponding 'instrument' whose level can be fixed *ex ante* at a single value across states while attaining the optimal domestic pricing rule implied by (16). The implications of such a constraint for the choice of instruments are best revealed if the three sources of disturbances are considered separately. These cases show the characteristics of the pricing rule and provide, where possible, a (second-best) ranking of the two most popular instruments—tariffs and quotas.[11]

2. Instrument rankings

2.1 *No foreign disturbances*

In this case the pricing rule requires that the domestic price respond to domestic disturbances of supply and/or demand but the world price is constant. Whether the level of protection should rise or fall with increases in θ depends on the

---

[11] In our analysis a quota is interpreted as a volume-based instrument. This is appropriate for many of the quotas imposed on internationally-traded commodities and it approximates quotas which are specified in terms of the market shares in the importing countries. A quota specified in terms of a fixed value of imports would have a very different effect as it would allow the volume of imports to increase proportionately as the world price fell. In the case, for example, where the sole disturbance is in the foreign price this would reverse the ranking of a quota and a tariff. However, it is hard to believe that a quota imposed to protect the domestic industry would be maintained in terms of a fixed value over periods in which the import price varied substantially.

sign of $R_{p\theta}$. While optimal instruments are difficult to determine in general, some definite results are forthcoming. Consider, for example, the issue of ranking a fixed tariff and a fixed non-tariff barrier. Given the constant world price, the fixed tariff (whether specific or *ad valorem*) results in a constant domestic price. The fixed NTB, on the other hand, implies that the domestic price will vary with fluctuations in domestic demand and supply. One might, therefore, conjecture that the tariff instrument will be ranked above (below) the NTB if the pricing rule requires that the domestic price move in the opposite (same) direction to that which naturally follows under the NTB.

The first part of this conjecture is true. This can be proven using a slightly modified version of Theorem 2 in Young and Anderson (1982).

Theorem: Suppose that when the instrument choice is constrained to a tariff policy that the tariff level which maximizes $E[R(p, \theta)]$ implies (fixed) domestic price $\bar{p}$. Then, if $R_{p\theta} < 0$ for all θ when $p = \bar{p}$, this fixed tariff yields a higher level of expected welfare than any other policy $\tilde{p}(\theta)$ for which $d\tilde{p}(\theta)/d\theta > 0$.

Proof: Since $R(p, \theta)$ is concave in p, the Second Mean Value Theorem implies that

$$R(\bar{p}, \theta) - R(\tilde{p}(\theta), \theta) \geqq R_p(\bar{p}, \theta).\{\bar{p} - \tilde{p}(\theta)\}$$

Since this inequality will be strict if $\tilde{p}(\theta) \neq \bar{p}$ on a set of positive measure, then

$$E[R(\bar{p}, \theta) - R(\tilde{p}(\theta), \theta)] > E[R_p(\bar{p}, \theta).(\bar{p} - \tilde{p}(\theta))]$$

With $R_{p\theta}(\bar{p}, \theta) < 0$, $d\bar{p}/d\theta = 0$ and $d\tilde{p}(\theta)/d\theta < 0$, $R_p(\bar{p}, \theta)$ and $\{\bar{p} - \tilde{p}(\theta)\}$ are non-negatively correlated as θ varies. Hence

$$E[R_p(\bar{p}, \theta)\{\bar{p} - \tilde{p}(\theta)\}] \geqq E[R_p(\bar{p}, \theta)]E[\bar{p} - \tilde{p}(\theta)] = 0,$$

given that the tariff is chosen so that $ER_p(\bar{p}, \theta) = 0$.

Thus $E[R(\bar{p}, \theta) - R(\tilde{p}(\theta), \theta)] > 0$, as required   Q.E.D.

In the converse case, where the pricing rule and the NTB move the domestic price in the same direction, the NTB will be the preferred instrument as long as it does not induce excessive flexibility in the domestic price.

Let $\tilde{p}(\theta)$ denote the domestic price regime under the NTB, and consider the case where $R_{p\theta} > 0$ and $d\hat{p}/d\theta > d\tilde{p}/d\theta > d\bar{p}/d\theta = 0$. Then one can readily demonstrate that the NTB will be preferred to the tariff as follows. The fixed tariff that maximizes political support will be selected so that $ER_p(\bar{p}, \theta) = 0$. Given that $R_{p\theta} > 0$, this implies that there exists some $\bar{\theta}$, such that $R_p(\bar{p}, \theta) \geqq 0$ as $\theta \geqq \bar{\theta}$. Now consider that value of the NTB which yields $\tilde{p}(\bar{\theta}) = \bar{p}$. Then since $d\tilde{p}/d\theta > 0$, one has that $\tilde{p}(\theta) \geqq \bar{p}$ as $\theta \geqq \bar{\theta}$. Given that $R_p(\hat{p}, \theta) = 0$ for all θ, by choice of $\hat{p}$, and that $d\hat{p}/d\theta > d\tilde{p}/d\theta > 0$, $R_p(\tilde{p}, \theta)$ has the same sign as $R_p(\bar{p}, \theta)$. Thus both $R_p(\tilde{p}, \theta).(\tilde{p}(\theta) - \bar{p}) > 0$ and $R_p(\bar{p}, \theta).(\tilde{p}(\theta) - \bar{p}) > 0$ for all $\theta(\neq \bar{\theta})$.

Political support is therefore higher at each $\theta(\neq\bar\theta)$ under this value of the NTB than under the maximizing tariff, so that the NTB will be the preferred instrument. One can also demonstrate the superiority of the NTB when $R_{p\theta} < 0$ and $0 < d\bar p/d\theta < d\hat p/d\theta$ in an analogous fashion.

But if the NTB induces excessive flexibility in the domestic price, the stable price generated by a tariff may still be preferred. This result is illustrated in Figure 1 for two possible states of nature $\theta_j, j = 1, 2$. The optimal price in each state are denoted by $\hat p_j, j = 1, 2$, with $\hat p_2 > \hat p_1$. The optimum (second best) tariff will involve an intermediate price such as $\bar p$ with $\hat p_1 < \bar p < \hat p_2$. From Figure 1 it is clear that if the optimum (second best) NTB leads to prices in the ranges $\bar p_1$ to $\bar p$ and $\bar p$ to $\bar p_2$ in the two states respectively, it will be preferred to the tariff. However, if the NTB induced so much price variation that one or both prices were outside these ranges then the tariff may still be the preferred instrument.

To illustrate the importance of parameters for instrument choice when there are domestic disturbances it is useful to consider the subcases with disturbances in domestic demand or domestic supply separately.

Suppose that the only disturbances in the domestic market are due to fluctuations in household income from other sources, θ_I. (These income changes must, with fixed preferences, be due to the effects of technological change or other supply side variations elsewhere in the economy). Then

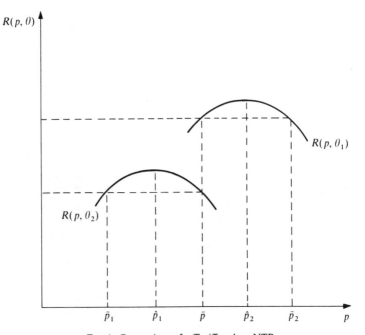

FIG. 1. Comparison of a Tariff and an NTB

$dI_i/d\theta_I = \beta_i + \psi_i T_I > 0$ and $d/d\theta_I(dI_i/dp) = \lambda_i T_{pI}$, so that (17) implies

$$\frac{d\hat{p}}{d\theta_I} = \frac{\sum_i \alpha_i U_I^i \{\gamma_i(\beta_i + \psi_i T_{pI}) - \psi_i T_I\}}{R_{pp}} \tag{18}$$

Since R_{pp} is assumed to be negative, the pricing rule reduces (or raises) the domestic price when domestic income increases and hence domestic demand shifts out as the numerator is positive (or negative).

As noted above, the direct income effect, which here is non-negative for all households, implies reduced protection is desired by net producers, while the position of net consumers is ambiguous depending on the tradeoff between income elasticity and risk aversion. The change in the marginal income effect of protection ($\psi_i T_{pI}$) also has the same sign for all households, which depends on the sign of T_{pI} (which is unknown, but most likely positive). The outcome for the pricing rule is therefore ambiguous, although assuming rent effects are negligible, if there is a presumption it must surely be that $d\hat{p}/d\theta_I < 0$.

Consequently, the ranking of a tariff versus a quota is, in general, ambiguous because the optimal instrument may require the domestic price to increase or decrease when domestic income increases.

The price adjustment under a quota policy ($\bar{m}$) can be determined by totally differentiating the market clearing constraint:

$$\sum_i x_i - \sum_i y_i = \bar{m} = \text{constant.}$$

This yields

$$\frac{dp}{d\theta_I}|\bar{m} = \frac{\sum_i \frac{x_i}{I_i} \varepsilon_I^i(\beta_i + \psi_i T_I)}{-\sum_i (dm_i/dp)} > 0 \tag{19}$$

which can be compared with (18) to determine the likelihood that the quota is the preferred policy.

Alternatively, suppose that the only disturbances in the domestic market are fluctuations in domestic output in this industry. Let $dy_i/d\theta_s = \rho_i \geq 0$, then $dI_i/d\theta_s = p\rho_i + \psi_i T_{\theta s}$, $d/d\theta_s(dI_i/dp) = \rho_i + \psi_i T_{p\theta s}$ and (17) becomes

$$\frac{d\hat{p}}{d\theta_s} = \frac{\sum_i \alpha_i U_I^i \{(p\gamma_i - 1)\rho_i + \psi_i(\gamma_i T_{\theta_s} - T_{p\theta_s})\}}{R_{pp}} \tag{20}$$

Again the outcome is ambiguous. Considering the coefficient on ρ_i an increase in domestic output increases the income gain resulting from any given price increase. On this basis those households who draw some income from the industry prefer higher domestic prices when domestic output is high (this influence is captured by the -1 term). Tempering this is the increase in a household's demand for the product as its income rises (as captured by the $(px_i/I_i) \varepsilon_I^i$ term, but note that $(px_i/I_i) \varepsilon_I^i - 1 = p\delta x_i/\delta I_i - 1 < 0$). On the other hand, if households are risk averse, variations in the domestic price can be used as a stabilizing device to (partially) offset the effects of output fluctuations on real income. Whether this requires an increase or reduction in the price as output rises depends on whether the household is a net consumer or net producer. In combination, considering this term alone, a net consumer clearly prefers $d\hat{p}/d\theta_s > 0$, while the outcome is ambiguous for a net producer.

Turning to the rental terms, an increase in output at constant prices can be expected to reduce import rents ($T_{\theta s} < 0$), but the change in the marginal rent is ambiguous (but most likely also negative). The implications of the rental changes for the optimal pricing rule are therefore unclear in general.

Again the ranking of the tariff and quota instruments will depend on the sign of $d\hat{p}(\theta)/d\theta_s$. Increases in domestic supply imply a falling domestic price under a quota which is to be contrasted with the constant domestic price under a tariff. If $d\hat{p}(\theta)/d\theta_s > 0$ is the optimal response under the pricing rule, one can apply our theorem to demonstrate that the optimal (second best) tariff will be preferred to any policy which induces a falling price as output expands (such as a quota). If $d\hat{p}(\theta)/d\theta_s < 0$, then a quota will be the preferred of the two instruments as long as it doesn't induce excessive price variation.

Finally, note the important implications of the source of domestic disturbances for policy choice. A tariff maintains a constant domestic price in either case, while under a quota an increase in domestic demand raises the domestic price and an increase in domestic supply reduces it. Rent effects aside, the optimal adjustment under the pricing rule depends primarily on the sign of the γ_i terms. If γ_i is positive, then $d\hat{p}/d\theta < 0$ is more likely. For domestic supply disturbances this implies a tariff is *less* likely to be preferred to a quota, while for domestic demand disturbances the tariff is *more* likely to be preferred to the quota.[12]

2.2 *No domestic disturbances*

Here, $dI_i/dp* = \psi_i T_{p*} < 0$ for all households, and $d/dp*(dI_i/dp) = \psi_i T_{pp*}$, so that

$$\frac{d\hat{p}}{dp*} = \frac{\sum_i \alpha_i U_I^i \psi_i (\gamma_i T_{p*} - T_{pp*})}{R_{pp}} \tag{21}$$

---

[12] It is also interesting to compare these results with those obtained by Young and Anderson (1982). Their problem involved selecting an instrument to maximize the expected utility of a risk averse representative consumer, subject to an upper bound on the expected volume of imports. A disadvantage of their approach is that since the country is a net importer, a representative consumer necessarily 'represents' only the interests of net buyers. The interests of net sellers, which presumably give rise to import restriction in the first place, can then only be captured by the rather arbitrary constraint on expected imports. Where the difference in approach proves important is in the consideration of domestic output disturbances. Young and Anderson find a tariff is always preferred to a quota, while in our case the outcome is ambiguous since either buyer or seller interests may dominate.

If the variation in rent is negligible or the weight of those who receive rent is zero in the political process which determine the choice and level of instrument in this commodity market, then $d\hat{p}/dp^* = 0$.[13] This implies a constant domestic price ($\bar{p}$) when the domestic market is protected. Since the world price fluctuates with disturbances in the world market the desired level of protection varies with the state of nature. In states when it is optimal to leave the domestic market unprotected (if there are any), domestic prices will all exceed $\bar{p}$ since R is concave is p. One instrument which would establish these outcomes is a variable import levy designed to maintain the desired minimum domestic price. If the variation in rent is negligible (i.e. $T_{p^*} = 0$) then an import quota will also achieve the same outcome.[14] The level at which the quota will be set and hence the implicit level of protection in each state (and on average) will depend on household attitudes to risk and their political weights, as indicated by equation (6).

In principle one can also rank any two or more alternative instruments which are fixed at the levels which would maximise political support from each. This ranking depends on how a fixed level of each instrument affects the distribution of the domestic price in relation to the fixed domestic price which is optimal under the circumstances. In general one would expect instruments that provide higher levels of protection at lower world prices to be preferred to a fixed *ad valorem* tariff, for example a multi-part or a sliding scale duty whose *ad valorem* tariff equivalent increases as the world price falls. Similarly, a specific tariff offers higher protection on the downside. This feature may explain the preference for such instruments over *ad valorem* tariffs when producers are downside risk-adverse, as is commonly supposed. (Menezes, Geiss and Tressler (1980) discuss income earners who exhibit increasing downside risk-aversion). This pattern of instrument preference is especially likely if downside risk-averse producers have a high political weight.

If rent effects are significant and the political weight of rent recipients is not zero, a constant domestic price ceases to be optimal since the income of those households which receive rent varies with the world price. However, the ambiguity with respect to the sign of γ_i remains. For a net producer ($\gamma_i > 0$), the rent reducing effects of an increase in p^* should be partially offset by an increase in p. For a net consumer the desired direction of any domestic price change depends on whether the income elasticity or risk aversion effect dominates. The overall outcome then depends on the relative weightings given to the various households and the sign of T_{pp^*}. However if there is a presumption

---

[13] A change in the terms of trade will also affect the real incomes of all households. For example, a fall in the terms of trade will reduce real household incomes and it may reduce domestic demand for the commodity. Consequently the optimal rule may require the domestic price fall when the foreign price falls, unless the real income derived from the production of this commodity is small. We assume this is so. This is a reasonable assumption for developed industrialized economics which have a well diversified bundle of export commodities but it would be inappropriate for an economy with one or a few dominant export commodities.

[14] Under the quota regime $(dp/dp^*)|_m = [\sum_i (x_i/I_i) \varepsilon_I^i \psi_i T_{p^*}/ - \sum_i (dm_i/dp)] = 0$ if $T_{p^*} = 0$.

it seems likely to be that $d\hat{p}/dp^* > 0$, i.e. the first-best policy implies a positive correlation between the domestic and world prices. In this case, however, the domestic price falls as the world prices rises under a quota regime (through the negative income effect of the declining rents on domestic demand), while a tariff regime implies the desired positive association between charges in domestic and world prices. One can then apply the arguments of the preceding section to show that the tariff regime is likely to be preferred in this case, unless it generates excessive flexibility.

3. Concluding remarks

This paper began by developing the general properties of a pricing rule that determined the optimal domestic price in each state of nature. The problem then was to find a protective instrument that matched this pricing rule—that is an instrument that translated the exogenously determined world price into the optimal domestic price in each state. In all cases this pricing rule could be satisfied by an arbitrary choice of instrument as long as its level could be varied as required from state to state.

The levels of many instruments—tariffs, quotas, purchasing preference margins, trigger price mechanisms, etc.—can rarely be varied with complete freedom. Hence the choice of instrument is important. When fixed at a particular level, different instruments do yield quite different distributions of the domestic price, and associated distributions of household welfare for a given distribution of foreign prices. The policy approach involves selecting that instrument which best approximates the domestic pricing rule.

In some circumstances the pricing rule can be satisfied by a recognizable instrument which was held constant at the appropriate level. A quota would perform this role under our assumptions if there were no domestic disturbances and if rent considerations are inconsequential. When the main disturbances are in foreign competitiveness and the foreign supply price, this implies a political preference for quantitative restrictions over tariffs. This preference for quotas stems from the fact that quotas allow the nominal rate of protection to vary across states in the way which maximises political support for protective intervention. Cases where a tariff, while not itself first-best, would still be preferred to an NTB were also demonstrated.

Finally, this analysis emphasizes that an industry's characteristics in terms of the sources of any disturbances in its market may be important in determining the instrument of protection as well as the level of protection it receives. This has implications for empirical attempts to explain protection levels. Empirical studies commonly focus on the (average) *ad valorem* equivalent levels only since these are readily quantified. However, one should take account of the whole distribution of these *ad valorem* rates across states. Ideally one should test for both the form and average level of protection simultaneously. Some of the commonly accepted stylized facts seem consistent with the model's predictions. One feature of the New Protectionism in the OECD countries is the increased use of NTBs, especially quotas and antidumping duties. There is growing concern in the US over the loss of *international* competitiveness due to the emergence of new competitors, especially Japan and the Asian NICs. The model predicts that downside risk-aversion will cause producers to push for levels of protection which are higher and which give more weight to the prevention of low prices. However, testing the predictions of the model will require a systematic econometric study.

* *Research School of Pacific Studies,Australian National University,*
** *University of Melbourne*

REFERENCES

ANDERSON, J. E. and YOUNG, L. (1982). 'The Optimality of Tariff Quotas under Uncertainty', *Journal of International Economics*, November, pp. 337–51.

BALDWIN, R. E. (1984). 'Trade Policies in Developed Countries', Chapter 12 in *Handbook of International Economics* Volume 1, R. W. Jones and P. B. Kenen (eds) North Holland, Amsterdam.

CASSING, J. H. and HILLMAN, A. L. (1985). 'Political Influence Motives and the Choice between Tariffs and Quotas', *Journal of International Economics*, 19, November, 279–90.

CASSING, J. H., HILLMAN, A.L. and LONG, N. V. (1986). 'Risk Aversion, Terms of Trade Uncertainty and Trade Policy', *Oxford Economic Papers*, 38, July, 234–42.

DE MEZA, D. (1987). 'The Optimum Tariff and Quota when the Terms of Trade are Random', *Oxford Economic Papers*, 39, June, pp. 412–7.

DIXIT, A. (1987). 'Trade and Insurance with Moral Hazard', *Journal of International Ecnomics*, November, pp. 201–20.

EATON, J. and GROSSMAN, G. M. (1985). 'Tariffs as Insurance: Optimal commercial Policy when Domestic Markets are Incomplete', *Canadian Journal of Economics*, May, pp. 258–72.

FISHELSON, G. and FLATTERS, F. (1974). 'The (Non) Equivalence of Optimal Tariffs and Quotas under Uncertainty', *Journal of International Economics*, 5, pp. 385–93.

HILLMAN, A. L. (1982). 'Declining Industries and Political Support Protectionist Motives', *American Economic Review*, 72, December, pp. 1180–7.

LLOYD, P. J. and FALVEY, R. E. (1986). 'The Choice of Instrument for Industry Protection' in R. H. Snape (ed.), *Issues in World Trade Policy*, Macmillan, London.

MAYER, W. (1984) 'Endogenous Tariff Formation', *American Economic Review*, 74, December, pp. 970–85.

MENEZES, C., GEISS, C. and TRESSLER, J. (1980). 'Increasing Downside Risk', *American Economic Review*, December, 921–32.

RAY, E. J. (1981). 'The Determinants of Tariff and Non-Tariff Trade Restrictions in the United States', *Journal of Political Economy*, 89, February, pp. 105–21.

RAY, E. J. and MARVEL, H. P. (1984). 'The Pattern of Protection in the Industrialized World', *Review of Economics and Statistics*, LXVI, August, pp. 452–8.

TURNOVSKY, S. J., SHALIT, H. and SCHMITZ, A. (1980). 'Consumer's Surplus, Price Instability, and Consumer Welfare', *Econometrica*, 48, January, pp. 135–52.

YOUNG, L. (1980). 'Optimal Revenue-Raising Trade Restrictions Under Uncertainty', *Journal of International Economics*, 10, pp. 425–39.

YOUNG, L. (1982). 'Quantity Controls vs Expenditure Controls in International Trade Under Uncertainty', *Journal of International Economics*, 12, pp. 143–63.

YOUNG, L. (1984). 'Uncertainty and the Theory of International Trade in Long Run Equilibrium', *Journal of Economic Theory*, 32, February, pp. 67–92.

YOUNG, L. and ANDERSON, J. E. (1982). 'Risk Aversion and Optimal Trade Restrictions', *Review of Economic Studies*, XLIX, pp. 291–305.

Protectionism

Protectionism, that is the advocacy of the protection of some domestic activities from foreign competition, is one of the oldest topics in the history of economic thought.[1] Its antithesis is free trade. The protection versus free trade debate played a central part in Adam Smith's *Wealth of Nations* whose bicentenary passed 13 years ago. However, the debate is much older than that. In *The Republic* Plato argues cogently for free trade because of the advantages of job specialization by individuals (see *Journal of Political Economy*, October, 1985, back page).

Since the time of Adam Smith the opinion of international trade theorists has been overwhelmingly in favour of free trade and opposed to protectionism. The case for free trade was formalized by David Ricardo in 1817. Ricardo derived the Principle of Comparative Advantage. This states that it benefits nations to specialize in the production of those goods and services in which they have a 'comparative advantage', that is, which they can produce relatively cheaply compared to the relative costs of production in other nations, just as it pays individuals to specialize and for the same reasons. In *The New Palgrave: A Dictionary of Economics*, which was published in 1987 to replace the old nineteenth-century Palgrave's *Dictionary of Political Economy*, this principle is lauded as '[the] deepest and most beautiful result in all of economics' (Findlay, 1987, p. 514).

Despite the antiquity and the beauty and the power of the case for free trade, protectionism is practised universally. The two island/city economies of Hong Kong and Singapore are the only states in the world currently to have adopted virtual free trade. This discord between the opinion of economists and the practices enacted by legislators is the phenomenon that needs to be explained.

In this context the case of New Zealand is a most interesting one for two reasons. First, until the 1960s, the New Zealand economy was an appendage of the British economy. Despite its being the most distant of the former colonies on the other side of the globe and in the Antipodes, the New Zealand economy was closely linked to the British economy by the mutual tariff preferences extended to each other under the Imperial Preference System set up by the 1932 Ottawa Agreement. These links had been strengthened by the purchase by Britain of the entire exportable surplus of agricultural products during the Second World War and by the bulk purchase agreements which succeeded those arrangements after the War and lasted until 1954. Furthermore, when New Zealand introduced import licensing in 1938 it gave an absolute margin of preference to imports of controlled items from the UK, chiefly to mollify the opposition of UK exporters to these new controls. More than one half of the combined commodity exports and imports of New Zealand were traded with the UK until 1959.

Secondly, New Zealand has had throughout the post-Second World War period the highest levels of protection for manufacturing industries of all the advanced industrialized countries who are now members of the Organization for Economic Cooperation and Development (OECD). However, in the 1980s it has reversed this policy and swung towards a much freer trade policy. In addition to lowering its border protection by unilateral reductions in tariffs, it has adopted other trade policies which are unusually adventurous. New Zealand is systematically and unilaterally replacing the import licensing system, which has been the basic instrument of industrial protection since 1938, by a regime of tariffs. It is doing so by rapidly increasing the value of licences and auctioning them and then converting the licences into 'global licences on demand' when the auction premia fall below the trigger level of 7.5 per cent then into licence exemption one year later. No other country has liberalized trade by this means before. This process should be complete by 1992. To take another example, it has, in cooperation with Australia, sharply accelerated the movement towards total free trade with Australia under the Closer Relations Agreement between the two countries. Bilateral free trade will occur in 1990 instead of the original date of 1995.

Thus in its recent history New Zealand has represented in an extreme form both the forces of protectionism and the forces of trade liberalization. I shall use this example to discuss some of the features and the effects of protectionism. Less frequently I shall draw upon the experience of the UK and of Australia.

The case for free trade
The case for free trade is simple and powerful. Free trade compared to no trade or restricted trade will increase the aggregate supplies of goods and services available for consumption by all households in the economy. It does so by taking advantage of the possibilities of specialization. A country may obtain final goods and services directly by producing them itself or indirectly by producing other goods and services and exchanging these with other countries for the goods and services it prefers to consume or invest. In a similar way countries also specialize in the production of intermediate inputs and exchange, some of which are for intermediate inputs or final goods and services produced by other countries. As a result countries consume a much greater range of goods and services than they produce themselves. This specialization lowers the opportunity cost of obtaining each good or service and maximizes aggregate consumption possibilities for the economy.[2]

There are two different versions of the argument for free trade. One is called the cosmopolitan view. It argues that free trade is the best policy for the *world* economy. That is, it maximizes the consumption possibilities for all households in the whole world. This proposition is accepted virtually universally by international trade theorists other than some neo-Marxists and others in developing countries who argue that the result does not hold because of widespread monopoly power exercised by large economies. The difficulty is that nations pursue national interests and it is nations that impose protection at their borders.

The second version applies to nations. It argues that free trade is the best trade policy for a *nation*. This holds in a world economy in which other nations impose tariffs and other barriers which distort the pattern of world trade. It is, therefore, a very strong argument that implies a nation should unilaterally adopt a policy of free trade, irrespective of the tariffs and barriers which other nations choose. There is a potential exception to this, as John Stuart Mill pointed out in 1848. If a country is not a small trader in the market for some of the commodities which it trades, it may do better than free trade by restricting trade in these commodities. For importable commodities this is the argument that the 'foreigner pays part of the tariff'. It implies an improvement in the terms of trade at which the country exchanges its goods and services and if the restriction is not excessively high the nation gains more from the improvement in the terms of trade, the price effect, than it loses from the reduction in the volume of trade.

It should be noted that this exception applies to exportable commodities as well as importable commodities and in the former case it is an argument for an export tax. Indeed, since all countries export a smaller range of commodities than they import and consequently their export sales constitute a larger proportion of the world markets on average than their purchases, there is a presumption that monopoly power will occur more frequently in export markets. (In Australia the only traded commodity for which it has been argued that the nation has some significant monopoly power is wool.)

However, there are a number of obvious and major practical difficulties with this qualification to free trade. In the first place, every traded commodity has substitutes whose existence severely limits the scope for welfare-improving restrictions on trade; for example, in the Australian wool case, there are clearly a number of synthetic and natural fibres which can be substituted for wool in any end use. Secondly, the imposition of optimal trade taxes requires detailed and accurate knowledge of demand and supply elasticities which, frankly, trade officials do not possess. They may, therefore, gravely miscalculate and make the nation worse off if they pursue such a policy. Third, this policy assumes that the other nations with which the trade-restricting nation trades do not retaliate. If other nations retaliate, there is a likelihood that they will all lose from the joint pursuit of this policy. For these reasons this argument is seldom advanced as a grounds for restricting trade (though it is still misleadingly given prominence in every textbook).

There are other arguments which purport to demonstrate that it is in the interests of the nation to protect certain industries or activities or producers, all based on some alleged market failure. The most celebrated of these is the Infant Industry argument which is normally based on some dynamic learning process. All of these market failure arguments have been severely circumscribed and it is now realized that they call for intervention in the factor market or the firm since they are specific to factor markets or firms rather than for border intervention which benefits all of the producers who add value to the product protected. The Infant Industry argument in particular is rarely advanced these days. In Australia, for example, the Industries Assistance Commission must enquire into any proposal to change the level of assistance by means of border protection. I do not know of a single recommendation in the last 30 years for increased or maintained protection by the Industries Assistance Commission or its predecessor, the Tariff Board, which appealed to this argument.

In the 1980s a new argument for protection, called 'strategic trade policy', has been espoused by some (see Helpman and Krugman, 1989 for a survey). It is based on oligopolistic behaviour in markets in which there are economies of scale which create a divergence between price and marginal cost. Under certain conditions it may be advantageous to a nation for its government to intervene by means of trade taxes or subsidies. But, as with earlier arguments, there are several qualifications. The economies of scale have to be large in relation to the aggregate world market. The policy recommendations are very sensitive to the market structure and the assumptions relating to the behaviour of the firms in the market. The information required by governments is not available to them. In any case trade policy is not the first-best intervention. This case turns out to be very circumscribed. It illustrates the fascination of intellectuals with qualifications to free trade which are logically valid but not relevant to most markets.

Thus modern opinion among international economists is firmly in favour of unilateral free trade. In this respect, opinion has not changed since Bastable wrote his survey in Palgrave's *Dictionary of Political Economy*. He cites approvingly the following statement by Professor Nicholson (Bastable, 1926, p. 235): 'These exceptions are simply part of the casuistry of economics; they are like the discussions by moral philosophers of the justification of occasional mendacity. Free trade like honesty still remains the best policy'.

Again one notes that the advice of international economists to adopt unilateral free trade liberalization is rarely heeded. There are periodic examples of nations unilaterally reducing their import trade barriers. Before accession to the EC the UK unilaterally reduced its tariffs. Australia had a major across-the-board reduction by 25 per cent of all tariffs in 1973 and some lesser reductions subsequently. On a world perspective unilateral reductions in trade restrictions are notable for being uncommon.

New Zealand began to liberalize imports subject to import licensing from 1981. When the Labour Government won the election of July 1984 it embarked on a very ambitious plan to accelerate the liberalization of imports subject to import licensing, to lower tariffs by a sequence of across-the-board tariff reductions and to abolish compensating assistance to export producers by means of various subsidies. (Trade liberalization was a part of a larger set of policies designed to increase efficiency in the private and public sectors. These included reforms of the financial and labour markets, regulatory reform and privatization and corporatization and the introduction of user charging in the public sector and other reforms. Most of these are discussed by other speakers at this conference.) Nevertheless, these recent events have been unique in New Zealand's economic history. In a book which reviews the trade liberalization experience of New Zealand, it is claimed that the tariff reductions in 1986 which initiated this programme were the first in the country's European history, though I have not had the resources to check this amazing claim[3] (Rayner and Lattimore, 1989).

The political economy of protectionism

International economists have not, of course, been oblivious to the stark contrast between their advocacy of free trade and the universal practice of protection. In the last 20 years a school of thought, called the Public Choice school, has evolved in the US to explain this contrast. It is based on the seminal work of Mancur Olson (1965) and Anne Krueger (1974).

The starting point of this view is that, while trade liberalization may increase the aggregate consumption possibilities of all households in an economy, it does not increase the real consumption of every individual household. Consequently it will be in the self-interest of those households which stand to lose from trade liberalization to oppose it. The essential idea is that trade liberalization will tend to yield large benefits which are dispersed over a large part of the population whereas the losses are concentrated on a few income earners. This idea is actually a fairly old piece of professional wisdom.

The gainers from trade liberalization will normally be the consumers/users of the commodities traded and importers, export industries in the home country, and the suppliers in the exporting countries. The losers will normally be owners of capital assets in protected industries and the workers employed whose assets or skills are 'specific' to the industry in that they cannot be employed in other industries, and exporters in other industries. The exact pattern of gains and losses will be complex and will vary from case to case. To take one example, businesses and individuals pay taxes to local or regional authorities and, if an industry is concentrated geographically, it is common to see the regional authorities join forces with the owners of firms and workers to oppose reforms which will hurt their region.

The ideas are given more precision by introducing Krueger's concept of rent-seeking. The rents which an individual supplier of some factor (a capital asset or a worker's labour skills) receives in the present occupation is the difference between the current income and the best alternative income in another occupation. Many individuals in protected industries receive rents. These include the owners of specific factors and workers who would be laid off and unable to find another equally paid job. This concept of rents defines precisely the losers and the gainers from any change in government protection.

The next component of the models which seek to explain protection is that all of the gainers from some act of trade protection will form a coalition to press their case. Similarly, all of the losers will form a coalition. Thus, there is a protectionist coalition and an anti-protectionist coalition. But there are asymmetries in the cost and benefits of coalition formation. In particular, it is much more difficult for consumers to form a coalition. Their numbers are much larger, they are geographically dispersed and each stands to gain or lose only a little from each change in protection policy. On the other hand, the producers are often few in number and have already formed industry or trade associations. Moreover, producers are often better informed of the threat or the possibility of government actions. That is, there are asymmetries of information which again favour the producer coalition over the consumer coalition.

The final component is that politicians use their legislative powers to maximize their own self-interests, the probability of re-election, by deciding in favour of that coalition group which can deliver the most votes. This is not in general the coalition with the most gainers or losers or the coalition with the most to gain or lose in the aggregate, for the reasons elaborated above. Consequently such political decisions are not in the interest of the nation. Moreover, we see that it is in the nature of the protectionist process that those individual income groups which are the least deserving because they are the highest cost producers have the greatest incentives to seek government assistance.

The prediction of this view of the world is that there will be protection and that the levels of protection will differ markedly among industries. Such protection will have an anti-trade bias which will cause losses to the whole economy of some of the gains from free trade. There will be further losses to the economy because it will distort the pattern of production within the trading sector of the economy.

This totally selfish view of the world reduces politics to a system of trading in property rights in which the politicians are the intermediaries. While it may have some appeal, it is plainly incomplete. It can be extended in many ways.

An alternative view of the world is that changes in levels of protection to various commodity groups come about as a *defensive* mechanism. They are designed to protect incomes already earned rather than to gain further increases in income. After all, the term 'protectionism' itself indicates that action is being initiated to protect something which already exists. This has considerable appeal for commodity groups such as textiles and clothing and footwear where traditional producers in all advanced industrialized countries have come under intense competition from new low-cost producers, first in the Asian NICs (newly industrialized countries), later in other industrializing countries in Asia and Latin America and most recently the People's Republic of China. The market shares of these new suppliers have steadily increased in this commodity group, despite very high levels of protection in many countries.

In this context, we could most generally interpret protectionism as rent protection. An important case of rent protection is government action which is motivated by job protection. That is, the government is concerned with the loss of income to those who derive their income from employment in the activities. This view of the political process is not necessarily in conflict with the Olson-type models. Rather it emphasizes that the politicians and governments weigh more heavily on some income changes than others. Politicians may still get electoral credit for such actions as the public sympathize with such groups whose incomes or jobs are at risk.

Attempts have been made to test empirically such political economy models of government behaviour in the area of protection and assistance to industries. These have been conducted chiefly in the US. There was a major study of assistance to manufacturing industries in Australia by Anderson (1980). This study included variables from the rent-seeking model such as the number of firms in the industry and the degree of concentration and variables which were intended to model defensive actions such as the change in the number of employees and the average wage of employees. It actually explained about 40 per cent of the inter-industry variation in effective rates of assistance from border protection including tariffs, quotas and subsidies in Australia for the years between 1968–9 and 1977–78. Given that many tariffs were fixed decades ago and have not been adjusted subsequently, this constitutes a remarkably successful attempt to explain the inter-industry pattern of assistance. This and other studies in the US indicate that the political economy view of the determination of protection must be taken seriously.

In a later book, *The Rise and Decline of Nations: Economic Growth Stagflation, and Social Rigidities*, Olson pushed his view of the world further and sought to explain the differences among nations in their rates of growth of incomes over time. He argued that countries which have well-developed interest groups – and he puts the UK, Australia and New Zealand in this category – will have lower growth rates as these interest groups will combine to oppose changes in market shares and other structural changes that are essential for a rapidly growing economy. After analysing the dismal growth experience of Australia and New Zealand, he states that 'the theory fits these countries like a pair of gloves' (Olson, 1982, p. 135). He argues that the long history of political stability and immunity from invasion due to geographic isolation allowed the formation of powerful interest groups and their linking to the two main political parties. On a grander scale he notes that the UK and the US as well as Australia and New Zealand, the group of English-speaking industrialized countries, which are characterized by stable two-party democracies, have all had rates of growth markedly below those of the European Community (EC) countries, Japan and several other industrialized countries.

With this background we can now consider the New Zealand experience.

Import substitution in New Zealand: 1938 to 1980

There is one feature of the New Zealand experience of protectionism over the last 50 years that distinguishes it from all other advanced industrialized countries. This is the reliance for all of that time on import licensing as the primary instrument of protection. Prior to 1938 New Zealand relied, like other countries, upon the tariff as the instrument of protection. In 1938 import licensing was introduced and remains today in the same basic form as an instrument of protection, though the commodity coverage and the severity of the individual import restrictions have waxed and recently waned. No other advanced industrialized country has used quantitative controls on imports for such a wide range of commodities or for so long. Australia abandoned its import licensing as a general instrument by 1962. To find comparable regimes in recent years one must look at countries like Israel, India and other developing countries.

The reliance on import controls has had a number of consequences. First, it has given very high average rates of effective protection to import-competing industries. Import licensing applied principally to manufacturing sector products, though initially all imported commodities were also subject to import licensing. These manufacturing products were also protected by tariffs. The General Agreement on Tariffs and Trade (GATT) has sytematically measured rates of protection due to tariffs as a preparation for recent multilateral trade and tariff negotiations. GATT (1972) was prepared for the Kennedy Round. It found that the average tariffs in New Zealand were higher than in any other industrialized country. This was still true in 1976 before the Tokyo Round cuts took effect. At that time the average tariff in New Zealand on dutiable imports (which is a better measure than the tariffs on all imports because duty-free access to imported materials and capital goods increases the effective protection for the value added in an economic activity) was 30.2 per cent. (As an Australian resident I note sadly that the second highest average tariff rate was for Australia with 26.4 per cent.)

For most commodities during the licensing period the import licensing restrictions, not the tariffs, were the binding constraint on imports. It follows inescapably that the regime of tariffs and import licensing was extremely restrictive by international standards. Recent estimates of the average rates are noted later.

This high average rate of effective assistance to import-competing sectors restricted trade. Anything which restricts import trade will restrict export trade, given a level of deficit or surplus in the balance of payments. Export industries are one of the groups in the economy which are inevitably harmed by protection to import-competing producers.

Second, it gave a highly differentiated structure of protection within the manufacturing sector. This differentiation introduces inefficiencies of production within the sector.

Third, it gave an unstable structure of protection. Unfortunately, we do not have estimates of the structure of protection in detail for successive periods in New Zealand but we can still be sure of this conclusion. If the import licence for a given category of goods subject to licensing is maintained over time the level of nominal protection which the licences imply will change over time as the demand for and/or supply of imports changes. For example, if there is an increase in demand because of a growth of incomes and the licensed good is a normal good with a positive income elasticity of demand, the implicit protection will rise. If the value of the licences is changed in a way other than that required to maintain the implicit rate of protection this too will change the implicit protection.

Several features of the New Zealand system of import licensing aggravated the problem of instability inherent in a quantitative regime. For much of the period of licensing the licences were issued every six months and they were subject to frequent adjustments up and down, depending on the availability of foreign exchange and other economic and political factors. Moreover, the categories of goods subject to each licence were defined very narrowly for most of the period. Narrow banding rules out the possibilities of offsetting changes which can occur within broader categories. For the period since the tendering of licences was introduced in 1981 instability is evident in the premia paid for goods in licensed categories, though it is compounded by the downward trend due to liberalization.

Fourth, the system of import licensing greatly restricted competition in the industries producing the protected goods and in the importing and retailing industries. Quantitative restrictions reduce the level of competition in several ways. They eliminate competition at the margin from all overseas producers. Potential new domestic entrants into the activity are restricted by the requirement for licences for essential imported materials or capital equipment. For 50 years the survival of many manufacturing establishments in New Zealand has been at the mercy of the annual or semi-annual decisions of officials in the former Departments of Industries and Commerce and of Trade and Industry who allocated these licences.

Fifth, rent-seeking has another cost to society because it consumes resources. A great deal of effort is expended by potential rent beneficiaries. Rent-seeking activities such as lobbying for licences are costly and the considerable costs imposed on the public sector must also be reckoned.

The effects of the licensing system on the long-run growth performance of the New Zealand economy are more difficult to assess. First, we need to consider the growth record.

The performance of the New Zealand economy in terms of growth in average real incomes has been abysmal. During a period in which real incomes have grown in the world economy at higher rates and for a longer sustained period than ever the real incomes of households in New Zealand have grown slowly. After 1951, the peak year of the Korean War wool boom which boosted the national income by 14 per cent, the real gross national profit (GNP) per capita has grown by around 1 per cent per annum. There have been long periods during which there has been stagnation. For example, for the latest quarter available at the time of writing, September 1988, the real GNP per capita was at virtually the same level as in 1974!

After the mid-1970s the macroeconomic performance of the New Zealand economy worsened. In 1978 the registered unemployment rate trebled from the figure of 0.6 per cent to 1.8 and it has increased steadily since then to levels which are normal in other industrialized countries (the unemployment rate at March 1989 is 7.4 per cent).[4] And in 1977 that most sensitive of indicators of national performance, the net migration rate, switched from a net inward migration of over 5,000 in 1976 to a substantial and negative net outward migration of over 16,000 in 1977.

The cumulative effect over decades of a relatively slow rate of growth of real incomes per capita has meant that New Zealand has fallen steadily in the ranking of countries by per capita incomes. Economic historians estimate that in the late nineteenth century New Zealand may have had the highest average real incomes in the world. In the early 1950s New Zealand ranked third after the US and Switzerland but there are now more than 20 countries with a per capita income higher than that in New Zealand.

The dismal record of almost stagnant real incomes, rising unemployment, wide fluctuations and rising net emigration became of more concern to New Zealanders in the late 1970s (see New Zealand Planning Council, 1978 for example). It is now evident that the problem was of much longer standing. One factor that disguised it is the unusually irregular path of GNP and GNP per capita in New Zealand noted above. Nevertheless, there does seem to have been a long recognition lag in policy formulation. The basic problem of the New Zealand economy should have been evident much sooner. I was living in New Zealand at the time an article appeared in *The Economist* (Anonymous, 1963) which lampooned the New Zealand growth performance. It was entitled 'How to Progress Backwards'. It caused considerable comment because it was written by an anonymous author who styled himself ambiguously as an 'economist in New Zealand' and there was speculation that it had been written by a prominent government adviser who did not wish to be identified. It is of interest now as an example of an early recognition and diagnosis of the trading difficulties of the economy. The author's judgement on import licensing was severe:

> Prohibition of competing imports (known euphemistically as 'import licensing') is the main method of enabling New Zealand manufacturers to cover their costs. This assists the transition by insulating domestic industry from increased efficiency overseas. Further, the dependence of industry on import licenses for raw materials and capital goods ensures that the major decisions on scale and method of manufacture will be made by public servants who have no financial interest in the outcome of their decisions. This divorce of decision-making from incentives, via import or other licensing, is a trick well worth imitating by any society which wishes to damp down the rate of economic growth.

It will not be possible without a major research project to ascertain the contribution which the high protectionism of the manufacturing sector may have made to the poor macroeconomic performance of the New Zealand economy. Such a project should be top priority in New Zealand and it would be of considerable interest to other countries. The difficulty is the standard one of isolating the effects of this factor from those of other policies or events. As a generalization the New Zealand economy has been highly regulated and there has been high average levels of direct taxation until the

1980s. In the trading sector, the terms of trade have trended downwards since the peak of the Korean War boom. Moreover, the access of New Zealand to the UK markets for butter and cheese and lamb products has been increasingly restricted since the UK accession to the European Economic Community (EEC) in 1973. All of these and other factors have contributed to the poor New Zealand performance.

The standard wisdom among international trade economists today is that restrictions on trade, especially on trade in manufactures which have grown much more rapidly in volume than trade in primary commodities or minerals, retard the growth performance of an economy. A large number of country studies sponsored by the World Bank, the National Bureau of Economic Research in the US and the OECD are all agreed that there is a consistent and strong positive correlation between trade liberalization, export performance and the rate of growth. New Zealand fits this statistical pattern – it has had a highly restrictive trade policy, a slow rate of growth in the volume of trade, and a very poor growth performance.

It is beyond dispute that the trade restrictions have reduced the size of the trade sector in the New Zealand economy. There is an old perception of New Zealand by its economists as a 'dependent economy' (see, especially, Simkin, 1951). One feature of trade dependence is a high ratio of the value of total exports and imports to national income. In this sense New Zealand was a dependent economy up to the 1960s. However, its failure to participate in the rapid growth of world trade in manufactures has meant that it ceased to be a dependent economy in this sense relative to other industrialized countries. Its trade ratio is now much lower than most industrialized countries and much lower than that of other small developed countries. It is true that the reduced access to EC and other markets for its traditional primary commodity exports and the downward trend in its terms of trade would, other things being equal, have reduced this ratio. On the other hand, transport costs which provide 'natural protection' and which especially inhibit trade for a country which is distant from its trading partners have trended downwards as a percentage of the value of internationally traded commodities. The relatively low trade ratio is the product of import trade restrictions to a significant extent.

Political economy in New Zealand

There is an interesting set of questions in how the extraordinary record of protectionism in New Zealand came about, why it persisted for so long and how it came to be reversed so suddenly.

The New Zealand political system is an oddity in terms of its overall structure. In the British tradition, elections to Parliament are made under the 'first past the post' method of voting. With all serious candidates associated with a party, voters who vote for a third-party candidate are unlikely to affect the election in the electorate in which they are voting. Consequently, it is difficult for third parties to obtain votes as even voters who rank them first must vote for one of the two main parties if their votes are to affect the outcome, unless the third party has reached a threshold level which makes it a credible threat. This discouragement of third parties is aggravated in New Zealand (and in Great Britain) by the automatic link between the party winning the majority of seats, which then constitutes the government, and the choice of the Prime Minister as the leader of this party. This means that a vote for a third-party candidate is unlikely to affect the national government as well as the choice of the voters' own representatives in their electorates. (By contrast, the 'separation of powers' in the US Constitution separates these two choices.) Moreover, the New Zealand system is non-federal, unicameral, and is based on no written constitution. In consequence New Zealand may be said to possess, for good or ill, the purest form of two-party government.

As in other countries which employ the 'first past the post' system, the New Zealand system has encouraged a very stable two-party contest. In fact, throughout most of the period of import licensing and protectionism which we are seeking to explain, elections have been essentially contests between the National Party and the Labour Party. The first Labour Party Government was elected in 1935 and the first National Party Government in 1949. Two minority parties in particular, the Social Credit Party (later the Democrats Party) and the New Zealand Party, did mount determined challenges to the two ruling parties but failed to get more than one or two members elected at their peak despite achieving a significant percentage of the national vote.

All of these features mean that the choice of all elected representatives depends solely upon a single set of elections for a single House held at intervals of not more than three years. This has two consequences. The first is that once the governing Party with a majority in the House of Representatives has decided upon a policy there is no obstacle to the immediate implementation of this policy. The second is that this system tends to intensify the opportunities for particular rent-seeking or rent-protecting groups to achieve real income gains. If these groups can form an effective coalition which may mean the loss or gain of a small number of marginal electorates, such groups may persuade one party to act as their agent, even though their numbers may be quite small.

Given the coincidence of a macroeconomic performance which is unique and a political system which is unique, it is tempting to attribute some of the former to the latter. Indeed, this association underlies the remarks of Olson quoted above. However, I do not think this is correct.

Significantly, the support for heavy protection of the import-competing sector has been bipartisan for most of the period. When it first came into office the National Party promised to 'overhaul' the system and it did substantially liberalize licences. Whereas in 1949 100 per cent of imports required licences by the time it lost office in 1956 the percentage had fallen to 40 per cent. When it regained office in 1960 the National Party did slowly reduce the commodity coverage of the system but it did retain the system. The National Party supported the objective of promoting import-replacing industries, though it also provided subsidies and assistance via price and income stabilization support and tax incentives to traditional farm exporters to compensate partially for the adverse effects of import replacement on these producers. Even more convincing against the Olson hypothesis, the National Party was, especially in the early days the party of the farmers, the only large group of exporters in the economy before the emergence of forest product exports and other manufacturing exports. If it had acted to protect the interests of this constituency the National Party would have opposed import replacement policies.

What then does explain the New Zealand experience? One important factor is the experience of the Great Depression. Import licensing was introduced by the newly victorious Labour Government after the Great Depression. New Zealand (and Australia) had suffered particularly badly from the contraction in world trade during the depression and there was a strong urge to 'insulate' the economy from the vagaries of world trade.

A second factor was the presence of a strong ideological belief in government intervention. The Labour Party was a planning party. The National Party rhetoric spoke of the party as the party of 'free enterprise' but it accepted a measure of state direction of economic activities and of state ownership of activities such as the statutory marketing boards for all of the major farm products which was extraordinarily high by comparison with other industrialized countries.

This belief in the role of the state guiding development of the economy was nurtured and supported by most professional opinion in New Zealand. Import licensing is a comprehensive system of quantitative controls on imports and all quantitative controls were proscribed by the GATT except under specified conditions. New Zealand justified its system to GATT under the article which applied to countries with chronic balance of payments problems. Throughout the period the belief that there was a foreign exchange gap which constrained growth possibilities in New Zealand was widespread among New Zealand economists until the 1980s, despite this theory of development having been discredited on both theoretical and empirical grounds in other countries. (One notable early critic of import licensing was Simkin (1962). The Monetary and Economic Council and some New Zealand economists were strongly critical of the administration of the import licensing system. In 1969 the National Development Conference recommended that licensing be replaced by tariff competition in order to encourage efficiency and competition and wider consumer choice.)

Thus Protectionists in New Zealand based their arguments on the national interest. In his earlier survey of Protectionism, Bastable emphasized that this was a standard feature of protectionist arguments. Earlier John Stuart Mill had stated this opinion (Mill, 1848, Book V, Chapter X, para 1):

> Protectionists often reason extremely ill, but it is an injustice to them to suppose that their protectionist creed rests on nothing superior to an economic blunder; many of them have been led to it much more out of consideration of humanity than by purely economic reasons.

This New Zealand case study shows that governments did not act purely as mediators between conflicting private interests. Rather they combined ideological views with the politics of interest groups.[5] This process was aided by arguments in favour of interventionism from economists and other intellectuals. Thus it was a conjuction of three factors which determined protectionist policy – party ideological views, interest groups and intellectual opinion.

One Olson-type factor helping to perpetuate the system once it had been put in place was the large rents accruing to licence-holders. When trade is restricted by the instrument of a quota or a system of import licensing, rents are likely to be particularly high. These rents accrued to two groups, the licence-holders and the domestic producers of commodities subject to tight licensing controls. The traditional method of allocating licenses among importers in all countries is to allocate them administratively, usually on the basis of the historical market shares of importers in some base period. This administrative allocation gives valuable property rights to the licence-holders and they have defended these rights vigorously.

The next interesting question is why this long-standing policy collapsed so suddenly. The collapse was not due to any dramatic change in the political order. It reflects a fundamental rethinking of the performance of the economy and the effects of government policies. It was led by staff in the Treasury (see Preston, 1978 and Carpinter, 1979, for example), the Reserve Bank and some others (for example, McClean, 1978). Pressure for trade liberalization and other reforms to free up the economy was also exerted by the OECD (1977) and the IMF. The latter was sharply critical of the heavily protected and heavily regulated economy in its 1980 Experts' Report. This author had his say in a report prepared for the New Zealand Planning Council (Lloyd et al., 1980). All of these authors favoured a movement towards a more market-oriented economy.

The unilateral trade liberalization was a part of this broader movement. In the trade sector this movement required a reduction in import barriers and a reduction in subsidies to exporters, the ending of import licensing and the establishment of an exchange rate which reflected the current demand and supply for foreign exchange. The case for trade liberalization reforms was aided by the success of the Closer Economic Relations negotiations with Australia which were completed in 1982 and showed that it was possible to achieve bilateral trade liberalization.

The trade liberalization reforms began in 1979 with the announcement of new policies towards import licensing including the intention to allocate them by tender, the adoption of a crawling peg exchange rate system and the establishment of Industry Plans for a number of industries to facilitate structural adjustment in these industries. However, it was the Lange Labour Government elected in 1984 which first embraced these policies wholeheartedly and had the political will to change policies. Thus, ironically, it was a Labour Government which took the decision in 1984 to dismantle the system of import licensing which had been introduced by the first Labour Government and to initiate the unilateral reduction in tariffs.

The United Kingdom experience
The United Kingdom experience is in broad terms much like that of the other major industrialized countries. Beginning with the first GATT Round in 1947 average tariffs have fallen steadily. The average nominal tariff rate has fallen from a pre-Second World War average of around 40 per cent to around 5 per cent. However, there has been an increase in quantitative restrictions on some commodity groups, especially clothing and textiles. In the UK there is the added factor that entry into the EEC in 1973 forced it to abandon the policy which it had followed since the repeal of the Corn Laws in 1846 of allowing duty-free and unrestricted entry for major foodstuffs.

To my knowledge there have been four empirical studies of the structure of nominal and effective protection in the UK.[6] Unfortunately, all of these are restricted to tariffs alone. They ignore non-tariff forms of protection and subsidies and other forms of assistance. Thus we know considerably less about the structure of protection in the UK than we do in Australia and New Zealand.

The latest results are those of Ennew et al. (1989) for the year 1986. The unweighted average nominal and effective tariff rates were 1.52 per cent and 1.20 per cent respectively. These rates are very low. It is also most unusual for the effective rate to be lower than the nominal rate. The authors note that this is due to the large number of negative effective rates; some 37 out of 101 industries have negative effective rates. In any case it is the dispersion of rates around the average and not the average itself which matters. A number of negative rates combined with a number of positive rates yields a differentiated structure, even if the average is close to zero. Some activities are relatively highly protected by tariffs, most notably agriculture and horticulture, electronic consumer goods, soft drinks, and a group of textile and clothing industries (hosiery and other knitted goods, clothing and furs, household and other made up textiles).

These results tell us that protection by means of tariffs is once again not important in the UK. However, this result does not imply a new era of free trade in the UK because of the growth of non-tariff forms of protection for some manufactures and the growth of agricultural protectionism under the Common Agricultural Policy (CAP). There is an urgent need for a systematic study of all forms of industry assistance in all sectors of the UK economy, like those which have been done for the Australian economy and more recently for the New Zealand economy (see below).

Aiding anti-protectionism

The New Zealand experience is of some help in explaining why a highly differentiated structure of industry assistance which yields considerable benefit to some industries and imposes considerable penalties on others can persist, and what might be done to reverse the protectionist pattern.

In the first place, the effects of the regime of import licensing on the structure of assistance to industries was obscure. A number of attempts had been made in New Zealand over the years to measure the structure of protection for manufacturing activities in single years.[7] Of these studies the first by Hampton (1965) and Candler and Hampton (1966) were especially commendable. They are based on direct price comparisons for a sample of commodities. This is the most reliable method of estimating nominal rates when protection is given by non-tariff instruments such as import licensing. Moreover, they estimated a version of the concept of 'effective protection' which had been introduced to international trade economists in that region of the world by Corden (1963). These estimates are among the very first estimates in the world of the implicit protection resulting from quantitative restrictions on trade and of effective protection. They were done at approximately the same time as estimates of effective protection for manufacturing industries in Australia in the Report of the Committee of Economic Enquiry (1965, II, Appendix L, iv). Max Corden was an adviser to this Committee. The first detailed estimates of effective protection for the US were published by Basevi (1966) and for the UK by Barker and Han (1971).

Candler and Hampton (1966, p. 52) went on to relate their measures to high levels of protection:

> The rates of protection which have been afforded different New Zealand industries varies greatly. It seems improbable that economic policymakers would intentionally provide protection ranging from zero to 177 per cent [for a selection of commodities which were items in the Consumer Price Index].

They recommended their measures as a method of quantifying the criteria which the New Zealand Tariff and Development Board could use in conducting enquiries for the purpose of deciding on the level of protection appropriate for particular industries. Unfortunately, this excellent suggestion was not taken up at the time.

The later studies of levels of protection differ in terms of commodity coverage, concepts and methods of measurement. The Economic Monitoring Group (1984) of the New Zealand Planning Council endeavoured to get consistent estimates to form a partial time series. These series show nominal and effective rates of protection for manufactures which were consistently very high over the 30 years from 1955 to 1985. The average nominal rate peaked in 1964–67 at 54 per cent and in 1982–82 at 50 per cent. The Economic Monitoring Group estimated that 'Clothing' industry received an effective rate of protection of 1,105 per cent at its peak in 1964–67 and the 'Vehicle Assembly' industry received 2,428 per cent during the period 1955–58.

The Report by Syntec Economic Services (1988) was the first set of measures in New Zealand of assistance to producers which was comprehensive in covering all manufacturing and agricultural producers and in terms of covering all tariffs, identifiable subsidies and import licensing instruments of assistance. It is very detailed as estimates of nominal and effective rates of assistance are calculated at the five-digit level of the New Zealand Standard Industrial Classification. 1981–82 is the earliest year covered by this report. The average nominal rate of assistance was 20 per cent and the average effective rate of assistance was 39 per cent. These are very high by OECD country standards. (The comparable figures for Australia in the same year were 9 per cent and 25 per cent respectively.) It is certain that these were the highest average levels of protectionism for the manufacturing sector among all industrialized countries. Some industries received very high rates of protection. At the two-digit level the most highly protected industries were the 'Textile, Wearing Apparel, Leather Industries' and 'Fabricated Metal Products, Machinery and Equipment' which had effective rates of assistance of 90 and 69 per cent respectively.

These statistics confirmed after many years that New Zealand was an extremely protectionist country in that year. Moreover, the year in question is after the trade liberalization reforms had begun and quite a long time after the peak of import licensing coverage in the 1950s and mid-1960s.

Across the Tasman, the Tariff Board, which was the statutory advisory board then responsible for recommending to the Australian Government levels of protection for commodity groups under review, produced the first detailed set of estimates of effective protection in the manufacturing sector of Australia in its 1970 Annual Report (Tariff Board, 1970, Appendix 2). Since then the Tariff Board and its successor, the Industries Assistance Commission, have refined and extended these studies of protection. Australia now has an annual time series of nominal and effective rates of protection. No other country has an official body which monitors the effects of government protection decisions in this way to my knowledge.

In recent years this goal of exposing the process of determining the levels of protection to more scrutiny has become known as 'transparency'. There are two alternative routes to making the policy determination system more transparent. One is by domestic surveillance and the other by multilateral surveillance. The measurement of the levels of protection discussed above is one aspect of domestic surveillance.

As a part of the present Uruguay Round the GATT established a group devoted to the 'functioning of the GATT system (FOGS)'. At the Montreal mid-term review earlier this year, GATT trade ministers were able to agree on the establishment of a 'Trade Policy Review Mechanism', the function of which is 'to examine the impact of a contracting party's trade policies on the multilateral trading system'. Periodic reviews are to be conducted by the GATT Council and they are to be based on two reports – one submitted by the countries under review and the other by the GATT secretariat. The focus of these reviews is on the effects of policies on other countries, and particularly on conformity to GATT rules. Given the complexity of GATT rules and the difficulties of reaching agreement among many countries with differing national interests, this route will be difficult.

In the last two years a new axis has developed between groups in the UK, Australia and New Zealand, all of which have been pressing for greater 'domestic transparency'. Since the establishment of the Tariff Board in 1921, Australia has had an independent statutory body charged with enquiring into proposals for changes in tariffs and later other forms of industry assistance. The Tariff Board and its successor, the Industries Assistance Commission, did not prevent some large increases in protection. However, the rates of industry assistance are lower and more rational than they would have been without this public scrutiny. In the longer term the Tariff Board and the IAC have brought about an enormous increase in the understanding of industry assistance, the necessity to view these instruments from the point of view of the economy as a whole, and who in the economy gains and who loses from protecting one industry.

In the UK the Trade Policy Research Centre has commissioned two studies on this subject, one headed by the former director-general of the GATT, Olivier Long and one by an Australian team which included two former chairmen of the Industries Assistance Commission. The Long Report (1987, p. (i)) stated its main premise with admirable clarity.

> This report is built on the premise that trade policy is the international dimension of national policies adopted primarily for **domestic** reasons. An additional ingredient, to make it possible for governments to **act** against the protection they have themselves introduced, is greater public awareness within protecting countries of the domestic costs of protection and subsidies. Governments have demonstrated that they are not likely to remove such measures just out of concern for their adverse effect on foreign producers. They are much more likely to do so out of concern for the costs they impose on domestic constituents.

New Zealand advocated to the FOGS group in 1987 that it develop criteria to assist contracting parties establish domestic surveillance bodies. Despite support from some nations, the FOGS group decided to concentrate upon international surveillance. The second report commissioned by the Trade Policy Research Centre has renewed advocacy of domestic surveillance carried out by an independent domestic agency (Rattigan, et al., 1989).

There is a third variant of these exposure models. A group of exporters in one country, who are harmed by restrictions on their access to another country, may go to the second country and attempt to convince the residents of that country that its own government is acting against their interests. This was suggested by Finger (1982, p. 376):

> The Argentineans would buy television time in Japan to show an Argentine family enjoying

a big roast beef and to show Japanese families how much of that roast beef they would have after the government of Japan took its slice.

One section of the Australian Government has adopted a policy of this type. The Australian Bureau of Agricultural Economics (1985) did a major study of the Common Agricultural Policy of the EC which became known popularly as The Red Book. This was targeted at the residents of the EC and sought to show the cost of the CAP to EC consumers and taxpayers.

Some conclusions

While the New Zealand Government has practised very protectionist policies towards much of the output of the manufacturing sector, one should also note that the levels of assistance for pastoral agricultural commodities – meat, wool and milk products – have been low. In 1981–82, the average nominal rate of assistance for this commodity group was 13 per cent. This is far below the OECD average for these commodities, and it has fallen to a mere 1 per cent in 1987–88 after the elimination of most agricultural subsidies in New Zealand (Syntec Economic Services, 1988). It is ironic that in the same period as New Zealand has abandoned its long-standing protectionist policies towards its non-competitive manufactures the UK has abandoned its long-standing free trade policies towards non-competitive agricultural products.

In giving high levels of protection to some of its non-competitive manufactures New Zealand has acted no differently than the EC countries, Japan and the US which have given high levels of protection to a range of high-cost agricultural commodities. When one looks at all sectors in the economies, New Zealand may not be the most protectionist country in the OECD. There is a Euro–Japan-centric bias in much of the global discussion of protectionism in that it has been preoccupied with protectionism of manufactures alone.

The essence of protectionism in all sectors in all countries is that rent-seekers seek an increase in their real incomes and thereby impose losses on others in the economy, and that the value of these losses exceeds the gains to the rent-seekers. Bhagwati (1982) has classified rent-seeking as one type of DUP-activity, that is, a Directly-Unproductive Profit-seeking Activity, pronounced 'dupe'. Such activities are profitable to the individuals pursuing them but not to the society. (Other examples of DUP activities are tax evasion and theft.)

Perhaps the greatest cost of protectionism is the attitudes it breeds among many agents in the economy. It breeds a kind of torpor that diverts effort from productive channels that increase the aggregate supplies of goods and services available to the economy. A famous enquiry into The Tariff in Australia expressed this felicitously:

> The most disquieting effect of the tariff has been the stimulus it has given for Government assistance of all kinds, with the consequent demoralising effect upon self-reliant efficiency through all forms of production. (Brigden Committee Report, 1929, p. 27)

Notes

1.   There have been other surveys of the subject. Two are notable. In the first *Palgrave's Dictionary of Political Economy* C.F. Bastable provided a very informative account of the origins of Protectionism in the nineteenth-century writings of Alexander Hamilton, Friedrich List and others. This emphasized

that Protectionism is based on the nationalist approach to trade policy. The second account I shall mention is the recent masterly survey by Bhagwati (1988).

2. The desirability of free trade does depend on markets for all commodities working efficiently. In particular, it requires competitive behaviour by all agents and prices which reflect the marginal social costs of production. If there is uncertainty in commodity markets it requires a complete set of markets for all contingencies.

3. Presumably this claim excludes the tariff changes due to tariff reclassifications and simplification.

4. This is the rate as measured by the Household Labour Force Survey which is now preferred to the registered unemployment rate because the former conforms to international conventions relating to the measurement of unemployment. This unemployment rate is less than the registered unemployment rate which was 9.1 per cent in the same month.

5. Quiggin (1989) is also critical of the Olson–Anderson political economy approach and claims that it does not explain inter-industry differences in industry assistance in Australia.

6. Barker and Han (1972), Kitchin (1976), Oulton (1976), and Greenaway (1988) and Ennew et al. (1989).

7. Hampton (1965) and Candler and Hampton (1966) provided estimates for selected commodities in the year 1955, Elkan (1972) had provided estimates for selected industries in the years 1955–58 and 1964–67, Elley (1976) provided estimates for 1972–73, and O'Dea and Hersfield (1981) for 1978–79.

References

Anderson, K. (1980), 'The Political Market for Government Assistance to Australian Manufacturing Industries', *Economic Record*, **56**, June, 132–44.

Anonymous (1963), 'How to Progress Backwards', *The Economist*, March 9, 874–76.

Barker, T.S. and S.S. Han (1971), 'Effective Rates of Protection for United Kingdom Production', *Economic Journal*, **81**, June, 282–93.

Basevi, G. (1966), 'The United States Tariff Structure: Estimate of Effective Rates of Protection of United States Industries and Industrial Labor', *Review of Economics and Statistics*, **47**, May, 142– 60.

Bastable, C.F. (1926), 'Protection, and Protective System' in H. Higgs (ed.), *Palgrave's Dictionary of Political Economy*, Macmillan, London, 234–36.

Bhagwati, J. (1982), 'Directly-Unproductive, Profit-Seeking (DUP) Activities', *Journal of Political Economy*, **90**, 988–1002.

Bhagwati, J. (1988), *Protectionism*, MIT Press, Cambridge, Mass.

Brigden, J.B. et al. (The Brigden Committee) (1929), *The Australian Tariff: An Economic Enquiry*, Melbourne University Press, Melbourne.

Bureau of Agricultural Economics (1985), *Agricultural Policies in the European Community, Policy Monograph No. 2*, Australian Government Publishing Service, Canberra.

Candler, W. and P. Hampton (1966), 'The Measurement of Industrial Protection in New Zealand', *Australian Economic Papers*, **5**, June, 47–58.

Carpinter, P. (1979), 'Trade, Protection and Growth – The New Zealand Experience', paper presented to the Australia and New Zealand Association for the Advancement of Science Congress, Auckland, January.

Committee of Economic Enquiry (1965), *Report on the Committee of Economic Enquiry* (Vernon Committee Report), 2 volumes, Commonwealth Government Printing Office, Canberra.

Corden, W.M. (1963), 'The Tariff', in A. Hunter (ed.), *The Economics of Australian Industry*, Melbourne University Press, Melbourne, Chapter 5.

Economic Monitoring Group (1984), *Strategy for Growth*, Economic Monitoring Group, New Zealand Planning Council, Wellington.

Elkan, P.G. (1972), *Industrial Protection in New Zealand 1952 to 1967*, Technical Memorandum No.15, New Zealand Institute of Economic Research, Wellington.

Elley, V. (1976), 'Effective Protection in Selected New Zealand Manufacturing Industries in 1972/73', Project on Economic Planning Occasional Paper No. 29, Victoria University of Wellington, Wellington.

Ennew, C., D. Greenaway and G. Reed (1989), 'Does Tariff Liberalisation Matter to the UK?', Centre for Research in Economic Development and International Trade, University of Nottingham.

Findlay, R. (1987), 'Free Trade and Protection', in J. Eatwell, M. Milgate and P. Newman (eds), *The New Palgrave: A Dictionary of Economics*, Macmillan, London, **2**, 421–22.

Finger, M. (1982), 'Incorporating Gains from Trade into Policy', *World Economy*, **5**, 367–77.

General Agreement on Tariffs and Trade (1972), *Basic Documentation for Tariff Study*, GATT, Geneva.

Greenaway, D. (1988), 'Effective Tariff Protection in the United Kingdom', *Oxford Bulletin of Economics and Statistics*, **50**, August, 313–24.

Hampton, P. (1965), *The Degree of Protection Accorded by Import Licensing to New Zealand Manufacturing Industry*, Agricultural Economics Research Unit Report No. 12, Lincoln College, Canterbury.

Helpman, E. and P. Krugman (1989), *Trade Policy and Market Structure*, MIT Press, Cambridge, Mass.

Journal of Political Economy (1985), 'The Divisions of Labour, IV: The Philosopher and the Yes Man', *Journal of Political Economy*, **93**, October, back page.

Kitchin, P.D. (1976), 'Effective Rates of Protection in UK Manufacturing for 1963 and 1968', in M.J. Artis and A.R. Nobay (eds), *Essays in Economic Analysis*, Cambridge University Press, Cambridge.

Krueger, A. (1974), 'The Political Economy of the Rent-seeking Society", *American Economic Review*, **64**, 291–303.

Lloyd, P.J. and others (1980), *New Zealand's Long Term Foreign Trade Problems and Structural Adjustment Policies*, New Zealand Planning Council, Wellington.

Long, O. and others (1987), *Public Scrutiny of Protection: A Report on Policy Transparency and Trade Liberalisation*, Trade Policy Research Centre, London.

McClean, I. (1978), *The Future for New Zealand Agriculture: Economic Strategies for the 1980's*, New Zealand Planning Council, Wellington.

Mill, J.S. (1852), *Principles of Political Economy with some of their Applications to Social Philosophy*, 3rd edition, Parker and Co., London.

New Zealand Planning Council (1978), *Planning Perspectives, 1978–83*, New Zealand Planning Council, Wellington.

O'Dea, D. and A. Hersfield (1981), 'Rate of Return on Capital Assets in Manufacturing and Agriculture, Adjusted for Protection' *New Zealand Institute of Economic Research*, Wellington.

OECD (1977), *New Zealand*, OECD, Paris.

Olson, M. ((1965), *The Logic of Collective Action*, Harvard University Press, Cambridge, Mass.

Olson, M. (1982), *The Rise and Decline of Nations*, Yale University Press, New Haven.

Preston, D.A. (1978) 'Restructuring the New Zealand Economy', *New Zealand Economic Papers*, **12**, 96–115.

Quiggin, J. (1989), 'The Role and Consequences of Special Interest Groups and Political Factors', in B. Chapman (ed.), *Australian Economic Growth*, Macmillan, South Melbourne.

Rattigan, G.A., W.B. Carmichael and G.R. Banks (1989), 'Domestic Transparency and the Functioning of the GATT System', a report prepared for the Trade Policy Research Centre, London.

Rayner, T. and R. Lattimore (1989), *The Timing and Sequencing of a Trade Liberalisation Policy: The Case of New Zealand*, World Bank, Washington, DC.

Simkin, C.G.F. (1951), *The Instability of a Dependent Economy: Economic Fluctuations in New Zealand 1840–1914*, Oxford University Press, Oxford.

Simkin, C.G.F. (1962), 'The Limits of Competitive Enterprise in New Zealand', in C.B. Hoover (ed.), *Economic Systems of the Commonwealth*, Duke University Press, Durham, NC.

Syntec Economic Services (1988), *Industial Assistance Reform in New Zealand*, Syntec Economic Services.

Tariff Board (1970), *Annual Report for the Year 1969–70*, Commonwealth Government Printing Office, Canberra.

PART III

UNILATERAL TRADE LIBERALIZATION

Introduction

N A

This section begins with a paper on the theory of lowering tariff barriers entitled 'A more general theory of price distortions in open economies'. While the theory of tariffs deals equally and symmetrically with tariff increase and tariff decreases, the theory has traditionally been approached from the point of view that, externalities and other strategic issues aside, tariffs impose a welfare loss on the tariff-imposing country. It usually, therefore, is couched in terms of the welfare effects of lowering tariff rates. This paper is concerned with the problems of piecemeal policy-making in which a government is considered to have a mandate to reform *partially* the structure of distorting border taxes, rather than move immediately to the first-best optimum of completely free trade. Some taxes are considered to be irremovable. This is a problem in the theory of the second-best. In particular, the paper was concerned with deriving simple rules which are sufficient for a welfare improvement. The two main rules considered were the reductions in extreme tariff rates and uniform reductions in all rates. Like most of the writings by international economists of the time, it uses the fiction of a single social utility function. Hatta (1977) provides a similar analysis of piecemeal policies.

The paper on 'Trade expenditure functions and gains from trade', co-authored with Albert Schweinberger, concerns basic issues of gains from trade as well as piecemeal reforms. The concept of a trade expenditure function turns out to be a very efficient one for the normative analysis of distorted economies. It provides a convenient money metric for changes in an economy in which there can be many households with distinct preferences and factor endowments. The function is $B(p^*,p,v,u)$ where p^* and p are the vectors of world prices and domestic prices respectively, v is the vector of primary endowments which are assumed constant and u is the vector of household utilities. Lloyd and Schweinberger were not the first to develop a trade expenditure function; compensated excess aggregate demand functions can also be found in Wan (1965) and more recently in Woodland (1982) and Bhagwati et al. (1983). Our conceptual contribution in this paper was to extend the function to the normative analysis of multi-household economies with distortions such as tariffs.

Since this paper was written other applications of the trade expenditure function to distorted economies have been made. The most important is probably the development by James Anderson and Peter Neary (see Anderson and Neary, 1994, 1996 and Anderson, 1995) of the concept of the Trade Restrictiveness Index. This is discussed in the first chapter and used in Chapter 7 in the analysis of unilateral reform in Australia.

Research on the topic of piecemeal national reforms continues today; for example, the problems of second-best piecemeal rules when the distortions take the form of quotas or a mixture of quotas and tariffs are analysed in the recent papers by Lahiri and Raimondos (1996) and Krishna and Panagariya (1997). The latter makes use of the trade expenditure function.

References

Anderson, J.E. (1995), 'Tariff Index Theory', *Review of International Economics*, **3**, June, 156–73.

Anderson, J.E. and J.P. Neary (1994), 'Measuring the Restrictiveness of Trade Policy', *World Bank Economic Review*, **8**, 151–69.

Anderson, J.E. and J.P. Neary (1996), 'A New Approach to Evaluating Trade Policy', *Review of Economic Studies*, **63**, 107–25.

Bhagwati, J.N., R. Brecher and T. Hatta (1983), 'The Generalised Theory of Transfer and Welfare: Bilateral Transfers in a Multilateral World', *American Economic Review*, **83**, 606–18.

Hatta, T. (1977), 'A Theory of Piecemeal Policy Recommendations', *Review of Economic Studies*, **44**, 1–22.

Krishna, P. and A. Panagariya (1997), 'A Unification of the Theory of Second Best', working paper no. 31, Center for International Economics, University of Maryland.

Lahiri, S. and P. Raimondos (1996), 'Correcting Trade Distortions in a Small Open Economy', *International Economic Review*, **4**, 287–99.

Wan, H.Y. (1964), 'Maximum Bonus: An Alternative Measure for Trading Gains', *Review of Economic Studies*, **32**, 49–58.

Woodland, A.D. (1982), *International Trade and Resource Allocation*, North-Holland, Amsterdam.

[5]

Journal of International Economics 4 (1974) 365–386. © North-Holland Publishing Company

A MORE GENERAL THEORY OF PRICE DISTORTIONS IN OPEN ECONOMIES*

P. J. LLOYD

Research School of Pacific Studies, Australian National University,
Canberra, A.C.T., Australia

1. Introduction

A standard welfare problem that has been considered is to maximise a social utility function $U = U(C_0, \ldots, C_n)$ with the aggregate consumption of the final consumable commodities as its arguments, subject to a transformation surface or production set and, in an open economy, the balance of payments requirement that total import payments not exceed total export receipts. The first-order conditions of this constrained maximisation are familiar. For tradable final consumable commodities, the marginal rates of substitution in consumption, transformation in domestic production and transformation through international trade must be equal to each other, for all pairs of commodities. Welfare losses are incurred whenever market prices diverge from the shadow price duals of this Pareto-optimal situation which they may do for several reasons.

The problems of piecemeal policy-making considered here are a particular kind of second-best optimisation and policy determination in which the sub-Pareto-optimal situations come about from additional constraints on relative prices. It is assumed there are unremovable taxes–subsidies[1] or monopolies which distort the relative prices of a subset of commodities while the relative prices of at least some of the remaining commodities are adjustable. In particular, there is a set of commodities, A_1, whose prices to consumers (p_i) are distorted away from the relative prices in world markets ($\bar{p}_i^*$),

$$p_i = \bar{p}_i^*(1+r_i), \qquad r_i = \bar{r}_i \neq 0 \text{ for } i \in A_1. \tag{1}$$

---

*I am indebted to Jeff Fishburn, Murray Kemp, Ted Sieper, Sundrum, Stephen Turnovsky and an unknown referee for valuable comments on an earlier draft.

[1]Domestic political and international commitments commonly rule out changes to some taxes–subsidies. Some tax–subsidy instruments are not adjustable simultaneously because different Government authorities are responsible by law for different instruments and they act independently of each other; for example, a Treasury may adjust commodity taxes while an independent tariff fixing authority adjusts tariffs periodically.

Instruments may also be alterable within limits but not removable. This kind of alteration is the basis of the conditions that are sufficient for a welfare increase.

There is a set of commodities, A_2, whose prices to producers (q_i) are distorted away from the relative prices on world markets,

$$q_i = \bar{p}_i^*(1+s_i), \qquad s_i = \bar{s}_i \neq 0 \text{ for } i \in A_2. \tag{2}$$

Bars denote distortions which are not alterable. We shall, following convention, assume that the degree of distortion for each commodity whose relative price is distorted is constant in ad valorem terms, except when considering reductions in all or some of the distortions themselves. These distortions may be due simply to taxes–subsidies on consumption or production or imports or exports, or to net combinations of these. In international trade models in which the domestically-produced and imported commodities are assumed to be perfect substitutes for each other and there are no quantitative constraints, there can be no domestic monopolies. However, the problems of unremovable monopolies and/or commodity taxes in a closed economy will emerge as a special case.

The term 'price distortions' has been adopted as a short hand to distinguish this area of policy-making and propositions from closely related areas of 'non-price distortions' which arise because of different additional constraints on variables other than the prices. One such area is the problem in public finance which arises because of the necessity to raise a total revenue through some levels of distortionary commodity taxes (to be decided) in order to pay for the provision of goods by the public sector [see Little (1951), Meade (1955, pp. 112–118), Diamond and Mirrlees (1971a, b), Dixit (1970), Lerner (1970) and Stiglitz and Dasgupta (1971)]. A second related area of discussion is the long search for optimal taxes to pay for losses of producers in industries subject to increasing returns to scale who sell their commodities at marginal cost [see Baumol and Bradford (1970) and references therein]. A third related divergence from Pareto-optimality arises when there are assumed to be non-economic objectives in the form of direct constraints on the *quantities* of goods produced, consumed or traded [see Bhagwati (1971) and references therein].[2] Finally, externalities in production or consumption and the terms-of-trade effects of trade restrictions may also provide market failures. All of the policy-making questions discussed here could be paralleled in each of the areas of 'non-price distortions'.

Three aspects of policy-making in the presence of unremovable price distortions are considered. (a) The sets of adjustable taxes–subsidies which are

[2]Relating this area to the theory of price distortions, Bhagwati (1971) noted the symmetry of the ranking of instruments between the situations with price distortions and the situations with additional constraints on corresponding production, consumption or trade. Ohyama (1972, pp. 56–58) and Lloyd (1973) proved the optimality of policies subject to constraints on the volume or value of production, consumption or trade of certain commodities carries over to a model with price distortions elsewhere in the economy.

implied by the first-order conditions of the constrained maximum are derived and some propositions concerning them are developed (section 2). An alternative interpretation of these results is given in terms of the Hicks–Allen (1934) concept of complementarity or substitutability, from the sign of the first partial derivatives of the inverse price functions. (b) The effects on welfare of pre-selected changes in the adjustable taxes–subsidies such as a uniform reduction in all distortions or a reduction of extreme distortions (section 3). (c) The ranking of alternative instruments for commodities whose relative prices are adjustable (section 4). We shall see that propositions for each of these three aspects of social welfare are related.[3]

2. Second-best rules

Formally the basic welfare problem is to maximise the social utility function

$$U = U(C_0, \ldots, C_n) \tag{3}$$

subject to

$$F(X_0, \ldots, X_n) = 0, \tag{4}$$

$$C_i = X_i + Z_i, \qquad i = 0, \ldots, n \tag{5}$$

$$\sum_i \bar{p}_i^* Z_i = 0, \tag{6}$$

[3]Elements of a general theory of price distortions have been emerging for several years. The first substantial attack on the theory of these problems was made by Meade (1955, ch. VII and Mathematical Supplement). Meade assumed the existence of a number of tariffs, domestic taxes–subsidies, monopolies and externalities and then enquired whether changing any one of them would increase or decrease welfare. The later more pragmatic approaches by Foster and Sonnenschein (1970), Bruno (1972) and Bertrand and Vanek (1971), the first two of whom examined the effect on national welfare of an across-the-board or radial reduction in all distortions and the last of whom examined the effects of reducing extreme distortions, are an extension of this method but they were all developed from the assumption of a social utility function rather than by following Meade's cumbersome method of retaining the utilities of individuals in a Bergson-type utility function. Similarly, the problem of whether the formation of a customs union increases the welfare of member countries is an application of this basic method. The literature on this subject is not considered.

Meade (1955, Mathematical Supplement) also made comparisons of pairs of instruments in different situations. Bhagwati and Ramaswami (1963), Bhagwati, Ramaswami and Srinivasan (1969), and Bhagwati (1971) developed independently and extended this approach by obtaining the best instrument and ranking other inferior instruments for several situations, given the social utility function.

The first attempts to devise second-best rules in the theory of price distortions were in the early general equilibrium discussions of monopoly. For the three-commodity model Lipsey and Lancaster (1956) and McManus (1959) derived the rules which Green (1961) extended to the multi-commodity case.

Bhagwati (1971) drew together some propositions concerning the welfare effects of single tax–subsidy changes and the ranking of instruments but he did not discuss any conditions which are sufficient for an increase in welfare and his analysis is severely restricted to only two commodities. The latter restriction does not permit any relations of net complementarity between two commodities.

and such domestic distortions as are given by eqs. (1) and (2). The social utility function is assumed to be continuous and twice differentiable and strictly quasi-concave. The transformation surface in eq. (4) is assumed to be continuous, twice differentiable and strictly concave from below. The assumption of a fixed transformation surface prevents us from examining distortions in relative input prices. Eqs. (5) and (6), respectively, define domestic aggregate consumption (C_i) equal to domestic production (X_i) plus net imports (Z_i) or less net exports, and the budget condition that import payments equal export receipts, both measured in foreign prices ($\bar{p}_i^*$). To isolate the problems due to price distortions we adopt the small country assumption that all prices are fixed on the world market independently of the demands and supplies of the country concerned. Commodity zero is taken as the numeraire commodity and we set $p_0^* = 1$.

Most authors assumed that the social utility function is derived from an individualistic Bergson-type social welfare function which weights the utilities of individual consumers and that an omniscient government makes ideal lump-sum transfers among consumers so as to maximise the social utility of any available set of commodities. With the added assumption of no externalities of consumption, the marginal rates of substitution between any two commodities must be equal among all consumers and equal to the social rate of substitution [see v.d. Graaff (1967, p. 54)]. Since we shall be concerned solely with cases in which the same distortion is assumed to apply to all consumers and lump-sum transfers are feasible, nothing is gained by retaining individual utilities as Meade (1955) originally did. Under analogous assumptions on the supply side we shall consider the aggregate supplies of each commodity rather than the supplies from each producer.[4]

We may consider all three welfare questions by deriving an expression for the change in utility in terms of total differentials which incorporates all of the constraints including the price distortions. This method of total differentials reduces the constrained maximisation to an unconstrained maximisation by successive substitution in the maximand. Differentiating totally eqs. (3)–(6):

$$dU/U_0 = dC_0 + \sum_i (U_i/U_0)\, dC_i, \tag{7}$$

$$dX_0 = -\sum_i (F_i/F_0)\, dX_i, \tag{8}$$

$$dC_i = dX_i + dZ_i, \qquad i = 0, \ldots, n \tag{9}$$

$$dZ_0 = -\sum_i \bar{p}_i^* dZ_i. \tag{10}$$

U_i and F_i are the first partial derivatives of U and F with respect to C_i and X_i. Unless otherwise indicated the summations are over $i = 1, \ldots, n$. Using

---

[4]The use of aggregated relations means that we can only consider one of the three sets of first-order conditions that are conventionally considered in welfare economics [see for example, Bator (1957)]; namely, the so-called production-cum-distribution conditions. We cannot in this model consider taxes on commodities which differentiate among individual consumers or producers, though the methods may be extended to these distortions.

eq. (9) for $i = 0$ and substituting eqs. (8) and (10) in (7) yields

$$dU/U_0 = \sum_i (\bar{p}_i^* - F_i/F_0) \, dX_i + (U_i/U_0 - \bar{p}_i^*) \, dC_i. \tag{11}$$

This form incorporates the constraint of the transformation surface and trading possibilities but no distortions. The control variables here are the amounts of all commodities produced and consumed. We assume that a unique interior solution exists in all distortion and distortion-free situations.[5]

The necessary (and sufficient) first-order conditions for Pareto-optimality are obtained by setting the coefficients of the total differentials equal to zero,

$$U_i/U_0 = F_i/F_0 = \bar{p}_i^*, \qquad i = 1, \ldots, n. \tag{12}$$

Eq. (12) states the familiar conditions that the marginal rates of substitution in consumption, transformation in domestic production and transformation through international trade be equal to each other, for all pairs of commodities.

Under the assumptions that consumers maximise utility and producers maximise profits and zero externalities, we have, respectively,

$$p_i = U_i/U_0, \qquad i = 1, \ldots, n, \tag{13}$$

and

$$q_i = F_i/F_0, \qquad i = 1, \ldots, n. \tag{14}$$

It is assumed that $p_0 = q_0 = 1$. With no price distortion or other additional constraints perfectly competitive behaviour realises Pareto-optimality.

The price distortions of eqs. (1) and (2) violate the two sets of conditions for Pareto-optimality in eq. (12) given competitive behaviour. It should be noted that the price distortions in eqs. (1) and (2) are derived from two assumptions; the assumption that there is some unremovable distortion in the price of commodity i and the assumption, implied by setting the price of the numeraire commodity equal to unity, that no offsetting tax–subsidy can be imposed on commodity zero. The second assumption and the choice of numeraire affect the solution of each problem.[6] This gives the following not-quite-trivial proposition.

Proposition 1. If there are unalterable taxes–subsidies of a particular kind or monopolies on a set of commodities, but the relative prices of these commodities may be varied by imposing other taxes–subsidies on the same commodities, the distortions of the prices of these commodities may be eliminated.

[5]Vanek (1965), Bhagwati (1968), and Foster and Sonnenschein (1970) established that multiple equilibria may arise with a given set of distortions if there are inferior goods. Foster and Sonnenschein (1970) derive some propositions concerning welfare changes in the presence of alternative equilibria by introducing different adjustment mechanisms. Sontheimer (1971) derives a very general set of conditions, including convexity of consumer preferences and the production possibility set, which are sufficient to prove the existence of a competitive equilibrium in the presence of tax–subsidy distortions.

[6]McManus (1959, pp. 210–211) criticised the original treatment of monopoly and related problems by Lipsey and Lancaster (1956) for their erroneous interpretation of the numeraire.

This has been well-known since the early controversy concerning proportionality of marginal cost and price when there are unremovable monopolies but commodity taxes may be levied [see, for example, v.d. Graaff (1967, ch. X)]. In this case Pareto-optimality may be restored by granting subsidies at the rate $e_i/1+e_i$ on the consumption of the commodities whose production is monopolised, where e_i are the Lerner degrees of monopoly. Another illustration is the use of uniform import tariffs and export duties to offset a fixed overvalued exchange rate. In fact, positive non-distortionary taxes–subsidies are required for the implied lump-sum transfers of the second-best.

With price distortions, substituting from eqs. (1)–(2) and (13)–(14) into (11) yields

$$\mathrm{d}U/U_0 = \sum_i \bar{p}_i^* s_i \, \mathrm{d}X_i + \sum_i \bar{p}_i^* r_i \, \mathrm{d}C_i. \tag{15}$$

In the presence of constraints on relative prices the solution is obtained most directly by setting up the relative prices as the control variables. Commodity demand functions with relative price arguments are obtained by maximising social utility for a given expenditure. Since these functions are homogeneous of degree zero we have, choosing commodity zero as the numeraire,

$$C_i = \psi_i(p_1, \ldots, p_n; y), \qquad i = 0, \ldots, n, \tag{16}$$

where $y = C_0 + \sum_i p_i C_i$ is real income in terms of the numeraire commodity.

From eqs. (14) and (4) we obtain the general equilibrium supply functions

$$X_i = X_i(q_1, \ldots, q_n), \qquad i = 0, \ldots, n. \tag{17}$$

Differentiating (16) and (17) and substituting in (15) yields

$$1/U_0 \, \mathrm{d}U = \sum_j \bar{p}_i^* r_i \left(\sum_j \partial \psi_i / \partial p_j \, \mathrm{d}p_j + \partial C_i / \partial y \, \mathrm{d}y \right)$$

$$- \sum_i \bar{p}_i^* s_i \sum_i \partial X_i / \partial q_j \, \mathrm{d}q_j.$$

Since

$$\mathrm{d}y = \left(\mathrm{d}C_0 + \sum_i p_i \, \mathrm{d}C_i \right) + \sum C_i \, \mathrm{d}p_i,$$

and in view of eq. (7), we have

$$m \, \mathrm{d}U = \sum_i \bar{p}_i^* r_i \sum_j \partial C_i / \partial p_j \, \mathrm{d}p_j - \sum_i \bar{p}_i^* s_i \sum_j \partial X_i / \partial q_j \, \mathrm{d}q_j, \tag{18}$$

where

$$\partial C_i / \partial p_j = \partial \psi_i / \partial p_j + C_j \partial C_i / \partial Y$$

is the income-compensated price change, and

$$m = 1/U_0 \left(1 - \sum_i \bar{p}_i^* r_i \partial C_i / \partial y \right)$$

is the marginal propensity to consume all commodities evaluated at world prices. The latter follows because

$$1/U_0 = p_0/U_0 = \lambda = \partial Y/\partial U,$$

where λ is the Lagrange multiplier in the consumers' problem of minimising expenditure (Y) for $U = \bar{U}$. Hence,

$$m = \partial Y/\partial U - \sum_i \bar{p}_i^* r_i \partial C_i/\partial U$$

$$= \sum_i \bar{p}_i^*(1+r_i)\partial C_i/\partial U + \partial C_0/\partial U - \sum_i \bar{p}_i^* r_i \partial C_i/\partial U$$

$$= \sum_i \bar{p}_i^* \partial C_i/\partial U + \partial C_0/\partial U. \tag{19}$$

Eq. (18) is the basic equation that may be used to examine different welfare questions by choosing the appropriate relative prices to adjust.

The question we consider in this section is the second-best level of all adjustable taxes–subsidies, given that there is a subset of some non-zero unalterable distortions. With fixed international prices, variations in domestic prices to consumers or producers now reflect solely variations in taxes–subsidies on domestic consumption and/or production. In eq. (18) setting the coefficients of the total differentials for those prices which are variable equal to zero yields the two systems of equations

$$\sum_i \bar{p}_i^* r_i \partial C_i/\partial p_j = 0, \qquad j \notin (A_1 \cup B_1),$$

$$\sum_i \bar{p}_i^* s_i \partial X_i/\partial q_j = 0, \qquad j \notin (A_2 \cup B_2). \tag{20}$$

B_1 and B_2 are, respectively, the sets of commodities whose consumer and producer prices are not distorted but because of domestic or international commitments cannot be varied by imposing consumer or producer taxes–subsidies. Transferring the terms involving fixed distortions to the right-hand side of each equation and applying Cramer's Rule, the system of equations yields the desired solution values for the taxes–subsidies on consumption and production, respectively,[7]

$$r_v = -\sum_j \left(\sum_{i \in A_1} \bar{p}_i^* \bar{r}_i \partial C_i/\partial p_j \right) D_{jv}/D, \qquad j \notin (A_1 \cup B_1), \tag{21}$$

where D is the determinant of the square matrix $[p_i^* \partial C_i/\partial p_j]$ and D_{jv} is the cofactor of the element $(p_v^* \partial C_v/\partial p_j)$, and

$$s_w = -\sum_j \left(\sum_{i \in A_2} \bar{p}_i^* \bar{s}_i \partial X_i/\partial q_j \right) E_{jw}/E, \qquad j \notin (A_2 \cup B_2), \tag{22}$$

where E is the determinant of the square matrix $[p_i^* \partial X_i/\partial q_j]$ and E_{jw} is the

[7]I am indebted to a referee for pointing out that Kolm (1971) has obtained a more general set of first-order conditions for constrained maximisation which includes this set in the presence of price distortions as a special case.

cofactor of the element $(p_w^* \partial X_w / \partial q_j)$.

This general formulation covers both the case in which all relative prices, other than those which are subject to non-zero unalterable distortions, are variable and the case in which the instrument set is further restricted because some of the tax–subsidy instruments on commodities not subject to non-zero distortions are assumed to be not variable, that is, committed at zero level. In the former case the sets B_1 and B_2 in eqs. (21) and (22) are empty. In the latter case the fixing of some taxes–subsidies at zero does impose a cost as the economy forgoes the opportunity of varying them to offset the harm of the distortions. Cases in which taxes–subsidies on production (consumption) of a set of commodities are constrained to be equal or otherwise fixed in relation to each other, may be handled by treating these commodities as a composite commodity in production (consumption) because of fixed world prices. Finally if tariffs–import subsidies are the only available instrument to compensate for distortions we set $dp_i = dq_i$ for these commodities.

While this rule and later rules are stated in terms of the determination of the levels of explicit taxes–subsidies they also provide shadow prices that a Government should use for commodity prices in cost–benefit analyses which evaluate Government projects and direct Government purchases in a distortion-ridden economy.

It is customary to define a pair of commodities as being substitutes or complements for each other in consumption according as the partial derivatives of the income-compensated commodity demand functions in eq. (16),

$$\partial C_i / \partial p_j \gtrless 0.$$

This is the Hicksian definition of net substitutes and complements. In an analogous way we define a pair of commodities as substitutes or complements for each other in production according as the partial derivatives of the general equilibrium supply function in eq. (17),

$$\partial X_i / \partial q_j \lessgtr 0.$$

Using this terminology the second-best tax–subsidy set given by eqs. (21) and (22) will in general depend on the relations of substitutability and complementarity between all commodities and those whose prices are adjustable, taken in pairs, and on the unalterable distortions. In fact, each adjustable consumption or production tax–subsidy may be written as a weighted average of the unalterable consumption or production distortions,

$$r_v = \sum_{i \in A_1} \bar{r}_i w_i, \qquad s_w = \sum_{i \in A_2} \bar{s}_i z_i, \qquad (23)$$

where the weights are

$$w_i = -\sum_j (\bar{p}_i^* \partial C_i / \partial p_j) D_{jv} / D, \qquad z_i = -\sum_j (\bar{p}_i^* \partial X_i / \partial q_j) E_{jw} / E.$$

One feature of the second-best tax–subsidy set emerges immediately from eqs. (21) and (22).

Proposition 2. If commodities are traded internationally at fixed prices, there is a second-best set of taxes–subsidies on consumption which depend only on the distortions of prices to consumers and the relations of Hicksian complementarity and substitutability in consumption between all pairs of commodities, and a second-best set of taxes–subsidies on production which depend only on the distortions of prices to producers and the relations of complementarity and substitutability in production between all pairs of commodities.

Thus the corrective taxes–subsidies on production and consumption are entirely separated. Utility maximisation is a two-layer optimisation because of the assumptions that inputs do not enter the utility function and final commodities do not enter production functions. The first layer is the maximisation of the value of national output which puts the economy somewhere on the highest budget surface. The second layer is the maximisation of utility given the value of national output.

One result of the separation of stages is that this consumption tax–subsidy problem with international trade at fixed prices is identical to the general equilibrium problem of monopoly which was considered by Lipsey and Lancaster (1956), McManus (1959) and Green (1961). They assumed there is no international trade and a linear transformation surface. With constant Lerner degrees of monopoly, creating the divergence between the marginal cost ratios and relative prices, this implies that the relative producer prices of all commodities cannot vary. The resulting second-best tax–subsidy set, obtained by Green (1961, p. 73) in a slightly different way, is then given by the eq. (21) alone. Thus the special feature of this sub-model is that the optimal tax–subsidy set depends only on the relations of complementarity and substitutability in consumption.[8]

Although the general expressions giving the optimal levels of taxes–subsidies in eqs. (21) and (22) are rather complex, useful propositions emerge when we consider restrictions on the form of the utility or transformation functions.

Proposition 3. If all pairs of commodities are Hicksian substitutes in consumption (or production) for each other, the taxes or subsidies on consumption (or production) on all commodities which are adjustable must lie between the largest and the smallest of the values of the unalterable distortions of consumer (or producer) prices.

---

[8]An alternative second-best set of taxes–subsidies on production in this case is given by eq. (22). The assumption of a fixed distortion is less satisfactory for the analysis of monopolies than it is for unremovable taxes–subsidies. Profit-maximising behaviour by a monopolist in a general equilibrium model implies a variable degree of monopoly; see Negishi (1961–62).

This theorem was proven by Green (1961, pp. 73–74) for consumption taxes–subsidies in the monopoly case, by proving the weights w_i in eq. (23) are positive and sum to unity, but it applies equally to production taxes–subsidies in this model.

Other propositions that follow from the restrictions on the utility or transformation function are derived later in this section.

The rules for the second-best sets of instrument values can be stated more simply through the use of the inverse price functions. Consider first the consumption taxes–subsidies. The partial derivatives in eq. (21), $\partial C_i/\partial p_j$, are the derivatives of the income-compensated commodity demand functions,

$$C_i = C_i(p_1, \ldots, p_n; U), \qquad\qquad i = 0, \ldots n. \qquad (24)$$

Inverting the last n equations of these equations we obtain n price functions,

$$p_i = p_i(C_1, \ldots, C_n; U), \qquad\qquad i = 1, \ldots, n. \qquad (25)$$

A sufficient condition for the inversion of the commodity demand functions is that the Jacobian does not vanish. Later we wish to invert the functions while holding some subset of prices constant. A sufficient condition for these inversions is that the principal minors of the Jacobian not vanish. This condition is satisfied under the assumed 'stability conditions' of consumer equilibrium, that is, by the strict quasi-concavity of U. Since C_i and p_i are inverse functions, their respective Jacobians are inverse matrices

$$[\partial C_i/\partial p_j] = [\partial p_j/\partial C_i]^{-1}, \qquad\qquad i, j = 1, \ldots, n. \qquad (26)$$

Eq. (21) can be rewritten, by reversing the order of summation, as

$$r_v = - \sum_{i \in A_1} \bar{p}_i^* \bar{r}_i (\sum_j \partial C_i/\partial p_j D_{jv}/D), \qquad j \notin (A_1 \cup B_1),$$

$$= - \sum_{i \in A_1} \bar{p}_i^* \bar{r}_i (\sum_j \partial C_i/\partial p_j K_{jv}/K p_v^*),$$

where K is the determinant of the $k \times k$ sub-matrix of Slutsky terms $(\partial C_i/\partial p_j)$ and K_{jv} is the cofactor of the element $\partial C_v/\partial p_j$ of this matrix. Using eq. (26),

$$r_v = - \sum_{i \in A_1} \bar{p}_i^* \bar{r}_i (\sum_j \partial C_i/\partial p_j \cdot \partial p_j/\partial C_v)/p_v^*, \qquad j \notin (A_1 \cup B_1).$$

Noting that from eq. (26),

$$\sum_j \partial C_i/\partial p_j \partial p_j/\partial C_v = 0, \qquad\qquad i \neq v, \qquad (27)$$

and that $\bar{p}_i^* \bar{r}_i = 0$ for $i \in B_1$ and rewriting the summations we now have

$$r_v = [\sum_{i \in A_1} (\sum_{j \in A_1} \bar{p}_j^* \bar{r}_j \partial C_j/\partial p_i) \partial p_i/\partial C_v]/p_v^*$$

$$= [\sum_{i \in A_1} \delta_i \partial p_i/\partial C_v]/p_v^*. \qquad (28)$$

The analogous expression for the second-best set of production taxes–subsidies is

$$s_w = \left[\sum_{i \in A_2} \phi_i \partial q_i / \partial X_w\right] / p_w^*. \tag{29}$$

It can be seen from eq. (18) that $\delta_i = m \partial U / \partial p_i$ and $\phi_i = m \partial U / \partial q_i$. These are the Lagrange multipliers associated with the constraints on the relative consumer and producer prices, respectively, of commodity i in the direct constrained maximisation of U.[9] Thus each expression for the second-best consumption or production tax–subsidy is a simple sum of terms involving the derivatives of the inverse price functions.

The interpretation of eqs. (28) and (29) requires the Hicks–Allen (1934) definition of substitutes and complements.[10] They defined a pair of commodities, i and j, to be substitutes or complements for each other in consumption according as the derivative of the utility surface,

$$\partial(U_j / U_0) / \partial C_i = \partial p_j / \partial C_i \lessgtr 0. \tag{30}$$

Analogously, a pair of commodities i and j may be said to be substitutes or complements for each other in production according as the derivative of the transformation surface,

$$\partial(F_j / F_0) / \partial X_i = \partial q_j / \partial X_i \gtrless 0. \tag{31}$$

The relationship between the Hicksian definition and the Hicks–Allen definition of substitutes and complements in consumption (or production) for a pair of commodities can be obtained by identifying elements on the right-hand and left-hand side of eq. (26) (or the analogous expression in terms of q_i). The relationship is in general complex. As with the Hicksian definition, the definition in terms of elements of inverse price functions is symmetric, but with

---

[9]These expressions for the second-best tax–subsidy set can be obtained directly by using the Lagrangian function with an indirect utility and an indirect transformation function [Lloyd (1973)]. However, the total differential method has the advantage that it can also be used to evaluate pre-determined or alternative instrument changes.

In their original formulation of the second-best theory, Lipsey and Lancaster (1956, pp. 28–31) did explore the relationships between the signs of the terms $\partial(U_i / U_0) / \partial C_j$ and the Edgeworth–Pareto definition of substitutes and complements in terms of the signs of the second derivatives of the utility function (U_{ij}) and the nature of the sub-optimal tax–subsidy set. The interpretation in the text follows from setting $U_i / U_0 = p_i$ and identifying these terms as the partial derivatives of the inverse price functions.

[10]The concept has been the subject of considerable confusion. Hicks and Allen (1934) and Hicks in the text of 'Value and Capital' (1939, p. 44) actually defined substitutes and complements in the theory on consumption in terms of $\partial(U_j / U_0) / \partial C_i$ for the case of three commodities with Hicks' money as the numeraire commodity. However, in his Appendix, Hicks (1939, p. 311) gives the 'Hicksian' definition in terms of the signs of the elements of the Slutsky matrix. These two definitions are now known not to be equivalent when $n > 3$ [for example, Samuelson (1950, p. 379, n.)].

The definition used in the text in terms of $\partial p_j / \partial C_i$ is equivalent to the Hicks–Allen definition [see Morishima (1955–56) for a formal proof].

$n > 3$ it is possible for two commodities to be substitutes in the Hicksian sense and complements in the Hicks–Allen sense. One convenient relationship can be readily established. If all pairs of commodities are net substitutes in the Hicksian sense then all pairs of commodities are net substitutes in the Hicks–Allen sense. These properties follow from the theorem of Mosak (1944) that if we have a Hicks matrix whose principal minors alternate in sign and if the off-diagonal elements are all positive, the inverse matrix is composed solely of negative elements.

The economic interpretation of the second-best rules in terms of the Hicks–Allen concept of substitutes and complements helps to explain the meaning of the more complex determinantal expressions. It is remarkable that almost all of the authors who have obtained determinantal expressions for optimal tax–subsidies whose elements are the partial derivatives of the income-compensated demand functions, have not attempted to explain the economic meaning of their results.[11] The reason may be found by considering an example such as the case of a good the consumption of which is reduced below the Pareto-optimal level because it is subject to an unalterable consumption tax. Welfare may be increased if we partially offset this distortion by taxing the substitutes of this commodity and subsidising its complements in the Hicksian sense. But this is not sufficient. Welfare may be further increased by taxing the complements of substitutes and subsidising the complements of complements and so on, taking account of the effects of each alterable instrument on the commodities whose prices are distorted. It is all these Hicksian relationships among commodities which are contained neatly in the Hicks–Allen concepts of substitutes and complements. Algebraically in this case the term of the constraint $(1+\bar{r}_i) > 1$ and $\delta_i < 0$; that is, social utility would be increased by a decrease in the relative price of the commodity. Failing a change in the distortion, utility will be increased by taxes on this commodity's Hicks–Allen substitutes and subsidies on its complements. If the price of a commodity is constrained below the free trade relative price, viz., $(1+\bar{r}_i) < 1$, the rule is reversed; the complements should be taxed and the substitutes subsidised.

In eq. (28) the summation terms average the relations of substitutability and complementarity between each commodity whose relative price is alterable and those whose relative prices are unalterable. The values of the Lagrange multiplier weights used in the averaging, δ_i, will depend on the extent of the distortion and the utility function. The production taxes–subsidies which are called for because of unalterable taxes–subsidies on the production of other commodities can be interpreted in the same way, after noting that lowering the relative price of a commodity to producers reduces domestic production.

With the Hicks–Allen definitions we can give an alternative economic interpretation of Proposition 2.

---

[11]A few have given explanations for the simpler cases of models with two or three commodities; for example, Green (1961, pp. 71–73) and Dornsbusch (1971).

Proposition 4. If commodities are traded internationally at fixed prices the second-best calls for (a) taxes on the consumption of those commodities which are Hicks–Allen complements (substitutes) for those commodities whose relative prices to consumers are constrained below (above) the free trade relative prices in the sense that $\sum \delta_i \partial p_i / \partial C_v > 0$, *and (b) taxes on the production of those commodities which are Hicks–Allen substitutes (complements) for those commodities whose relative prices are constrained below (above) the free trade relative prices to producers in the sense that* $\sum \phi_i \partial q_i / \partial X_w > 0$.

The use of inverse price functions in eqs. (28) and (29) leads to another proposition.

Proposition 5. (a) If the utility surface is separable into two or more subsets of variables, one of which contains all commodities whose prices to consumers are unalterably distorted, the optimal tax–subsidy on the consumption of any commodity which is not in this set and whose price is variable, is zero. (b) If the transformation surface is separable into two or more subsets of variables, one of which contains all commodities whose prices to producers are unalterably distorted, the optimal tax–subsidy on the production of any commodity which is not in this set and whose price is variable, is zero.

This proposition was stated by Lloyd (1973).[12] A function $f(x_i, \ldots, x_s)$ is said here to be separable with respect to two sets of variables, $(x_1, \ldots, x_h)$ and $(x_{h+1}, \ldots, x_s)$, if

$$\partial \left(\frac{\partial f / \partial x_i}{\partial f / \partial x_j} \right) / \partial x_k = 0, \tag{32}$$

where i and j, but not k, belong to the same set and movement is constrained to a level surface of the function. Alternatively, the function is separable if the partial derivatives of the inverse compensated price functions of the commodities subject to unalterable distortions with respect to commodities in the other group are zero. Hence, the second-best does not call for corrective taxes–subsidies on commodities whose prices are variable but which are separable in production or consumption from the commodities whose prices are unalterably distorted.

3. Welfare effects of pre-selected changes

Propositions concerning the effects on welfare of arbitrary changes in the values of unconstrained instruments can easily be obtained.

[12]The importance of separability in second-best theory was first noted by Davis and Whinston (1965). However, they assumed the strongest form of separability, namely, additivity, and did not constrain movements to the level surface of a function. The definition in the text may not be invariant with respect to the choice of numeraire. It is an application of Leontief's concept at 'functional' (or weak) separability [Leontief (1947)] to a case where $f(x)$ is a surface.

Consider that changes can be made only to taxes–subsidies on consumption; that is, under the assumption that all international prices are fixed, the relative prices of all commodities to producers are fixed. If variation in only one consumption tax–subsidy is considered, the effect on welfare is, from eq. (18),

$$m \, dU = \left[\sum_i \bar{p}_i^* r_i \partial C_i / \partial p_v\right] dp_v.$$

By analogy, a change in only one tax–subsidy on production has the following effect on welfare,

$$m \, dU = \left[\sum_i \bar{p}_i^* s_i \partial X_i / \partial q_v\right] dq_v.$$

Differentiating eqs. (1) and (2) and substituting

$$m \, dU = \left[\sum_i (\bar{p}_i^* r_i) \partial C_i / \partial p_v\right] \bar{p}_v^* \, dr_v,$$

and   (33)

$$m \, dU = \left[\sum_i (\bar{p}_i^* s_i) \partial X_i / \partial q_v\right] \bar{p}_v^* \, ds_v.$$

The necessary and sufficient condition for a welfare improvement by a single tax–subsidy change is that the relevant square bracketed terms be positive (negative) for a tax increase (decrease). These terms represent weighted average relationships of substitutability or complementarity with the weights being the specific values of the taxes–subsidies. Thus welfare is increased if a (small) consumption tax is imposed on a commodity which is on average in this sense a Hicksian substitute in consumption for all commodities whose consumer prices are distorted upwards ($\bar{r}_i > 0$). The sign of the tax change is reversed if the prices are distorted downwards by means of subsidies ($\bar{r}_i < 0$), or the commodity is a complement for the commodities whose prices are distorted.

It is convenient now to write eq. (33) in another form[13]

$$m \, dU = \left[\bar{p}_v^* r_v \partial C_v / \partial p_v + \sum_{i \neq v} \bar{p}_i^* \bar{r}_i \partial C_i / \partial p_v\right] \bar{p}_v^* \, dr_v$$

$$= \left[\sum_{i \neq v} \bar{p}_i^* (\bar{r}_i - r_v) \partial C_i / \partial p_v\right] \bar{p}_v^* \, dr_v / (1 + r_v),$$

and   (34)

$$m \, dU = - \left[\sum_{i \neq v} \bar{p}_i^* (\bar{s}_i - s_v) \partial X_i / \partial q_v\right] \bar{p}_v^* \, ds_v / (1 + s_v).$$

The most important application of these equations is the following proposition concerning extreme distortions. A distortion of consumer prices, for example, is the extreme if $|r_v| > |r_i|$ for all i other than v. A reduction in this distortion requires $dr_v \lessgtr 0$ as $r_v \gtrless 0$.

---

[13]This utilises the well-known relation among Slutsky terms

$$\sum_i p_i \partial C_i / \partial p_v + \partial C_0 / \partial p_v = 0.$$

Note that $r_0 = 0$.

Proposition 6. If all pairs of commodities are Hicksian substitutes in consumption (or production) and the aggregate marginal propensity to consume evaluated at world prices is positive, a sufficient condition for an increase in welfare is that the single most extreme distortion of consumer (or producer) prices be reduced.

Proposition 6 was hinted at by Meade (1955, pp. 103–104) and proven by Lipsey and Lancaster (1956, p. 25) for the case of a change in relative consumer prices due to taxes–subsidies with a Cobb–Douglas utility function which has the sufficient properties that all commodities are net substitutes and all goods are superior. Vanek (1964) proved a related proposition for trade liberalisation in a multi-country world. All of these authors considered only positive distortions due to monopoly or tariffs but one can see by inspection of eq. (34) that the proposition can be generalised to include negative distortions. However, as noted by Meade (1955, p. 103, n. 1), welfare is not necessarily increased under the same circumstances if the distortion is reduced to zero. This result is implied by Proposition 3.

Alternatively, Proposition 6 provides a generalisation of the proposition, noted by Bhagwati (1971, p. 84) and Foster and Sonnenschein (1970, p. 284) for a model with only two commodities, that if there is only one distortion in an economy a reduction in this distortion by any amount necessarily increases welfare.[14] Both Proposition 6 above and Bhagwati's proposition include as a special case the propositions of Kemp (1962) that restricted trade is superior to no trade and that a lower tariff is superior to a higher tariff, provided as Bhagwati (1968) noted and is evident from Proposition 6 there are no other distortions due to consumption or production taxes–subsidies, and no commodity is inferior (and hence there is no possibility of multiple equilibria).[15] An interesting case arises with international trade when we consider the effect of changing a tariff which distorts prices to both consumers and producers. From eq. (18), in this case

$$m \, dU = [\sum_{i \neq v} \bar{p}_i^*(\bar{r}_v - r_v)\partial C_i/\partial p_v - \sum_{i \neq v} \bar{p}_i^*(\bar{s}_i - s_v)\partial X_i/\partial q_v]\bar{p}_v^* d\tau_v/(1 + \tau_v).$$

(35)

If the prices to both consumers and producers of the commodity subject to the most extreme of all tariffs are the most distorted of all relative prices then a reduction in this tariff must increase welfare (by Proposition 6 a fortiori, provided all commodities are net substitutes in consumption *and* production).

[14]It is apparent, as Bhagwati (1971, p. 86) noted in another proposition, that if one among multiple distortions is reduced, welfare is not necessarily increased. This is a straightforward application of Lipsey and Lancaster's basic theorem of the second-best. However, other propositions developed above indicate that we can make useful generalisations when Pareto-optimality is not attainable.

[15]The assumption of no inferiority plays a dual role. It ensures that the aggregate marginal propensity to consume is positive and it eliminates the possibility of multiple equilibria.

Bertrand and Vanek (1971) proved this result for a version of this model which incorporated tariffs but no other distortions. But if there are taxes–subsidies on production or consumption in addition to the tariffs on the trade of commodities, it is no longer true that a reduction in the most extreme *tariff* will necessarily increase welfare because the prices of some other commodities may be more distorted.

The effect of a simultaneous change in more than one pre-selected instrument is the sum of the effects of each instrument taken singly, some of which are likely to be positive and some negative. Differentiating eqs. (1) and (2) and subsitituting in eq. (18),

$$m \, dU = \sum_i \bar{p}_i^* r_i [\sum_v \partial C_i / \partial p_v p_v^* \, dr_v] - \sum_i \bar{p}_i^* s_i [\sum_v \partial X_i / \partial q_v p_v^* \, ds_v]. \quad (36)$$

Assuming $m > 0$ the change in the set of taxes–subsidies will increase or decrease welfare as the right-hand side of eq. (36) is positive or negative.

Alternatively:

Proposition 7. Any pre-selected set of changes in taxes–subsidies will increase or decrease social utility as that part of the resulting change in total net revenue from all taxes–subsidies which is due to the change in the quantities of goods consumed and produced, is positive or negative.

The two double summations in eq. (36) represent the corresponding changes in total net revenue from taxes–subsidies on production and consumption respectively. Consider the total net revenue-payment from any consumption tax–subsidy. This is

$$T_i = \bar{p}_i^* r_i \psi_i(p_1, \ldots, p_n; y).$$

Hence,

$$dT_i = \bar{p}_i^* r_i (\sum_j \partial \psi_i / \partial p_j \bar{p}_j^* \, dr_j + \partial \psi_i / \partial y \, dy) + \bar{p}_i^* C_i \, dr_i. \quad (37)$$

Ignoring the last term and summing over all commodities gives the second term of eq. (15) or, multiplying by (m/U_0), the first term of eq. (36). Ohyama (1972, sect. VII) using set theory has also shown how the total net revenue change in this sense can be used to rank any two or more situations with different tax–subsidy regimes; but he does not consider the second-best tax–subsidy problem of sections 1 and 2 above nor the problems of this section, except to show that a uniform reduction in tariffs with no other distortions will improve welfare if the revenue change is positive. While the set theory method can deal readily with discrete changes the quantity changes which determine these revenue changes and the price elasticities which determine the quantity changes reflect the total adjustment simultaneously to all the prices which are varied as a result of the tax–subsidy changes. The determinants of these total elasticities are not revealed.[16] The form of eq. (36) has the advantage of exposing the demand and production determinants of the changes in net revenue and social utility. With caution one may use these expressions as approximations for discrete changes.

The case of uniform reductions in *all distortions* is perhaps the most interesting pre-selected change because, like that of a change in a single extreme distortion, it involves changes in instruments that appeal to common-sense and are easily put into practice. These policies do not require estimates of the degrees of complementarity and substitutability among commodities in production and consumption, as do the second-best taxes–subsidies. If there is an equal percentage reduction in all distortions, $dr_i/r_i = ds_i/s_i = \mu < 0$. The distortions themselves as defined in eqs. (1) and (2) were ad valorem distortions. Thus, we are considering what Foster and Sonnenschein (1970) called 'radial' changes in ad valorem distortions. In this case, eq. (36) becomes

$$m\, dU = [\sum_{i \in A_1} \bar{p}_i^* r_i \sum_{v \in A_1} \partial C_i/\partial p_v \bar{p}_v^* r_v - \sum_{i \in A_2} \bar{p}_i^* s_i \sum_{v \in A_2} \partial X_i/\partial q_v \bar{p}_v^* s_v]\mu$$

$$= [\sum_{i \in A_1} \sum_{v \in A_1} (p_i - \bar{p}_i^*)(p_v - \bar{p}_v^*)\partial C_i/\partial p_v]\mu$$

$$- [\sum_{i \in A_2} \sum_{v \in A_2} (q_i - \bar{p}_i^*)(q_v - \bar{q}_v^*)\partial X_i/\partial q_v]\mu < 0. \tag{38}$$

The first term in brackets is negative because of the strict convexity of the utility surface [Hicks (1939, p. 311)], given the linearity of real incomes in terms of foreign prices and domestic prices, $y = \sum p_i C_i$ and $y^* = \sum \bar{p}_i^* C_i$, which constrain utility maximisation. Similarly, the second term is negative.

Proposition 8. If the aggregate marginal propensity to consume evaluated at world prices is positive a sufficient condition for an increase in welfare is that there be a radial reduction in all distortions.

Moreover, a radial reduction in all production *or* all consumption distortions is sufficient because of the two-stage maximisation in this model. Earlier Foster and Sonnenschein (1970) had proved the same result for the more restricted case of no trade, a linear transformation surface and no inferior commodity. The condition of a positive marginal propensity to consume is implied by that of no inferiority. Bruno (1972) proved the result for the open economy case in which the only distorting instruments are tariffs. The proposition above is more general in that it encompasses any combination of positive and negative production and consumption distortions, though it is less general in that it applies locally whereas Bruno (1972) and Foster and Sonnenschein (1970) obtained global results using set theory.

---

[16]One can also define the second-best tax–subsidy set as that which maximises the expressions Ohyama (1972, eqs. (15″)–(17″)) gives for the change in revenue but this too does not reveal functional determinants.

The case of a radial reduction in all *prices* which are distorted produces a different result. In this case $|dr_i/(1+r_i)| = |\bar{p}_i^* dr_i/\bar{p}_i^*(1+r_i)| = |ds_i/(1+s_i)|$ for all commodities whose consumer or producer prices are distorted. From eq. (36) and using the Slutsky relation $\sum_{i=0}^{n} p_i \partial C_i/\partial p_v = 0$,

$$m \, dU = -[\sum_{i \in A_1} \bar{p}_i^* r_i(\sum_{v \notin A_1} \partial C_i/\partial p_v p_v^*(1+r_v))]\mu_i$$
$$+[\sum_{i \in A_2} \bar{p}_i^* s_i(\sum_{v \notin A_2} \partial X_i/\partial q_v p_v^*(1+s_v))]\mu_i^1,$$

where $\mu_i \lessgtr 0$ as $r_i \gtrless 0$ and $\mu_i^1 \lessgtr 0$ as $s_i \gtrless 0$. A sufficient condition for a welfare increase in this event is that the group of commodities whose consumer prices are distorted and the group whose producer prices are distorted be weighted average substitutes in consumption and production, respectively, for the groups of commodities whose consumer and producer prices are not distorted. Again a radial reduction in all consumer *or* all producer prices which were distorted will increase welfare if the corresponding groups of commodities whose prices are distorted are on average substitutes for the group of commodities whose prices are not distorted. Alternatively, these results may be looked upon as an application of Proposition 6 since the groups in this event are Hicks composite commodities.

4. Ranking of instruments

Meade (1955, Mathematical Supplement) had used the total differential method to compare pairs of instruments, and Bhagwati and Ramaswani (1963) had, using geometry, ranked several instruments in situations with certain distortions and externalities. With only two commodities in the model, Bhagwati, Ramaswami and Srinivasan (1969), derived the expression, in my symbols,

$$m \, dU_0 = (p_1^* - q_1) \, dX_1 - (p_1 - p_1^*) \, dC_1 + (X_1 - C_1) \, dp_1^*. \tag{39}$$

This is the two-commodity version of eq. (11) above, plus a term for the terms of trade effect since international prices were variable in their model. Among the cases they considered was that of a production externality and that of producers charging a premium over the cost of domestic and imported supplies. The former is analogous to a monopoly and the latter to a consumption tax. From eq. (39) they concluded that the first-best instrument to adjust for the former case was the production tax–subsidy and the second-best was a tax–subsidy on either trade or on input. In the latter case, they concluded that the first-best was a consumption tax–subsidy, the second-best a trade tax–subsidy and that a production or factor tax–subsidy were of no help.

These results can be generalised to the multi-commodity model using eq. (18),

$$m \, dU = \sum_i \bar{p}_i^* r_i \sum_j \partial C_i/\partial p_j \, dp_j - \sum_i \bar{p}_i^* s_i \sum_j \partial X_i/\partial q_j \, dq_j. \tag{18}$$

Consider the case where some relative producer prices are distorted. As with Bhagwati, Ramaswami and Srinivasan (1969) the first-best instrument, if it is available, is the production tax–subsidy. This coincides to Proposition 1. In deriving eq. (18) this possibility has been ruled out by considering that the distortions of the producer prices are unalterable. In this event, as established by Proposition 4, the second-best is a set of taxes–subsidies on the commodities substitutes–complements. This alternative was not considered by the previous authors because of the severe limitations of the two-commodity model. The third and only other available instrument in this situation is a set of taxes–subsidies on the trade of other commodities. This is clearly inferior to production taxes–subsidies which were calculated in section 2 because a tariff or import subsidy or export tax, being a tax–subsidy on both domestic production and domestic consumption, causes a welfare loss due to the additional distortion of prices to consumers which it creates and which partially offsets the benefits of correcting the distortions of production. The commodities which should be subject to the trade taxes–subsidies and the levels of these instruments can be obtained by setting $dp_i = dq_i = d\tau_i$ in eq. (18). This yields the system of equations

$$\sum_i \bar{p}_i^*(r_i \partial C_i/\partial p_j - s_i \partial X_i/\partial q_j) = 0, \tag{40}$$

which has as many equations as there are trade taxes–subsidies which are considered variable. The solutions to these equations can be interpreted in much the same manner as the second-best levels of production and consumption taxes–subsidies considered in section 3. We should impose trade taxes (subsidies) on any commodity whose domestic production should be increased (decreased) or consumption decreased (increased). The solutions to the eq. (40) average the distortions in production and consumption, each weighted by the magnitude of the cross-price substitution and complementarity in production and consumption, respectively.

Using these methods all possible instruments can be ranked for different situations in this model or any other model.

Proposition 9. In any situation in which there are some unalterable distortions, it is possible to rank all of the alterable tax–subsidy instruments according to their effects on welfare.

It should be noted that these instruments are ranked by taking the effect on welfare for each instrument of the *best* level of that instrument. For example, in some situations the best level of a set of production subsidies may improve welfare more than the best level of the set of tariff-export subsidies which are considered adjustable, but some other higher or lower levels of these production subsidies may be inferior to the best level of tariff-export subsidies. This ranking therefore of alternative *instruments* still requires that we have an approximate idea at least of the magnitudes. One could if desired rank any number of different *levels* of each instrument using eq. (18).

5. Concluding remarks

These propositions have been established for a model whose behavioural assumptions are severely limited in many respects. However, the important point is that we have established the close links between several propositions concerning the best levels of taxes–subsidies or shadow prices, the effect on welfare of pre-selected tax–subsidy changes and the ranking of alternative instruments which have hitherto been considered separately. These rules for the choice of tax–subsidy instruments from among those which are variable and the best levels of these instruments or of shadow prices are important because they provide policy guidelines for the kind of situation where a government or policy-making authority has limited freedom to make changes which arises commonly in economic policy-making. Propositions 1, 3, 6, 7, 8 and 9 would carry over to more complex models with intermediate commodities, non-tradable commodities, variable international prices and some other variations.[17] The separation propositions 2, 4 and 5, would not carry over in their present form but they exemplify the general principle of confining intervention in the economy to commodities which are related in production and/or consumption to those whose prices are distorted.

---

[17]A few special cases of some of the propositions under more relaxed assumptions have been developed in the literature. In particular the terms of trade argument for tariffs in the presence of production and/or consumption taxes has been examined by Friedlaender and Vandendorpe (1968), Dornsbusch (1970) and Vandendorpe (1972), and in the presence of a divergence between the marginal rate of transformation and producer prices, by Ohyama (1972a). Many aspects of distortions in factor markets have been considered [see Magee (1973) for a survey] and Lloyd (1973) included taxes–subsidies on imported inputs in his model.

References

Bator, F.M., 1957, The simple analytics of welfare maximisation, American Economic Review 47, 22–59.

Baumol, W.J. and D.F. Bradford, 1970, Optimal departures from marginal cost pricing, American Economic Review 60, 265–283.

Bertrand, T.J. and J. Vanek, 1971, The theory of tariffs, taxes and subsidies: Some aspects of the second best, American Economic Review 61, 925–931.

Bhagwati, J., 1968, The theory and practice of commercial policy: Departures from unified exchange rates, Special Papers in International Economics, no. 8 (International Finance Section, Princeton University).

Bhagwati, J., 1971, The generalized theory of distortions and welfare, in: J. Bhagwati et al., eds., Trade, balance of payments, and growth: Papers in international economics in honor of Charles P. Kindleberger (North-Holland Amsterdam).

Bhagwati, J. and V.K. Ramaswami, 1963, Domestic distortions, tariffs and the theory of optimum subsidy, Journal of Political Economy 71, 44–50.

Bhagwati, J., V.K. Ramaswami and T.N. Srinivasan, 1969, Domestic distortions, tariffs and the theory of optimum subsidy: Some further results, Journal of Political Economy 77, 1005–1010.

Bruno, M., 1972, Market distortions and gradual reform, Review of Economic Studies 34, 373–383.

Davis, O. and A. Whinston, 1965, Welfare economics and the theory of second best, Review of Economic Studies 32, 1–14.

Diamond, P.A. and J.A. Mirrlees, 1971, Optimal taxation and public production: I, American Economic Review 61, 8–27.

Diamond, P.A. and J.A. Mirrlees, 1971, Optimal taxation and public production: II, American Economic Review 61, 261–278.

Dixit, A.K., 1970, On the optimum structure of commodity taxes, American Economic Review 60, 295–301,

Dornsbusch, R., 1971, Optimal commodity and trade taxes, Journal of Political Economy 79, 1360–1368.

Foster, E. and H. Sonnenschein, 1970, Price distortion and economic welfare, Econometrica 38, 281–296.

Friedlaender, A. and A. Vandendorpe, 1968, Excise taxes and the gains from trade, Journal of Political Economy 76, 1058–1068.

Graaff, J. v.d., 1957, Theoretical welfare economics (Cambridge University Press, Cambridge).

Green, H.A.J., 1961, The social optimum in the presence of monopoly and taxation, Review of Economic Studies 29, 66–78.

Hicks, J.R., 1939, Value and capital (Clarendon Press, Oxford).

Hicks, J.R. and R.G.D. Allen, 1934, A reconsideration of the theory of value, Economica N.S. 1, 52–76.

Kemp, M.C., 1962, The gain from international trade, Economic Journal 72, 803–819.

Kolm, S., 1971, La theorie des constraintes de valeur et ses applications (Dunod, Paris).

Leontief, W.W., 1947, Introduction to the theory of the internal structure of functional relationships, Econometrica 15, 361–373.

Lerner, A.P., 1970, On optimal taxes with an untaxable sector, American Economic Review 60, 284–294.

Lipsey, R.G. and K. Lancaster, 1956, The general theory of second best, Review of Economic Studies 24, 11–32.

Little, I.M.D., 1951, Direct versus indirect taxes, The Economic Journal 61, 577–584.

Lloyd, P.J., 1973, Optimal intervention in a distortion-ridden open economy, Economic Record, Sept., 377–393.

McManus, M., 1959, Comments on the general theory of second best, Review of Economic Studies 26, 209–224.

Magee, S.P., 1973, Factor market distortions, production and trade: A survey, Oxford Economic Papers 25, 1–43.

Meade, J., 1955, Trade and welfare (Oxford University Press, London).

Morishima, M., 1955/6, A note on definitions of related goods, Review of Economic Studies 23, 132–134.

Mosak, J.L., 1944, General equilibrium theory in international trade (The Principia Press, Bloomington, Ind.).

Negishi, T., 1961/2, Monopolistic firm competition and general equilibrium, Review of Economic Studies 28, 196–201.

Ohyama, M., 1972, Domestic distortions and the theory of tariffs, Keio Economic Studies 9, 1–14.

Ohyama, M., 1972, Trade and welfare in general equilibrium, Keio Economic Studies 9, 37–73.

Samuelson, P., 1950, The problem of integrability in utility theory, Economica N.S. 17, 355–385.

Samuelson, P., 1956, Social indifference curves, The Quarterly Journal of Economics 70, 1–22.

Sato, K., 1968, A two-level constant-elasticity-of-substitution production function, Review of Economic Studies 34, 201–218.

Sontheimer, K.C., 1971, The existence of international trade equilibrium with trade tax–
    subsidy distortions, Econometrica 39, 1015–1035.
Stiglitz, J. and P. Dasgupta, 1971, Differential taxation, public goods and economic efficiency,
    Review of Economic Studies 38, 151–174.
Vanek, J., 1964, Unilateral trade liberalization and global world income, The Quarterly
    Journal of Economics 78, 139–147.
Vanek, J., 1965, General equilibrium of international discrimination (Harvard University
    Press, Cambridge, Mass.).
Vandendorpe, A., 1972, Optimal tax structures in a model with traded and non-traded goods,
    Journal of International Economics 2, 235–256.

[6]

Journal of International Economics 24 (1988) 275–297. North-Holland

TRADE EXPENDITURE FUNCTIONS
AND THE GAINS FROM TRADE

P.J. LLOYD

University of Melbourne, Melbourne, Victoria, Australia

A.G. SCHWEINBERGER*

Australian National University, Canberra, ACT 2601, Australia

Received August 1985, revised version received April 1987

This paper develops a number of concepts of trade expenditure functions for an internationally trading economy with many households which differ in tastes and factor endowments. These concepts are then applied to the analysis of gains from trade in undistorted economies with and without governmental intervention. We generalise and extend a number of propositions concerning sufficient, and necessary and sufficient conditions for individual households and groups of households to gain from trade in economies which are subject to trade taxes and subsidies.

1. Introduction

The subject-matter of the present paper is one of the oldest and most central topics in trade theory – the analysis of gains from trade in multihousehold economies with and without governmental intervention.

In order to analyse these issues we develop concepts which we call trade expenditure functions. A trade expenditure function can be defined for an individual household, a group of households, a country, or a number of countries. Essentially it relates the net cost of 'producing' a given utility level or utility vector of households to parameters such as technology, factor endowments, tastes, given distortions, etc. We were not the first to invent a trade expenditure function. It appears that trade expenditure functions have been derived independently by a number of economists.[1] We have extended

---

*We are grateful to an unknown referee and to Richard Brecher for comments. Any remaining shortcomings are the sole responsibility of the authors.

[1]Wan (1965) stated the function in terms of the maximum balance of payments surplus and called it the 'maximum bonus'. Chipman (1970) derived it as the envelope function which is dual to the direct trade utility function and called it the 'minimum income function'. Woodland (1982, p. 170) defined a 'net revenue' function, and Bhagwati, Brecher and Hatta (1983) defined an 'overspending function' in the same manner as our economy-wide trade expenditure function of definition (III). All of these derivations are apparently independent and we were not aware of any when we first derived our economy-wide trade expenditure function.

and adapted these concepts to a number of issues concerning the gains from trade in multihousehold economies. These applications have led to several new propositions and provided a more unified treatment of gains from trade.

We distinguish between the *implicit goods trade model* and the *implicit factor trade model*. This distinction, which is apparently new, lies at the heart of trade theory and gives it a distinctive flavour as compared with the standard general equilibrium theory. In trade theory, households are endowed with factors which do not enter the utility function directly. They sell factors to firms and use the resulting income to buy goods from firms. This model may be reduced in two distinct ways:

(1) one may calculate the vector of goods which is embodied in the vector of factors sold by households to firms, or

(2) one may calculate the vector of factors which is embodied in the goods consumed by the household (and purchased from firms).

The first reduction gives rise to the implicit goods trade model and the implicit goods trade expenditure function and the second to the implicit factor trade model and the implicit factor trade expenditure function. The derivation of the basic trade expenditure functions is presented in section 2.

In section 3, using these two distinct approaches, we derive a number of new results:

(1) We show that for any factor ownership each household will have at least one true friend and one true enemy among goods.

(2) We extend and generalise a condition of Bhagwati and Brecher (1980) which is necessary and sufficient for a subset of households to gain from trade.

(3) We show that a household which is in an implicit autarky factor trade equilibrium must gain from international trade, provided that a certain condition of nonspecialisation in production is satisfied.

These results hold in multihousehold economies which are opened up to foreign trade without any form of governmental intervention. Our approach can also be used to confirm existing propositions such as the proposition of Dixit and Norman (1980, 1986) that, with appropriate government taxes, any movement to free trade from autarky can be a Pareto improvement.

In section 4 we prove a necessary and sufficient condition for gains from trade in the aggregate if the trading equilibrium is characterised by trade taxes and subsidies. This extends the results of Eaton and Panagariya (1979).

2. Trade expenditure functions

Assumption 1. The preferences of all H households are representable by utility functions, $U^h(x^h), h = 1, \ldots, H$, where each of these functions is a real valued, continuous, twice differentiable, weakly increasing and strictly quasiconcave functions of $x^h = (x_1^h, \ldots, x_n^h) \geqq 0$.

Assumption 2. The technology can be described by a multiple output production function, $F(x-m,v)\leqq 0$ where $x=\sum_h x^h$ and $m=(m_1,\ldots,m_n)\geqq 0$ is a vector of imports $(m_i>0)$ and exports $(m_i<0)$ and $v=(v_1,\ldots,v_k)>0$ is a vector of endowments of fixed factors. Hence, $y=(x-m)=(y_1,\ldots,y_n)\gtreqless 0$ is a vector of net outputs $(y_i\geqq 0)$ or net inputs $(y_i\leqq 0)$ which are technically feasible given the endowments and technology. $F(x-m,v)$ is continuous, twice differentiable, non-decreasing in y, non-increasing in v and convex in y. This specification of technology allows for joint outputs and pure and impure intermediate inputs.

Assumption 3. Unless otherwise indicated we assume perfect competition and a small open economy with all goods traded.

One of the advantages of trade expenditure functions is their flexibility. They can be defined for any group in any economy, with or without distortions. (They can also be applied to temporary or intertemporal equilibria.)

Our first concern is to derive trade expenditure functions for undistorted economies. We derive and interpret the following three functions:

(1) The trade expenditure function for an individual household.

(2) The trade expenditure function for the economy with multiple households. In this function a vector of household utilities is treated exogenously. It is therefore suitable for the analysis of Pareto improving changes in the economy.

(3) The social trade expenditure function. This function can be derived only if a well-defined social utility function exists.

2.1. The trade expenditure functions of households

To derive the trade expenditure function for the individual household it is necessary to make some assumptions about the factor ownership of households and the structure of production. We assume that each household is endowed with a vector v^h of primary factors, such that $\sum_h v^h = v$. In common with most trade models, we also assume that households supply all their factors to firms and use their factor income to buy goods from firms. The role of firms is only to organise 'national' production and thereby to create economy wide factor markets. Factors do not enter directly the utility function of households. The fact that households sell factors to firms and buy goods from firms implies that there are two reduced form interpretations of this model of a multihousehold economy:

(1) the implicit goods trade model, and

(2) the implicit factor trade model.

The key feature of the implicit goods trade model is that the vector of factors sold by each household to firms is reduced to the vector of goods embodied in this vector of factors. Even though households do not carry out any production in this model, one can define a vector of outputs imputed to each household such that the sum of all the imputed or implicit outputs of all the households is equal to the outputs produced by the firms. By contrast, the key feature of the implicit factor trade model is that the vector of goods bought by each household from firms is reduced to a vector of factors embodied in the vector of goods. This approach is well known from the factor content theory of trade between countries [see, for example, Deardorff (1982) and Neary and Schweinberger (1986)]. Both these approaches have advantages, as will be explained below.

First, we derive the *trade expenditure functions of individual households.* For household h, the trade expenditure function in its most general form is defined as:

$$b^h(p, w, v^h, u^h) \equiv e^h(p, u^h) - v^h w \tag{1}$$

where

p = the given vector of prices of goods,
w = the given vector of factor prices,
v^h = the given vector of factor endowments of household h,
u^h = the given utility level of household h,
e^h = the expenditure function of household h.

b^h may be regarded as the net transfer to household h which ensures that the household can attain a utility level u^h, given goods prices p, factor prices w, factor endowments v^h. The inner product of the vectors v^h and $w(p, v)$ is written as $v^h w(p, v)$. Alternatively, b^h may be interpreted as the net cost of 'producing' a given utility level u^h. Since the household earns factor income which is endogenously determined in a general equilibrium, it is the net expenditure which is required as a transfer to maintain utility.

Under a standard set of assumptions (as, for example, differentiability), the following set of functions may be derived from the national product function [see Dixit and Norman (1980) and Woodland (1982)]. Let:

$g(p, v)$ = the national product function,
$g_p(p, v) = y(p, v)$ = the competitive (optimal) outputs, and
$g_v(p, v) = w(p, v)$ = the competitive factor prices.

Subscripts are used throughout to denote partial derivatives.

Substituting $w(p, v)$ into (1) gives:

$$B^h(p, v, v^h, u^h) \equiv e^h(p, u^h) - v^h w(p, v). \tag{I}$$

This is the first of the trade expenditure functions which we shall employ. It is the *household trade expenditure function* associated with the implicit goods trade model. Its main properties are:

I(1) It is linearly homogeneous in p.

I(2) It is increasing in u^h.

I(3) The first-order derivatives with respect to prices are equal to the household compensated implicit excess demand functions for the goods, m^h.

I(4) The function B^h may or may not be concave in p. However, the compensated implicit excess demand curve for each good is downward sloping for at least one household.

Proof. Properties I(1) and I(2) are obvious. Property I(3) is implied by differentiating $v^h w$ with respect to p, summing over households, and using the properties of the national product function:

$$\sum_h v^h w_p(p, v) = v w_p(p, v). \tag{2}$$

We may, therefore, regard

$$y^h(p, v, v^h) \equiv v^h w_p(p, v) \tag{3}$$

as the output vector imputed to household h. The ith element of this vector is $y_i^h = \sum_j v_j^h \, \partial w_j / \partial p_i$. The output vector imputed to household h is therefore defined as the product of the vector v^h and the matrix $w_p(p, v)$, i.e. $v^h w_p(p, v)$. These implicit outputs may be positive or negative. However, it follows from (2) that the implicit output of at least one household must be positive for each good. Property I(4) follows because

$$\sum_h y^h \equiv y \quad \text{and} \quad \sum_h y_p^h \equiv y_p. \tag{4}$$

Even though y_p is a matrix which is (semi) definite positive, one cannot conclude that one or more of the matrices y_p^h are (semi) definite positive. However, it follows that since all the diagonal elements of the matrix y_p are positive or zero that the corresponding diagonal element of at least one of the matrices y_p^h must be of the same sign.

With the concept of the household implicit output vector it is possible to define a vector of excess demands or imports for the household and a household product function which are analogous to those of the nation. From (I), using (3) and Hotelling's Lemma, the vector of *implicit excess demands for a household*, household h, is:

$$B_p^h = x^h - y^h = m^h, \tag{5}$$

whose *i*th element $m_i \gtreqless 0 (m_i > 0$ denotes an implicit import and $m_i < 0$ denotes an implicit export good). The *household product function* is:

$$g^h(p, v, v^h) = p y^h(p, v, v^h) = v^h w(p, v). \tag{6}$$

If there is no implicit factor price equalisation among households,[2] i.e. $v^h w(p, v) > v^h w(p, v^h)$, any change in the prices p will have effects on the gains accruing to household h from the existence of firms. This is the source of the possibility of non-convexity in p of the function $v^h w(p, v)$. Furthermore, from (6):

$$B^h(p, v, v^h, u^h) \equiv e^h(p, u^h) - g^h(p, v, v^h) \tag{7}$$

and

$$g(p, v) = \sum_h g^h(p, v, v^h) = v w(p, v). \tag{8}$$

Thus, household product functions have the desirable property that their sum is the national product function.

There is, however, one special case in which the trade expenditure function, B^h, must be concave in prices. This is the case when a household holds factor endowments in the same proportions as the economy. Denoting by α^h the share of economy endowments held by such a household, one has:

$$v^h w(p, v) = \alpha^h v w = \alpha^h g(p, v).$$

Consequently, in this case, $g^h(p, v, v^h)$ is convex and $B^h = e^h(p, u^h) - g^h(p, v, v^h)$ is concave in p.

Differentiating the household trade expenditure function B^h with respect to prices and noting that the compensated implicit excess demand functions of household h are homogeneous of degree zero in prices, we obtain:

$$dB^h = [x^h(p, u^h) - y^h(p, v, v^h)] \, dp. \tag{9}$$

Assuming that household utility is endogenous, so that $B^h(\cdot) = 0$ it follows from (9) that, for any good which is in implicit excess demand, an increase in the price of this good alone will reduce the household's utility and,

[2]Assuming all households have the same technology, we can define an *autarky* household production possibility locus and a corresponding autarky household product function $v^h w(p, v^h)$. Clearly, we can never have $v^h w(p, v) < v^h w(p, v^h)$ because in this case households would not supply any factors to firms and would prefer to produce on the autarky household production possibility locus. Whenever we have implicit factor price equalisation, i.e. $w(p, v) = w(p, v^h)$, the household is indifferent between supplying factors to firms and producing on the autarky household production possibility locus.

conversely, for any good which is in implicit excess supply by the household an increase in its price will increase its utility. Such goods may be described as true friends and true enemies of households h because the existence of true friendship or enmity is the necessary and sufficient condition for a household to gain or lose from a single price change.[3] As mentioned before, in the absence of transfers, u^h must be such that $B^h = m^h p = 0$. This in turn implies that each household will have at least one good which is in implicit excess demand and one which is in implicit excess supply unless it is in a state of implicit goods autarky equilibrium, i.e.

$$x^h(p, u^h) = y^h(p, v, v^h). \tag{10}$$

This state of autarky equilibrium is implicit because in this model of the multihousehold economy households sell factors to firms and buy goods from firms (unless there is implicit factor price equalisation). One may note that, from (2) and (9), autarky equilibrium of an economy is implied by autarky equilibrium of all households but that the converse will hold only in very special circumstances.

From these definitions and from (9) we can derive the following proposition.

Proposition 1.   In the absence of transfers every household will have at least one true 'friend' and one true 'enemy' among goods, except in a state of implicit autarky equilibrium.

Proposition 1 extends a well-known generalisation of the Stolper–Samuelson theorem [see, for example, Ethier (1984)] to households which own many different factors. It has the additional advantage that it holds whatever the pattern of specialisation in production for the economy.

At this point it may be tempting to conjecture that a state of implicit autarky equilibrium represents a welfare minimum with respect to p. From property I(4) and (4) it is known that there may not exist even one household whose trade expenditure function B^h is concave is prices. Therefore, a state of implicit autarky equilibrium may not represent a local welfare minimum for even one household. In fact, surprisingly, it may represent a local welfare maximum for one or more households. These results highlight the differences between the properties of the aggregate concepts and the corresponding concepts for individual households. Contrary to intuition, the aggregate concepts will be shown in this case to have stronger properties than the corresponding disaggregated (household) concepts.

[3]Our friends and enemies are not identical to those of Jones and Scheinkman (1977). Their 'natural friends and enemies' are a sufficient condition only for groups of households who own a single factor to gain from trade. Lloyd (1987) has previously used the concepts of true friends and enemies for a model in which households own only one factor.

We turn briefly to the implicit factor trade model. Assuming non-specialisation in production and linearly homogeneous single-output production functions, one can substitute the unit cost functions $c = c(w)$ for the prices p in the expenditure function of (1). [For a related approach, see Neary and Schweinberger (1986).] This yields our second trade expenditure function for a household:

$$C^h(w, v^h, u^h) \equiv e^h[c(w), u^h] - v^h w. \tag{II}$$

This is called the *household factor trade expenditure function* to distinguish it from the household trade expenditure function defined in (I). C^h has the following main properties:

II(1) It is linearly homogeneous in the factor prices w.

II(2) It is increasing in u^h.

II(3) Its partial derivatives with respect to factor prices w are the compensated implicit excess demand functions for the factors of household h,

II(4) It is concave in the factor prices w.

Proof. Properties II(1), II(2), and II(3) are easy to prove and their proofs have therefore been omitted.

The proof of property II(4) is as follows. From the concavity of the cost functions:

$$\theta c(w_1) + (1 - \theta)c(w_2) \leqq c(w_3),$$

where $w_3 = \theta w_1 + (1 - \theta)w_2$. Taking these as row vectors we postmultiply by the column vector $x_3 = x_3(p_3)$, where $p_3 = c(w_3)$ and x_3 denotes the consumption of the goods at the prices p_3:

$$\theta c(w_1)x_3(p_3) + (1 - \theta)c(w_2)x_3(p_3) \leqq c(w_3)x_3(p_3),$$

where $x_3(p_3)$ refers to a constant utility level.

From the minimisation property of the expenditure function:

$$c(w_1)x_3(p_3) \geqq c(w_1)x_1(p_1), \quad \text{where } p_1 = c(w_1),$$

and

$$c(w_2)x_3(p_3) \geqq c(w_2)x_2(p_2), \quad \text{where } p_2 = c(w_2).$$

Hence,

$$\theta c(w_1)x_1[c(w_1)] + (1 - \theta)c(w_2)x_2[c(w_2)]$$

$$\leqq \theta c(w_1)x_3(p_3) + (1 - \theta)c(w_2)x_3(p_3) \leqq c(w_3)x_3(p_3).$$

Rewriting this we have, for any u^h:

$$\theta e[c(w_1)] + (1 - \theta)e[c(w_2)] \leqq e[c(w_3)]. \quad \text{Q.E.D.}$$

One can compare the properties of the implicit goods trade expenditure function B^h, with the properties of the implicit factor trade expenditure function C^h. As noted, one cannot be certain that the former function is even locally concave for one household. However, the corresponding implicit factor trade expenditure function is, subject to the assumption of non-specialisation in production, globally concave in the factor prices w. The reason for this result is that although the functions $c(w) = p$ are concave in the factor prices, the inverse functions $w = w(p)$ are not normally convex in the product prices p.

Utilising C^h, a household h is said to be in an *implicit factor autarky equilibrium* if and only if, for some factor prices:

$$e^h_w[c(w), u^h] = v^h. \tag{11}$$

If factor prices are such that a household is in an implicit factor trade autarky equilibrium it follows from the property II(4) that, subject to the assumption of non-specialisation in production, the implicit factor trade expenditure function reaches a global maximum at the implicit autarky factor prices. Hence, any change in factor prices w cannot reduce welfare (and normally will increase welfare). This result contrasts sharply with the agnostic conclusion derived from the implicit goods trade expenditure function. It is, therefore, clear that we have here two distinct approaches which lead to different conclusions. We note that we have treated exogenously goods prices in the former and factor prices in the latter. Making use of implicit excess demand functions for goods or implicit excess demand functions for factors one can easily endogenise product and factor prices, respectively.

To conclude section 2.1, we summarise the relationship between the household and the economy as captured by the following three production possibility loci.

(1) *The autarky household's production possibility locus.* Assuming that all households have the same knowledge of technology and that the household's technology sets are convex, we can define a corresponding *autarky* household product function:

$$g^{\Delta h}(p, v^h) \equiv \left\{ \underset{y^h}{\text{maximise}} \, py^h; (y^h, v^h) \, \text{feasible}, \, y^h \geqq 0 \right\}.$$

The autarky household product function is relevant if and only if

$$w(p, v^h) = w(p, v),$$

i.e. if and only if there is implicit factor price equalisation between households when the household's factor endowments lie within the diversification cone spanned by the economy endowments. The vector y^h refers to the actual outputs of household h. In this case there cannot be gains from factor trade or the existence of firms.

(2) *The implicit household production possibility locus.* The corresponding product function is given by (6). Whilst the *autarky* household product function is convex in prices, the household production function $g^h(p, v, v^h)$ may or may not be convex in prices. The derivatives of g^{Ah} with respect to prices are the *actual* outputs of household h, whilst the derivatives of $g^h(p, v, v^h)$ with respect to prices are the *implicit* outputs [see (3)]. The distinction between the autarky household product function $g^{Ah}(p, v^h)$ and the household product function $g^h(p, v, v^h)$ is crucial if and only if:

$$v^h w(p, v) > v^h w(p, v^h).$$

It therefore follows that the implicit household production possibility set [from which the function $g^h(p, v, v^h)$ is derived] contains as a subset the autarky household production possibility sets, which can be used to derive $g^{Ah}(p, v^h)$, the *autarky* household product function. The implicit household production possibility set is defined as:

$$\{y^h : y^h = g^h_p(p, v, v^h); p \geq 0, v \geq 0, v^h \geq 0\}.$$

It is clear that an *implicit* autarky equilibrium of household h based on either the implicit good or the factor trade model must be distinguished from the *actual* autarky equilibrium of household h.

(3) *The economy production possibility locus.* The national product function, which can be derived from it, is given by $g = g(p, v)$ as in (8) and it is necessarily convex in prices.

This paper combines these various products functions with expenditure functions to yield the relevant trade expenditure functions. Several of our main results follow from relating the properties of the relevant household trade expenditure functions to known properties of the relevant economy trade expenditure function (see especially Proposition 2).

2.2. The multihousehold trade expenditure function

To derive the multihousehold goods trade expenditure function, we simply sum the implicit goods trade expenditure functions in (I) over all households. (Alternatively, one may add the implicit factor trade expenditure functions of all households.) From (7) and (8):

$$B^e(p, v, u) \equiv \sum_h e^h(p, u^h) - g(p, v), \tag{III}$$

where u now denotes the vector of utility, $u = (u^1, \ldots, u^H)$.

The economic interpretation of (III) is clear. The function B^e expresses the net transfer from outside the economy which is required to 'produce' a utility vector u, given tastes, the technology, product prices p and the vector endowments v.

The most important properties of this function are:

III(1) It is linearly homogeneous and globally concave in prices.

III(2) It is increasing in the u^h's.

III(3) Its partial derivatives with respect to prices are the compensated market excess demand functions for the goods.

III(4) The function reaches a global maximum at the (economy) autarky prices.

Proof. Properties III(1)–III(3) are easy to prove. We simply note that $vw(p, v) \equiv g(p, v)$ which is convex in prices. To prove property III(4) we use the Kuhn–Tucker theorem. Since the function is concave in prices it follows from the Kuhn–Tucker theorem that the function B^e reaches a maximum at prices p^A (autarky prices) if and only if

$$B_p^e(p^A, v, u^A) = \sum_h e_p^h(p^A, u^A) - vw_p(p^A, v) \leqq 0 \tag{12}$$

where u^A denotes the autarky utility vector and, from Walras' Law:

$$B^e(p^A, v, u^A) = 0.$$

However, the inequalities under (12) express the autarky equilibrium conditions.   Q.E.D.

Eq. (12) is a global result because of the global concavity of B^e in p.

The trade expenditure functions defined in (I), (II) and (III) are powerful tools in the analysis of Pareto-improving changes in the paramenters of the model. Definition (III) may be used if lump-sum transfers betwen households are possible. In the absence of lump-sum transfers one has to utilise the trade expenditure functions of individual households. To derive optimal policies we need the social trade expenditure function.

2.3. The social trade expenditure function

Samuelson (1956) obtained the direct social utility function whose arguments are the aggregates of consumption across all households. Formally, the direct social utility function is:

$$Z(x) \equiv \underset{x^1, x^2, \dots, x^n}{\text{maximise}} \left\{ W[U^1(x^1), U^2(x^2), \dots, U^n(x^n)] \colon \sum_{h=1}^{n} x^h \leqq x \right\},$$

where $x =$ the aggregate consumption vector, and $W[U^1(x^1), U^2(x^2), \dots, U^n(x^n)] =$ the Samuelson–Bergson social welfare function.

Recently, Pollak (1981) has defined the dual of the social utility function:

$$e^s(p, z) \equiv \min_{x} [px \colon Z(x) \geqq z].$$

The function $e^s(p, z)$ is referred to as the social expenditure function. We obtain the *social trade expenditure function* by subtracting the national product or revenue function from the social expenditure function:

$$B^s(p, v, z) \equiv e^s(p, z) - g(p, v). \tag{IV}$$

This function is associated with the implicit goods model. [In complete analogy to (IV) one can also define a social factor trade expenditure function.]

To clarify the roles of the multihousehold and social trade expenditure functions in normative analysis we relate the former to the latter. Assume a given reference utility vector $\bar{u}$, and prices such that

$$B(p, v, \bar{u}) = 0. \tag{13}$$

Find the implied level of social utility from $\bar{z} = W(\bar{u})$. This gives $B^s(p, v, \bar{z})$. Now we have:

$$B^s(p, v, \bar{z}) \leqq B^e(p, v, \bar{u}). \tag{14}$$

This result simply reflects the fact that the derivation of the social trade expenditure function allows for substitution among utilities, whereas such substitutions are ruled out in the case of multihousehold trade expenditure functions.

3. Results

First we address the question of gains from trade for households without governmental intervention (see Proposition 2). Later we comment on a recent result by Dixit and Norman (1980) concerning gains from trade without lump-sum compensation. The important issues of gains from trade in distorted economies is taken up in section 4.

When one consults the literature with regard to gains from trade in economies with multiple households but without governmental intervention one is struck by the agnostic nature of the results. Free trade will not generally maximise the utility possibilities of a subset of persons or factors within a country [see Samuelson (1962)].

Our first result is a restatement of the well-known fact that, subject to the standard assumptions, at least one household must gain from free trade and this household could compensate the losing households and still gain.

An immediate implication of property III(4) of the multihousehold trade expenditure function is that:

$$B^e(p^*, v, u^A) \leqq B^e(p^A, v, u^A) = 0,$$

where u^A is the autarky utility vector of households and an asterisk denotes the free trade situation. Since $B(p^*, v, u^*) = 0$ from Walras' Law, we know that:

$$B(p^*, v, u^A) - B(p^*, v, u^*) \leqq 0. \tag{15}$$

This implies that at least one element of $(u^A - u^*)$ is non-positive as the multihousehold trade expenditure function is increasing in the u^h's. As the multihousehold trade expenditure function is defined as the sum of the household trade expenditure functions, (15) can be written as:

$$\sum_h [B^h(p^*, v^h, v, u^{hA}) - B^h(p^*, v^h, v, u^{h*})] \leqq 0. \tag{16}$$

The gainers from free trade are indexed by $h = 1, \ldots, p$ and the losers by $k = p+1, \ldots, s$. It then follows from (16) that:

$$\sum_h [B^h(p^*, v^h, v, u^{h*}) - B^h(p^*, v^h, v, u^{hA})]$$

$$\geqq \sum_k [B^k(p, v^h, v, u^{k*}) - B^k(p^*, v^h, v, u^{kA})]. \tag{17}$$

This equation shows the precise sense in which the gainers can compensate the losers.[4] This result is of limited applicability because, in general, one

---

[4]Another result which is interesting, and new as far as we know, follows directly from the fact that the multihousehold trade expenditure function, reaches a maximum at autarky prices and at the autarky utility level:

$$\sum_h e^h(p^*, u^{hA}) - \sum_h e^h(p^A, u^{hA}) \leqq g(p^*, v) - g(p^A, v).$$

expects that some households will gain and some lose from any set of international prices.

For a small change in a single price, one may obtain from (9) above a condition that all households gain. Consider an initial set of prices, $p=p^*$. Given our definition of the implicit excess demand or imports of a good by a household, one can state the condition that all households be on the same side of the market for this good in the sense that the implicit excess demand for the good be of the same sign for all households. That is, all households are *implicit net sellers (buyers)* if and only if $m_i^h < (>)0$ for all h. This definition of net sellers/buyers is an alternative to the Weymark Condition [Weymark (1979)]. This condition implies that all households will gain (lose) from a small increase in the price of a good if and only if they are all implicit net sellers (buyers) of the good.

This condition will be satisfied by goods that are produced wholly for foreign consumption or commodities that are supplied wholly by foreign producers. However, it will not be satisfied for all goods in an economy with multiple distinct households and, therefore, cannot be extended to gains from the opening of trade.

The following proposition states a necessary and sufficient condition which ensures a household will gain from international trade, for any international prices, p^*.

Proposition 2.   Household h gains from international trade if and only if the implicit goods trade expenditure function of household h, $B^h(p,v,v^h,u^h)$, is a strictly increasing transformation in prices of the multihousehold trade expenditure function $B^e(p,v,u) = \sum_h B^h(p,v,v^h,u^h)$; that is, for all p and given v and u, $B^h = T(B^e)$ with $T' > 0$.

This is a global result. It may be applied to any subset of households.

Proof.

Necessity.   From (15), $B^e(p^*,v,u^A) \leq 0$. Suppose, contrary to Proposition 2, that the fall in the value of the multihousehold trade expenditure function resulting from a change from autarky to free trade prices is associated with a

---

The economic interpretation of the last expression is that, if the cost of achieving the autarky utility vector is higher at international prices than at autarky prices, the value of output at international prices must exceed the value of output at autarky prices. On the other hand, if the value of output at autarky prices is in excess of the value of output at international prices, the cost of achieving the given autarky utility vector must be lower at international prices, than at autarky prices. If we define $g(p^*,v) - g(p^A,v)$ as the production gains and $\sum_h e^h(p^A,u^{hA}) - \sum_h e^h(p^*,u^{hA})$ as the consumption gains, we can see from the last inequality that the production gains plus the consumption gains must be non-negative. The usual definitions of consumption and production gains are, of course, quite different.

rise in the value of the trade expenditure function of household h. That is,

$$B^h(p*, v^h, v, u^{hA}) > 0.$$

But, in the free trade equilibrium,

$$B^h(p*, v^h, v, u^{h*}) = 0.$$

This implies $u^{hA} > u^{h*}$.

Sufficiency. Since any increasing transformation preserves concavity, we know that if the condition of Proposition 2 holds, the household trade expenditure function is concave in prices. Moreover, a state of economy autarky clearly implies a state of implicit goods trade autarky equilibrium of household h. The property of concavity and implicit autarky equilibrium of household h at the economy autarky prices imply that the household trade expenditure function of household h reaches a maximum at the economy autarky prices. Q.E.D.

A monotonic relationship between the household and the economy trade expenditure exists only if:

Condition 1. The implicit compensated excess demand curves for household h are downward sloping.

And if and only if:

Condition 2. The sign pattern of implicit excess demands of household h is, at free trade prices, the same as the economy pattern of excess demands. The latter condition can be extended to groups of households. If it applies to all households we have a condition which is an alternative to the Weymark Condition. Proposition 2 makes it clear that the Weymark Condition would have to hold for all goods.

This approach to gains from international trade for households via trade expenditure functions can be compared with an alternative approach via the household product functions which is closer to the standard literature. Suppose that the product function of household h, $v^h w(p, v)$, is a monotonic transformation of the national product function because, for example $v^h = \alpha v$. Suppose, furthermore, that household h is in an implicit autarky equilibrium before the economy is opened up to foreign trade. In this case the standard chain argument proves that household h must gain from international trade:

$$e^h(p*, u^{hA}) \leqq p* y^{hA}(p^A, v, v^h) \leqq p* y^{h*}(p*, v, v^h) = e^h(p*, u^{h*}), \tag{18}$$

where y^{hA} and y^{h*} denote the vectors of implicit outputs of household h in the economy autarky equilibrium and the free trade equilibrium respectively. The implicit outputs of household h must be non-negative. In comparing (18) and Proposition 2 the latter must be judged preferable to the former. Trade expenditure functions, by definition, take into account consumption gains as well as production gains or losses. The chain argument given above focuses on the production side and hence can only yield sufficient conditions, whereas the trade expenditure function yields necessary and sufficient conditions. As far as we are aware, there is only one article which deals with some of these issues and it does so in a different analytical framework. Bhagwati and Brecher (1980) have examined the question of national gains from trade or improvements in the terms of trade, when some factors are owned by foreign households. More specifically, they are concerned with the derivation of a set of conditions under which all domestic households experience a welfare improvement as the economy is opened up to trade. The main result of Bhagwati and Brecher (1980) is that, in the absence of a 'differential trade pattern', that is, a different sign pattern of excess demands, domestic households will gain from international trade. This can be regarded as the special case of Proposition 2 when there are only two goods, two factors, and two households. If it is assumed, following Bhagwati and Brecher, that foreign households spend their income in the home economy and domestic households do not supply facotrs to the foreign economy, their model is isomorphic to the trade model we employ. In this context the reader is also referred to an article by Svensson (1981) which presents an alternative generalisation of the results by Bhagwati and Brecher.

Of course if the government intervenes by means of lump-sum transfers all households can gain from trade. Recently Dixit and Norman (1980) have put forward a proof that free trade may be made Pareto superior to autarky by means of commodity and factor taxes instead of lump-sum compensation. The issue is of great importance because lump-sum compensation and transfers are generally not incentive-compatible [see Hammond (1979)]. Since commodity and factor taxes are anonymous and incentive compatible, it follows that they must be judged superior to lump-sum compensation. The Dixit and Norman result requires production gains, i.e. an increase in the value of output at world market prices as the economy moves from autarky to free trade. Such a production gain may not materialise even in a perfectly competitive model, as Kemp and Wan (1986) noted.

It is also clear from its derivation that the Dixit–Norman proposition relies upon the existence of firms as production units. Households sell factors to firms and firms sell goods to households and therefore the Weymark Condition must be satisfied.

We explore this issue in more detail making use of our concepts. If we ignore consumption gains or losses, we can decompose the welfare gains or losses of household h resulting from a move from economy autarky equilibrium to free trade equilibrium into three components:

$$\Delta u^h = [v^h w(p^A, v) - v^h w(p^A, v^h)] + [v^h w(p^A, v^h) - v^h w(p^*, v^h)]$$

$$+ [v^h w(p^*, v^h) - v^h w(p^*, v)]. \tag{19}$$

The first term measures the welfare gains from the existence of firms or from factor trade in the economy autarky equilibrium. The second term represents the gains or losses from the changes in prices as the outputs of household h moves along the autarky household production possibility locus. Finally, the third term is equal to the losses which would result from restricting the household to its autarky production possibility locus at free trade prices. It follows from the above decomposition that

$$v^h w(p^A, v) - v^h w(p^*, v^h) < 0$$

is a sufficient condition for a welfare loss and

$$v^h w(p^A, v^h) - v^h w(p^*, v) > 0$$

is a sufficient condition for a welfare gain.

We now focus on one special case which is of particular interest in the context of the Dixit and Norman result. Suppose that at prices p^A and p^*, the endowments of all households, v^h, and therefore endowments v are in the same diversification cone. As is well known, this will guarantee that

$$w(p^A, v^h) = w(p^A, v), \quad \text{for all } h, \tag{20}$$

and

$$w(p^*, v^h) = w(p^*, v), \quad \text{for all } h.$$

In this special case the welfare effects on all households of changes in production can be analysed as movements along the autarky household production possibility locus. In these circumstances, firms have no role to play in our multihousehold economy. The same applies, of course, to factor trade. Moreover, since the autarky household production possibility set is convex it follows that in this case the implicit goods trade expenditure function of household h is concave. An implicit autarky equilibrium is therefore an actual autarky equilibrium.

What are the implications of this for the Dixit and Norman result? Formally, there are no problems if we regard the household as a consumption-cum-production agent. This agent then faces different prices for goods and factors as a consumption unit from the prices it faces as a production unit. In what sense if any it is practicable to tax a household for factor services which it sells to itself is an open question.

In essence, Dixit and Norman have shown that a production and exchange economy cannot be reduced to an exchange economy in the presence of commodity and factor taxation. It follows from the implicit goods and factor trade models of section 2 that in the absence of factor and commodity taxation a production and exchange economy can always be reduced to an exchange economy and this is the key theme of the traditional trade theory.

4. Further applications and conclusions

This section applies trade expenditure functions to the analysis of gains from trade in the presence of distortions. As is well known [see, for example, Corden (1984)] the literature on gains from trade with distortions suffers from two main weaknesses:

(1) Generally, most of the results present only sufficient conditions.

(2) The approach is generally piecemeal, deriving different conditions for different distortions.

Making use of the concept of a trade expenditure function suitably redefined for the various distortions, we can, subject to some relatively weak assumptions, provide (a) a unified approach and (b) a set of necessary and sufficient conditions. The key idea underlying our approach is that there will be aggregate gains from trade if and only if the distorted multihousehold trade expenditure function reaches a regular maximum at goods autarky prices (and distortions). Our approach to the analysis of gains from trade in distorted economies is therefore a direct extension of the approach to gains from trade in undistorted economies. Section 3 showed that the multi-household goods trade expenditure function, definition (III), reaches a maximum at autarky prices. Clearly, this is a necessary and sufficient condition for gains from trade in an aggregate sense.

For lack of space we concentrate on the case of distortions brought about by the existence of taxes and/or subsidies on trade. To analyse gains from trade in the presence of trade distortions one requires the concept of the *distorted economy multihousehold trade expenditure function*. This is obtained by deducting the trade tax revenue from the multihousehold trade expenditure function:

$$B^{\mathrm{d}}(p, p^*, v, u) \equiv B^{\mathrm{e}}(p, v, u) - (p - p^*)B^{\mathrm{e}}_p(p, v, u). \tag{V}$$

The function $B^{\mathrm{d}}(p, p^*, v, u)$ is useful for welfare analysis because it measures the total value of compensation payments to households which is required to sustain or 'produce' a given utility vector, given (p, p^*, v). From the linear homogeneity of $B^e(p, v, u)$ in p^* it follows that:

$$pB^e_p(p, v, u) = B^e(p, v, u). \qquad (21)$$

Hence,

$$B^d(p, p^*, v, u) = p^*B^e_p(p, v, u) = p^*m(p, v, u), \qquad (22)$$

where m is the vector of competitive imports at prices p.

Thus, (V) values the compensation payments at the social opportunity costs. Moreover, B^d is the sum across households of the differences between the value of spending and the value of income from production and trade tax income distributed to the households:

$$B^d(p, p^*, v, u) = \sum_h [e^h(p, u^h) - v^h w(p, v) - \beta^h(p - p^*)m(p, v, u)], \qquad (23)$$

where β^h is the share of household h in tariff revenue.

The most important properties of this function are:

V(1) It is homogeneous of degree zero in p and degree one in p^*.

V(2) Its partial derivatives with respect to p^* are the compensated excess demand functions.

V(3) It reaches a global minimum at $p = p^*$.

Proof. Properties V(1) and V(2) follow directly from the properties of the trade expenditure function for an undistorted economy. To prove V(3) we note that, by construction,

$$B^e(p^*, v, u) = p^*B^e_p(p^*, v, u)$$

and that $B^e(p^*, v, u)$ is minimised with respect of p^*. Hence,

$$p^*[B^e_p(p, v, u) - B^e_p p^*, v, u)] \geqq 0. \qquad (24)$$

For quasi-concavity relative to $p = p^*$, we must prove that:

$$B^d[\theta p^1 + (1 - \theta)p^2, p^*, v, u] \geqq \min [B^d(p^1, p^*, v, u), B^d(p^2, p^*, v, u)].$$

Setting p^1 or p^2 equal to p^* this weak inequality follows because $B^d(p, p^*, v, u)$ reaches a minimum at $p^1 = p^*$ or $p^2 = p^*$. Furthermore, we assume that $B^d(p, p^*, v, u)$ is strictly increasing in at least one element of the vector u (Assumption A). This is a weak assumption and follows from boundedness of the utility possibility set.

From these properties, it follows that any domestic prices vector, p^1, which can be expressed as a convex combination of some other domestic prices vector p^2 and the international prices p^*, cannot be Pareto inferior to the price vector p^2. Thus, a proportionate reduction in trade distortions will improve welfare. This is a well-known result. It can be found, for example, in Dixit (1985). However, the present proof is more general because it does not require differentiation.

We now turn to the analysis of gains from tariff- and/or subsidy-ridden trade. Initially, we assume lump-sum compensation of households.

Our main result is contained in the following proposition.

Proposition 3.   Subject to Assumption A and lump-sum compensation of households, tax-ridden trade is strictly Pareto superior to autarky (no trade) if and only if the trade expenditure function $B^d = B^d(p, p^*, v, u^A)$ reaches a regular maximum at autarky prices, i.e.

$$B^d(p, p^*, v, u^A) < 0, \text{ for all } p \text{ other than } p^A \text{ (autarky prices).}$$

Proof.   At autarky prices, clearly $B^d(p^A, p^*, v, u^A) = B^e(p^A, v, u^A) = 0$ from Walras' Law. Hence,

$$B^d(p, p^*, v, u^A) < 0$$

if and only if B^d reaches a maximum at p^A. This implies that tax-ridden trade is strictly Pareto superior because $B^d(p, p^*, v, u^T) = 0$ from Walras' Law (where u^T is the utility vector with trade). Assumption A implies that at least one element of the vector u^T is greater than the corresponding element of the vector u^A. This proves sufficiency.

To prove necessity, we assume, contrary to Proposition 3, that

$$B^d(p, p^*, v, u^A) \geqq 0.$$

But, since

$$B^d(p, p^*, v, u^T) = 0$$

and Assumption A holds, we know at least one element of u^A is either greater or equal to the corresponding element of u^T.

Proposition 3 can be compared with the well-known sufficient condition of gains from distorted trade which was originally derived by Ohyama (1972) and generalised by Eaton and Panagariya (1979). This condition is that the net trade tax revenue is positive. This can be shown to be one case of Proposition 3 using our notation:

$$B^d(p, p^*, v, u^T) = B^e(p, v, u^T) - (p - p^*)B_p^e(p, v, u^T) = 0. \tag{25}$$

And, from the condition that net trade tax revenue is positive:

$$B^e(p, v, u^T) > 0. \tag{26}$$

Furthermore, from Walras' Law,

$$B^e(p^A, v, u^A) = 0.$$

Hence, since $B^e(p, v, u^A)$ reaches a maximum at autarky prices:

$$B^e(p, v, u^A) < 0. \tag{27}$$

From (26) and (27) it follows that at least one element of u^T must exceed the corresponding element of u^A.

Our approach is superior because (26) is only a sufficient condition for gains from trade, whereas we have derived a necessary and sufficient condition. We can have

$$B(p, v, u^T) < 0$$

and still have gains from trade provided that

$$0 > B^e(p, v, u^T) > B^e(p, v, u^A). \tag{28}$$

If, as an extreme case, there is no substitution on either the consumption or production side, then it follows that even though the function $B^e(p, v, u^A)$ reaches a maximum at autarky prices, we shall have:

$$B^e(p^A, v, u^A) = B^e(p, v, u^A) = 0, \quad \text{for all } p. \tag{29}$$

In this extreme case we can see from (26), (28) and (29) that (26) would represent a necessary and sufficient condition for gains from trade. More generally, if there is any substitution in the economy,

$$B^e(p, v, u^A) < 0$$

and, in this case, there may be gains from tax-ridden trade even if the net trade tax revenue is negative.

Until now, the analysis of this section has been based upon the assumption of lump-sum compensation. It would, however, be straightforward to extend the Dixit and Norman result to open economies which are tax ridden.[5]

There is a large number of further applications of trade expenditure functions which could be developed. They could be applied to economies with all forms of distortions but particularly to models with variable returns to scale and imperfect competition. The advantage of applying trade expenditure functions in these cases is clear. It forces us to consider potential production *and* consumption gains. This approach therefore naturally leads to the derivation of necessary and sufficient conditions rather than sufficient conditions for gains from trade in the presence of distortions. Finally, these functions can be used to derive true trade price and true trade quantity indices.

[5]As expected, the Dixit and Norman result can be generalised to tax-ridden economies if and only if the value of output increases at world market prices. This last result holds whether or not the change in outputs is brought about by an opening up of the economy to tax-ridden trade or through changes in the structure of taxes.

References

Bhagwati, J.N. and R.A. Brecher, 1980, National welfare in an open economy in the presence of foreign-owned factors of production, Journal of International Economics 10, Feb., 103–115.

Bhagwati, J.N., R. Brecher and T. Hatta, 1983, The generalised theory of transfers and welfare: Bilateral transfers in a multilateral world, American Economic Review 83, 606–618.

Chipman, J., 1970, Lectures on the mathematical foundation of international trade theory, Mimeo., Institute of Advanced Science, Vienna, Austria.

Corden, W.M., 1984, The normative theory of international trade, in: R.W. Jones and P.B. Kenen, eds., Handbook of international economics, vol. 1 (North-Holland, Amsterdam) 63–130.

Deardorff, A.V., 1982, The general validity of the Heckscher–Ohlin theorem, American Economic Review 72, 683–694.

Dixit, A. 1985, Tax policies in open economies, in: A. Auerbach, ed., Handbook of public economics, vol. 1 (North-Holland, Amsterdam).

Dixit, A. and V. Norman, 1980, Theory of international trade (James Nisbet, Welwyn, UK).

Dixit, A. and V. Norman, 1986, Gains from trade without lump sum compensation, Journal of International Economics 21, 111–122.

Eaton, J. and A. Panagariya, 1979, Gains from trade under variable returns to scale, commodity taxation, tariffs and factor market distortions, Journal of International Economics 9, 481–502.

Ethier, W., 1984, Higher dimensional issues of trade theory, in: Handbook of international economics, vol. 1 (North-Holland, Amsterdam) 131–184.

Hammond, P., 1979, Straightforward individual incentive compatibility in large economics, Review of Economic Studies 46, 263–282.

Jones, R.W. and J. Scheinkman, 1977, The relevance of the two sector production model in trade theory, Journal of Political Economy 85, 909–936.

Kemp, M.C. and T. Negishi, 1970, Variable returns to scale, commodity taxes, factor market distortions and their implications for trade gains, Swedish Journal of Economics 72, 1–11.

Kemp, M.C. and W.H. Wan, Jr., 1986, Gains from trade with and without lump sum compensation, Journal of International Economics 21, 99–110.

Lloyd, P.J., 1987, Protection policy and the assignment rule, in: H. Kierzkowski, ed., Protection and competition in international trade: Essays in honour of Max Corden (Basil Blackwell).

McKenzie, L.W., 1954, Specialisation and efficiency in world production, Review of Economic Studies 21, 165–180.

Neary, P.J. and A.G. Schweinberger, 1986, Factor content functions and the theory of international trade, Review of Economic Studies 53, 421–432.

Ohyama, M., 1972, Trade and welfare in general equilibrium, Keio Economics Papers 9, 37–73.

Pollak, R.A., 1981, The social cost of living index, Journal of Public Economics 15, 311–336.

Samuelson, P.A., 1956, Social indifference curves, Quarterly Journal of Economics 70, 1–22.

Samuelson, P.A., 1962, The gains from international trade once again, Economic Journal 72, 820–829.

Svensson, L.E.O., 1981, National welfare in the presence of foreign-owned factors of production: An extension, Scandinavian Journal of Economics 83, 497–507.

Wan, H.Y. 1965, Maximum bonus: An alternative measure for trading gains, Review of Economic Studies 32, 49–58.

Weymark, J.A., 1979, A reconciliation of recent results in optimal tax theory, Journal of Public Economics 12, 171–189.

Woodland, A.D., 1982, International trade and resource allocation (North-Holland, Amsterdam).

Unilateral and regional trade policies of the CER countries

1 Introduction

While Australia and New Zealand are sovereign states, they have in the 1980s and 1990s pursued sets of trade policies which share many elements and which together represent a style of trade policy that is distinctive. Among the common elements are a fast rate of unilateral reductions in barriers to trade with other nations, a sharp movement away from reliance on quantitative restrictions and other non-tariff instruments of trade restriction, membership of a regional trading arrangement that has achieved virtually complete freedom of bilateral trade and deepened the integration of the two economies, and a strong commitment to multilateralism.

These policies were quite different from those followed by Australia before the mid-1970s and by New Zealand in the period before the 1980s. Yet, from a long-term point of view, the trade policies of Australia and New Zealand also exhibit remarkable similarities. By the 1920s, both countries had average tariffs that were high compared with those of other high-income countries (see Anderson and Garnaut, 1987, Table 2.1) and they were increased for many manufacturing industries in the following decades. Given these initial levels and a low level of participation in the early rounds of tariff-cutting under the General Agreement on Tariffs and Trade (GATT), Australia and New Zealand by 1970 had average tariff rates which were the highest of the member countries of the Organization for Economic Cooperation and Development (OECD). In addition, Australia and New Zealand introduced comprehensive import licensing in 1939 and 1938 respectively, and used them as wartime measures, but they extended and continued these schemes long after the end of the war. In Australia, import licensing continued until 1962, and selective tariff quotas and quotas were reintroduced after 1973. In New Zealand, import licensing continued until the mid-1980s. While no exactly comparable statistics are available for protection from both tariff and non-tariff measures in other countries, we can safely say that, among the OECD countries, Australia and New Zealand had the highest average levels of protection for their import-competing manufacturing producers during the 1970s and early 1980s.[1] Thus the history of trade policies in Australia and New Zealand in the last two decades or so represents a triumph of anti-protectionist or pro-free-trade views over a long-standing and deeply rooted protectionism.

This chapter reviews these policies. It is necessary to review the events in Australia and New Zealand separately as the timing and nature of their reforms differ in some respects. The first and second sections provide a potted history of these policies in Australia and New Zealand, respectively, emphasizing the movement away from high trade barriers as a result of unilateral reductions; and section 1 includes the first estimates of the Trade Restrictiveness Index (TRI) (that is, true utility-constant levels of trade barriers) for Australia. The third section then examines the regional aspects of trade policies, and the fourth examines multilateral aspects of trade policies in the two countries, including the approach of both countries to the Asia Pacific Economic Co-operation Forum (APEC). Section 5 offers some concluding remarks and hypotheses concerning the trends in these trade policies and their convergence.

2 Industry assistance in Australia

One of the features of the Australian debate about protection is the availability of excellent data measuring the extent of the distortions caused by government border interventions. Under the influence of Max Corden, the report of the government-appointed Vernon Committee (1965, Appendix L) produced the first official estimates of effective protection (and subsidy equivalents) for the manufacturing sector in Australia. These related to the year 1961–2 and were made for seven industry groups and for some subgroups and individual commodities within these groups. Beginning with its Annual Report for 1969–70, the Tariff Board (Tariff Board, 1970, Appendix 2) and its successors, the Industries Assistance Commission and the Industry Commission, have produced annual estimates of nominal and effective assistance for the manufacturing sector and later for the agricultural and the mining sectors. The estimates cover the major Commonwealth Government interventions, which apply selectively to some activities only. The instrument coverage is quite comprehensive; it includes assistance provided by tariffs, and the major non-tariff border instruments (quantitative import restrictions, production bounties, local content schemes and certain export incentives) and, for agricultural commodities, domestic pricing arrangements and tax concessions from the Commonwealth government and from state government interventions of national significance. For this reason, the term 'rates of assistance' has been preferred in Australia to the term 'rates of protection'.

Consistent times series for these rates are now available for the manufacturing sector from the year 1968–9, or the agricultural sector from 1970–1 and for the mining sector from 1986–7. For the manufacturing sector, these estimates are available at the two-, three-, and four-digit classifications of industries and for the agricultural sector for 26 commodity groups (for the latest series see Industry Commission, 1995) and for the mining sector for 16 subindustry groups (Industry Commission, 1992). Indeed, for more than 25 years, the Australian Government has had in this area of policy-making the best data available to any government.

Figures 1 and 2 show the average nominal and effective rates of assistance for the manufacturing and agricultural sectors, respectively, from the beginning of these series. For the manufacturing sector, the discontinuities reflect the periodic rebasing of the estimates to account for changes in the structure of activities in this sector, and the figures include forecasts based on the announced phased reductions up to the year 2000–1. These figures show a downward trend for assistance to the manufacturing sector from 1973 which is strong and continues steadily to the year 2001. There is a downward trend for the agricultural sector which holds for the period as a whole, but this is due to the sharp reductions in 1970 and 1971 and is subject to wide annual fluctuations because many of the instruments giving assistance to agricultural producers vary with prices or incomes and are, therefore, not constant in *ad valorem* terms.

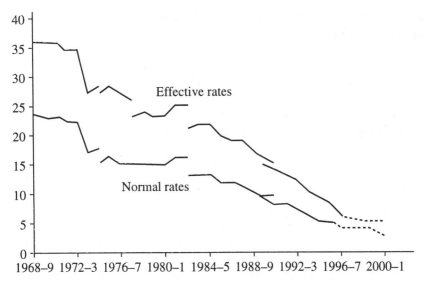

Notes: ᵃ The discontinuities in the series reflect the periodic rebasing of the estimates to account for changes in the structure of the manufacturing sector.

Source: As indicated in the text.

Figure 1   Average nominal and effective rates of assistance for the manufacturing sectorᵃ: 1968–9 to 2000–1 (per cent)

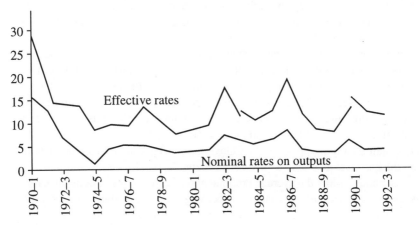

Source: As indicated in text.

Figure 2   Average nominal and effective rates of assistance to agriculture: 1970–1 to 1992–3 (per cent)

The estimates of assistance to the mining sector relate to 1990–1 and selected earlier years (Industry Commission, 1992, Table K10). These show that the mining sector has had negative average assistance, since mining outputs receive almost no assistance and many of the inputs are subject to tariffs and other forms of assistance which raise their prices above world prices. There are no estimates of rates of assistance for the services industries, though the Australian Government imposes substantial impediments to international trade in services, chiefly through the regulation of industries such as coastal shipping, banking and civil aviation (Industry Commission, 1995, Appendix G).

Thus the effect of assistance in Australia over the period has been to penalize exporters in the agricultural and mining sectors (and probably also in the services sector). There is a long tradition of the analysis of the costs of protection, and their burden on exporters in particular, which dates back to the 1929 Brigden Report. This analysis will not be reviewed here; instead, I shall present at the end of this section new estimates of the TRI for Australia.

The reductions in assistance to manufacturers have resulted from an almost continuous programme of reform.[3] This began in a systematic way with the Tariff Review, which was a review of the highly protected areas of manufacturing. It was proposed by the Tariff Board in its 1966–7 Annual Report but was not implemented until the Minister for Trade and Industry, in May 1971, finally forwarded to the Board the references it had requested to begin it. On 19 July 1973, without any notice and following a report from a confidential committee appointed a month earlier, the Government cut by 25 per cent all tariffs except those applying to goods which were subject to excise duties. This is the largest single reduction in levels of assistance in Australian history and marks the beginning of the period of reduced levels of assistance. It lowered the average effective rate of assistance for the sector by about 8 percentage points. (There were only a few imports subject to quantitative restrictions at that time.) The chief concern of the Government that appointed the committee was to reduce aggregate excess demand and the rate of inflation, not to reform the pattern of assistance to industry. After the event there was vigorous debate as to whether this tariff cut was responsible for the subsequent rise in the unemployment rate, and this led to speculation that there could never again be an across-the-board cut in rates of assistance in Australia.

Piecemeal reforms of the assistance to some industries which received above-average assistance, such as the passenger motor vehicles (PMV), the textile, clothing and footwear (TCF), and the white goods' industries, continued under references sent by the Government to the Industries Assistance Commission. Then, in the May 1988 Economic Statement, the Government announced a programme of tariff reductions for most imports, to continue until 1992. The method of cutting tariffs applied greater percentage cuts to higher rates. With some exceptions, tariffs greater than 15 per cent were phased down to 15 per cent and those between 15 and 10 per cent to 10 per cent by 1992. In addition, the 2 per cent revenue duty, which had applied to all imports from January 1980, was removed from 1 July 1988. One must note, however, the exceptions to the tariff cuts related to certain imports covered by industry plans for PMV and TCF products and also to tariffs on some agricultural products subject to commodity stabilization or other schemes. These were the most highly assisted product groups. Under the April 1988 amendments to the motor vehicle plan, tariffs were reduced and import quotas abolished on these products.

In its Industry Policy Statement of March 1991, the Government announced the continuation of this programme of tariff reductions beyond 1992. Most tariffs were phased down to 5 per cent by July 1996. In this programme, the tariffs on both PMV and TCF industry products, the two areas with relatively high rates of assistance remaining in the 1990s, are to be reduced annually to levels of 10, 15 or 25 per cent by the year 2000. Despite efforts by these industries to slow down this timetable, the Labour Government that instituted the programme stuck to it. The coalition government elected in 1996 has not yet revealed its policies with respect to the substantive tariffs. In the election campaign it had announced that the Tariff Concession Scheme, which gives duty-free entry to most imported business inputs not made in Australia and to some consumer goods for which there is no close substitute made in Australia, would be abolished. This change was proposed as a revenue measure but in May, following strong pressure from industry lobby groups, the Government announced that concessions would be reduced to 40 per cent of the tariff costs rather than being eliminated.

Almost all these reductions in assistance, shown in Figures 1 and 2, were carried out unilaterally. Widespread tariff reductions were introduced in January 1977 as the Australian commitment to the Tokyo Round of Multilateral trade negotiations (MTN). These tariff reductions were not across-the-board but were instead designed specifically to cause minimal disruption to Australian industries and mainly represented the removal of unused assistance to lightly assisted industries. They did not, therefore, lessen the dispersion in rates of assistance; and even these reductions were made in part as a response to the devaluation of the Australian dollar in November 1976. It has been estimated that these 1977 MTN reductions lowered the average effective rate for the manufacturing sector by three percentage points during the 1976–7 and 1978–9 years (Industries Assistance Commission, 1979, p. 80). Hence, of the reduction in the average effective rate of assistance to the manufacturing sector from 36 per cent in 1968–9 to 8 per cent in 1995–6, the MTN reductions have contributed only three percentage points (that is about 11 per cent of the total) and the corresponding contributions to the reductions in the agricultural sector would be proportionately less.

Two other features of the reduction in tariff assistance are noteworthy. These are the trend to substitution of tariff for non-tariff measures of assistance since the early 1980s, and the reduction in the inter-industry variation in nominal and effective rates.

Quantitative restrictions on imports, chiefly under the regime of import licensing, were the main instrument of assistance to the import-competing industries after the Second World War. Import licensing ended in Australia in the early 1960s and tariffs again became the instrument of protection for all but a few highly regulated industry groups. Beginning in December 1974 and continuing in 1975 tariff quotas, quotas and other quantitative restrictions were reintroduced in Australia for several commodity groups. Although originally applied as temporary measures for periods of one or two years, they became the main instruments of protection for the two industries receiving the highest levels of assistance, the PMV and the TCF groups. In the early 1980s the government moved to reform some aspects of the administration of these quotas and later to dismantle them. Imports of motor vehicles ceased to be subject to quotas from 13 April 1988. From 1 March 1989, assistance for TCF products by means of quotas was reduced, through the device of gradual reductions in the rate of penalty duty applying to imports outside quotas. This programme was accelerated under the March 1991 Statement and all TCF products became free of quotas on 23 February 1993. Moreover. the local content scheme for motor vehicles manufactured in Australia, which was a part of the agreement reached in 1945 between the Australian Government and General Motors Holden to promote the local production of chassis and engines and was formalized in 1965, terminated at the end of 1988, and that for the tobacco industry, which was a part of the marketing arrangements for growers and dated back to 1936, terminated on 1 January 1995. The area of production now assisted by content-based schemes is the services industries such as television and films (see Industry Commission, 1996, Appendix G) but there are no measures of the incidence of these restrictions.

It was this return to assistance by means of tariffs that made it possible to project accurately the rates of assistance until the year 2000 shown in Figures 1 and 2.

The Industries Assistance Commission has split up the assistance provided to manufacturing industries by 'form': that is, by instrument. This was done by calculating the subsidy equivalents of each instrument. In 1983–4, quantitative restrictions accounted for 15 per cent of the total assistance to outputs, and tariffs for 84 per cent. This statistic understates the significance of quantitative restrictions, as the assistance for the two highly protected industry groups, TCF and PMV; came mainly from quotas. By 1992–3, tariffs accounted for 97 per cent of the assistance to manufacturing industries (Industry Commission, 1995, Table 4.2). Today, the remaining non-tariff barriers affecting the manufacturing sector consist of a few bounties (mainly on ships, computers, textile yarn and books) and selective export subsidies (mainly the Export Market Development Grants Scheme and the Automotive Export Facilitation Scheme), but the agricultural sector still receives support from a variety of schemes, most of which are commodity-specific (see Industry Commission, 1995, Appendix F). Australia has also been one of the main users of the anti-dumping provisions of Article VI of the GATT, which is sometimes classified as a non-tariff barrier because of the protective effect of these duties, but the number of new cases has declined considerably since the early 1990s.

In substituting tariffs for quotas, Australia introduced one major modality of reform that is noteworthy. It was the first country, to my knowledge, to auction import quotas. In 1980 the Government of Australia introduced a tender for about 11 per cent of the quota for imports of passenger motor vehicles. It reverted to a historical allocation of import quotas for 1981 but, in January 1982, the Government introduced a similar scheme for tendering for 15 per cent of the quotas for imports of TCF products. Quota tenders were introduced partly in order to reveal the structure of protection implicit in quotas which covered broad categories of goods and partly to collect rent otherwise accruing to the quota-holders; the rent earned from property rights inherent in quota allocations became more transparent when transferability of quotas was allowed and large transfer prices were paid. The tender premiums that were paid for the TCF commodity groups in each category varied widely in any one year from zero to well over 100 per cent and, within the tender categories, they varied widely over the years.[4] These were on top of the basic duty rates applying to the same goods, which were generally high, most being 50 per cent or more. Thus they revealed implicit rates of assistance which were very high and unstable over time.

Regarding the inter-industry variation in effective rates, the Tariff Board and its successors have been aware that it is the variation around the average of the rates of nominal and effective rates of assistance for different groups of producers that imposes distortions on the economy. They have used the standard deviation as the measure of variation. While there is no measure of variation that is a predictor of the magnitude of welfare losses from inter-industry variation in these rates in general, Anderson (1995) has shown that a mean-preserving reduction in the variance of nominal rates is welfare-improving under certain conditions.

For the manufacturing sector, time series of the standard deviation of the nominal and effective rates of assistance, measured at the four-digit level, is available from 1968–9 (Industry Commission, 1995, Table A6.7–8). This shows that the reductions in the average nominal and effective rates of assistance for this sector were generally, but not always, accompanied by reductions in the variances of this assistance. Having remained constant at around 30 per cent from the beginning of the series in 1968–9, the standard deviation of the effective rates fell in 1973–4 as a result of the across-the-board tariff cut to 23 per cent; with a 25 per cent cut, the variance after the cut was only 9/16 (= $[3/4]^2$) of the level before the cut. The measure then rose with the introduction of highly selective quotas in the mid-1970s to a peak of 48 per cent in 1984–5, although the average nominal and effective rates in this sector were falling over this period. It fell after the reduction in quotas and has fallen steadily since the phased reductions in tariffs began in 1991, though not after the 1988 programme, because of the exemptions for some highly assisted industries (Industry Assistance Commission, 1989, Table A7.8). The results in 1973 and 1991 illustrate that a widespread reduction in (nominal) rates reduces the variance.[5]

There are estimates of the variance of nominal and effective rates of assistance to the agricultural sector in Australia. These show again that the variance of the effective rates is much higher than that of the nominal rates. Intra-sectoral variance in the agricultural sector is higher than that in the manufacturing sector and has not declined over the period. Given that the manufacturing sector has been the most assisted of the sectors throughout the period, and that the variance of rates in this sector has fallen, the interactivity variance across all sectors has almost certainly fallen.

Since, in some periods, the trends in the average levels of assistance to the manufacturing and agricultural sectors and in the standard deviations of the assistance for these sectors have moved in opposite directions, the overall trend in the extent of distortions in the economy is ambiguous. This problem of measuring the height of restrictions to international trade has long been recognized in Australia (see, for example, Crawford, 1934). It is an index number problem in a general equilibrium context.

Anderson and Neary have recently resolved this problem. In a series of papers (see, in particular, Anderson and Neary, 1994; and Anderson 1995), they constructed the Trade Restrictiveness Index (TRI). The index is derived from the Trade Expenditure Function for a distorted economy which was first developed by Lloyd and Schweinberger (1988). This function provides a money metric for welfare changes in the economy. The function is $B(p^*, p, v, u)$ where p^* and p are the vectors of world prices and domestic prices respectively, v is the vector of primary endowments, which are assumed constant, and u is the vector of household utilities. If all border interventions are *ad valorem* tariffs/export subsidies or equivalents, p can be replaced by the vector of these tariffs, t. The Trade Restrictiveness Index, τ, is then given from the equation:

$$B(p^*, t, v, u) = B(p^*, \tau, v, u) \tag{1}$$

where $1_i = (\tau, \ldots \tau)$, is the vector of uniform tariff rates. This index is a true utility-constant index of the distortions. It captures all the general equilibrium demand and supply responses to changes in the structure of border interventions. It has the desirable property that, for a given economy, a decrease in the index must increase the welfare of the economy in the sense of a Pareto improvement.

This index has been calculated from the Monash general equilibrium model of the Australian economy. Table 1 reports the results for the year 1986–7, which is roughly in the middle of the period represented in Figures 1 and 2. For all sectors, the index is the solution to equation (1). This shows that the pattern of border interventions in the Australian economy in 1986–7 was equivalent to a uniform *ad valorem* tariff of 21.80. This compares to an import-weighted index of the actual non-uniform distortions of 13.69. Thus, the latter conventional index is a considerable understatement of the true utility-constant index.

Table 1   A comparison of average levels of trade restriction, Australia, 1986–7

Sector	Import-weighted average	Trade restrictiveness index
Manufacturing	16.98	24.62
All sectors	13.69	21.80

The same utility-constant calculation has been done for the subset of border interventions relating to the manufacturing sector only. This shows that the TRI for this sector was 24.62, which is higher than that for all sectors as the manufacturing sector was the most heavily assisted sector. Again, the TRI is much higher than the import-weighted index of 16.98. The Industry Commission also calculates the average nominal rate of assistance to output of the manufacturing sector using the (unassisted) value of production as weights. In 1986–7 the average nominal rate of assistance was 12 per cent (Industry Commission, 1995, Table A6.4), which is an even greater underestimate.

Evidently the weighting of the index used to calculate the height of trade restrictions is extremely important. It has been shown that, in the neighbourhood of the initial tariffs, the TRI is an arithmetic mean of the individual tariff where the weights are the marginal welfare weights given by the effects of the changes in each tariff on the value of the function B relative to the effects of changing all border prices (Anderson, 1995, equation 6), namely:

$$\tau = \sum_i^n t_i [(\partial B/\partial p_i \; p_i / \sum_i^n \partial B/\partial p_i \; p_i)] \tag{2}$$

These weights may be positive or negative in a distorted economy These marginal weights were calculated for the Australian economy at the two-digit level. A few of the export industries had negative weights. The industries with the highest weights are reported in Table 2, together with the import weights for comparison. The results are very clear. Sub-industries in the TCF and PMV industries with high rates of assistance have much higher marginal welfare weights; indeed, the first three subindustries alone account for 70 per cent of the weights in the TRI. All the heavily weighted subindustries are in the manufacturing sector. These results show the high costs imposed on the economy from the extremely high rates of assistance given to a few producers.

Table 2   Import-weighted average and the weights in the import trade restrictiveness index

	Import-weighted average	Trade restrictiveness index
Motor vehicles and parts	0.184	0.351
Footwear	0.031	0.198
Clothing	0.053	0.169
Knitting mills	0.028	0.048
Electronic equipment	0.142	0.043
Manufacturing machinery and equipment	0.078	0.042
Construction machinery	0.026	0.030
Wire products and other metal products	0.024	0.016
Wine and spirits	0.006	0.016
Electrical machinery and batteries	0.045	0.016
Rubber products	0.022	0.015
Man-made fibres, yarns and broadwoven fabrics	0.044	0.015
Cotton yarns and household textiles	0.031	0.015
Sporting equipment and other manufacturing	0.020	0.014

3   Industry assistance in New Zealand

New Zealand is the only developed country in the last 30 years to have used quantitative restrictions, in the form of a comprehensive import licensing system, as the primary instrument of protection for its manufacturers. This system led to a structure of effective rates of protection characterized by very high average levels of assistance to import-competing activities, very wide variations among and within industries, and an unstable structure.

For New Zealand, unlike Australia, there is no annual time series of these effective rates. Hampton (1965) and Candler and Hampton (1966) made among the first estimates anywhere of the nominal rates of protection for goods subject to import licensing (by making direct price comparisons) for the year 1955, and also estimated a version of effective rates, following Max Corden. They found nominal rates of protection ranging from zero to 177 per cent for a selection of commodities that were items in the Consumers Price Index. The Economic Monitoring Group of the New Zealand Planning Council (1984) constructed a fragmented time series of rates of protection from 1955 to 1985. These series showed nominal and effective rates of protection for import-competing producers which were consistently very high over the 30 years. The average nominal rate peaked in 1964–7 at 54 per cent and the average effective rate in 1981–4 at 50 per cent. They estimated that the 'clothing' industry received an effective rate of protection of 1105 per cent at its peak in 1964–7 and the 'vehicle assembly' industry 2428 per cent during the period 1955–8. Other estimates of nominal and effective protection were made, but they are limited in commodity and instrument coverage.

Syntec Economic Services (1988), following the methods of the Industries Assistance Commission in Australia and employing some IAC staff as consultants, provided the first set of measures of assistance in New Zealand which were comprehensive in terms both of covering all manufacturing and most agricultural producers and of including all tariffs, identifiable subsidies and import licensing instruments of assistance. In the manufacturing sector, they estimated rates of assistance down to the five-digit level. Some estimates have been made subsequently, but they used a different classification of industries and method of estimation.

Table 3   Nominal and effective rates of assistance in New Zealand

	1981–82	1985–86	1987–88
Manufacturing			
Average nominal rate	20	19	14
Average effective rate	39	37	26
Pastoral agriculture			
Average nominal rate	13	4	1

Source: Syntec Economic Services (1988).

The Syntec Economic Services estimates are of particular value as they cover the years in which the major reforms occurred and are directly comparable with the Australian estimates. They made detailed estimates of the average nominal and effective rates for three years: 1981–2, 1985–6 and 1987–8 (see Table 3).

In 1981–2 the average nominal rate of assistance to manufacturing industries was 20 per cent and the average effective rate 39 per cent.[6] The comparable figures for Australia in the same year were 16 per cent and 25 per cent, respectively. Some manufacturing industries received very high levels of assistance, largely due to the import licensing system. In 1982, some 22 per cent of total merchandise imports were subject to import licensing. At the two-digit level, 'textiles, wearing apparel, leather industries' and 'fabricated metal products, machinery and equipment' had effective rates of assistance of 90 per cent and 69 per cent respectively. The average rates had fallen to 14 per cent and 26 per cent respectively by 1987–8. (The comparable figures for Australia in that year were 11 per cent and 19 per cent.)

On the other hand, the rates of assistance for agricultural producers were much lower than those for producers in the manufacturing sector. In 1981–2 the average nominal rate of assistance to the main pastoral group of agricultural commodities – meat, wool and milk products – was only 13 per cent. This fell to a mere 1 per cent in 1987–8 after the elimination of most agricultural subsidies in New Zealand.

The New Zealand experience in reducing protection is remarkable for the speed of the reforms and for the modality of the shift from reliance on quantitative restrictions to reliance on tariffs. The trade liberalization reforms began in 1979 with the announcement of the intention to allocate quotas by tender, and some other minor reforms, but it was the election of the Labour Government in 1984 that began the process in earnest. In April 1984, the Government adopted an import liberalization programme centred on the conversion of the import licensing regime into a regime of *ad valorem* tariffs (see Rayner and Lattimore (1991) for a review of the early reform years).

As with the Australian schemes in the PMV and TCF industries, the central idea was to use the tenders to provide information on the price distortions. The method of implementing the liberalization of quantitative restrictions differed from that used in Australia. In addition to existing licences, further licences were issued under the Import Licensing Tendering System, up to 5 per cent of the annual domestic production less exports (by value) and, as a general rule, import licences were to be removed when the tender premiums fell to 7.5 per cent or less over a two-year period. The method of allocating the tender quotas resembled that in Australia except that the duty levied was equal to the individual bids and, therefore, at non-uniform rates within the tender quotas.

In fact, New Zealand accelerated and liberalized this timetable in a number of ways. In July 1984 it increased global import access for goods subject to licensing to a minimum of 10 per cent (previously a maximum of 5 per cent) of the estimated domestic production less exports, and future annual allocations of licences were set at 5 per cent (previously 2.5 per cent). A year later, in September 1985, extra tenders equal to a 5 per cent increase in access were granted. The import licensing system ended on 1 July 1988 for industries that were not subject to industry plans, which constituted about 70 per cent of the manufacturing sector. The remaining import licences were to be removed by 1992 but were in fact removed in 1990, six years after the import liberalization programme began.

Over the same period that import licensing was being liberalized, the tariff rates on all commodities were liberalized by across-the-board cuts in rates, 5 per cent on 1 July 1986 and 10 per cent a year later. These were the first (unilateral) reductions in New Zealand tariff history, according to Rayner and Lattimore (1991, p. 98). There were some additional cuts in tariffs on non-competing imports. In 1987 the New Zealand Government conducted the first comprehensive review of the country's tariffs. As a result, a programme of phased annual tariff cuts over the period 1 July 1988 to 1 July 1992 was announced in the General Tariff Reduction programme. This programme used the 'Swiss formula' devised in the Tokyo Round of multilateral trade negotiations and which results in a greater proportionate reduction of higher tariff rates.[7] It leads, therefore, to a more rapid narrowing of the dispersion of rates than does an across-the-board uniform percentage cut. In addition, all specific duties were converted to *ad valorem* rates by 1 July 1992. (In Australia many specific rates, once commonly applied to the TCF goods, have been replaced by *ad valorem* rates. Specific rates now apply mainly to excisable commodities. These rates collected 3.6 per cent of all import duty in 1994–5, compared, for example, to 19.1 per cent in 1979–80.) Since 1992 phased tariff cuts have continued but, as in Australia, special provisions have been necessary for delayed cuts to industries subject to industry plans. This includes the groups of footwear, carpet and apparel, and motor vehicles – the same two groups as in Australia. New Zealand committed itself to reducing the maximum tariff on most products to 10 per cent by 1996. Performance-based export incentives and the export market development incentive were phased out in 1990 and most assistance to agricultural producers, including the important Supplementary Minimum Prices schemes for meat and wool producers and input subsidies for fertilizers, were ended. On 16 December 1994, the New Zealand Government announced a further unilateral tariff reduction plan for the period 1 July 1997 to 1 July 2001. By the year 2000, the maximum tariff will be 15 per cent.

Following the method of the IAC in Australia, Syntec Economic Services estimated the share of total assistance provided by each form of assistance. In 1981–2, import licensing accounted for 22 per cent of the gross-subsidy-equivalent measure of assistance to the manufacturing sector and tariffs for 78 per cent, but by 1987–8 the share of import licensing had fallen to 1 per cent for the year (Syntec Economic Services, 1988, Table 2.1).

By the end of 1992 the only major form of assistance to New Zealand's industry was *ad valorem* tariffs. Thus it had radically reformed the form of assistance at the same time as it had rapidly reduced assistance. Indeed, New Zealand now probably has the purest system in the world in terms of almost total reliance on (*ad valorem*) tariffs for assistance to merchandise commodities[8] (apart from Singapore and Hong Kong which are free ports). Even the US Trade Representative, in his annual review of foreign trade barriers facing US exporters, found little to complain of and concluded '... New Zealand's increasingly open trade and investment policy is a bell-wether for regional and global trade and investment liberalization' (United States Trade Representative, 1996, p. 251).

Syntec Economic Services also estimated the standard deviation of the nominal and effective rates for the manufacturing sector. For the three years surveyed in the 1980s, there were 122, 110 and 94 per cent respectively (Syntec Economic Services, 1988, Table A.2.3). These standard deviations are four and five times higher than those in Australia. They also find very high standard deviations within the two-digit industries. It was this extreme inter- and intra-industry variability in rates of assistance, largely due to the import licensing system, that created such large distortions in the incentives to produce commodities in the New Zealand economy. These extreme distortions persisted until 1990. However, the dispersion of these rates as measured by the standard deviation had declined substantially by 1987–8 and must have fallen sharply since that time. The sweeping and extremely rapid trade reforms carried out since 1983 have greatly improved national resource allocation.

It is possible to compare (unweighted) average tariffs and the frequency index of non-tariff barriers in New Zealand with those in Australia and other APEC countries using data recently collated by the Pacific Economic Cooperation Council (PECC) (1995b). The data relating to 1993 show that both average tariffs and non-tariff barriers to imports have declined more rapidly in New Zealand and Australia over the five-year period 1988 to 1993 than those of other APEC countries. (Chile is the one country that broadly matches the rate of reform in the CER countries.) This five-year period omits the substantial reforms in both countries in the early 1980s. At the end of this period, the unweighted average tariffs of 9 per cent and 8 per cent in Australia and New Zealand, respectively, were a few percentage points higher than those in the USA (6.8 per cent), Canada (6.7 per cent) and Japan (6.5 per cent). The index of non-tariff barriers in New Zealand was much lower than the indices of these countries and less than those of other APEC countries, with the exceptions of Hong Kong, Singapore and Chile; and the same is true of Australia, though again its index is higher than that of New Zealand. Both countries have reduced tariffs considerably in the years since 1993, to levels that are now about the same as those of other OECD countries. Overall, therefore, the levels of import restrictions are less in New Zealand and Australia than the OECD average.

While no internationally comparable measures of disparities in rates of assistance are available, it is possible to compare the standard deviations of applied tariff rates in Australia and New Zealand with those of other APEC countries in 1993 and 1995. For all sectors, the standard deviations of these rates in the CER countries were about the average of the APEC countries (PECC, 1995b, Figure 4.1). Some data on the standard deviations are also available for OECD countries (OECD, 1996). The standard deviations of tariff rates in Australia and New Zealand were above the OECD average in 1993 but lower than those in Japan and Switzerland. Given the elimination of most non-tariff barriers in the CER countries, it may be that the disparities in nominal rates of assistance are now less than the OECD average.

4   The closer economic relations agreement

On 1 January 1983 the Closer Economic Relations Agreement between Australia and New Zealand (CER) replaced the 1966 New Zealand Australian Free Trade Area (the original NAFTA). In a short time, the provisions of the agreement have been substantially widened and deepened so that the area is now more closely integrated than any regional trading arrangement other than the European Union (EU). This section will concentrate on the main features of the Agreement and the relationships between the bilateral freeing of trade and the unilateral actions described in the sections above. Recent reviews of the progress of CER are provided by Lloyd (1995), PECC (1995a), and Holmes (1996).

CER was planned to bring about a complete free trade area by 1995 – that is, all border restrictions were to be ended within 12 years. Tariffs were to be phased out by 1988, performance-based export incentives by 1987, and quantitative import restrictions and tariff quotas by 1995. In fact, this target for the ending of these forms of assistance was achieved on 1 July 1990, some five years ahead of the schedule. In addition, anti-dumping actions against the trans-Tasman partner ceased from the same date.

The first Review of the Agreement in 1988, among other extensions, widened the liberalization of border trade to trade in services, including national treatment in relation to all laws, regulations and practices as well as free market access. This took effect from 1 January 1989. There was a 'negatives list' of services not covered. Although the number of services on this list has been reduced as a result of annual reviews and the 1992 and 1995 reviews, some significant areas are still inscribed, mainly in Australia, where the telecommunications, aviation and shipping industries are still subject to a high degree of domestic regulation. Complete equality of access for government purchases of goods was achieved when New Zealand joined the Australian National Preference Agreement between the Commonwealth and Australian States on a nil preference basis from 1 June 1989, with New Zealand reciprocating the benefits. This was extended to all government purchases of services in July 1991. From this time, all trans-Tasman trade in goods and most trade in services has been completely free of border barriers.

CER has also resulted in a substantial reduction of non-border barriers. The most notable and important of these is that, as a part of the 1988 Agreed Minute on Industry Assistance, the two countries have ceased to pay bounties and other production subsidies that would affect international trade. There has also been a growing harmonization of policies in several areas, including customs and quarantine procedures, technical and food standards and, most notably in this context, competition law and some other areas of business law. Following the example of the EU the Australian Commonwealth and State Governments have implemented a Mutual Recognition regime for standards and occupations from 1 March 1993. As a result of the 1995 review of CER, a Trans-Tasman Mutual Recognition Arrangement for both goods and occupations was added, with effect from 1 January 1997.

In 1992, from an initiative by the then Australian Prime Minister, Mr Paul Keating, a Memorandum of Understanding on Air Services was signed on 1 August 1992. This was to establish a single aviation market covering the two countries from 1 November 1994, but it lapsed when the Australian government withdrew from the agreement a week before it was due to take effect. The new coalition government, which came to power in 1996, has stated its intention to resume negotiations on the single aviation market. In May 1996, the Australian and New Zealand stock exchanges have reached an agreement in principle to establish a single trans-Tasman market covering share options and derivatives. This is intended as the first step towards a single securities market. It will require enabling legislation in both countries; and there are some outstanding areas that negotiations have been unable to resolve, chiefly the tax treatment of trans-Tasman equity and the incorporation of foreign investment into the agreement. There are no provisions in the CER agreement relating to factor movements between the two countries. (Residents move without restriction between the two countries under a separate Trans-Tasman Travel Arrangement dating back to the 1920s.) Thus the free trade area is moving unevenly towards a single market form of integration.

One feature of this progress is that it has been achieved with simple rules and no formal institutions, not even a secretariat. This is in marked contrast to the EU, with its complex structure of institutions and large bureaucracy, and NAFTA, which has a growing set of institutions, and even the Association of South East Asian Nations (ASEAN), which has a secretariat. CER was planned as an agreement that would require low maintenance and a minimum of bureaucratic resources.

Another notable feature of the Agreement is that it has been accompanied by strong unilateral movements towards free trade (and deregulation) in both countries. As noted in the previous sections, both Australia and New Zealand have achieved substantial unilateral liberalization since the Agreement came into effect in 1983. CER is the most outstanding example of 'open regionalism', interpreting that term in the sense of a regional liberalization of trade in goods and services, accompanied by a liberalization *vis-à-vis* countries outside the region. The only other regional trading arrangement in the world that has achieved substantial regional liberalization accompanied by substantial unilateral liberalizations is ASEAN.

The dual liberalization by means of unilateral and regional action is no coincidence; and in New Zealand's case its unilateral liberalization almost coincides with the period of CER regional liberalization. Fundamentally, both countries have sought to open their economies to increased trade with the rest of the world and have followed both the bilateral and the unilateral route.

There have been some positive interactions between these two routes to liberalization. Both Australia and New Zealand see the bilateral freeing of trade in goods and services as a way of making the countries more competitive in world markets. There has also been a desire, especially in New Zealand, to reduce possible trade diversion to the trans-Tasman partner. Australian irritation with import licensing restrictions on access to New Zealand markets after tariffs had been reduced led the two countries to put a firm timetable for the elimination of quantitative restrictions on bilateral trade into the CER Agreement, thus paving the way for the New Zealand decision two years later to phase out the import licensing system. Similarly, the realization by both countries that their export incentive schemes and subsidies distorted bilateral trade led them in general to reduce these incentives substantially. In these ways, bilateral liberalization has aided the unilateral liberalization *vis-à-vis* all trading partners.

5   Australia and New Zealand in the GATT

The multilateral trading system is very important to Australia and New Zealand, as two trading countries which are small and not members of a larger economic group, and they were foundation members of the GATT in 1947 and the World Trade Organization (WTO) in 1994. The multilateral trade policies of the two countries are reviewed briefly, followed by some comments on APEC.

Australia has generally abided by the rules of the GATT as it believed that the multilateral organization provided protection for smaller trading countries against aggressive unilateral actions by larger and more powerful countries. Although its tariffs have been higher than those of most other developed countries, it has made relatively little use of non-tariff barriers for most of the last 25 years and has therefore come closer than many other GATT contracting parties to the GATT principle that countries should use tariffs rather than quantitative restrictions or other measures to restrict trade. During the period between 1974 and 1993, when quantitative restrictions were again used in Australia to protect major industries, it preferred to use the more transparent quotas and tariff quotas rather than the voluntary export restraints and orderly marketing agreements used by many other countries. It has taken complaints about other contracting parties to the GATT, principally in the area of agricultural trade; and sometimes in concert with New Zealand. But the Australian record in abiding by the rules of the GATT and the WTO is not unblemished. In the first 11 months of the existence of the WTO, 2 of the 21 complaints to the organization were against Australia, both against quarantine measures applying to imports of Atlantic salmon, brought by the USA and Canada jointly (WTO, 1995).

The Australian record in relation to tariff bindings has not been good. Prior to the Uruguay Round, Australia had bound only about 20 per cent of its tariff lines, which was a much lower percentage than for any of the other OECD countries, most of whom had bound 90 per cent or more. Historically, the non-binding of tariffs has been important as it has given Australian governments the freedom to raise tariffs when they wished to increase protection of producers of certain goods.

Its record in subscribing to those parts of the GATT that were voluntary is also not particularly good. When the Tokyo Round introduced nine supplementary and voluntary Codes and Agreements in 1979, Australia did not accede to those relating to technical barriers to trade, subsidies and countervailing duties, trade in civil aircraft, and to government procurement. It signed the subsidies code later in 1981. Australia has still not acceded to the WTO Agreement on government procurement, which is the most important of the four remaining voluntary agreements.

In terms of the reduction in Australia's own border barriers, the GATT multilateral trade negotiations have been less important than either unilateral or regional policies. In the earlier rounds, Australia made few concessions and received a largely free ride from the USA and other major industrialized countries in relation to tariffs restricting its access to foreign markets. The last two rounds, the Tokyo Round and the Uruguay Round, were by far the most important of the multilateral negotiations during the life of the GATT. As the major part of its participation in the Tokyo Round, Australia made widespread tariff reductions in January 1977 but, as noted in section 1, these did not reduce the rates of assistance to the most highly assisted industries.

The Australian contribution to the Uruguay Round, signed in April 1994, included an average tariff cut of 44 per cent relative to the 1986–7 levels, and changes to tariffs in the local content scheme and stabilization plan in the tobacco industry, along with minor changes to non-tariff restrictions – the tariff quota on cheese imports and sales-tax concessions on fruit and vegetable juices – and the termination of export subsidies for the dairy industry. These tariff cuts compare with the cuts under the announced phased programmes of 70 per cent. They do not, therefore, add to the scheduled unilateral reductions over this period. On the other hand, Australia did agree to bind 95 per cent of the tariff lines; and although, in many cases, the bound rates are above the levels that will apply after the implementation of the present schedule of tariff cuts, this is a historic change.

Australia made at least one significant contribution to the success of the Uruguay Round as a whole. It created the Cairns Group, so named because the first meeting was held in Cairns in 1986. The Cairns Group was a coalition within the GATT of agricultural exporting countries (but not including the USA and the European Community) whose agricultural sectors were generally low-cost and lightly assisted compared with those in the USA, the EC and Japan. It insisted that, as laid down in the Punta del Este Declaration, the world agricultural trading system should be reformed through a reduction in border protection and subsidies, and it targeted especially the major industrial nations. Australia chaired all sessions of the Group. The Group is generally credited with having had a major influence on the Agreement on Agriculture and the outcome of the Uruguay Round in general, though the extent of the reforms in the Agriculture Agreement fell well short of proposals put forward by the Cairns Group during the multilateral negotiations (see Tyers, 1993).

The history of New Zealand activities in the GATT is rather different from that of Australia, until the liberalization of the 1980s. As a small country whose exports have been heavily concentrated in primary products, chiefly temperate foodstuffs, New Zealand had a high stake in the observance of GATT rules by other countries which were potential importers of these products or competitors in third-country markets. Indeed, it is likely that, between the time of the accession of the UK into the EC in 1973 and the present, New Zealand exports have been more severely restricted than those of any other GATT contracting party by import barriers in the major markets of the industrial countries and by export subsidies which reduced its markets in third countries. Not surprisingly, New Zealand was a strong supporter of the Cairns Group during the Uruguay Round; and New Zealand and Australia were the major proponents of the extended Trade Policy Review Mechanism of the WTO.

New Zealand's own observance of the GATT rules was, however, far from exemplary until the mid-1980s. During the long continuous period of comprehensive import licensing, New Zealand was the outstanding example of a developed country which relied on quantitative restrictions rather than tariffs as the main instrument of industry assistance and it made no reductions in tariff rates. However, this situation changed dramatically and swiftly after 1984, to the point that New Zealand is now the outstanding example among the developed countries of a country which relies almost entirely upon tariffs as the instrument of industry assistance and which has reduced its import trade barriers and its subsidies to export industries unilaterally.

Because the binding constraint on most restricted import commodities was quantitative controls during the period of import licensing, the small tariff concessions that New Zealand made in multilateral negotiations before the Uruguay Round did not significantly reduce assistance to the highly protected industries. In the Uruguay Round, New Zealand cut tariffs on some product groups, but this concession was dwarfed by the programme of phased unilateral tariff cuts which it announced at the conclusion of the Round.

Prior to the Uruguay Round, the New Zealand Government had bound only 48 per cent of tariff lines. This was the lowest percentage of the OECD countries apart from Australia. However, as a part of its commitments in this Round, New Zealand agreed to bind all tariff lines, except those for used motor vehicles and used clothing.

Another important part of the external trade strategies of both Australia and New Zealand is APEC. This organization was an Australian initiative, having been first proposed by the former Prime Minister, Mr Bob Hawke, in a speech in Seoul in January 1989, and the first ministerial meeting was held in Canberra later that year. The Eminent Persons Group (EPG), which proposed a goal of free trade in Asia-Pacific and introduced the concept of 'open regionalism' into APEC discussions of trade liberalization, also followed from an Australian suggestion. The proposals for regional trade liberalization contained in the Bogor Declaration and the Osaka Action Agenda have been very strongly supported by the Australian and New Zealand Governments. My own interpretation of this support in Australia is that the government has seen APEC as a counter to the formation of large continent-based regional trading arrangements in Europe and the Americas, and possibly also in East Asia, and to the dangers of discrimination against the exports of countries which are not members of these emerging blocs. New Zealand has an explicit purpose of pursuing unilateral, regional and multilateral trade liberalization.

It remains to be seen whether and, if so, how APEC proposals for trade liberalization will be implemented. At the time of writing, they are due to be discussed again at the Manila Meeting of Economic Leaders in 1996, and it is too early to make a definite judgement about the contribution of APEC to regional and global trade liberalization. Yet APEC has already had a major influence on the debates in the Asia-Pacific region and elsewhere, with its vision of ultimate complete free trade and its discussion of new modalities of trade negotiations such as 'concerted unilateral actions'. It should also be remembered that it is still less than three years since the appearance of the First Report of the EPG which precipitated the present proposals.

6 Concluding remarks

This brief history of the trade policies of the CER countries in the last 25 years or so reveals a number of interesting features and raises some questions.

First, while the assistance to import-competing producers in the manufacturing sector in Australia and New Zealand has been the highest of the OECD countries, this comparison overstates the importance of trade distortions in these economies relative to other economies. In heavily protecting some uncompetitive producers in this sector, Australia and New Zealand behaved no differently from the European, North American and Japanese governments in protecting their uncompetitive producers of some high-cost agricultural commodities and, one should note, many mineral products (such as coal), which are very heavily protected in Europe and some other OECD countries. All countries have concentrated their assistance on industries or subindustries in which the national producers have a strong comparative disadvantage. The misfortune of Australia and New Zealand is that they reduced international trade and specialization in the commodity group for which international trade and technology developed most rapidly.

Second, one observes a frequent imitation of trade policies initiated by the trans-Tasman partner. During the period reviewed in this chapter, New Zealand imitated Australia several times; across-the-board tariff cuts, the auctioning of quotas, the introduction of industry plans (which was a strategy first used by the Whitlam Government for the steel industry), the measurement of rates of assistance in the manufacturing and agricultural sectors.[9] This borrowing has been a major factor in the formation of trade policies, especially since the early 1980s, and it has produced convergence of Australian and New Zealand trade policies.

Third, both Australia and New Zealand have become fairly aggressive trade reformers. The sharp and rapid reductions in average levels of assistance and in the dispersion of these rates among industries has led to the opening up of these economies once more to higher levels of international trade in goods and services (and, one should note, to cross-border capital flows). The trade ratios of these countries have increased since the new opening of their economies, but they are still not high relative to those of many other countries of comparable size and income.

This fundamental reversal of protectionist policies raises the basic question of why it has taken place. Consider first Australia. While the structure of the economy and the associated pattern of rents received from the structure of assistance have changed somewhat, the changes have not been great. The relative importance in production and exports of agricultural producers, who historically have been a coalition calling for lowering of assistance to manufacturers, has declined, and the importance of mining and service-sector exporters has increased. Although the mining and service sectors have been discriminated against, and this effect has increased towards the end of the period studied here as these sectors have become more important in the Australian economy, they have had little to say about assistance policies. By the 1990s the average rate of assistance to manufacturers barely exceeded that given to agriculture producers on average. This may have weakened the historical opposition of the agricultural sector to assistance for the manufacturing sector. But it is difficult to explain much of the decline of protectionism in terms of these changes.

My own explanation of the historic shifts that have occurred relies more upon two non-coalition factors. The first is the slow but eventually dominant influence of a steady drip of anti-protectionism. This came initially from academics, percolating to the civil servants and eventually transforming public attitudes towards differential industry assistance policies. It began with the 1929 Report of the Brigden Committee, but the major debates can be dated from the work of the Tariff Board and of Max Corden on effective protection in the 1960s. This represents one area where the contribution of academic economists in Australia has been profound. Sound ideas are eventually irresistible. The second factor is the growing transparency of the pattern of assistance and its effects on exporters, consumers and other groups who have been adversely affected. In Australia, the Industry Commission and its predecessors have played a very honourable part, constantly pointing out, in a number of reports since 1968–9, the implications of complex patterns of assistance to the PMV and TCF industries in particular, and providing systematic measures of this assistance.

The New Zealand history is somewhat different. While an increasing number of economists in the New Zealand Treasury, the Reserve Bank and outside the New Zealand public service challenged the traditional protectionism from the late 1970s, the critical factor was a financial crisis coupled with a deep disillusionment with reliance on state assistance in many areas: the welfare state, government-owned enterprises, overseas marketing and other areas as well as industry assistance. If New Zealand had had a Tariff Board and a more vigorous academic group of trade analysts, the reforms might have come earlier, but they might not have been as far-reaching.

There are lessons to be learnt from Australian and New Zealand experiences, I believe, for other countries with slower rates of reform of trade policies, especially in relation to the role of independent enquiries, transparency and changes in the instruments of assistance. Similarly, the CER is the cleanest regional trading arrangement in the world, with virtually no exceptions to free trade in goods and services and an absence of bureaucracy, and both countries are now model members of the WTO in terms of their observance of both its rules and its spirit.

Notes

1. Mancur Olson (1982, p. 135) cited Australia and New Zealand as two slow-growing countries with high levels of protection and an inability to adjust to changes. In 1981, the prime minister of Singapore described the Australian government as 'more restrictive, conservative and backward-looking [in its

industrial protection policies] than the meanest of the EEC countries' (cited by Anderson and Garnaut, 1987, p. 1).

2. The part of the second section (on the TRI) is taken from a joint paper with Professor Peter Dixon and Dr Philip Adams of Monash University.

3. For a review of the earlier post-war history of protection and the tariff debate, see the excellent survey by Corden (1963). For the period from the mid-1960s to the mid-1970s, which includes the period of the Tariff Review and the 1973 tariff cut, see Lloyd (1978). For the period up to 1985, see Woodland (1992). The best source of information for later years is the annual reports of the Industries Assistance Commission and the Industry Commission.

4. The tender quotas were offered for sale by a tender in which the bidders indicated the *ad valorem* premium over the base tariff rates which they were prepared to pay, and the number of units bid. The tender quotas were then allocated to the highest bidder, the second highest bidder and so on until the total bids equalled the total tender pool available. The duty paid by all successful bidders is the sum of the basic rate applicable and the tender premium, the bid rate at which the total bids equal the total tender pool available.

   When only a portion of the quota is sold by tender, the tender premium is an upper bound of the true *ad valorem* equivalent – that is, the *ad valorem* tariff which, if substituted for the quota, would yield the same quantity of imports (Gibbs and Konovalov, 1984). The Australian experience is that the *ad valorem* equivalents derived from tender premiums correspond closely with estimates based on other methods such as direct price surveys and quota transfer sale prices (Industries Assistance Commission (1985, Appendix 6)).

5. Strictly speaking, this proposition applies to the variance of the nominal rates and holds only if all rates of assistance are cut equi-proportionately. This was the case in the 1973 reductions. It does not hold exactly in the later phased reductions because of some exemptions and, offsetting this, the somewhat uneven extent of the reductions in those tariffs that were cut. While the variance of effective rates depends on the pattern of input–output coefficients as well as the variance of the nominal rates, the pattern of the variance of the effective rates follows that of the variance of nominal rates.

6. Syntec followed the IAC in using as weights the unassisted value of production. Consequently, the New Zealand estimates are lower than their TRI but no estimates have been made of the TRI in New Zealand.

7. Let t^0 and t^1 be the tariff rates before and after the cut and α the parameter determining the size of the cut. With the Swiss formula $t^1 = \alpha t^0/(\alpha + t^0)$.

8. The only blot on the New Zealand copybook is the continued use of anti-dumping actions. Along with Australia and a small number of other countries (chiefly the USA, the EU and its member countries, Canada and Mexico), New Zealand has been a frequent user of anti-dumping measures.

9. In more recent years, New Zealand has made a number of policy innovations in areas outside trade policies; for example, the Reserve Bank Act of 1989, the Employment Contracts Act of 1991 and the Fiscal Responsibility Act of 1992, all of these in the area of the macro-management of the economy. Australia, the big sister, seems reluctant to admit the wisdom of its little sister in any of these areas.

References

Anderson, J.E. (1995), 'Tariff Index Theory', *Review of International Economics*, vol. 3, June, pp. 156–73.

Anderson, K. and R. Garnaut (1987), *Australian Protectionism: Extent, Causes and Effects*, Sydney: George Allen & Unwin.

Anderson, J.E. and J.P. Neary (1994), 'Measuring the Restrictiveness of Trade Policy', *The World Bank Economic Review*, vol. 8, pp. 151–69.

Candler, W. and P. Hampton (1966), 'The Measurement of Industrial Protection in New Zealand', *Australian Economic Papers*, vol. 5, June, pp. 47–58.

Corden, M. (1963), 'The Tariff', in A. Hunter (ed.), *The Economics of Australian Industry*, Cambridge University Press.

Crawford, J.G. (1934), 'Tariff Level Indices', *Economic Record*, vol. 11, pp. 213–21.

Gibbs, I. and V. Konovalov (1984), 'Volume Quotas with Heterogeneous Product Categories', *Economic Record*, vol. 60, September, pp. 294–303.

Hampton. P. (1965), 'The Degree of Protection Accorded by Import Licensing to New Zealand Manufacturing Industries', Agricultural Economics Research Unit Report No. 12, Lincoln College, Christchurch, New Zealand.

Holmes, Sir F. (1996), *The Trans-Tasman Relationship*, Wellington: Institute of Policy Studies.

Industries Assistance Commission (1979), *Annual Report for 1978–79*, Canberra: Australian Government Publishing Service.

Industries Assistance Commission (1985), *Annual Report 1984–85*, Canberra: Australian Government Publishing Service.

Industries Assistance Commission (1989), *Annual Report 1988–89*, Canberra: Commonwealth Government Printer.

Industry Commission (1992), *Annual Report 1991–92*, Canberra: Australian Government Publishing Service.

Industry Commission (1995), *Assistance to Agricultural and Manufacturing Industries*, Information Paper, Canberra: Australian Government Publishing Service.

Industries Assistance Commission (1996), *Annual Report for 1995–96*, Canberra: Australian Government Publishing Service.

Lloyd, P.J. (1978), 'Protection Policy', in F.H. Gruen (ed.), *Surveys of Australian Economics*, Sydney: George Allen & Unwin.

Lloyd, P.J. (1995), 'The Future of Trans-Tasman Closer Economic Relations', *Agenda*, vol. 2, pp. 267–80.

Lloyd, P.J. and A.G. Schweinberger (1988), 'Trade Expenditure Functions and the Gains from Trade', *Journal of International Economics*, vol. 24, pp. 275–97.

New Zealand Planning Council, Economic Monitoring Group (1984), *Strategy for Growth*, Wellington: New Zealand Planning Council.

Olson, M. (1982), *The Rise and Decline of Nations: Economic Growth, Stagflation, and Social Rigidities*, New Haven, Yale University Press.

OECD (Organization for Economic Cooperation and Development) (1996), *Indicators of Tariff and Non-tariff Barriers to Trade*, Paris: OECD.

PECC (Pacific Economic Co-operation Council) (1995a), *Milestones in APEC Liberalisation: A Map of Market Opening Measures by APEC Economies*, Singapore: PECC.

PECC (Pacific Economic Co-operation Council) (1995b), *Survey of Impediments to Trade and Investment in the APEC Region*, Singapore: PECC.

Rayner, A.C. and R. Lattimore (1991), 'New Zealand', in D. Papageorgiou, M. Michaely and A.M. Choksi (eds), *Liberalizing Foreign Trade*, Vol. 6, Oxford: Basil Blackwell.

Syntec Economic Services (1988), *Industrial Assistance Reform in New Zealand*, Sydney: Syntec Economic Services.

Tariff Board (1970), *Annual Report for Year 1969–70*, Canberra: Commonwealth Government Printing Office.

Tyers, R. (1993), 'The Cairns Group and the Uruguay Round of International Trade Negotiations', *Australian Economic Review*, First Quarter, pp. 49–60.

United States Trade Representative (1996), *1996 National Trade Estimate Report on Foreign Trade Barriers*, Washington, DC: US Government Printing Office.

Vernon Committee (Committee of Economic Enquiry) (1965), *Report of the Committee of Economic Enquiry*, Melbourne: Wilke and Co.

Woodland, A.D. (1992), 'Trade Policies in Australia', in Salvatore, D. (ed.), *National Trade Policies*, New York: Greenwood Press.

WTO (World Trade Organization) (1995), 'WTO's First Year: "An Encouraging Start"', *WTO Focus*, December.

PART IV

REGIONAL TRADE LIBERALIZATION

Introduction

The first selection on '3 × 3 theory of customs unions' is a survey of the post-Viner models of customs unions which related to a world in which there are three countries and three goods, hence '3 × 3'. It provides a synthesis of the customs union analysis in these models, emphasizing the diversity of results and the importance of the prior restrictions on the patterns of trade among the countries forming a customs union.

With the steady growth of regional trading arrangements and especially in the last decade, there is a common perception that world trade has become more regionalized. This issue is addressed in the paper on 'Regionalization and world trade', using commodity import trade data for RTAs among OECD countries. The findings do not support this perception. In this paper, I defined regional integration in terms of the establishment of the 'Law of One Price' regionally (see Flam, 1992) but again this definition had been anticipated by Cooper (1976).

Associated with the geographic spread of regional trading arrangements, there have been marked changes in the scope of these arrangements in terms of the taxes and other instruments of government intervention and regulation which are covered by them. Regional trading arrangements have been extended beyond border barriers to include many non-border barriers such as industrial standards, subsidies, commodity tax rates and competition policies. This process is referred to as 'deepening' in contrast to 'widening' the coverage of an agreement in terms of its commodity coverage. Extension of policy measures to non-border taxes and regulations is based on the realization that complete equality of access for producers in all member countries to each other's markets requires more than the removal of border barriers. In the terminology used above, these agreements can be described as pursuing a goal of regional integration rather than just regional free trade. As with a fully integrated global economy, a fully integrated regional economy is one in which the law of one price holds for the region. This requires more than borderless trade. These trends are reviewed in 'The changing nature of regional trading arrangements'.

In this context, the case of the regional trading arrangements between Australia and New Zealand, known in the region as the Closer Economic Relations Agreement or just CER, is particularly interesting. CER is second to the European Union (EU) in terms of the scope of instruments covered and the degree of integration of the member economies. In the paper reproduced, this author recommended the formation of a single market in the region, following in broad terms the precedent of the EU. It is argued that progression from a free trade area to a fully integrated single market would bring efficiency gains to the two economies.

References

Cooper, R. (1976), 'Worldwide Regional Integration: Is there an Optimal Size of the Integrated Area?', in Fritz Machlup (ed.), *Economic Integration Worldwide, Regional and Sectoral*, Macmillan, New York.
Flam, H. (1992), 'Product Markets and 1992: Full Integration, Large Gains', *Journal of Economic Perspectives*, **6**, 7–30.

166- 88

[82]

[8]

Journal of International Economics 12 (1982) 41–63. North-Holland Publishing Company

4112 F13

F12

3×3 THEORY OF CUSTOMS UNIONS

P.J. LLOYD*

Australian National University, Canberra, A.C.T., Australia

Received November 1980, revised version received April 1981

Four recent models (those of Berglas, Corden, Meade and Riezman) which have extended the theory of customs union to 3 × 3 dimensions are reviewed. The reasons for both apparent and real differences among the welfare propositions from these models are explained. Some new extensions are derived. The main conclusions are that the family of 3 × 3 models introduce several effects which cannot be present in 3 × 2 models and that the distinctions among the models are due mostly to diverse assumptions concerning the trilateral pattern of trade which are not readily apparent.

1. Introduction

While the theory of customs unions has a venerable history the formal theory has been couched predominantly in terms of models with three countries and only two commodities. These are 3 × 2 models. The early exception was the model of Meade (1955, ch. III) which has been reconsidered by Vanek (1965, appendix), Lipsey (1970, chs. 5 and 6) and McMillan and McCann (1981). Corden (1976) has a model with three commodities. Recently and almost simultaneously several authors [Berglas (1979), Collier (1979) and Riezman (1979)] have introduced new models with three commodities. These constitute a family of 3 × 3 models. International economists will welcome these extensions since it is now recognised that the limitation of the dimensionality of models yields some results which do not extend to higher dimensions.[1]

One difficulty has quickly emerged with the 3 × 3 extensions of customs union theory. They have yielded a welter of new propositions which are distinct from those yielded by 3 × 2 models but they are also distinct from

*This paper was written while the author was visiting the Institute for International Economic Studies at the University of Stockholm. I wish to thank Eitan Berglas, John McMillan, Raymond Riezman and Lars Svennson for comments on a draft.

[1]This has been demonstrated for models of international trade with non-discriminating trade barriers by Jones (1976) and Jones and Scheinkman (1977). Similar results concerning the non-robustness of propositions relating to exchange rate adjustments in 2-dimensional monetary models occur when a third asset is added to the model [see Van Duyne (1979) and Brillembourg and Schadler (1979)].

each other. In several cases they appear to be unrelated and in some to be actually contradictory. In his model Meade showed that a small reduction in the tariff on the commodity which one country imports from its customs union partner will increase the national welfare if it increases the quantities of imports from both the union partner and the outside country and only if the aggregate volume of imports measured in constant international prices increases. A welfare gain is the more likely the higher the pre-union (uniform) tariffs. In this model the two member countries are affected by the union in the same way. In Berglas's model when the tariff reductions are small one country loses if the commodities which it imports from its partner and the non-union country are both normal. However, the welfare of the other union country is affected differently and it may increase or decrease even when all goods are normal. In the Corden (1976) model when the union eliminates trade barriers within the union one member of a customs union may gain or lose if there is Vinerian trade diversion. Corden does not consider the welfare of the second member country. Moreover, the one country (and perhaps the other) is the more likely to gain from joining a customs union the lower the external tariffs on those goods where imports from the country outside the union remain and the more non-uniform the initial pre-union tariffs. In his model Riezman (1979) establishes that, in general, the change in intra-union trading upon the formation of a customs union will benefit one member at the expense of the other. Both countries will gain if their bilateral trade is small. In this model, unlike those of Meade and of Berglas, this result holds for both small mutual reductions in trade barriers and for their total elimination.

In the Meade model there is the added complication that there are distinct propositions for the one model. Lipsey stated that a welfare increase is the more likely the larger is the proportion of total expenditure devoted to the commodity produced by the country in relation to the proportion devoted to the commodity imported from the country outside the union [Lipsey (1970, ch. 6)]. McMillan and McCann (1981) show that a small reduction in the tariff on the commodity which the country imports from its union partner will increase the national welfare if and only if this commodity is a net substitute in demand for the commodity which it produces and exports. They also show that a customs union which eliminates the trade barriers will increase the welfare if the demand for the commodity it imports from its partner is independent of the third commodity which it imports from the country outside the union.

Several authors have also stated propositions relating to endogenous variables other than country welfare. Some of these are distinct and some apparently contradictory. For example, when Berglas relaxes the constant external price assumption, he concludes that 'it is impossible to determine a priori which way the terms of trade will change' [Berglas (1979, p. 328)]. By contrast, Riezman states that, subject to certain 'regularity conditions', the terms of trade between the member countries and the third country outside the union must improve [Riezman (1979, theorem I)].

The marked differences among these propositions and some apparent contradictions are bewildering. Certain differences are obviously due to the fact that some of the propositions are sufficient conditions for a welfare improvement in one member country, some are necessary conditions and some are likelihood conditions. And some relate to small changes in tariffs and some to their total removal. It should be possible to reconcile these differences. Likelihood propositions can be stated as sufficient conditions.

Yet, after the conditions have been expressed in comparable forms there remain many distinctions and some propositions still appear contradictory; for example, the Riezman proposition has a *small* intra-union trade as a sufficient condition for a welfare increase (in both countries) whereas the Lipsey proposition has a *large* intra-union trade as a sufficient condition. Truly distinct propositions must be traceable to differences in assumptions concerning the structure of the economic models used but which of the multiple differences is or are crucial?

The purpose of this paper is to resolve apparent differences and elucidate real differences and to discuss the gains from moving to 3 × 3 models. This requires that we first construct a more general model which is at least general enough to encompass all of the models studied. Four models are examined; those of Meade, Riezman, Berglas and Corden. Section 2 derives the criterion of welfare gain or loss in several equivalent forms. Section 3 discusses the differences in assumptions concerning the pattern of trade among the three countries. Section 4 presents the results of the four models in comparable form and considers the role of differences in assumptions. Section 5 considers some general aspects of the dimensionality of the models. Some of the results are extended. For example, the Lipsey proposition concerning the shares of consumer expenditure is readily extended to any utility function and sufficient conditions for an increase in welfare in the Berglas model are derived. The main conclusions are that 3 × 3 models introduce several effects which cannot be present in 3 × 2 models and that the distinctions between individual models within this family are due mostly to diverse assumptions concerning the pattern of trade among the countries.

2.

The world economy of the model consists of three countries (A, B, C) of which two (A and B) are assumed to form some customs union. These three countries trade three final commodities (1, 2, 3). It is not possible to make a prior assignment of the commodities as the export or import commodities of particular countries without restricting the model.

Consider one of the three countries. We use the following notation for variables of the country:

$x = (x_1, x_2, x_3)$ = a non-negative vector of aggregate consumption,

$y = (y_1, y_2, y_3)$ = a non-negative vector of aggregate production,

$e = (e_1, e_2, e_3)$ = a vector of aggregate excess demand (a positive element denotes imports, a negative element denotes exports) = $(x - y)$,

$p = (p_1, p_2, p_3)$ = a non-negative vector of domestic prices,

$p^* = (p_1^*, p_2^*, p_3^*)$ = a non-negative vector of the prices ex-trade taxes,

$t = (t_{1k}, t_{2k}, t_{3k})$ = a vector of ad valorem taxes on trade flows between the country and country k (a positive element denotes a tariff or export subsidy and a negative element denotes an import subsidy or export tax),

Y = national income (at domestic market prices).

These variables in the three countries describe the equilibrium for the tax-distorted world economy. All of the authors of the four models considered tariffs as the only taxes but taxes-subsidies on exports have been included. All trade taxes are expressed with foreign prices as the tax base. Rates may be zero.

The theory concerns the comparisons of the economy in two situations, the pre-union and the post-union situations. The term 'customs union' is a short-hand generic title for any geographically discriminating reductions in trade taxes. It encompasses post-union situations in which trade taxes vis-a-vis the outside country are uniform across commodities or not, and situations in which the taxes are uniform across countries (such as a common external tariff) or not, whichever multiple rates are relevant to a model.

With international trade the prices in one member, say A, of each commodity are related to the prices in the other two countries, B and C. In any situation, one or more of the following holds in A

$$p_i = p_{iA}^* \qquad\qquad \text{if produced,}$$

$$= p_{iB}^*(1 + t_{iB}) \leq p_{iC}^*(1 + 1_{iC}) \qquad \text{if traded with } B,$$

$$= p_{iC}^*(1 + t_{iC}) \leq p_{iB}^*(1 + t_{iB}) \qquad \text{if traded with } C. \tag{1}$$

In the pre-union situation $t_{iB} = t_{iC}$ for all i and if the commodity is traded with both countries $p_{iB}^* = p_{iC}^*$. In the post-union situation $t_{iB} < t_{iC}$ for all i with $t_{iC} \neq 0$, and if the commodity is imported from both countries B and C, $p_{iB}^*(1 + t_{iB}) = p_{iC}^*(1 + t_{iC})$ with $p_{iB}^* > p_{iC}^*$.

All of the models assume the existence of a Samuelson-type social utility function in each country. This plays the dual role of generating aggregate country-wide commodity demand functions and of evaluating the consequences of the union for the countries. We concentrate on the effects on welfare in the two member countries. The welfare of a union member country, say A, in any situation is given by its indirect social utility function

$$W = V(Y, p). \tag{2}$$

This function is the dual of the direct social utility function, $U(x)$.[2] Utility is maximised for any set of commodity prices, subject to the budget constraint,

$$\sum_i p_i x_i = \sum_i p_{iA}^* y_i + \sum_i p_{iB}^* t_{iB} e_{iB} + \sum_i p_{iC}^* t_{iC} e_{iC} + T \equiv Y. \tag{3}$$

National income is the sum of producer income, tax revenue and unilateral transfers (T). Tax revenues are assumed to be returned in a lump-sum to the country's consumers. $V(Y, p)$ is homogeneous of degree zero,[3] strictly increasing in Y and strictly decreasing in p_i and it is assumed to be continuous and differentiable.

Differentiating totally eq. (2) and using Roy's Identity gives the first expression for the change in the welfare of the country,

$$a\,\mathrm{d}V = \mathrm{d}Y - \sum_i x_i \mathrm{d}p_i, \qquad a = (\partial V/\partial Y)^{-1} > 0. \tag{4}$$

This expression holds strictly only for small changes in taxes and prices. Its usefulness is that it shows how the changes in utility which follow the formation of the customs union can be traced to those which operate through the change in the national income of the country and those which operate through changes in the consumer prices.

The change in income and prices are obtained by differentiating eqs. (3) and (1) respectively and substituting in eq. (4). This gives the second general expression for the change in national welfare

$$a\,\mathrm{d}V = \sum_i p_{iA}^* \mathrm{d}y_i - \left(\sum_i e_{iB} \mathrm{d}p_{iB}^* + \sum_i e_{iC} \mathrm{d}p_{iC}^* \right)$$

$$+ \left(\sum_i p_{iB}^* t_{iB} \mathrm{d}e_{iB} + \sum_i p_{iC}^* t_{iC} \mathrm{d}e_{iC} \right) + \mathrm{d}T. \tag{5}$$

[2]In addition to assuming the existence of the direct social utility function, the derivation of the indirect function implies the assumptions that there exists a unique set of commodity demand functions, $x_i(Y, p)$. Multiple equilibria may arise in these tax-distorted equilibria, as Vanek (1965) noted. Uniqueness implies certain regularity conditions on marginal expenditures [Riezman (1979)].

[3]The homogeneity implies that only relative (consumer) prices matter. With trade taxes which change in a discriminatory manner, changes in the relative prices of commodities differ between countries. One may use the price of one commodity in the outside country as the numeraire.

This expression is useful to identify the several components of the changes in welfare. The first is the change in the national output. The next two are terms of trade effects. The Vinerian term $(\sum_i e_{iB} dp^*_{iB})$ is the change in the terms of trade due to the change in the import or export price at which the commodity was previously traded with the union partner in the pre-union situation. The term $(\sum_i e_{iC} dp^*_{iC})$ is due to the changes in the prices at which commodities are traded with the outside country. This term is zero under the assumption that member countries are small. Under this assumption, however, the first terms of trade effect need not be zero. Hence, smallness does not imply constant terms of trade in the presence of discriminatory trade tax changes. The term $(\sum_i p^*_{iB} t_{iB} de_{iB} + \sum_i p^*_{iC} t_{iC} de_{iC})$ is a weighted average change in volume of trade. It represents the changes in the costs of the tariff distortions upon which Meade (1955) concentrated. For example, if an imported commodity is subject to a high tariff it will be underimported compared to the free trade situation. If the changes in prices increase the quantity of imports the cost of the distortion is reduced. The summation sums these expressions over all commodities, weighting each by the specific equivalent of its ad valorem tax. Alternatively, it can be seen to be that part of the change in the trade tax revenue which is due to the change in the quantities traded. Each of these terms may be positive, negative, or zero.

Under the assumptions of consumer utility maximisation and producer income maximisation there are sets of commodity demand and supply functions

$$x_i = x_i(Y, p), \qquad i = 1, 2, 3, \tag{6}$$

$$y_i = y_i(p), \qquad i = 1, 2, 3. \tag{7}$$

Differentiating these equations and substituting in eq. (5) gives

$$adV = \sum_i p^*_{iA} \sum_j \partial y_i / \partial p_j dp_j - \left(\sum_i e_{iB} dp^*_{iB} + \sum_i e_{iC} dp^*_{iC} \right)$$

$$+ \sum_i \left\{ [p^*_{iB} t_{iB} \alpha_i + p^*_{iC} t_{iC} (1 - \alpha_i)] \left[\sum_j (\partial e_i / \partial p_j dp_j \right. \right.$$

$$\left. \left. + \partial x_i / \partial Y d Y) \right] \right\} + dT, \tag{8}$$

where

$$\partial e_i / \partial p_j = \partial x_i / \partial p_j - \partial y_i / \partial p_j \text{ and } \alpha_i = de_{iB} / (de_{iB} + de_{iC}),$$

α_i mostly takes values of 0 or 1 in the models below. In eq. (8) the change in welfare depends solely upon the changes in prices and income and the derivatives of the demand and supply functions. These derivatives express the relationships of gross substitutability and complementarity in demand and supply. The change in income is itself a function of the price changes. From the Slutsky equation

$$\partial x_i/\partial p_j = \partial \phi_i/\partial p_j - x_j \partial x_i/\partial Y,$$

where $\partial \phi_i/\partial p_j$ is the income-compensated derivative. Substituting in eq. (8) and using the relations $dY = \sum_i p_i dx_i + \sum_i x_i dp_i$ and $dV/(\partial V/\partial Y) = \sum_i p_i dx_i$ yields

$$m dV = \sum_i p_{iA}^* \left(\sum_j \partial y_i/\partial p_j dp_j \right) - \left(\sum_i e_{iB} dp_{iB}^* + \sum_i e_{iC} dp_{iC}^* \right)$$

$$+ \sum_i \left\{ [p_{iB}^* t_{iB} \alpha_i + p_{iC}^* t_{iC} (1-\alpha_i)] \left[\sum_j \partial \psi_i/\partial p_j dp_j \right] \right\} + dT, \tag{9}$$

where

$$m = (\partial V/\partial Y)^{-1} \left(1 - \sum_i [p_{iB}^* t_{iB} \alpha_i + p_{iC}^* t_{iC} (1-\alpha_i)] \partial x_i/\partial Y \right) \tag{10}$$

and

$$\partial \psi_i/\partial p_j = \partial \phi_i/\partial p_j - \partial y_i/\partial p_j. \tag{11}$$

From eq. (3), $\sum_i p_i \partial x_i/\partial Y = 1$. Hence

$$m = \left(\sum_i [p_{iB}^* \alpha_i + p_{iC}^* (1-\alpha_i)] \partial x_i/\partial Y \right) (\partial V/\partial Y)^{-1}$$

is the marginal propensity to consume all commodities evaluated at weighted average world prices. It is assumed to be positive.[4] The derivatives $(\partial \psi_i/\partial p_j)$ in eq. (11) is the change in the excess demand for commodity i when the price of commodity j changes and the utility is constrained to the initial level of utility by appropriate income adjustments and the production is constrained to the transformation surface. For the first component, a pair of commodities (i,j) are net substitutes (complements) in demand as $\partial \phi_i/\partial p_j > (<)0$. For the second component, the pair are net substitutes or complements in supply as $\partial y_i/\partial p_j < (>)0$. We shall define a pair of commodities as being net substitutes (complements) as $\partial \psi_i/\partial p_j > (<)0$. The

---

[4]Positivity of this marginal propensity is satisfied if all commodities are superior, as in the Riezman (1979) conditions.

usefulness of this third expression is that it gives the welfare change solely in terms of changes in prices and the relationships of substitutability and complementarity among commodities.[5]

Thus eqs. (5), (8) and (9) provide three alternative expressions for the change in welfare. All three have been used by various authors. (Some terms disappear because of further special assumptions in each model.) Berglas (1979) uses a form of eq. (5) whereas Meade (1955) and Lipsey (1970) use a form of eq. (8) and McMillan and McCann (1979) use a form of eq. (9). Vanek's (1965) geometric analysis is equivalent locally to eq. (9). The equivalence of the three expressions will permit us to relate the propositions of different authors.

Eq. (5) (or (8) or (9)) gives the necessary and sufficient conditions for welfare gain. The necessary and sufficient condition is that the sum of the terms on the right-hand side be positive. Some sufficient conditions take the form that the individual terms or groups of them be all positive. The likelihood conditions take the form that one (or more) of the terms is an increasing function of some variable and, therefore, provided the other terms are not affected negatively, a gain is more likely under some condition. Such likelihood conditions can be expressed more conveniently for the purposes of model comparison as sufficient conditions.

In reality customs unions involve large, not small, changes in tax rates and associated changes in commodity prices. The effect on welfare may be obtained by integration of eq. (8)

$$\Delta V = \int_P dV = \int_P \partial V / \partial Y R, \tag{12}$$

where R is the right-hand of eq. (8) and P is the price path. This integral may be difficult to evaluate.[6] One alternative is to find whether a path exists such that the marginal expression in one of eqs. (5), (8) or (11) is positive at all times as trade taxes within the union are reduced to zero. This was the method used by Riezman (1979). Such a path provides a sufficient condition for welfare to be increased by eliminating trade barriers within the union. In general, no such path exists. Another alternative is to obtain the indirect social utility function by substituting for the income argument and to

---

[5]This expression is closely related to that which has been used to analyse the welfare effects of piecemeal changes in trade (and other) taxes. The expression used, for example, by Lloyd (1974) and Hatta (1977), to consider piecemeal non-discriminatory changes in trade taxes may in fact be derived from eq. (9) by setting the rates of trade taxes equal across countries.

[6]Berglas (1979, p. 322 n. 9) uses the integral $\int_P adV$ but this is only approximate unless the utility function is homothetic. Non-homotheticity poses another problem. When more than one price in the country changes this integral is a line integral whose value is not invariant with respect to the price path because the marginal utility of income is a function of prices (and income) [for example, Burns (1977)].

evaluate the function in two situations. This is in effect the method used by Lipsey (1970, appendix to ch. 6) but it is only tractable for the simplest models.

3.

There are basic differences among the four models in the assumptions concerning the pattern of commodity trade among the three countries. This is not obvious since none of the authors other than Collier (1979) considered alternative patterns and several seem unaware of the possibility of patterns other than the one adopted and, therefore, of the peculiarity of the one adopted. The number of permissible patterns is greater than any of the authors contemplated.

Fig. 1 produces a flow diagram of the trilateral pattern of trade assumed in each of the Meade, Riezman, and Berglas models and three others. In this diagram the arrow indicates the direction of the flow. First, compare the Meade pattern with that of Riezman. Both are symmetrical but the two are very different. In the Meade model each country *exports* one commodity and imports the other two commodities and each commodity can be identified as the export commodity of one of the three countries. Thus commodities 1, 2, 3, are the export commodities of countries A, B, and C respectively. By contrast, in the Riezman model each country *imports* only one commodity and exports the other two commodities and each commodity can be identified as the import commodity of one of the three countries. Thus commodities 1, 2, 3 are the import commodities of countries A, B and C respectively.

The Berglas pattern is asymmetrical. Countries A and B each have one export and two import commodities but country A exports its export commodity to both B and C and imports one commodity from both B and C whereas country B exports its export commodity to A only and imports each of the other two commodities from a separate country.

Corden (1976) considers the trading pattern of only one member country rather than the full trilateral pattern. His model is consistent with any pattern in the post-union situation in which one country imports two commodities and exports one commodity, as in the Meade pattern or Berglas for either country or in others.

These trading patterns may apply to the pre-union situation as well as the post-union situation or they may not. This is assumed to be the case in the Meade model [Lipsey (1970, p. 32)], the Riezman model [Riezman (1979, p. 343)] and in the Berglas model [Berglas (1979, p. 318)]. Corden is alone in allowing the union to change the trade pattern.

There are many more possible trading patterns than those listed above. Subject to the restrictions that each country must export at least one and

50   *P.J. Lloyd, 3 × 3 theory of customs unions*

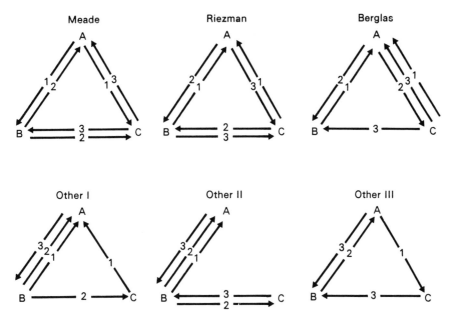

Fig. 1. Some permissible trading patterns.

import at least one commodity, must not export and import the same commodity, and the two member countries have at least one export commodity not in common and these commodities are traded between them, I have enumerated 11 permissible trading patterns.[7] Three more are given in fig. 1. The labelling of countries and commodities in fig. 1 is arbitrary. Any pattern which replicates another by an appropriate interchange of labels for two or more countries or commodities has been considered the same pattern. Most patterns, such as that of the Berglas model, are asymmetrical so that the number of patterns permissible for individual countries exceeds the number of patterns permissible for the three countries. Asymmetry has the important consequence that the welfare of two countries may be affected in different ways by a customs union.

In all patterns the assumptions concerning the ratio of the number of import to export commodities in each member country and those concerning the country of supply predetermine the changes in relative prices and income

[7]The three models which specified a trilateral trading pattern all have these charateristics. The second rules out, among other possibilities, the transhipment of any commodity from one union member to another. One might add or subtract other restrictions. For example, one might add the restriction that every commodity be traded by every country (which is not true of Other I, II and III in fig. 1) or that every country trade with the other two (which is not true of Other II).

With any restrictions the determination of the number of permissible patterns is a complex problem. For the analysis of a similar problem in consumer theory which uses combinatorial graph theory see Mosenson and Dror (1972).

which can occur and therefore the welfare effects in each member country. When comparing two distinct trading patterns it is possible for the price effects in one pattern for *one* of the customs union partners to be identical to that of one of the countries in the other pattern. In the Meade and Corden models the pattern of trade is also linked to fixed patterns of production which further restrict the substitution effects of the price changes. The assumption of only one import commodity in the Riezman model rules out any Corden 'import pattern' effects in either member country.

Properly the pattern of trade in both the pre- and the post-union situations should emerge endogenously as part of the solution of the competitive equilibrium for the world economy. Lipsey (1970, ch. 9) was the only author to demonstrate that the assumed pattern of trade can emerge from a competitive solution to the whole model. Indeed, the disturbance to the equilibrium of the world economy may result in a commodity in some country switching from exporting to importing a commodity or vice versa [Kemp (1969)]. Most multi-commodity models yield, realistically, solutions in which each country imports more commodities than it exports [Jones (1976, pp. 37–38)] but Riezman assumes the opposite.

4.

In section 2 the only assumptions imposed on the model (apart from the 3×3 dimensionality) were the existence of the social utility function, the absence of taxes other than trade taxes and the lump-sum distribution of taxes revenue. All four models make these assumptions. All four also assume that the production transformation surface is fixed which reduces the national output term ($\sum_i p_{iA}^* \mathrm{d}y_i$) to zero. All, apart from Berglas, assume that international transfers are zero and that trade taxes vis-a-vis the outside country are fixed. These two assumptions will be made for all four models to make the results comparable.

Table 1 sets out the differences among the models with regard to assumptions. Each set of assumptions puts restrictions on the elasticities of demand and supply and therefore excess demand, and on the price changes which can occur.

4.1. The Meade model[8]

Because of the symmetry of the trading and production patterns it suffices to consider only one member, say country *A*. The customs union reduces *A*'s

---

[8]The assumptions are those of Vanek (1965, pp. 189–192) and Lipsey (1970, pp. 32–33). Meade did not make the small country assumption. Despite his brilliant insights and historical importance Meade can be criticised for his failure to make his supply constraint explicit [Vanek (1965, p. 15)]. It was not clear that his volume index was an effect which supplements rather than substitutes for the Vinerian price effect.

Table 1

Assumptions of the four models.

	Meade	Riezman	Berglas	Corden
Trading pattern	As in fig. 1	As in fig. 1	As in fig. 1	Country *A* exports one and imports two commodities, one or both of which are switched to *B* in the post-union situation
Production pattern	*A* and *B* completely specialised in their export commodities	No restriction	No restriction	Supply of export commodity fixed
Smallness	*A* and *B* small	None small	*A* and *B* small	*A* small
Uniformity of tariffs across commodities in pre-union situation	Uniform in *A* (and *B*)	Not relevant	No restriction	Non-uniform
Other	—	—	—	No domestic consumption of export commodity

tariff on imports of commodity 2 from *B* and *B*'s tariff on its imports of commodity 1 from *A*.

From eq. (5), given the assumptions, the welfare change in country *A* reduces to

$$a\mathrm{d}V = p_{2B}^* t_{2B}\mathrm{d}e_2 + p_{3C}^* t_{3C}\mathrm{d}e_3, \qquad a > 0. \tag{13}$$

The assumption of the Meade trading pattern before and after the union rules out trade diversion and that of smallness rules out changes in p_{iC}^*. A sufficient condition for a small change in tariffs to increase the welfare of the member country *A* is that there be an increase in the quantity of all imports [Meade (1955, ch. IV)]. Starting from the initial pre-union situation of uniform tariffs ($t_{2B} = t_{3C} = t > 0$), the change in welfare is

$$a\mathrm{d}V = t(p_{2B}^*\mathrm{d}e_2 + p_{3C}^*\mathrm{d}e_3). \tag{14}$$

The necessary and sufficient condition for an increase in welfare is that the volume of trade evaluated at world prices increase [Meade (1955)].

It is more fruitful to use eq. (9) rather than (5) or (8). Substituting $\mathrm{d}p_2 = p_{2B}^*\mathrm{d}t_{2B}$ and using the additional assumption of complete specialisation

$(\partial\psi_i/\partial p_j = \partial\phi_i/\partial p_j)$ one obtains

$$md V = [p^*_{2B}t_{2B}\partial\phi_2/\partial p_2 + p^*_{3C}t_{3C}\partial\phi_3/\partial p_2]p^*_{2B}dt_{2B}. \tag{15}$$

In the absence of trade diversion, only the reduction in its own tariff on commodity 2 affects country A's welfare. Furthermore, from the homogeneity of the income-compensated demand functions,

$$p^*_{1A}\partial\phi_1/\partial p_2 + p^*_{2B}(1+t_{2B})\partial\phi_2/\partial p_2 + p^*_{3C}(1+t_{3C})\partial\phi_3/\partial p_2 = 0. \tag{16}$$

Eliminating $\partial\phi_3/\partial p_2$ from eq. (15) gives

$$md V = [-p^*_{1A}t_{3C}\partial\phi_1/\partial p_2 + p^*_{2B}(t_{2B}-t_{3C})\partial\phi_2/\partial p_2]p^*_{2B}dt_{2B}/(1+t_{3C}). \tag{17}$$

In the initial situation $t_{2B}=t_{3C}$. Hence, a small reduction in the initial tariff on the commodity imported from the partner country increases welfare if and only if this commodity is a net substitute in demand for the home-produced commodity [McMillan and McCann (1981)].

These propositions relate to marginal tariff changes. As Meade (1955, pp. 110–113) first showed, the reductions may first increase and then beyond some level decrease welfare and the effect of their reduction to zero is ambiguous. From eq. (15), continuous reduction in the tariff on commodity 2 will increase the welfare of country A if commodities 2 and 3 are independent commodities, that is $\partial\phi_3/\partial p_2=0$ (since $\partial\phi_2/\partial p_2<0$). The optimum tariff reduction (given the tariff on imports from the outside country) is obtained from eq. (15) by setting $md V=0$,

$$t^{opt}_{2B} = -p^*_{3C}t_{3C}\partial\phi_3/\partial p_2/p^*_{2B}\partial\phi_2/\partial p_2. \tag{18}$$

Independence of these two commodities is the necessary and sufficient condition for a zero tariff on commodity 2 to be optimal [Vanek (1965, p. 205) and McMillan and McCann (1981)].

Lipsey (1970, ch. 6) states that a customs union is the more likely to increase the welfare of country A the larger the proportion of the consumer budget spent on commodity 1 relative to that spent on commodity 3. Commodity 3 is the commodity imported from the outside country whose price remains constant. He proves this proposition for the special case of the Graham model. It may be proven simply and extended by using the indirect utility function. In the Meade model, the total output of the home-produced commodity is fixed and one can obtain a simple expression for the national income argument of the indirect utility function. From eq. (3)

$$Y = p_{1A}^* \bar{y}_1 + p_{2B}^* t_{2B} x_{2A} + p_{3C}^* t_{3C} x_{3A}$$

$$= p_{1A}^* \bar{y}_1 / [1 - \beta_2 t_{2B}/(1 + t_{2B}) - \beta_3 t_{3C}/(1 + t_{3C})], \tag{19}$$

where $\beta_i = (x_i p_i/Y)$ is the proportion of the budget spent on commodity i. One must evaluate

$$F = V(Y'', p'')/V(Y', p'),$$

where $''$ and $'$ denote the post-union and pre-union situations respectively. Now, the indirect utility function is an increasing function of the income argument and a decreasing function of the price arguments. By definition $\sum_i \beta_i = 1$ and in the pre-union situation $t'_{2A} = t'_{3A}$ and in the post-union situation $t''_{2B} = 0$. Hence,

$$(Y''/Y') \gtreqless 1 \quad \text{as} \quad \beta_1'' + \beta_2'' \gtreqless \beta_2' + \beta_3'. \tag{20}$$

In the Graham model $\beta_i'' = \beta_i'$. Lipsey used the result $\beta_1 \gtreqless \beta_3$ to state a likelihood condition but eq. (20) provides a more general sufficient condition for welfare improvement which holds for any level of initial tariffs. It is not a necessary condition since $\Delta p = (p_{2B}^* \Delta t_{2B}) < 0$ which itself increases welfare.

The effects of the customs union on the second member country, country B, are symmetrical. B is affected only by the reduction on the tariff on the commodity it imports from A, commodity 1. All of the results above follow by interchanging commodities 1 and 2. Thus, commodities 1 and 2 being net substitutes is a sufficient condition for a small reduction to increase the welfare of country B. From the symmetry of the Slutsky matrix $\partial\phi_2/\partial p_1 = \partial\phi_1/\partial p_2$. If countries A and B have the same utility functions, this condition is *sufficient* for an increase in welfare in both countries. But the other conditions are not identical. Therefore, it is possible for one country to gain and one to lose from a marginal or total mutual reduction in tariffs.[9]

These propositions derived from eq. (15) can be extended very easily. They carry over if one allows production of all commodities and replaces the net substitution or independence in demand relations with net substitution or independence in excess demand, that is, $\partial\psi_1/\partial p_2 > 0$ or $\partial\psi_3/\partial p_2 = 0$. This reveals that it is the assumptions of smallness and trading patterns rather

[9]For example, the sufficient condition for country A to gain from the elimination of tariffs, namely, that commodities 2 and 3 be independent, has its counterpart for country B, namely, that commodities 1 and 3 be independent. However, it is impossible for both commodities 1 and 2 to be independent of commodity 3.

than complete specialisation which are important. However, the Lipsey proposition requires complete specialisation.

4.2. The Riezman model

As in the Meade model, the customs union involves a mutual reduction in one tariff in each member, now t_{1B} in country A and t_{2A} in country B. This simplicity is due to the fact that each imports only one commodity in the pre-union and post-union situations rather than to the fact that it must source each import from a different country as in the former model. Moreover, the import commodities differ. Hence, there is no question of uniformity across commodities or countries. Riezman also assumes that in each country

$$\partial x_i/\partial p_j > 0, \quad \text{and} \quad \partial y_i/\partial p_j < 0,$$
$$\partial x_i/\partial p_i < 0, \qquad \qquad \partial y_i/\partial p_i > 0, \qquad i \neq j.$$

The first states that all pairs of commodities are gross substitutes in demand and supply. Therefore, $\partial e_i/\partial p_j > 0$ for $i \neq j$ and $\partial e_i/\partial p_i < 0$.

From eq. (5) and the assumed trading pattern, the welfare change for country A is

$$adV = -\left(\sum_i e_{iB} dp_{iB}^* + \sum_i e_{iC} dp_{iC}\right) + (p_{1B}^* t_{1B} de_{1B} + p_{1C}^* t_{1C} de_{1C}). \quad (21)$$

Riezman concentrates on the terms of trade effects. These are explicitly broken up into the intra-union and the extra-union effects for the member country, as in the equation. Although the foreign prices on which the import taxes are based are not fixed, it is still true that the mutual reduction in tariffs reduces the domestic prices of these commodities in the union member countries. This occurs because certain 'regularity conditions' imply that the own-price effects dominate the cross-price effects. Using the price of the imported commodity 3 in country C as the numeraire and holding constant the tariffs in the outside country, it follows that the import price of the commodity imported by the member country from the outside country must fall relative to its export price. Hence, the extra-union terms of trade must improve for both countries. However, the changes in the prices p_{2A}^* and p_{1B}^* and, therefore, in the intra-union terms of trade are indeterminate. Moreover, the regularity assumptions ensure that as the price of the import commodity falls, the volume term $(p_{1b}^* t_{1B} de_{1B} + p_{1B}^* t_{1C} de_{1C})$ is positive. Provided the intra-union imports of country A from B are small, the welfare in country A must increase.

Because of symmetry the second member country's welfare is affected in the same way. Thus, if the intra-union trade of the two countries is small both countries will benefit from the union [Riezman (1979, theorem 2)]. Clearly, however, it is possible for one country to gain and one to lose despite the symmetry of the structure of the model, as in the Meade model.

The sufficiency proposition applies to marginal changes in tariffs. Riezman also showed that if the mutual tariff reduction takes the form of equal constant percentage reductions in t_{1B} and t_{2A} utility continually increases along the resulting price path. Hence, under the same conditions, a customs union which eliminates intra-union trade barriers yields welfare gains to both member countries.

4.3. The Berglas model

Unlike the first two models, this trading pattern is asymmetrical and one must consider the effects on the two member countries separately.

In country A the customs union lowers the price of the commodity it imports from country B, commodity 1. From eq. (5) and (8), for country A,

$$a d V = -e_{1B} d p_{1B}^* + p_{1B}^* t_{1B} d e_{1B} + p_{1C}^* t_{1C} d e_{1C} + p_{3C}^* t_{3C} d e_{3C}$$

$$= -e_{1B} d p_{1B}^* + [p_{1B}^* t_{1B} \alpha_1 + p_{1C}^* t_{1C} (1 - \alpha_1)] \partial x_1 / \partial Y d Y$$

$$+ p_{3C}^* t_{3C} \partial x_3 / \partial Y d Y, \qquad \alpha_1 = d e_{1B} / (d e_{1B} + d e_{1C}). \qquad (22)$$

Because of the joint assumptions that commodity 1 is imported from both B and C and that A and B are small, the tariff reduction does not lower the price in country A but the supply price of imports of commodity 1 from its partner is increased. This gives rise to a loss of tariff revenue and a fall in this component of national income, as stated in the first two terms of the first equation. If commodities 1 and 3 are normal the last two terms of eq. (22) must also be negative; that is, national income falls. Normality of the commodities provides a sufficient condition for a welfare loss for country A.

In country B the domestic price of its export commodity, commodity 1, rises and that of its import commodity, commodity 2, falls as a result of the mutual tariff reductions and that of commodity 3 which it imports from country C remains constant because of the small country assumption. From eq. (8) the corresponding expression for country B is

$$a\mathrm{d}V = -e_{1B}\mathrm{d}p_{1B}^* + p_{2A}^* t_{2A}\mathrm{d}e_{2A} + p_{3C}^* t_{3C}\mathrm{d}e_{3C}$$

$$= -e_{1B}\mathrm{d}p_{1B}^* + p_{2A}^* t_{2A}\left(\sum_{j=1,2}[\partial e_2/\partial p_j\mathrm{d}p_j + \partial x_j/\partial Y\mathrm{d}Y]\right)$$

$$+ p_{3C}^* t_{3C}\left(\sum_{j=1,2}[\partial e_3/\partial p_j\mathrm{d}p_j + \partial x_j/\partial Y\mathrm{d}Y]\right). \tag{23}$$

The first term represents the gain in income due to the increase in its export price to country A. The second term will be positive if commodity 2 is normal and a gross substitute for commodities 1 and 3 in demand and supply but the sign of the last term is ambiguous under the same assumptions since the price of commodity 3 falls relative to that of commodity 1 and rises relative to that of commodity 2. Berglas observes that, as in the Meade model, a small reduction in the initial tariffs may increase the welfare of country B whereas a large or total reduction may decrease it.

The relationship between these results for country B and those of the Meade model may be seen more clearly if the third welfare expression is used. From eq. (9),

$$m\mathrm{d}V = -e_{1B}\mathrm{d}p_{1B}^* + p_{2A}^* t_{2A}\left(\sum_{j=1,2}\partial\psi_2/\partial p_j\mathrm{d}p_j\right)$$

$$+ p_{3C}^* t_{3C}\left(\sum_{j=1,2}\partial\psi_3/\partial p_j\mathrm{d}p_j\right). \tag{24}$$

In this expression the complications of the income terms are removed. The joint assumptions of normality and gross substitutes imply that pairs of commodities are net substitutes in demand. Assuming the commodities are net substitutes in supply, then $\partial\psi_i/\partial p_j \geq 0$. Because of homogeneity of ψ_i, $\sum_i p_i\partial\psi_i/\partial p_j = 0$. Eliminating $\partial\psi_3/\partial p_2$ from eq. (24) gives

$$m\mathrm{d}V = [-e_{1B}\mathrm{d}p_{1B}^* + p_{2A}^* t_{2A}\partial\psi_2/\partial p_1\mathrm{d}p_1 + p_{3C}^* t_{3C}\partial\psi_3/\partial p_1\mathrm{d}p_1]$$

$$+ [-p_{1B}^* t_{3C}\partial\psi_1/\partial p_2 + p_{2A}^*(t_{2A}-t_{3C})\partial\psi_2/\partial p_2]p_{2B}^*\mathrm{d}t_{2B}/(1+t_{3C}). \tag{25}$$

Commodities 1 and 3 being net substitutes for commodity 2 and uniform initial tariffs are sufficient for a small reduction in the initial tariffs to increase welfare. Moreover, under the net substitute assumption, the second term of eq. (24) $(p_{2A}^* t_{2A}\sum_j\partial\psi_2/\partial p_j\mathrm{d}p_j)$ is positive but the third term

$(p_{3C}^* t_{3C} \sum_j \partial \psi_3 / \partial p_j \mathrm{d}p_j)$ is ambiguous in sign. If, instead, it is assumed for commodities 2 and 3 that they are net independents, the last term is also positive. The independence of commodities 2 and 3 (and net substitutability of commodities 2 and 3 with commodity 1) is another sufficient condition for a welfare increase. These two conditions parallel those of the Meade model. The reason is that in both models the country imports one commodity from its partner only and another from country C only. The necessary conditions also differ because of the additional positive effects in the Berglas model due to the rise in the price of the commodity exported to its union partner.

4.4. The Corden model

For the one country concerned, which we shall call country A, there are two import commodities. One or both of these are imported from the outside country in the pre-union situation but in the post-union situation one or both are switched to the union partner. The import commodities are commodities 1 and 2.

From eq. (5) we have

$$a\mathrm{d}V = -(e_{1B}p_{2B}^* \mathrm{d}t_{1B} + e_{2B}p_{2B}^* \mathrm{d}t_{2B}) + \left(\sum_{k=B,C} \sum_{i=1,2} p_{ik}^* t_{ik} \mathrm{d}e_{ik} \right). \qquad (26)$$

The combination of zero elasticity of supply of the export commodity and zero consumption of this commodity and a fixed export price imply that the value of exports are fixed $(X = \bar{X})$. Hence, the last term is subject to the constraint that $(\sum_{k=B,C} \sum_{i=1,2} p_{ik}^* \mathrm{d}e_{ik}) = 0$. Initial tariffs are assumed to be non-uniform among commodities and to be eliminated within the union. The first trade diversion term is negative by construction. The second term $(\sum_{k=B,C} \sum_{i=1,2} p_{ik}^* t_{ik} \mathrm{d}e_{ik})$ is the 'import pattern' effect. This is the effect of the change in the pattern of imports due solely to the change in their relative price. It is positive if all imports come from the union partner in the post-union situation and ambiguous in sign if the outside country continues to supply one commodity. A welfare gain is more likely the more non-uniform the initial tariff rates because the 'import pattern' terms increase with tariff non-uniformity.

Terms due to change in import trade may occur in any model with two importables. In general they arise because of changes in production as well as consumption and are due to changes in several prices. With non-uniform initial tariffs and without the constraint of constant exports the 'import pattern' becomes only a part of the generalised terms in eq. (5) showing the effect of changes in distortions, $(\sum_k \sum_i p_{ik}^* t_{ik} \mathrm{d}e_{ik})$.

Nothing can be said about the change in welfare in the partner country except that the trade diversion component will be positive and welfare may increase or decrease, unless a model of trade and production in the three countries is fully specified.

All four models have considered only tariffs. Yet, the expressions obtained in section 2 allow both export and import taxes-subsidies. In all models there may be export diversion terms. In the Riezman and other models with two export commodities there may be Meade-type distortion effects, including Corden-type 'export pattern' effects.

Thus the 3 × 3 models generate many distinct propositions. Some of the propositions involve assumptions which are not mutually exclusive. For example, Corden's likelihood proposition relates to the differences between the non-uniform pre-union tariffs whereas Lipsey's relates to the height of the (uniform) tariffs. These propositions complement each other and could be combined in one model. Other assumptions are mutually exclusive. The specialisation assumption of the Meade model does not affect the propositions for this model other than the Lipsey proposition and that of the Corden model is unessential. Smallness and non-smallness are mutually exclusive but the non-smallness is more general and can be added to any trading pattern and other assumptions. Thus mutually exclusive differences in the assumption concerning trading patterns account for most of the irreducible differences among the four models.

Two other aspects of the structure of models have been used to obtain propositions. For country *B* in the Berglas model and countries *A* and *B* in the Meade model a sufficient condition was derived in terms of the independence between the commodity imported from the partner country and that imported from the outside country. The economic explanations in both models is that the mutual tariff reduction drives the price of the commodity imported from the union partner relative to the price of that imported from the outside country from the optimal free trade level. This will normally, by itself, worsen welfare but if the two commodities are independents this term goes to zero. Both propositions are examples of the use of separability to obtain stronger qualitative results.

The Riezman proposition is an example of the use of regularity conditions to sign the terms of trade effect. Weaker regularity conditions on cross-substitution effects were used in the Meade and Berglas models.[10]

5.

For a long time in the development of the theory of customs unions it was commonly believed that 3 × 2 models were adequate. As one example, 'To

---

[10]One may conjecture that acceptable regularity conditions would also allow one to prove that the terms of trade effect vis-a-vis the outside country must benefit both in the modified Meade, Berglas and Corden models in which no country is small. For the Meade model, both Meade (1955, p. 95) and Vanek (1965, p. 208) presumed this to be so.

properly pose the problems associated with preferential trading and investing arrangements, however, one need recognize only three trading countries and two traded commodities (other than the services of capital)' [Kemp (1969, p. 21)].

The authors of the 3 × 3 models have given different reasons for increasing the dimensions of the model.[11] The first feature which attracted some authors is the possibility of trading patterns different from those of the 3 × 2 models. With only two commodities one must be the export and one the import commodity in each country and if the customs union is to be relevant country *A*'s export commodity must be country *B*'s import commodity. These characteristics imply that the trading pattern must be asymmetrical and one member country cannot trade with the outside country. The effect of the union on the welfare of a member country depends on whether it is the country which trades with the outside country [see Kemp (1969, chs. 2 and 4)]. Asymmetrical patterns are not necessary in 3 × 3 models, as Vanek (1965, p. 13) and Collier (1979, p. 86) stressed, though they are still permissible as in the Berglas model. Presumably it was this feature which led Riezman (1979, p. 342) to state 'The three-country-three-good model has the advantage that there is not the asymmetry that exists in the three-country-two-good model'. On the other hand, Berglas (1979, p. 317) claimed that 'This asymmetry in the 3 × 3 model exists whenever we exclude the possibility that a country will export and import the same commodity'. The earlier Meade and the Riezman models serve as counter-examples.

A second related feature was stressed by Corden. In order to have differential tariffs on imports and changes in the structure of imports it is necessary to have two import commodities, that is, at least three commodities. This feature also puts an additional restriction on the permissible trading patterns.

A third feature was stressed by Berglas and by McMillan and McCann, namely that the extension to three commodities permits relations of complementarity as well as substitutability in demand (and one should add in supply). Berglas used gross substitutability relations whereas McMillan and McCann used net relations. In both the Berglas and Meade models section 4 revealed the further usefulness of the possibility of independence. Independence, as well as complementarity, is ruled out with only two commodities for net relations in demand (and supply).

Fourth, Lipsey (1960, 1970) emphasised that three commodities increases the number of relative prices to two and introduces the possibilities of divergences between these two marginal rates of substitution in consumption

---

[11]Each of these aspects of higher dimensionality occurs in trade models with non-discriminatory tariffs [see the survey of Jones (1976)]. In this respect, as in others, the theory of discriminatory tariff reductions is an extension of the basic theory.

on the one hand and the marginal rates of transformation, either through domestic production or through international trade, on the other. This gives rise to many more second-best possibilities. It led Lipsey to the view: 'The general problems raised by customs unions must, however, be analysed in a model containing a minimum of three types of commodities: domestic commodities, imports from the union partner and imports from the outside world.' [Lipsey (1960, p. 503)]. Similarly, Berglas (1979, p. 317) stresses that 'the existence of a third commodity introduces very important considerations which are absent in the two-commodity model'.

The operation of the second, third and fourth features depends on the assumed trading patterns. Thus the trading pattern assumption is central to all propositions.

These features of the 3×3 models have yielded welfare results which differ from those of the 3×2 models. The larger number of relative price changes and the possibilities of complementarity give rise to more ambiguities. In different ways, each of the four 3×3 models yields effects and propositions which differ essentially from those of 3×2 models. It is clearly a great handicap to limit the theory of customs unions to models with two commodities.

The question now arises as to whether there are further gains in extending the commodity dimensions beyond 3×3. The expression of welfare change obtained in section 3 carry over to n commodities merely by extending the range of the summations. Other assumptions concerning the uniformity of pre-union tariffs, smallness, and specialisation in production can be made and varied in a $3 \times n$ model in precisely the same way as in the 3×3 models.

The relation of the permissible trading patterns to the number of commodities is more complex. Berglas (1979, p. 89) noted that in his asymmetrical pattern the difference between the effects of the union on A and B arises because the commodity which A imports from B is also imported from C in the post-union situation and therefore there is no change in prices within country A whereas B imports commodity 2 only from country A. A $3 \times n$ model would permit a fourth commodity (or a fourth group) that is exported from B to both A and C and, therefore, imported by A from country B only [see Berglas (1979, appendix)]. Collier (1979) makes much the same point more strongly. He considers three patterns: The 'Berglas' pattern, the 'Berglas' pattern with countries A and B interchanged and the 'Meade' pattern. He argues that one model which handles all three cases requires five commodities: each member country has two export commodities one of which is exported only to the partner, and country C exports the fifth commodity to both A and B. These commodity classifications are associated with different trading patterns. To encompass all in one model simultaneously would require a model with five or more commodities. All of the possibilities can be accommodated individually in the family of 3×3 models. Indeed, it is these possibilities which make the 3×3 trading world so much richer than the 3×2 models.

There is one aspect of trade that cannot be fitted into the 3×3 model without sacrificing some of these gains. All of the models have maintained the assumption that the three commodities are final consumable commodities. One very important aspect of the structure of tariffs in most countries is that the tariffs on traded intermediate materials and inputs are differentiated from those on final commodities. A customs union which reduces the tariffs on these inputs as well as tariffs on final commodities may shift the production transformation surface and give rise to important positive and negative national output effects. Similarly, the introduction of capital mobility between countries requires an additional intermediate commodity, the service payments on foreign-owned capital. The treatment of commodities which are tradeable inputs would require a further increase in the dimensionality of the model.[12]

With the caveat of the last paragraph one may conclude that 3×3 are the minimum dimensions for models of customs unions. Yet, every 3×3 model is a very special case. The basic importance of alternative trading patterns has not been appreciated. The individual propositions, being special cases, cannot be considered as general indicators of the effects of a customs union. Any specific customs union proposal can be evaluated by considering the structural aspects which appear germane to the specific proposal, using the building blocks of the 3×3 models.

[12]These factors would shift the transformation surface between the pre- and post-union situations. With the exclusion of these — and other input productivity effects — the only change in the value of national income which can occur in the four models is that due to the change in prices and tax revenues!

References

Berglas, E., 1979, Preferential trading theory: The n commodity case, Journal of Political Economy 87, 315–331.

Brillembourg, A. and S.M. Schadler, A model of currency substitution in exchange rate determination 1973–78, IMF Staff Papers 26, 513–542.

Burns, M.E., 1977, On the uniqueness of consumer's surplus and the invariance of economic index numbers, Manchester School 45, 41–61.

Collier, P., 1979, The welfare effects of customs unions: An anatomy, Economic Journal 89, 84–95.

Corden, W.M., 1976, Customs union theory and nonuniformity of tariffs, Journal of International Economics 6, 99–106.

Hatta, T., 1977, A recommendation for a better tariff structure, Econometrica 45, 1859–1869.

Jones, R.W., 1976, Two-ness in trade theory: Costs and benefits, Special Papers in International Economics, no. 12.

Jones, R.W. and J. Scheinkman, 1977, The relevance of the two-sector production model in trade theory, Journal of Political Economy 85, 909–935.

Kemp, M.C., 1969, A contribution to the general equilibrium theory of preferential trading (North-Holland, Amsterdam).

Lloyd, P.J., 1974, A more general theory of price distortions in open economies, Journal of International Economics 4, 365–386.

Lipsey, R.G., 1960, Theory of customs unions: A general survey, Economic Journal 70, 496–513.

Lipsey, R.G., 1970, The theory of customs unions: A general equilibrium analysis (Weidenfelt and Nicolson, London).

McMillan, J. and E. McCann, 1981, Welfare effects in customs unions, Economic Journal 91, 697–703.

Meade, J.E., 1955, The theory of customs unions (North-Holland, Amsterdam).

Mosenson, R. and E. Dror, 1972, A solution to the qualitative substitution problem in demand theory, Review of Economic Studies 39, 433–441.

Riezman, R., 1979, A 3 × 3 model of customs unions, Journal of International Economics 9, 341–354. .

Van Duyne, C., 1979, The macroeconomic effects of commodity market disruptions in open economies, Journal of International Economics 9, 559–582.

Vanek, J., 1965, General equilibrium of international discrimination (Harvard University Press, Cambridge, MA).

Viner, J., 1950, The customs union issue (Carnegie Endowment for International Peace, New York).

[9]

OECD Economic Studies No. 18, Spring 1992

F02
F13
F14

REGIONALISATION AND WORLD TRADE

Peter J. Lloyd

CONTENTS

The author is Professor of Economics at the University of Melbourne, Australia. He wrote this article as Consultant to the Resource Allocation Division, Economics and Statistics Department of the OECD, most of it in Paris during May and June 1991. At the time of writing the Uruguay Round had not concluded. He is grateful to Andrew Dean, Serge Devos, Henry Ergas, David Henderson, Grant Kirkpatrick, John P. Martin, Anne Richards, Jeffrey R. Shafer, Nick Vanston and Robert York for many helpful comments. Florence Spiesser and Stefano Cavaglia did the computations reported in Sections II and V.

INTRODUCTION

There has been a concern among international trade economists and government officials that the growth of regional trade blocs poses a threat to multilateral trading relations. This concern was evident after the decision of the European Community in 1985 to adopt measures to complete the creation of a Single Market in 1992. It has increased substantially in recent years with the United States and Canada agreeing in 1988 to form a Free Trade Area, which may now be extended to a North American Free Trade Agreement including Mexico, and with the uncertainty as to the prospect of a satisfactory conclusion of the Uruguay Round. The main concerns have been over the further erosion of the principle of non-discrimination and, more particularly, over the danger of trade wars between trading blocs.

It is taken for granted by many commentators in this debate that world trade has become more "regionalised", whatever that term may mean. Certainly a number of regional arrangements have been formed or extended. These are reviewed briefly in Section I. However, over the same period multilateral and unilateral reductions in trade barriers have also occurred. Section II considers whether the net effect of all these changes in trade policies has indeed led to greater regionalisation of world trade over the period 1961-1989. Section III reviews the literature on the effects of forming regional arrangements, emphasising the relationship of these effects to the observed trade flows and the effects on third countries. Section IV considers how the regional arrangements have affected the multilateral trading system and Section V examines the tripolar view of regional developments. Some conclusions are set out in Section VI.

I.   REVIEW OF REGIONAL TRADE ARRANGEMENTS

The General Agreement on Tariffs and Trade (GATT) is based on the principle of non-discrimination among the Contracting Parties. Article 24 provides for regional trading arrangements provided they do not restrict trade with other countries and satisfy other conditions. From the time of its establishment in 1947 until 1990, more than 80 regional arrangements had been notified to the GATT under Article 24 or other Articles[1]. Many of these arrangements are preference schemes and association agreements. These should be separated from reciprocal regional trade arrangements because they are rather different in nature. Preference schemes are non-reciprocal,

Table 1.　**Regional trade arrangements notified to the GATT, 1947-1990**

Title	Members	Date signed
France-Italy Interim Customs Union [This was incorporated into the EC in 1957]	France, Italy	13 September 1947
South African-Southern Rhodesian Customs Union	South Africa, Southern Rhodesia	December 1948
Nicaragua and El Salvador Free Trade Area [This was incorporated into the Central America Free Trade Area in 1958]	El Salvador, Nicaragua	9 March 1951
European Coal and Steel Community [This was incorporated into the EC in 1957]	Belgium, France, western Germany, Italy, Luxembourg, Netherlands	
European Economic Community (including European Atomic Energy Community)	1. Belgium, France, western Germany, Italy, Luxembourg, Netherlands 2. Denmark, Ireland, United Kingdom joined in 1973 3. Greece joined in 1981 4. Portugal and Spain joined in 1986	25 March 1957
Central American Free Trade Area [This was incorporated into the Central American Common Market in 1960]	Costa Rica, El Salvador, Guatemala, Honduras, Nicaragua	10 June 1958
European Free Trade Association	1. Austria, Denmark, Norway, Portugal, Sweden, Switzerland, United Kingdom 2. Denmark and United Kingdom seceded and joined the EC in 1973 3. Iceland acceded in 1970 4. Finland became a full member in 1986 5. Portugal seceded and joined the EC in 1986	4 January 1960
Latin American Free Trade Area [This was replaced by the Latin America Integration Association in 1980]	1. Argentina, Brazil, Chile, Mexico, Paraguay, Peru, Uruguay 2. Colombia and Ecuador acceded in 1961	18 February 1960
Central American Common Market	Costa Rica, El Salvador, Guatemala, Honduras, Nicaragua	1960
Arab Common Market	United Arab Republic	13 August 1964
Central African Economic and Customs Union	Congo (Brazzaville), Chad, Gabon, Central African Republic	8 December 1964
Canada-U.S. Automative Agreement [This was incorporated into the Canada-United States Free Trade Area in 1988]	Canada, United States	1965
New Zealand-Australia Free Trade Agreement [This was replaced by the Australia-New Zealand Closer Economic Relations Agreement in 1983]	Australia, New Zealand	31 August 1965

9

Table 1. *(continued)*

Title	Members	Date signed
United Kingdom-Ireland Free Trade Agreement [This was incorporated into the EC in 1973]	Ireland, United Kingdom	14 December 1965
Caribbean Free Trade Agreement [This was replaced by the Caribbean Community and Common Market in 1974]	Barbados, Guyana, Jamaica, Trinidad and Tobago	1968
Andean Pact	Bolivia, Colombia, Ecuador, Peru, Venezuela	1969
Caribbean Community and Common Market	1. Barbados, Guyana, Jamaica, Trinidad and Tobago 2. Other countries joined in 1974	4 July 1973
ASEAN Preferential Trading Arrangements	1. Indonesia, Malaysia, Philippines, Singapore, Thailand 2. Brunei joined in 1988	24 February 1977
Latin American Integration Association	Argentina, Bolivia, Brazil, Chile, Colombia, Ecuador, Mexico, Paraguay, Peru, Uruguay, Venezuela	1979
Australia-New Zealand Closer Economic Relations Trade Agreement	Australia, New Zealand	28 March 1983
Free Trade Agreement between Israel and the United States	Israel, United States	22 April 1985
Single European Act [This replaces the European Coal and Steel Community, the European Economic Community and the European Atomic Energy Community]	Belgium, Denmark, France, western Germany, Greece, Ireland, Italy, Luxembourg, Netherlands, Portugal, Spain, United Kingdom	1986
Canada-United States Free Trade Area	Canada, United States	2 January 1988

Note: These arrangements were notified under Article 24 or in a few cases Article 1 or other Articles. The table does not include preference schemes and association agreements notified to the GATT.
Sources: GATT, *Basic Instruments and Selected Documents,* Supplements 1-36. GATT, *Activities,* various issues.

10

usually provide for a reduction in tariff rates or implicit protection but not their elimination, and are available to developing countries only, many of which are outside the region concerned. Association agreements are usually reciprocal but some are not. For example, those between the EC on the one hand and the EFTA countries and Cyprus, Israel, Malta, Turkey and Andorra on the other are reciprocal. These associations are really an extension of the EC free trading area but they are limited in commodity and instrument coverage. The term "Regional Trading Arrangement" (RTA) is used below to cover all forms of regional trading except preference schemes and association agreements. Excluding the preference and association agreements, there have been more than 20 RTAs. These are listed in Table 1. (In addition, there have been a number of other reciprocal trading arrangements among developing countries, especially in Africa, which do not have to be notified to the GATT.)

A. Different forms of RTAs

The first major RTA under the aegis of GATT was the European Economic Community established by the Treaty of Rome in 1958. The EEC was a customs union in the terminology of GATT, as it involved the establishment of a common external tariff. It was described in the Treaty as a Common Market as it provided for free trade in capital and labour as well as in goods and services. This precedent and the importance of the six countries concerned led to the formation of EFTA in 1960 and a number of other regional arrangements followed in rapid succession during the 1960s. These included the Latin American Free Trade Area (which came into effect in 1960), the Central American Common Market (1960), the Canada-U.S. Automotive Agreement (1965), the New Zealand-Australia Free Trade Area (1965), the U.K.-Ireland Free Trade Agreement (1965) and a number of less important agreements among developing countries in Africa, the Middle East and the Caribbean. The United Kingdom and Denmark moved from EFTA to the EC in 1972.

During the 1980s there was a second burst of new trading agreements. These included the Second Enlargement of the EC (which added Greece in 1981, and Portugal and Spain in 1986), the commitment to form a Single Market in the EC by 1992, the Closer Economic Relations (CER) Agreement between Australia and New Zealand in 1983, and the Canada-U.S. Free Trade Agreement in 1989. All of these involved countries which are members of the OECD, and all were extensions of earlier agreements. Thus, they may be referred to as second-generation agreements. In 1991, two agreements were reached in Latin America which promise more substantial trade liberalisation than previous agreements in the area; these are the Southern Cone Common Market of Brazil, Argentina, Uruguay, and Paraguay and the Act of Caracas which has set up a new free trade area for the Andean countries (Bolivia, Colombia, Ecuador, Peru and Venezuela). Geographically, these arrangements have been concentrated in Europe, Africa, and the Americas. The first and only agreement in the Asian region was the 1977 ASEAN agreement.

The regional freeing of trade in commodities proceeds in two ways. It may proceed by extending geographically through forming new agreements or accepting new members into an existing agreement. Alternatively, it may proceed by increasing the extent of intra-area free trade for each agreement through lowering restrictions on the commodities covered or by extending the commodity coverage.

11

Evidently there has been a continued increase in the number of regional agreements and in the total number of member countries[2]. However, some have replaced earlier agreements between the same countries. Hence, the proliferation of arrangements is exaggerated by the number notified. The most important new arrangement is the Canada-U.S. Free Trade Area.

The geographic extension of existing RTAs is easily traced too. To date the only major instance of geographic extension of an existing arrangement is the expansion of the EC from the original six members to nine, then 10 and now 12. (One could count the unification of the former East Germany with the Federal Republic of Germany in 1990 as the addition of a thirteenth country because it became *de facto* a part of the EC customs territory.) The European Economic Area accord between the EC and EFTA which was signed in October 1991 will, when implemented in 1993, effectively extend the EC Single Market to 19 countries. ASEAN was extended from the original five to six members with the inclusion of Brunei in 1988.

B.   The extent of RTA liberalisation

The extent of intra-RTA trade liberalisation is much more difficult to measure. All of these arrangements have led or will lead to the removal of some barriers to intra-area trade in commodities but some agreements have achieved a much greater degree of liberalisation than others. There is a bewildering array of different kinds of "free trade areas", "customs unions", "common markets", "single markets" and other arrangements. Some exclude agriculture (e.g. EFTA and the Canada-U.S. Free Trade Area). Most exclude trade in services, although the EC '92, the Canada-U.S. FTA, and the CER Agreement between Australia and New Zealand include trade in specified services. Some have no provision for factor movements (e.g. ASEAN), some cover free movement of capital (e.g. Canada-U.S. FTA) or labour (e.g. CER)[3] or both (EC '92). Some harmonise selected non-border instruments (EC and CER) but most do not. The term "Regional Trading Arrangement" (RTA) is used below to cover all forms of regional trading except preference schemes and association agreements.

Most of these RTAs were approved by GATT as free trade areas which result in the freeing of "substantially all" commodity trade between members rather than customs unions. Many of the "free trade areas" were severely restricted in commodity coverage, however, and for those commodities covered they frequently did not provide for the complete elimination of all tariffs. For example, the Canada-U.S. Automotive Agreement was restricted to one sector of the economy and the New Zealand-Australia Free Trade Area was based on trade in forest products. The agreements among developing countries generally involved relatively little commodity and factor trade liberalisation.

Only two RTAs come close to removing all barriers to trade in goods and services, namely the EC and CER. All tariffs and quantitative restrictions were eliminated on the intra-EC trade of the original six by 1968. The Single Market measures will eliminate many other non-tariff barriers when they are implemented; for example, preferences on government procurement across national borders will be lifted and the technical and product standards will be harmonised through mutual recognition. In the case of the CER, all tariffs, import licensing and quantitative restrictions, export incentives and subsidies restricting trade between the two countries were removed by 1 July 1990 and harmonisation of other instruments is proceeding.

For all other RTAs it is not possible to measure with any degree of precision the extent of intra-area trade liberalisation. In this respect, as in other aspects of trade policies, empirical research is severely restricted by the absence of systematic measurement of national trade barriers. Ideally, one needs time series of an aggregate measure of support for all industries in all countries *vis-à-vis* third countries and of the margins of preference *vis-à-vis* member countries. The only comprehensive multi-country series of levels of support is that of producer subsidy equivalents produced by the OECD for most major commodities in the agricultural sector. These data are available on an annual basis since 1979 and measure support *vis-à-vis* all countries. There are no time series of the margins of preference in any RTA.

In the absence of measures of intra-regional trade barriers, one can merely note broad trends. The commodity coverage of most RTAs has been extended; for example, the coverage of the Canada-U.S. FTA and CER greatly exceeds that of the agreements between the countries which they replaced. More agreements now have a timetable which provides for the elimination of tariffs among members, e.g. the Canada-U.S. FTA, the Southern Cone Common Market and the Andean Agreement. Increasingly over the last ten years or so, RTAs have included provisions for eliminating barriers due to non-tariff border measures which have provided an increasing portion of national protection. Hence, though one cannot gauge the extent of intra-area trade liberalisation, one can safely conclude that it has risen substantially in the 1980s under the second generation of more ambitious agreements.

C. Recent developments in RTAs

Trade liberalisation within some RTAs has recently been extended to barriers to trade deriving from non-border measures. Article 24 of the GATT relates solely to border restrictions on trade among members and with outside countries. Most RTAs have been preoccupied with the reduction among members of tariffs, quotas and other border restrictions on trade among members[4]. As an RTA progresses towards the achievement of *complete free trade* within the area in the sense of the total absence of border restrictions, other non-border instruments continue to restrict or distort trade. These include differences in rates of national subsidies and bounties, and in excise, VAT and other commodity tax rates. These distortions can be reduced or removed by harmonisation of policies. These include the harmonisation of standards and business law regulations and competition policy, where differences between member countries inhibit competition. They also include the substitution of an area policy for a border restriction such as the replacement of anti-dumping actions on imports from members of the area by area-wide competition policy.

Extension of the policy measures to non-border taxes and regulations is based on the realisation that *complete equality of access* within an area requires more than the removal of border restrictions. The removal of the border restrictions itself increases the relative importance of the remaining instruments which restrict or distort trade among members. Thus, once the freeing of trade has progressed substantially, there is a force within the agreement which leads to further liberalisation[5]. The two RTAs which have exhibited this progression in a number of areas to date are the EC and more recently

13

the CER. This progression is also evident in the Canada-U.S. FTA in areas such as the recognition of the need for a new anti-dumping regime[6]. The goal of complete freedom of access is, like that of free trade, a means to the end of promoting more efficient production. The ultimate goal is higher real incomes for the residents of these areas.

This leads one to ask when the complete freedom of trade in the sense of equal access to markets is achieved. The EC uses the term a "Single Market". A Single Market is manifestly not a Common Market but what precisely is it? In introducing the Single Market measures, the White Paper began with the statement:

> "Unifying the market (of 320 million) presupposes the member States will agree on the abolition of barriers of all kinds, harmonisation of rules, approximation of legislation and tax structures, strengthening of monetary cooperation and the necessary flanking measures to encourage European firms to work together." (Commission of the European Communities, 1985).

This conveys the essential idea that there should be no barriers to the operation of a single Community-wide market.

Perhaps the best conception of a single market is one in which the Law of One Price prevails. This means that in a competitive market, for either a produced commodity or a factor, there is only one price, allowing for transport and other transfer costs which prevent perfect arbitrage. This concept could be used to measure the degree of achievement of completely free access within RTAs.

These developments in relation to the instruments of government policy and the methods of eliminating restrictions on market access have created new forms of economic integration. With the removal of non-border barriers among members, trade among the members of the EC is now more free than trade between any other countries, including bilateral trade involving partner countries such as Singapore or Hong Kong which have virtually no border restrictions[7]. EC '92 has progressed beyond the conception of free trade in the rules of GATT. Furthermore, the development of some RTAs is associated increasingly with proposals for monetary union and even federation or political union among members. These developments are not considered in this paper.

One may conclude that the number of RTAs and of member countries, and the extent of intra-area trade liberalisation within them, have all steadily increased. The effect on world trade patterns is considered in the next section. RTAs also have important effects on foreign investment and other factor flows and on competition but these are not examined in this paper.

II.   HAS THE WORLD ECONOMY BECOME MORE REGIONALISED?

There are two distinct versions of the claim that world trade has become more regionalised. One relates to trade within RTAs and the other to trade within more broadly defined regions such as Europe and the Pacific Rim. This section considers

RTAs as regions, while Section V considers the broader groupings as a part of the multilateral trading system.

RTAs are of primary interest because they are the regional units which operate trade policies which discriminate against third countries and thereby change the distribution of world trade. However, non-regional trade interventions and transport costs also affect the distribution of trade, and these too have not remained constant. Consequently, the spread of RTAs does not imply a growing regionalisation of world trade. The Tokyo Round, whose last reductions took effect in 1987, has led to further multilateral reductions in tariffs and some non-tariff measures such as government procurement. These reductions have had the dual effect of increasing non-discriminatory trade among GATT Contracting Parties and, as these have applied to the RTAs or their members, of reducing discrimination in these arrangements. In addition, a number of Contracting Parties have undertaken major unilateral reductions in trade barriers. These include over the last decade Japan, Australia, New Zealand and Turkey among OECD Members and a number of developing countries such as Chile, Mexico and Thailand. Conversely, some countries have increased tariffs or non-tariff measures and so too have some regional arrangements, e.g. anti-dumping actions and VERs have increased in the EC countries. The latter interventions only reduce trade flows between the RTA which imposes them and non-member countries since they do not apply to intra-RTA trade.

A. Import trends in four OECD RTAs

To consider the effects of RTAs on trade flows in the presence of multilateral and unilateral changes in trade policies, a preliminary study was made of import trends in the four current RTAs whose member countries are all in the OECD (the EC, EFTA, Canada and the United States, Australia and New Zealand). These high-income RTAs cover "substantially all trade" for the whole or at least part of the period, as in the GATT criterion for a free trade area or customs union. The EC and EFTA countries alone have accounted for 40 per cent or more of total world imports since EFTA was formed in 1960. Moreover, the degree of intra-area freedom of trade and discrimination *vis-à-vis* non-member countries is higher in all four of these RTAs than for any RTA among the non-OECD countries. Consequently, any effects of regionalisation are more likely to show up in these groupings.

Import data are used in preference to export data because trade discrimination policies are applied to imports and because non-zero balances of trade imply that the import shares for some countries and groups of countries diverge from the corresponding export shares. The import data relate to total commodity trade, the broad commodity groups of "Manufactures" and "Non-energy products", and to a small sample of four industries as defined at the two-digit level of the SITC ("Food", "Clothing and textiles", "Iron and steel" and "Passenger motor vehicles"). The broad aggregate of "Manufactures" was chosen because liberalising trade in manufactures has been the major focus in most RTAs, and "Non-energy products" was chosen to exclude the influence of large changes in energy prices relative to prices of other goods. The four two-digit industries were selected because of the importance of trade flows in these areas and the high degree of regional discrimination in the commodities of these industries which results from the combination of free or near-free trade between member countries with relatively high protection against third countries. If discrimination affects the direction of trade flows, one would expect it to show up in time series for such industries. The details of the groupings of countries and commodities are given in the Appendix. The time period of the sample is 1961-89 inclusive. This covers a 30-year period of almost uninterrupted expansion in world trade and it follows the formation of the EEC and EFTA.

Two measures of regionalisation are used. The first is the share of the group in world imports. Because of changes in the membership of some groups (the EC and EFTA) over the period, two definitions of the group are used. When the group is "as at the time" (or ASAT), the series shows the growth of regional trade in the sense of the change in the share of the group in world trade. This measure combines the influences of greater trade liberalisation among member countries with that of an expanding membership. To isolate the effects of intra-area trade liberalisation *per se,* one examines the trend in the shares of a fixed group such as the original members. The import trade shares are also affected by other factors, such as increases in factor productivities in fast-growing countries, which are independent of trade policy. These shares are useful as a measure of the importance of the group in international trade.

The results for this measure are reported in Chart 1. As this measure is regarded as an indicator of the importance of the region in world trade, it is calculated only for all commodities. The data bases provided this measure only for the EC, EFTA and Canada-United States (since 1989) but these are the three most important regional

Chart 1. **OECD RTA'S shares of world imports, 1960-1989**

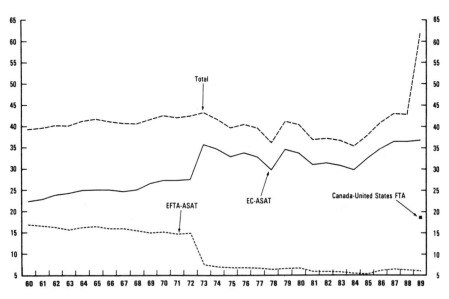

arrangements. Chart 1 shows that the combined shares in world import trade of the EC and EFTA have not tended to increase over the 30-year period. The share of the EC "as at the time" has increased substantially from 22 per cent at the beginning of the period to almost 37 per cent at the end but this is almost wholly due to the addition of the United Kingdom in 1973 and Portugal and Spain in 1986. The total ASAT series for all three groups including North America jumps upwards in 1989 because of the formation of the Canada-U.S. FTA in that year.

The second measure of regionalisation is the share of intra-group trade in the total import trade of the group in the commodities concerned. The intra-group share is the measure commonly used as an indicator of regionalisation, although the share of export trade is sometimes used. The intra-group share of total import trade would increase as a result of the introduction of discrimination within RTAs if there were no changes in trade policies *vis-à-vis* third countries and no other disturbances. In the presence of multilateral and unilateral changes in trade restrictions over the period, this measure captures the combined effects of unilateral, regional and multilateral policy changes. It also captures the effects of differences in the growth rates of countries on import demand and export supply, the effects of major price changes and changes in national preferences and technologies. An increase in the intra-group share is, there-fore, weak evidence of the effects of RTAs on trade patterns. (See Section III for discussion of the interpretation of this measure.)

The intra-group shares of RTA group trade are reported in Charts 2A to 2G[8]. Consider first the EC, EFTA and CER as these three groups have experienced sub-stantial intra-group trade liberalisation over the whole period in the case of the EC and EFTA and since 1965 in the case of CER. The EC and EFTA have had changing membership over the period. For the EC, the most useful definition of the group here is the *original* membership – referred to as EC-6 – as they have been in the group for the whole period. For EFTA, the most useful definition is the original eight (including Finland) plus Iceland less the United Kingdom, Denmark and Portugal which have joined the EC[9]. This group will be called the EFTA-6.

For all merchandise commodities, Chart 2A shows an upward trend in the intra-group share for the EC-6 in the 1960s and early 1970s following the Treaty of Rome, and in the CER. In EFTA-6 the trend is upward until the early 1970s and then down-wards. The same trends are evident in all three regional groups for the series for Non-energy products (Chart 2B), except in the CER where there is no clear trend, and for Manufactures in the case of EFTA. There is no trend in Manufactures in the case of the EC-6 and CER groups, despite the importance of intra-group preferences for this commodity group (Chart 2C).

The peaking of EC-6 and EFTA-6 intra-group import shares around the time the United Kingdom and Denmark moved from EFTA to the EC could be the result of the original formation of the EC and EFTA with the effect of the new members reducing the shares of the intra-EC-6 group. Alternatively, the decline in shares after the early 1970s could be the result of global freeing of trade and/or the declining competitiveness in some industries. To cancel the effects of the shift of members between EFTA and EC, the shares were also considered for the group of EC-12 throughout the period. This shows an upward trend for all commodities in the intra-EC-12 import shares but it is stronger in the period up to 1973, indicating that both the change in membership of the EC and EFTA and the decline in competitiveness contributed to the later fall in these shares.

Chart 2. **Intra-area imports as share of total group imports**

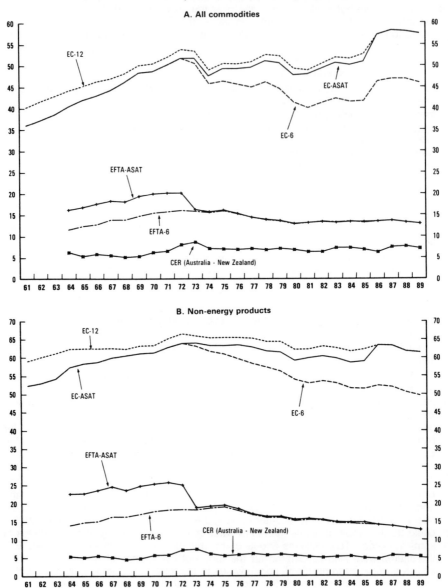

A. All commodities

B. Non-energy products

Chart 2. (continued)

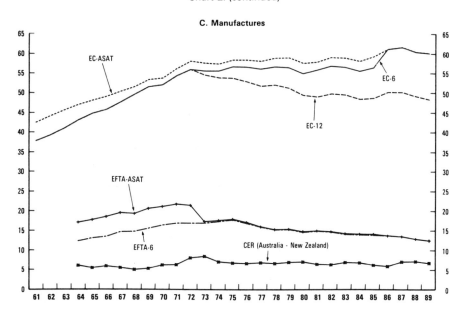

C. Manufactures

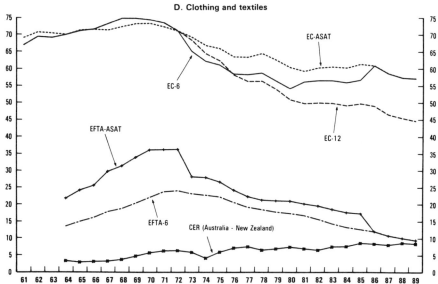

D. Clothing and textiles

19

Chart 2. (continued)

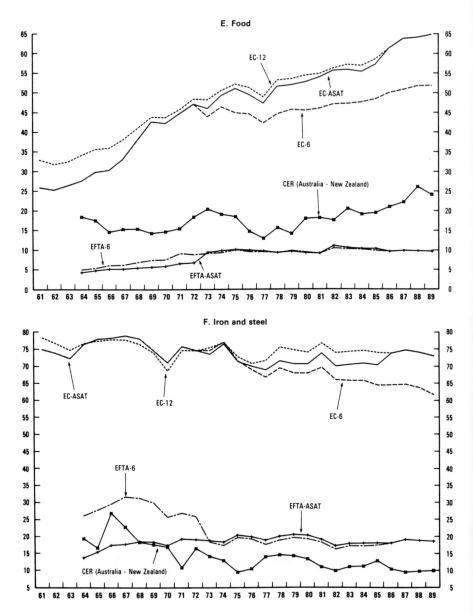

20

Chart 2. (continued)

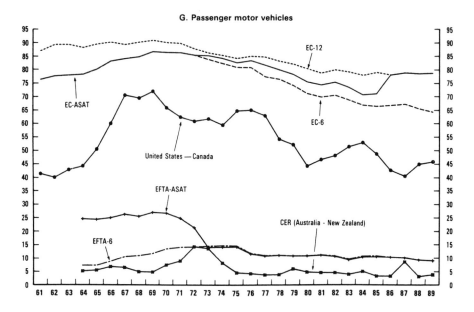

G. Passenger motor vehicles

Data at the disaggregated two-digit level relate to the four industry groups of particular interest and rule out the effects of changes in the composition of import trade by commodity groups. At this level the evidence is very mixed. For both the EC-6 and EC-12, there is a distinct and substantial upward trend in the group share for Food only (Chart 2E). For the other three industrial products, there is an upward trend until the early or middle 1970s, followed by a downward trend. This is especially marked in the case of Clothing and textiles (Chart 2D) which probably reflects the declining competitiveness of the EC-6 and EC-12 for this commodity group relative to the NICs and later a broader group of developing countries which emerged as low-cost producers of these commodities.

For the EFTA-6, there is no trend after the 1960s in the case of Food and no trend in the case of Iron and steel (Chart 2F) and Passenger motor vehicles (Chart 2G). In the case of Clothing and textiles, there is an early upward trend followed by a downward trend, again reflecting the declining competitiveness of the regional group in these commodities.

For the CER, there are upward trends in both Food and clothing and textiles. In the cases of Iron and steel and Passenger motor vehicles, there is a downward trend although the tariff preferences were substantial for most of the period. This reflects primarily the importance of import licensing in New Zealand and secondarily the substantial unilateral liberalisations in both countries.

21

For Canada and the United States, the only commodity group considered is Passenger motor vehicles because substantially free trade has not yet been achieved for other industries. This group shows some upward trend in the early years of the Agreement but a steady downward trend since the share peaked in the mid-1970s, due principally to the increase in imports from Japan.

Overall, these series provide only very weak support for the hypothesis that RTA intra-group preferences increase the share of imports for traded commodities once allowance is made for extensions of membership of the RTAs over time. There is weak evidence at the level of all commodities or broad commodity groups for the OECD groups, mainly in the early years following the formation of the RTAs, but this trend did not continue into the 1980s. At the disaggregated level, the evidence is consistent with the hypothesis only for a few observations of the sample, particularly Food in the EC and CER and Clothing and textiles in the CER.

B. Possible explanations of import trends

The first factor that may explain the contradiction between the expected increase in intra-group import shares and the observed trends for the OECD RTAs is the countervailing influence of multilateral and unilateral reductions in trade barriers. This non-regional liberalisation may be greater than commonly believed. (For this purpose one should include the introduction of non-reciprocal trade preferences to developing countries and association agreements, although in most cases they have had only a small effect on trade flows.) Second, there is also a tendency to exaggerate the restrictiveness of non-tariff measures which apply exclusively or predominantly to third countries. The series of NTM's compiled by UNCTAD and the World Bank relate to the incidence of these measures, not to the height of the barriers. Some of the measures which receive a lot of publicity affect only small volumes of trade, e.g. anti-dumping duties. Some NTMs are rather ineffective in restraining total imports of the commodity groups concerned. Those which apply selectively to individual countries, such as VERs, induce substitution towards imports from other non-restricted countries. Those which apply to narrowly defined commodity groups induce substitution of closely related commodities. Quantitative restrictions induce quality and unit value upgrading (see Baldwin, 1982, for a general thesis that NTMs are ineffective). Geographically, the increasing use of NTMs in the EC and United States has received publicity but the decline in levels of protection in Japan and the Asian region as a whole (see Stoeckel, Pearce and Banks, 1990, Chapter 2) has received less attention. Finally, one needs to recall that the extent of regional freeing of trade can be exaggerated as all RTAs retain some distortions of intra-RTA trade.

A second factor in interpreting these results is the effect on import shares of changes in competitiveness and comparative advantage, as in the cases of Clothing and textiles and of Passenger motor vehicles noted above. In such cases it may be that the crude group import share decreased reflecting a loss of competitiveness, but the share would have increased in the absence of changes in competitiveness. Hence, the intra-group preferences (and in some cases unilateral increases in protection) may have limited the decrease in the group shares. Viewing these trends from the point of view of third countries, one could say that the intra-group preferences did not prevent some growth in the level of imports from low-cost suppliers in third countries.

To derive the relative importance of regional freeing of trade one would need to regress the country/region shares of individual commodity markets on variables reflecting multilateral, regional and unilateral trade policy changes and such changes in prices, incomes or technologies and other non-price factors as are considered important. This would be a major and difficult research project which is beyond the scope of the present study.

The next section considers how to interpret the change in shares due to the introduction of discrimination within RTAs and other effects of RTAs on trade and welfare, especially in third countries.

III.   THE DIRECT EFFECTS OF RTAs ON WORLD TRADE AND WELFARE

The formation of an RTA is a major perturbation of the economies of the member countries and sometimes of third countries because it changes many relative commodity prices. These commodity price changes induce changes in factor prices and in market competition. An RTA, therefore, affects the welfare of households in these economies in a complex way, both as consumers and as income earners. There is a large literature which analyses these effects. The classic survey of the earlier literature is by Lipsey (1960). A recent survey is provided by Pomfret (1988, Chapters 7 and 8). In order to interpret the trends noted in the previous section, this section concentrates on the effects of regional trade liberalisation on trade and third-country welfare. The discussion is restricted to Developed Countries. (Langhammer and Hiemenz, 1990, provide an excellent survey of the theory and empirical studies for Developing Countries.)

A.   Trade creation, trade diversion and other effects

Viner (1950) introduced the concern over the effects of "trade diversion" on countries' welfare which has remained central to the analysis of RTAs ever since. The term was used before Viner but there was no clear definition or perception of its implications. Viner described "trade diversion" as a shift in the location of production from a low-cost source of supply outside the RTA to a high-cost source in another member country within the RTA. He contrasted it with the second type of trade effect, "trade creation", which is a shift in the location of production from a high-cost domestic source to a lower-cost source within the RTA. This distinction arises only because of the discriminatory nature of reductions in an RTA which will sometimes affect commodity markets in the same manner as a non-discriminatory reduction but will at other times divert the pattern of trade from that which would occur in the absence of discrimination. Viner's conclusion was definite:

"Where the trade-creating force is predominant, one of the members at least must benefit, both may benefit, the two combined must have a net benefit, and the world

23

at large benefits; but the outside world loses, in the short run at least ... Where the trade-diverting effect is predominant, one at least of the member countries is bound to be injured, the two combined will suffer a net injury, and there will be injury to the outside world and to the world at large." (Viner, 1950, p. 44).

Vinerian trade diversion is a terms-of-trade effect due to the switch of sources of import supply. When increasing costs are introduced, third countries may continue to supply some of the imported country in the post-RTA situation along with the member country. The quantity of trade diverted is ambiguous. The decrease in the market shares of third countries exaggerates the value of trade diverted, even in a partial equilibrium context, because the consumption effect increases total imports. Furthermore, in a world characterised by globalised production and trade, trade creation may benefit third-country firms operating in the region and trade diversion may harm member country firms with production facilities in third countries and exporting to the region "... indicators such as trade creation or trade diversion may lose much of their significance in the context of globalisation" (Julius, 1990). The concepts of trade creation and trade diversion are of no use in the presence of decreasing costs as trade liberalisation causes substantial changes in the set of commodities produced by countries.

As models with a more complex structure and higher dimensions in terms of the number of traded commodities were constructed, it became clear that the formation of an RTA has a number of other effects which may outweigh those of trade diversion for a member country or third countries. There are induced changes in the volume of trade with both members and non-members, changes in the terms of trade with the Rest of the World and in the value of national output. All of these may be positive or negative for a country. It is not necessary that the value of imports from third countries falls even if trade diversion predominates. The changes in relative prices and the growth in real income of the RTA may induce new trade with non-members. This has been called "external trade creation". Nor is it necessary that the terms of trade of the Rest of the World will decline, as commonly supposed, though this occurs under plausible assumptions (Mundell, 1964 and Riezman, 1979). This terms-of-trade effect is crucial to the welfare of outside countries.

With some hindsight, the early emphasis placed on the theory of trade diversion and trade creation can be seen to have been misplaced. The phenomenon of trade diversion was recognised as a problem of the Theory of the Second Best and it was shown that the importing country does not necessarily lose in such instances. Kowalczyk (1990) argues that the concepts of trade diversion and trade creation should be abandoned and be replaced by the terms-of-trade and trade volume effects which are used in other areas of the theory of distorted economies. Vinerian trade diversion is just one kind of terms-of-trade effect. The concept of trade diversion focused on the importing member country excessively and biased the analysis against finding welfare gains for the members and the third countries.

Most of the formal literature has assumed that the real value of national output (as distinct from real national income) of member countries is fixed and therefore unaffected by the formation of an RTA. Lipsey's influential survey mentioned the possibilities of increasing real output due to greater exploitation of economies of scale, improvements in input productivity and faster growth but these were treated as an afterthought. These factors received some attention in the earlier literature on European integration (see especially, Scitovsky, 1956, and Balassa, 1961) but the analysis was simplistic because of the inability of general equilibrium theory at that time to handle production with economies of scale and/or imperfect competition. Moreover, changes in factor prices associated with the changes in national output interact with the commodity price effects and may change the pattern of commodity trade.

B. Empirical studies

Many empirical studies have attempted to identify the signs of the effects which economic theory predicts are ambiguous. Until recently, most have been limited to the effects on trade rather than estimating directly the effects on countries' welfare, have failed to distinguish between trade volume and terms-of-trade effects and have been partial equilibrium in nature, not taking account of changes in factor prices and incomes.

The EC-6 is by far the most studied of the actual RTAs. There are several surveys of this literature, including Balassa (1975), Robson (1984, pp. 192-203) and Pomfret (1988, Chapter 8). Robson (1984, p. 200) concluded that:

"... for manufactured products (to which most of the studies are limited) the trade created was considerable and far outweighed trade diverted .... Secondly, several of the studies suggested that the formation of the EEC has resulted in a good deal of external trade creation. From both points of view it may be concluded that the effects of the EEC have been favourable to allocative efficiency at a global level."

This positive view of trade in manufactures is shared by most empirical researchers, though Pomfret (1988, Chapter 8) disputes it, denying in particular that there is any evidence of "external trade creation". With respect to agriculture, the consensus is that the CAP has resulted in substantial trade diversion and losses of income for agricultural exporting countries through a fall in world prices for commodities covered by the CAP. With respect to the growth effects, Pomfret (1988, pp. 134-135) concludes:

"There is no empirical evidence that additional scale economies or X-efficiency gains have resulted from the customs union. There is some evidence that the EC benefited from additional direct foreign investment and especially from terms-of-trade gains, but both of these involve redistribution rather than net gains to the world."

Balassa (1975) estimates that the welfare gain to the EC, after netting out the trade diversion in agricultural products, was less than one-tenth of 1 per cent of the members' GNP. Incorporating economies of scale in manufacturing industries but still using essentially partial equilibrium analysis, Owens (1983) obtained much larger benefits of between 3 and 6 per cent of the GDP of the original six.

C. Computable general equilibrium modelling results

In the last decade the techniques available for analysing RTAs have improved dramatically with the advent of multi-country, multi-sector computable general equilibrium (CGE) models. These were pioneered by Whalley (see especially, Whalley, 1985). He concludes:

> "... geographically discriminating protection that leaves average protection levels much the same seems to have small effects on the protecting region, with the largest effects detrimental to the region discriminated against and to the advantage of the region favoured by discrimination." (Whalley, 1985, p. 215).

This reaffirms the importance of terms-of-trade effects. The advent of CGE methods is undoubtedly a significant advance but some economists believe that the low foreign trade substitution elasticities usually adopted with the Armington assumption concerning nationally differentiated commodities in the Whalley model exaggerate the magnitude of these terms-of-trade effects (for example, Harrison and Rutstrom, 1991, footnotes 1 and 7).

The latest advance in CGE modelling has been the incorporation of economies of scale and imperfect competition. These models were first used to study unilateral or multilateral trade liberalisation, beginning with the pioneering studies of Canada by Harris (1984) and Harris and Cox (1984). Trade liberalisation in this class of models has been surveyed by Richardson (1989) and Norman (1990).

CGE models with economies of scale and imperfect competition have now been adapted to measure *ex ante* the effects of prospective or proposed RTAs. The prospective completion of the European Single Market in 1992 has been studied by Smith and Venables (1988). The Canada-U.S. Free Trade Area was studied extensively at the time of its proposal in models of this type by Brown and Stern (1988), Canada (1988), Hazeldine (1989) and Markusen and Wigle (1988). The GET model, which descended from the earlier work in Canada by Harris and Cox, was commissioned and used by the Canadian Government in its negotiation of the Canada-U.S. Free Trade Area and to convince the Canadian public of the benefits of the FTA proposal. The Australian Government's Bureau of Industry Economics (1989) used a Harris and Cox-type model to evaluate the effects of CER.

These models have generally predicted larger gains to the member countries than were obtained from traditional competitive industry versions of the general equilibrium models. Regional trade liberalisation in these models leads to gains in the form of increased competition, reduced unit costs and greater product variety which are additional to those quantified in standard models. When these gains are measured by the percentage increase in real income, they are often two or three times larger than those estimated under perfect competition. For example, Smith and Venables (1988) predict that the completion of the EC's internal market will lead to more than three times the gain from trade liberalisation alone. This is due to the increased competition as production for a single market eliminates the ability of domestic firms to charge higher prices on nationally segmented markets. Curiously, this effect tends to reduce the value of intra-EC trade because it lowers the price of domestically-produced goods *vis-à-vis* imported goods.

One difficulty with these imperfectly competitive models is that the quantitative results are very sensitive to variations in the specifications of the models such as the form of strategic interaction between oligopolistic firms or the presence of free entry and exit from industries. Very few of the model parameters are estimated econometrically. Consequently, they should be regarded as indicative thought experiments rather than reliable predictions but they have changed the perception of the benefits and costs of RTAs. In particular, they have emphasised the benefits of increased competition.

The predicted effect of RTAs from the viewpoint of third countries seems now to be regarded more positively, though there is still concern over terms-of-trade effects. This is partly due to the accumulated consensus that trade diversion is less important and partly to the increased emphasis on the real income effects. These real income effects, unlike the price effects of discriminatory border protection reductions, are almost certain to benefit the outside countries collectively because of the increased demand for most goods and services. It is possible that they could favour third countries over other members and lead to an increase in the extra-area share of trade. These effects may be substantial. For example, the European Commission's own estimates of the Single Market in Cecchini (1988) and Emerson *et al.* (1988) predicted an increase in real Community GDP of between 2.5 to 6.5 per cent, most of which is attributed to the realisation of economies of scale and increased competition. Baldwin (1989) suggests even more optimistically that the reforms could lead to a permanent increase in the EC GDP growth rate of at least 0.6 percentage points a year. The effects will differ among third countries, depending chiefly upon the links of the third-country economy and firms with the region and the world economy.

The concern now has shifted to the possibility that the RTAs may adopt restrictive trade policies *vis-à-vis* third countries or they may engage in trade wars with other blocs. The next section considers the long-term effects of RTAs on the multilateral trading system.

IV. IS THERE A CONFLICT BETWEEN REGIONALISATION AND MULTILATERALISM?

All RTAs are discriminatory by definition. Indeed, that is their distinguishing feature. Since its formation the GATT has been primarily concerned with the effects of regional arrangements on third-country producers. Under Article 24 the GATT recognised free trade areas and customs unions as acceptable exceptions to the principle of non-discrimination, provided they met certain conditions. They must not adopt tariff duties or other border restrictions which are more restrictive on average than those previously applied, they must have a plan and schedule for the formation of the customs union or area and, in the case of a free trade area, they must apply to "substantially all the trade" between members. Article 24 states "... The purpose of a customs union or of a free trade area should be to facilitate trade between the constituent territories and not to raise barriers to the trade of other contracting parties with such territories."

Of the more than 70 arrangements under Article 24 which have been reviewed by the GATT, only four were declared fully compatible with the Article and all of these were lesser agreements among non-OECD countries. However, no agreement was declared incompatible with the Article. [The 1979 Decision on Differential and More Favourable

Treatment for Developing Countries (known as the Enabling Clause) exempted these countries from the requirement to meet the criteria of Article 24.] Other GATT members have raised concerns over the "substantially all trade" requirement, the failure in some cases to meet the timetable requirement, external trade policies and other features. A number of suggestions have been made in the Uruguay Round negotiations to tighten the application of Article 24 and in particular to reduce the adverse effects of discrimination on third countries.

A.   Tariff wars and game theory

The direct effects of discriminatory trade policies were considered in the previous section. RTAs may also affect the multilateral trading system in a number of ways other than the direct effects. For example, formation of trading blocs may lead to conflict among them and even to an outbreak of restrictions on trade between two or more RTAs or members of such RTAs and to retaliatory actions. This could be precipitated by RTAs or large member countries seeking to use their bargaining power to obtain policies in trading partners which they consider fairer. It could also be precipitated by a desire to improve the terms of trade of a trading group.

There is a recent literature, confined almost exclusively to the United States and Canada, which applies game theory to trade between blocs and the formation of blocs. The earlier customs union literature proceeded on the assumption that the common external tariff is fixed, i.e. it cannot be adjusted. In a well-known paper Johnson (1958) analysed the optimal tariff for two countries (or two trading blocs) to maximise the welfare of members when each can retaliate repeatedly in a tariff war. This produced the result that both countries normally lose from a tariff war, although the country initiating the war can gain. (The world as a whole, of course, is always best off under free trade.) This result went unchallenged for a long time. Johnson's tariff war equilibrium was later recognised as the solution of a two-person non-zero-sum game in which the countries or blocs are the players. Using a more general two-player game model, Keenan and Riezman (1988) found that if one country is substantially bigger than the other, it can expect to gain from retaliation – big countries win trade wars. In doing so, they impose losses on the smaller countries. Keenan and Riezman (1990) extended the model to three players. This introduces the possibility of different coalitions of two players (there are three possibilities with three players). The game becomes a two-stage game, the first stage being the choice of partner and the second the choice of optimal tariff for each player. This is a much richer game. The prospects of countries gaining from the formation of customs unions are greater with three players, and again the larger the union the more likely it is to gain.

These game theory models can also be used to compare free trade areas, which do not have a common external tariff policy, with customs union which do. Keenan and Riezman (1990) compare the advantages to two countries of forming either a free trade area or a customs union when there is a third country. They show that a customs union has two advantages in this context. It is a larger bloc for the purpose of setting optimal tariffs, and it internalises a "tariff externality" which exists when both members import the same good. The latter effect is due to the induced improvement in the terms of trade which benefits both countries when only one imposes a tariff on imports from the third outside country.

28

Such game theory models are grossly simplified in structure and they assume an ability to retaliate which is not realistic in the present multilateral system. They are also based on the assumption that countries act in the interest of the country as a whole rather than in that of particular groups of producer or consumer agents. This implies too that the country ignores the interests of the Rest of the World. These assumptions may not be realistic. For example, it is a notable fact that for approaching 200 years the leading economy in the world (first the United Kingdom and then the United States) has vigorously promoted trade liberalisation.

Nevertheless, these models are suggestive. They highlight the importance of terms-of-trade effects and, following from that, the importance of the external tariff policy of RTAs. They will have more real world appeal if the world trading system becomes less co-operative, and in this respect they parallel the development of "strategic trade policies" based on the market power and strategies of large oligopolistic firms.

B. Possible coalescence of RTAs

It has also been suggested that the extension of RTAs may inhibit multilateral trade liberalisation by providing an alternative for some trade partners that is faster than the protracted GATT multilateral negotiations.

A central question is whether RTAs will proliferate or, alternatively, whether they will be a way of progressing towards global freeing of trade by extending the country coverage. In the latter case they could extend until possibly the world economy is one bloc, the so-called grand coalition. Progress towards completely free global trade could occur via continual multilateral trade reductions, or unilateral reductions, or the coalescence of areas that have achieved intra-area free trade, or some combination of these.

The coalescence prospect is predicted by Kemp and Wan (1976). They showed that a customs union could be beneficial to all its members if the common external tariff is adjusted so that the terms of trade are unchanged and members who would lose are compensated by lump-sum payments among members of the group. The obvious problem with this optimistic scenario is the difficulty of arranging payments among members, whether lump-sum or not, though Grinols (1981) has proposed a method of compensation. There are also problems of which partners to select.

The predicted outcome is very different in the game theory models without compensation payments and with competitive tariff-fixing. These models show that countries have a motive for forming a customs union and moving away from global free trade if they can adjust their external tariffs. (Other motives for RTAs are surveyed by Pomfret, 1988, Chapter 9.)

C. RTAs and multilateral trade negotiations

On the other hand, it is possible that regional trade liberalisation may reinforce multilateral trade liberalisation. It could do so in a number of ways. By making member countries more competitive and international trade-oriented, it might reduce protectionist pressures. RTAs can act as a model for multilateral trade liberalisation, especially in areas of non-tariff measures and services trade where the GATT record in achieving multilateral reduction has been less successful. The costs of transacting agreements may be lower in RTAs with few countries and less diverse preferences and cost structures than in many-country multilateral negotiations. Member countries may reduce import barriers for third countries to avoid trade diversion and to gain access to the lowest-cost imported inputs. Third countries may pursue unilateral liberalisation as they press for multilateral liberalisation in order to gain from the opportunities of trading with an expanding RTA. The EC, NAFTA and CER members have at times exemplified all of these aspects.

Work done at the OECD has concluded that there appears to be a strong case in favour of regionalism in pushing forward the multilateral liberalisation process, though it adds that this result hinges on the RTAs having an outward orientation. After a survey of the historical experience of the EC and 10 RTAs involving Developing Countries, the World Bank (1991, pp. 107-108) emphasised the dangers of inward-looking agreements and stressed that unilateral and multilateral liberalisation are preferable to the formation of trading blocs. One may note that many RTA member countries in more recent years have simultaneously pursued unilateral and regional trade liberalisation, e.g. Australia, Chile, Mexico, New Zealand and Thailand.

Practical questions of market access to major trading partners may also be decisive. Countries which are left out of blocs fear that their access to major markets will deteriorate. They may seek to join an RTA, preferably with one or more large fellow members, in order to improve their market access as well as their bargaining power. The developing countries as a group fear that they may lose market access if they are not part of a major group or if trade wars between blocs occur (see Emmerij, 1989).

Numerous proposals have been put forward for new arrangements in recent years, especially in the Pacific and North American regions. Over the last five years or so proposals have been made for new bilateral RTAs between the United States on the one hand and Australia, ASEAN, Japan, Korea and Taiwan on the other. In the cases of Japan, Korea, Taiwan and ASEAN, these advanced as far as the preparation, at the request of the U.S. Congress, of reports by the U.S. International Trade Commission on the "pros and cons" of each proposal. There have been other proposals for trilateral RTAs. The most important of these is the proposed North American Free Trade Area. The President of the United States has put forward an Enterprise for the Americas Initiative whose ultimate objective is a free trade zone embracing North and South America. There have also been proposals for multi-nation Pacific groupings. These began with the proposal in 1966 for a free trade area involving the five developed Pacific countries, the United States, Japan, Canada, Australia and New Zealand (Kojima, 1966). The latest proposal is one by Malaysia for an East Asian Economic Group including the ASEAN countries and possibly Japan and other Asian countries. (For a discussion of these proposals up to 1988, see Schott, 1989a,b).

The proximate cause of the proposals to form free trade areas with the United States was the ending by the United States in the early 1980s of its previous opposition to new geographically discriminatory trade arrangements. This *volte face* in its attitude and its current interest in bilateral free trade areas is attributed mainly to two factors: *i)* U.S. disillusionment with GATT progress in achieving multilateral improvements in market access; and *ii)* the concern over "unfair" trading practices overseas which many U.S. politicians blame for their persistent balance of payments deficits (see Schott (1989a) and Pomfret (1988, pp. 89-93). Another general concern is the fear of competition with other RTAs and the economic security from largeness.

The attractiveness of regional arrangements will depend significantly upon the outcome of the Uruguay Round and the future of the GATT system. Many of the proposed RTAs are defensive in character. In the Pacific Rim the RTAs are fewer in number and less advanced in form. United States acceptance of the Canada-U.S. FTA was largely based on frustration with the difficulties of launching the Uruguay Round and as a vehicle for underlining the significance which it attached to the new issues of trade in services, intellectual property and investment. This is even more true of the various Pacific Rim proposals. While the Pacific countries are concerned about the possible emergence of "Fortress Europe", the prevailing opinion in all Pacific countries, at least in official pronouncements, has been strongly in favour of the multilateral route towards trade liberalisation. For example, the 1989 Asia Pacific Economic Cooperation (APEC) agreement among 12 countries is not an RTA and one of its basic principles is that "cooperation should be directed at strengthening the open multilateral trading system; it should not involve the formation of a trading bloc" (APEC, 1989, p. 6).

D.   RTAs may reinforce the decline of non-discrimination

A third aspect of the relationship between RTAs and the multilateral trading system is the indirect effects on the principle of non-discrimination via other discriminatory practices. Several of the RTAs or countries which are members of RTAs operate additional preferences for non-member countries. The EC maintains a multi-layer system of trade preferences which gives preferences to most of its trading partners outside the EC. (In this context the reciprocal association agreements with the EFTA countries, four Mediterranean countries and Andorra should be excluded as they are an extension of the EC free trading area.) There is the Lome IV Convention with more than sixty countries, the Community GSP, the co-operation agreements with seven North African countries and Yugoslavia, and the Agreements with six central and eastern European countries[10]. The Canada-U.S. and Australia-New Zealand RTAs operate similar though less extensive multi-layer systems. The United States introduced new non-reciprocal preferences for Caribbean countries in 1963 (and a reciprocal agreement with Israel in the same year) and Canada has a co-operation agreement with the Caribbean Common Market. Both the United States and Canada operate GSP schemes. Australia and New Zealand grant non-reciprocal preferences on a wide range of imports to 11 members of the South Pacific Forum under the 1981 SPARTECA Agreement, both countries operate GSP-type schemes for developing countries, and Australia grants additional preferences to Papua Niugini. In total, these amount to a network of preferences associated with RTAs that has been spreading continually.

The principle of non-discrimination has also been breached with increasing frequency by actions under the MFA and Article 19 of the GATT, the growth of voluntary export restraint agreements and other non-global quantitative restrictions outside GATT regulations. In this context, the discriminatory nature of RTAs themselves and the further discriminations through RTA-based preferences and association agreements and RTA-operated discriminatory NTMs have contributed to the decline in the commitment to non-discrimination in the multilateral system.

V. THE TRIPOLAR VIEW OF THE WORLD

Much of the recent discussion is in terms of a tripolar view of the world, with the United States, Japan and the EC being the three poles (see, for example, Aho and Ostry, 1990; Lorenz, 1990; and Stoeckel, Pearce and Banks, 1990). These three are the biggest traders in the world economy and each is the centre of trading for many other countries based on geographical ties, preference systems and investment links. A more recent concern is over the possibility that the world economy could become essentially bipolar if the United States, Japan and other Pacific Rim countries formed a new bloc.

A. A test of the hypothesis of polarisation

The hypothesis that the world is becoming more polarised in terms of trade flows is tested in the same manner as the RTA version of the regionalisation view of the world was examined in Section II. For this purpose, only the total commodity trade of each "region" is considered since all commodities form part of the influence of the pole and the region. The country groups relevant here are OECD Europe, North America (the United States and Canada) and Asia (Japan, Hong Kong, Korea, Taiwan and the ASEAN countries).

Data on the crude shares of world imports for these three "regions" are reported in Chart 3. They show that the import share of western Europe has been remarkably constant throughout the period at just over 40 per cent and that of North America has been roughly constant at around 15-17 per cent, with some increase in the second half of the 1980s. The Asian share of world imports has almost doubled over this period reflecting the impressive economic performance of this group of countries.

The intra-area import shares as a measure of the concentration of trade within these areas are reported in Chart 4. For OECD Europe, this measure has tended to increase throughout the period, from 56.4 per cent in 1964 to a peak of 69 per cent in 1987. For North America, this share is much lower and has fallen from a peak of 40.5 per cent in 1969 to only 27.5 per cent in 1988. For Asia, the intra-region share roughly doubled between 1964 and 1988 from 20 to 41 per cent[11]. However, this is primarily due to the fact that the total (import) trade of countries in the region has grown faster than trade in other countries and not to regionally discriminatory trade policies as there has been much less trade discrimination in the Asian region than in Europe and North America. If there were no change in trade policies and competitiveness, faster growth within a region would itself increase the share of intra-area trade, even if the shares of export markets were constant.

Thus, one may conclude from the evidence in Chart 4 that there is a tendency for world trade to become more regionalised in terms of broadly-defined regions as western Europe and Asia have tended to trade increasingly within their own area. Earlier studies for the post-World War II period (see Pomfret, 1988, pp. 180-83) and the pre-World War II period (see Sautter, 1983), showed no tendency towards regionalisation.

32

Chart 3. **Shares of world imports accounted for by the three poles**

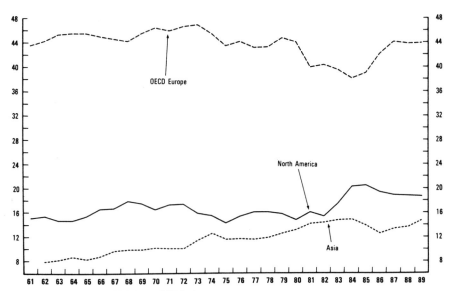

Source: North America and OECD Europe: OECD database;
Asia: UN Comtrade database.
Note: The data for Asia contain some missing observations
for certain countries.

However, the changes in the Asian region at least are not attributable to discriminatory trade policies.

One feature of the more broadly-defined regions is the change in the definitions of the broad groups themselves. Since 1960 several major groupings have collapsed and disappeared. These include the Sterling Area countries, the system of British Imperial (later British Commonwealth) Preferences and most recently the COMECON. These collapses were associated with the decline of the polar power in the grouping, namely, the United Kingdom and the USSR, respectively. Similarly, some RTA groupings in Africa and the Caribbean have collapsed or merged with others. This long-term instability in the groupings reinforces the conclusion that there is no clear polarisation of the world economy.

B.   Greater integration of the world economy

The GATT (1990, p. 36) has concluded that the world economy has become more "integrated" in each of the post-war decades. Their main indicator of integration is the trend in the rate of growth of the volume of trade relative to the rate of growth of real

33

Chart 4. **Intra-area imports as share of total imports:
all commodities**

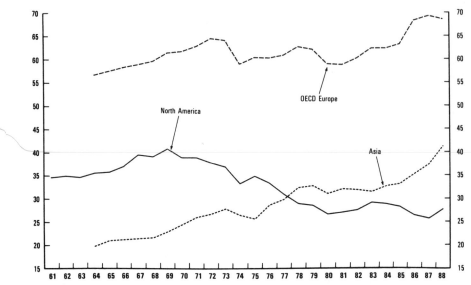

Source: North America and OECD Europe: OECD Database;
Asia: UN Comtrade database.
Note: The data for Asia contain some missing observations
for certain countries.

output in the world economy. As the world as a whole is a closed economy, this implies an increase in the ratios of imports/consumption and of exports/production on average, though not necessarily for all countries. These ratios are more relevant for the welfare of countries than intra-group shares in group trade or group shares of world trade as they reflect directly the benefits of more efficient global production resulting from greater specialisation in the world economy. Integration in this sense could occur at the same time as regionalisation or polarisation, but the sustaining of this trend over decades indicates that the benefits of increased international exchange have been widespread and have dominated the trend towards regionalisation and polarisation.

VI. CONCLUSIONS

The numbers of both RTAs and the countries which are members of them have been growing steadily. The extent of the intra-area liberalisation of trade barriers has also increased for both tariffs and non-tariff measures alike. Some RTAs are now addressing non-border measures which distort intra-area production and trade and harmonising other policies which affect trade. The second generation of RTAs among the OECD members (EC, CER and Canada-United States FTA) are evolving towards the achievement of single markets with completely free access and a greater degree of co-ordination of policies within the arrangements.

These moves have led to a widespread perception of a growing regionalisation of world trade. However, the empirical evidence for four major OECD RTAs does not support this view. There is only weak evidence that the intra-group shares of total group imports for the four RTAs considered have increased over the last 30 years, and this applies to the OECD groupings mainly in the years following the agreements. Similarly, for individual commodity groups with significant discrimination which could be expected to show these trends more clearly, there is again only weak evidence of regionalisation with the exception of trade in agricultural products. The shares of RTAs in total world trade have increased but this is explained in large part by the increase in membership of the RTAs and in any case it is a measure of the importance of these countries in world trade rather than of regionalisation.

A central question is whether the formation of RTAs conflicts with multilateralism and threatens the world multilateral trading system. There are several aspects to this question. RTAs are by definition discriminatory, but this does not itself imply that the direct trading effects harm third countries and the world trading system.

RTAs affect the multilateral system in a number of ways other than the direct effects of discrimination. One concern is that they could lead to retaliatory actions or even to trade wars. Recent applications of game theory confirm this is a danger if countries were free to retaliate and the co-operation involved in the multilateral system were absent. Larger countries or blocs could win trade wars at the expense of small countries. On the other hand, RTAs may progress towards global free trade by coalescing and encouraging multilateral reductions. The predictions of economic theory differ on these aspects depending on the availability of intra-area compensation and other factors. There is evidence that some RTAs have assisted multilateral trade liberalisation. A third aspect is the spread of preferences from RTAs or countries which are members of RTAs to third countries. The growth of RTAs and other RTA-associated trade discrimination has contributed to the decline in the commitment to the principle of non-discrimination in the multilateral system. These systemic effects may be the most serious consequence of the spread of RTAs.

The question of regionalisation is sometimes put in terms of the growing importance of more broadly-defined regions. Currently this view is in terms of the groups around three poles, the United States, Japan and the EC. There has been a tendency for world trade to become more regionalised in the OECD Europe and Asian regions but in the case of Asia this cannot be attributable to discriminatory trade policies.

Moreover, over the longer term, the major groupings have changed as some groupings have collapsed.

There is a current spate of new arrangements and a number of prospective candidates for future RTAs are being considered. There may, therefore, be a greater danger of regionalisation in the future. The United States in particular has abandoned its historical opposition to new discriminatory arrangements. Many of these current proposals are defensive, showing a concern over the dangers of trade conflicts and seeking economic security from largeness. The attractiveness of regional arrangements will depend significantly upon the outcome of the Uruguay Round and the future of the GATT-based system.

A number of aspects of regional trade need to be investigated further. The extent and timing of changes in intra-area trade policies within regional trade arrangements should be carefully tracked. The same should be done for actions with respect to third countries to ascertain whether these arrangements have restricted trade with outside countries. Article 24 of the GATT which covers regional trade arrangements needs to be examined, especially from the point of view of the effects of RTAs on third countries. An attempt might be made to estimate the net effect of regional variables *vis-à-vis* other variables in a sample of markets subject to regional discrimination[12]. These studies could be extended to more RTAs and regions and to a longer time period, and a detailed examination of the history of RTAs could reveal more of the economic and political motivations for forming and expanding them. The effects of harmonising domestic policies and the movement towards monetary and political union in some RTAs should be investigated. Increasing freedom of movement of factors within RTAs will have direct productivity effects and may substantially change the patterns of production and trade among members in ways which are poorly understood at present. The conclusions presented in the previous paragraphs, therefore, may be sharpened or modified as further research throws more light on the way in which RTAs have developed. And the future may not repeat the past.

NOTES

1. This excludes the earlier preference schemes, such as the British Imperial Preferences, which were accepted under the grandfather clause of the GATT. Schott, 1989*b*, Annex A provides an incomplete list up to 1988. The very first was an interim customs agreement between France and Italy concluded in 1947.

2. This takes no account of the collapse of COMECON in 1989-90. The economies of the COMECON countries were essentially closed to trade with western economies and the agreement was outside the GATT.

3. Technically, the free movement of labour between Australia and New Zealand was provided by a separate agreement, the Trans-Tasman Travel Agreement, which preceded the trade agreement.

4. The Treaty of Rome contained some features which went beyond the removal of border restrictions. These included the provisions relating to the harmonisation of standards and the approximation of commodity taxes and competition law, but they were limited in effectiveness.

5. It can be argued that restrictions on trade set up the same form of momentum in reverse, leading to further restrictions on substitute or downstream commodities which are adversely affected.

6. There are few studies of this aspect of RTAs. The EC history is well known. For an account of the evolution of the CER, see Lloyd (1987). Hart (1989) reviews the treatment of dumping in free trade areas and customs unions.

   A second related trend is the development of new means of harmonising national instruments. The EC'92 measures contain a "new approach" to harmonisation based on the principle of Mutual Recognition of each others' standards. The EC has also used this method in the area of recognition of professional training, for certification in professional bodies. The *Cassis de Dijon* decision of the European Court in 1978 ruled that a product which was sold legally in the market of one member country can enter without restriction the markets of another member country, even if it does not meet the standards of this country. This made a policy of Mutual Recognition enforceable.

   The adoption of mutual recognition in place of attempts to achieve harmonisation by agreement among all members on a single uniform standard has, in turn, changed the process of harmonisation and the legal and political structure of policy making. In the longer term it will lead to the convergence of standards because of competition between government jurisdictions. Siebert (1989) refers to this as "*ex post*" harmonisation in contrast to "*ex ante*" harmonisation by prior agreement.

7. Agriculture in the EC is an exception as intra-EC trade is still distorted by "green rates" which differ from market exchange rates and by other regulations.

8. The time-series data on the import shares in these figures are available from the author on request.

9. Wijkman (1991) gives a detailed account of the trade patterns of the EFTA and the EC countries.

10. These arrangements are conveniently described in GATT (1991, Chapter II.8). This does not include the Agreement with East Germany. Since October 1990 Community law has applied to the territory of the former East Germany.

11. The data for Asia contain some missing observations for certain countries. In particular, there was no observations for imports into the Philippines in 1987 and Korea in 1988 in the data supplied by the UN.

12. One difficulty with empirical studies is that the great majority of countries do not have adequate estimates of trade restrictions *vis-à-vis* the rest of the world because of the absence of measures of non-tariff protection or assistance. However, there are statistics for some commodity groups (e.g. the OECD PSE series for agricultural commodities) and for some countries (e.g. the United States, Australia and

37

New Zealand) and some instruments (e.g. VERs and other export restraints). The data problem is even more severe for discriminatory trade policies such as partial tariff preferences or special partner country import quotas. Fortunately, discrimination in regional trading arrangements is increasingly associated with the removal of all tariff and NTM restrictions on trade among member countries so that the rate of protection *vis-à-vis* third countries measures the intra-area margin of preference.

Appendix

NOTES ON DATA AND DEFINITIONS

A. Definition of a region

Two concepts of a region are used in the study.

1. *Regional trading arrangements*

Four such groups are examined:

i) The European Community (EC)
Period:1958-72 (inclusive): the original six (Belgium, France, Italy, Luxembourg, Netherlands, western Germany)
1973-80: six + Denmark, Ireland, United Kingdom
1981-85: nine + Greece
1986-present: 10 + Portugal and Spain.

ii) The European Free Trade Area (EFTA)
Period: 1960-72: the original eight (Austria, Denmark, Norway, Portugal, Sweden, Switzerland, United Kingdom) plus Finland
1972-85: nine **less** United Kingdom and Denmark
1986-present: nine less United Kingdom, Denmark and Portugal.

iii) North America (Canada and the United States)
Period: 1989-present.
Although the Canada-U.S. Automotive Agreement came into effect in 1965, and was approved by the GATT as a "free trade area" under Article 24, it was a sectoral free trade area which covered only a small percentage of the total bilateral trade. Therefore, the formation of the North American area is dated from the Canada-United States Free Trade Area in 1989. This covers most trade in merchandise, though it excludes almost all agriculture and does not cover all NTMs on the remaining trade.

iv) Australia and New Zealand
Period: 1965-present.
The New Zealand-Australia Free Trade Area covered most actual goods traded between the two countries although it excluded agriculture and permitted the retention of NTMs, particularly the comprehensive import licensing system which New Zealand maintained until it was dismantled progressively from 1983. The Closer Economic Relations (CER) Agreement which came into effect in 1983, covered all goods trade (and most services) and has led to the elimination of all NTMs on bilateral trade.

2. *Broad regional groups*

Three broad regional groupings have been used:

OECD Europe;

North America (United States, Canada);

Asia (Japan, Hong Kong, Korea, Taiwan plus ASEAN countries).

These groups correspond to geographic regions which have a recognisable identity because of the formation of RTAs among some countries in the group and other links due to proximity and regional

39

preferences and closer investment ties. They correspond to the three poles of trade centred on the EC, United States and Japan, respectively. The choice of members for the "Asian" group is most difficult. China was omitted because it is still a more closed economy with a distinct commodity pattern of trade. The remaining countries of East and South-East Asia have closer trade and investment ties that have been increasing more rapidly in the last years of the 1980s.

B. Time and commodity coverage

The period of the sample is 1961-1989 or a sub-period if the data is restricted.

The merchandise trade commodities have been examined at three levels; those of trade in all commodities, trade in the groups of "manufactures" and the broader group of "non-energy products," and a small selection of industries. These commodity groups are defined in terms of SITC as follows:

"Manufactures": Sections 5-8 less Division 68 ("Non-ferrous Metals").

"Non-Energy Products": Total less Section 3 ("Fuels").

"Food": Section O "Food and Live Animals".

"Clothing and Textiles": Divisions 65 ("Textile Yarns, Fabrics and Made-up Articles n.e.s.") and 84 ("Articles of Apparel and Clothing Accessories").

"Iron and Steel": Division 67 ("Iron and Steel").

"Passenger Motor Vehicles": Division 78 ("Road Vehicles").

C. Database

OECD database for all but the data on import shares for Asia which are taken from the UN Comtrade database.

BIBLIOGRAPHY

Aho, C.M. and S. Ostry (1990), "Regional trade blocs", in W. Brock and R.D. Harmat (eds.), *The Global Economy: America's Role in the Decade Ahead*, W.W. Norton and Company.

Asia Pacific Economic Cooperation (APEC) (1989), Summary Statement by the Chairman, Conference Secretariat, Department of Foreign Affairs and Trade, Canberra.

Balassa, B. (1961), *The Theory of Economic Integration*, Irwin, Homewood, Illinois.

Balassa, B. (ed.)(1975), *European Economic Integration*, North Holland, Amsterdam.

Baldwin, R. (1989), "On the growth effects of 1992", *Economic Policy*, 9, (Autumn), pp. 247-81.

Baldwin, R.E. (1982), "The inefficacy of trade policy", Princeton University International Finance Section, Essays in International Finance, No. 150, (December).

Brown, D.K. and R.M. Stern (1989), "Computational analysis of the U.S.-Canada Free Trade Agreement: the rate of product differentiation and market structures", in R.C. Feenstra (ed.), *Empirical Methods for International Trade*, MIT Press, Cambridge.

Bureau of Industry Economics (1989), "Trade liberalisation and Australian manufacturing industry: the impact of the Australia-New Zealand Closer Economic Relations Trade Agreement", Research Report No. 29, Australian Government Publishing Service, Canberra.

Canada, Department of Finance, Fiscal Policy and Economic Analysis Branch (1988), *The Canadian-U.S. Free Trade Agreement: An Economic Assessment*, Ottawa.

Cecchini, P. *et al.* (1988), *The European Challenge 1992: The Benefits of a Single Market*, Wildwood House, Aldershot.

Commission of the European Economic Communities (1985), *Completing the Internal Market*, White Paper for the Commission to the European Council, Office for Official Publications of the European Communities, Luxembourg.

Dell, S. (1963), *Trade Blocs and Common Markets*, Constable, London.

Emerson, M. *et al.* (1988), *The Economics of 1992: The EC Commission's Assessment of the Economic Effects of Completing the Internal Market*, Oxford University Press, Oxford.

Emmerij, L. (ed.) (1989), *One World or Several*, Development Centre of the OECD, Paris.

GATT (1990), *International Trade 89-90*, GATT, Geneva.

GATT (1991), *Trade Policy Review – European Communities*, GATT, Geneva.

Grinols, E.L. (1981), "An extension of the Kemp-Wan theorem on the formation of customs unions", *Journal of International Economics*, 11, pp. 259-66.

Harris, R.G. (1984), "Applied general equilibrium analysis of small open economies with economies of scale and imperfect competition", *American Economic Review*, 74, (December), pp. 1016-1032.

Harris, R.G. and D. Cox (1984), *Trade, Industrial Policy and Canadian Manufacturing*, Ontario Economic Council, Toronto.

Harrison, G.W. and E.E. Rutstrom (1991), "Trade wars, trade negotiations and applied game theory", *Economic Journal*, 101, (May), pp. 420-435.

Hart, M. (1990) "Dumping and free trade areas", in J.H. Jackson and E.A. Vermulst (eds.), *Antidumping Laws and Practice: A Comparative Study*, Harvester Wheatsheaf, London.

Hazeldine, T. (1989), "Industrial organisation foundations of trade policy". *Australian Journal of Agricultural Economics*, 33, (April), pp. 1-19.

Johnson, H.G. (1958), "Marshallian analysis of discriminatory tariff reductions: an extension", *Indian Journal of Economics*, 6, pp. 177-82.

Julius, D. (1990), *Global Companies and Public Policy: The Growing Challenge of Foreign Direct Investment*, The Royal Institute of International Affairs, London.

Keenan, J. and R. Riezman (1988), "Do big countries win tariff wars", *International Economic Review*, 29, (February), pp. 81-85.

Keenan, J. and R. Riezman (1990), "Optimal tariff equilibria with customs unions", *Canadian Journal of Economics*, 23, (February), pp. 70-83.

Kemp, M.C. and H. Wan (1976), "An elementary proposition concerning the formation of customs unions", *Journal of International Economics*, 6, pp. 95-97.

Kojima, K (1966), "A Pacific economic community and Asian developing countries", *Hitotsubashi Journal of Economics*, 7, (June), pp. 17-37.

Kowalczyk, C. (1990), "Welfare and customs union", NBER Working Papers No. 3476, Cambridge, Mass.

Kreinen, M.E. (1989), "EC-1992 and world trade and the world trading system", Paper presented to the Conference on 1992, Europe and America, Reading, England.

Langhammer, R.J. and U. Hiemenz, (1990), "Regional integration among developing countries", Kieler Studies No. 232, University of Kiel, Kiel.

Lipsey, R.G. (1960), "The theory of customs unions: a general survey", *Economic Journal*, 70, (September), pp. 496-513.

Lloyd, P.J. (1987), "Australia-New Zealand trade relations: NAFTA to CER", in K. Sinclair (ed.) *Tasman Relations, New Zealand and Australia, 1788-1988*, Auckland University Press, Auckland, pp. 142-163.

Lloyd, P.J. (1991), *The Future of CER: A Single Market for Australia and New Zealand*, CEDA and Institute of Policy Studies, Wellington.

Lorenz, D. (1991), "Regionalisation versus regionalism – problems of change in the world economy", *Intereconomics*, (January/February), pp. 3-16.

Markusen, J.R. and R.M. Wigle (1989), "Nash equilibrium tariffs for the United States and Canada: the roles of country size, scale economies, and capital mobility", *Journal of Political Economy*, 97, (April), pp. 368-386.

Mundell, R.A. (1964), "Tariff preferences and the terms of trade", *Manchester School of Economics and Social Studies*, 32, (January), pp. 1-13.

Norman, V.D. (1990), "Assessing trade and welfare effects of trade liberalisation: a comparison of alternative approaches to CGE modelling with imperfect competition", *European Economic Review*, 34, pp. 725-751.

Owen, N. (1983), *Economies of Scale, Competitiveness and Trade Patterns within the European Community*, Clarendon Press, Oxford.

Pomfret, R. (1988), *Unequal Trade: The Economics of Discriminatory International Trade Policies*, Basil Blackwell, Oxford.

Richardson, J.D. (1989), "Empirical Research on trade liberalisation with imperfect competition: a survey", *OECD Economic Studies*, No. 12, (Spring), pp. 7-50.

Riezman, R. (1979), "A 3x3 model of customs unions", *Journal of International Economics*, 9, pp. 341-54.

Riezman, R. (1982), "Tariff retaliation from a strategic point of view", *Southern Economic Journal*, 48, pp. 583-93.

Robson, P. (1984), *The Economics of International Integration*, George Allen and Unwin, London.

Sautter, H. (1983), *Regionalisierung und komparative Vorteile im internationalen Handel*, Tübingen.

Schott, J.J. (ed.) (1989a), *Free Trade Areas and US Trade Policy*, Institute for International Economics, Washington, D.C.

Schott, J.J. (ed.) (1989b), *More Free Trade Areas?*, Institute for International Economics, Washington, D.C.

Scitovsky, T. (1956), "Economies of scale, competition and European integration", *American Economic Review*, 46, (March), pp. 71-91.

Siebert, H. (1990), "The harmonisation issue in Europe: prior agreement or a competitive process?" in H. Siebert (ed.), *The Completion of the Internal Market*, J.C.B. Mohr, Tübingen.

Smith, A. and A.J. Venables (1988), "Completing the internal market in the European Community: some industry simulations", *European Economic Review*, 32, pp. 1501-1525.

Stoeckel, A., D. Pearce and G. Banks (1990), *Western Trade Blocs*, Centre for International Economics, Canberra, Australia.

Thorbecke, E. (1960), *The Tendency Towards Regionalisation in International Trade 1928-56*, Martinus Nijhoff, The Hague.

Viner, J. (1950), *The Customs Union Issue*, Carnegie Foundation for International Peace, New York.

Whalley, J. (1985), *Trade Liberalization Among Major World Trading Areas*, MIT Press, Cambridge, Mass.

Wijkman, P.M. (1991), "Patterns of production and trade in Western Europe: looking forward after thirty years", in W. Wallace (ed.) *The Dynamics of European Integration*, Royal Institute of International Affairs, London.

[10]

The Changing Nature of Regional Trading Arrangements

Peter Lloyd

Many governments have stated their view that the barriers to world trade are best reduced by means of multilateral negotiations under the aegis of the GATT, rather than by the development of discriminatory regional trading agreements. I share the commitment to a multilateral system of trading. However, the number of regional trading arrangements has continued to grow in recent years, and their nature has changed substantially in several respects. The Uruguay Round settlement will achieve a significant multilateral reduction in border barriers to international in goods and, for the first time, discipline in services trade. As a result of these regional and multilateral developments, new issues in international trade policy have become more important; these include trade in services and factors, international competition policy, and cross-border environmental problems. Regional integration must, therefore, be considered in a broad context which goes beyond the traditional issues of discrimination in border barriers to the international trade in goods.

The first section reviews the expanding country and commodity coverage of regional trading arrangements (RTAs) and then reviews trends in the Asia-Pacific region. Asia exemplifies the importance of capital movements as well as trade in goods and services. We then consider the current view of regional liberalisation of trade in goods and services, the traditional focus of regional trade analysis. The third section addresses the issue of whether the reductions in border trade barriers by means of regional arrangements are complementary to multilateral liberalisation of trade in goods and services, or whether they hinder and threaten the multilateral system. The role of foreign direct investment within regional arrangements is then examined. The fifth section discusses the extension of regional arrangements beyond border trade instruments. This leads to an examination of the meaning of regional integration. It also considers cross-border environmental and competition policies and other new issues. Some general remarks about these developments conclude the chapter.

Trends in the World Economy and in the Asia-Pacific Region

It is taken for granted by many commentators that world trade has become more 'regionalised'. However, this term is ill defined. Significant multilateral and unilateral reductions in commodity trade barriers have occurred in recent decades, as well as regional liberalisation through the formation of RTAs. We need also to consider factor movements. Consequently, the extent of reorganisation in the world economy is an open question, and the claim of reorganisation should be treated as a testable hypothesis. This empirical question of reorganisation of the world economy will not be pursued further, as is examined in Chapter 2 by Pomfret.

The expanding scope of regional trading arrangements

Conceptually, a movement towards greater trading within discriminatory regional arrangements can occur in three main ways. The scope or coverage of RTAs may increase due to an increase in the *country* coverage or the *commodity* coverage or the *instrument* coverage of the arrangements. There is a fourth dimension, namely, the depth of cuts in tariffs and other barriers to trade for those commodities covered by RTAs if the initial depth is less than 100 per cent.

Most of those concerned over reorganisation point to the growing number of regional trading arrangements, and the growing number of *countries* which are members of them. This growth can result either from the expansion in the membership of existing RTAs or from the formation of new ones. The EU has expanded from the original six signatories of the Treaty of Rome in 1957 to fifteen countries in 1995. The Canada–USA Free Trade Agreement (CUSTA), which came into force on 1 January 1989, added substantially to this concern, partly because of the economic size of this trading bloc and partly because it marked a movement away from its historic opposition to regional trade discrimination by the USA. After this, there was a new wave of regional trading agreements. Over the three years 1991–3, twenty-seven agreements were signed and notified to the GATT. These include the North American Free Trade Agreement (NAFTA), which came into effect on 1 January 1994 and which extended the USA–Canada bloc to include Mexico.

However, this growth in the number of arrangements exaggerates the extent of reorganisation for several reasons. Certainly more than 100 regional or preferential trading arrangements have been notified to the GATT since 1947. (See World Trade Organisation, 1995, for a review of these arrangements.) But many of these are non-reciprocal preference schemes and association agreements, designed to improve the market access of the preference-receiving countries. Excluding preference schemes and non-reciprocal association agreements, the number notified to GATT over the period 1947-93 is less than fifty.

Moreover, a number of these RTAs are replacements for earlier ones that applied to the same or substantially the same group of countries; for example, the 1992 Treaty on European Union (the Maastricht treaty) established the EU in place of the European Economic Community; CUSTA replaced the Canada–USA Automotive Agreement; and the 1983 Closer Economic Relations Agreement (CER) between Australia and New Zealand replaced the earlier New

Zealand–Australia Free Trade Agreement. These might be called second-generation agreements.

Another feature of the emerging RTAs is that they have moved beyond associations of neighbouring countries that are small relative to the aggregate size of the
world economy. The EU and NAFTA are continent-based associations, with
enormous economic and political power. This exacerbates the concerns over
trade discrimination and trade frictions in the world economy.

Within an RTA, the extent of the discrimination may increase over time. The
extent of the discrimination at any one time depends on both the extent of
regional preferences and the level of barriers *vis-à-vis* outside countries. To measure the degree of intra-area commodity trade discrimination, one requires time
series in each member country of an aggregate measure of support for all industries *vis-à-vis* outside countries, and a separate series *vis-à-vis* member countries.
The aggregate measure of support should include support from both tariff and
non-tariff measures in each commodity group. The difference between these two
series then gives a series of the margins of preferences. Unfortunately, there are no
time series of the margins of preference in any RTA, as few countries have series
of aggregate measures of support for all or most industries *vis-à-vis* all other countries, and none has a series of measures *vis-à-vis* member countries.

In the absence of measures or preference margins, we can consider the trends
in the depth of cut of trade barriers and in the *commodity* coverage within individual regional trading arrangements.

In relation to the depth of tariff cuts for those commodities which are subject
to the provisions of RTAs, the tariff preferences for members are less than 100 per
cent in some agreements, and some non-tariff barriers remain when tariffs have
been eliminated on intra-area trade. However, more agreements now have a
timetable which provides for the elimination of tariffs among members.

The depth of cuts in the barriers to trade among the members of an RTA also
depend on the reduction or elimination of non-tariff barriers to trade among the
members. More non-tariff *instruments* have been included in recent arrangements, such as CUSTA, NAFTA and CER. Under CUSTA, Canada and the
USA agreed that existing quantitative restrictions on imports and exports will
be eliminated, either immediately or according to a timetable, unless they are
grandfathered or permitted by the GATT. There are limits on some other non-
tariff, barriers, such as the elimination of direct export subsidies on bilateral
agricultural trade. There are commitments in other areas, such as government
procurement, which deepen the governments' undertakings under GATT, but
they are generally rather weak. NAFTA followed the lines of CUSTA in these
areas. The CER agreement, unlike its predecessor, contained a timetable to
eliminate all quantitative restrictions on trade between the two countries
within twelve years, that is, by 1995. (In fact, they were ended by 1990.) As a
result of the 1988 review of the agreement, the two countries agreed to eliminate all subsidies distorting trade between them, and to remove restrictions on
government purchasing across the Tasman Sea. The same review agreed that

the members would no longer apply anti-dumping duties on imports from each other. This makes the CER, along with the EU and the European Economic Area, one of the three RTAs which have ended anti-dumping actions among members.

Hence, for those commodities which are covered, the depth of the cuts of tariff and non-tariff barriers has certainly increased for the trade among the members of the arrangements.

With the exception of the EC, for which the Treaty of Rome guaranteed complete freedom of trade for all goods and services, all other arrangements had less than complete commodity coverage at their inception. The commodity coverage of most other RTAs has been extended. For example, the commodity coverage of the tariff cuts in CUSTA and in CER greatly exceeds that of the agreements between the countries which they replaced: the Canada–USA Automotive Agreement which preceded CUSTA was restricted to automotive products, and the New Zealand–Australia Free Trade Agreement which preceded CER was based on forest products, with a very limited coverage initially of other manufactures.

Most RTAs have no provisions relating to intra-area trade in services, and service trade has been increasing relative to goods trades; the exceptions are the EU, CER, CUSTA and NAFTA. From the outset, the Treaty of Rome provided for free international trade in all services as well as goods among its members, including the rights of establishment for all service providers. Despite this principle, some barriers remained because of non-border regulations. The 1985 White Paper stated, 'Despite the provisions of Articles 59 and 62 of the Treaty, progress on the freedom to provide services across internal frontiers has been much slower than the progress achieved on free movement of goods.' (Commission of the European Communities, 1985, p. 26). The single-market measures adopted by the White Paper included some measures relating to service trade, chiefly transport and financial services.

CUSTA contained provisions liberalising trade in some services, including the rights of establishment and national treatment for service providers. It utilised the device of a 'positives' list, that is, the liberalisation applied only to those services listed. The list included financial services, architecture, tourism, enhanced telecommunications, and computer services; but many areas were not covered, including transport, basic telecommunications, and most professional and government-provided services. NAFTA followed the CUSTA model of services quite closely. In the CER, there was no provision in the 1983 agreement for liberalising trade in services. But the 1988 Protocol on Trade in Services established free trade in most services, including national treatment in relation to all laws, regulations and practices as well as free market access. To handle sensitive areas, CER used the device of a 'negative' list, that is, the exemption from the provisions only of services specified by each country. Australia exempted substantially more services than New Zealand, partly on the grounds that a number of these were subject to inquiries and proposals for deregulation or reform, though some areas have been added subsequently.

As of the beginning of 1994, only two RTAs come close to removing most barriers to trade in all goods and services, namely the EU and CER.

One can safely conclude that intra-area commodity trade liberalisation has risen in the 1980s, at least under the second generation of more ambitious agreements, because of the expansion of the commodity coverage of RTAs and increased depth of cut of trade barriers. But it is not possible to compare this quantitatively with the effects of multilateral and unilateral changes in trade barriers *vis-à-vis* outside countries. One cannot, therefore, determine whether regional discrimination has worsened.

Trends in the Asia-Pacific region

Asia is of particular interest, because it is the geographic region of the world in which trade and real output have been growing most rapidly. The definition of the Asia-Pacific region is unclear because economists in different countries tend to use different groupings. The essence of the grouping is that countries border the Pacific, that is, they are Pacific Rim countries. I shall define it as all of the East Asian economies, Australia and New Zealand, Canada and the USA.[1] The term *Asia-Pacific* also indicates that it consists of two halves, with different characteristics in some respects at least.

The Asia-Pacific region is distinctive in a number of ways which are relevant to trade policies. As we have said, it is the region of the world economy in which trade and investment and technology transfers are growing most rapidly. Consider the shares of the three major regions in world commodity trade for the thirty-year period from 1960 to 1990. These regions are OECD Europe, North America (USA and Canada), and Asia (Japan, Hong Kong, South Korea, Taiwan and the ASEAN countries). The import share of OECD Europe has been remarkably constant throughout the period, at just over 40 per cent. That of North America has been roughly constant at around 15–17 per cent, with some increase in the second half of the 1980s. The Asian share has almost doubled from under 8 per cent at the start of the 1960s to 14.8 per cent in 1989. This reflects the impressive economic performance of this group of countries. If we add the Asian and the North American shares, we find that they have together increased from around 23 to 32 per cent over this interval.

This trend in capital flows is more marked because of the rapid increases in the surpluses of Japan and the emergence of surpluses on the current accounts of the balance of payments of Taiwan, South Korea and Singapore in the late 1980s. Garnaut (1989, p. 81 and Table 4.1) notes that the countries of North-East Asia are much more important in total world savings and investment than they are in total world trade, because of their very high savings rates. These statistics relate to net flows and to the net investment in all forms: foreign direct investments, portfolio and other investments. From the point of view of the link between investment and trade flows, perhaps the most useful series are those relating to the gross outwards flows in the form of direct investment abroad. By 1990 Japan alone accounted for 21 per cent of the reported direct investment abroad in the world economy (International Monetary Fund, 1991, Table C. 17), whereas in 1985 it accounted for only 11 per cent.

Furthermore, the flows of trade have been increasingly within the region, and this preference (statistically speaking) for intra-regional trading has, unlike Europe, become more marked. Consider the intra-regional share of imports of commodity trade for the same three regions. For OECD Europe, this measure has been high and tended to increase slowly throughout the period, from 56.4 per cent in 1964 to 69 per cent in 1987. For North America, this share is much lower: it has fallen from a peak of 40.5 per cent in 1969 to only 27 per cent in 1988. For Asia, the intra-regional share of import trade has roughly doubled between 1964 and 1988, from 20 to 41 per cent. For the combined Asia-Pacific region, the share of intra-regional imports has also increased rapidly throughout the period, and it is now about the same as that in Europe.

The share of Japanese investment abroad going to North-East and South-East Asia has actually declined in recent years, as the Japanese have invested heavily in the USA. However, the share of the inflow of foreign direct investment coming from Japan has increased for the ASEAN countries and for Taiwan (but not South Korea) in the second half of the 1980s (Department of Foreign Affairs, 1992, Appendix 5).

The increase in intra-regional commodity trade (and trade in services, investment and technology transfers) is all the more remarkable because this region is the least regionalised in the sense of the formation of RTAs which discriminate in trade flows and therefore tend to increase the intra-regional share of trade compared to what it would be in their absence. Until the formation of CUSTA in 1989,[2] the only RTAs in the Asia-Pacific region were the ASEAN Free Trade Agreement (AFTA, formed in 1977) and the agreements between Australia and New Zealand (the New Zealand–Australia Free Trade Agreement of 1965 and its successor, the CER Agreement of 1983). In Asia, ASEAN remains the only regional trading arrangement, and there is none in the North Asia sub-region. By contrast, there have been many arrangements in Europe, Africa, Latin America and the Caribbean. (See de la Torre and Kelly, 1992, chapter V, for the development of these arrangements.)

There has been significant freeing of trade in the Asian region over the last two decades. GATT (1992, Appendix Table) provides a list of sixty-three countries which have undertaken unilateral reductions in protection *vis-à-vis* all trading partners since the start of the Uruguay Round of GATT in 1986, nine of these being in East Asia and four in South Asia. The East Asian countries are Japan, South Korea, China, Macau, Indonesia, Thailand, the Philippines, Malaysia and Singapore. The South Asian countries are Bangladesh, India, Pakistan and Sri

Lanka. In addition, Japan has taken measures to free trade in certain commodities after bilateral negotiations with the USA; for example, the 1988 negotiations on beef between the USA, Australia, and Japan, and the 1990 Structural Impediments Initiative. Many of the reductions in Asian countries have been substantial. By comparison, the non-discriminatory reductions in the EU and the USA have been much less comprehensive.

As we have said, the Asian region generally and the East Asian region in particular is remarkable in being the least 'regionalised' of the world regions in the sense of customs unions and free trade areas notified under the articles of the GATT. These RTAs discriminate in commodity trade flows, and therefore tend to increase the intra-regional share of trade compared to what it would be in their absence. In East Asia, AFTA remains the only RTA. While there has been intense discussion of the Malaysian proposal for an East Asian Economic Caucus and the Australian-led proposal for an Asia-Pacific Economic Cooperation forum and other proposals for bilateral or trilateral trade links in South Asia and Melanesia, no trade preference arrangements have resulted to date from these discussions. This is in contrast to the picture in the rest of the world.

However, there has been substantial movement towards freer trade on a local or sub-regional basis in the East Asian region outside the conventional customs unions and free trade areas that are approved under GATT. This has taken several forms, including export-processing zones, Growth Triangles, and bilateral or multilateral trade and investment arrangements.

Export-processing zones began in the 1970s in Asia, largely following Japan's relaxation of investment abroad, as a way of attracting foreign investment and technology transfers to take advantage of the low labour costs in these countries and boost exports of manufactures. (See World Bank, 1992a). They spread throughout Asia and the Pacific islands, and also to several Latin American and Caribbean countries and some countries in Africa. There are now thirty in China alone. Indeed, Asia is the region in which this form of organisation has been concentrated. Much of the growth of exports of manufactures from Asia has originated in these zones.

More recently a new kind of zone spreading across two or more countries has emerged. These are known variously as Growth Triangles or sub-regional economic zones. In 1989 the Growth Triangle between Singapore, the southern part of the Malaysian State of Johore and the islands of the Riau Province of Indonesia was recognised by the governments of Singapore, Malaysia and Indonesia (see Chapter 14). The Asian Development Bank (1992, p. 64) describes this triangle as a 'concept [which] exploits complementarities between geographically contiguous areas of different countries to gain greater competitive edges in export promotion'. It is intended to shift labour-intensive industries from Singapore to Johore and the Riau Islands as Singapore unit costs increase because of rising per capita output.

The concept of a Growth Triangle is a distinctly Asian form of cooperation which has evolved from the experience with industrial estates and economic zones. Like the export-processing zones, it was mooted as a means of establishing regional cooperation without requiring the participation and formal agreement of all six ASEAN countries (see Chapter 14).

There is a similar though less formal inter-government arrangement, involving the triangle formed by Hong Kong, Taiwan and southern China. This has been described as an informal Growth Triangle (Asian Development Bank, 1992). There are several special economic zones in the Guangdong and Fujian Provinces of China as one leg of the triangle. There has been substantial Hong Kong and Taiwan investment in southern China to take advantage of low labour costs, complemented by substantial infrastructure development by the Chinese government to promote growth in the area. These developments have led to a high degree of economic integration in the area. Jones, King and Klein (1993) refer to it as the Chinese Economic Area. There are informal arrangements known as the Baht Zone in the areas bordering Thailand, Laos, Cambodia and Vietnam, and the Yellow Sea Zone in north-east China, North and South Korea and Japan, and several other sub-regional zones are under discussion in East Asia.

Thus, Asia is the region of the world economy which has seen the largest number and the greatest variety of what might be called 'non-GATT' regional trade and investment arrangements. This is another part of the explanation of the paradox of an increasing intra-regional trade combined with a low and stagnant level of intra-regional trade preferences.

The fast rate of growth in the region and the unilateral trade reductions may explain the increase in intra-regional goods trade. If there were no change in trade policies or in competitiveness, fast growth within a region would itself increase the share of intra-regional trade, even if the shares of export markets were constant. (This evades the question of the causal relationship between freeing trade and the rate of growth of economies.) Similarly, if the economies of the region are more complementary with each other in terms of relative cost differences, due to wide differences in resource endowments and technologies, as found by Drysdale and Garnaut (1989a), unilateral reductions in trade barriers *vis-à-vis* all trading partners will increase the share of intra-regional trade.

There is a strong link over time between the trends in the expansion of trade and the growth of direct foreign investment in this region. For example, the Asian Development Bank (1992, p. 63) has observed:

> The importance of this increased intra-regional foreign direct investment goes much beyond an increase in financial flows to the developing countries in Asia. The new pattern of investment has in fact assisted in extensive industrial restructuring and the development of a sophisticated regional division of labour in Asia. Intra-regional FDI has been an important instrument for the realization of the so-called 'flying geese' pattern of industrial

development in Asia, i.e. the relocation of industries from one tier of economies to the next tier in response to changing comparative advantage.

The Flying Geese model is based on a view of comparative advantage which changes quite rapidly over time. It was devised by Japanese economists on the basis of the Japanese experience (see Yamazawa, Hirata and Yokota, 1991). Initially, the relocations were from Japan to South Korea, Taiwan, Hong Kong and Singapore. Footloose manufactures such as textiles, steel, electronics and automobiles are now being transferred from these economies to the second-tier East Asian countries, such as Thailand, Malaysia, Indonesia, the Philippines and China, as these latter countries diversify their export bundles from a heavy reliance on exports of commodities based on natural resources. These manufacturing activities have been export-oriented in their new locations. Empirical support for the Flying Geese model is provided by Fukasaku (1992).

This Asia-Pacific example shows that many factors besides commodity trade liberalisation on a regional basis affect the trading patterns of regions. In particular, it shows we must consider regional factor trade as well as commodity trade.

Effects of Regional Liberalisation of Commodity Trade

Member countries

With regard to regional freeing of commodity trade, the traditional concern in the theory of free trade areas and customs unions has been on the effects of this liberalisation on the countries which are members of the regional trading arrangement. Since Viner (1950) the focus has been on the effects in creating or diverting trade. According to Viner (p. 44), 'Where the trade-diverting effect is predominant, one at least of the member countries is bound to be injured, the two combined will suffer a net injury, and there will be injury to the outside world and to the world at large.'

With some hindsight, the emphasis placed on these effects can be seen to have over-emphasised the negative effects of RTAs. They reflect the proximate terms of trade effects due to the changes in sources of import supply, and under the assumption of integrated processes and constant returns to scale. It is now well understood that trade diversion is not necessarily harmful to the country whose trade has been diverted, because of changes in consumption and/or national income which accompany the diversion. The creation or diversion of trade is only one type of terms-of-trade effect. An RTA has many other effects on the prices and volume of goods traded and national tax revenues, which are the factors which will determine the change in welfare of a country.[3] Much of the focus now is on the direct and indirect effects on national income of member countries, which are generally perceived as positive.

Recent computable general equilibrium (CGE) modelling has emphasised the effects of changes in factor prices, competition and the product varieties available to consumers, especially in models with increasing returns to scale and non-perfect competition. (See Richardson, 1989; Norman, 1990; and Srinivasan, Whalley and Wooton, 1993, for surveys of such models.)

CGE models with economies of scale and imperfect competition have now been adapted to measure *ex ante* the effects of prospective or proposed RTAs. The prospective completion of the European Single Market in 1992 has been studied by Smith and Venables (1988). CUSTA was studied extensively at the time of its proposal in models of this type. The GET model, which descended from the earlier work in Canada by Harris and Cox (1984), was commissioned and used by the Canadian government in its negotiation of the agreement and to convince the Canadian public of the benefits of the proposal. In Australia, the Bureau of Industry Economics (1989) used a model based on that of Harris and Cox to evaluate the effects of CER.

These recent CGE models have generally predicted larger gains to the member countries than were obtained from traditional competitive industry versions of the general equilibrium models. Regional trade liberalisation in these models leads to gains—in the form of increased competition, reduced unit costs, and greater product variety—which are additional to those quantified in the traditional models. For example, Smith and Venables (1988) predict that the completion of the single market will lead to more than three times the gain from trade liberalisation alone in terms of the percentage increase in real incomes. This is due to the increased competition as production for a single market eliminates the ability of domestic firms to charge higher prices on nationally segmented markets.

One difficulty with these imperfectly competitive models is that the quantitative results are very sensitive to variations in the specifications of the models, such as the form of strategic interaction between oligopolistic firms or the presence of free entry and exit from industries. For example, Burniaux and Waelbroeck (1992) have reworked the scenario of Smith and Venables by varying the specification of trade elasticities. The calculated welfare gains, while substantial, are much smaller than those predicted by Smith and Venables. Very few of the parameters are estimated econometrically in any of these models. Consequently, they should be regarded as indicative thought experiments rather than reliable predictions, but they have changed the perception of the benefits and costs of RTAs to member countries, mainly by emphasising the benefits of increased competition.

Non-member countries

The general concern in the world trading community and in the GATT is with the effects of regional trade discrimination in the RTAs on non-member countries. For a given program of liberalisation of the intra-regional trade, this will depend upon two things: the height of the trade barriers facing outside countries exporting to the area, and the effects induced by the liberalisation of trade within the area.

The height of the barriers into the area will be unaffected by the formation of the RTA itself if the agreement creates only a free trade area and leaves responsibility for external trade policy with the individual countries. In the case of customs unions, it will depend initially upon the common external trade barriers, and subsequently upon the decisions by the area with respect to external trade policy. Article XXIV of the GATT specifies that the external trade barriers shall not on the whole be higher or more restrictive than those of the individual countries before union. In the important case of the EC, the common external tariffs for each item were set at the level of the arithmetic average of the pre-existing tariff rates of the member countries, and subsequently reduced as a result of the Dillon and Kennedy Rounds of multilateral reductions. Since its formation, the EU has raised some barriers by means of introducing quantitative restrictions and contingent protection for some commodity groups, such as textiles and automobiles.

For a given external trade policy, the effects of the RTA on outside countries depend primarily upon the induced changes in the terms of trade of these countries, and secondarily upon the changes in trade tax revenues. According to Viner (1950), trade diversion will reduce the demand for exports from the country outside the RTA from which trade is diverted. Such trade diversion has a direct and adverse effect on the terms of trade of non-members, which is the cause of the welfare loss to them. However, for non-member countries as well as member countries, trade diversion is only one of the effects on non-member countries' terms of trade. The terms-of-trade effect captures all of the effects identified by Viner and other direct effects, and all of the indirect effects through the changes in national income and competition and prices of the member countries. When these are taken into account, it is not necessary that the terms of trade of an outside country decline, as commonly supposed.[4] Real income effects on member countries are almost certain to benefit outside countries collectively, because of the increased demand for goods and services. If the effects of an RTA on the national incomes and competition are strongly positive, as many recent simulations suggest, there is a presumption that these areas will benefit outside countries collectively. However, some individual outside countries may lose.

In summary, the theorists' views of RTAs have tended to become more positive. Since Viner's book, theoretical developments have predicted an increase in regional real output from a number of effects. These real output effects, unlike the price effects of discriminatory border protection reductions, are almost certain to benefit the outside countries collectively because of increased aggregate demand for most goods and services. The main concerns now are over the possibilities of trade wars and negative terms of trade effects on third countries if the agreements are not outward-looking.

Effects on the World Commodity Trading System

The effects of regional trading arrangements go beyond the effects on the member and non-member countries of an individual RTA. Because of the spread of these arrangements and the precedents set in individual cases, they have had systemic effects.

Regional and multilateral reductions in trade barriers are linked in several ways. Progress towards completely free global trade could occur in several ways: by means of continual multilateral trade barrier reductions, or the freeing of trade regionally combined with coalescence of regions that have achieved intra-regional free trade, or independent unilateral reductions in all countries, or some combination of them. Until we reach global free trade, regional and discriminatory reductions could either aid or hinder multilateral reductions.

With growth in the number of RTAs and the number of members of existing agreements, the issue of whether the RTAs will coalesce in the long run or remain separate is important. Coalescence can occur from a merger of two (or more) RTAs or the expansion of the membership of an RTA (which is effectively the coalescence of the pre-existing RTA and an RTA with a membership of one). The European Economic Area is an example of the first form, and the continually expanding example of the EC and later the EU is the outstanding example of the second form.

Krugman (1991b) analyses the effect on world welfare of increasing the size, and thereby reducing the number, of trading blocs in the world economy. Plotting world welfare as a function of the number of such blocs, he finds that the function is U-shaped. World welfare is minimised when there are three blocs. This result is particularly suggestive, since there is an argument that the world is dividing into three centres, or 'poles'—Europe, North America and Asia—which are increasingly resembling blocs.

Krugman's result depends, in part at least, upon several features of his model. Every country is a member of a bloc. The utility function (Armington, 1969) assumes that every country trades every product and produces a high level of trade initially with countries outside the bloc, thereby increasing the scope for trade diversion. Each bloc has a common external tariff and fixes its tariffs optimally and without restraint; hence, trade barriers *vis-à-vis* outside member countries rise as the number of blocs falls. It is not clear that this result is general. The result will depend on the extent to which blocs are formed by countries which trade with each other because of proximity and reduced transport costs ('natural trading blocs'), as Krugman noted, and, in a more general model, on other factors—such as the complementarity of production between members—as well as the level of the external tariffs.

Some models predict coalescence and some do not. For example, Kemp and Wan (1976) showed that a customs union could be beneficial to all its members if the common external tariff is adjusted so that the terms of trade are unchanged and members who would lose are compensated by lump-sum payments among members of the group. On the other hand, there are game theory models, which usually assume no compensation payments and the ability to adjust without restraint external tariffs *vis-à-vis* non-members. These models predict that countries have a motive for forming more exclusive arrangements and moving away from global free trade. All of these models are restrictive in their structures and assumptions, and the results are inconclusive.

Another systemic effect relating to the formation of new RTAs arises when one country enters into individual trading arrangements with two or more other countries. Suppose, for example, there are three countries, A, B, and C. Country A concludes separate regional arrangements with B and C, but B and C do not conclude an arrangement with each other. This has become known as the 'hub-and-spoke system'. Country A is the hub, and B and C are the spokes. It is possible that the hub can itself be a RTA. The system comprises a series of bilateral agreements among the countries, rather than a single multilateral agreement.

The hub-and-spoke system has been discussed in the USA and Canada. The USA formed free trade areas with Israel and then Canada, making it the hub. More recently, there has been discussion of the possibility that NAFTA could be expanded by concluding separate arrangements with a number of countries.

Such systems have been seen by some commentators as undesirable, because they do not give equal access among all the members of system. (See, for example, Kowalczyk and Wonnacott, 1992). Assuming for simplicity that all of the individual arrangements ensure free commodity trade between the members, the hub country has free access to all countries in the system, but the spoke countries have free access to the markets of the hub country only. An added fear is that the favoured position of the hub country may divert investment to this country at the expense of the spoke countries.

A hub-and-spoke system does not itself introduce any barriers to trade, but it does introduce an additional layer of discrimination between the hub country and the set of spoke countries. This would not arise if all of the countries in a system joined the one regional arrangement (see Chapter 4).

Such arrangements are more common than is generally realised.[5] Europe is now a complex web of hubs and spokes. Both the EU and the European Free Trade Area (EFTA) are hubs with many spokes. By the beginning of 1994, the European Union had concluded reciprocal free trade agreements with the members of EFTA individually and with nine countries in Eastern Europe. EFTA had concluded reciprocal agreements with seven countries in Eastern Europe and with Israel. In addition, four of the countries which are members of EFTA (Finland, Norway, Switzerland and Sweden) have formed agreements with the three Baltic states (Estonia, Lithuania and Latvia). Finally, there is a European Economic Area spanning the EU and EFTA countries. This creates a partial free trade area among the nineteen countries which are members of this agreement.

All of these hubs—the EU, the USA and EFTA—are large economies. The smaller spoke countries are anxious to secure their market access to the hub. This creates a piecemeal fashion of regional trade liberalisation, with the prospect for considerable friction among the members of the system.

Besides the spokes surrounding it, each of these hubs has a maze of non-reciprocal preferences with other developing countries outside the hub-and-spoke system. These have been introduced partly under the Generalised System of Preferences, and partly under the Lomé Convention between the EU and African, Caribbean and Pacific countries, and other treaties. The reciprocal and non-reciprocal agreements together have enveloped almost all the countries which are contracting parties of the GATT. At the end of 1993, the EU alone had discriminatory trade agreements of some kind with all but five of the contracting parties of the GATT (the USA, Canada, Japan, Australia and New Zealand). This spread of discrimination has threatened the principle of non-discrimination on which the global trading system is supposedly founded.

Regional, multilateral and unilateral reductions do, of course, proceed simultaneously and should not be thought of as mutually exclusive. Both regional and unilateral reductions have occurred over the same period. Some of the countries which have made recent unilateral reductions are members of regional trading arrangements; in the Asia-Pacific region these countries are Thailand and Indonesia, which are members of AFTA, and Australia and New Zealand, which are the two members of CER.

A number of practical considerations suggest that regional trade liberalisation may reinforce multilateral trade liberalisation. It could do so in a number of ways. By making member countries more competitive and more oriented to international trade, it might reduce protectionist pressures. Regional arrangements can act as model for multilateral liberalisation. This has occurred in areas of non-tariff measures and services trade, where the GATT has been less successful in achieving multilateral reductions. The liberalisation of service trade between countries began with the EC in 1957 and the 1988 CUSTA. In the latter case, US dissatisfaction with the failure of the GATT to tackle service trade issues was one of the reasons for the formation of this agreement.

The costs of transacting agreements relating to tariff and non-tariff measures may be lower in regional arrangements that have fewer members and less diverse preferences and cost structures. Member countries may reduce import barriers for third countries in order to avoid trade diversion and to gain access to the lowest-cost imported inputs.

On the other hand, the formation of RTAs poses a risk of trade wars between RTAs or members of them, and they may reinforce the decline in non-discrimination in the GATT system. The games-theory models are based on the assumption that the players (countries) can increase their external tariffs in a tariff war. This ignores the bindings of tariffs on most commodities and the commitments of free trade areas and customs unions not to increase external tariffs under the GATT system. These aspects are surveyed by Lloyd (1992).

The OECD (1995) has concluded that there appears to be a strong case that regionalism pushes forward the multilateral process, though it adds that this result hinges on the arrangements having an outward orientation. On the other hand, after a survey of the historical experience of the EC and ten arrangements involving developing countries, the World Bank (1991, pp. 107-8) emphasised the danger of inward-looking agreements; it stressed that unilateral and multilateral liberalisation is preferable to the formation of trading blocs. The survey for the IMF by de la Torre and Kelly (1992, p. 41) reached a similar anxious conclusion:

> The recent trend towards regionalism, however, may be qualitatively different from past efforts and may carry greater risks of becoming a substitute for, rather than a complement to, multilateralism. Apart from the potentially distorting effects of these arrangements on the allocation of world resources, a number of important elements unique to current regionalism seem to pose a greater threat to multilateralism.

The successful conclusion of the Uruguay Round of GATT may slow down the formation of RTAs. The reduction in most-favoured-nation trade barriers achieved by the Uruguay Round diminishes the incentives to form new RTAs, because it diminishes the (maximum) regional preferences that member countries enjoy over non-member countries. Nevertheless, as the Uruguay Round dragged on, a large momentum towards the formation of further RTAs built up, and this may not diminish. There are still incentives to join a regional bloc, especially if the bloc contains a large country. There are some industries in which the barriers will remain quite high. Moreover, membership may give greater protection from the imposition of contingent protection, such as safeguard or anti-dumping action.

Factor Trade

We need to devote more attention to the links between capital flows and commodity trade. The second section of this chapter noted the importance of capital flows in the Asia-Pacific region and their links to trade flows. Surprisingly little work has been done on measuring the extent of intra-regional freedom of movement of factor or on analysing the effects of freeing factor movements within regions.

The Treaty of Rome was unique in giving complete freedom of movement within the EC to capital and labour, as well as to goods and services. However, the 1985 White Paper of the Commission of the European Communities identified a number of restrictions on the movement of people or the recognition of their qualifications, and it introduced policies such as mutual recognition to overcome these restrictions.

Other free trade areas or customs unions have generally had no provisions, or weak ones, relating to factor trade. Most countries have substantially liberalised the entry of foreign capital by unilateral actions, but have kept some residual control on private direct foreign investment. Some RTAs, such as CUSTA, NAFTA and CER, have provided for national treatment of foreign capital.

In relation to the movement of people or labour, CUSTA and NAFTA contain provisions relating to the temporary entry for business purposes of residents of the other country. The great majority of RTAs have continued to make residents of the member countries subject to the same restrictions on entry for immigration or employment as the residents of outside countries. In the case of the CER countries, there is free movement of citizens and residents between Australia and New Zealand. This is guaranteed under a different agreement, known as the Trans-Tasman Travel Arrangements; it was adopted formally in the 1920s, long before the formation of the CER. The CER and Trans-Tasman Travel Arrangements are unique in having achieved free trade in goods, services and labour, but not in capital, within the area.

Factor movements interact with commodity flows in several ways. In a justly famous paper, Mundell (1957) pointed out that in the Heckscher–Ohlin model of international trade, under certain conditions, the free movement of capital *and* labour could substitute for commodity movements, and could lead to the equalisation across countries of both commodity prices and factor prices, that is, to the same effect as free commodity trade. The conditions of the Heckscher–Ohlin model include, most importantly, the assumption that the technologies of all countries are identical.

Similar but not identical results hold for the regional freeing of commodity trade and factor movements. For example, there is less likelihood of the equalisation of factor prices with free trade in commodities alone within a regional arrangement. Nevertheless, free regional movement of factors may partially substitute for free regional movement of trade. For example, when the free trade area between the USA, Canada, and Mexico was proposed, there was an element of choice between freeing commodity markets or labour markets. 'If Mexico cannot export its goods, it will export its people.'

However, if barriers to commodity trade with third countries remain and factor prices are not equalised, it is well known that foreign direct investment may be immiserising to the recipient countries because of the loss of gains from trade. This would apply to foreign direct investment from either a regional partner or a third country if it were directed to areas which are more heavily protected or assisted.

Wooton (1988) and Michael (1991) examined a related issue, namely, the movement from a customs union to a common market by the addition of free movement of factors after trade has already been freed. This situation corresponds roughly to the effects of mutual recognition and other measures which are freeing factor movements in the EU. Their results have shown that capital (or labour) flows within a common market may be harmful if there is a non-zero common external tariff, or if factor tax rates are not harmonised. In the former case, the loss comes about because of the reduction in trade tax revenue, which indicates a loss of gains from trade. In the latter case, factors move to the location where the return net of taxes is greatest, but this is not necessarily the location in which the marginal product is greatest in the presence of differences in factor tax rates. The same result may apply if commodity taxes or income taxes are not harmonised. These are all further examples of second-best (regional) liberalisations which may be welfare-harming to the liberalising countries.

Like the application of second-best trade-diversion effects to the analysis of commodity trade, these results are excessively negative. The countries gain if the tax rates are harmonised, as Michael (1991) showed for factor taxes.

Economic theory provides a strong and surprisingly general result concerning the aggregate production when the production sectors of two (or more) countries are united by the removal of restrictions on intra-regional factor mobility and factor tax differences, that is, the establishment of a single regional market for factors. The proposition is that the aggregate production using the sum of the resources is greater (or no less) than the sum of the production of the member countries separately.[6] This proposition is quite distinct from considerations of comparative advantage and gains from freeing commodity trade, as it is based on a given set of prices. There is a gain from freeing trade in primary factors over and above the gain from freeing commodity trade, assuming the latter does not equalise factor prices. This result derives from differences in the countries in terms of the productivities of factors. If there are differences in technologies between the countries, and if the factors migrating to the country with the higher productivity—due, say, to superior management methods—take on the productivity (for a given factor intensity) of the receiving country, the result holds *a fortiori*. However, it is not true that the real incomes of all factor-owners in the region will increase.

Links between Factor Trade and Commodity Trade

Factor trade is linked to commodity trade in both directions and in a number of ways.

There are trade-related investment restrictions—TRIMs in the language of the GATT since the Uruguay Round—which affect the pattern of trade associated with foreign investment flows. These may affect both imports and exports of the country in which the foreign investment and production occurs.

Conversely, when production facilities in one country are owned by foreign investors from another country or countries, trade creation and diversion will produce international income flows which may partly offset the effects on commodity trade flows. For those commodities in which trade is created, part of the production may be in countries outside the area which supply intermediate inputs into the production of the goods created; similarly, for those commodities in which trade is diverted, part of the production may occur outside the area.

In the mid-1990s, attention has been directed towards the ways in which changes in market access for commodities may affect the allocation of foreign investment flows around the world. For example, a case of commodity trade diversion may lead to further diversion of foreign direct investment to an RTA if the expanded production facilities are financed by foreign investors. Indeed, all of the final general equilibrium effects in the world economy may induce changes in the allocation of foreign direct investments. An RTA which is expanding in commodity coverage or country membership or deepening may attract new investments to its area if it is perceived as offering new opportunities in an environment of greater real growth.

If the RTA is a free trade area with no common external tariff, there may be similar reallocations of foreign direct investments within it. In this context, the choice of rules of origin by the RTA are crucial. Strict rules of origin imposed by one or more countries will tend to divert foreign investments to that country or countries. For example, the Hondas produced in Canada have not satisfied the US rules of origin and have been treated, therefore, as imports from outside CUSTA. This is likely to induce new investments and production by Honda in the USA rather than in the member country, Canada. In such cases, we need to consider trade and investment effects together. These effects are likely to be particularly important in a hub-and-spoke regional system.

In relation to the transfers of technology, there may be restrictions based on regional preferences for transfers of technology or associated intellectual property rights in an RTA, though these flows are largely unrestricted in most countries today. By joining an RTA, a country may also indirectly affect these flows by changing the pattern of trade in goods and services and foreign investment.

Non-Border Instruments and New Issues

Non-border instruments

Second-generation agreements have progressed beyond the removal of border trade restrictions to cover some non-border restrictions or distortions which affect international (or cross-border) trade. These include differences in rates of national subsidies and bounties, and in rates of excise, value-added tax, and other commodity taxation. They also include the harmonisation of standards, business law regulations and competition policy where differences between countries inhibit competition.

The impetus for most of these developments has come from the EU, most particularly from the set of measures known as the European Single Market which were announced in 1985 (Commission of the European Communities, 1985) and completed at the end of 1992. In relation to trade in both commodities and factors, the EU has set a number of precedents in integrating the economies of its members. For example, its 1992 measures contain a 'new approach' to harmonisation, based on the principle of mutual recognition of each other's standards. The EU has also used this method in the area of recognition of professional training and certification in professional bodies. Mutual recognition has several advantages over the traditional choice of negotiation of common regulations. It avoids protracted government negotiations; it gives agents more time to adjust; it reduces the cost of the bureaucracy; and it may, in some cases, be more responsive to the preferences of economic agents. It also avoids the necessity of courts or agencies to enforce arbitrary area-wide standards.

Some other recent second-generation agreements have followed the EU in seeking to harmonise selected policy instruments. Article 12 of the CER Agreement declared that the two countries shall 'examine the scope for taking action to harmonize requirements relating to such matters as standards, technical specifications and testing procedures, domestic labelling and restrictive trade practices'. The approach adopted to harmonisation in the CER is to provide a framework for cooperation between relevant authorities in the two countries, and to use 'best endeavours' towards this end, rather than requiring harmonisation. There has been considerable debate in Australia and more in New Zealand, as in the EU and in the USA and Canada, about the meaning of the concept of harmonisation. The prevalent view is that harmonisation shall not mean 'uniformity' or 'replication'.

This view has been reflected in the areas to which harmonisation has been applied; these are the agreements on customs procedures and industrial standards before the 1988 review of CER and the areas of quarantine administrative procedures, customs policies and procedures, technical barriers to trade and business law which were included in the 1988 review. For example, Article 8 of the Memorandum of Understanding on Harmonisation of Business Law states explicitly that 'Both Governments recognize that effective harmonisation does not require replication of laws, although that may be appropriate in some cases.' However, the Joint Understanding on Harmonisation of Customs Policies and Procedures states that the countries shall adopt 'common approaches wherever appropriate'. The outcome has been a considerable convergence of policies and procedures in the areas covered by these harmonisation agreements.

These developments in relation to the instruments of government policy and the methods of eliminating restrictions on market access have created new forms of regional cooperation. With the removal of non-border barriers among members, market access among the members of the EU is now more free than trade between any other countries, including bilateral trade involving partner countries which have virtually no border restrictions on commodity trade, such as Singapore or Hong Kong. Extension of the policy measures to non-border taxes and regulations is based on the realisation that *complete equality of access* within an area requires more than the removal of all border restrictions, that is, more than *complete free trade*.

When is complete equality of access to the markets of some area achieved? The old terminology used by international economists of free trade areas, customs unions and common markets is now inadequate. The EU uses the term *single market*. A single market is manifestly not a common market, but what precisely is it? In introducing the measures for the European Single Market, the White Paper began with the statement:

> Unifying the market (of 320 million) presupposes the member States will agree on the abolition of barriers of all kinds, harmonization of rules, approximation of legislation and tax structures, strengthening of monetary cooperation and the necessary flanking measures to encourage European firms to work together. [Commission of the European Communities, 1985, p. 4.]

This conveys the essential idea that there should be no barriers to the operation of a single market across the whole of the EU; there is completely free access in a single market. But the idea is still vague.

The best definition of a single market is one in which the law of one price prevails (Lloyd, 1992; Flam, 1992). This means that in a competitive market, for either a produced commodity or a factor, there is only one price, allowing for transport and other transfer costs which prevent perfect arbitrage. It implies the removal of all border and non-border restrictions on commodity trade, and the harmonisation of commodity taxes and other measures which affect access to markets. In factor markets, it implies the removal of all border restrictions, the harmonisation of factor taxes, and the introduction of rights of establishment and national treatment for foreign-owned factors. This concept of a single market is more useful than the old concept of a common market: it is more precise, and it provides a standard against which one can measure the degree of integration of markets within a region.

Using this definition of a single market for a commodity, one can say that an RTA is a single market if and only if all commodity markets are single, that is, if the law of one price prevails in all markets. This applies to both commodity and factor markets. Alternatively, we can say that the national economies of the group of countries are completely integrated. Thus, complete regional integration requires complete free trade for both commodities and factors, and the removal of other non-border regulations and taxes which prevent the establishment of single markets.

With this concept of a single market, one can say that the second-generation agreements represent a progression towards regional integration rather than towards regional free trade. However, many regional agreements are still concerned entirely or essentially with progression towards regional free trade. For this reason, I prefer to retain the term *regional trading agreement* as a descriptor rather than the term *regional integration agreement* which is used in, for example, Anderson and Blackhurst (1993).

New Policy Issues

The second revision of the Treaty of Rome by means of the Treaty on European Union, known generally as the Maastricht treaty and signed in February 1992, has progressed beyond a single market. It seeks to establish a *full economic union* of members. The EU concept of a full economic union entails a fiscal and monetary union and common policies in many other areas, such as the environment and social policy.

A monetary union entails a single currency and a single central bank, that is, true unification of the monetary system. A fiscal or 'tax' union does not entail a single set of taxes within the area. Rather, it entails equal tax treatment within member countries of all taxpayers in the sense that there is no geographic discrimination among member citizens or corporations. (The standard reference is to Shibata, 1967.) This is national treatment in the fiscal area. Tax rates may be different in each member country. The further step of unifying the tax rates may be called a *unified fiscal system*. Thus, with respect to the treatment of domestic taxes, a fiscal union stands in relation to a unified fiscal system in the same way, with respect to border taxes, as a free trade area stands in relation to a customs union. The EU is essentially a fiscal union, not a unified fiscal system, though it is taking steps to harmonise the value-added tax rates in the EU, and its budget expenditures are growing.

No other RTAs have moved towards a complete union. There are, however, signs that some of them are expanding to encompass some of the other new issues. One such area is environmental policy. Mexico's environmental policies were a concern for the USA, and NAFTA embodies some convergence of the environmental policies of its members. Another area is labour standards. Again, this was a major concern in the NAFTA negotiations. Both environmental issues and labour standards pose the problem that they are partly national problems which impinge indirectly and often unintentionally on international trade and they are partly genuine cross-border problems. Only the latter category is suitable for bilateral or multilateral regional cooperation.

Competition policy is another area of emerging activity in RTAs. This is more clearly an area where cross-border problems can and do arise. The principal difficulty lies in developing ways in which any policies that might be agreed upon by the governments can be enforced. Bilateral agreements relating to competition policies, such as the Agreement on Anti-trust Cooperation between the USA and the EC, depend entirely for enforcement upon the remedies available to the individual nations under national legislation, but these are palpably inadequate to deal with international disputes. The EU and the CER[7] have developed regional competition policies, and both of these involve members with common or similar laws and a high degree of integration and government policy coordination generally.

Conclusion

Evidently, the scope of RTAs has expanded continually though unevenly over the last three decades. There has been an increase in the depth of cuts in tariff and non-tariff barriers to trade within these arrangements, and a steady extension in the commodity coverage. Some of these effects of trade discrimination have been mitigated by multilateral and unilateral reductions in the barriers to entry into these regional markets. Most of the concern now is with the effects on third countries and on the global trading system. This is exacerbated by the increase in the size of the trading blocs.

Countries which are not members of any large bloc are still fearful of the role of RTAs and the possibilities of discrimination against outside countries. This applies to Australia as an example. Its earnestness in the cause of multilateralism is demonstrated by the formation of the Cairns Group and by the major unilateral reductions (consistent with GATT) in its own tariff and non-tariff restrictions on imports which it announced in 1973, 1988 and 1991, and the lesser piecemeal reductions for individual industries.[8] It also proposed the establishment of APEC in 1989 as a regional organisation committed to multilateralism. Similarly, the East Asian countries, which have not been members of any regional trading arrangements apart from ASEAN, are strong advocates of global reductions in trade barriers (Young, 1993).

Despite the successful conclusion of the Uruguay Round, regional trading arrangements continue to proliferate. This may be partly because there are still substantial barriers to trade within regions for some more highly protected commodity groups, and partly to prevent or reduce the possibilities of being subject to contingent protection.

Another possible explanation of the proliferation of RTAs is the desire for greater integration within regions. The freeing of commodity trade within RTAs by removing border restrictions seems itself to have prompted the member countries to examine non-border policies that restrict or distort international trade. This, in turn, has led to consideration of other policies such as standards and tax policies, and eventually to fiscal and monetary union in the case of the EU. There is a natural progression, as the removal of one set of barriers has highlighted the importance of other barriers or restrictions which remain.

The focus of policies in RTAs has changed substantially since the mid-1980s. They are now concerned with many issues beyond the removal of border barriers to trade in goods, which is the subject of the GATT articles. In particular, the EU has progressed far beyond the conception of free trade in the GATT.

This poses a question regarding the international regulation of regional trading arrangements. The Uruguay Round did result in the General Agreement on Trade in Services: this contains provisions relating to the formation of free trade areas and customs unions, but these are separate from and parallel to those of Article XXIV. Similarly, the Uruguay Round extended the powers of the GATT/WTO in some areas such as intellectual property, but it does not cover many areas of policy which have been increasingly subject to regulation or harmonisation in RTAs. And with minor exceptions, such as TRIMs and some aspects of intellectual property, GATT/WTO does not cover international trade or movement of factors. It is hoped that the new WTO will reconsider the articles of the agreement which relate to regional trading arrangements, because they are now outmoded.

Notes

1 On the basis of the physical region, it should also include all of the Central and South American countries. This group is frequently omitted by economists in Asia and the non-Asian English-speaking countries (USA, Canada, Australia and New Zealand), principally on the grounds that the economies of these countries are not as well integrated into the region. By convention, this sub-region also does not include the area of the former USSR or the current Russia which borders the Pacific Ocean. I shall follow these conventions.

   This definition of the Asia-Pacific region coincides with the grouping of countries in APEC before Mexico was admitted, but the countries of the Asian region were not selected on this basis. Rather, the formation of APEC itself represents a feeling of common interests among its members and a desire to explore these interests collectively.

2 The Canada–USA Automotive Agreement was a sectoral agreement only, though it was important in beginning the process of the integration of the Canadian and US economies by means of formal discriminatory agreements.

3 For a discussion of the effects of regional trading arrangements, see Wooton (1986).

4 In early general equilibrium models of the effects of customs unions, Mundell (1964) and Riezman (1979) showed that the terms of trade of outside countries will decline under plausible assumptions. These models, however, are static and do not include many of the sources of increased national income in the member countries from improved efficiency of factor use, increased competition and economies of scale.

5 One might note that the old British Imperial Preference Scheme and its later variant, the British Preferential Scheme, were of the hub-and-spoke type, with the added complication that many of the countries at the ends of the spokes formed supplementary agreements with each other.

6 The only source of this proposition I know of is Wegge (1974, pp. 169–70), where the proof is in terms of production possibility sets.

   A simpler proof can be provided from the properties of the national product function. Under standard conditions (in particular, the production possibility set of the nation is convex and there is perfect competition in all markets), each trading country has a well-defined national product function. This function is $g(p,v)$, where p is the vector of market prices and v is the vector of national endowments.

   Moreover, this function is concave and linearly homogeneous in v, as Wegge showed. Now a function which is concave and linearly homogeneous in its arguments is super-additive in these arguments (Sharkey and Telser, 1978, p.36). Therefore, if the two countries have the same technologies and $g(p,v^1)$ and $g(p,v^2)$ are the national product functions of the two countries, countries 1 and 2 respectively, then

   $g(p,v^1 + v^2) = g(p,v^1) + g(p,v^2)$.

   This proposition is a global result compared to the local result obtained by Michael (1991). Moreover, this proof can be extended to a world with increasing returns to scale. Increasing returns to scale make the national product function super-additive in v.

7 See Vautier, Farmer and Baxt (1990).

8 This view has not prevented it from developing a free trade area with New Zealand in its own region (CER), maintaining a preferential tariff agreement with Canada, and

P. LLOYD

expanding the non-reciprocal arrangements with Papua New Guinea and the South
Pacific Forum island state and its own Developing Country Preference Scheme. But it
does not see these preferences as inconsistent with multilateralism. For example, 'Australia is outside the framework of major bloc concepts and has the strongest interest in
ensuring … that trading arrangements develop in ways that support the open multilateral trading system.' (Department of Foreign Affairs, 1992, p. 42).

References

Anderson, K., and Blackhurst, R. (eds) (1993), *Regional Integration and the Global Trading
System*, Harvester Wheatsheaf, London.
Armington, P. S. (1969), 'A Theory of Demand for Products Distinguished by Place of
Production', *IMF Staff Papers*, 16: 1, 159–78.
Asian Development Bank (1992), *Asian Development Outlook 1992*, Asian Development
Bank, Manila.
Australia. Bureau of Industry Economics (1989), 'Trade Liberalization and Australian
Manufacturing Industry: The Impact of the Australia-New Zealand Closer
Relations Trade Agreement', Research Report No. 29, Australian Government
Publishing Service, Canberra.
Australia, Department of Foreign Affairs, East Asia Analytical Unit (1992), *Australia and
North-East Asia in the 1990s: Accelerating Change*, Australian Government Publishing
Service, Canberra.
Burniaux, J. M., and Waelbroeck, J. (1992), 'Preliminary Results of Two Experimental
Models of General Equilibrium with Imperfect Competition', *Journal of Policy
Modeling*, 14, 65–92.
Commission of the European Communities (1985), *Completing the Internal Market: White
Paper for the Commission to the European Council*, Office for Official Publications of the
European Communities, Luxembourg.
De la Torre, A., and Kelly, M. (1992), *Regional Trade Arrangements*, International
Monetary Fund, Washington, DC.
Drysdale, P., and Garnaut, R. (1989a), 'A Pacific Free Trade Area?', Pacific Economic
Papers, No. 171, Australia-Japan Research Centre, Australian National University.
Flam, H. (1992), 'Product Markets and 1992: Full Integration, Large Gains', *Journal of
Economic Perspectives*, 6, 7–30.
Fukasaku, K. (1992), *Economic Reorganization and Intra-industry Trade: Pacific-Asian
Perspectives*, OECD Development Centre Technical Papers, No. 53, OECD
Development Centre, Paris.
Garnaut, R. (1989), *Australia and the Northeast Asian Ascendancy*, Australian Government
Publishing Service, Canberra.
Harris, R. G., and Cox, D. (1984), *Trade, Industrial Policy and Canadian Manufacturing*,
Ontario Economic Council, Toronto.
International Monetary Fund (1991), *Balance of Payments Yearbook*, IMF, Washington,
DC.
Jones, R., King, R. E. and Klein, M. (1993), 'Economic Integration between Hong
Kong, Taiwan and the Coastal Provinces of China', *OECD Economic Studies*, Spring,
1, 115–45.
Kemp, M., and Wan, H. (1976), 'An Elementary Proposition Concerning the
Formation of Customs Unions', *Journal of International Economics*, 6, 95–7.
Kowalczky, C., and Wonnacott, R. J. (1992), 'Hubs and Spokes, and Free Trade in
the Americas', Working Paper no. 92–14, Department of Economics, Dartmouth
College, New Hampshire.

Krugman, P. (1991b), 'Is Bilateralism Bad?', in E. Helpman and A. Razin (eds), *International Trade and Trade Policy*, MIT Press, Cambridge, Mass.

Lloyd, P. J. (1992), 'Regionalisation and World Trade', *OECD Economic Studies*, 18, Spring, 7–43.

Michael, M. S. (1991), 'From a Customs Union to a Common Market: The Need for Factor-tax Harmonization', *Canadian Journal of Economics*, 25, May, 493–9.

Mundell, R. (1957), 'International Trade and Factor Mobility', *American Economic Review*, 47, 321–37.

Mundell, R. (1964), 'Tariff Preferences and the Terms of Trade', *Manchester School of Economic and Social Studies*, 32, January, 1–13.

Norman, V. D. (1990), 'Assessing Trade and Welfare Effects of Trade Liberalization: A Comparison of Alternative: Approaches to CGE Modelling with Imperfect Competition', *European Economic Review*, 34, 725–51.

OECD (1995), *Regional Integration and the Multilateral Trading System: Synergy and Divergence*, OECD, Paris.

Richardson, J. D. (1989), 'Empirical Research on Trade Liberalization with Imperfect Competition: A Survey', *OECD Economic Studies*, 12, Spring, 7–50.

Riezman, R. (1979),'A 3x3 Model of Customs Unions', *Journal of International Economics*, 9, 341–54.

Sharkey, W. W., and Telser, L. G. (1978), 'Supportable Cost Functions for the Multiproduct Firm', *Journal of Economic Theory*, 18, 23–37.

Shibata, H. (1967), 'The Theory of Economic Unions: A Comparative Analysis of Customs Unions, Free Trade Areas, and Tax Unions', in C. S. Shoup (ed.), *Fiscal Harmonization in Common Markets*, Columbia University Press, New York.

Smith, A., and Venables, A. J. (1988), 'Completing the Internal Market in the European Community: Some Industry Simulations', *European Economic Review*, 32, 1501–25.

Srinivasan, T. N., Whalley, J., and Wooton, I. (1993), 'Measuring the Effects of Regionalism on Trade and Welfare', in K. Anderson and R. Blackhurst (eds), *Regional Integration and the Global Trading System*, Harvester Wheatsheaf, New York.

Vautier, K., Farmer, J., and Baxt, R. (eds) (1990), *CER and Business Competition*, Commerce Clearing House, Auckland.

Viner, J. (1950), *The Customs Union Issue*, Carnegie Foundation of International Peace, New York.

Wegge, L. L. (1974), 'Notes on the Regional Product Function,' *Tijdschrift voor Economie*, 19, 165–86.

Wooton, I. (1986), 'Preferential Trading Arrangements: An Investigation', *Journal of International Economics*, 21, 81–97.

Wooton, I. (1988), 'Towards a Common Market: Factor Mobility in a Customs Union', *Canadian Journal of Economics*, 21, 525–38.

World Bank (1991), *World Development Report 1991*, Oxford University Press, Oxford.

World Bank (1992a), *Export Processing Zones*, World Bank Policy and Research Series No. 20, March, Washington, DC.

World Trade Organization (1995), *Regionalism and the World Trading System*, World Trade Organization, Geneva.

Yamazawa, I., Hirata, A., and Yokota, K. (1991), 'Evolving Patterns of Comparative Advantage in the Pacific Economies', in M. Ariff (ed.), *The Pacific Economy: Growth and Stability*, Allen & Unwin.

Young, S. (1993), 'East Asia as a Regional Force for Globalism', in Anderson and Blackhurst (1993).

The future of the CER Agreement: a single market for Australia and New Zealand

Closer economic relations

The Closer Economic Relations (CER) Agreement came into effect on 1 January 1983. It replaced the New Zealand–Australia Free Trade Agreement, which had come into effect on 1 January 1966. In terms of the usual economists' classification of regional trading agreements, the CER denotes a free trade area, whereas its predecessor, although formally recognized by GATT (General Agreement on Tariffs and Trade) as a 'free trade area', was restricted to freeing trade in products of the forest products sector and a quite limited range of manufactures.

The objectives of the CER Agreement, as stated in Article 1, are:

(a)   to strengthen the broader relationship between Australia and New Zealand;

(b)   to develop closer economic relations between the member states through a mutually beneficial expansion of free trade between Australia and New Zealand;

(c)   to eliminate barriers to trade between Australia and New Zealand under an agreed timetable and with a minimum of disruption; and

(d)   to develop trade between New Zealand and Australia under conditions of fair competition.

Objectives (b) and (c) state unmistakeably that the trade objective is ultimate free trade. The first objective, and the preamble to the Agreement, declare that the free trade provisions are part of a more basic desire to maintain closer economic relations, and the preamble refers to 'strengthening and fostering links and cooperation in such fields as investment, marketing, movement of people, tourism and transport'.

The CER Agreement was a major accomplishment, given the long history of failed attempts at freeing trade between the two countries and the climate of opinion at the time.

The Ministerial Review of the Agreement in June 1988 reached agreement on a 'comprehensive package of arrangements designed to accelerate the implementation of the full free trade area and open a new chapter in the closer economic relationship between the two countries'. Free trade in commodities was achieved on 1 July 1990, by which time all tariffs, import licensing and quantitative restrictions, and export incentives restricting trade between the two countries were removed. This was five years ahead of the date specified in the Agreement. The other principal features of this important review were the extension of Australian state preferences to trans-Tasman government purchasing, an agreement on trade in services which freed trade in services except those specified by 1 January 1989, the termination of anti-dumping measures from I July 1990, the agreement on avoiding industry assistance policy which impacts on competition within the free trade area, and the agreement to harmonize policies and practices in a number of areas. The areas of harmonization included business law, customs policies and procedures, quarantine administration, and technical barriers to trade. In the important area of competition policy it was agreed that competition policies in each country should be amended so that dominance was defined as a dominant position in the market of either country or the combined market. This review was another notable and praiseworthy achievement in bilateral trading relations.

As a result of the procedures agreed to in the 1988 review there has been further progress in removing impediments to trade. In particular, a comprehensive review of the scope for harmonization of business laws identified a number of areas where harmonization would be beneficial to the business communities (Steering Committee of Officials, 1990). To implement the 1988 agreement on dominance in competition policy, both Australia and New Zealand in May–June 1990 altered the laws relating to enforcement of orders and judgements to allow their courts to sit in each other's jurisdictions to determine competition law cases. Also an Agreement on Standards, Accreditation and Quality was signed by the two governments in October 1990.

The CER has been accompanied by a rapid expansion of trade between Australia and New Zealand. Table 1 contains series of imports into Australia and New Zealand from the Tasman partner for the period immediately preceding the CER until the latest available year. It also includes 1965, the year where the New Zealand–Australia Free Trade Agreement was introduced, and five-yearly intervals until 1980 for comparison.

Table 1   Australia–New Zealand commodity trade, 1965–93

	Australian imports from NZ		NZ imports from Australia	
	Total US$m	% total imports	Total US$m	% total imports
1965	55.99	1.51	199.98	18.36
1970	117.60	2.35	247.04	19.38
1975	288.01	2.62	600.01	19.05
1980	761.24	3.41	1 011.36	18.48
1981	853.50	3.27	1 079.36	18.81
1982	803.23	3.03	1 102.58	19.02
1983	753.52	3.54	1 028.79	19.29
1984	963.42	3.75	1 252.38	20.38
1985	1 052.09	4.08	1 025.67	17.25
1986	1 010.16	3.86	980.14	16.33
1987	1 220.78	4.13	1 474.63	20.28
1988	1 608.98	4.41	1 587.46	21.60
1989	1 827.95	4.09	1 829.93	20.96
1990	1 886.84	4.40	1 930.55	20.19
1991	1 947.73	4.59	1 848.81	22.02
1992	2 064.30	4.63	1 941.13	21.19
1993	2 225.08	4.93	2 003.72	21.68

Note: This table replaces that in the original source, which provided local currency data up to 1990.

Source: International Economic Database, Australian National University, Canberra.

These trade statistics are in current price US dollars. Most of the increase in trade throughout the period of the New Zealand–Australia Free Trade Agreement and the CER is due to inflation rather than to increases in the volume of trade. Nevertheless, trade in real terms has increased steadily, particularly since the formation of the CER.

Another indication of the effects of a preferential reduction in trade barriers is the change in the percentage of trade which is with the CER partner. The New Zealand share of Australian imports has steadily increased for New Zealand throughout the period of the New Zealand–Australia Free Trade Agreement and CER but the Australian share of New Zealand imports has been roughly constant. New Zealand seems to have gained more from the trade agreements than Australia.

The CER is a successful and far-reaching trade liberalization agreement. It is a more advanced form of trade liberalization than the Canada–US Free Trade Agreement of 1989, which has a number of exclusions and exceptions that substantially limit the extent to which trade in both goods and services will be freed. It is second only to the European Community (EC) in terms of the range of measures which relate to or bear upon trade that is covered.

Yet there is still no free trade in a number of important services, notably shipping between the two countries and entry into Australia for New Zealand exports of civil aviation and telecommunications; there is no common external tariff, no common commodity taxes/subsidies. and a number of domestic policies relating to technical standards and business laws inhibit trade in goods and services. Furthermore, the CER Agreement is unique among regional trading arrangements around the world in that it has freed completely trade in all goods and most services, and there is free movement of residents of both countries under the long-standing Trans-Tasman Travel arrangements, but there are still significant restrictions on capital movements, especially from New Zealand to Australia.

Another feature of the restrictions on trade which remain between the two countries is that the Australian restrictions on imports of goods and services and capital flows are (at the time of writing) in 1991 more comprehensive in extent than the New Zealand restrictions on imports from Australia. This is especially true in services where the New Zealand exemptions are less than the Australian, in agriculture (where trade is still inhibited by regulations on trade across state borders) and in the area of capital flows. It is the reverse of the situation which prevailed throughout the period of the New Zealand–Australia Free Trade Agreement and it is the result of the extensive and rapid liberalization of trade and the removal of assistance for agricultural producers and manufacturers which New Zealand began in 1984 with its global trade liberalization programme, and the deregulation of the service sector in New Zealand.

However, this difference in the extent of barriers does not imply that imports into New Zealand from Australia are restricted more in value than Australian imports from New Zealand as the effects of freeing trade bilaterally depend on the *margins of preference* for all goods and services. When bilateral trade has been freed totally the margins of preference are measured simply by the difference between the rates for the rest of the world countries and the zero rate for the partner. Unfortunately, it is not possible to compare the structure of industry assistance *vis-à-vis* third countries. In Australia, the Industry Commission (and before it the Industries Assistance Commission and the Tariff Board) has prepared an annual set of estimates for all commodity groups, including in recent years agricultural and mining industries (see Industry Commission 1990a, Appendixes 9–11) and there are estimates for some service industries. Unfortunately, there is no comparable series in New Zealand. The first set of measures in New Zealand of assistance to producers which were comprehensive in covering all manufacturing and agricultural production were in Syntec Economic Services (1988). These revealed that in 1987–88 for the manufacturing sector the average effective rate of industry assistance, which is the best single summary measure of the assistance, was 26 and 18 per cent for manufacturing and pastoral agriculture respectively. The comparable figures for Australia in the same year were 19 and 49 per cent respectively.

Since 1987–88 the New Zealand rates have fallen in the manufacturing sector under the trade liberalization programme. The reductions will end in 1996, by which time the maximum tariff will be 10 per cent. Post- 1992 the average rates of assistance to domestic producers *vis-à-vis* third countries in New Zealand will be lower than that in Australia for the agricultural and service sectors and possibly for the manufacturing sector too. This means that the margins of preference which New Zealand enjoys because of the freeing of bilateral trade will in the future be greater on average than those which the Australian producers receive.

The last feature of the CER Agreement that should be noted is that the freeing of trade between the two countries since 1983 has been accompanied by a significant liberalization of trade *vis-à-vis* third countries over the same period. This is especially true of New Zealand but it is also true of Australia.

This fact has two important implications. It means that the standard dangers of welfare losses to the two countries, given that the preferences divert import (and export) trade from the lowest cost sources of supply and deflect trade because of differences in the nominal rates of protection for materials and other inputs, are reduced. It also means that the Agreement is outward-looking in the sense that the discrimination against third countries has been reduced and the total trade with these countries has been expanded by global assistance reductions. Indeed, in the case of New Zealand, the bilateral freeing of trade was only undertaken by the smaller country because it adopted this strategy of avoiding the cost of increased trading with a country that is a high cost supplier of many commodities. The CER was a part of a larger set of trade liberalization strategies.

Trends in world trade
Both governments have expressed the view that the CER should be an outward-looking agreement which should not restrict the trade with third countries. Both have expressed the view that the CER should provide a base for the development of enterprises which are competitive on the global marketplace. This is a reflection of the growing concern of both the Australian and New Zealand governments that they have been losing competitiveness in world markets which are becoming increasingly competitive and more closely integrated. They share this concern with other countries such as the USA. This concern was also a fundamental factor behind the EC movement to the measures of the EC '92.

The added feature of the Australian and New Zealand economies that needs to be considered is that, on the world stage, these two nations are two small and peculiar trading economies. Their peculiarity is that they are high-income countries with a specialization in primary commodities.

This pattern of commodity trade is an oddity among developed market economies. Unfortunately, it is a specialization in markets which have the features that the world demand for the products has grown less rapidly than that for manufactures and services and the world markets are more heavily restricted. The pattern has been exacerbated historically by remoteness, which is not easily changed, and by the highly protectionist policies towards manufactures in the two countries, which are changeable and have recently been changing rapidly. The central question for both economies is how they can become more closely linked to the markets which are growing more rapidly. The governments of both countries are strongly in favour of a multilateral approach to those barriers to world trade which result from border protection and are strong supporters of GATT.

A comparison of the CER with the EC Single Market

In order to appreciate what the establishment of a single market across Australia and New Zealand would imply, Table 2 compares the (1991) CER with the Single Market measures in EC '92. A +(−) sign indicates that the measures in the EC have, or at least will have, by 1992, progressed further (less) towards a single market than the corresponding provisions of the CER, provided the measures are implemented by all EC members. An = sign indicates that the progress is roughly equal in the EC '92 and in the CER. An ± sign indicates approximate equality of single-marketness, some features in the EC being more single and some less single than in the CER. The measures in the EC relating to road transport are not applicable to the CER because of the separation by the Tasman Sea. One should also note that the single market features of a common external tariff and freedom of movement of capital do not appear in this table as they were achieved in the original Treaty of Rome.

There is a preponderance of = or ± signs, indicating that in many respects the degree of single-marketness in the CER is about equal to that of the EC. However, the EC '92 has progressed further towards a single market than the CER in a number of areas, notably the common market for all services, the common excise and value added taxes, and freedom of movement of capital. In two significant areas the CER has progressed further than the EC '92. These areas are the important areas of subsidies and bounties to producers ('state aids' in the EC terminology) and 'Proposals for Cooperation in Training and Education'. The first reflects the agreement reached in the 1988 Ministerial Review of the CER under which the two governments agreed to avoid the adoption of industry-specific measures which have an adverse effect on competition between industries in the free trade area. This was based on the principle that 'bounties and subsidies providing long-term competition can no longer be regarded as viable instruments of industry policy' in a free trade area. The second is the result of cooperation between the two governments in recognizing the qualifications of professionals trained in the other country which precedes the CER but has been recognized as a principle in the Agreement.

Overall, the general conclusion is that the CER experience parallels that of the EC in many respects but that the EC is advancing more rapidly than the CER towards a single market.

Table 2   A comparison of the EC '92 and CER internal market measures

Market measures	Goods	Services	Labour	Capital
Removal of border protection and restrictions	+ (abolition of frontier controls) = (liberalization of public procurement)	= (liberalization of public procurement) Not applicable (abolition of quotas at border (road transport))	+ (abolition of intra-EC frontier controls on individuals (elimination of obstacles to the movement and residence of migrant workers and unemployed)	+ (monitoring of exchange controls and restrictions on capital movements)
Removal of discriminatory non-border taxes/ and discriminatory subsidies/regulations	+ (fiscal approximation) − (state aids) + (harmonization of standards in sectors)	+ (common market for financial services) + (common market for transport) + (common market for new technologies and services) + (harmonization of income tax transactions in securities)	+ (right of establishment for professionals with higher education diplomas based on mutual recognition = (European vocational training card) + (harmonization of income tax provisions for migrants)	=+ (European company statute) + (European interest grouping) ± (proposals on cross-border mergers and takeovers)
Measures to improve functioning single activities	± (company law framework) ± (harmonization of intellectual and industrial property law) ± (company policy)	± (company law framework) ± (harmonization of intellectual and industrial property law) ± (company policy)	− (proposals for cooperation in training and education	± (company law framework) ± (harmonization of intellectual and industrial property law) ± (company policy)

From the point of view of the future development of the CER one sees that the CER is an advanced form of regional trading arrangement with many features of a single market. In a few ways the CER is very advanced; these include the abolition of export incentives affecting bilateral trade, the agreement to abolish subsidies and bounties which affect bilateral trade, and in the area of business law generally but particularly in competition policy with the extension of dominance to the single trans-Tasman market and the legislation to allow the courts to sit in the jurisdiction of the other country. On the other hand, there are some areas in which current taxes/subsidies/regulations fall significantly short of a single market; these include the absence of a common external tariff, the absence of a common market for some services, inter-country differences in commodity and value-added tax rates, and the absence of an agreement on capital flows.

The advantages and disadvantages of a single market

The appeal of a single market is that it removes all differences between the member countries in the rates of taxes/subsidies/regulations which discriminate between producers or consumers according to their location. Since the time of Adam Smith at least, economists have known that all such differences distort the choices of consumers and producers. This simple but powerful idea applies to distortions in all markets, that is, to the markets for goods and services and factors alike.

As examples, consider two of the measures of the EC '92 which go beyond the traditional concern of free trade areas and customs unions with that subset of discriminatory instruments which apply at the border. These are the harmonization of standards and the 'approximation' of tax rates.

The loss of efficiency in production due to inter-country differences in standards applying to industrial safety, health, transport, goods specifications, labelling, and so on is obvious. The primary loss is the distortion due to differences in costs. The costs of meeting the different standards will differ between the two countries and thus consumers will buy the products at different prices in the two countries. These costs include the costs due to the loss of consumer welfare because the standards may prohibit the sale of goods in one country but not in the other.

Now there may be a justification for standards which, say, protect the consumer from products which are unsafe in ways which the consumer cannot perceive as a buyer. In such cases, however, there is no reason in general to expect that the standards should differ between countries. Either they are too stringent in one or too lax in the other or both too stringent or too lax but by differing degrees. Both producers and consumers will benefit if the standards are harmonized, provided of course that the harmonization moves in the direction of the country with the better standards (or, more generally, the optimal standards).

The second general source of welfare loss is that differences in standards between jurisdictions impose extra costs of compliance. Harmonization which results in simplification will yield benefits by reducing the costs of production.

The second example is the equalization of commodity tax rates. Inter-country differences in tax rates on a commodity or group of commodities distort the pattern of consumption and trade in these commodities because they lead to differences in relative consumer prices between the countries concerned as tax differences are passed on to consumers/users, and usually to the same extent in different countries as the elasticities of demand and supply which determine the incidence will not in general differ systematically between countries. Article 99 of the Treaty of Rome specifically provided for the approximation of indirect taxes. Accordingly, in 1967 the EC member estates decided that the existing turnover taxes must be replaced by a value-added tax levied on a common basis, and the broad principles of the harmonized common tax base were laid down in 1967. Indeed, the White Paper stated that 'It is clear . . . that the harmonization of indirect taxes has always been regarded as an essential and integral part of achieving a common market' (Commission of the European Communities, 1985, p. 42). However, the Commission lacked the means of enforcing common value-added tax rates. In 1989 there were wide differences of many percentage points among the 12 members for each of the three rates permitted – the normal rates, the reduced rates and the high rates (see Siebert 1990, p. 55). These will be eliminated by 1992 under the European Single Market.

Another advantage of a single market is that it would increase competition. Commodity trade liberalization by itself will increase competition. A study by Australia's Bureau of Industry Economics (1989) indicated that the gains from trade liberalization are likely to be much greater than previously estimated because of economies of scale and increased competition effects. The full extent of potential competition can only be reached if all barriers due to non-border restrictions, standards, and the territorial limitation of competition law and other business laws are removed.

The disadvantages of a single market relate to the fact that the equalization of rates (or equivalent) rates of taxes or subsidies across the members of the area will generally result in the creation of new differences between the rates which apply within the area on the one hand and the rates which apply to trade with other countries outside the area on the other. This is exemplified by the classic problem of trade diversion when the rates of taxes are due to tariffs at the border. The gains due to the equalization of rates within the area for some commodities will be offset by losses due to the differentiation of the rates between the member countries and the non-member countries on other commodities where the discriminatory tariff reductions induce some countries within the area to substitute imports from members for imports from other countries which produce them at a lower real cost ex-tariff. Such trade diversion may apply to export trade as well as import trade, and to capital flows when the source or destination of investment flows are distorted by trade preferences.

Precisely the same problem arises with other equalizations in a single market which create new differences between the members and non-members. Perhaps the most important such case which would be involved if Australia and New Zealand were to form a single market is that of a common external tariff. All of these are examples of the theory of the second best which arises with any piecemeal reforms.

In the case of equalization of rates of *non-border* taxes/subsidies such as excise or value added rates, the creation of a single market with a single rate for each commodity across the whole area would not create new differences between the rates at which the goods are traded across borders. But it would create new differences in the rates across commodities which give rise to analogous gains and losses. However, the danger of losses can be reduced by various strategies of harmonization.

It is likely that the gains from the formation of a single market would be greater for New Zealand simply because it joins with a larger market with more market opportunities and more suppliers. It is also true that the greater orientation of the Australian economy towards trading with third countries means that the potential gains from increased trading with third countries may be proportionately larger for New Zealand. Nevertheless, the gains will not be negligible for Australia. If it is to progress with trade liberalization and industry deregulation it is better to do so in the context of a single market and to gain the benefits of a simultaneous improvement in market access and efficiency of production with the trading partner.

Implementing a single market for Australia and New Zealand
The argument for a common market for services is a standard case of establishing a common market for any commodity. The fact that a market is for a service rather than a commodity does not change the gains and losses of trade liberalization. The CER has accepted the merits of freeing trade in all physical commodities and many services and the remaining services are an anomaly that should be corrected. The exemptions on the Australian and New Zealand lists are all industries or commodity groups which are highly regulated in the exempting country. The freeing of international trade in commodities which are subject to domestic regulation is more complicated and requires more legislative changes but one should note that many of the physical commodities for which trans-Tasman trade was liberalized in July 1990 had been subject to industry plans or other forms of regulation including state trading monopolies (for example, the former New Zealand Wheat Board). These commodity groups were put in Annex E of the Agreement for special negotiation and a delayed timetable but this did not prevent the freeing of trade. Free trade tends to undermine domestic regulations and bilateral freeing of trade therefore requires a large measure of deregulation. Those interest groups which gain rents from the present national regulations will protest vigorously at suggestions to free trade and deregulate the markets concerned but the fundamental case for free trade is not essentially different from that of non-regulated commodities.

The absence of free trade in capital is also an anomaly in the factor markets. There was no provision for free trade in capital in the CER, unlike the Treaty of Rome for instance. During the CER negotiations the question of investment policy arose but it was considered inappropriate. The essential argument for free movement of the factor capital is based on the increase in factor productivities. The elimination of barriers to the movement of capital will allow capital to move to the location in the free trade area where it can earn the highest rate of return (allowing for possible differences in risk). In the absence of distortions, this is the location where the marginal productivity of the factor capital is greater. The liberalization of commodity trade within a free trade area itself changes factor productivities and creates incentives to reallocate production between as well as within the two countries. This reallocation of production requires takeovers, joint ventures, mergers and other inter-company stock transactions to rationalize the location of plants. These can only be realized in full if there is free movement of capital within the area.

Since both countries still restrict capital movements into their markets from all foreign countries, the freeing of capital within the free trade area would give a capital preference to the capitalists in the other member country over all other third countries. To enforce the preferences, the governments would have to introduce a content rule similar to that which governs trade within free trade areas in order to prevent the preference being received by investors of third countries through entering the country with the less restrictive barriers and then reinvesting in the second country.

The Australian government has repeatedly stated that the Nara Treaty between Australia and Japan prevents the introduction of investment policies which diminish Japan's MFN (Most-Favoured Nation) status. The obvious resolution of this problem is to approach it in the same way as the GATT treats discriminatory tariff reductions in free trade areas; namely, to ensure that the agreement on foreign investments does not impose new restrictions on the investments from third countries and is outward-looking in encouraging investment flows.

The real difficulty is not one of law but of the possibility that the freeing of capital which is bilateral and therefore discriminatory will, like that of commodity trade, produce new distortions that result in a net loss associated with capital movements. For example, it might encourage investment in New Zealand by some Australian company to take advantage of the new opportunities when this company is technologically inferior and a higher cost producer than some other producer from a third country. As both countries have liberalized capital flows greatly in recent years this danger has been greatly reduced. Where it might occur, the obvious action is to reduce restrictions on capital inflows from all countries.

The absence of a common external tariff and differences in commodity tax rates are two examples of the issue of harmonization of policy instruments which affect the bilateral trade flows indirectly. Articles 12 and 14 of the CER Agreement recognized some of these. Article 12 declared that member states shall 'examine the scope for taking action to harmonise requirements relating to such matters as standards, technical specifications and testing procedures, domestic labelling and restrictive trade practices . . .'. Agreements were reached to begin harmonizing standards on foods, consumer products and other standards and labelling. Article 14 recognized the 'intermediate goods problem' which arises because of the absence of a common external tariff on intermediate goods.

The CER did not recognize the generality or the extent of the harmonization issue. Subsequently, there has been considerable debate in Australia and especially in New Zealand about the meaning of harmonization. This has arisen in several contexts, including external tariffs, taxation, business laws, standards, and exchange rates (see, especially, Holmes et al., 1986). The problem is, however, a universal one which applies to all areas of government intervention in the economies which impinge on bilateral trade. In all areas of policy the two countries as sovereign states have made policies which differ in at least some material respects.

The view which is predominant in New Zealand seems to be that 'harmonization' of a policy instrument should not mean 'uniformity' or 'replication'. Sir Frank Holmes and his colleagues at the Institute of Policy Studies opted for 'approximation rather than unification of policy' (Holmes et al., 1986, p. 91). Similarly, Professor Farrar (1989), in his commentary on the harmonization of business laws which is proceeding under the 1988 Memorandum of Understanding between the two governments, argues that 'harmonisation is simply a means to an end' and cites other legal authorities who believe that harmonization does not mean necessarily the adoption of identical policies. Indeed, the Memorandum of Understanding is quite explicit in stating under Article 8 that 'both governments recognise that effective harmonisation does not require replication of laws, although that may be appropriate in some cases'. The former Prime Minister of New Zealand, Mr Geoffrey Palmer, cited these views with approval (Palmer, 1990).

It is true that harmonization is a means to an end, that end being efficient production and exchange. It should, therefore, mean what is in the best interests of the economies rather than a dogma. However, there is a very strong logic based on efficiency of production and exchange which implies the two economies should move towards unification or approximation of the major policies which impinge upon bilateral trade.

As the first example, consider the common external tariff: that is, a common external tariff on all items. It is useful to consider the tariffs on two sets of goods, those on intermediate inputs and those on final goods.

The existence of differences in tariffs or tariff equivalents on raw materials, components and capital equipment give the producers of the country which imposes the lower tariffs or tariff equivalents upon the input goods an advantage in bilateral competition. Under the CER this is regarded by industries in which it occurs as unfair competition but we shall see that the real issue is efficiency of production.

Article 14 provides for several responses – a common external tariff, compensating export duties, compensating input duties or countervailing subsidies, variation of area content requirements, cancellation of drawback or tariff concession, or acceleration of trade liberalization – on the items concerned. Of these, the only instrument which completely and permanently removes the advantage is the common external tariff.

The objection that has been raised in New Zealand to the common external tariff is that it would result in New Zealand having to accept the higher Australian levels for many intermediate goods (see Holmes et al., 1986, pp. 71–7; and Australia–New Zealand Business Council, 1990, Session Four). This is so because more intermediates and capital goods enter New Zealand at zero or low concessional rates of duty than in Australia. It is also based on the premise that the harmonization would proceed by averaging the rates or at least would result in some rates which are higher than their lower pre-harmonization levels. The GATT rules require that the common tariff be no higher than the pre-harmonization trade-weighted average.

This objection can be overcome. The obvious method of overcoming it is to harmonize in such a way that the post-harmonization level is lower than the simple average of the pre-harmonization levels of the tariffs on an item. This method shifts the adjustment to the country with the higher pre-harmonization level. It is likely to encounter the objection in that country that the harmonization in the trading arrangement is undermining the level of protection given by the general tariff rate. While this is true, it is a merit of the common external tariff, and in any case the levels of tariffs are generally falling in both countries.

There is a second variant of this strategy. That is to reduce the tariffs on all intermediates in both countries from all sources to zero. Such a reduction would automatically harmonize the rates (at zero) and remove the discrimination *vis-à-vis* third countries for these imports. The justification for this policy is that efficient production requires that there be no distortion of input prices (Diamond and Mirrlees,

1971). Any tariffs or other taxes on inputs result in a loss of aggregate production. This powerful theorem means that there should be no tariffs on inputs.

This proposition is neither as novel nor as radical as it seems at first. Both the Australian Tariff through its by-laws and commercial tariff concessions and the New Zealand Tariff through Part II and other end-user concessions have long allowed duty-free or concessional entry for intermediates not produced in the country. These concessions have always been based on the realization that tariffs on inputs increase the real costs of production. Numerical simulations of the Australian economy done by the Industry Commission indicate that these concessions do provide significant benefits to the Australian economy by reducing industries' costs of production (Industry Commission, 1990b, Appendix F).

The common external tariff on final goods avoids another distortion in the economies. If there is a difference between the (effective) rate of assistance on a final commodity between the two countries, there is another violation of Pareto efficiency in the regional trading area as a whole. Consequently, the elimination of this difference would permit an increase in the aggregate production of the region. This argument has already been recognized loosely in the CER provision under Article 13 that a common external tariff on the outputs as well as the inputs may be used to promote rationalization in an industry. The argument holds generally for all industries.

For most final goods tariff items, the establishment of a common external tariff would not have a major impact because the differences in rates are small or the tariffs are protective in only one of the two countries. However, there are a small number of industries in both countries which are heavily protected by tariffs. In Australia these are the groups of clothing, textile and footwear, passenger motor vehicles and tobacco products; and in New Zealand the same groups less tobacco products. Even if the area continues to protect these groups heavily, production within the area should be efficient; that is, minimize the real costs of area production. This requires a common tariff. As with the difference on intermediate inputs, it is best if the rates are harmonized downwards.

Thus there should be a common external tariff on the tariff items for all traded goods. Once tariffs were harmonized it would then be essential to harmonize other forms of assistance which inhibit trade or efficiency. It would also mean that future changes in tariff rates and other forms of assistance would have to be decided by both countries jointly. While this was seen as a disadvantage by the Australia–New Zealand Business Council (1990), it is really an advantage because it would in practice act as a form of rate binding which would inhibit future rate increases but not decreases.

The second issue of the harmonization of commodity and value-added taxes poses very similar issues. Consider excise taxation as a form of commodity taxation that is common to both countries and which, indeed, has a common historical origin in British excise taxation, which was transplanted to the colonies in the nineteenth century. The nature of the harmonization problem in this area and its relationship to the harmonization of tariffs is best appreciated if we regard an excise tax as a tax levied on the unit of production of the commodity at an administratively convenient stage of manufacturing production, such as the brewery or distillery for alcoholic beverages, or the refinery for petroleum products. In Australia and New Zealand excise taxes are specific duties but the *ad valorem* equivalent can be easily calculated.

An excise tax is a negative subsidy on production, expressed in *ad valorem* equivalent terms. As with a subsidy, part of the tax is passed forward to the buyer or backward to the supplier, depending on market conditions, in the usual way. Thus the system of excise taxation discourages the production of excisable commodities in precisely the same way as the use of subsidies and bounties encourages the production of the subsidized commodities. The argument for harmonizing the rates of excise within a free trade area is precisely the same as the argument for harmonizing subsidy and bounty rates, namely to avoid distortions of production within the area which move the economies away from efficient production.

The case for harmonizing other commodity taxes such as wholesale sales taxes, the goods and services tax or financial services duties is precisely the same as that of harmonizing excise tax rates.

Furthermore, we can relate the issue of harmonizing production taxes/subsidies to the issue of harmonizing tariffs by using the familiar equivalence relation in tax theory. An *ad valorem* tariff is equivalent to the combination of an *ad valorem* subsidy on the production of the commodity and an *ad valorem* tax on the consumption of the commodity, provided all of the tax rates are levied at the same rate and under very general conditions. The first component affects production in precisely the same way as the *ad valorem* subsidy on production. This is the protective effect of the tariff. Again we see that the essential argument for harmonizing excise taxes and other taxes levied directly on commodities and subsidies/bounties is the same as that for harmonizing tariffs (and all other forms of border protection).

This argument can readily be extended to value-added taxation. At the present time New Zealand has a value added tax, the Goods and Services Tax (GST). Australia does not have a value added-type tax but the desirability of introducing a broad-based commodity tax and quite possibly a value added tax has been canvassed repeatedly since the Tax Summit of 1985. Value added taxes use as a base of the tax the value added rather than the volume of production at each stage of production but inter-country differences in rates of value added taxation distort production within a free trade area in the same way as differences in production taxes or subsidies/bounties. Therefore, there is an argument for their harmonization.

In all of the four areas of harmonization discussed so far – the common markets for services and capital, the common external tariff, and harmonization of commodity tax rates – the argument for harmonization of the relevant instruments has also produced an argument for unification or replication. This is essentially due to the nature of these instruments, all of which are expressible in terms of *ad valorem* rates of assistance (in the case of services and the external tariff) or subsidy/taxation. Inter-country differences in tax/subsidy rates give an incentive for producers to change the location of production or for consumers to change their consumption choices and these differences are removed if and only if the rates are equated. In the case of capital flows the incentive comes directly from the restrictions on capital flows.

The feature of unification is not inevitable and general. An important counter-example is standards. The experience of the EC is germane here. For many years the Community attempted to eliminate technical barriers through harmonization, by which was meant the adjustment of national regulations to conform to a single common Community standard. The process proved to be slow, bureaucratic and time consuming.

The 'new approach' to harmonization of standards in the White Paper is based on the principle of 'mutual recognition' of each other's standards. The Cassis de Dijon decision of the European Court in 1976 ruled that a product which was brought legally into the market of one member country can enter without restriction the markets of the other member countries. This made a policy of mutual recognition enforceable. However, harmonization in the form of agreed community standards will still be required for two types of standards, those for 'essential requirements' and those in high technology areas where the inter-operability of equipment is necessary for the rational development of new products and the maintenance of free competition.

The reason for the preference for a non-uniform approach in the area of standards lies in the difficulty of comparing standards and the need to trade off the desirability of uniformity with the costs of negotiating and enforcing 'uniformity' when the standards are not readily comparable. Moreover, the Community is seeking to avoid the creation of new barriers by requiring member states to notify the Commission in advance of proposals for new regulations. This will lead to a high degree of uniformity in the long run.

The method of 'mutual recognition' may also be applicable in other areas. For example, the EC has also used this method in the area of recognition of professional training for certification in professional bodies. As a result of the Australian Prime Minister's initiative on cooperative federalism in 1990, the Commonwealth and State governments agreed to adopt mutual recognition of regulations. The New Zealand government wishes to be involved in this process, which could see mutual recognition of regulations extended throughout the area.

A single market will also require ultimately the harmonization of other policies. One obvious example is income tax regimes. Substantial differences between countries in either the tax base or the tax rate payable on an income will provide a distortion of economic activities. Perhaps the clearest way of seeing this is to regard the labour income after tax of an income taxpayer as the price of leisure foregone. Differences in the tax base and/or tax rates lead to a differential in the price of leisure and, therefore, violate the 'law of one price'.

The final area of harmonization I shall consider is the idea of a common currency. This has been discussed by Holmes et al. (1986, Section 3.8), Lloyd (1990) and the Australia–New Zealand Business Council (1990, Session Three). Sir Frank Holmes and his colleagues recommended against a common currency and the Australia–New Zealand Business Council recommended that this be put on the agenda of the 1992 review of the CER. The issue of a common currency or, more generally, of exchange rate policy is undoubtedly a very important one that has been debated since the formation of the New Zealand–Australia Free Trade Agreement. However, a common currency is not conceptually a part of a single market. It is an aspect of a larger set of issues concerning macroeconomic policy coordination between the governments of a free trade area or simply between any governments. It involves a trade-off of the gains from the elimination of exchange rate risk and the reduction in transactions costs against the losses in the form of the loss of an instrument of macroeconomic policy. The theory of optimal currency areas suggests that the primary consideration should be the extent to which the two national economies are subject to similar or dissimilar shocks from the rest of the world (see Kawai, 1987).

This list of measures which may be harmonized is not exhaustive. In a single market it would also be necessary to examine other areas of economic policy which restrict efficiency of production in the area such as transport and energy policies, technology development, other taxes, and labour market policies.

The inevitability of greater unification

Market forces will inexorably drive the two economies towards a greater degree of unification and ultimately towards complete unification of the major policies which impinge on trade between the two countries.

The first set of market forces stems from the pressures which will be put on governments to unify policies between the two economies by the removal of all border barriers for traded commodities. For example, the freeing of tariffs on final commodities has quickly led to pressures to remove non-tariff barriers. The freeing of all trade in final commodities has shown that truly free competition between two producers who add value in the two countries requires in addition equal access to raw materials and components and other intermediate inputs. Complete freedom of trade for all commodities including intermediates demonstrates that assistance by means of bounties/subsidies and other non-border assistance also has a significant effect on the competitiveness of country producers. The awareness of the importance of these differences then leads the producers in the disadvantaged country to lobby their politicians for equality of opportunity and fair competition.

This sequence of discovery is evident in the progress made under the New Zealand–Australia Free Trade Agreement and the CER, and in the progress of the EC. The most dramatic expression of it was the realization in the EC that a 'common market' was not an integrated single market because of the existence of other domestic impediments. Indeed, the whole history of free trade areas which have progressed to a substantial freeing of trade is a realization that the freeing of trade in one area of potential trade reveals that other policies which were not previously thought to be important are now a more important impediment which prevents the full realization of potential trade.

The second way in which harmonization of policies can come about is through the incentives which the differences give to the governments themselves to make the change because the government is losing fiscal revenue or business or the migration of its citizens which induces the governments to act. The essential ingredient is the arbitrage of firms and households as consumers and factor suppliers and asset-owners. In response to price differentials due to differences in tax/subsidy rates or regulations or conditions for market entry, agents will respond by shifting their purchases or sales or assets to the market with the more favourable conditions.

Consider, for example, differences in a commodity or value added tax. If the goods are freely tradable after taxes are paid, arbitrage will occur in many forms such as direct mailing or purchases on tourist or business travel. This then leads to competition between the governments fixing the tax rates. A similar process can occur in the regulation of industries via licensing or other regulations, leading to the phenomenon known as 'regulatory competition'. The phenomenon applies broadly to differences in all policies where there is some scope for agents to avoid the higher taxes or the more restrictive regulations by arbitraging. Siebert (1990) has called it *ex post* harmonization.

Arbitrage requires that the agents are free to contract. Hence, in a particular market, development of inter-government competition may require the removal of barriers which restrict commodity trade and other forms of contracting. The importance of the adoption of the policy of 'mutual recognition' of standards is that it permitted trade which had been banned.

The phenomenon of arbitrage followed by convergence of policies between jurisdictions is observable for some policy differences among the Australian states. Trade across the border of neighbouring states occurs when there are significant differences in the level of state taxation of commodities such as alcoholic beverages or when gambling is prohibited in one state but permitted in a neighbouring state. The most dramatic example in Australia occurred when the former Premier of Queensland, Sir Joh Bjelke-Petersen, abolished death duties in Queensland. Within a short time all other Australian states were forced to follow suit because of the flow of migration of elderly citizens to avoid the duties in their home states.

A similar process has occurred in the CER when differences in the treatment of some items of income for corporate tax assessment led to a large loss of revenue to the Australian government. In both Australia and New Zealand there is a long practice of travellers returning to their country of residence loading themselves up with duty-free goods.

The phenomenon has another fundamental implication in that it provides an alternative route to harmonizing some policies by government negotiation and agreement. The alternative is to remove the barriers to arbitrage and allow competition to produce convergence in the longer run rather than the governments trying to agree upon the level of the instruments and all other legislative change required to enforce them. The conspicuous example is the EC policy of 'mutual recognition' of standards. A similar policy could be applied in other areas.

An important example is the possibility of the establishment of an Australasia without a frontier, parallel to the Europe without frontiers. A single market requires the abolition of all restrictions on travellers and on the transport of goods within the area; that is, the abolition of the customs controls at the frontier. There can be little doubt that the removal of trans-Tasman restrictions on the transport of dutiable goods and all duties on goods transported across the Tasman would increase this form of arbitrage. An obvious example is the transport of automobiles that would occur between the two countries with differential commodity taxes. For tax instruments the abolition of the frontier would require the substitution of the country-of-origin basis of taxation (where the tax is levied in the country of origin and paid to the government in this country) for the country of destination basis, as in the example of commodity taxes above.

This approach to harmonization could even be applied to a common currency. In this instance the governments would only have to legislate to declare that the currency of each member country is legal tender throughout the free trade area. Currency substitution may then result in individuals declaring a distinct preference for one currency.

A policy of *ex post* harmonization could not, however, be applied in all areas. It would not be applicable to competition policy, which is designed to ensure competition among all producers, or to areas such as environmental problems, which involve spillover effects from one country to the next.

This policy of *ex post* harmonization has several advantages over the traditional choice of *ex ante* negotiation of common or harmonized levels or regulations. It avoids protracted government negotiations, can take place over a longer time, reduces considerably the cost of the bureaucracy, and may in some cases be more responsive to the preferences of the economic agents or decision-makers and less responsive to the pressure of industry lobbies. It also avoids the necessity of courts or other agencies to enforce arbitrary area-wide standards and thereby avoids the infringements on the sovereignty of the two countries. This method of harmonization is gaining more proponents in the EC (see Lal, 1990; Pelkmans, 1990; Siebert, 1990), including the UK.

Conclusions

The existing CER is a far-reaching and highly successful trade agreement. The two economies are approaching the status of a free trade area though there are still some exceptions to free international trade, notably in the markets for services and capital.

This paper concludes that there is a strong case that Australia and New Zealand should proceed to form a single market; that is, that the two countries should remove all impediments to trade and competition and harmonize major policies that impinge on trade and competition across the Tasman. We should unashamedly emulate in general (though not in all detail) the policies of the Single European Market. These measures include a common market for all services, a common market for capital, a common external tariff and a common regime for commodity taxation. They also include an Australasia without a frontier.

The essential justification for these measures is that they are required if the two economies are to realize the full potential gains from the freeing of trade under the CER. A second advantage is that the increase in efficiency and in competition that will occur throughout the single market will improve the competitiveness of the two economies in global markets.

An additional substantial argument in favour of the adoption of the concept of a single market is that it provides a standard by which to evaluate alternative proposals and positions during negotiations. Without such a standard there is a considerable danger that the negotiations will be *ad hoc* and directionless.

The harmonization of instrument levels will require in some cases, such as the common external tariff and the common market for services, the unification of instruments or measures. However, in other cases where the instruments are not easily expressible in terms of percentage rates or other measurements, harmonization will mean approximation rather than unification. This applies to measures such as standards and the recognition of professional and educational qualifications and industry regulations.

Harmonization may occur either by the negotiation of common tax/subsidy regimes and regulations or the convergence of tax/subsidy rates and regulations as a result of competition between governments in pursuit of the welfare of their citizens. The two governments should consider the extension of the EC principle of 'mutual recognition' to standards and other areas of policies.

The issue of a common currency is not a part of a single market but it should be addressed by the two governments.

The process of forming a single market could begin with the compilation of a list of measures needed for implementation, like the list compiled by the Commission of the European Communities (1985) in its White Paper. It is not necessary that the single market be achieved by a single date. A common target date could be set for the achievement of measures which require *ex ante* harmonization. For those measures which are subject to 'mutual recognition' and evolution towards a common level, the progression towards a single market could take place over a longer time.

The single market would require new institutional arrangements for some measures such as the abolition of the frontier and the institution of common trade policies *vis-à-vis* third countries. These need careful attention.

The formation of a single market involves many complex issues which have scarcely been debated in either country. The two governments should promote a debate in the community at large which extends beyond consultations with the main industry associations and unions as the extension of the CER will substantially affect all residents of both countries.

References

Australia–New Zealand Business Council (1990), *Proceedings of the Annual Conference*, 14–15 November.

Bureau of Industry Economics (1989), *Trade Liberalisation and Australian Manufacturing Industry: The Impact of the Australia–New Zealand Closer Economic Relations Trade Agreement*, Research Report No. 29, Canberra: Australian Government Publishing Service.

Commission of the European Communities (1985), *Completing the Internal Market: White Paper for the Commission to the European Council*, Luxembourg: Office for Official Publications of of the European Communities.

Diamond, P.A. and J.A. Mirrlees (1971), 'Optimal taxation and public production – production efficiency', *American Economic Review*, **61**, pp. 8–27.

Farrar, J.H. (1989), 'Harmonisation of business law between Australia and New Zealand', *Victoria University of Wellington Law Review*, **19**, pp. 435–63.

Holmes, Sir Frank et al. (1986), *Closer Economic Relations with Australia: Agenda for Progress*, Wellington: Victoria University Press.

Industry Commission (1990a), *Annual Report 1989–90*, Canberra: Australian Government Publishing Service.

Industry Commission (1990b), *The Commercial Tariff Concession and By-Law System, A Draft Report*, Canberra: Industry Commission.

Kawai, M. (1987), 'Optimal currency area', in J. Eatwell et al. (eds), *The New Palgrave: A Dictionary of Economics*, Vol. 3, London: Macmillan.

Lal, D. (1990), 'Comment', in H. Siebert (ed.), *The Competition of the Internal Market*, Tubingen: J.C.B. Mohr.

Lloyd, K. (1990), 'An Australia–New Zealand currency union?', *Policy*, **6**, Winter, pp. 9–12.

Palmer, G. (1990), 'International trade blocs: New Zealand and Australia: beyond CER', Address to the Ninth Commonwealth Law Conference, Auckland.

Pelkmans, J. (1990), 'Regulation and the single market: an economic perspective', in H. Siebert (ed.), *The Competition of the Internal Market*, Tübingen: J.C.B. Mohr.

Siebert, H. (1990), 'The harmonization issue in Europe: prior agreement or a competitive process?', in H. Siebert (ed.), *The Competition of the Internal Market*, Tübingen: J.C.B. Mohr.

Syntec Economic Services (1988), *Industry Assistance Reform in New Zealand*, Syntec Economic Services.

PART V

MULTILATERAL TRADE LIBERALIZATION

Introduction

'The Uruguay Round, WTO and Asia-Pacific liberalization' contains an evaluation of the Uruguay Round using the version of Global Trade Analysis and Policy (GTAP) used at the World Bank. As a multi-country computable general equilibrium model, GTAP is suitable for the analysis of multilateral reductions in tariffs and other trade barriers. In the simulations covered here the Uruguay Round experiment covers reductions in tariffs and export subsidies committed in the Round. In a previous paper Martin and Winters (1995) graphed the magnitude of a country's gains from the Uruguay Round against a measure of the reduction in the own country average level of protection. In their graph there is a strong positive association between the average reduction in the country's own levels of protection and the magnitude of the gains. They concluded that the countries with the larger welfare gains were those which made the larger reductions in their own import barriers. However, this correlation could be due to an association of own country tariff cuts with other countries' trade barriers or other factors which are related to gains and, therefore, spurious. The paper reproduced here tests this interesting relationship by decomposing the effects of the Uruguay Round, as calculated from the model, into those due to own reductions and those due to other country reductions separately. It finds that the larger welfare gains are indeed due principally to own country 'concessions'. Thus, multilateral reductions provide a means of persuading countries to reduce their own barriers.

The second selection is an overview of the First Ministerial Conference of the World Trade Organization (WTO) which was held in Singapore in December 1996 and the evolution of the WTO since it came into being on 1 January 1995. It highlights the same issues of regionalism and new issues that are discussed elsewhere in the book.

References

Martin, W. and L.A. Winters (1995), 'The Uruguay Round and Developing Countries', paper presented to the Pacific Economic Cooperation Council Trade Policy Forum VII, Taipei.

12

The Uruguay Round, World Trade Organization and Asia–Pacific trade liberalization

Christian F. Bach, P.J. Lloyd and Will Martin

1 Introduction

The 1990s have seen sweeping changes to global trading conditions. The conclusion of the multilateral Uruguay Round is the single most important change. At the regional level, 31 regional trading agreements came into operation over the four years from January 1991 to January 1995 (WTO, 1995b, Appendix Table 1). These include, in the Asia-Pacific region, the ASEAN Free Trade Area (AFTA) which came into effect on 1 January 1993 and the North American Free Trade Area (NAFTA) which came into effect on 1 January 1994. At the national level, an increasing number of countries have unilaterally reduced trade barriers *vis-à-vis* all trading partners. The newly formed World Trade Organization (WTO) has also begun from 1 January 1995 to oversee the new rules for the world trading system.

The volume of world merchandise trade has grown in every year of the 1990s, even when world output turned down in the recession years of 1992 and 1993, and the increase of 9 per cent in 1994 is the largest annual percentage increase since 1976 (WTO, 1995b). These increases in the volume of international trade are partly the effect of the reductions in trade barriers but they have also fed back into the policy changes as nations are keen to share in the expansion of international trade in goods and services.

This paper seeks to assess the main effects of the Uruguay Round and the formation of the WTO on the world economy and the Asia-Pacific region. Section 2 examines the path of trade liberalization in the Asia-Pacific region. This path exhibits some features which make this region distinctive in terms of trade policy. Section 3 provides a general assessment of the Uruguay Round. Section 4 provides a new decomposition of the gains to individual countries from the Uruguay Round. The total gains to an individual country are broken down into those which are due to the reduction in own country barriers to trade and those which are due to the reduction in other countries' barriers. These may be called the 'unilateral' and the 'multilateral' components of the Uruguay Round package. In Section 5, we look at the future evolution of the world trading system. There is a need for a strong multilateral organization to oversee the system.

2 Asia-Pacific trade liberalization

The Asia-Pacific region consists of two sub-regions with different characteristics from the point of view of trade policy and trade patterns, that is, the Asian and the Pacific sub-regions. 'Asia' will be taken to mean East Asia. Russia is omitted because its economic centre is in Europe. South Asia and the Central Asian republics of the former Soviet Union are a part of the geographic area of Asia but they have different historical ties and trade patterns than the East Asian countries, though the links between them and the rest of East Asia are beginning to increase. The Pacific countries are taken to be the four English-speaking Pacific countries – the United States, Canada, Australia and New Zealand – and Mexico.

East Asia

There has been significant unilateral freeing of trade in the East Asian region over the last two decades.The General Agreement on Tariffs and Trade (GATT, 1992, Appendix Table) provides a list of 63 countries which have undertaken unilateral reductions in protection *vis-à-vis* all trading partners since the start of the Uruguay Round in 1986, nine of these being in East Asia. The East Asian countries are Japan, South Korea, Peoples' Republic of China (and Macau), Indonesia, Thailand, Philippines, Malaysia and Singapore. In addition, Japan has taken measures to free trade in certain commodities after bilateral negotiations with the US; for example, the 1988 US–Australia–Japan beef negotiations and the 1990 Structural Impediments Initiative. Many of the reductions in Asian countries have been substantial.

The East Asian geographic region is the least 'regionalized' of the world regions in the sense of customs unions and free trade areas notified under the articles of the GATT. These regional trading arrangements discriminate in commodity trade and therefore tend to increase the intra-area share of trade compared to what it would be in their absence. In East Asia, AFTA remains the only regional trading arrangement of importance. (The 1975 Bangkok Agreement among the Developing member countries of the Economic and Social Commission for Asia and the Pacific and the 1991 Trade Agreement between Thailand and the Lao Peoples' Democratic Republic have not produced significant trade liberalization.) Starting on 1 January 1993 intra-ASEAN tariffs on manufactured goods were to be phased out over a 15-year period but this has been accelerated to 10 years. After the announcement of the AFTA schedule, many of these commitments have been multilateralized by the countries extending these commitments to all MFN traders. (Pangestu, 1995, gives a detailed analysis of the unilateral and AFTA liberalizations in the ASEAN countries.)

None of the countries in North Asia are members of any regional trading arrangement and this includes Japan and Peoples' Republic of China which are the third and fourth largest trading countries of the world if one lumps together the countries of the European Union (EU) and includes Hong Kong with the Peoples' Republic of China. There has been discussion of the Malaysian proposal for an East Asian Economic Caucus and the ASEAN meeting in Singapore in July 1993 recognized the East Asian Economic Caucus as a subgroup within APEC. To date, however, no trade preference arrangements have resulted from these discussions. By contrast, all of the countries in Western Europe, North America and South America (with the sole exception of Cuba) and most of those in Africa are members of at least one reciprocal regional trading arrangement (WTO, 1995b, Table 1, lists all regional trading arrangements notified to the GATT and in force as of January 1995).

Thus the East Asian region is a geographic region with a low level of trade in discriminatory regional trading arrangements and a strong record of unilateral reduction in trade barriers. No other region of the world economy has remained as faithful to the fundamental GATT principles of MFN (Most-Favoured Nation) trading. One can make an even stronger statement about the absence of discriminatory trade in East Asia. The East Asian countries have a much lower participation in non-reciprocal preference arrangements as well as reciprocal regional arrangements. Japan has a preferential scheme for developing countries based on the Generalized System of Preferences. The East Asian Newly Industrialized Countries (NICs) are no longer beneficiaries of some preference schemes as they have been graduated out of the schemes of the US and some other preference-granting countries.

On the other hand, there has been substantial movement in the East Asian region towards freer trade on a local or sub-regional basis outside the conventional GATT-approved customs unions and free trade areas and preference schemes. This has taken several forms including export processing zones, free trade zones, Growth Triangles and bilateral or multilateral trade and investment arrangements.[1]

Some of these zones, such as export-processing zones and free trade zones, are areas within national borders and might be called sub-national zones. East Asia has been the main area of the world for the growth of these types of trade liberalization zones. There are now more than 50 sub-national zones in East Asia.

Other zones cross national borders. Unlike GATT-approved free trade areas and customs unions, they do not cover all of the territories of the countries concerned. These have come to be known as sub-regional economic zones. The emphasis in these zones is on regional technical cooperation and infrastructure construction rather than the liberalization of trade. The main geographic location of these zones is in South East Asia. ASEAN is unique among the GATT-approved regional trading arrangements in that it contains a provision for the establishment of sub-regional zones. There are now three sub-regional zones which involve ASEAN countries – the IMS Growth Triangle, IMT Growth Triangle and BIMPEAGA.[2]

Sub-national and sub-regional zones have played a major role in the freeing of commodity trade flows and the expansion of exports from the region. This means that the measures of liberalization based on unilateral MFN and regional liberalization understates the extent of trade liberalization in the region. These zones also exhibit the East Asian propensity for cooperation and consensus-building.

USA–Canada–Mexico–Australia–New Zealand
These countries split into two groups from the point of view of both unilateral and regional trade policies as well as trade patterns, namely, the pair of neighbours – the USA and Canada and Mexico, and Australia and New Zealand.

Neither the USA nor Canada has engaged in systematic unilateral trade liberalization outside the GATT rounds in the last decade but they have formed a close regional association. The Canada US Free Trade Agreement (CUSTA) is a free trade area which came into effect on 1 January 1989. All merchandise trade will be tariff-free by 1998. There is freedom of trade for some services and an investment chapter provides for freedom of movement of capital with some exceptions. Mexico was incorporated into the free trade area under the North America Free Trade Agreement (NAFTA) from 1 January 1994. All trade between Canada and Mexico will be tariff-free by 2003 but a limited number of products traded between Mexico and the US will not be tariff-free until 2008. Mexico has unilaterally reduced tariffs and non-tariff barriers.

By contrast, Australia and New Zealand have both engaged in major unilateral trade liberalizations over the last 10 years and longer and they have formed a close regional association. In both countries, the highest levels of protection historically have been for the less efficient and mostly import-competing manufacturing sector. As a result of the tariffication of quotas and the reduction in tariffs in both countries during the 1980s and 1990s, average levels of protection in this sector have been halved in the last decade.[3] Australia and more particularly New Zealand have also greatly reduced the assistance provided to agricultural industries. These two countries are the only members of the Organization for Economic Cooperation and Development (OECD) to have done so.

The Closer Economic Relations Agreement (CER) between Australia and New Zealand came into effect on 1 January 1983. All border barriers to trade between the two members were eliminated by 1 July 1990. A review of the Agreement in 1988 has extended the free trade provisions to services. CER, like NAFTA and the EU, has introduced a wide range of harmonization of non-border regulations and factor flows that go much beyond the multilateral rules. (Lloyd, 1995, reviews the Agreement.)

Open regionalism
When the unilateral and regional reductions are considered together, no other regional trading arrangements have lowered trade barriers *vis-à-vis* third countries to the same extent as the countries of the CER and AFTA. These two regional arrangements are the outstanding examples in this respect of the 'open regionalism' which is advocated in the Asia–Pacific Economic Cooperation (APEC) forum. The main requirement of 'open regionalism' is a lowering of barriers and trade facilitation *vis-à-vis* third countries (see Garnaut and Drysdale, 1994). Both Australia and New Zealand have regarded regional trade liberalization as a supplement to their unilateral liberalizations and in particular as a way of making their economies more competitive in global markets. The ASEAN economies have adopted a similar view and have introduced the modality of multilateralizing many of their regional trade liberalizations.

Pre-Uruguay Round level of trade restrictions
The outcome of these unilateral and regional policy changes has been a substantial reduction in trade barriers since the conclusion of the previous GATT round, the Tokyo Round.

As a part of the Work for the Uruguay Round, the GATT has constructed a database of tariff levels which provides a much better assessment of the levels of restrictions on international trade due to tariffs than has previously been available. There are no comparable data for the level of restrictions on international trade due to non-tariff barriers. The levels of MFN tariffs before the Uruguay Round reductions take effect are reported in François et al. (1995, Table 1). In this table, the figures are reported for the US, Canada and Japan separately, and for Australia and New Zealand combined, and for East Asia. Further details for the individual countries are available from the database.

In broad terms, the tariffs of the developed countries are now mostly below 5 per cent. The exceptions to this are Australia and New Zealand where they are generally below 10 per cent (and falling because of the current programmes of tariff reductions in both countries). In all countries the tariff rates are highly differentiated with some high peaks, most notably in all developed countries in the textiles and clothing area where they average from 10 to 30 per cent with many above these levels.

In East Asia (excluding Japan) the tariff rates range mostly from 5 to 15 per cent. This makes them higher than the developed countries but substantially lower than any of the other regions of developing countries (Latin America, Africa, Middle East and South Asia). There is great variation among commodity groups and countries. Singapore and Hong Kong have the distinction of being the only two countries in the world which are virtually tariff free.

3   A General assessment of the Uruguay Round

The Uruguay Round is by far the most comprehensive of the eight Rounds of negotiations of trade barriers and trade rules which have been conducted by the GATT since its establishment in 1947. It covered both tariffs and non-tariff restrictions and it addressed for the first time the restrictions in the two areas which had been largely exempt from previous GATT rounds negotiations, namely, agriculture and textiles and clothing. For the first time, these multilateral rules extend to trade in services under the General Agreement on Trade in Services (GATS) Agreement and to intellectual property under the TRIPS Agreement.

At the conclusion of the negotiations in December 1993, the Director-General of the GATT, Mr Peter Sutherland, gave a euphoric interpretation of the Round:

> Seven years of hard work today come to a successful conclusion . . . It is a truly remarkable achievement, from any perspective. The result will mean more trade, more investment, more jobs, and larger income growth for all. Economic operators across the globe will benefit; producers and consumers, investors and traders everywhere will gain. I am convinced that today will be seen as a defining moment in modern economic and political history.

Since that time the agreements of the Round have been subject to detailed analyses (see the OECD, 1994 and the World Bank, 1995). For industrial products the reductions in MFN tariff levels was on average 40 per cent. In the developed countries, the average tariff on industrial products will fall from the pre-Uruguay Round average of 6.3 per cent to an average of only 3.8 per cent at the end of the five-year transition period. In the developing countries, the corresponding pre- and post-UR average MFN levels are 10 and 7.1 per cent respectively. The distribution of these levels when the reductions have taken place in full is available for commodity groups from the GATT database (see François et al., 1995, Table 1). However, the true extent of the liberalization resulting from the Agreements which relate to non-tariff barriers and to the agriculture and services sectors are much harder to evaluate.

In broad terms, a general consensus view of the qualitative effects has emerged. The conclusions are:

- substantial liberalization of trade in manufactures was achieved, both in the area of tariffs and through the abolition of non-tariff barriers such as Voluntary Export restraints, and in particular the phasing out of quotas imposed under the

Multifibre Arrangement (MFA) should lead to a more substantial liberalization of trade in textiles and clothing

- the Agreement on agriculture was important in developing a set of rules and the tariffication of import barriers to agricultural trade but it achieved much less trade liberalization than expected, largely because the base period, 1986-88, was a period of very low world prices and generally high rates of agricultural protection and because of the 'dirty' tariffication of quotas in several countries
- GATS is a landmark in terms of creating discipline in services trade but it achieved little in terms of trade liberalization
- unlike previous GATT multilateral rounds, many developing countries in the Uruguay Round made significant market access offers and tariff bindings which will substantially liberalize trade in these countries
- the establishment of the WTO with new responsibilities than the GATT for service trade, intellectual property, trade-related investment measures and other new areas and the Single Undertaking, which brings almost all of the codes and agreements under one agreement which is binding on all members of the WTO, have greatly strengthened the rules of the world trading system
- the new dispute settlement procedures, which are more automatic and are binding on all parties after a dispute have gone through an appeal process unless there is a consensus against the adoption of the report of the appellate body, should lead to much greater enforceability of the rules of international trade.

Thus, the Uruguay Round will, when implemented, lead to a major reduction in barriers to international trade in goods and services. In addition, the tariffication of many non-tariff barriers in both agricultural and non-agricultural trade and tariff bindings will make the barriers more transparent, more secure from future increases in tariff or tariff equivalent rates and more stable over time.

While the general assessment of the outcomes of the Uruguay Round is quite positive, one cannot expect that all countries will gain, as the Director-General of the GATT had claimed. Any set of policy-induced changes in relative prices will mean that some individuals gain and some lose. When these gains and losses are aggregated to the level of countries, some countries will lose and some will gain. In the longer run, as the growth effects increase demand for goods and services and the new rules benefit the international trade of all countries, all countries could gain.

The quantitative effects of multilateral trade liberalization are extremely difficult to measure because of the interdependence of individual commodity markets through input–output relations and the simultaneous actions in many countries. In recent years new techniques of multi-country computable general equilibrium modelling have enabled economists to handle these complexities. A number of authors have used computable general equilibrium models of the world economy to estimate the effects on the incomes and welfare of countries of the Final Act of the Uruguay Round.

François et al., 1995, Table 9 provide a summary of the structure and coverage of these computable general equilibrium (CGE) models and their estimates of the effects. (See also Harrison et al., 1995.) These models yield different estimates because they differ in terms of the policy scenarios which they simulate and in terms of model structure. They predict an increase in the volume of world trade in goods and services which is mostly in the range of 8 to 10 per cent of base period exports if the Armington assumption of national product differentiation and constant returns to scale is made and 20 to 30 per cent or more if firm-level product differentiation with imperfect competition is assumed. They predict an increase in real income for the world as a whole within the range of 0.2 to 1 per cent. Here it should be noted that the liberalization of service trade and some non-tariff barriers are excluded and most models exclude the long-run effect of higher real incomes leading to more rapid capital accumulation and all exclude the benefits which will derive from a more stable and more enforceable regime of border restrictions on international trade. The models also show that the great majority of both developed and developing countries gain.

In this paper the multiple-country computable general equilibrium model studied is the GTAP (Global Trade Analysis Project) model which has been used at the World Bank for the analysis of the Uruguay Round outcome. (See Hertel et al., 1995 and Hertel, 1995, for information on the GTAP model itself.) The base year is 1992. The model projects the changes in population, labour force, capital stocks and total factor productivity until the year 2005, the terminal year, and computes the equilibrium in the world economy in that year. It then shocks the world by introducing the Uruguay Round changes to border restrictions on international trade.

In the simulations which are reported here, the Uruguay Round experiment covers the reductions in tariffs and export subsidies to which the countries have committed themselves in the Uruguay Round. It excludes the abolition of the MFA (Multi-Fibre Agreement), as well as the changes in service trade and world trade rules, because the welfare effects of the MFA are different than that of other reductions in border restrictions. The abolition of the quotas under the MFA are equivalent in their primary effects to a cut in export taxes in the exporting countries rather than a cut in tariffs in the importing countries because the quotas give most of the rent to the exporting countries. Simulations of the Uruguay Round show that some of the countries which export goods restricted by the MFA arrangements lose when the MFA is abolished and their market access is improved. It was thought, therefore, that the exclusion of the MFA component of the Uruguay Round should give a clearer picture of the effects of multilateral reforms.

Table 1 reports the cuts in tariffs and export subsidies and the weighted average cuts called 'liberalizations' in each of the 15 countries or groups of countries. These are all measured in percentage terms. The average of the tariffs and export subsidies is the trade-weighted average. The use of trade-weighted average biases the measures downwards as duty-free imports receive a large weight and prohibitive tariffs or restrictions receive a zero weight, and it may also distort the relative measures among the countries. (Ideally one should use the Trade Restrictiveness Index proposed by Anderson and Neary, 1994. This is a true or constant utility measure of the average level of restrictions. The World Bank is currently calculating these measures but they are not available at the time of writing.)

Table 2 reports the changes in welfare for these countries. The measure of gain/loss is the equivalent variation. This is reported in US dollars and as a percentage of the gross domestic product (GDP) of the country or countries. In absolute terms, the large gainers are the EU, Japan, Korea and Malaysia. In percentage terms, the large gainers are Malaysia, the Republic of Korea, Thailand, and Hong Kong – all East Asian

Table 1 Uruguay Round liberalizations

	Tariffs		Export Subsidies		Total Distortion (t)		Liberalization
	Before	After	Before	After	Before	After	(dt/(1 + t))
USC	0.043	0.031	0.003	0.002	0.045	0.033	1.181
EU	0.069	0.054	0.018	0.012	0.088	0.066	2.027
JPN	0.180	0.125	0.000	0.000	0.180	0.125	4.710
KOR	0.272	0.171	0.000	0.000	0.272	0.171	7.912
TWN	0.105	0.105	0.000	0.000	0.105	0.105	0.000
HKG	0.000	0.000	0.000	0.000	0.000	0.000	0.000
CHI	0.000	0.000	0.000	0.000	0.000	0.000	0.000
IND	0.138	0.127	0.000	0.000	0.138	0.127	0.942
MYS	0.163	0.095	0.000	0.000	0.163	0.095	5.832
PHL	0.277	0.209	0.000	0.000	0.277	0.209	5.288
THA	0.370	0.276	0.000	0.000	0.370	0.276	6.863
LTN	0.138	0.123	0.000	0.000	0.139	0.123	1.384
SSA	0.094	0.089	0.000	0.000	0.094	0.089	0.449
SAS	0.350	0.264	0.000	0.000	0.350	0.264	6.378
ROW	0.090	0.079	0.000	0.000	0.090	0.079	1.025

Key: USC – US–Canada, EU – European Union, JPN – Japan, KOR – Republic of Korea, TWN – Taiwan, HKG – Hong Kong, CHI – People's Republic of China, IND – Indonesia, MYS – Malaysia, PHL – Philippines, THA – Thailand, LTN – Latin America, SSA – Sub-Saharan Africa, SAS – South Asia, ROW – Rest of World.

Table 2 Change in welfare from Uruguay Round

	Change in Welfare (US$m)	Change in Welfare/GDP (%)
US–Canada (USC)	2,304	0.0256
European Union (EU)	28,682	0.3195
Japan (JPN)	41,183	0.8507
Republic of Korea (KOR)	31,844	5.4257
Taiwan (TWN)	10,885	2.3390
Hong Kong (HKG)	1,404	3.0160
China, P.R. (CHI)	14,214	0.9515
Indonesia (IND)	3,504	1.3424
Malaysia (MYS)	31,731	
Philippines (PHL)	5,172	5.8273
Thailand (THA)	8,770	3.4490
Latin America (LTN)	2,471	0.1339
Sub-Sahara Africa (SSA)	–563	–0.2074
South Asia (SAS)	7,962	1.2484
Rest of world (ROW)	11,189	0.2854
Global total	200,753	0.61

Source: World Bank simulation

countries. The only loser is Sub-Sahara Africa. For the world as a whole, the gain when the Uruguay Round is fully implemented is 0.61 per cent of the global product.

As these utility changes are the result of the movement from one competitive general equilibrium to another for all regions in the world economy, it is difficult to know why some countries gain and some lose. The decomposition in the next section gives some insights into this question as well as providing us with a further breakdown of the gains and losses.

4   A decomposition of the gains to individual countries

Martin and Winters (1995) considered the Uruguay Round package including the abolition of the MFA. They graphed the magnitude of a country's gains from the UR against a measure of the reduction in the own country average level of protection. Their measure of the average reduction in import protection is a simple unweighted average of the reduction in the prices of agricultural products and manufactures in the country. Their measure of gain is the increase in equivalent variation as a percentage of the country GDP. There are 10 regions reported in their model. In their graph there is a strong positive association between the average reduction in the country's own levels of protection and the magnitude of the gains. They concluded '. . . it is clear that the regions with the larger reductions in import prices generally achieved larger welfare gains' (Martin and Winters, 1995, p. 30). This is a most interesting result.

However, one cannot infer from this association between the extent of the country gains and the extent of the own country trade liberalization that the own country liberalization is the main source of the gains from the multilateral round. The correlation may be spurious. It may be that the countries with the greatest own country reductions in trade barriers were also those which faced the greatest barriers to their own exports and, therefore, gained most from the reduction in other country barriers or had the largest improvements in their commodity terms of trade in the post-Uruguay Round competitive equilibrium of the world economy or gained most from economies of scale and increased competition.

To settle this issue, this paper breaks down the sources of gain and loss in the Uruguay Round. The Uruguay Round is a concerted set of country liberalizations. From the point of view of a single country, one can regard the UR reductions in border barriers to international trade as the sum of two parts, the own country trade liberalization and the concerted liberalization of all other countries.

This partition of the Uruguay Round means that we can divide the gains/losses to individual countries into two corresponding parts. The gains/losses from the first part, the own country liberalization, are the standard gains from unilateral reform of the border restrictions of a country plus a terms of trade effect as the terms of trade are endogenous for all countries in the model. The standard gains are due to the increased efficiency of the production and consumption allocations. Exceptional second-best cases which produce efficiency losses from piecemeal reforms are unlikely for large reductions with a substantial across-the-board component. The own country terms of trade effects are expected to be negative. The sum of these effects for own country liberalization are expected to be positive unless the terms of trade effect is large.

The gains/losses from the second part depend to a greater extent on the direction of change in the country's commodity terms of trade. This measure picks up the net effects of changes in world prices. These changes may have a positive or negative effect on country welfare for individual countries. (For the world economy as a whole the gains the terms of trade effects are zero since one country's gain or loss must be the loss or gain of the rest of the world.) Favourable terms of trade effects may come directly from improved market access for its export commodities or indirectly from higher export prices as real incomes increase demand or possibly lower import prices. Unfavourable effects may come in some cases from higher world prices of imports which result directly from the elimination of export subsidies or indirectly from growth in real incomes which push up some commodity prices or possibly lower export prices. In addition, the changes in prices may have efficiency effects as they will change the total revenue collected from tariffs and other border distortions and thereby change the costs of the existing distortions.

This twofold division of the gains is constructed in the following manner. For one country, we simulate the former by lowering its border restrictions as agreed in the Uruguay Round but holding all other country restrictions at the pre-UR level. This gives a hypothetical calculation of the effects when each country acts 'unilaterally' as if the other countries were not changing their trade policies. We then lower the border restrictions of all other countries as agreed in the UR, holding the single own country trade restrictions constant at the pre-UR level. At each stage the effects of the policy changes are recorded from the model. This simulation exercise is repeated for all individual countries in the model. In this way, for each country individually and for all countries collectively, one can break down the country gains into a 'unilateral' component and a 'multilateral' component. The resulting numbers provide an exact quantitative division of the gains into the two components.

Figure 1 shows the plot of the gains/losses ('Welfare change as a percentage of GDP') from the Uruguay Round reductions in border distortions excluding the MFA against the extent of own liberalization which each country undertakes in the Uruguay Round ('Own liberalization'). The size of own liberalization through the reform of tariffs and export subsidies is reported for each country in Table 1. Hong Kong, Taiwan and China have zero reductions in trade distortions as they did not participate in the Round. They should be dropped from the figure for the purpose of plotting own country liberalizations against welfare gain/loss.

This figure shows a positive relationship between the extent of own liberalization and gains but it is less striking than the figure in Martin and Winters (1995). Martin and Winters use the unweighted average of the cuts in tariffs and the reductions in agricultural export subsidies. The reductions in agricultural export subsidies generally result in greater gains because the losses from distortions increase with the square of the distortions and consequently cutting highly distorting agricultural export subsidies yields higher gains. Consequently, the unweighted average may be a better approximation of the true trade restrictiveness index than the trade-weighted average used in this paper.

Table 3 presents the decomposition for this simulation of the outcome of the Uruguay Round. The first two columns show the results from the liberalization of 'own' country and 'other' country reductions in trade distortions and 'sum' is the sum of these two components. 'Global' is the effect of doing both components simultaneously as in the Uruguay Round package. In a few cases, there is a discrepancy between 'sum' and

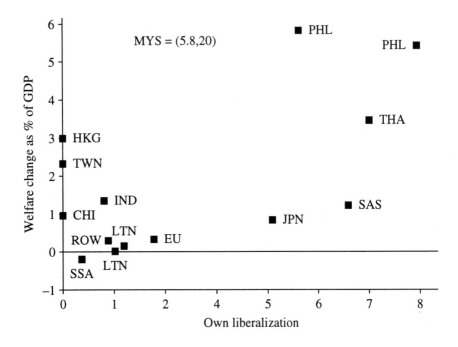

Figure 1   Gains from the Uruguay Round

'global' because there is an interaction between the two components, indicating that the gains/losses from the simultaneous changes by all countries is not exactly equal to the sum of the two components. However, in all cases this is small. We can therefore split the total effect of the package into these two components.

Table 3 reveals the proportion of the total gains which derive from 'own' country effects. We can express these proportions by calculating, for each country, 'own' and 'other' as a proportion of 'sum'. Six of the countries or groups of countries gain more from the 'own' liberalizations and six gain more from the 'other' liberalizations, leaving out the three countries which did not make any reductions for this calculation. Three of the four large gainers in absolute dollar terms – Japan, Korea, and Malaysia – have 2/3 or more of the total gains from the 'own' component. The EU is the one country whose gains come mostly from multilateral reduction in border distortions in the rest of the world.

The countries that gain most from the 'own' component, notably the Philippines, Korea, Malaysia, Thailand and Japan, are also the countries with the largest reductions in the distortions and the countries that derive the largest overall gains from the experiment. Latin America and Indonesia do not get large unilateral gains as they make relatively small reductions in their border restrictions. The US and Canada lose from unilateral liberalization but the adverse movement of the terms of trade plays a larger role for these countries due to their importance in international trade. This may explain in part why the US is a strong advocate of reciprocity in APEC

Table 3 Summary table

	Welfare change (US$m)				Terms of trade (% Change)		
	Own	Other	Sum	Global	Own	Other	Global
USC	−6,153	8,111	1,958	2,304	−0.540	0.557	0.023
EU	6,007	23,026	29,033	28,682	−0.670	0.671	0.008
JPN	27,895	13,121	41,016	41,183	−0.680	0.766	0.069
KOR	30,525	6,519	37,044	31,844	−1.318	0.606	−0.821
TWN	0	10,885	10,885	10,885	0.000	1.264	1.264
HKG	0	1,404	1,404	1,404	0.000	0.553	0.553
CHI	0	14,214	14,214	14,214	0.000	0.945	0.945
IND	1,347	2,162	3,509	3,504	−0.130	0.666	0.533
MYS	25,200	4,131	29,331	31,731	−2.796	0.904	−1.988
PHL	5,977	257	6,234	5,172	−1.180	0.535	−1.216
THA	6,576	2,446	9,022	8,770	−2.578	0.434	−2.109
LTN	435	2,153	2,588	2,471	−0.484	0.135	−0.352
SSA	170	−598	−428	−563	−0.184	−0.034	−0.271
SAS	1,984	6,394	8,378	7,962	−2.786	1.735	−1.203
ROW	−280	12,974	12,694	11,189	−0.376	0.640	0.271
Total	99,683	107,199	206,882	200,753			

Key: USC – US–Canada, EU — European Union, JPN – Japan, KOR – Republic of Korea, TWN – Taiwan, HKG – Hong Kong, CHI – People's Republic of China, IND – Indonesia, MYS – Malaysia, PHL – Philippines, THA – Thailand, LTN – Latin America, SSA – Sub-Saharan Africa, SAS – South Asia, ROW – Rest of world.

and other negotiations. However, the loss from unilateral action is small in relation to GDP.

The notable exceptions to this pattern are the EU and South Asia. In the case of the EU, relatively large overall gains go hand in hand with relatively small unilateral gains. The EU manages to capture large gains from liberalizations in other countries. In South Asia a quite high reduction in the distortions fails to yield large unilateral gains.

The correlation of large gains with large cuts in own country border distortions proves that the correlation observed between large gains from the total package and large cuts in own country border distortions, which was observed by Martin and Winters, can indeed be attributed to the effect of the own country reforms with the EU and the US–Canada group as the significant exceptions.

The columns for the terms of trade associated with the 'own' and 'other' components give us further insight into the pattern of gains and losses from the Uruguay Round. First, all countries which reduce their border distortions suffer an adverse movement in their terms of trade from the 'own' component, as standard economic theory predicts, ruling out pathological and improbable cases. However, not all countries can suffer an adverse movement in their commodity terms of trade from the total package of course. Korea, Malaysia, Thailand and South Asia lose the most from adverse movement of the terms of trade from the whole package of the Uruguay Round. Despite the adverse movement of the terms of trade, Korea, Malaysia and Thailand gain from own country cuts because they receive larger efficiency gains from larger cuts in these distortions. Both the US and Canada, and the EU lose substantially or gain little respectively from cutting their own border distortions, apparently because they suffer a substantial deterioration in their terms of trade and because they gain little in efficiency as the tariffs were already low pre-UR and the extent of the reduction in agricultural subsidies was small (Table 1).

These results have important implications for trade liberalization strategies. The gains from the 'own' component would accrue to the country if it alone changed its border restrictions but the multilateral round provides a stronger incentive to make these changes. Almost all governments, whether they gain or lose from unilateral liberalization, regard own country changes as a 'concession' which is a price to be paid for access to the gains due to the reductions in the restrictions of other countries. All of the countries which gain from unilateral liberalization except sub-Sahara Africa receive an extra gain from the liberalization of other countries. To a large extent, multilateral rounds provide a device for countries to effect reform of their own border restrictions on international trade.

5   The future evolution of the global trading system

The world trading system will no doubt continue to change rapidly but it is difficult to predict most changes.

One change is easy to predict because many of the main developments are already in the pipeline of policy negotiations: regional trading arrangements will continue to grow in areas. It is likely that the main growth will take the form of an expansion in already existing arrangements. The EU has been having discussions with a number of countries about future membership. The US Congress has begun hearings related to the accession of Chile to NAFTA. At the Summit of the Americas held in December 1994 in Miami 33 countries agreed in principle to form the Free Trade Area of the Americas (FTAA) by 2005. This would cover every western hemisphere country except Cuba. Trade ministers of the countries are to meet in Denver in July 1995. Vietnam is to become the seventh member of ASEAN in November and Cambodia, Laos and Burma may join subsequently. Other regional trading arrangements are planning to expand.

Regional trading arrangements will also increasingly engage in 'deeper' integration of markets through the reduction and harmonization of non-border measures which inhibit trade. This movement has been one of the attractions of the formation and extension of regional trading arrangements in the 1980s and 1990s.

Links between regional trading arrangements

Quite suddenly, the growth of regional trading areas which has been going on for the last 10 years or so is entering a new phase of links between these areas.

The movement towards the FTAA is to be achieved in the first instance by means of a new link between the Mercosur (Brazil, Argentina, Paraguay and Uruguay) and NAFTA regional trading agreements. Alarmed by discrimination against it that would result from this link, the EU has put more emphasis on the negotiations which had been proposed in 1994 for a new fee trade agreement between the EU and Mercosur. The EU has offered to create a free trade area with Mercosur by 2001, provided Mercosur frees trade internally and establishes a common external tariff. In April 1995 the EU Council of Ministers approved the progress of trade negotiations with Mercosur and scheduled the signing of a preliminary cooperation agreement in late 1995. In 1994 the Canadian Prime Minister called for a free trade area between North America and Europe which would link the NAFTA and the EU. This has become known in 1995 as the Trans-Atlantic Free Trade Area (TAFTA). Another possible link in the Asia-Pacific region is the AFTA-CER link which was raised by Thailand with Australian and New Zealand ministers in 1993 and then enthusiastically promoted by the Australian Prime Minister during his visit to Thailand in early 1994. The ASEAN Ministerial Meeting in April issued an invitation to the trade ministers of the countries involved in the two areas to consult. It has been agreed that, in the initial stages, the discussions will be limited to APEC-style agenda items relating to trade facilitation rather than trade liberalization.

Finally, we need to consider APEC. The Bogor Declaration in November 1994 set out a vision of a 'community of Asia-Pacific economies' and proposed a 'long-term goal of free and open trade and investment in the Asia-Pacific'. They announced a commitment to complete these arrangements by the year 2010 for the industrial countries and 2020 for the developing countries in the region. APEC includes the members of NAFTA, AFTA and CER. If the APEC proposal took the form of a free trade area, it would be in effect a multiple link.

The imperative for a strong multilateral system
The EU and NAFTA are now continent-sized areas and other regional trading arrangements such as ASEAN may become large. There has been growing concern over the inadequacies of the GATT rules relating to regional trading arrangements and of their enforcement, especially the failure of most arrangements to conform to the timetables and 'substantially all trade' provision and, most particularly, the possible harmful effects of trade discrimination inherent in these arrangements on outside countries.

Despite discussion in the Uruguay Round negotiations on the need to tighten GATT rules relating to regional trading arrangements, the Round avoided the main issues in this area. The Final Act of the Uruguay Round contained an Understanding on the Interpretation of Article XXIV which clarified some aspects of the article but left the main provisions unchanged. In particular, it did nothing to protect the interest of third countries.

A number of studies have examined the question of whether the world economy is becoming more regionalized as a result of the growth of regional trading arrangements. They have rejected this claim. Recent studies by the WTO (1995) itself and the OECD (1995) confirm this view. Within their respective spheres of application, both multilateral and regional agreements have liberalized trade between nations and they have reinforced each other in a number of ways. Some countries which have joined regional trading arrangements have also unilaterally liberalized trade. Many modalities of trade liberalization have been developed in one sphere and then applied in the other. For example, the EU and CUSTA have contributed a number of new modalities and ideas into the multilateral negotiations of service trade, technical barriers, dispute settlement and investment measures in the Uruguay Round (see OECD, 1995, pp. 62–66.

Notwithstanding the sanguine view of the effects of regional trading arrangements on world trade, the increase in the size of these areas may pose problems. Large regions welded by regional trading arrangements may see themselves as rivals in some contest of trade policy, and countries which are excluded from them have reduced bargaining power in any negotiations or dispute.

Links between regional trading arrangements may resolve the problems of discrimination between the linked areas but they increase the discrimination against outsiders.

Another possibility is a revision of the rules of GATT/WTO relating to regional trading arrangements. A number of possible ways in which the Article and its administration might be strengthened are discussed in WTO (1995b, Chapter V).

If APEC trade liberalization takes some form of concerted liberalization under which the lowering of trade barriers by each country is extended unconditionally to all members of the GATT/WTO, it will serve to liberalize trade on an MFN basis. If instead, it liberalizes trade on a conditional MFN basis within an APEC free trade area, it will greatly extend the area of non-MFN trade.

Better still, further multilateral trade liberalization under the aegis of the WTO would reduce discrimination due to the regional trading arrangements as an automatic by-product of the general lowering of barriers to international trade. The WTO should also carry out further multilateral liberalization of trade restrictions as soon as possible in order to keep up with 'deeper' integration within regional trading arrangements.

Best of all, unilateral reductions in border distortions by the countries which are members of discriminatory regional trading arrangements would ensure that both the members and outsiders gain more from regional integration. The countries of the CER and AFTA regional agreements have done this. The decomposition in section 4 above clearly demonstrated that reciprocity is not required for many individual countries to gain from trade reforms and the case for lowering external trade barriers is even stronger when it accompanies a regional lowering of barriers. This applies particularly to those countries which have relatively high tariffs or trade barriers or export subsidies.

In this environment, the continuation of multilateral reductions in trade restrictions and the enforcement of the rules of the WTO and especially its new dispute settlement procedures are vital to the development of a world trading system. The growing integration of national economies through international trade in goods and services and intellectual property depends on the establishment of a strong WTO.

Notes

1. A number of Asian countries also offer extensive duty exemptions and drawbacks for imports outside the sub-national zones. In China, for example, these exemptions are more important than those obtained through the zones.
2. The IMS Growth Triangle comprises parts of Indonesia and Malaysia and the whole of Singapore, the IMT Growth Triangle comprises parts of Indonesia, Malaysia and Thailand, and BIMPEAGA comprises parts of Brunei, Indonesia, Malaysia and the Philippines.
3. For Australia, the average effective rate of assistance for all manufactures in 1982–83 was 23 per cent. As a result of the tariffication of quotas and a series of unilateral reductions in tariffs, this fell to only

12 per cent in 1992–93, the latest year available (Industry Comission, 1995, Table A1). After a change in government in 1983, New Zealand has undertaken a rapid programme of tariffication of the comprehensive system of quotas and reduction in the tariff rates. The more limited measures which are available for New Zealand show that the average effective rate of assistance for the manufacturing sector fell from 39 per cent in 1981–82 to 26 per cent in 1987–88 and it has fallen sharply since then. (Syntec, 1988 and Ministry of Commerce, 1991.

For the measures of assistance provided to agricultural producers in Australia, see Industry Commission (1994, Appendix L).

References

Anderson, J.E. and J.P. Neary (1994), 'Measuring the Restrictiveness of Trade Policy', *The World Bank Economic Review*, **8**, May, 151–69.

François, J., B. McDonald and H. Nordstrom (1995), 'Assessing the Uruguay Round', paper presented to the World Bank Conference on The Uruguay Round and the Developing Countries, The World Bank, Washington, DC.

Garnaut, R. and P. Drysdale (1994) (eds), *Asia Pacific Regionalism: Readings in International Relations*, Harper Education, Sydney.

General Agreement on Tariffs and Trade (1992), *International Trade and the Trading System*, GATT, Geneva.

Harrison, G.W., T.F. Rutherford and D.G. Tarr 1995), 'Quantifying the Uruguay Round', paper presented to the World Bank Conference on The Uruguay Round and the Developing Countries, The World Bank, Washington, DC.

Hertel, T. (ed.) (1995), *Global Trade Analysis using the GTAP Model*, forthcoming.

Hertel, T., W. Martin, K. Yanagishima and B. Dimaranan (1995), 'Liberalizing Manufactures Trade in a Changing World Economy', paper presented to theWorld Bank Conference on The Uruguay Round and the Developing Countries, The World Bank, Washington, DC.

Industry Commission (1994), *Annual Report 1993–94*, Australian Government Publishing Service, Canberra.

Industry Commission (1995), *Australian Manufacturing Industry and International Trade data 1968–69 to 1992–93*, Australian Government Publishing Service, Canberra.

Lloyd, P.J. (1995), 'The Future of Trans-Tasman Closer Economic Relations', *Agenda* (forthcoming).

Martin, W. and L.A. Winters (1995), 'The Uruguay Round and the Developing Countries', paper presented to the Pacific Economic Cooperation Council Trade Policy Forum VIII, Taipei, 20–21 April 1995.

Ministry of Commerce (1991), *Official Report on the post-1992 Tariff Review*, Ministry of Commerce, Wellington.

OECD (1994), *The New World Trading System: Readings*, OECD, Paris.

OECD (1995), *Regional Integration and the Multilateral Trading System*, OECD, Paris.

Pangestu, M. (1995), 'Trade and Investment Facilitation through Free Trade Areas: AFTA', paper presented to the Second APEC Roundtable Facilitating Interdependence in the Asia-Pacific, Singapore, 23–24 June 1995.

Syntec (1988), *Industry Assistance Reform in New Zealand*, Syntec, Sydney.

World Bank (1995), Conference on the Uruguay Round and the Developing Countries, The World Bank, Washington, DC.

World Trade Organization (WTO) (1995a), Press Release, 28 March 1995, WTO, Geneva.

World Trade Organization (1995b), *Regionalism and the World Trading System*, WTO, Geneva.

[13]

The Australian Economic Review, vol. 30, no. 1, pp. 71-4

Policy Forum: The WTO Post-Singapore

The Singapore Ministerial Conference: An Overview

P. J. Lloyd
Department of Economics
The University of Melbourne

On 1 January 1995, the World Trade Organisation (WTO) replaced the GATT, a temporary arrangement created in the turmoil of the immediate post-Second World War period. The WTO has been heralded as the first major international institution to be created in the post-Cold War era. It is much more ambitious in scope than its predecessor as it covers services as well as goods and trade-related aspects of intellectual property and investment measures.

The WTO joins the World Bank and the IMF as one of the three Bretton Woods Sisters, a reference to the Bretton Woods Conference in 1944 which planned the multilateral institutions to oversee the post-Second World War world trading system. The WTO bears a much closer resemblance to the International Trade Organisation which was planned as the third leg of the system but which never came into being because the US Congress failed to ratify the agreement. Indeed, the WTO is already the more important of the three. Whereas the World Bank and the IMF are troubled by changes in the world economy which have substantially removed the original justification for these institutions, the WTO has a clear and expanding role in managing international trade in goods and services. The main questions relate to how far its powers should be extended.

The 1996 Singapore Ministerial (SM) Conference was the first biennial Ministerial Conference of the WTO. It was a major event which was to consider the future course of the organisation. The Singaporean Minister for Trade and Industry and the Chairman of the Ministerial Conference, Mr Yeo Cheow Tong,

declared in his conclusion of the Conference that 'The Singapore Ministerial Conference has been an outstanding event in all respects'. At the same time, the Australian Minister for Trade declared 'The Singapore Ministerial has been a case of five days of hard effort delivering five years and more of progress toward a new millennium of free world trade.' (Deputy Prime Minister and Minister for Trade 1996).

The purpose of this Policy Forum it to provide an early assessment of the SM. This overview presents some general comments on the scope of the discussions at the SM and the outcome. Dr Sampson looks at the issue of regionalisation, that is, the spread of regional trade arrangements which discriminate against non-members. While these arrangements are permitted under Article XXIV, the Enabling Clause and other articles of the GATT, they are widely regarded as a threat to the principle of non-discrimination which is the foundation of the GATT and the WTO. Professor Milner looks at the four 'New Issues'—labour standards, trade and the environment, investment and competition policy—which were on the agenda of the SM. All of these represent a potential expansion of the responsibilities of the WTO into areas of policy which have traditionally been regarded as domestic (non-border) policy. Professor Yamazawa looks at the APEC process of trade liberalisation and discusses how the APEC process may facilitate WTO trade liberalisation.

The SM was a solid outcome which did achieve some concrete results, although it was disappointing in some areas of trade negotiations.

Among the concrete outcomes which are expected to lead to further liberalisation of world trade in goods and services one can list the continuation of negotiations in services (Basic Telecommunications, Maritime Transport Services, Financial Services and Accountancy) and the agreement on future negotiations on Agriculture, aspects of TRIPS, and the reviews of Antidumping, Customs Valuation, Dispute Settlement Understanding and several other areas. Most of these have arisen from the so-called Built-in Agenda of issues left unresolved or listed for review in the Uruguay Round. In fact, the Agreement on Telecommunications Services was concluded in February 1997, as planned at the SM.

Another area of liberalisation was the Information Technology Agreement (ITA). The ITA is not technically part of the SM. In Singapore 28 WTO members and countries seeking to accede to the WTO agreed to free substantially all trade in information technology products such as computers, software, semiconductors and telecommunications equipment by 2000. This Agreement will take effect from 1 July 1997, provided enough countries accounting for 90 per cent of world trade in these products sign the Agreement. ITA is essentially an agreement reached by the European Union and the United States: 15 of the 28 countries are the members of the European Union. A further group of countries indicated they might join.

While the ITA has been hailed widely, including in Australia, as a major breakthrough, it poses two problems. First, it is an example of an increasing tendency, led by the United States, to negotiate issues on a sectoral basis. This may lead to gains in the chosen sectors but it may also make it more difficult to achieve gains in remaining sectors, especially if the sectors chosen are those in which gains are easier and sectors such as agriculture with high barriers are left behind. Sector by sector negotiations have been tried in earlier GATT rounds with little success. ITA may not be a precedent that can be followed in many sectors because it was not a highly protected industry and the three main markets—the United States, European Union and Japan—all wanted the agreement. (There are some sector-specific arrangements in the WTO relating to agricultural products, textiles and clothing, and to civil aircraft and other plurilateral agreements on bovine meat and dairy products but these are all monuments to the lack of success in negotiating barriers in these sectors. The inclusion of the Agreements on Agriculture and on Textiles and Clothing as part of the Uruguay Round with their more limited liberalisation was done at the insistence of exporters of these products who were not prepared to sign other agreements in the multilateral negotiations without some progress in these areas.) Second, it is not clear whether the reduction in tariffs and other barriers in the ITA will be universally applied on an MFN basis; the United States has indicated that it will introduce completely free trade in these products for participating countries.

Perhaps the major achievement of the SM lies in what it did not do. Here I refer to the discussion on Labour Standards and on Trade and the Environment, two of the 'new issues'. Both of these areas had been subject to an enormous amount of discussion in various fora before the meeting. In the area of labour standards, the WTO renewed its commitment to the observance of internationally recognised core labour standards but determined that the International Labour Organisation is the competent body to set and deal with these standards, and rejected the use of labour standards for protectionist purposes and agreed that the comparative advantage of countries, particularly low-wage countries, must in no way be put into question. This has effectively ruled out incorporation of labour standards into the rules of the WTO, although as Milner notes, some US officials continue to believe that it leaves open the possibility of actions in the WTO on the grounds of labour standards. It represents a victory for Developing Countries such as India and other small countries such as Australia which opposed the introduction of labour standards into the WTO. Similarly, the agreement that the WTO Committee on Trade and Environment would carry out its work under its existing terms of reference rejected the call for the use of trade instruments as a means of achieving environmental goals.

Two important Working Groups were set up which may have a major impact on the nature of the WTO in future. These were the Working Group which is to examine the relationship between trade and investment and the Working Group to study issues relating to interaction between trade and competition policy, including anticompetitive practices. These Working Groups are to deal with the other two new issues. The former was pressed very hard by the European Union which is keen to see a multilateral agreement on investment embedded in the WTO. If this were done, it would be a major extension of the role of the WTO. It would effectively create an organisation with powers to regulate government actions in the field of foreign investments parallel to those it currently possesses in the fields of trade in goods and services.

However, there is no certainty that investment or competition policy will be addressed systematically in the WTO. A Multilateral Agreement on Investment has been drafted by the OECD, and UNCTAD too has a substantial role in setting standards and monitoring developments in the area. An agreement on competition policy poses quite different problems as competition policy is mostly concerned with the regulation of the actions of private producers, not the actions of governments. The Singapore Ministerial Declaration stated 'It is clearly understood that future negotiations, if any, regarding multilateral disciplines in these areas, will take place only after an explicit consensus decision is taken among WTO members regarding such negotiations'.

These discussions regarding multilateral rules relating to investment and competition policy are further illustrations of the broadening scope of discussions and negotiations of world trade issues. They arise because of changes in the structure of the world economy. In particular, both reflect the fact that cross-border or international competition among producers takes place through two distinct but competing modes.

First, producers in different countries compete with each other by the direct shipment of their goods and services to markets in foreign countries. The GATT was founded on the regulation of this mode of competition. Second, producers of one country may compete in foreign markets by establishing production facilities in the countries in which the markets are located. This requires foreign investments in these countries. Such multinational firms engage in what is sometimes usefully called international production. (They may also establish affiliates in a third country and export the outputs to other foreign markets.) Efficient world production requires that production be neutral between the two modes, that is, it calls for free (unrestricted and non-discriminatory) world investment as well as free international trade. The situation is more complicated in services as some service providers can compete in foreign markets only establishing a commercial presence in these markets involving foreign investment and/or the movement of 'natural persons' associated with international production. This was recognised in the General Agreement on Trade in Services (GATS) in the Marrakesh Agreement that established the WTO. The growth in foreign investment and international production is requiring multilateral bodies such as the WTO to consider these issues. For example, the Telecommunications Services Agreement reached two weeks ago includes provisions for the right of establishment of foreign competitors as well as provision for free trade in services.

Some commentators have expressed disappointments with the outcome of the SM. The Developing Countries and especially the Least Developed Countries are not generally happy with progress on trade issues of relevance to them, despite the failure of labour standards and the rather pious statement in the Declaration regarding the importance of the integration of these countries into the multilateral trading system. There are continuing complaints about the implementation of the Uruguay Round Agreement on Textiles and Clothing which include the backloading of commitments and new barriers, and major disagreements among members on future negotiations relating to agriculture.

The statement on Regional Agreements reaffirmed the primacy of the multilateral trading system and endorsed the work of the new Committee on Regional Trade Agreements. It dodged the essential need to rewrite Article XXIV to prevent harmful effects of regional discrimination on non-member countries.

Given the fact that regional trade agreements are burgeoning in numbers and country coverage and are a major threat to the fundamental principle of non-discrimination in Article I of GATT (1947), this is a disappointment. However, Sampson notes that the new Committee on Regional Trade Agreements which was created in the WTO in 1996 will enable these problems to be addressed systematically.

The European Union and some other countries had sought agreement on another round of negotiations by 2000 but there was no general support for this. The Uruguay Round negotiations had taken 7 years and most countries are not ready for general negotiations, apart from those which are already on the Built-in Agenda, such as agriculture.

More ambitiously, some economists had recommended that the WTO take a leaf out of the APEC book and establish an ultimate goal of border-free trade for all members; for example, the Stockholm Declaration (1996) which was written by a group of international economists. The declaration of a goal of free trade and target dates is a major contribution of APEC to global trade liberalisation. The APEC process of trade liberalisation is discussed in the article below by Yamazawa. The Preamble to the GATT in 1947 stated the goal of 'a substantial reduction of tariffs and other barriers to trade and to the elimination of discriminatory treatment in international commerce' and the Preamble to the Marrakesh Agreement establishing the WTO repeats this language. There is no reference to a goal of free trade, though the Governments of the United Kingdom and Canada have advocated it and the Director-General of the WTO, Mr Renato Ruggerio, has supported the adoption of this goal (Ruggerio 1996). However, these more ambitious hopes for a new round before 2000 and a declared goal of free trade were, it seems to me, unrealistic for a Ministerial meeting lasting five days, especially given the effort spent on labour standards and trade and the environment. The Singapore Ministerial Conference achieved more than previous GATT Ministerial meetings.

For the first time in world economic history the goal of global free trade is being openly discussed and is a real possibility. There is significant movement in virtually all countries. Yet, there is still significant opposition to trade liberalisation in many of the world's major markets. The most important question is how can this momentum be maintained. The Built-in Agenda, Working Groups and Committee programs and the ITA should propel the WTO towards further multilateral trade liberalisation, pending a new round of comprehensive negotiations some time after 2000.

Looking ahead to the long term future of the organisation, what the SM did was to reaffirm the WTO as the multilateral body which has the primary responsibility to regulate world trade in goods and services but it does not have the primary responsibility for labour standards and the environment. Possibly in the future it will also have a primary or major responsibility for related areas of investment and competition policy. We may end up with a World Trade and Investment Organisation or something even broader as policy changes frequently induce further policy changes.

February 1997

References

Deputy Prime Minister and Minister for Trade 1996, *Media Release*, 13 December.

Ruggerio, R. 1996, 'Beyond borders: Managing a world of free trade and deep interdependence', address to Argentinian Council on Foreign Relations, WTO Press/55, 10 September.

Stockholm Declaration 1996, 'Stockholm Declaration for Free Trade', *Business Times*, 9 December.

World Trade Organisation 1996, *Singapore Ministerial Declaration*, WT/MIN (96)/ DEC/W, World Trade Organisation, Geneva.

Yeo Cheow Tong 1996, 'Concluding remarks by H. E. Mr Yeo Cheow Tong Chairman of the Ministerial Conference and Minister for Trade and Industry of Singapore', WTO.

PART VI

TRADE AND INVESTMENT LIBERALIZATION IN THE ASIA–PACIFIC REGION

Introduction

This section examines a number of aspects of the liberalization of trade in goods and services and capital in the Asia-Pacific region. As the most rapidly liberalizing and the most rapidly growing region in the world during the 1970s and 1980s and most of the 1990s, much attention has been paid to this region. One may regard the liberalization of trade in goods and factors which has occurred as a process of integration. These papers deal with the integration of the economies of the region or the consequences of this integration. The region is also of special interest because of the formation of the Asia-Pacific Economic Cooperation (APEC), a unique type of regional forum which has greatly stimulated debate about liberalization of trade in goods and factors and the harmonization across countries of national policies which affect trade.

The first paper on 'East Asian export competitiveness: new measures and policy implications' documents the remarkable competitiveness of the East Asian economies in the world economy. It considers the factors which account for a high and rising share of the global markets for manufactures by the East Asian countries. The constant market share analysis is applied to total apparent consumption in the industrialized countries whereas hitherto it has been applied to imports only. The results show that it is 'competitiveness' in the sense of an increasing share of individual product markets in individual countries rather than the concentration on growing markets or product groups which explains the growth of the market share of these countries.

In the 1990s increasing attention has been played to foreign direct investment as a factor which increases exports of goods and improves total factor productivity. The second paper, 'The role of foreign investment in the success of Asian industrialization', looks at the important role of foreign direct investment in the industrialization of the East Asian region.

The growth of foreign direct investment flows has led to proposals for the conclusion of a regional agreement on investment in the Asia-Pacific region under the aegis of the APEC forum. 'An APEC or multilateral code?' considers whether rules relating to national government regulation of investment flows are best conducted at the regional or the multilateral level. The choice of regional or multilateral basis for rules parallels that in the liberalization of trade in goods and services but, unlike regional trading arrangements, the regional proposals for investment rules would not discriminate among countries. Nevertheless, there are reasons why a more comprehensive agreement under the Organization for Economic Cooperation and Development (OECD) or the World Trade Organization (WTO) might be preferable to an Asia-Pacific agreement.

APEC is also considering the development of rules relating to competition policies in the region. These proposals focus on the development of national competition law in all the member countries in the first instance and the possible harmonization of such national rules. 'Competition policy in APEC: principles of harmonization' examines these proposals. It also puts forward a new multilateral version of the index of similarity of the competition policies of pairs of countries devised by Bollard and Vautier (1998).

The last paper deals with the crises in financial and foreign exchange markets of East Asia after July 1997. This paper illustrates an aspect of the formation of the global economy not discussed elsewhere, namely, the integration across countries of markets for financial capital. The paper, written with University of Melbourne colleague Kym Sawyer, attributes the crises to a number of factors. These include an increase in capital inflows – itself due partly to the liberalization of capital movements into the region and partly to high interest rate differentials favouring offshore borrowing – long-run convergence of growth rates and the failure to liberalize financial markets in East Asia. The interaction of international movements of goods, fixed capital and financial capital markets illustrates the complexity of new interdependencies in a global economy.

References
Bollard, A. and K.M. Vautier (1998), 'The Convergence of Competition Law within APEC and CER', in Rong-I Wu (ed.), *Business Markets and Government in Asia and the Pacific*, London: Routledge.

[14]

East Asian Export Competitiveness: New Measures and Policy Implications

P. J. Lloyd* and Hisako Toguchi*

South Korea

China

Indonesia

This paper demonstrates the remarkable competitiveness of East Asian countries in world export markets for manufactures and develops some policy implications, both for developed and other developing economies. Using constant market share analysis, applied to data for exports from three East Asian countries—Korea, China and Indonesia—to markets in the industrially advanced economies (IAEs), it shows that East Asian countries have increased their share, not merely in IAE imports, but in total IAE market sales at the expense of exporters from other countries and of domestic IAE producers.

Introduction

The rapid growth of exports of manufactures from East Asian countries over the last three decades is a phenomenon that is now well known. It has been recognised as an important factor in the rapid overall economic growth of these economies (World Bank 1993). From this point of view, it is the envy of many other developing countries and might provide a strategy for accelerating their rate of economic growth. It has also been stressed by the United States, the European Union and other industrially advanced economies (IAEs) to which most of these exports of manufactures have been directed. Increasing imports from East Asia have been blamed by several of their economists for de-industrialisation, falling real wages and rising unemployment, and worsening income distribution (Wood 1994). Other economists have, however, attributed these effects to technology shocks and other variables (for example, Krugman and Lawrence 1993 and Lawrence 1994 and the

surveys of this literature in the *Journal of Economic Perspectives* 1995). It is important for policy purposes to understand the source of this rapid growth of exports.

Constant market share analysis of imports

This paper looks at the pattern of growth of exports from East Asian countries using a decomposition known as constant market share analysis. It discusses past studies of East Asian exports using this method, develops an extension of the method using data on total market sales rather than imports alone, and comments on the policy implications for exporting and importing countries. Constant market share analysis provides a breakdown of the proximate sources of growth in competitiveness in individual country and commodity markets. It has been applied to East Asian exports (cf. Chow and Kellman 1993; Low 1994 and Lloyd 1994).

* Asian Business Centre, The University of Melbourne.

One country's exports may grow more rapidly than total world exports for three reasons: (1) its exports may be more concentrated in commodities for which world trade has grown relatively rapidly; (2) its exports may be concentrated on countries whose imports have grown relatively rapidly; (3) it may have increased its share of the imports of commodities in individual country markets.[1]

This data set has been constructed using a concordance of the international trade data classified according to the Standard International Trade Classification (SITC) and the national data according to the International Standard Industrial Classification (ISIC). With this concordance, the apparent consumption of some commodity group in some country is given by national production plus imports less exports of the commodity. Although this measure ignores changes in stocks, it is a good approximation of the true foreign country shares of total final sales to consumers and producers. The first two effects may be referred to as the country and commodity effect respectively. The third effect will be referred to as the competitiveness effect. It needs to be understood that this term does not refer to the overall export performance of economies but to the competitiveness of a country's exports of individual commodities in individual country markets.

What this three-fold decomposition highlights is that an increasing share of world export markets does not necessarily imply increased competitiveness in this narrower sense. It may be due to the pattern of specialisation in either the country of destination or in the particular commodity bundle exported. If a country is fortunate in exporting to countries whose

> *All constant market share studies of East Asian countries have shown that the major explanation for the increase in the exports of manufactures has been a steady increase in the contribution of the competitiveness effect*

imports are growing relatively rapidly or in exporting commodities for which world total imports are growing relatively rapidly, it may increase its overall or average competitiveness without increasing its share of individual markets.

Decomposition permits us to identify the contribution of each of these three sources to the difference between an individual country's export performance, on the one hand, and that of all the foreign suppliers to a given market, on the other (Leamer and Stern 1970). Thus it provides a very useful descriptive decomposition of the Asian export performance.

Some US economists have suggested that the Asian export strategy has deliberately targeted the US market because it has grown rapidly and has allowed increased market penetration for imports from all foreign countries, as shown in Appendix Tables 1 and 2. Lester Thurow (1992:62) declares

> All of the successful developing countries in the past half century have gone through a phase where they sent most of their exports to the United States. The United States has effectively been the open market of first resort on which any country that wished to join the industrial world focused its attention during the takeoff phase of economic growth. Between 1981 and 1986, 42 per cent of Korea's growth and 74 per cent of Taiwan's growth could be traced to exports to the American market ...

This argument predicts that the country effect will be important.

All constant market share studies of East Asian countries have shown that the major explanation for the increase in the exports of manufactures from East Asian countries has been a steady increase in the contribution of

---

1 The exports of one commodity by one country to another country or group of countries are of course the imports of the commodity by the importing country or countries, neglecting differences in valuation and timing. In the constant market share analysis of apparent consumption in Table 1, we have used the imports into the IAEs as these relate more closely to the apparent consumption in the IAEs in the same year whereas in the constant market share analysis of imports in Table 2 we have used the export data, following other studies. It makes no significant difference whether one uses the export or import data.

what we have called the competitiveness effect. This is much more important than either the country or the commodity effects. There is some variation in the results of these decompositions according to the time period and the sample of countries. In their study of the four Asian NIEs, Chow and Kellman (1993) find some cyclical variation in the country and commodity effects. Although these were small in all periods relative to the individual market-share effect for the four countries, the country effect tended to be small but negative in periods of slow growth or decline in world imports and small but positive in other periods, whereas the reverse held for the commodity effect. In his study of the exports of Korea, the People's Republic of China and Indonesia over the period 1980–91, Lloyd (1993) confirmed the dominance of the individual market-share effect for Korea and found it was even stronger in the case of the People's Republic of China. However, the results for Indonesia were very different. The value of Indonesian total exports grew more slowly than world exports during this period, owing to a large negative commodity effect as the price of petroleum and petroleum products fell on world markets. This pattern was more typical of the experience of primary product exporters.

Growing import penetration of apparent consumption in the IAEs

Empirical study of market shares has so far been confined to the analysis of changes in the share in imports of manufactures. However, import shares do not represent true market shares. Commodity markets in all countries include the domestic supplies to the markets as well as the imports. When examining issues of competitiveness and market penetration, markets should be measured in terms of total sales, that is, imports plus domestic supplies. This paper provides for the first time, to the

authors' knowledge, a decomposition of the penetration of the total sales for manufactures in the IAEs by East Asian countries.

Import shares may behave differently, and for different reasons, from total market shares. It is the total market shares which are of concern to both the exporting and the importing countries. From the point of view of the exporting countries, a growing share of the total market is a very different prospect from a growing share of imports, if the share of imports in the total market is contracting or expanding. From the point of view of the importing country, a growing share in imports of some manufacturing commodity has different implications for domestic sales and employment if the import share of the market is expanding or contracting. For example, if the share of imports from all countries in total sales in the US market is rising, changes in the share in imports from East Asia underestimate the growth in the market share of East Asian countries.

Unfortunately, data on total market shares for all goods and services are not generally available. For manufacturing commodities in the markets of the IAEs, however, data are available from the International Economic Databank (IEDB) of the Australian National University for 'apparent consumption'.[2] When imports from a specific country are divided by apparent consumption, the percentage shares are called 'import penetration' ratios or shares.

This paper looks at East Asian exports as a share of apparent consumption in the IAEs over the period 1980 to 1993, the latest year for which the statistics of apparent consumption are available. The East Asian countries are the countries of the East Asian region less Japan, which is a developed country and a high technology exporter, and the transition economies which have not yet established full market economies. They therefore include the newly industrialised economies (NIEs: Hong Kong, Korea, Taiwan and Singapore), plus the countries of the ASEAN 6 other than Singapore

---

2   This data set has been constructed using a concordance of the international trade data classified according to the Standard International Trade Classification (SITC) and the national data according to the International Standard Industrial Classification (ISIC). With this concordance, the apparent consumption of some commodity group in some country is given by national production plus imports less exports of the commodity. Although this measure ignores changes in stocks, it is a good approximation of the true foreign country shares of total final sales to consumers and producers.

and Brunei, and the People's Republic of China. These are the countries whose recent export performance has been outstanding.

The International Standard Industrial Classification (ISIC) Section 3 statistics on manufacturing have been reported at the 2-digit level to provide the detail of broad industry groups. For the importing countries, statistics are reported for three groups—the USA, Japan and other IAEs, principally the European Union (EU).

Appendix Tables 1 and 2 show the import penetration ratios of East Asian countries for the individual 2-digit manufacturing industries in 1980 and in 1993. The rows report the results separately for imports into the USA, Japan and other IAEs. The second to last column of each table shows the import penetration ratio for all of East Asia collectively. For comparison the last column shows the import penetration from all foreign sources.

In 1993, for the IAEs as a whole, 3.7 per cent of the markets were supplied from East Asia. (This, one should note, is still only 15 per cent of the total imports of all manufactures from all foreign countries into these markets.) The largest single supplier was China, followed by Taiwan and Korea. (If Japan were added into East Asia as a supplier, the share would rise to 6.6 per cent). Industries which have import penetration ratios much higher than the average include 'Textile wearing apparel and leather', 'Fabricated metal products', 'Machinery and equipment', and the miscellaneous group 'Other manufacturing industries'.

These data confirm the growing penetration of these markets by exports from the East Asian countries over the period 1980–93. For East Asia as a whole and for 'All manufacturing', the import penetration ratio rose from 1.2 per cent in 1980 to 3.7 per cent in 1993. This is a very large increase over a relatively short period of 13 years. Moreover, every one of the East Asian exporting countries listed in this table had a substantial increase in its penetration ratio into the IAEs.

Looking at the pattern in the importing countries over the period, there is a large increase in the East Asian import penetration of all three markets. In the USA, the ratio rose from 1.3 to 3.9 per cent, in Japan from 1.2 per cent to 2.0 and in the other IAEs from 1.0 to 7.0 per cent. One can compare the corresponding cells for a 2-digit group in each of the three markets in Appendix Tables 1 and 2. There are nine East Asian countries which export nine 2-digit manufacturing groups to the three individual markets. This gives a total of 243 individual cells in these tables, ignoring the row aggregates for the whole manufacturing sector and the column aggregates for East Asia and the world. As many as 207 of these, or 85 per cent, showed an increase in the import penetration ratio of the individual markets between 1980 and 1993.

This pattern shows an increased penetration of the markets of the IAEs by the East Asian exporters. This is amazingly consistent in all of these importing countries and in all commodity markets.

Constant market share analysis of apparent consumption

It is important to understand the reasons for this East Asian penetration of the markets of the IAEs. Increased import penetration means that the rate of growth of exports of these commodities by the Asian countries has exceeded the rate of growth of apparent consumption in these IAEs' markets by a wide margin. Using the methods developed by constant market share analysis, this difference between the rates of growth of Asian exports and that of apparent consumption can be decomposed into its three components, the country effect, the commodity effect and the competitiveness effect.

The method of decomposition (described in the Appendix) is precisely the same as that used in the decomposition of shares of imports, except that the relevant market is total apparent consumption rather than total imports as used in previous studies. The decomposition permits us to identify the share of each of these three sources in explaining the difference between the

Table 1
Decomposition of the growth of apparent consumption of manufactures in the IAEs, 1980–1993

	Korea	China	Indonesia
Exports to IAEs, 1993 ($'000)	38,805,084	72,050,607	14,363,233
Exports to IAEs, 1980 ($'000)	9,905,380	4,965,256	3,124,553
Growth in exports (%)	291.8	1351.1	359.7
Growth in IAEs apparent cons.(%)	46.6	46.6	46.6
Difference to be explained	+245.2	+1,304.5	+313.1
Components due to:			
commodity composition	-6.0	-1.7	-8.7
country composition	+10.7	+1.5	+10.9
increased market share	+95.3	+100.2	+97.8

Source: Authors' calculations.

export performance of a country or group of countries on the one hand and that of all (foreign and domestic) suppliers to these markets on the other.

A decomposition of export growth performance is carried out for a sample of three individual Asian countries: the Republic of Korea (hereafter Korea), the People's Republic of China (hereafter China) and Indonesia. Korea is taken as a representative of the first generation NIEs. Indonesia is taken as a representative of the second generation NIEs and China is chosen because of its size and importance, the latest of the East Asian countries to storm the markets of the IAEs. The export destinations were again divided into the three major countries or groups of countries— the USA, Japan, and other IAEs—and broken down into the 2-digit commodity groups. Imports from all three Asian countries grew much more rapidly than the total sales in the IAE markets. In the case of China, the supplies from this country grew at an extraordinary 30 times the rate of growth of the market for the 13 year period. In the cases of Korea and Indonesia, the growth rates were 6 and 8 times that of the market respectively. (The increase in their market shares is shown in the Appendix tables.)

The decomposition of the growth of apparent consumption in the IAEs is reported

in Table 1. It produces results which are clear and uniform across all three countries. The commodity and country effects are small for all three countries and offsetting in sign. Consequently, the increase in individual market shares accounts for very close to 100 per cent of the growth in market share for all three countries! The closeness to 100 per cent is fortuitous, due to the country and commodity effects being small and almost cancelling each other. Thus, the growth of overall import shares is not a story of a fortunate specialisation in commodity groups or of countries with above-average growth or of the ability to switch comparative advantage to those markets which exhibit rapid growth. Rather, the increase in the market share of these countries is due to an increase in their market shares across the board, that is, across the nine industry groups and the three countries or country groups.

These results can be compared with the standard constant market share analysis of imports. Constant market share analysis of apparent consumption differs from constant market share analysis of imports only in terms of the variable whose distribution is being examined. To obtain the decomposition of import shares for manufactures, one merely substitutes in equation A.1 (see p.11), the growth rate of imports of manufactures into

Table 2
**Decomposition of the growth of imports of manufactures
to the IAEs, 1980–93**

	Korea	China	Indonesia
Exports to IAEs, 1993 ($'000)	38,730,701	71,495,408	12,732,169
Exports to IAEs, 1980 ($'000)	9,994,234	4,886,082	2,252,592
Growth in exports (%)	288	1363	465
Growth in IAEs imports (%)	129	129	129
Difference to be explained	+158	+1234	+336
Components due to:			
commodity composition	+1.9	-0.8	-14.1
country composition	+48.4	+3.9	+6.5
increased market share	+49.7	+96.9	+107.6

Source: Authors' calculations.

these markets for the growth rate of apparent consumption used above. As these growth rates differ, the decompositions will also differ.[3]

In general, one would expect the contributions of the three factors in the decomposition of total sales (apparent consumption) to differ from that of imports. For example, a country's exports may grow relatively rapidly, in part at least because it specialises in exporting to a country with relatively rapid growth of imports, perhaps because the country is reducing barriers to imports in these markets. If, however, the total sales of these countries are not increasing rapidly because of, say, slow economic growth in the country, the country effect will not explain as much, if any, of the relatively rapid growth of exports.

In order to compare the constant market share analysis of apparent consumption of manufactures in the IAEs with a constant market share analysis of imports of manufactures into the IAEs, we have replicated the method used above for the same three countries and the same time period but used total imports into the IAEs in place of apparent consumption of the IAEs. The decomposition appears in Table 2.

Again, competitiveness is the dominant factor for China and for Indonesia, and the largest single factor in Korea. The results for Indonesia are noteworthy since a constant market share analysis of all Indonesian merchandise exports by Lloyd (1994) showed different results. For the period 1980–91, Indonesia had a large negative commodity effect because of the fall in the price of its large exports of petroleum and petroleum products, as noted above. However, when one examines Indonesian exports of manufactures only, its behaviour is not significantly different from that of the other East Asian exporters.

The decomposition of apparent consumption is quite similar to the decomposition of imports. The general similarity of these results means that there has been an increase in the competitiveness of exports of manufactures from these three countries to the IAEs which has resulted in the simultaneous displacement

3   The relationship between these growth rates is simple. Consider the market for some commodity i in country j, the importing country. Let p denote the share of imports from country k in this market. (That is, imports from country k divided by total sales, or consumption.) Let s denote the share of country k in the total imports of commodity i by country j and m_{ij} the share of imports in the total sales of commodity i in country j. Then

$$p^k_{ij} = s^k_{ij} m_{ij} \qquad (1)$$

That is, the share of country j in this market in country k is the product of its share of imports and the import share of the total market. Hence, differentiating (1) totally,

$$dp^k_{ij} / p^k_{ij} = ds^k_{ij} / s^k_{ij} + dm_{ij} / m_{ij} \qquad (2)$$

That is, the change in the import penetration of the total market, for a particular commodity in a particular country, depends on the change in the share of imports from all sources in apparent consumption as well as on the change in the import share of the country k.

of both imports from other countries and home supplies.

However, for Korea there is a large country effect because of the importance for Korea of the growth in sales to the US market. This example shows that the use of apparent consumption in place of imports may give different results. For the purposes of analysing market shares, the decomposition of total sales is preferable to that of imports only.

Comprehensive East Asian competitiveness

We have shown that East Asian countries have increased their share of the total markets of the IAEs, not just their share of total imports into the IAEs, and that the increase in competitiveness of East Asian exports in the markets for manufactures in the IAEs is surprisingly comprehensive. It holds for all of the sample export countries and for the three major groups of IAEs. Moreover, it holds for a large majority of the manufactured commodity groups in each of these groups of countries: that is, it holds for most of the individual country markets for manufactures in the IAEs.

An increasing share of the markets for individual commodities in individual countries plainly cannot hold for all countries. The gain in the market share of one group of countries must mean a decline in the market share of some other suppliers, either other countries or the home country itself.

In the importing countries, where some alarm has been expressed over the growth in the share of imports from East Asian countries, what matters for domestic producers is not the growth in the import share from these countries alone. Rather, it is the growth of the share in apparent consumption of imports from all countries. If imports from one group of countries merely replace imports from another group who had previously had a larger share of the market, this change would not be of general concern to domestic producers. But if the domestic producers in (say) the USA or Europe, lose out in their home markets to both

East Asian and other importers, there is bound to be concern. And the cause of these changes and the policy implications would differ greatly between these two situations.

What factors account for East Asian competitiveness?

'Cheap labour'?

The continued increase in East Asian competitiveness cannot be due to cheap labour, the explanation often espoused by politicians in the importing countries.

At the end of the period examined here, East Asian labour was much less cheap than it was a decade ago. High and sustained rates of growth of real output in the East Asian countries have led to rapid increases in real wages. Real wage rates have risen sharply, relative to the USA and Europe, in most East Asian countries, particularly over the last decade. Some of the countries which have been most successful in increasing their exports of manufactures to the IAEs, such as Singapore and Hong Kong, now have real wages higher than those of several OECD countries. Import penetration has increased even though relative real wages have risen. Rather, it was the opening of these economies, together with measures that increased the productivity of labour, that improved their competitiveness.

The last two columns of Tables 1 and 2 show that the problem is fundamentally not increased East Asian competitiveness in the markets of the IAEs but rather a loss of competitiveness of the IAE countries, *vis-à-vis* the rest of the world. These columns report the combined East Asian shares of apparent consumption in the USA, Japan and other IAEs for 1980 and 1993. In both years imports from East Asia are a small part of total imports; about 7 and 15 per cent respectively. The share of imports from all countries increased for the IAEs collectively from 16.32 per cent to 25.51 per cent over the period. Increased imports from East Asia accounted for only 28 per cent of the increase in total imports of the IAEs.

Appendix 3 gives the import penetration ratios for the UK, which is one of the countries in the group of IAEs excluding the USA and Japan. This shows a similar pattern and trends. The share of imports in total apparent consumption in the UK increased from 1.02 per cent for all manufacturing in 1980 to 2.53 per cent in 1992. Over the same period the share of imports from all countries into the UK increased from 23 per cent to almost 31 per cent. Again the increase in the share of apparent consumption supplied by East Asia as group was more rapid than that of the other foreign countries but it accounted for only 19 per cent of the increase in imports of the UK.

Thus, what we observe is a systematic increase in imports from all sources which reduces the share of home country suppliers. While the Asian exporters have been among the more active gainers in market share and have increased their market share on average, the fundamental problem is one of declining competitiveness of the importing countries— the systematic loss of their own suppliers' market shares.

IAE trade liberalisation?

One possible cause of the increase in import penetration is liberalisation by the IAEs of access to their markets. But the period 1980–93 which predates the conclusion of the Uruguay Round did not bring across-the-board liberal- isation in the IAEs. Mutual liberalisation, moreover, would lead to mutual interpenet- ration of markets across liberalising countries, that is increased imports generally matched by increased exports. Of the latter there is no evidence. IAE trade liberalisation, therefore, cannot explain the widespread changes in import penetration ratios.

Technological catch-up?

A systematic increase in import shares of manufactures might also reflect a loss of comparative advantage in this commodity group due to the technological catch-up in exporting countries. Some of this may be associated with the role of foreign direct investment (FDI) in the East Asian countries.

The IAEs in Europe and North America, along with Japan, have been the main foreign direct investors in East Asia. FDI has played an important role in the Asian economies, providing additional resources for capital formation and transferring technology, knowhow and manage- ment methods.

For the IAEs, there is a partial offset to increased imports associated with the relocation of industries in the form of a share in the increase in incomes generated by the growth of exports from the East Asian economies. This shows up in increased factor service receipts in Japan, the USA and European countries. The IAEs have also benefited from increased sales of capital goods to the countries catching up. Paul Krugman and others have suggested that convergence will slow down the rate of growth of factor and technology accumu- lation in the fast-growing economies, but there is little evidence of this at present. The gaps between the technology levels of the USA, Japan and other leading IAEs and countries in East Asia and the rest of the world are still large, with much room for further technological catch-up.

Exchange rate changes?

Another possible cause of systematic changes in market shares is a downward shift in real exchange rates of the successful exporters. A conspicuous example of the effects of exchange rate realignment was the Plaza Accord of 1985. The large appreciation of the yen led to major changes in the pattern of commodity trade of Japan and to a huge surge in Japanese foreign direct investment in East Asia.

Of the three exporting countries examined in this paper, two—Indonesia and Korea—have had a large real devaluation *vis-à-vis* the US dollar over the period 1980–93, but the Korean *won* has moved little when adjustments are made for relative prices (APEC Economic Committee 1995, Table 5). All three countries have had a large devaluation *vis-à-vis* Japan and some, but not all, European countries. The appreciation of the yen alleviated the pressure of imports from Japan and other IAE markets. Thus the pattern of real exchange rate changes for these IAEs is mixed.

Lessons for the IAEs

There are a number of measures the importing IAEs can consider to arrest the decline in competitiveness and the rising share of imports in total apparent consumption. One approach to which they might be tempted to resort but which would certainly be unhelpful, indeed counter-productive, is further protection of their import-competing industries. An implication of the pervasive nature of the increase in market shares of these East Asian and other exporting countries is that it will not be reversed by such measures as anti-dumping and safeguard clause actions in the industrialised countries. These actions are limited by the WTO to specific imports and to specific circumstances and there is already growing concern about the over-use of this type of contingency measure. In any case, East Asian experience shows that it is a reduction in import barriers, not the raising of new barriers in a simple-minded defence strategy, together with appropriate macroeconomic policies, that leads to competitiveness in world markets.

Another possible line of action is devaluation of currencies subject to rising import pressure. An upward adjustment of the exchange rate when a country has become less competitive in world markets encourages exports and discourages imports of all goods and services. With the shift towards flexible exchange rate regimes, changes in exchange rates have come to reflect market conditions, changes in the demand and supply of tradable goods and services and international capital movements. It is doubtful whether government-induced changes in nominal exchange rates can, in contemporary conditions of volatile capital movements, bring about a lasting change in real effective exchange rates.

When current account deficits have become unsustainable, they call for measures to reduce aggregate expenditure on goods and services, to increase domestic savings by restraints on government budget deficits and other macroeconomic policies, and such measures need to be supplemented by microeconomic policies in the IAEs to increase the competitiveness of

industry and to facilitate structural adjustments. There is a diverse range of such policies, and the mix will vary among countries. In some, such as European countries and Australia, a major ingredient will be increased flexibility in wages and other labour market conditions. In others, infrastructure development or the introduction of competition into government-owned enterprises, especially those which supply essential inputs such as power, telecommunications and water to other industries. Tax reforms are needed in some countries to lower the cost of business capital. In all IAEs international competitiveness is most likely to be enhanced in the longer run by emphasis on human capital formation and R&D.

Lessons for developing economies

The success of East Asian countries in export-led growth provides lessons for other developing economies. The comprehensive character of increased import penetration of the markets of the IAEs, in terms of both countries and commodity groups, suggests that common supply-side factors have been operating in these exporting economies.

For all successful East Asian exporters, export growth was part of a general strategy of opening up the economy. All of them made substantial unilateral reductions in import trade barriers. Sachs and Warner (1995), who have recently provided a general chronology of these events, put the date of opening up at 1968 for Korea and 1970 for Indonesia. They consider that China has not yet opened up by their criteria, but the Chinese economy is now clearly very much more open than it was at the beginning of the period, 1980. Relaxation of barriers to trade in goods and services was accompanied by a relaxation of restrictions on foreign investment, both portfolio investment and foreign direct investment. Many commentators believe the encouragement of foreign direct investment played an important role in the growing export success of these countries by facilitating the transfer of technologies and of other production and marketing skills. (The Asian Development Bank 1996, Parts I and III, has provided a comprehensive survey of these issues.)

Trade policies alone cannot adequately explain the export success of East Asian countries. In particular, the accumulation of human capital is often emphasised in these discussions. Human capital accumulation has made a major contribution to increased productivity of labour generally. We have already mentioned prudent fiscal policies, high rates of national saving and capital formation, and macroeconomic stability. It is notable that several of the fast-growing East Asian economies have an overall surplus in their central government budgets (for example, Singapore, Malaysia and Thailand) and the other fast-growing economies have deficits which are small in relation to their GDP whereas all of the OECD countries except Japan and New Zealand have government deficits. But the general openness of these economies has been essential to their competitiveness in export markets.

Greater openness in the world economy as a whole has led to a greater share of the world's output of goods and services being traded internationally. This in turn has increased the responsiveness of nations to the policies adopted by other nations. It has become more important than ever before for nations to respond to changes in international markets which affect their competitiveness.

Appendix
Decomposition of Relative Market Performance

Consider one country (or group of countries) which exports manufactures to the IAEs. We can call this country k but, as all of the values of exports below relate to this country, it is not necessary to index this country. We define a market to be the market of a particular commodity group in a particular country or group of countries, including domestic supplies to the market. Let

X_{ij} = the value of exports of commodity i by the country to the country or group of countries j

$X_{.j}$ = the value of exports of all commodities by the country to the country or group of countries j

$$= \sum_j X_{ij}$$

$X_{i.}$ = the value of exports of commodity i by the country to all IAEs

$$= \sum_j X_{ij}$$

$X_{..}$ = the value of the exports of all commodities by the country to IAEs

$$= \sum_{ij} X_{ij}$$

These values are the annual flows from the country. We are interested in the percentage changes between a base period (1980) and the current period (1993). The base and current periods are denoted by the superscripts 1 and 2 respectively.

We are seeking to explain, for the country, $[(\Delta X_{..}/X_{..} - r]$, that is, the difference between the percentage growth in the total value of exports of the country and the percentage growth of the value of total sales (= apparent consumption) in all IAEs over the period (r).

It can be shown (Leamer and Stern 1970, ch. 7) that this difference is given by the expression

$$[(\Delta./X..) - r] = \sum_i (r_i - r) X^1_{i.} + \sum_{ij} (r_{ij} - r_i) X^1_{ij} + \sum_{ij} (r^k_{ij} - r_{ij}) X^1_{ij}$$

(A.1)

where

r = the rate of growth of IAEs apparent consumption of manufactures over the period

r_i = the rate of growth of IAEs apparent consumption of commodity i over the period

r_{ij} = the rate of growth of IAEs apparent consumption of commodity i in country j over the period

r^k_{ij} = the rate of growth of the country k's sales to the market for commodity i in country j.

The first term on the right-hand side of this equation is the component which is due to the commodity composition effect. The second term is the component which is due to the country (of destination) composition of the country's exports. The third term depends on the rate of growth of exports to the market of the country concerned compared to the rate of growth of imports from all countries into this market. Any difference between these two rates will change the market share of the country. Hence, this may be called the market share or competitiveness component. Each of these terms may be positive or negative.

Appendix Table 1
Import penetration from East Asia into USA, Japan and IAEs
(excluding USA and Japan), and IAEs in 1980: 2-digit manufacturing industries

	China	Hong Kong	Indonesia	Korea	Malaysia	Philippines	Singapore	Taiwan	Thailand	East Asia	World
USA											
31 - Manuf Food, Bevgs Tobacco	0.03	0.02	0.02	0.02	0.05	0.20	0.01	0.06	0.04	0.45	4.69
32 - Text, Wearing, Apprl, Leathr	0.40	1.92	0.01	1.26	0.04	0.26	0.15	1.61	0.09	5.74	10.13
33 - Man Wood + Wood Products	0.03	0.03	0.05	0.28	0.12	0.24	0.05	0.78	0.03	1.61	8.15
34 - Man Paper, Prods, Printing	..	0.10	..	0.04	..	..	0.01	0.11	..	0.27	4.62
35 - Man of Chemls + Products	0.07	0.12	0.12	0.19	0.04	0.02	0.04	0.37	..	0.95	7.35
36 - Man Non-Metal Min Prods	0.04	0.08	..	0.07	..	0.01	..	0.31	..	0.52	5.39
37 - Basic Metal Industries	0.04	0.01	0.08	0.38	0.20	0.06	0.01	0.08	0.21	1.07	12.78
38 - Fab Met Prds, Mach + Eqp	..	0.24	0.01	0.17	0.15	0.07	0.21	0.39	0.02	1.25	10.68
39 - Other Man Industries	0.24	1.53	..	0.89	0.02	0.25	0.05	1.71	0.34	5.03	15.81
3 - Manufacturing	0.05	0.26	0.04	0.23	0.09	0.09	0.10	0.39	0.04	1.29	8.58
Japan											
31 - Manuf Food, Bevgs Tobacco	0.22	0.03	0.05	0.06	0.11	0.30	0.02	0.44	0.19	1.42	6.66
32 - Text, Wearing, Apprl, Leathr	1.25	0.35	0.04	1.75	0.04	0.04	0.02	0.62	0.10	4.22	7.85
33 - Man Wood + Wood Products	0.08	0.03	0.12	0.24	0.20	0.19	0.04	0.52	0.05	1.45	5.34
34 - Man Paper, Prods, Printing	0.01	0.02	..	0.02	..	0.01	..	0.05	..	0.11	3.02
35 - Man of Chemls + Products	0.28	0.01	0.56	0.21	0.01	0.03	0.65	0.18	0.01	1.94	7.80
36 - Man Non-Metal Min Prods	0.04	..	..	0.15	..	..	0.01	0.05	..	0.25	1.10
37 - Basic Metal Industries	0.05	..	0.28	0.34	0.32	0.10	..	0.03	0.11	1.24	6.15
38 - Fab Met Prds, Mach + Eqp	..	0.05	..	0.13	0.02	0.02	0.04	0.12	..	0.40	3.77
39 - Other Man Industries	0.48	0.60	0.02	0.60	0.06	0.13	0.05	0.80	0.45	3.17	9.06
3 - Manufacturing	0.18	0.05	0.16	0.26	0.07	0.07	0.16	0.21	0.05	1.22	5.45
IAES excluding the USA, Japan											
31 - Manuf Food, Bevgs Tobacco	0.12	0.01	0.09	0.01	0.10	0.10	0.01	0.06	0.05	0.53	14.78
32 - Text, Wearing, Apprl, Leathr	0.68	1.86	0.04	0.96	0.11	0.13	0.14	0.62	0.18	4.73	34.72
33 - Man Wood + Wood Products	0.05	0.03	0.21	0.12	0.63	0.26	0.26	0.33	0.04	1.94	19.98
34 - Man Paper, Prods, Printing	0.02	0.13	..	0.03	..	..	0.02	0.06	..	0.27	17.71
35 - Man of Chemls + Products	0.09	0.08	0.03	0.09	0.02	0.01	0.14	0.15	..	0.63	28.51
36 - Man Non-Metal Min Prods	0.04	0.03	..	0.10	..	0.02	..	0.15	0.02	0.35	15.30
37 - Basic Metal Industries	0.03	0.04	0.11	0.09	0.11	0.02	0.02	0.03	0.15	0.59	31.64
38 - Fab Met Prds, Mach + Eqp	0.02	0.22	..	0.09	0.05	0.02	0.14	0.18	0.01	0.71	31.69
39 - Other Man Industries	0.70	1.95	0.01	0.89	0.07	0.42	0.20	1.13	0.36	5.74	67.97
3 - Manufacturing	0.11	0.26	0.04	0.14	0.08	0.05	0.10	0.18	0.04	1.00	26.90
IAES											
3 - Manufacturing	0.10	0.22	0.06	0.20	0.08	0.07	0.11	0.26	0.04	1.15	16.32

Data Source: IEDB Trade and Production Data, International Economic Data Bank, The Australian National University.

LLOYD AND TOGUCHI — *EXPORT COMPETITIVENESS*

Appendix Table 2
Import penetration from East Asia into USA, Japan, IAEs (excluding USA and Japan) and IAEs in 1993: 2-digit manufacturing industries

	China	Hong Kong	Indonesia	Korea	Malaysia	Philippines	Singapore	Taiwan	Thailand	East Asia	World
USA											
31 - Manuf Food, Bevgs Tobacco	0.09	0.03	0.03	0.02	0.04	0.10	0.01	0.04	0.20	0.55	4.48
32 - Text, Wearing, Apprl, Leathr	4.65	2.37	0.71	1.88	0.53	0.79	0.29	1.77	0.72	13.72	25.53
33 - Man Wood + Wood Products	0.60	0.06	0.60	0.06	0.39	0.17	0.07	1.12	0.22	3.28	13.85
34 - Man Paper, Prods, Printing	0.83	0.13	0.01	0.05	0.02	0.02	0.05	0.20	0.05	1.36	6.29
35 - Man of Chemls + Products	1.22	0.06	0.20	0.34	0.10	0.04	0.13	0.45	0.12	2.66	12.21
36 - Man Non-Metal Min Prods	0.86	0.05	0.09	0.12	0.06	0.10	0.01	0.68	0.19	2.18	10.45
37 - Basic Metal Industries	0.18	0.03	0.04	0.43	0.02	0.00	0.01	0.42	0.02	1.16	15.45
38 - Fab Met Prds, Mach + Eqp	0.68	0.25	0.06	0.74	0.61	0.17	0.81	1.17	0.27	4.73	21.56
39 - Other Man Industries	5.76	1.26	0.20	1.68	0.20	0.40	0.06	1.89	1.67	13.14	31.28
3 - Manufacturing	1.00	0.29	0.13	0.53	0.32	0.15	0.39	0.79	0.24	3.85	15.72
Japan											
31 - Manuf Food, Bevgs Tobacco	0.46	0.02	0.04	0.09	0.08	0.04	0.05	0.59	0.40	1.77	6.55
32 - Text, Wearing, Apprl, Leathr	6.30	0.33	0.37	2.17	0.13	0.11	0.04	0.51	0.41	10.36	14.94
33 - Man Wood + Wood Products	0.70	0.01	2.85	0.15	1.10	0.08	0.07	0.57	0.29	5.84	12.32
34 - Man Paper, Prods, Printing	0.12	0.02	0.01	0.02	0.01	0.01	0.01	0.06	0.01	0.28	2.02
35 - Man of Chemls + Products	0.47	0.02	0.20	0.44	0.10	0.04	0.25	0.28	0.09	1.89	7.26
36 - Man Non-Metal Min Prods	0.32	0.00	0.03	0.30	0.02	0.02	0.02	0.13	0.08	0.92	2.21
37 - Basic Metal Industries	0.27	0.01	0.21	0.85	0.04	0.05	0.01	0.36	0.03	1.84	6.38
38 - Fab Met Prds, Mach + Eqp	0.17	0.06	0.03	0.23	0.13	0.04	0.16	0.23	0.15	1.20	4.17
39 - Other Man Industries	1.80	0.77	0.06	0.99	0.04	0.15	0.09	0.79	0.92	5.62	11.63
3 - Manufacturing	0.59	0.06	0.16	0.38	0.13	0.05	0.12	0.31	0.18	1.98	5.72
IAEs excluding the USA, Japan											
31 - Manuf Food, Bevgs Tobacco	0.35	0.05	0.24	0.02	0.24	0.11	0.05	0.03	0.37	1.46	41.56
32 - Text, Wearing, Apprl, Leathr	6.78	4.46	1.73	1.71	0.74	0.43	0.32	1.15	1.24	18.57	90.57
33 - Man Wood + Wood Products	0.70	0.13	1.77	0.10	1.68	0.23	0.33	0.81	0.37	6.13	54.29
34 - Man Paper, Prods, Printing	1.19	0.60	0.07	0.06	0.07	0.04	0.16	0.29	0.09	2.58	42.38
35 - Man of Chemls + Products	1.63	0.32	0.49	0.73	0.23	0.07	0.27	0.70	0.34	4.78	100.09
36 - Man Non-Metal Min Prods	1.12	0.22	0.11	0.19	0.12	0.13	0.03	0.69	0.30	2.90	56.03
37 - Basic Metal Industries	0.38	0.06	0.08	0.34	0.20	0.04	0.04	0.41	0.05	1.59	94.84
38 - Fab Met Prds, Mach + Eqp	1.33	0.89	0.13	1.38	1.00	0.20	1.68	2.27	0.42	9.29	118.72
39 - Other Man Industries	11.04	5.77	0.51	2.56	0.56	0.67	0.92	3.67	3.28	28.99	119.56
3 - Manufacturing	1.73	0.91	0.41	0.82	0.58	0.17	0.71	1.17	0.45	6.95	87.51
IAEs											
3 - Manufacturing	0.99	0.32	0.20	0.53	0.30	0.12	0.35	0.68	0.26	3.74	25.51

Data Source: IEDB Trade and Production Data, International Economic Data Bank, The Australian National University.

Appendix Table 3
Import penetration from East Asia into the UK, 1980 and 1992: 2-digit manufacturing industries

	China	Hong Kong	Indonesia	Korea	Malaysia	Philippines	Singapore	Taiwan	Thailand	East Asia	World
UK											
1980											
31 - Manf Food,Bevgs,Tobacco	0.06	0.01	0.06	0.01	0.13	0.02	0.01	0.01	0.01	0.32	14.19
32 - Text,Wearing Apprl,Leathr	0.41	3.56	0.05	1.05	0.07	0.13	0.16	0.13	0.45	6.01	27.85
33 - Man Wood + Wood Products	0.04	0.04	0.12	0.12	0.49	0.40	0.37	0.04	0.38	2.00	21.26
34 - Man Paper,Prods,Printing	0.02	0.25	..	0.03	..	..	0.03	..	0.06	0.39	15.99
35 - Man Of Chemls + Products	0.06	0.15	..	0.09	0.04	0.01	0.03	..	0.10	0.48	19.76
36 - Man Non-Metal Min Prods	0.02	0.03	..	0.03	..	0.01	..	..	0.16	0.25	7.66
37 - Basic Metal Industries	0.04	0.17	0.05	0.09	0.03	..	0.03	0.07	0.03	0.51	31.84
38 - Fab Met Prds,Mach + Eqp	0.02	0.32	..	0.08	0.05	0.03	0.13	0.01	0.14	0.78	26.91
39 - Other Man Industries	0.50	2.67	..	0.84	0.04	1.39	0.22	0.23	1.24	7.13	118.77
3 - Manufacturing	0.07	0.43	0.02	0.14	0.07	0.05	0.08	0.03	0.13	1.02	23.01
1992											
31 - Manf Food,Bevgs,Tobacco	0.07	0.03	0.06	..	0.07	0.01	0.02	0.01	0.08	0.35	15.37
32 - Text,Wearing Apprl,Leathr	1.43	4.43	1.13	1.12	0.52	0.27	0.49	0.76	0.69	10.84	47.15
33 - Man Wood + Wood Products	0.16	0.15	1.03	0.06	0.85	0.35	0.32	0.52	0.25	3.17	25.900
34 - Man Paper,Prods,Printing	0.22	0.65	0.01	0.02	0.02	0.01	0.12	0.12	0.06	1.23	18.48
35 - Man Of Chemls + Products	0.16	0.25	0.09	0.17	0.07	0.02	0.10	0.23	0.10	1.19	26.69
36 - Man Non-Metal Min Prods	0.18	0.15	0.01	0.04	0.04	0.05	0.03	0.25	0.05	0.80	15.85
37 - Basic Metal Industries	0.10	0.04	0.04	0.11	0.04	0.02	0.02	0.11	0.01	0.49	37.78
38 - Fab Met Prds, Mach + Eqp	0.19	0.61	0.03	0.39	0.59	0.06	0.61	0.67	0.17	3.32	41.96
39 - Other Man Industries	2.06	5.47	0.15	1.28	0.08	0.25	2.61	1.82	0.90	14.62	46.90
3 - Manufacturing	0.25	0.65	0.14	0.26	0.30	0.06	0.32	0.39	0.16	2.53	30.83

Data Source: IEDB Trade and Production Data, International Economic Data Bank, The Australian National University.

References

APEC Economic Committee. 1995. *Foreign Direct Investment and APEC Economic Integration*, APEC Secretariat, Singapore.

Asian Development Bank. 1996. *Asian Development Outlook 1996*, Asian Development Bank, Manila.

Chow, P. C. Y. and Kellman, M. H. 1993. *Trade: the engine of growth in East Asia*, Oxford University Press, New York and Oxford.

Journal of Economic Perspectives. 1995. 'Symposium on Income Inequality and Trade', *Journal of Economic Perspectives*, 9(1):15–80.

Krugman, P. and Lawrence, R. Z. 1993. *Trade, jobs and wages*, Working Paper No. 4836, National Bureau of Economic Research, Cambridge MA.

Lawrence, R. Z. 1994. *The Impact of Trade on OECD Labor Markets*, Occasional Paper No. 45, Group of Thirty, Washington DC.

Leamer, E. E. and Stern, R. M. 1970. *Quantitative International Economics*, Allyn and Bacon, Boston.

Lloyd, P. J. 1994. 'Intraregional trade in the Asian and Pacific region', *Asian Development Review*, 12(2):1–27.

Low, L. 1994. 'The east ASEAN growth area or polygon: some perspectives', Paper presented at the International Seminar on Polygonal Economic and Business Partnership and its Role to Participate and Accelerate the Development of Indonesia's Eastern Region, Manado, Indonesia, 24–26 October 1994.

Sachs, J. D. and Warner, A. 1995. 'Economic reform and the process of global integration', *Brookings Papers on Economic Activity*, Vol. I:1–118.

Thurow, L. 1992. *Head to Head: the coming economic battle among Japan, Europe and America*, Allen and Unwin, Singapore.

Wood, A. 1994. *North-South Trade, Employment and Inequality: changing fortunes in a skill-driven world*, Clarendon Press, Oxford.

The World Bank. 1993. *The East Asian Miracle*, Oxford University Press, Oxford.

312-38
[96]

F21
014
019

asia

[15]

The Role of Foreign Investment in the Success of Asian Industrialization

P. J. LLOYD

There has been a tremendous upsurge of foreign direct investment into Asia, chiefly East Asia, since the mid-1980s. Much of this is intra-Asian investment, starting with Japanese investment in the NIEs and other countries and more recently foreign direct investment from the NIEs in other East Asian economies.

This paper looks at foreign investment as a source of savings to the Asian economies and at FDI as an agent of technology transfer and transformation of the structure of the economies. Much of the investment has been in export-oriented industries and this has association of FDI and exports has been called the foreign investment-led export growth.

Looking at the regional economy, FDI has led to a relocation of productive activities among the countries of the region. This aspect has come to be called the Flying Geese pattern. It is an important part of the structural adjustments of the source and host countries and it has enabled these countries to sustain rapid growth for long periods.

In the longer run, several of the high income countries in Asia have gone through a Savings-Investment Transition which has converted them from net borrowers to net lenders or investors. This Savings-Investment Transition can be linked to the Migration Transition which has caused these and some other Asian countries to switch from net exporters of labor to net importers of labor. Together these transitions define new relationships among the countries which are an important part of the growth process in Asia.

I. INTRODUCTION

One of the characteristics of the fast-growing East Asian economies is a relatively high level of foreign investment, particularly foreign direct investment. Moreover,

*P.J. Lloyd** Asian Business Centre, Faculty of Economics and Commerce, The University of Melbourne, Parkville, Victoria 3052, Australia <p.lloyd@ecomfac.unimelb.edu.au>.

Journal of Asian Economics, Vol. 7, No. 3, 1996 pp. 407-433
ISSN: 1049-0078

this foreign investment has increased steadily in the 1980s and 1990s. More Asian countries[1] are recipients of large capital inflows than ever before and the Asian share of the global foreign direct investment stock has increased sharply from 7 per cent to 13 per cent over the period 1980 to 1994 (UNCTAD, 1995, Annex Table 3). Several authors have associated the rapid growth of Asian exports and output with this growth of Asian foreign investment inflows (for example, Asian Development Bank, 1992; Petri, 1995; APEC Economic Committee, 1995).

From the point of view of a recipient country, foreign investment affects the macroeconomic performance of the country in many and complex ways. Foreign investment is a source of savings to increase the rate of capital formation. It is a mechanism for technology transfer from overseas producers. It is an agent for the transformation of the industrial structure of the economy and the commodity composition of its exports. It may increase the productive capacity of the economy in other ways too; for example, it may lead to human capital formation or the development of activities based on natural resources.

In the relationship between foreign borrowing and the domestic rate of capital formation, it is the aggregate economy-wide level of borrowing in all forms which matters most. However, to understand the relationships between foreign borrowing on the one hand and technology transfers and the transformation of the economy on the other, one must recognise the many different forms of international borrowing and lending by the government and private sectors of an economy. In the relationships between foreign borrowing and international trade in goods and services, foreign equity investment flows are of more interest than other investments such as private bank loans and export credits, and official development assistance and other borrowings by the government sector.

This paper explores the relationships between foreign investment in Asia and the growth of exports and output. It concentrates upon the effects of foreign borrowing on the rate of capital formation, technology transfers and the transformation of the Asian economies. The final section takes a long term view of the growth process and highlights the transition from net borrowers to net lenders which has occurred in some East Asian economies and its relationship to the Migration Transition which has also been observed in these economies. These turning points in the historical growth path of these economies highlight important changes which affect trade and investment among the Asian countries.

II. FOREIGN INVESTMENT

A. Foreign Investment as a Source of Savings

It is usual to take the deficit or surplus on the current account of the balance of payments as the measure of net aggregate foreign borrowing, that is, net borrowing by both the public and private sectors and covering loan and equity capital movements.

TABLE 1. Balance of Payments on Current Account
(percent of GDP)

	1990	1991	1992	1993	1994	1995	1996	1997
Newly Industrializing Economies	2.3	1.4	1.6	1.8	1.8	1.3	1.7	1.8
Hong Kong	—	—	—	—	—	—	—	—
Korea	-0.7	-2.8	-1.2	0.3	-1.0	-1.9	-1.2	-0.8
Singapore	9.1	11.1	12.4	9.0	17.3	16.3	16.5	16.4
Taipei, China	6.7	6.7	3.8	3.0	2.6	2.8	2.8	2.6
People's Rep. of China and Mongolia	3.1	3.2	1.3	-2.0	1.3	2.4	0.5	0.1
China, People's Rep. of	3.1	3.2	1.3	-2.0	1.3	2.4	0.5	0.1
Mongolia	-28.7	-20.0	-7.7	-7.5	-5.9	-7.3	-10.4	-11.4
Central Asian Republics	—	—	—	—	—	—	—	—
Kazahstan	—	—	-10.0	-7.6	-8.0	-7.3	—	—
Kyrgyz Republic	—	—	-10.1	-6.5	-8.2	-7.2	—	—
Southeast Asia	—	—	-9.2	-14.8	-6.7	-7.9	—	—
Cambodia	-4.8	-5.3	-3.3	-3.9	-4.1	-5.7	-5.7	-5.1
Indonesia	-3.4	-1.3	1.6	1.0	-1.9	-5.4	-7.5	-7.5
Lao People's Democratic Rep.	-2.6	-3.3	-2.0	-1.3	-1.6	-3.8	-3.8	-2.8
Malaysia	-9.0	-4.3	-3.5	-3.2	-6.9	-5.2	-8.6	-9.1
Myanmar	-2.0	-8.9	-3.8	-4.5	-5.9	-8.9	-8.0	-7.0
Philippines	-1.8	-0.9	-0.6	-0.5	-0.4	-0.3	—	—
Thailand	-6.1	-2.3	-1.9	-6.0	-4.4	-2.8	-3.1	-3.2
Viet Nam	-8.5	-7.7	-5.7	-5.6	-5.9	-7.5	-7.6	-7.6
	-4.2	-1.9	-0.1	-6.7	-6.2	-8.9	-8.9	-7.9

(continued)

TABLE 1. (continued)

	1990	1991	1992	1993	1994	1995	1996	1997
South Asia	-3.3	-1.0	-1.6	-1.0	-1.5	-2.1	-2.2	-2.5
Bangladesh	-2.0	0.3	0.7	1.4	0.9	0.3	1.6	-2.8
Bhutan	-8.1	-4.7	-7.5	-24.8	-14.0	-15.6	—	—
India	-3.2	-0.4	-1.3	0.1	-0.8	-1.6	-1.7	-2.0
Maldives	5.9	-5.5	-10.3	-21.0	-6.1	-11.2	—	—
Nepal	-8.2	-9.4	-5.2	-6.3	-7.7	-7.1	-8.2	-7.6
Pakistan	-4.1	-3.1	-3.8	-5.7	-5.6	-5.1	-4.7	-4.3
Sri Lanka	-3.7	-6.7	-4.7	-3.7	-4.7	-4.0	-3.1	-3.4
Pacific Islands	0.5	-4.8	0.6	9.9	9.3	6.6	—	—
Cook Islands	—	—	—	—	0.0	—	—	—
Fiji	-3.3	-0.1	0.7	-4.2	34.9	—	—	—
Kiribati	34.8	37.9	21.6	26.5	4.5	13.7	—	—
Marshall Islands	34.1	5.8	-10.8	—	-1.2	5.2	—	—
Micronesia, Federated States of	18.4	4.9	0.4	-0.1	10.6	-0.2	—	—
Papua New Guinea	-2.3	-4.1	2.2	12.6	0.9	7.1	—	—
Solomon Islands	-16.6	-19.4	-0.8	-1.5	-0.3	2.4	—	—
Tonga	60.0	-1.8	2.4	2.0	10.6	-8.1	—	—
Tuvalu	16.9	2.8	50.8	2.2	-10.4	—	—	—
Vanuatu	7.7	-10.8	-9.9	-9.7	2.8	-5.7	—	—
Western Samoa	4.9	-18.5	-47.0	-34.0	-0.2	5.7	—	—
Average for DMCs	-0.2	0.0	-0.1	-0.9	-0.2	-0.5	-0.9	-0.8

As a group, the Asian countries (excluding Japan) are net borrowers. However, in relation to the aggregate GDP of the region, the deficit on the current account of the balance of payments is small, only 0.5% in 1995 and in one year, 1991, there was a negligible surplus for the region (Asian Development Bank, 1996, Appendix Table A16).

There is considerable variation among the countries of East Asia in terms of the deficit/surplus of the balance of payments. Table 1 reproduces the latest calculations of the Asian Development Bank of the balance of payments deficit/surplus as a percentage of the GDPs of the Asian countries.

The NIEs have persistent and substantial annual surpluses on current account. Singapore and Taiwan are members of the small group of countries in the world which are significant sources of net lending to the other economies of the world. The Peoples' Republic of China has had a small surplus as a percentage of GDP in most recent years.

All of the countries of South and South East Asia (excluding Singapore which is in the NIEs) except Bangladesh, on the other hand, have persistent annual deficits on the current account. Apart from India, these deficits are large as a percentage of the GDP, ranging up to 15.6 per cent in the case of Bhutan.

These figures record the *ex post* net lending. An *ex post* balance of payments deficit represents a transfer of resources to the borrowing country but it does not necessarily represent a corresponding increase in the rate of capital formation. Borrowed resources may be used to finance either capital formation or an increase in consumption in the public or private sectors of the economy. Foreign borrowing may increase capital formation by the full amount of the borrowing or a lesser amount if the borrowing by itself reduces the aggregate domestic savings ratio in some way. Indeed, foreign borrowing may increase the rate of capital formation by more than the borrowing if it shifts the domestic savings ratio upwards.

To ascertain whether foreign borrowing has increased the capital formation of the borrowing country and by how much, one requires a model of the savings and investment in the economy. Unfortunately, the literature on the determinants of both the savings ratios and investment is rather confused. Asian countries have extremely high rates of both savings and capital formation, especially when adjustment is made for the average levels of per capita income (see, for example, The World Bank (1993, chapter 5) and Prescott (1995). Savings rates for Developing Asian economies have increased by more than 10 percentage points since 1970. Some East Asian economies that have maintained high rates of growth have doubled their savings rate over this period; for example, Korea, Malaysia and Thailand. By contrast, savings rates have tended to fall in the developed industrialised countries over the period.

Attempts to estimate savings functions in Asian economies have generally produced results which are poor statistically in that they leave much of the savings behaviour unexplained and frequently do not confirm the standard life cycle, dependency ratio and other hypotheses about savings behaviour. Harrigan (1995) provides a survey and new estimates of the savings functions for Southeast Asian countries. He finds a correlation between income growth and the private savings rate which is statistically robust but numerically weak; his estimates suggest an acceleration in income growth of one percent increases the private savings rate by only 0.26%. Growth may increase aggregate savings in other indirect ways. It may reduce the dependency ratio and the studies confirm that a reduction in this ratio increases private savings. Or it may increase the rate of savings in the public sector which will increase aggregate savings, provided public saving does not completely crowd out private savings.

However, the rate of growth of real incomes is in turn partly determined by the rate of capital formation and by the improvements in technology which stem from foreign borrowing. In the presence of this circularity, the net effect of foreign borrowing on aggregate savings and investment can only be determined by the estimation of a full model of the growth process. It can be safely stated that foreign borrowing has increased the rate of capital formation in Asian economies since there is no suggestion that it has depressed savings rates in either the private or public sectors in Asian countries,[2] however, one cannot state by how much capital formation has increased. It is possible the direct and indirect growth effects may be an important part of the explanation of the increase in Asian savings rates. Causality tests indicate that it is the growth of incomes which raises savings rate (The World Bank, 1993, chapter 5; Carroll and Weill, 1994; Prescott, 1995).

If one takes a long term perspective, all of the fast-growing Asian economies have been net borrowers in the earlier stages of their period of fast growth. This includes Taiwan and Singapore which, along with Japan in the Asian region, are now net lenders. These two countries (and Japan before them) have switched from a status of net borrowers to a status of net lenders in the years 1981 and 1988 respectively. This may be called the Savings-Investment Transition in these economies. This transition is itself primarily the product of a period of sustained rapid growth in factor incomes. The links between the Savings-Investment Transition and other aspects of the pattern of growth are discussed in the last section of the paper.

The next section examines the pattern of foreign direct investment as a prelude to consideration of the effects of this form of borrowing on technology transfer and the transformation of the economies of Asia.

III.   THE PATTERN OF FOREIGN DIRECT INVESTMENT

Attention has focused in recent years on foreign direct investments as an important form of international lending. In quantitative terms, foreign direct investment along with private portfolio investment have become the major forms of capital inflows since the late 1980s for a growing number of East and South East Asian countries. In qualitative terms, FDI represents the internationalisation of the production activities of multinational corporations. Foreign direct investments are, therefore, part of the decisions of these corporations relating to the location of production and the sales of the outputs of the goods produced and the sources of the inputs used in their production. Capital movement in the form of foreign direct investment is also an important device for the international transfer of knowledge, know-how and management methods.

Foreign direct investment, as with other forms of international asset transactions, is a two-way flow as almost all countries are both host and source countries for foreign direct investment. As a group the East Asian countries are net recipients of foreign direct investment whereas Japan is a net supplier. There has been a tremendous upsurge of outward FDI from Japan since the mid-1980s which was precipitated by the large appreciation of the Yen following the Plaza Accord in September 1985 and aided by deregulation of financial outflows in Japan. In the late 1980s and the 1990s the Asian NIEs have also become major sources of foreign direct capital flows. For the period 1990-94 outflows of direct capital from the NIEs exceeded the inflows into these countries. The ASEAN-4 and South Asia are net recipients of foreign direct investment.

Table 2 shows the levels of foreign direct investment inflows for Asia over the period 1989 to 1994. Asia is here defined as the Developing Member countries of the Asian Development Bank as the table is taken from the just released Asian Development Outlook published by the ADB (1996, p.20).

The first notable feature is the rapid rate of growth. Flows of foreign direct investment across national borders have increased at about four times the rate of growth of world commodity trade and those in East Asia (including Southeast Asia) have grown even faster. East Asian inflows of foreign direct investments rose sharply from an annual average of less than $US 4,000 million in 1982-85 to an estimated $US 50,269 million in 1994.

East Asia dominates FDI flows into the region. The major host countries have been the Asian NIEs followed by the ASEAN countries. The PRC shows a phenomenal increase in annual FDI inflows from $US 3798 million in 1982-85 to $US 33,787 million in 1994. From 1992 the PRC has been the largest host of FDI in Asia or in the developing countries, accounting for about one half of the total inflows into Asia in 1993 and 1994, and the second largest in the world after the US. According to the latest available statistics for 1994, Singapore, Malaysia, Indonesia and Taipei, China in that order were the other main recipients.

In 1994, the inflows into South Asia were not much more than one quarter of those into the 4 NIEs or the ASEAN-4 individually. The fundamental reason for the difference between South Asia on the one hand and the countries of East and South East Asia which have received large capital inflows in the late 1980s and the 1990s on the other has to do with the strategies adopted by the two groups of countries. All of the South Asian countries were much later than the East and South East Asian countries in adopting policies to open up their markets for both commodities and capital according to the dating of the opening up of economies by Sachs and Warner (1995).[3] As for the source of these flows, the South Asian countries have all drawn their inflows of FDI from North America and Europe to a much greater extent than have the

TABLE 2.   Foreign Direct Investment in Selected DMCs, 1989-1994
($ million)

	1989	1990	1991	1992	1993	1994	1989-1994
Newly Industrializing Economies	5,609	7,693	7,330	3,957	6,521	7,772	38,882
Korean	1,118	788	1,180	727	588	809	5,210
Singapore	2,887	5,575	4,879	2,351	5,016	5,588	26,290
Taipei, China	1,804	1,330	1,271	879	917	1,375	7,376
China, People's Republic of	3,393	3,487	4,366	11,156	27,515	33,787	83,704
Central Asian Republics							
Kazakhstan	—	—	—	—	473	445	918
Kyrgyz Republic[a]	—	—	—	—	1	42	43
Southeast Asian	4,668	8,399	8,038	9,304	9,499	8,223	46,151
indonesia	682	1,093	1,482	1,777	2,004	2,109	9,147
Malaysia	1,668	2,332	3,998	5,183	5,006	4,348	22,535
Philippines[b]	563	530	544	228	763	1,126	3,754
Thailand	1,775	2,444	2,014	2,116	1,726	640	10,715
South Asia	580	455	454	805	1,155	2,140	5,589
Bangladesh	—	3	1	4	14	11	33
India[c]	350	165	148	344	600	1,314	2,921
Pakistan	210	244	257	335	346	649	2,041
Sri Lanka	20	43	48	122	195	166	595
Pacific Islands	232	258	258	382	101	112	1,343
Fiji	8	80	15	50	49	69	272
Papua New Guinea	203	155	203	291	1	4	857
Solomon Islands	12	10	15	14	24	9	83
Vanuatu	9	13	25	27	27	30	131
Total	14,502	18,293	20,446	25,604	45,264	52,521	176,630

Note: a. Data include portfolio investment.
        b. Data for 1994 refer to foreign direct investment for the first two quarters of the year only.
        c. Data refer to net foreign direct investment.

Source: Asian Development Bank (1996)

East Asian countries. Japan has not been a substantial source of FDI for South Asia. The distribution and the level of FDI inflows into South Asia reflect the historical preference for import substitution rather than export promotion strategies, though these barriers to FDI have been aggravated by political and economic instability.

In looking at the matrix of flows between countries, analysis of FDI is severely handicapped by the paucity of data. The only data showing the distribution of inflows and outflows for the Asian economies by source and host country are the stock data recently compiled by PECC (1995) and APEC Economic Committee (1995) for the APEC countries. Table 3 is taken from PECC (1995).

This table shows the growth of intra-Asian capital flows. As of 1993, 51.8% of the total value of the stock of foreign direct capital in East and South East Asia had come from the Asian region. The major recorded source is surprisingly the Asian NIEs, followed by Japan, but the figure for the Asian NIEs is dominated by investment from Hong Kong into the PRC. Some of this is a return of a capital outflow from the PRC itself, a phenomenon known as "roundtripping." Japan has been the dominant investor in the Asian developing countries in recent years with the Asian NIEs becoming increasingly important. The main destinations of Japanese and NIE FDI into Asia have been the ASEAN-4, chiefly Thailand and Indonesia.

This growth in intra-Asian foreign direct investment flows parallels the growth of intra-Asian commodity trade but, unlike the trade shares, the intra-Asian FDI shares of inward and outward capital flows have declined slightly because of the growth of extra-regional FDI flows. However, the share of intra-Asian FDI may not be a good indicator of regional bias in FDI. This is because the shares combine the influences of the total size of the national FDI flows and the complementarity between economies in these FDI.

One way of addressing these issues is to use a measure of the bilateral investment intensities. The intensity of FDI can be measured using the same measure as that used in the analysis of commodity trade flows (Drysdale and Garnaut, 1995, survey these measures.) In the FDI intensity measure, the countries (or regions) are the host and source countries rather than the importing and exporting countries, and stock rather than flow data must be used because of the unavailability of data on the distribution of flows. For a country investing in another country, the index of FDI intensity is measured by the share of the investing or source country's investments in the host country relative to the host country's share in total world FDI (less that of the source country itself). If this index is greater than unity, the source country has a bias towards the host country in locating its investments as its share of FDI in that country is greater than can be explained by the importance of the host country in world FDI stocks.

The index of FDI intensity for Asian countries as a source of foreign direct investment are shown in Table 4. The rows of the table show the FDI intensities for outward FDI of the countries concerned. This table shows that the intensities of foreign direct investment inflows among the Asian countries are very high. The average intensity for East Asian countries investing in other East Asian countries is 4, that is, the FDI flows between these countries are four times as high as the importance of

TABLE 3. Foreign Direct Investment to Pacific Asia, 1982-93
(outstanding stock and $ millions)

From/to:	Hong Kong	Singapore	Chinese Taipei	Korea	ANIEs	Indonesia	Malaysia	Philippines	Thailand	ASEAN4	China	Vietnam	Asia PECC
USA													
1982	581	1453	1060	418	3512	664	159	1077	578	2478	NA		5990
1986	1032	2355	1720	1073	6180	1216	280	1552	1732	4780	1022		11982
1990	1216	4322	3290	2258	11086	2197	877	1771	2985	7830	2286		21202
1993	1487	6516	4357	3090	15450	3701	3509	2457	7648	17315	5202	223	38190
EC													
1982	177	1649	320	188	2334	1380	290	219	1585	3474	NA		5808
1986	274	1927	760	346	3307	1900	801	332	1432	4465	472		8244
1990	617	3146	2068	1219	7050	4762	2379	365	1893	9399	1027		17476
1993	653	4264	2612	2439	9968	8787	5499	869	5518	20673	2054	1241	33936
Japan													
1982	375	763	731	676	2535	4344	348	402	1598	6692	NA		9227
1986	514	1542	1487	1901	5444	5251	624	372	1859	8106	989		14539
1990	1252	3255	3871	3793	12171	9645	3930	502	9086	23163	2780		38114
1993	1803	4675	5105	4329	15912	13937	6977	759	13025	34698	5498	690	56798
Canada													
1982		1	14	14	15	661	34			695			710
1986	19	894	14	14	941	809	34			843			1784
1990	19	1546	139	51	1755	742	92			834			2589
1993	8	1683	161	74	1926	644	126			770			2696
Hong Kong													
1982		NA	290	NA	290	1193	51	131	232	1607	NA		1897
1986		NA	344	131	475	1881	120	163	291	2455	3505		6435
1990		NA	606	226	832	3731	537	224	1509	6001	12201		19034
1993		NA	1117		1117	5683	822	253	8322	15080	40802	1551	58550

TABLE 3.   (continued)

From/to:	Chile	Colombia	Mexico	Peru	LA PECC	LDC PECC	USA	Canada	Australia	New Zealand	Japan	Industrial PECC	PECC Total
Singapore													
1982	21		NA	NA	21	NA	106	NA	244	350	NA		371
1986	34		NA	5	39	314	288	NA	253	855	28		922
1990	39		129	58	226	993	1220	NA	958	3171	220		3617
1993	121		454	NA	575	3895	2002	92	2318	8307	896	1055	10833
Chinese Taipei													
1982	16	NA		NA	16	NA	22	NA	467	489	NA		505
1986	NA	NA		NA	0	144	57	NA	561	762	NA		762
1990	28	NA		NA	28	2302	3611	NA	1793	7706	NA		7734
1993	15	NA		NA	15	4035	5859	20	3008	12922	NA	1901	14838
Korea													
1982	NA	NA	NA		NA	NA	6	NA	15	21	NA		21
1986	NA	NA	NA		NA	215	32	NA	8	255	NA		255
1990	NA	NA	NA		NA	1864	360	NA	159	2383	NA		2383
1993	NA	NA	NA		NA	3622	1103	92	NA	4817	NA	860	5677
ANIES													
1982	37	NA	290	0	327	1193	185	131	958	2467	NA		2794
1986	34	NA	344	136	514	2554	497	163	1113	4327	3533		8374
1990	67	NA	735	284	1086	8890	5728	224	4419	19261	12421		32768
1993	136	NA	1580	313	2029	17235	9786	457	13648	41126	41698	5367	90220
Total													
1982	1245	4492	3495	1436	10668	11777	1600	2228	6819	22424	NA		33092
1986	2506	6421	5893	3633	18453	15809	3217	2722	9076	30824	6538		55815
1990	3971	11547	13215	7873	36606	38678	15610	3303	25687	83278	20452		140336
1993	5287	16607	17667	10552	50113	67625	31233	4897	54738	158493	64180	10934	283720

(continued)

TABLE 3. (continued)

From/to:	Chile	Colombia	Mexico	Peru	LA PECC	LDC PECC	USA	Canada	Australia	New Zealand	Japan	Industrial PECC	PECC Total
USA													
1982								44141	6369	152	2008	52678	
1986	2606	2189	13716		15915	27897		48237	9096	352	3555	61240	89137
1990	4450	2473	19080	572	24731	45933		69362	19258	737	8573	97930	143862
1993		2742	26621	628	34441	72631		77437	23638	2539	12174	115788	188419
EC													
1982							83193	11054	5769		546	100561	
1986	1852	272	3929		4201	12445	144181	13072	10912		1057	169223	181668
1990	1519	392	6303	78	8625	26101	247320	26643	26604		3367	303934	330035
1993		430	8389	2090	12428	46364	270767	27916	27734		8823	335240	381604
Japan													
1983							9677	1087	1187	66		12017	
1986			1170		1170	15709	26824	1649	2787	86		31348	47057
1990	162	40	1456	41	1699	39813	83091	3546	11033	290		97960	137773
1993	483	73	1690	39	2285	59083	96213	4231	13240	344		114028	173111
Canada													
1982							11708		474	55	79	12316	
1986		63	290		353	2137	20318		1897	63	126	22404	24541
1990		56	417	50	523	3112	29544		2499	32	329	32404	35536
1993	1449	78	654	37	2218	4914	39408		2341	284	1330	43363	48277
Hong Kong													
1982							229				105		
1986							605	95	0	18	310		
1990							1511	307	354	29	515		
1993							2015	1122	721	254	644		

TABLE 3. (continued)

From/to:	Chile	Colombia	Mexico	Peru	LA PECC	LDC PECC	USA	Canada	Australia	New Zealand	Japan	Industrial PECC	PECC Total
Singapore													
1982							97	15	0				
1986							169	37	732	−1			
1990							1289	95	654	−26			
1993							228			521			
Chinese Taipei													
1982							80	0	0				
1986							177	16	0				
1990							836	8	49	5			
1993							1272			11			
Korea													
1982							−55		0				
1986							383		28	1			
1990							−1009		147	1			
1993							795						
ANIES													
1982							351	109	0	0	105		
1986							1334	360	1114	17	310		
1990							2627	1225	1571	9	515		
1993							4310			787	644		
Total													
1982							124677	59021	16239	842	4162	204941	402580
1986	6303	2992	20930	1254	23922	79737	220414	66499	26730	1861	7339	322843	780105
1990	9975	3500	30310	3920	41367	181703	394911	108493	72201	4364	18433	598402	1030244
1993		4389	42375		60659	344379	445268	113100	87959	9605	29933	685865	

TABLE 4. Foreing Direct Investment Intensities for Asian Countries: 1992

From/To	Canada	US	Japan	China	Korea	Hong Kong	Taipei, China	Singapore	Indonesia
Japan	0.55	.54	—	—	78.00	3.61	50.50	16.00	1,212.00
China	0.13	1.08	0.26	—	—	29.52	—	0.63	—
Korea	0.02	0.37	0.17	—	—	1.05	—	5.13	1,790.00
Hong Kong	0.23	0.08	0.24	1,055.50	16.25	—	416.50	99.13	2,595.00
Taipei, China	—	0.97	0.13	—	9.75	4.64	—	43.81	888.00
Singapore	—	.04	—	—	—	13.06	38.50	—	230.00
Indonesia	0.18	-0.05	—	11.50	—	—	777.00	476.63	—
Malaysia	0.03	0.07	—	—	—	0.27	710.50	417.13	521.00
Thailand	—	1.02	—	—	—	54.88	—	37.69	—
Philippines	—	0.57	—	49.00	—	3.89	3,123.00	—	—
NIEs	4.05	0.10	0.20	835.00	13.00	2.11	335.50	79.44	2,172.00
ASEAN	4.01	0.25	—	17.50	—	2.36	1,357.50	275.69	792.00
East Asia	0.49	0.49	0.02	101.50	68.25	3.47	110.50	28.75	1,318.00

From/To	Malaysia	Thailand	Philippines	Australia	New Zealand	North America	NIEs	ASEAN	East Asia
Japan	17.80	—	28.17	12.35	7.00	0.59	9.23	98.06	3.05
China	4.00	—	—	—	—	0.99	23.43	2.35	3.11
Korea	0.50	—	17.83	2.88	16.40	0.34	1.61	137.41	2.69
Hong Kong	121.50	—	22.50	9.31	—	0.09	23.66	250.59	10.43
Taipei, China	30.60	—	162.83	1.85	—	0.88	10.71	155.65	4.47
Singapore	60.80	—	19.17	7.71	—	0.04	11.06	318.59	8.75
Indonesia	49.50	—	—	5.63	—	-0.05	87.73	35.76	11.36
Malaysia	—	—	1.33	15.56	—	0.07	77.31	46.59	10.29
Thailand	—	—	—	—	—	0.93	48.17	—	7.00
Philippines	1.80	—	—	—	—	0.52	54.84	97.18	8.56
NIEs	187.80	—	24.67	8.69	0.60	0.11	20.66	263.00	9.77
ASEAN	3.20	—	0.83	9.46	—	.23	69.72	60.59	9.68
East Asia	38.10	—	27.00	13.92	6.00	0.52	11.84	117.12	4.00

Note: —Data are either zero, negligible, or unavailable.

Source: Bors (1995, Table 2.5).

these countries in the world flows would suggest. The main interest is in Japan and the NIEs as they are the major sources of FDI in the region. Japan has a strong bias towards investing in the East Asian region with an index just over 3 and the bias is stronger in the cases of Hong Kong (10.4), Singapore (8.8) and Taiwan (4.5). The small but increasing flows from Indonesia and Malaysia have an even stronger bias towards the region. None of the Asian countries shown in the table has an index below 3 whereas none of these countries register a level as high as 3 for intra-Asian goods trade. Unfortunately, it not possible to measure the change in these country intensities over time because there are no comparable statistics of the distribution of the stocks of FDI for earlier years.

There are no comprehensive statistics for Asian countries of the distribution of FDI inflows or stocks by the industry in which the investments are made. The only level of disaggregation is the sectoral level. Apart from the Indonesia and the Philippines in which the Primary sector accounts for 82% and 29% respectively of the total value of the inward FDI stock, FDI is predominantly in the Manufacturing and Service sectors (APEC Economic Committee, 1995, Table 10). Most of the foreign direct investments in the Asia (excluding Japan) are in intermediate goods production; for example, the export propensity of US affiliates, calculated as the share of international sales of foreign affiliates in their total sales, in Singapore in 1992 was 62.4 per cent for US affiliates located in South, East, South East Asia and the Pacific in 1992 (UNCTAD, 1995, Table IV.4). Many of these exports are intra-firm transactions in intermediate inputs.

This growth of intra-Asian FDI may be explained by several factors: (1) The growth of the real output of the Asian economies has undoubtedly made them a more attractive location for investors including investors from other Asian countries. (2) The relaxation of controls on inward FDI has been rapid and probably more rapid than in other regions of the world. This relaxation involved several elements: greater rights of establishment for foreign investors through relaxation of approval procedures, greater realisation of national treatment through the removal of performance requirements on foreign corporations, privatisation and other reductions in administrative controls on capital and factor income movements. (3) The pattern of exchange rate adjustments beginning with the Plaza Accord in 1985 has encouraged the transfer of some manufacturing activities from Japan and more recently from the Asian NIEs to lower wage countries in the region. (4) Asian countries have liberalised their commodity trade more rapidly than other countries in the world over the last 10 years.

It is not easy to determine the relative importance of these factors. All have probably played a part. Empirical studies of the distribution of merchandise trade indicate that the rapid growth of outputs in the region is the major factor explaining the increase in intra-Asian commodity trade commodity (see Asian Development Bank, 1996, Part III). The Asian Developing countries have generally been ahead of developing countries in other regions in recognising possibilities of new production and exports associated with foreign direct investments. Some Asian countries have adopted measures such as export processing zones and performance requirements to direct incoming foreign direct investments into export activities. Many Asian governments promote foreign investments through financial incentives.

The liberalisation of the commodity and the capital markets in the Asian economies have been super-additive. That is, the combined effect has been greater than the sum of the effects singly. There would have been less FDI in the region if commodity trade had not been liberalised. Part of the explanation of the growth of acquisition of capital assets by foreign corporations is the liberalisation of trade in goods and services and the new profit opportunities which this has created. Conversely, in the presence of capital market liberalisation, the effects of trade liberalisation in stimulating trade flows have been greater than they would have been in isolation. For example, much of the export trade would not have occurred if there had been no export-oriented FDI. Consequently, part of the explanation of the growth of trade in goods and services in Asia is, therefore, the very rapid liberalisation of foreign direct investment which has taken place in all countries in Asia and the associated trade in producer and intermediate goods as well as the exports of the final goods from the new foreign-owned enterprises.

A. FDI as an Agent of Technology Transfer

There are many references in the literature on FDI to the multinational firm as the agent of technology transfer but, unfortunately, there is little modelling of this process and no hard firm-level empirical evidence for Asian economies.

One needs to distinguish two aspects of technology transfer by multinationals. First, there is the direct effects on the affiliate in the host country and on the host economy itself of technology transfer by the parent company. Second, it is sometimes claimed that foreign direct investments have additional positive spillover effects through the demonstration to other producers in the host economy of new technologies and management methods. There is a third area of technology development, namely the deliberate development of new technologies by R & D. This is not restricted to multinationals. For a recent survey of the literature on this area, see Grossman and Helpman (1995).

In relation to the direct effects of technology transfer by the multinational firm, the dominant model in the contemporary literature is the Dunning eclectic or Ownership, Location and Internalisation (OLI) model. The reasons why foreign countries choose to serve local markets by direct foreign investment are the subject of an excellent survey by Markusen (1995). In these models multinationals arise endogenously as part of the solution to a general equilibrium for the global (multi-country) market. They are, therefore, genuine models of the globalisation process.

What drives these models is the existence of economies of multi-plant operation. These are due to the public goods characteristic of assets which are firm-specific and non-rivalrous across plants. Firm-specific assets such as product patents and processes and knowhow can be used at no extra cost in more than one plant and therefore in more than one country. They give rise to firm-level fixed costs. Furthermore, the preference for internal rather than arm's length transfer of technology across countries may be explained by the same public goods characteristic of knowledge capital that explains multi-plant production; for example, the non-excludability property which makes it easily transferred to potential competitors, or reputation effects.

Such models are a distinct improvement over earlier models of foreign direct investment. The multinational is a firm with distinctive characteristics in the models. These models can explain the foreign direct investments and multi-plant activities of multinationals and the pattern of international trade. Multinationals reduce the costs of production in the host country because of the transfer at zero cost within the multinational of firm-specific assets and therefore benefit the host country economy.

These models are particularly useful in the context of examining intra-Asian foreign direct investment and trade because of the wide differences in technologies between the technologically advanced countries such as Japan and increasingly the Asian NIEs on the one hand and the other countries of Asia which have older technologies and low wages on the other, and high rates of capital formation. They may provide an important part of the explanation of the establishment of new industries which would not evolve without the advantages of multinational production. Similarly, they can explain the development of new products within industries and the technological upgrading that has gone on within some industries. In effect multinational firms supply missing inputs, that is inputs of knowledge, management knowhow and marketing access which are not available in the local economy and which in some cases cannot be purchased in arm's length markets.

The notion that knowledge spills over from one firm to others has become popular in recent years (see Blomstrom, 1989). Looking at it from the receiver firm, firms gain from the experience of other firms. But, what is the set of others from which a given firm learns and how exactly is this knowledge transmitted? The standard way of incorporating this notion into economic models is to assume that the firm level production is a function of an index of accumulated knowledge or knowhow. This index in turn can be a function of the cumulative national output of the good, or the cumulative world output or sometimes of the output of a group of related outputs in an industry at the national or international level. This generates a family of learning by doing spillovers (see Grossman and Helpman, 1995, Section 2 for a survey of these models).

In these models, spillovers occur as a function of cumulative aggregate industry output at some level. It does not matter whether the output is produced by home or by foreign firms. Yet, the level of spillovers in an economy may still be related to the level of foreign direct investment. Suppose foreign investment results in the establishment of new industries or activities in which national spillovers occur and, as is often presumed, that spillovers are limited to the producers of a good within the nation. Once an industry or activity is established, it generates spillovers which would not otherwise occur. If, furthermore, the rate of spillovers in the newly-established industries is greater than the national average, there is a gain to the economy in addition to the direct effects of FDI. Thus, when we link the ideas of proprietary knowledge specific to the multinational firm with national spillovers, the gains from direct foreign investment to the host country are increased. The operations of an affiliate may become more cost competitive over time and lead to rapid increases in output of the industry and to higher national product. Similar results hold if R & D is combined with national spillovers.

Alternatively, we might make some spillovers a function only of foreign investments or of national output produced by affiliates of foreign companies, or even of particular technology-leading foreign companies. For example, in the case of Japanese foreign investors, the output of Japanese affiliates may incorporate the benefits of Japanese production techniques such as Just-In-Time or Quality Circles or labour training methods and these techniques may spread among other national producers as Japanese affiliates in a country increase their output. This again leads to a higher national product.

Regrettably, but perhaps understandably, empirical research has lagged far behind the development of theories of FDI and multinational behaviour. There are some descriptive case studies of the transfer of technologies by foreign multinationals to Asian industries; for example, the account of the development of the electronics industries in Korea and Taiwan in UNCTAD (1995, pp. 250-256) and that of the same industry in Penang in Malaysia and in Guadalajara in Mexico by Palacios (1995), and UNCTAD (1994, chapter V.B). There are, however, no systematic studies of technology transfer. Earlier literature emphasised local conditions relating to the education and skills of the labour force and other factors which were necessary for the successful transfer of technologies. More recent literature emphasises the necessity of the host economy being open to foreign investment and to international trade in goods and services for successful transfer.

Narayanan and Wah (1996) provide a rare example of firm-level data of the extent of technology transfer from foreign parent companies to their affiliates in Malaysian electronics and electrical industries. They use a Japanese model of the technology transfer process which distinguishes between adoption, rooting and diffusion of foreign technologies and looks separately at operations, maintenance, repair and R&D. They find that, in a significant proportion of firms sampled, local personnel are able to undertake independent operations, maintenance and repair functions but the final phase of rooting in R&D has been attained by local staff in only 5% of the sample firms. They also find a slower pace of technology transfer in Japanese firms compared to their US counterparts.

I know of no microeconomic studies of spillovers resulting from FDI in Asia, though spillovers are mentioned as a possible source of benefit; for example, Athukurola and Menon (1996). Haddad and Harrison (1993) used firm-level data to test for spillover effects of foreign direct investment in Morocco. Their evidence suggests that foreign investment is associated with a once-only increase in the total factor productivity of domestic firms but it does not raise the rate of growth of factor productivity. There have been studies of R&D spillovers; for example, Coe, Helpman, and Hoffmaister (1995) find that developing countries total factor productivities are larger the larger the foreign R&D capital stock and conclude that R&D spillovers from the North and South are significant and substantial. See also Bernstein and Yan (1995).

Although most commentators seem to have become sanguine about the transferability of foreign technologies and the benefits of technology transfer, we should demand more reliable evidence.

B.   FDI as an Agent for Transformation of the Economies

To consider the role of FDI as an agent of the transformation of the macro-economy, one needs to look at the activities of the multinationals in the context of the world economy. That is, one needs a global comparative advantage framework. In particular, trends in FDI must be related to developments in the markets for commodities as FDI is a production-related decision and the foreign affiliates in East and South East Asia are very export-oriented, as noted above.

From the point of view of the East and South East Asian countries, these foreign corporations have been a major force in the development of exports, especially of manufactures. For example, in the late 1980s and early 1990s, shares of foreign affiliates in national exports were as high as 57% in Malaysia (all industries), 91% in Singapore (non-oil manufacturing), and somewhat less at 24% in Hong Kong (manufacturing) and 17% in Taiwan (manufacturing) UNCTAD (1995, p. 214).

There has been increasing acceptance of the Flying Geese model of this process of transformation of the structure of industry and exports. The modern interpretation of this hypothesis is one of a pattern of comparative advantage in Asia which has been changing over time, linked to foreign direct investment as a deliberate strategy to relocate activities from the source countries which no longer have a comparative advantage in the production of certain goods to host countries which do (UNCTAD, 1995, chapter V.B.1) reviews the literature on what it calls "transnational-assisted restructuring").

Japan was the original lead goose in the Asian formation. It has gone through a sequence of structural upgrading in its manufacturing industries, progressing from the labor-intensive industries such as textiles to a second tier of heavy capital-intensive industries such as steel and shipbuilding to a third tier of assembly-oriented industries such as motor vehicles, electronics and machine tools to a fourth tier of high technology industries such as biotechnology and super-conductors. There is a similar process of restructuring <u>within</u> industries from low-technology low-productivity and frequently labour-intensive activities to higher-technology higher-productivity less labour-intensive activities within industries. In the later stages of structural change, some of these latter industries or activities have been relocated by the Japanese firms to the Asian NIEs and more recently to the ASEAN-4 countries.

426   JOURNAL OF ASIAN ECONOMICS 7(3), 1996

The Asian NIEs countries then became the new lead goose in Asia. Korea, Singapore and Taiwan (but not Hong Kong) have, like Japan, experienced a sharp appreciation of their exchange rates since 1986 and all the NIEs have experienced rapidly rising labour costs in the last decade. In their turn the Asian NIEs have begun to transfer some of the more labour-intensive and less technology-intensive manufacturing activities in lower tiers which have become non-competitive to new locations in the ASEAN-4 countries and the PRC which can now carry out these activities at lower cost.

The geographic pattern of relocation has differed among the Asian NIEs. In the case of Taiwan and Singapore much of the relocation has been to neighbouring countries. This aspect has been captured by the concept of Sub-Regional Economic Zones (SREZs). The IMS Growth Triangle is an agreement among the countries of Indonesia, Malaysia and Singapore. It a triangle consisting of the Riau Islands of Indonesia just South of Singapore, Johor Province of Malaysia across the Singapore-Malaysia Causeway and Singapore. Similarly, the South China SREZs comprises coastal areas of the provinces of Guangdong and Fujian which border Hong Kong and which are close to Taiwan. Recent literature on these SREZs has emphasised the complementarity of these neighbouring areas in terms of factor availabilities and the advantages of agglomeration in areas which are close to each other (see Pomfret, 1996). These two zones are centred on the city-states of Singapore and Hong Kong respectively. The industries of these cities have spilled across the borders when the rising prices and shortages of labour have made older labour- or capital-intensive industries no longer competitive.

By contrast, in the case of Korea, multinational corporations such as Samsung, Hyundai and Daewoo have relocated plants to diverse locations, including Mexico and the US and other industrialised countries to a significant extent.

In this process of restructuring, multinational corporations have played a central role in developing the production capacities of the host countries. Often they have done this by relocating some of their own production from the NIEs to new locations in other Asian countries. The global general equilibrium perspective of this section indicates that to the micro gains from technology transfer and national spillovers, we must add gains from trade of a classic comparative advantage type. Foreign direct investments have helped the rapidly growing Asian economies establish and diversify into areas of manufacturing and service sector outputs which have been opening to world trade.

As it is a dynamic hypothesis and involves links between the patterns of commodity trade and of FDI, the Flying Geese hypothesis is difficult to prove. There has been no systematic investigation of the hypothesis. However, the individual observations of trading patterns are consistent with the hypothesis. Shifts in the pattern of comparative advantage have been verified from empirical studies of revealed comparative advantage. For example, Bora (1996) shows large shifts in the revealed comparative advantage in "technology-intensive" and "labour-intensive" industries in particular, the two industry groups at the extremes of the technology ladder, for Japan,

Hong Kong, Korea, Singapore and Taiwan during the period 1980 to 1993. The distribution of FDI by these countries among the other countries of the Asia-Pacific region and outside it are also consistent with the hypothesis (see Table 3).

In this process of shifting comparative advantage, growth in foreign direct investment has partly followed the growth in trade in goods and services and partly led to a growth of trade in goods and services. The dominant modern view is that international trade in goods and services is complementary with rather than a substitute for international flows of capital, especially if trade is due to differences in technology (see Ethier, 1996, for a survey). In the case of Asia, much of the foreign direct investment has been directed towards activities which are export-oriented and whose outputs are destined mainly to third country markets outside the host and source Asian countries. As inputs, these activities have used capital goods and upstream intermediate inputs supplied by Japan and other foreign investors. Thus, the foreign direct investments are associated with both import and export trade in goods. Much of the FDI into East Asia has come from Japan and the Asian NIEs and it has been associated with inputs of capital and intermediate goods. Empirical studies by Petri (1995) and APEC Economic Committee (1995) find positive effects of FDI on the exports of the source countries. Jin (1995) verifies statistically the positive effect of Taiwan's outward FDI on its exports. Consequently, the joint operation of these changes in the commodity and the capital goods markets provides a link between the growth in the intra-Asian imports of goods and services and of FDI. That is, there has been investment-led export growth. It may be equally true to describe the process as export-led investment growth.

IV.   A LONG TERM VIEW OF INVESTMENT AND GROWTH IN ASIA

If one takes a long term view of savings and investment in Asia, a main event is the transition of some of the Asian economies from net borrowers to net lenders. In fact, looking at the broad sweep of developments in the Asian economies over the last three decades, one can distinguish three turning points in the evolution of these economies which are linked to each other.

One turning point is the opening to international trade of a growing number of Asian economies over this period, beginning with the Asian NIEs in the mid-1960s. A second turning point is the transition of some Asian economies from net capital-importing to net capital-exporting economies. A third turning point of some Asian economies is a transition from net labour-exporting to a net labour-importing economy.

The turning points are important events in the economic history of these economies. The shift to openness and the success of the open Asian economies is well known (see, in particular, the excellent review by Sachs and Warner, 1995). The entry of Japan into Asia as a major foreign investor has had profound effects on the pattern of production and specialisation in the region and the subsequent entry of the NIEs is

TABLE 5.   Transition Years in Asian Economics

	Year of Opening of Economics	Years of Migraton Transition	Years of Savings Investment Transition
Hong Kong	Always	Early 1970s	1984
Thailand	Always	Mid-1990s	—
Taipei, China	1963	Late 1960s	1981
Malaysia	1963	Late 1980s	—
Japan	1964	Mid-1960s	1981
Singapore	1965	Early 1970s	1988
Korea	1968	Late 1980s	—
Indonesia	1970	—	—
Philippines	1988	—	—
Nepal	1991	—	—
Sri Lanka	1991	—	—
India	1994	—	—

Sources: Column 1: Sachs and Warner (1995)
               Column 2: Freeman and Mo (1996)
               Column 3: Calculated from ADTs data

having major effects on the source and host countries. Similarly, the switch from net emigration to net immigration, together with the intra-Asian pattern of this trade in labour, is changing the relationships among the labour markets and national economies in Asia.

Some time after the opening of their economies, a subset of seven of the Asian economies which have opened to the rest of the world have gone through a turning point at which they have changed from being a net exporter of labour to a net importer of labour. This too has been reported and studied by migration specialists (see the special issue of the *Asian and Pacific Migration Journal* (1994) and the Asian Development Bank (1996, Part III). The turning point marking the change from the status of a net recipient of capital flows from the rest of the world to that of a net supplier of capital to the rest of the world has been noted for individual countries.

The turning point with respect to openness is a policy-induced turning point whereas the other two are transitions reflecting the behavioural response of producer and household agents in the economies. The transition relating to the net labour exporting status has been called the *Migration Transition.* The transition relating to the net saving status might be called the *Savings-Investment Transition.* Turning points relating to openness and the two transitions are set out in the Table 5 for the 12 Asian economies which are judged to be now relatively open. The dates of the transitions have been recorded in the three columns of the table. The countries have been listed in the order given by the date of the transition to openness.

The dates of the shift to openness are taken from Sachs and Warner (1995). They are estimates, based on several indicators of restrictions to trade in both commodity and capital markets, of the dates at which these countries became open relative to those in the countries which are regarded as being open.[4] In any case, there has been a close correspondence in most countries between the liberalisation of capital flows and of trade in goods. Indeed, the steps to open a country are usually part of a more general movement towards greater freedom of economic activity with elements of reform of taxation and government expenditures, deregulation of many industries and, in more recent years, privatisation of government-owned enterprises. In the cases of Malaysia and Singapore, the dates of opening are the dates of independence of the countries as they are considered to have been open since independence.

The dates of the two transitions which involve changes in the direction of net flows of primary factors are problematical because capital and labour markets are heterogenous. Investments in productive enterprises differ in terms of the mixes of loan and equity and of industry knowledge, risks and other variables that affect the choice of investments. Some countries, such as Korea and Japan, have had a much smaller proportion of their borrowings in the form of FDI than other Asian countries such as Singapore and Malaysia. Similarly, there are markets for many types of labour, not a single labour market, in each country. As growth proceeds, a rapidly growing economy will have excess demand emerging for some kinds of skilled or specialised labour which cannot be filled from national labour supplies at the same time as there may be a national excess supply of other types of labour. As a consequence of this heterogeneity, capital and labour flows between one economy and the rest of the world are two way. The date for the transition to a capital-exporting economy is the date from which the balance of payments current account has been in persistent surplus. This criterion simply adds all the different capital transactions, on public and private account, by value.[5] It reflects the savings-investment gap *ex post* for the economy. Similarly, the dates of the transition to a labour-importing or net immigrant economy are based on the difference between observed or *ex post* total emigration and total immigration.

For both transitions, the dates were taken to be the years or periods from which the economy has remained continuously in the new state. The existence of such dates indicates that the switches have been permanent in all cases, at least until the present time.

In all cases the shift to an open economy preceded the transitions relating to international factor flows. And in all cases of countries which have passed through a Savings-Investment Transition, this has occurred some 10-15 years after the Migration Transition. The four East Asian economies which have passed through both transitions—Japan, Hong Kong, Singapore and Taiwan - have been transformed from labour-exporting and capital-importing countries to labour-importing and capital-exporting economies.

Causal observation of other countries indicates that the transition to a capital exporter is not inevitable. Open high income resource-rich countries outside Asia, such as Canada and Australia, have remained capital importers for a hundred years (Clarke and Smith, 1996). Similarly, the transition to a net immigration country is not inevitable, though it seems to be more widespread. A few developed countries such as Ireland and the United Kingdom have continued to be net exporters of labor for a very long time.

The lags between the timing of the opening of the economies on the one hand and the Migration Transition and the Savings-Investment Transitions are variable. This variability in the timing of the transitions is not surprising as there is no theory which predicts a sequence or timing of these transitions.[6] The Migration Transition literature ascribes this transition to the effect of growth in household incomes or demographic changes associated with these growth in incomes. There is no theory of the Savings-Investment Transition. There is accumulating evidence that sustained growth increases the national savings rate. If the rate of capital formation does not increase as rapidly, a change in the net savings status will occur.

These transitions are not independent of each other. They are parts of the process of the growth of real output in these economies which has been sustained and, compared to all other regions of the world, extremely rapid.

It is generally accepted that the opening of economies, or more generally the freeing up of all markets in these economies, has been the trigger which put them on a higher long term growth path, though the exact relationship between opening and faster growth is debatable (Frankel and Romer, 1995). Following the opening up of these economies, the very rapid rate of growth of exports of goods and services has enabled them to achieve rates of growth of output which could not have been achieved if the output had had to be sold on domestic markets alone.

I shall sketch a theoretical framework which considers the relationships between the growth of the economy on the one hand and the Savings-Investment Transition and the Migration Transition on the other. These relationships can be explained by a Neoclassical growth model for an economy which is open to trade in both commodities and factors. New Growth Theory gives additional insights as it emphasises the international diffusion of technologies through international movement of factors.

Rapid growth has been associated with changes in factor proportions. Most of the open Asian economies have had a rate of capital formation which has been high relative to those of almost all countries outside the region, as noted above. On the other hand, the rate of growth of labour inputs has slowed down over time, though in some countries the increased labor force participation of women has delayed this effect. (In Hong Kong large scale immigration has maintained a rapid increase in the stock of labor.) Consequently, for all countries, the stock of capital has risen relative to the stock of labor. The open Asian economies which have had sustained rapid growth have moved sharply from being very labour-abundant economies to being capital-abundant.

By itself, this change in factor proportions has raised the marginal productivity of labour and lowered that of capital. This in turn has raised the real price of labour substantially, although the rate of growth of this index has usually lagged the rate of growth of the index of real output per capita.

As each of these economies is open, these intra-national changes in factor endowments and prices have changed the incentives for the international migration of capital and labour. Differential growth for long periods of one or two decades has changed substantially the real wages in these economies relative to those of other Asian countries which have not grown so rapidly and also relative to those in Western countries which have been the destination of Asian emigration outside the region. These changes in factor prices, along with the changes in incomes, have affected the quantities and direction of net flows of factors between the countries. Capital moves to less developed capital-scarce economies and labour seeks to move to countries with significantly higher real wage incomes. There has been a great increase in intra-Asian labour migration as well as in intra-Asian capital movements in the last decade, much of this between neighbouring countries, as noted above.

Viewed from the long run perspective, the increased intra-Asian movements of capital and, tc a lesser extent labour, have aided the transformation of the economies and the development of new industries and products. They are playing an increasing role in the maintenance of high rates of growth of exports and real output in Asia.[7]

Acknowledgment: *Parts of this paper have used material prepared for the Asian Development Bank as a consultant for the Asian Development Outlook 1996. I wish to acknowledge my gratitude to the Bank for the opportunity to work on these subjects and the assistance it provided me.*

NOTES

1.   Asia is taken to be East Asia, Southeast Asia and South East. Some statistics taken from Asian Development Bank or other sources which include the Pacific Islands but these islands account for a tiny fraction of the total.

2.   Giovannini (1985) finds some empirical evidence of a negative relationship between domestic savings and foreign savings in non-Asian developing countries.

3.   Nepal and Sri Lanka did not open their economies until 1991, India until 1994 and Pakistan and Bangladesh have never opened their economies though Bangladesh began a liberalisation in the mid-1980s and Pakistan took up a fairly elaborate liberalisation program in 1991. All of the countries of South Asia retain some exchange controls, including controls on capital transactions, as well as comprehensive restrictions on the establishment of foreign direct investments, and they have much higher border barriers to trade in goods.

4.   The criteria of openness relate to both current and capital account transactions as the indicators include the level of the exchange rate premium in the black market over the official rate. Under exchange control regimes both current and capital account transactions are restricted.

5.   The dates of the transitions to an "open" economy are arbitrary as openness is really a continuous variable with degrees of openness running from zero for a completely closed autarchic economy to infinity for a completely open economy with zero restrictions on transactions with other countries. The dates should be treated as approximate.

6.   An alternative, based on the important role of direct foreign investment, would be to look at the transition in terms of net foreign direct investment. Dunning (1981) outlined stages of an investment-development path. Some Asian countries have gone through a transition in terms of net FDI.

7.   The relationship between net FDI and net total foreign borrowing/lending is complex. Some FDI does not lead to international capital flows as the purchase of assets in the host country may be

financed by the sale of proprietary technology or management expertise or by borrowing on the local markets.

8.   There are significant differences among the open Asian economies in terms of natural resources which may play a role in these transitions. For example, Malaysia is a resource-rich Asian country whereas Japan and the NIEs have few natural resources.

9.   The variable lags may also be due in part to the crudity of the dating of turning points of the three transitions. One of the countries which has not yet reached the turning point for the movement of capital, Korea, has been oscillating between annual surpluses and deficits in the current account of the balance of payments. Thailand seems to be an outlier in terms of the long lags to the Migration and Savings-Investment Transition turning points but the dating of the Thailand opening is generous as Thailand had and still has tariff rates for many commodity groups which are higher than those in its ASEAN nations and other countries which opened later according to the chronology.

10.   They are also are a force producing greater integration of the economies and the convergence of per capita incomes. In tending to equalise factor proportions (and product) prices, they also tend to equalise incomes among the countries. This convergence force is additional to short-run convergence produced by the freeing of trade in goods and services and in capital.

11.   The role of technological change is also important in this context and little understood. Through foreign direct investment and related research and development and human capital formation these economies have been reaching higher levels of technology. The increase in factor productivity due to technological change is not equal in all countries. This may be a factor which causes divergence of real incomes among the Asian countries, even when there are increasing levels of factor flows and trade among the countries of the region.

REFERENCES

APEC Economic Committee. 1995. *Foreign Direct Investment and APEC Economic Integration.* Singapore: APEC Secretariat.

Asian Development Bank. 1992. *Asian Development Outlook 1992.* Manila: Asian Development Bank.

Asian Development Bank. 1996. *Asian Development Outlook 1996 and 1997.* Manila: Asian Development Bank.

Asian and Pacific Migration Journal. 1994. "Turning Points in Labor Migration," *Asian and Pacific Migration Journal,* 3(Special Issue).

Athukorala, P. and Menon, J. 1996. "Foreign Investment and Industrialization in Malaysia: Exports, Employment and Spillovers," *Asian Economic Journal,* 10(March): 29-44.

Bernstein, J. and Yan, X. 1995. *International R & D Spillovers between Canadian and Japanese Industries,* NBER Working Paper No. 5401.

Blomstrom, M. 1989. *Foreign Investment and Spillovers.* London: Routledge.

Bora, B. 1996. "Trade and Investment in the APEC Region: 1980 to 1993." In *International Trade and Migration in the Asia-Pacific Region,* edited by P.J. Lloyd and L. Williams. Melbourne: Oxford University Press.

Carroll, C. and Weill, D.N. 1994. "Savings and Growth: A Reinterpretation," *Carnegie-Rochester Conference Series on Public Policy,* 40(June): 133-192.

Clarke, H. and Smith, L. 1996. "Labour Immigration and Capital Flows: Long-term Australian, Canadian and United States Experience," *International Migration Review* (forthcoming)

Coe, S., Helpman, E. and Hoffmaister, A. 1995. *North-South Spillovers.* Centre for Economic Policy Research Discussion Paper No. 1133.

Drysdale, P. and Garnaut, R. 1994. "Trade Intensities and the Analysis of Bilateral Trade Flows in a Many-country World: A Survey." In *Asia Pacific Regionalism: Readings in International Economic Relations,* edited by R. Garnaut and P. Drysdale. Pymble, Australia: Harper Educational.

Dunning, J.H. 1981. "Explaining the International Direct Foreign Investment Position of Countries: Towards a Dynamic or Developmental Approach," *Weltwirtschaftliches Archiv*, 119: 30-64.

Ethier, W.E. 1996. "Are Trade in Goods and Factors Substitutes or Complements?" In *International Trade and Migration in the Asia-Pacific Region*, edited by P.J. Lloyd and L. Williams. Melbourne: Oxford University Press.

Frankel, J.A. and Romer, D. 1995. *Trade and Growth: An Empirical Investigation*. National Bureau of Economic Research Working Paper No. 5476.

Giovannini, A. 1985. "Savings and the Real Interest Rate in LDCs," *Journal of Development Studies*, 18(August): 197-217.

Grossman, G.M. and Helpman, E. 1995. "Technology and Trade." In *Handbook of International Economics*, Vol. 3, edited by G.M. Grossman and K. Rogoff. Amsterdam: North Holland.

Haddad, M. and Harrison, A. 1993. "Are there Positive Spillovers from Direct Foreign Investment? Evidence from Panel Data for Morocco,"*Journal of Development Studies*, 42: 51-74.

Harrigan, F. 1995. *How Much do we Know about the Private Saving in Southeast Asia?* Paper presented to the Sixth ICSEAD International Workshop, Kitakyushu, July 1995.

Jin, An-loh. 1995. "Trade Effects of Foreign Direct Investment: Evidence from Taiwan for four ASEAN Countries," *Weltwirtschaftliches Archiv*, 131: 737-747.

Markusen, J.R. 1995. "Incorporating the Multinational Enterprise into the Theory of International Trade," *Journal of Economic Perspectives*, 9(Spring): 169-190.

Narayanan, S. and Wah Lai Yew. 1996. *Sources of Technology Inflow to Malaysia: U.S. Firms Versus Japanese Firms*. Paper presented to the 20th ACAES Conference on Asian Economies, Selangor, Malaysia, May 14-17 1996.

Pacific Economic Co-operation (PECC). 1995. *Pacific Economic Outlook: Capital Flows in the Pacific Region: Past Trends and Future Prospects*. Singapore: PECC Secretariat.

Palacios, J.J. 1995. "Multinational Corporations and Technology Transfer in Penang and Guadalajara." In *Corporate Links and Foreign Direct Investment in Asia and the Pacific*, edited by E.H.Y. Chen and P. Drysdale. Sydney, Australia: Harper Educational.

Petri, P.A. 1995. "The Interdependence of Trade and Investment in the Pacific." In *Corporate Links and Foreign Direct Investment in Asia and the Pacific*, edited by E.Y. Chen and P. Drysdale. Sydney: Harper Educational.

Prescott, R.F. 1995. *Prospects for World Saving*. Paper presented to the Sixth ICSEAD International Workshop, Kitakyushu, July 1995.

Pomfret, R. 1996. "Sub-regional Economic Zones." In *Regional Integration and the Asia-Pacific*, edited by B. Bora and C. Findlay. Melbourne: Oxford University Press.

Sachs, J.D. and Warner, A. 1995. "Economic Reform and the Process of Global Integration," *Brookings Papers on Economic Activity*, 1: 1-118.

Thant, M., Tang, M. and Kazaku, H. 1994. *Growth Triangles in Asia: A New Approach to Regional Economic Cooperation*. Manila: Asian Development Bank.

United Nations Conference on Trade and Development. 1994. *Transnational Corporations and Technology Transfer to Developing Countries*. New York: Author.

United Nations Conference on Trade and Development. 1995. *World Investment Report*. New York: Author.

The World Bank. 1993. *The East Asian Miracle: Economic Growth and Public Policy*. Oxford: Oxford University Press.

[16]

AN APEC OR MULTILATERAL INVESTMENT CODE?

P. J. LLOYD

This paper considers whether there should be an international investment code and, if so, whether it should be a regional code for the Asia Pacific Economic Cooperation (APEC) countries or a multilateral code. The APEC Eminent Persons Group recommended to APEC in October 1993 that there should be an Asia—Pacific Investment Code to regulate direct foreign investment in the region. On the other hand, there is already substantial regulation of international investment at the bilateral, regional and multilateral levels and other proposals for increased regulation are under consideration in the OECD and other fora. This paper argues that, in the long term, a Code under the World Trade Organisation would have the advantages of greater country coverage, links to other investment-related provisions of the WTO and greater enforceability. In the interim, APEC can develop and promote the principles of transparency and non-discrimination in the treatment of foreign direct investments. *JEL Classification: F21.*

I. INTRODUCTION

In the last three years interest in a code to regulate aspects of government control of investment flows in the Asia Pacific region has been growing steadily. Guisinger (1991) proposed an investment code for the Asia-Pacific region. This proposal was discussed by the Pacific Economic Cooperation Council (PECC) at the May 1991 plenary session in Singapore in 1992 and in August it was referred to the Investment Study Group of the PECC Trade Policy Forum (TPF). The TPF produced a final Draft Asia Pacific Investment Code (PECC, 1993). While this draft code was received favourably, it was not adopted or endorsed by PECC (see Bora, 1994). The idea of a code was, however, picked up by the Eminent Persons Group of the Asia Pacific Economic Cooperation (APEC) forum in its report to the October 1993 APEC Ministerial Meeting in Seattle. Recommendation 3 of this Report was that "APEC should adopt

P. J. Lloyd • Asian Business Centre, Faculty of Economics and Commerce, The University of Melbourne, Parkville, Victoria 3052, Australia.

Journal of Asian Economics, Vol. 6, No. 1, 1995 pp. 53-70
ISSN: 1049-0078

an Asia Pacific Investment Code [APIC] to reduce the uncertainties and transactions costs of trade and investment in the region" (APEC, 1993).

This paper considers the proposal and looks at the alternative of a multilateral investment code under the auspices of the new World Trade Organization or some other group. Section II describes some trends in foreign direct investment flows and the deregulation at the national level of these flows as background to the subsequent examination of proposals for a code. Section III looks at the existing international regulation of international investment. There are bilateral agreements, regional agreements contained within some regional trade arrangements such as the European Union and the North American Free Trade Agreement and, at the multilateral level, some aspects of international investment flows are regulated by the OECD, the GATT and the World Bank. In the light of existing national, bilateral and multilateral regulation, Section IV examines the PECC/APEC proposal for a code. Section V considers the desirability of the APEC Code. Existing regulation by other bodies is more extensive than is commonly realized and other proposals for increased regulation are under consideration in the OECD and other fora. In the long term, a multilateral code has a number of advantages over the proposed Asia-Pacific code.

II. TRENDS IN FOREIGN DIRECT INVESTMENT

World flows of capital between countries have increased rapidly in the 1980s and 1990s. From the point of view of the relationships with international trade in goods and services, the direct foreign investment flows are of more interest than portfolio and other investments. The International Monetary Fund collates statistics of direct foreign investment. They show that total direct investment abroad has increased from $US 49 billion in 1983 to $US 149 billion in 1992 (International Monetary Fund, 1993, Table C.17). This is an average rate of growth of around 25 percent, though the flows are subject to large annual fluctuations.

The US, Japan, Germany, and France and other industrial countries are the principal sources of the direct foreign investment flows. A feature of the international movement of capital by direct foreign investment is that it is two-way trade. Most countries are both a source and destination of direct foreign investment in any one year. For example, there was a surge of direct foreign investment in the US in the mid 1980s whereas previously the US had been a heavy foreign investor with little matching inflow. At the end of the decade the US had replaced Canada as the largest host investment nation in terms of the cumulative value of foreign-controlled investments. "Thus, rather than the one-way process, foreign direct investment had come to resemble trade in goods and services, with substantial flows in both directions." (McCulloch, 1991) One is interested in the gross flows rather than the net flows as the gross flows affect production while the net flows are largely influenced by the balance of payments situation of the individual countries.

Table 1 records the inflows into reporting or destination countries for the APEC region and, for comparison, the world total. (Statistics for Brunei, Hong Kong, and Taiwan are not reported.)[1] As destination countries, the APEC region over the period of the late 1980s and early 1990s has declined sharply in importance. This is due almost entirely to the sharp fall in foreign direct investment into the United States. (There is a similar fall in foreign direct investment into Australia and New Zealand though it is much smaller in absolute terms.) This probably reflects the combined and interactive results of the recession in these countries and their reduced attractiveness as FDI destinations with a poor record of productivity growth. However, the Asian group of countries has seen steadily increasing inflows and has become more important on the world scene. China in particular has had a very rapid growth of FDI inflows and it is expected that the statistics for 1993 and 1994 will show another large increase.

Looking at the two-way flows, a high proportion of the foreign direct investment flows in the Asia-Pacific region are intra-regional. Unfortunately, it is not possible to obtain a general picture of the two-way intra-regional flows in the Asia-Pacific region because the IMF does not report the breakdown of flows out of and into countries by the partner countries, but details are available for some countries from national sources, including the two most important source countries, the US and Japan. (Yamazawa, 1993, Table 6-3) construct a matrix of intra-APEC direct investment flows for 1980, 1985, and 1989. These show substantial intra-APEC flows but the data are dated. In the case of Japan, considerably more than one half of its direct foreign investment has been destined for other APEC countries, chiefly the US but increasingly other East Asian countries. In the case of the US, a third or a quarter is destined to other APEC countries with Canada the single most important destination and only 10-20 percent directed to East Asia.

The rapid expansion of direct foreign investment flows globally and in East Asia in particular may be explained in large part by the fact that the movement of capital around the world has become much freer in recent years, chiefly as a result of national policies of deregulation of financial markets. Regrettably there are no quantitative measures of the extent of the reduction in barriers to inward flows to my knowledge.

A number of features of the national regulations of foreign direct investment make it difficult to measure the extent of these restrictions. Restrictions should be viewed as discrimination against foreign domestic investors but there are multiple dimensions to discrimination against foreigners in the movement of capital.[2]

First, a capital investor requires the right of establishment and this is frequently denied foreign investors, in some sectors at least.

Second, Outward transfers of capital and capital income after establishment may also be restricted.

Third, even when there are no restrictions on capital movements across borders, there may be significant non-border differences in treatment between the operation and taxation of non-resident owned companies as distinct from the treat-

TABLE 1.   Foreign Direct Investment into APEC Countries

	\$US millions						
	1986	*1987*	*1988*	*1989*	*1990*	*1991*	*1992*
Industrial Countries							
United States	35,630	58,220	57,270	67,870	45,140	23,972	2,370
Canada	1,217	4,198	3,795	2,626	7,638	6,592	7,757
Japan	230	1,170	-520	-1,060	1,760	1,370	2,720
Australia	3,484	3,920	8,013	7,770	6,884	4,763	4,968
New Zealand	283	293	441	1,365	1,754	682	70
Total, Industrial Countries	40,844	67,801	68,999	78,571	63,176	37,379	17,885
Asia							
China, P. R. of	1,875	2,314	3,194	3,393	3,487	4,366	11,156
Indonesia	258	385	576	682	1,093	1,482	1,774
Korea	435	601	871	758	715	1,116	550
Malaysia	489	423	719	1,668	2,332	4,073	4,118
Singapore	1,710	2,836	3,655	2,773	5,263	4,395	5,635
Thailand	263	352	1,105	1,775	2,444	2,014	2,116
Total - Asia	5,030	7,011	10,120	11,049	15,334	17,446	25,349
Mexico	1,160	1,796	635	2,648	2,548	4,742	5,366
Total - APEC	47,034	76,608	79,754	92,268	81,058	59,567	48,600
Total - World	78,826	123,568	151,343	192,361	203,969	158,350	149,928
APEC as percentage of World Total	60	62	53	48	40	38	31
ASIA as percentage of World Total	6	6	7	6	8	11	17

Source: IMF, Balance of Payments Statistics Yearbook, 1993, Part 2

ment of resident companies. For example, as a condition of the establishment or operation of such FDI activities, some governments impose taxes or limit access to imports of these enterprises or impose other performance requirements such as labor training and R & D which do not apply to like domestically controlled enterprises. These are equivalent to a discriminatory tax on the inputs used in these activities. The elimination of such practices is called national treatment. It is the commitment by countries to accord to foreign-controlled enterprises operating in their territories treatment under their national laws, regulations and administrative practices which is no less favorable than that accorded to domestic enterprises.

Fourth, host governments may also discriminate among the *countries* of origin of the foreign investment in terms of the rights of establishment and transfer or national treatment, giving more favourable treatment to some countries. The absence of this form of discrimination is called Most Favored Nation (MFN) treatment.

Free access to foreign markets for investors means the removal of barriers and discriminations in all four dimensions. This provides the standard of completely free movement of capital against which one may measure restrictions.

On top of the multiple dimensions, there is another measurement problem. Unlike trade in goods, there are no taxes levied directly on cross-border capital movements. Instead, in all countries, decisions to allow a foreign direct investment across national borders are decided administratively, often with few guiding rules or principles, and the restrictions may be more severe for some industries than others. Most of the restrictions on inflow have been of the all-or-nothing kind which are equivalent to total prohibitions when there is a decision to disallow an application for foreign investment and to free movement when the application is allowed.

Despite the absence of measurement, we can be certain that the barriers to international flows of direct investment have fallen as almost all countries have removed or relaxed restrictions on capital movements in the 1980s and 1990s (see OECD, 1990, 1993, chapter IV). Throughout the OECD countries and most of the Third World and recently in the countries of the former Soviet Union there has been a deregulation of financial markets and a steady relaxation of national restrictions on the inward (and in some cases outward) movement of capital flows and capital income service payments, and they have moved towards national treatment. All of the APEC countries have liberalized the movement of foreign capital in some respects at some time in the 1980s or 1990s, some of them quite strongly; for example, Canada, Korea, the Peoples' Republic of China, and New Zealand.

Some governments have given incentives to foreign corporations to locate their activities and invest in the country which are not available to the domestic investors. These include tax holidays, duty-free imports of intermediate and capital inputs, and the subsidised sale of land, infrastructure and other services. Hence, there is, in some individual investments, discrimination in *favor* of foreign investors. Overall, it is possible that some countries on average discriminate in favor of foreign investors in the economy *vis-à-vis* domestic investors.

What has caused the widespread reductions in barriers to foreign direct investment? When it was established in 1960, the OECD adopted a program of expansion of liberalization of international trade and international investment. Those members which signed the 1961 OECD Code of Liberalization of Capital Movements (OECD, 1992a) gave a general undertaking to "progressively abolish between one another, in accordance with the provision of Article 2, restrictions on movements of capital to the extent necessary for effective economic cooperation." This included a commitment to national treatment which was expanded in the National Treatment for Foreign Controlled Enterprises Instrument (OECD, 1993). Although the role of the OECD as the regulator of capital flows among its members has been restricted to non-binding rules relating to non-discrimination, it has played an important part in promoting liberalisation of capital movements between nations. Similarly, both the World Bank and the International Monetary Fund have promoted liberalization of capital movements in

developing countries; for example, they have made liberalization of capital movements a condition of loan agreements with some countries.

The main reason for capital liberalization has been a marked change around the
world during the last two decades in perceptions of the benefits of direct foreign
investment. Prior to this, many economists had emphasized negative aspects of foreign investment such as the effects of foreign monopolies on market sharing and
export franchising, the possibility of immiserizing growth and avoidance of corporate
income taxation by transfer pricing. Many governments were suspicious of foreign
investors and doubted the benefits of foreign investment. Today foreign investment is
seen by governments as an important agent of economic growth through the transfer
of technology and management skills, improved access to export markets and
increased competition.

A third factor in recent years is the fear of "investment diversion." As other countries liberalized their restrictions and sought to attract foreign investors, those with
greater restrictions became fearful that investment would be diverted to the former
group of countries. The fear of investment diversion has been most pronounced in
association with the regional freeing of commodity trade and foreign investment. In
particular, East Asian countries are fearful that the preferential access to commodity
markets in the US granted to Canada and Mexico under the NAFTA will divert investment by countries such as Japan from countries outside NAFTA to the US, Canada,
and Mexico.

Some of the simultaneous inward and outward direct foreign investment is within
the same production industries. This two-way intra-industry investment parallels the
intra-industry trade flows for commodity trade and may indeed by related to it, as
noted by Grubel (1979). This suggests too that the growth of direct foreign investment may be due in part to the reduction in border restrictions on commodity trade as
well as to the liberalization of the capital flows themselves.[3] From 1980 to 1992
world merchandise trade expanded steadily at an average compound rate of five percent per year in nominal terms. This is impressive but much slower than the increase
in FDI. In particular, it appears that the regional reduction in trade barriers and other
measures to achieve equal access for all producers within regions such as the European Union and NAFTA have led to a surge of direct foreign investment into these
regions.

III.   INTERNATIONAL REGULATION
OF DIRECT FOREIGN INVESTMENT

The international regulation of national government actions relating to investment
flows between nations takes place at three levels—bilateral, regional, and multilateral
or plurilateral. There are agreements made at each of these levels which seek to regulate in some way the restrictions which individual countries impose on investment
inflows and outflows. Fortunately for the purposes of this paper, APEC (1993) has

published details of the investment regimes of 15 APEC countries (not including Mexico, Papua New Guinea, and Chile) in 1993. This publication was designed to improve the transparency of the national investment procedures and regulations as a way of increasing foreign investment in the region.

Bilateral agreements come in several different forms. Some are binding treaties, such as bilateral investment treaties or investment protection treaties or investment guarantee treaties as they are variously known, and friendship treaties. Some are of less than treaty status such as framework agreements or other statements of general principles. Typically bilateral investment agreements provide for rights of establishment and national treatment, sometimes with exceptions or exclusions, and some provide guarantees for the free transfer of profits and capital funds in and out of the countries, compensation in the event of expropriation and other matters. Friendship, commerce, and navigation treaties are broader and cover trade and consular and navigation and other matters besides investment. There other bilateral agreements which are restricted to particular aspects of these flows such as double taxation treaties or agreements on international competition or dispute settlement.

All of the countries in the APEC region survey except Brunei have bilateral agreements with one or more countries. These agreements are of most concern to the investing source country and are almost always initiated by it. The United States had signed 24 Bilateral Investment Treaties and 47 Friendship, Commerce and Navigation Treaties by 1993. "By the early 1980s, however, the U. S. government decided that because of lack of established multilateral rules governing the treatment of investment it was necessary to develop a bilateral treaty instrument to provide protection for U.S. investment abroad" (APEC, 1993). The countries with which the US has signed bilateral agreements include some APEC countries such as Korea, Thailand and Indonesia. Japan has fewer bilateral agreements. Within the APEC region, it has a Friendship, Commerce and Navigation Treaty with Australia and a Bilateral Investment Treaty with China.

Regional trading agreements sometimes contain provisions relating to foreign investment as the free movement of capital is desirable to obtain the maximum benefit from the free trade provisions. The European Union (formerly the European Community) has provided the precedent for other such agreements. The 1957 Treaty of Rome provided for the free movement of capital among members as one of the "four freedoms" but many barriers to the free movement of capital remained. Subsequently and most importantly after the 1985 White Paper, policies have evolved to establish a Single Market. The Single Market includes a single market for capital in which all investments of all members are treated alike in all respects. This covers tax treatment, competition policy, and other business laws as well as national treatment and rights of establishment. The guarantee of the free movement of capital and access to markets in the EU are the most comprehensive and binding of international agreements at any level. Under the European Economic Area, these freedoms have been extended effectively to the EFTA countries.

Within APEC, the most important regional agreements from the point of view of investment as well as trade are the Canada-U.S. Free Trade Agreement and the North American Free Trade Area. Both of these contain a number of provisions relating to direct foreign investment. One of the objectives of NAFTA is to "increase investment opportunities" and the Agreement contains an Investment Chapter. For the member countries (Canada, US, and Mexico) and from 1 January 1994, this provides national treatment including rights of establishment, most-favored-nation treatment, free movement of funds and binding international arbitration, prohibits expropriation except for "public purposes" and a number of performance requirements such as domestic content and domestic sourcing and exclusive supplier requirements. There are some important exclusions; for example, Canada retains the right of review of direct acquisitions. NAFTA also contains a chapter on regional competition policies.

Regional agreements relating to investment have been signed by the ASEAN (Association of Southeast Asian Nations) members but they are limited to the promotion of joint ventures and industrial cooperation under several schemes—ASEAN Industrial Project, ASEAN Industrial Complementation, and ASEAN Joint Ventures. They do not provide explicitly for national treatment. The Singapore Declaration of 1992 declares that "ASEAN recognizes the complementarity of trade and investment opportunities and therefore encourages, among others, increased cooperation and exchanges among the ASEAN private sectors, and the consideration of appropriate policies for greater intra-ASEAN investments" but this has not yet been translated into concrete measures. The only other regional trading arrangement in the APEC region, the Closer Economic Relations Agreement between Australia and New Zealand, is unusual in that it contains no provisions relating to the movement of capital or investments, though the possibility has been discussed since the formation of the agreement.

Bilateral and regional investment agreements in the APEC region together provide investment protection in the form of rights of establishment and national treatment and some other benefits for a small fraction of intra-APEC direct foreign investments.[4]

At the multilateral level, the main attempt at regulation of government actions has been made by the OECD. The OECD rules and guidelines are contained in several documents. In 1961, as part of its program to liberalize the movement of capital internationally, the OECD members agreed upon the Code of Liberalization of Capital Movements and the Code of Liberalization of Current Invisible Operations. The Code of Liberalization of Capital Movements (OECD, 1992a) sets out member countries' obligations with respect to the right of establishment in foreign countries and the movement of capital. It encourages members to liberalize capital movements and states that no member shall discriminate among countries. It also provides a statement that members shall endeavor to give national treatment to all non-resident-owned assets. The Code of Liberalization of Current Invisible Operations (OECD, 1992b) provides the same rules for "current invisible operations" which include, inter alia, all movements of income from capital, that is, dividends and shares and profits and interest payments. It encourages member countries to liberalize the international movement of income from capital. Between them these two codes cover all investment transactions, both for direct investments and portfolio investments, and three dimensions of non-discrimination. However, member countries were permitted to lodge reservations and temporary derogations to both Codes.

The National Treatment for Foreign-controlled Enterprises was introduced in 1976 as one element of a broader agreement, the Declaration on International Investment and Multinational Enterprises[5] which was adopted by the OECD Ministers in 1976, and strengthened in December 1991. All members of the OECD have adopted the National Treatment Instrument. National Treatment is intended to avoid discrimination against foreign-controlled enterprises and is a vital part of free and equal access to the markets of other countries. Exceptions are permitted for public order, national security, and other exceptions lodged by member countries.

The revision of the OECD National Treatment rules in 1991 introduced a requirement for notification and transparency of all non-conforming measures.

The World Bank has also played a role in the development of principles relating to flows of foreign direct investment. In 1992 theWorld Bank adopted a set of Guidelines on the Treatment of Foreign Direct Investment (World Bank, 1992). Like the OECD principles, these are a set or principles for implementation on a voluntary basis. They cover rights of establishment and transfers of capital and capital income, MFN and national treatment, and expropriation and the settlement of disputes.

In relation to the settlement of foreign investment disputes, the US, Japan, and most APEC countries are parties to the International Centre for Settlement of Investment Disputes (ICSID) Convention . This is an international organization under the aegis of the World Bank. The United Nations Commission on International Trade Law (UNCITRAL) may also be used to resolve disputes. Both of these institutions require that the parties agree to use the facility and that decisions are not binding.

The GATT also deals with measures that breach national treatment through some government measures relating to imports and exports of goods. Article III of the GATT deals with National Treatment on Internal Taxation and Regulation and dates back to 1947. It proscribes the use of import measures such as taxes and restrictions on the purchases of imports which are used to provide protection to domestic production and discriminate against foreign-controlled enterprises if they are a part of the conditions on which they are allowed to operate. GATT articles are binding on all members of the GATT.

The recently concluded Uruguay Round includes two further agreements relating to aspects of foreign investments, the Agreement on Trade-related Investment Measures or TRIMS and the Agreement on Trade-Related Aspects of Intellectual Property Rights (TRIPS) (GATT, 1994). TRIMS is the name now given to trade-related measures which are inconsistent with Article III of the Agreement. Article III of this TRIMS Agreement proscribes such measures: an illustrative list cites such examples as domestic content provisions and restrictions on the use of imported intermediate inputs which had become quite widespread. The Article covers exports as well as imports and it also contains a reaffirmation of the commitment of the Contracting Parties of the GATT to obligations of transparency under Article X of the GATT.

Intellectual property rights are rights relating to the use of private intellectual property. They are important in the transfer internationally of knowledge through foreign investments. TRIPS guarantees national treatment and most-favored-nation treatment with regard to the protection of intellectual property.

There are other bilateral, regional, and multilateral agreements on other aspects of government control of international investment or business. For example, there are many bilateral double taxation agreements and a much more limited number of bilateral agreements on competition policy; for example, the US-EC Agreement on Antitrust Co-operation (see Lloyd & Sampson, 1994, personal communication, for a review of international competition policies.)

In summary, there are numerous bilateral, regional, and multilateral agreements which regulate or restrict in some way national government actions relating to international investments. However, the coverage of these agreements is uneven in terms of the countries which are covered, the principles on which the agreements are based and the enforceability of the provisions. There is undoubtedly a need for a more uniform set of rules.

IV. THE APEC/PECC PROPOSAL

The Report to APEC Ministers of the Eminent Persons Group (1993) included among its recommendations that APEC should adopt an Asia Pacific Investment Code or APIC. It declares that the Code should be based on the fundamental principles of transparency, non-discrimination, right of establishment, and national treatment. The Eminent Persons Group did not seek to draft a Code, but suggested that the PECC draft Code could be used as one basis for developing the APEC Code. The PECC draft Code is therefore the only detailed proposal that can be considered.

There are two sections of the draft PECC Code which contain substantive guidelines. The first and central section deals with the responsibilities of the signatory nations and the second with the responsibilities of the investors. There are also sections dealing with dispute resolution, extensions of the Code, relations to other agreements and institutions, and participation. The Code is intended to apply to all forms of international investment. It is described as voluntary and non-binding, that is, participation is voluntary and the code is non-binding for participants.

The section of the PECC (1993) draft Code dealing with the "responsibilities" of signatories contains eight such responsibilities. These are

1. Transparency
2. Most-Favored-Nation Treatment

3. Establishment of Investments
4. National Treatment
5. Transfers
6. Nationalization and Compensation
7. Performance Requirements
8. Taxation and Investment Incentives

The very first is the principle that, whatever is done by national governments to restrict or regulate foreign investments, it should be transparent.

Responsibilities 2, 3, 4, and 5 deal with what has been called above the four dimensions of non-discrimination in investment. Incentives under Responsibility 8 are the reverse forms of industry intervention which discriminate in favor of foreign investors if they are not offered to domestic investors and Performance Requirements under Responsibility 7 are listed separately from National Treatment though they are a breach of national treatment since they are not normally required of domestic investors. Finally, Nationalization is in effect disestablishment by transfer of ownership to the government of the host country and in most cases domestic enterprises are not simultaneously nationalized. All eight Responsibilities may, therefore, be considered as a set of policies which pursue non-discrimination and transparency.

The Introduction to the draft Code states that "International investment is recognized by all regional economies to be mutually beneficial. Promoting investment based on market-consistent commercial decisions is a positive sum game." (PECC, 1993, p. 5). This is a strong pro-foreign investment statement.

In relation to non-discrimination, it is helpful to consider this term in its broad sense with the four dimenstions listed above. Responsibilities 2 and 5 of the Code contain simple statements of the desirability without exceptions of the principles of most-favored nation treatment and outward transfers of capital and capital income. (If there were restrictions on the movement of capital or current funds by domestic investors out of the country, this would give foreign investors in such instances a right not enjoyed by domestic investors. Such restrictions exist in some countries with exchange control systems, but they have been removed in most industrial countries.)

The most basic of all four aspects of non-discrimination is the right of establishment. The establishment of a foreign investment activity is the first aspect of non-discrimination with national treatment becoming relevant after establishment and the right of establishment is the right of entry into the markets of the host country which is important to promote competition in these markets. Responsibility 3 of the draft Code states "Signatories will *facilitate* foreign investment in all commercial fields and activities *other than those explicitly specified...*" (italics added). It does not, therefore, adopt the principle of unrestricted rights of establishment. There are a number of economic and non-economic grounds on which governments in many countries restrict the entry of foreign owners, especially in such industry as the media, real estate, and financial enterprises.

Responsibility 4 of the draft Code permits exceptions to national treatment which are explicitly specified by each signatory.

The remaining responsibilities are weak. The Responsibility with regard to nationalization lays downs the responsibility that nationalization be carried out on a non-discriminatory basis (that is among foreign nations), in accordance with the due process of law and on payment of compensation. Payment of compensation is an important principle. But the draft Code would permit nationalization "for a public purpose" which is broad enough to permit almost any act of nationalization. The Responsibilities with respect to Performance Requirements and to Taxation and Investment Incentives are merely an undertaking to list them explicitly and make information available to all interested parties, as a consequence of transparency, and to encourage the harmonization of tax and incentive policies. There is no standstill and rollback provision relating to these responsibilities.

The remaining sections are also weak. With respect to dispute settlement, the signatories would undertake to reduce the likelihood of disputes and to consider becoming parties to international legal conventions which are designed to reduce uncertainty and costs involved in international commercial transactions and to facilitate the settlement of investment disputes. With respect to Extensions and Relation to Other Agreements and Institutions, the signatories would merely agree to reconvene for a full review of the Code within five years and to accept the importance of not entering into subsequent obligations whose provisions are not consistent with the Code.

Similarly, the section dealing with the Responsibilities of Investors would commit signatories merely to encourage foreign investors to accept a range of responsibilities and standards of corporate behavior including contributing to the development of science, technology, and human resources of host economies and to sensitivity to local community values and compliance with local laws and regulations.

Hence, the draft Code is essentially a statement of the two general principles of transparency and non-discrimination as principles which should guide the actions of host country governments. The most-favored-nation and transfer aspects of non-discrimination would hold without exception, but the signatories would be permitted to make exceptions in relation to rights of establishment, national treatment, nationalization, and incentives. It does not, therefore, advocate or pursue completely free movement of capital

There is nothing in the draft Code to which exception can be taken on the grounds that it would produce a less efficient allocation of resources in the world economy, though the provisions relating to National Treatment, Performance Requirements, Taxation and Investment Incentives, Nationalization, and to the Responsibilities of Investors seem so weak that they accomplish little.

The fundamental argument in favor of non-discrimination is that discrimination of all forms will, in general, lead to loss of output because it prefers less efficient producers or encourages the use of less efficient methods of production. There is general acceptance of *economic* gains from foreign investment, provided unfair competitive practices and other potential abuses such as transfer pricing are avoided. Much of the recent literature on New Growth Theory emphasizes the positive spillover effects of foreign direct investment on technology transfer and labor training from foreign investments. If there are government taxes or regulations or the absence of regulations in areas such as the environmental effects of production which create negative externalities or distortions, the standard advice is that these should be removed directly for both domestic and foreign investors. There may, however, be other social or non-economic objectives which justify restrictions on foreign ownership of certain assets through restrictions on the rights of establishment; for example, "cultural" industries. The argument for exceptions to national treatment after establishment seem weaker.

Economists question the wisdom of some such restrictions. It is the prerogative of governments to make such decisions. However, it is desirable for governments to develop clear and consistent principles on which the right of establishment or national treatment is denied.

The limitations on nationalization are acceptable. In any case, nationalization of industries has declined greatly in recent years. In many countries governments are now reversing the earlier trend towards more government ownership of enterprises which produced marketable goods and services by offering government owned enterprise for sale. Since the early 1980s the number of acts of nationalization have been outnumbered by the number of acts of privatization (United Nations, 1994, Box I.1) The important issue in privatization cases is whether foreign investors have the right to bid, that is, to establish themselves.

With regard to the responsibilities of foreign investors, it is questionable whether the Code should attempt to influence the behavior of foreign investors in this way. Foreign investors are subject to the laws and regulations of the host country and compliance with these laws is the responsibility of the host country government. It is also the responsibility of host country governments to frame the laws and regulations so that corporate behavior, by both domestic and foreign investors, does not inflict substantial harm on any other parties. Nations do not impose a code of behavior on domestic investors, other than that implicit in national laws and regulations. Consequently, the introduction of such a code could discriminate against foreign investors.

The important issues are what aspects of government actions relating to international investment need better rules or enforcement and whether APEC or some other international body or group of nations is the best forum to pursue the codification of the responsibilities of nations hosting foreign investments.

V. ASSESSMENT OF THE APEC PROPOSAL

Given the unexceptionable nature of the principles in the proposed APIC, the first question is whether the Agreement should go further in terms of the scope of the

Agreement. Section IV noted that the provisions relating to National Treatment, Taxation and Investment Incentives, Performance Requirements, and Nationalization are weak. The draft might strengthen these provisions. And the scope of the Agreement might be widened to include a number of related aspects of investment policies.

In considering the scope of the proposed Agreement, economists commonly regard foreign direct investment as a package of inputs which are transferred to the host country. This package includes technology and intellectual property rights, management practices and marketing skills, and management personnel as well as the transfer of real resources through the capital funds. Hence, the draft Agreement might be extended to include the protection of intellectual property rights and the international movement of business personnel. It might also be extended to include domestic takeover and other competition policies and to international competition policies which seek to regulate the cross-border competitive practices of firms but the latter is probably better treated as a separate problem.

The wider the scope of a proposal the more difficult it will be to achieve multi-country agreement. It seems sensible to limit the scope of the agreement to the main principles of non-discrimination and transparency. There will be differences of opinion among the APEC countries and none has yet considered the proposal.

Various groups other than APEC have called recently for review of some aspects of international investment. The OECD has been considering the possibility of an investment instrument which would bring together its existing Codes and the National Treatment Instrument and possibly add other elements such as competition policy and intellectual property protection. The World Investment Report of the United Nations (1993) called for new international agreements on investment issues. The European Business Roundtable, a group of business leaders, revived the idea current in the early eighties of a GATT for Investment which would extend the trade covered by this body to capital movements, like the Uruguay Round extension of the GATT to trade in services. (The Economist, 1993).

All of these proposals and the APIC are principally concerned with the basic rights of establishment and other aspects of non-discrimination. Thus, there is widespread agreement that the present rules relating to non-discrimination are not adequate, though they are adhered to much more frequently than was the case a decade and more ago.

The two OECD Codes lay down the principles of non-discrimination with respect to rights of establishment and most-favored-nation treatment and transfers, though they permit reservations with respect to rights of establishment. The GATT Article on National Treatment is binding on all contracting parties, but it is not clear how far this extends beyond national treatment relating to import measures. Similarly, the OECD National Treatment Instrument lays down the principle of national treatment and allows for exceptions and has been adopted by all members of the OECD. The GATT and the OECD have also been pressing strongly in recent years for transparency.

Hence, APIC would not add significantly to existing OECD and GATT principles of transparency and non-discrimination. Similarly, the coverage of principles in the

PECC proposal is almost the same as that in NAFTA. Indeed, the APEC document has drawn on the principles contained in these earlier international agreements and codes as well as bilateral agreements.

An APEC Code could, however, considerably strengthen the world rules relating to direct foreign investment in a number of ways. It could develop principles which would limit the permitted exceptions to rights of establishment and national treatment (including performance requirements). It could similarly develop principles limiting national subsidies and incentives which are proliferating as competition for foreign direct investment intensifies and which are, in my opinion, now one of the major problems with national government actions relating to direct foreign investment flows. The proposed APIC "standstill and rollback" provision for the exceptions to rights of establishment and national treatment strengthens the standstill and rollback provisions of the OECD Codes which apply to rights of establishment but not to the national treatment instrument.

The second question is how the basic principles on which there has been agreement for quite a long time can be adopted by more countries and enforced. The difficulties of achieving international agreement on a principle increase as the number of countries increases.

One choice in the promotion of these principles is between action at the regional level or the multilateral level. It has been argued by some academic writers that regional level agreements are likely to achieve greater scope because there are fewer countries involved (see Bora, 1992 and Guisinger, 1993). Countries in a region may also be more similar in terms of their laws and policy orientation. It is notable that the two agreements which have gone furtherest in scope and binding commitments, the European Union and NAFTA, are regional agreements among contiguous countries within a comprehensive regional trading arrangement.

From this point of view of a regional or a multilateral agreement, the APEC countries are not a region in either the sense of a group of contiguous countries which trade heavily with each other or in the sense of a regional trading arrangement in the form of a customs union or free trade area. The APEC should be considered as a group of diverse and widely separated countries, essentially similar to the OECD and overlapping substantially in country membership with that group. (The discussion below is based on the premise that APEC will not become a regional trading arrangement.[6]) The intention of PECC and the Eminent Persons Group is that the rights accepted by members under a Code be extended to all trading partners. APIC is a multilateral[7] rather than a regional code.

The simultaneous discussions in the OECD and APEC of new investment guidelines or rules pose a danger of new parallel multilateral rules which will complicate the international regime. PECC itself stated emphatically that "Any new code should avoid creating a new layer of rules; it should encourage the simplification, or reduction, of rules in order to facilitate international investment" (PECC, 1993). Possible overlap and conflict between OECD and APEC proposals could be avoided if APEC and the OECD cooperate.

Both the OECD and the draft APIC are trying to achieve the same general principles but the country membership differs substantially: The East Asian countries other than Japan and Korea are not members of the OECD and conversely the European countries are not members of APEC. Asian countries which are not members of the OECD should have a say in the evolution of international rules relating to foreign direct investment. On the other hand, the OECD has valuable experience in the administration of national treatment and other aspects of non-discrimination through the work of the Committee on International Investment and Multinational Enterprises which is responsible for the implementation of the National Treatment Instrument and other measures and the Committee on Capital Movements and Invisible Transactions which is responsible for the implementation of the two Codes of Liberalization. Hence, both institutions should cooperate in the development of principles and rules for foreign investment.

At present, as noted in Section IV, the OECD, the GATT, and the World Bank all play an important part in the present regulation of government actions relating to international investment. There is an advantage to having only one multilateral organization regulating national governments in this area.

In the long run, the new World Trade Organization may be the best institution in which to embed the principles and law relating to international investment. Both the PECC draft Code and the Eminent Persons report were drawn up when the prospect that the Uruguay Round would be satisfactorily concluded were uncertain. This uncertainty has been removed though the Final Act has not yet been ratified by the US and other countries.

The existing GATT and the WTO are based upon the principles of non-discrimination including MFN and national treatment in relation to trade in goods and these principles have been extended to services under the GATS in the WTO. They could be extended to international investments within the one agreement. The WTO already contains the Agreement on TRIMS which covers what are called "trade-related" aspects of performance requirements in the APIC, and the Agreement on TRIPS. In addition, the WTO may consider international competition policy as a part of its future work agenda once it is established.

The GATT/WTO has other advantages. The country coverage of the GATT is already much larger than that of the OECD or APEC regions. It now exceeds 125 and is growing rapidly as more developing and transition economies, many of which refrained from joining or withdrew from the GATT, are joining after the completion of the Uruguay Round negotiations.

More importantly, the GATT is hard binding law, unlike the OECD codes and the proposed APIC. The Final Act of the Uruguay Round distinguishes between multilateral and plurilateral agreements. Multilateral Agreements are agreements which are binding and in the context of the GATT are signed by all parties or members. (These include the GATS and TRIPS and TRIMS.) By contrast, plurilateral agreements are not binding and are accepted only by those parties or members which agree to sign them. One of the most important achievements of the Uruguay

Round was that some of the previous non-binding codes were incorporated into the "single undertaking" and made binding on all contracting parties. In addition, the new dispute settlement procedures agreed upon in the Uruguay Round greatly strengthen the enforcement of its rules.

PECC itself saw APIC as a basis for a subsequent set of binding multilateral guidelines, possibly in the GATT. The addition of comprehensive rules for non-discrimination in capital movements within the GATT/WTO will, however, be a major task that will take many years, even if the members of the WTO agree upon the issues.

In the interim, APEC can certainly develop and promote the principles of a transparent and non-discriminatory treatment of foreign investment in the region and work towards the establishment of a binding multilateral agreement on investment. An APEC Code could assist the evolution of the principles, but it is doubtful that a code which is non-binding, restricted in its country coverage and scope and whose main provisions duplicate that of the OECD codes and instruments and to a considerable extent the GATT/WTO, will strengthen the observance of these principles.

ACKNOWLEDGEMENTS: I would like to acknowledge the suggestions made by Bijit Bora.

NOTES

1.   Although they are equal conceptually, there is a substantial shortfall of the total inflows into the reporting countries compared to the total outflows from the source countries.

2.   There is no agreed way of classifying these aspects of discrimination. For example, the rights of establishment may be regarded as an aspect of national treatment, as in the NAFTA chapter on foreign investment. Or, non-performance requirements may be separated from other aspects of national treatment, as in the draft APIC.

3.   Some barriers may attract foreign investment as access to the markets via exports is difficult with high barriers, but such defensive foreign investment is less important now.

4.   It is not possible to be more precise as the information given in the APEC volume about bilateral investment arrangements by one party sometimes conflicts with that given by the other party.

5.   The Declaration on International Investment and Multinational Enterprises (reproduced in OECD, 1993c, Annex I) contains Guidelines for Multinational Enterprises. These seek to lay down principles which will be observed by the multinational enterprises rather than the governments. They are voluntary and not legally enforceable.

6.   If more recent proposals from the Prime Minister of Australia and others to convert the APEC into a regional trading arrangement should eventuate this would substantially strengthen the case for an APEC Code. The commitment of the members to regional integration in this event and the development of rules relating to trade and possibly also intellectual property rights and TRIMS and other investment-related policies would increase the likelihood of acceptance and the effectiveness of an investment agreement within a regional trading arrangement.

7.   The term multilateral is used here in the common sense of an agreement which includes many countries and is not restricted in its membership. In the new Uruguay Round terminology of the GATT, it is a plurilateral code since it is a voluntary non-binding code. See the text below.

REFERENCES

Asia Pacific Economic Cooperation. (1993). Guide to the investment regimes of the fifteen APEC member countries (First Edition). APEC Informal Group on Regional Trade Liberalization. Singapore: APEC.

Bora, B. (1992). Conceptualizing the issues regarding alternative investment arrangements. In Pangestu, M. (Ed.), *Pacific initiatives for regional trade liberalization and investment cooperation.* Singapore: Pacific Economic Cooperation Council.

_____ . 1994. Investment cooperation in the Asia-Pacific region: The PECC Asia-Pacific investment code. In *New directions in regional trade liberalization.* Taipei: Taiwan Institute for Economic Research.

Eminent Persons Group. (1993). *A vision for APEC: Towards an Asia Pacific economic community, report of the eminent persons Group to APEC Ministers.* October. Singapore: APEC.

General Agreement on Tariffs and Trade. (1994). Uruguay round final act. Geneva: United States Government Printing Office.

Grubel, H. G. (1979). Towards a theory of two-way trade in capital assets. In H. Giersch (Ed.), *On the economics of intra-industry trade.* Tubingen, Germany: J. C. B. Mohr.

Guisinger, S. (1991). Foreign direct investment flows in East and Southeast Asia: Policy issues. *ASEAN Economic Bulletin, 8,* 29-46.

Guisinger, S. (1993). A pacific basin investment agreement. *ASEAN Economic Bulletin, 19,* 176-183.

International Monetary Fund. (1993). Balance of payments yearbook 1993, Part 2. Washington, D. C: Author.

McCulloch, R. (1991). Foreign investment in the United States. *The Annals of the American Academy of the Social Sciences, 516,* 169-182.

Organization for Economic Cooperation and Development. (1990). *Liberalization of capital movements and financial services in the OECD area.* Paris: Author.

_____ . (1992a). Code of liberalization of capital movements. Paris: Author.

_____ . (1992b). Code of liberalization of current invisible operations. Paris: Author.

_____ . (1993). National treatment for foreign-controlled enterprises. Paris: Author.

Pacific Economic Cooperation Council (PECC). (1993). Encouraging international investment in the Asia Pacific region: A draft Asia Pacific code. Jakarta, Indonesia: Centre for Strategic and International Studies.

The Economist. (1993). A new GATT for investment. *The Economist, 18*(Sept.), 73.

United Nations. (1993). World investment report. New York: Author.

United Nations. (1994). World investment report. New York: Author.

The World Bank. (1992). *Legal framework of the treatment of foreign investment: Vol. II. Guidelines.* Washington, D. C.: Author.

Yamazawa, I. (1993). *Economic integration in the Asia-Pacific region and the options for Japan.* Tokyo: Japanese Ministry of Foreign Affairs.

Received: August, 1994; Revised: January, 1995

[17]

Competition policy in APEC

Principles of harmonisation

P. J. Lloyd

The international dimensions of competition policy have become a 'new issue' in international economic policy in recent years.[1] The proximate cause of this growing concern is an increasing frequency of disputes among governments or producers over alleged anticompetitive behaviour that involves two or more nations. In the World Trade Organisation (WTO), the primary concern is that anticompetitive behaviour by producer agents may restrict international trade in goods and services and reduce the benefits of the General Agreement on Tariffs and Trade (GATT) liberalisation of government barriers to this trade. In the Organisation for Economic Cooperation and Development (OECD), the concern is with the growing problems of national competition authorities in administering their national competition laws. There is, however, an underlying reason for these concerns — namely, the increasingly international nature of competition which has resulted from the reduction in border barriers to international trade in goods, services and capital. This trend is likely to continue. Consequently, the international dimensions of competition policy are certain to become more prominent in the international forums.

The Asia Pacific Economic Cooperation (APEC) debate on competition policies reflects this wider concern. Competition policy is one of the 15 specific areas designated in the 1995 Osaka Action Plan. The focus in these plans is on the development of national competition policies in all member countries and cooperation among members.

The second section of this chapter discusses the nature of the new issues in competition policy. The third section reviews the APEC work programme and the fourth section outlines the diversity among APEC countries in their national competition policies. The fifth section examines how these diverse national policies might be harmonised and the sixth section considers whether harmonisation is desirable. Some conclusions are presented in the final section.

THE INTERNATIONAL DIMENSION OF COMPETITION POLICY

Globalisation has raised new issues of competition policy. Many markets which were previously segmented are now imperfectly accessible. Foreign producers have become less tolerant of behaviour which they see as anticompetitive and as posing a threat to their access to foreign markets, either through direct exporting or through the establishment of foreign affiliates. As the perception of these barriers to competing in foreign markets has increased, private producers and governments, acting as the agents of producers, have sought ways of reducing anticompetitive behaviour in other countries.

Increasingly in the OECD, and now the WTO, the notion of the international contestability of markets is being used as a framework for analysing issues of international trade and competition.[2] This use of the notion of contestability has been adopted from industrial organisation theory. A contestable market requires the absence of restrictions, in the public or private sector, on entry and investment as well as access to the markets of the products. In the case of those services which involve a commercial presence or the movement of natural persons, market access can only be achieved by market presence and this requires free movement of capital and persons.

The fundamental difficulty in developing cross-border competition policies to make markets more contestable is that competition policies are based on national competition laws.[3] There has been no multilateral organisation and no substantial multilateral rules relating to cross-border competition. While the WTO contains some international law relating to some areas of competition, the coverage is still extremely limited. In particular, the WTO is confined to regulating the activities of governments, not private producers. It is not an adjudicating body for actions involving competition polices; it has no powers of investigation and no fines or remedies can be imposed on governments, let alone private agents, and private persons cannot bring actions.[4]

National laws differ in the extent to which they cover conduct beyond their national borders, but in all cases the ability to pursue actions in other countries is limited. Countries may base the jurisdiction on the doctrines of territoriality, or nationality or effects. Under the principle of territoriality a state may exercise its jurisdiction over all persons (including corporations), whether local or foreign, within its territory. This prevents the reach of its laws beyond its jurisdiction unless the government can persuade the governments of other countries to take actions in their territories to support the actions of the competition authorities of the home government. The principle of nationality allows a state to exercise its jurisdiction within its territory over its nationals who reside abroad. This extends the jurisdiction to a subset of persons residing outside the home country. Under the effects doctrine, a state claims the right to take actions against persons outside its jurisdiction for conduct which has effects within its borders. This extends the jurisdiction to the subset of persons residing outside the home country whose actions affect residents of the home country.

The most prevalent doctrine is territoriality. Some countries extend the reach of their competition laws to their citizens resident in other countries. A few, most notably the

United States and in some respects the European Union and Canada, apply the effects doctrine.[5]

It is this coexistence of *global* markets with *national* jurisdictions which causes the search for mechanisms to cover cross-border competition problems. These mechanisms range from an extension of national powers through bilateral agreements based on cooperation among nations at one end of the spectrum of powers to the development of an international competition law administered by a multilateral authority at the other. The options will not be reviewed here.[6]

A consensus seems to be emerging, in some countries at least, that it will not be feasible or desirable at the present time to seek a multilateral form of international competition policies. The Chairman of the US Federal Trade Commission has recently stated that a world antitrust code 'is not going to happen in the near future' (Pitofsky 1996). Another US author states his beliefs even more strongly:

> The opinion of this author is that it is highly unlikely that countries will agree in my own lifetime to the creation of an EU-like mechanism in the domain of competition policy at the level of the WTO, i.e. one where an agency along the lines of DG [Directorate General] IV [of the European Union] is given powers to implement and enforce competition applicable to all WTO member nations (Graham 1995, p. 112).

A growing number of authors are recommending a more gradual approach.[7] Looking forward to the debate at the Singapore Ministerial Meeting of the WTO, the European Union commissioned a group of independent experts to consider the role of competition policy in the WTO. The report of this group (European Union 1996) preferred a gradual building-block approach, recommending the development of national competition policies in all countries, a core of common principles and cooperation under bilateral agreements and through the OECD recommendations. A similar view has been put forward in Australia (see Productivity Commission 1996; and Lloyd 1996). In Canada, Crampton and Witterick (1996) have advocated a two-track approach, one track being bilateral cooperation and the development of a set of minimum standards, and the other being international dispute settlement. Bliss (1996) reaches similar conclusions.

A gradual approach is usually associated with a preference for plurilateral (non-binding) agreements rather than multilateral (binding) agreements. A plurilateral agreement may be a stepping stone to an eventual multilateral agreement.

In this environment, the harmonisation of national laws is an important component of the gradualist options. This term encompasses the development of national policies in countries which have none and the development of a core of common principles or minimum standards, but there are many options within harmonisation.

THE APEC WORK PROGRAMME ON COMPETITION POLICIES

At the Osaka meeting in December 1995, the APEC economic leaders adopted an Action Plan. The plan included action in 15 specific areas, of which 'competition policy' was one. The objective of the plan in this area read:

> APEC economies will enhance the competitive environment in the Asia–Pacific region by introducing or maintaining effective and adequate competition policy and/or laws and associated enforcement policies, ensuring the transparency of the above, and promoting cooperation among the APEC countries, thereby maximizing, inter alia, the efficient operation of markets, competition among producers and traders, and consumer benefits (APEC 1995, p. 19).

The guidelines called upon the member countries to review their competition policies, to implement technical assistance in regard to policy development among them as appropriate and to establish appropriate cooperation arrangements among the APEC economies with regard to competition policies.

Under the Action Plan, members are to develop both 'collective action plans' and individual country 'action plans' for this area, as with other areas. The collective action plan will encourage cooperation among the competition authorities of APEC economies with regard to information exchange, notification and consultation and examination of the interrelationships between competition policies and laws and other policies related to trade and investment. It provides for the development of a training programme in the area. Perhaps of most importance in the long run, it asks members to consider developing non-binding principles on competition policy and laws in APEC.

The APEC Committee on Trade and Investment (CTI) has coordinated the development of the collective action plans in this area. To carry out this function, it held two workshops on competition policy and was working towards the establishment in 1997 of an APEC database on competition policies, laws and regulations. The CTI meeting in February 1996 agreed to merge the work areas of competition policies and deregulation in the APEC countries but the collective action plans for the two areas would be separate. The workshop noted the central role of competition policy in enhancing economic efficiency and observed that the globalisation of business is creating new challenges for competition policy. The collective action plan which incorporates these developments was presented to the Leaders' Meeting in Subic Bay but this was not a priority area for delivering immediate actions at the meeting. A decision was made to hold a further workshop on competition policy and deregulation in 1997 with a view to continuing the exchange of ideas and policy dialogue in these areas.

Thus the outcome of this process to date has been to establish a dialogue among members on competition policies and laws. The emphasis on cooperation and the consideration of a set of non-binding principles may lead to the harmonisation of competition policies in the APEC region on a plurilateral basis.

APEC DIVERSITY IN COMPETITION LAWS

Before examining inter-country differences in competition policy, it is necessary to define these competition policies. There is some difficulty in defining the scope of these policies. A broad definition would encompass all government policies which affect competition in markets. However, this is open-ended and too broad as many government policies which are not addressed at competition in markets do affect competition incidentally in some industries; such policies include, import restrictions, foreign investment regulations and industrial policies. More narrowly, one can define competition policies as those which are intended to promote free competition among producers. These policies plainly include antitrust law and exclude government policies such as privatisation, foreign investment regulation and regulation or deregulation. (Some commentators express this difference by referring to competition law as distinct from competition policy in the broad sense.) There are grey areas such as subsidies or state aid and consumer protection which are regarded as part of competition policy in some countries but not in others.

A narrow definition is preferable as it contains the scope of the discussion and makes agreement among countries more achievable. For the same reasons, it would be better, at least in the early stages, to omit grey areas.

APEC has adopted the narrower definition with the addition of consideration of the links between competition policies on the one hand and other policies related to trade and investment. The CTI meeting in February 1996 agreed to merge the work areas of competition policies and deregulation in the APEC countries.

As part of the preparation for the CTI work programme, the New Zealand officials conducted a survey of the competition policies of APEC member countries in 1994.[8]

There is great diversity among the APEC countries in terms of their national competition policies, much greater in fact than in their policies with respect to international trade in goods and services or foreign investment. In East Asia at the present time, six member countries — Hong Kong, Indonesia, Malaysia, Papua New Guinea, the People's Republic of China and Singapore — do not have comprehensive competition policies. All have some policies which can be regarded as elements of a competition policy. For those countries which do have comprehensive competition policies, the coverage of these policies differs greatly.

The difficulty in the description of these competition policies is that they are multi-dimensional. One dimension or element is the specific rules which apply to outcomes. In the case of competition policies, these are types of horizontal or vertical restraints or mergers — price fixing, bid rigging, market sharing, retail price maintenance, and so on. Another element is remedies. Other elements are the territorial application of the rules and the extent of private actions. Yet other elements are the objectives of competition policy, the principles and the methods of analysis of competition policies.

Enforcement of policies is as important as the substance of the policies. Lack of enforcement is one of the major causes of disputes between countries in the area of competition policies, such as the Kodak–Fuji dispute, for instance. Some have also suggested a form of dispute settlement for this area.

The tabulation of national competition policies done for APEC by the New Zealand government classifies the competition policies of the APEC countries according to types of horizontal and vertical restraints, sanctions 'enforcement, remedies and penalties' and 'international application'.

In Chapter 6 of this volume, Bollard and Vautier have taken seven aspects of elements of competition policies from these tables and tabulated the results. From this information, they have constructed a novel index of similarity of the competition policies of a pair of countries. This index has a maximum value of 100 (or 1 if each element is scored on the interval from 0 to +1). Hence, it measures the extent to which two countries have adopted the same competition policy rules in their competition law. For a pair of countries, an increase in this index over time represents convergence.

There are 11 APEC countries which have comprehensive competition policies and Bollard and Vautier have considered seven elements of competition law. These pair-wise indexes differ greatly. They range from a low of 14 for New Zealand–Thailand and Mexico–Philippines, indicating little similarity between these pairs of countries in their competition policies, to a high of 77 for Australia–New Zealand, indicating a close similarity for this pair.

One can construct a multilateral index of the similarity of competition policies among a group of countries by averaging the bilateral indexes (see Appendix 7.1). A multilateral index can be used to measure similarity across a set of countries such as APEC. An increase in the multilateral index over time would represent multilateral convergence of competition policies. For the countries in Bollard and Vautier's sample, the multilateral index is 36, which is a rather low figure, indicating little similarity among those APEC countries which do have competition policies.

Tabulations of elements of competition law can be interpreted in different ways. Levinsohn (1966, p. 331) partitions the competition policies of nations into five groups according to the degree of liberality. These range from the lax or *laissez-faire* (such as Singapore and Hong Kong) to the most strict, with no or few exemptions and with *per se* prohibitions in all markets. In between these extremes are the groups of countries which apply the rule of reason to some or all markets. One group applies the rule of reason to domestic but not to export markets, a second group applies it to both domestic and export markets; and a third group applies strict *per se* rules to domestic but not to export markets. This is a useful but rough categorisation which emphasises the distinctions between the rule of reason and strict rules and between export and domestic markets.

There are examples of these types in the Asia Pacific region. At the most lax extreme lie Singapore and Hong Kong and other countries with no comprehensive competition policy. At the strictest end of the spectrum generally is the United States. In between, Japan is an example of a country which enforces a fairly strict policy in domestic markets but is lax in export markets.

HARMONISATION — WHAT IS IT?

The notion of harmonisation is vague. 'Harmonization can be loosely defined as making the regulatory requirements or government policies of different jurisdictions identical, or at least similar' (Leebron 1996, p. 43). That is, harmonisation is convergence of requirements or policies. Harmonisation of domestic policies across countries has been debated in several areas of policy as an adjunct of international trade liberalisation.[9] These areas include all of the 'new issues' in the WTO — environmental standards, labour standards and competition policies — and tax policies (see Bhagwati and Hudec 1996). The literature on the harmonisation of competition policies is sparse.

In some policy areas, the notion of harmonisation is straightforward as there is only one object to be harmonised and this object has a parameter or value which can be located on a single dimensional continuum. This applies, for example, to harmonisation of the tariff rate for some tariff item or to the excise tax rate for some excisable commodity. For a group of countries, each country has a single parameter which might be harmonised among them, as in a Common External Tariff or a common schedule of excise tax rates. In all such cases, there will be debate about the level at which the rates should be harmonised but the concept of harmonisation is unambiguous.

In the area of competition policy, there are examples of elements which can be measured on a line. Where there is discretion, competition tests may apply, such as tests of dominance or market power and merger thresholds. These concepts are, in principle at least, measurable on a continuum. Tests of dominance use market shares or concentration ratios which lie on an interval of the real line (from zero to one). Merger thresholds are in value terms (zero to infinity).

Most elements of competition policy, however, cannot be portrayed on a line or continuum. Some restraints are binary variables; for example, either there is price fixing or collusion or exclusion or whatever, or there is not. A country may have a competition policy in regard to some restraint or it may not. Some authorities apply the rule of reason whereas other authorities prohibit them *per se*. For some restraints, there are exemptions for some industries or enterprises (such as state-owned enterprises or exporters or intra-state traders). All such elements can be regarded as a binary variable which takes on two values — one if some property holds and zero if it does not.

Where the elements are binary variables, harmonisation takes the form of all countries agreeing to one of the two alternatives. For example, they might all agree to have competition policies relating to price fixing and to ban the practice *per se* or to make it authorisable. Or, they might all agree on common objectives of competition policies (such as efficiency in the allocation of resources) – that is, to include rather than to exclude a list of objectives. Or they might agree on common principles (such as national treatment, non-discrimination, transparency and the rule of law). Or they might agree on common methods of analysis (such as market definition and analysis and the identification and analysis of entry barriers). Or they might agree on common enforcement procedures. This type of harmonisation might be called qualitative harmonisation as distinct from the harmonisation of, say, tariff rates, which might be called quantitative harmonisation. Harmonisation of competition policies is predominantly qualitative harmonisation.

For any one element, the most extreme form of multilateral harmonisation would be for all APEC countries to agree to adopt the same values, either qualitative (0 or 1) or values on some line interval. Complete convergence across countries would be achieved if all agreed to adopt the same standard for all elements — that is, a single uniform law among all nations. This could be achieved in several ways. All countries could agree to adopt a uniform law. Alternatively, the establishment of a multilateral competition authority would result in a single uniform law among all nations. Another possibility which has been discussed in the literature on harmonisation of competition policies is the development of some 'model', a composite of the laws of several countries perhaps. All of these forms of multilateral harmonisation are extremely unlikely, given the diversity of policies and views among countries. Partial convergence could be achieved by uniformity among a subset of countries or uniformity among a subset of elements of competition policy.

There are so many elements of competition policy that even partial harmonisation could not, at least initially, address all of them. Hence harmonisation will inevitably be restricted to a limited number of elements. This form of harmonisation of competition policies is known as 'minimum standards' (or what might be called weak qualitative harmonisation). It may be achievable and is the most likely form.

There are two aspects to minimum standards. First, there is the choice of the set of elements which is to be included. They might be restricted to a small set, a 'core'.[10] Second, there is the choice of standard for each element which is included.

In relation to the choice of elements of competition policy to be included, discussions of harmonisation of competition policy tend to produce lists of items which are believed to be more important or more easily implemented. For example, Crampton and Witterick (1996, p. 5) single out five restraints as forming the core of any competition policy: these are exclusionary behaviour by dominant firms, price fixing, bid rigging, market allocations and boycotts of distributors carrying products of foreign or other low-cost suppliers. Crampton and Witterick call these 'the most egregious of private anticompetitive restraints'. One can add objectives, principles or instruments/remedies or jurisdictions to the list of selected items.

In relation to the choice of common standards for each element of competition policy which is included in the set, such standards may already exist in one member government. It is extremely unlikely that any single country's policies would be chosen given the diversity of views among APEC countries. Alternatively, a standard could be a composite or model standard.

For any set of elements and any chosen standard for each element, the competition policies of a group of countries will become harmonised as the countries adopt these minimum standards. (The Index of Similarity developed in Appendix 7.1 has the desired properties that it will increase as partial convergence occurs and will reach unity with uniformity of policies.)

There is a danger that harmonisation could result in a lowering of efficiency through the adoption of the lowest common denominator by all countries. This problem has arisen with environmental standards and tax rates, in what has been called the 'race to the bottom' — see Bhagwati and Hudec (1996, Chs 10–11). In the context of harmonisation of competition policies where most standards are binary variables, the objections of some countries could result in the omission of some aspects of competition policy from the core, but it is unlikely to result in those countries which already have policies in these areas following the example of those which do not.

In principle, the choice of standards should be that which maximises the gains from harmonisation. This requires an understanding of the benefits and costs of harmonisation.

THE BENEFITS AND COSTS OF HARMONISATION

Harmonisation is not an end in itself. Harmonisation of competition policies is generally believed to have two primary benefits.

The first benefit is a reduction in transactions costs, including uncertainty. This refers specifically to the compliance and enforcement costs associated with doing business across jurisdictions. Leebron (1996, p. 53) notes that the elimination of these costs does not require uniformity of policies. Rather, this can be achieved instead by deciding which jurisdiction the policies and laws apply to.

The second benefit relates to an increase in the efficiency of markets. This should be interpreted as Pareto-efficiency in the world economy and as such it includes improvements in efficiency due to improvements in the allocation of production among producers and commodities and improvements in the allocation of aggregate world production among consumers. The ultimate concern is with the welfare of consumers or users, though this includes income effects as well as price effects.

The size of the benefits from harmonisation will depend on the pattern of harmonisation and, in particular, the standards or levels which are chosen. If the best standards are adopted for any element, it would seem that the region will gain from harmonisation since this implies the replacement of inferior competition standards by superior standards. But what is the 'best'? Is the standard which is best from the point of view of one country also the best from the point of view of other countries and the world?

The 'best' policy depends upon the effects of the choice on market efficiency since any harmonised standards will eliminate the costs of doing business across jurisdictions with different policies — the costs of disharmony.

An issue here is whether there is a single best choice for every element of competition policy. Principles of economic behaviour and analysis are universal — that is, the same principles apply to all countries. Certain restraints may be universally condemned as unquestionably harmful in all markets in all countries: for example, price fixing and bid rigging. These should be prohibited *per se* in all countries under the harmonised standard. In cases where the rule of reason applies, the same principles should be used to analyse each case. This implies that if the same circumstances arose with respect to actions in two (or more) countries, the same competition policy decisions would be taken, but it also allows the circumstances of the individual country markets to be taken into account where they differ. For other restraints, however, it may be necessary to have some variation among countries in best choices to allow for local conditions and differences in legal or regulatory sophistication.

In some cases the question of the best choice is uncertain because the benefits and costs may be distributed so that one or more countries will gain and one or more will lose from the adoption of a harmonised standard. Is 'best' defined from the point of view of the world? This choice would be analogous to the national interest provision at the level of competition policy decisions by a national competition authority. This world view has been advocated by Crampton and Witterick (1996) and Fox and Ordover (1995), subject to preservation of some national autonomy in the latter case.

We need to analyse possible cases of cross-country harmonisation, using economic models of the industries concerned. A large literature has emerged in the last ten years which models international trade in markets that are imperfectly competitive. This draws heavily on recent developments in the theory of industrial organisation. A basic problem with the literature from the point of view of considering the effects of harmonisation of national competition policies is that the outcome in any market is highly sensitive to the particular specification of the model. It makes a great difference as to whether the products traded are homogeneous or differentiated, whether there are constant or decreasing unit costs and whether the oligopolies are

Cournot or Bertrand competitors, and so on. There is a second body of literature in which models with imperfectly competitive markets have been used to analyse the effects of trade policies such as the introduction of tariffs or export subsidies. This is the so-called 'new trade theory'.[11]

However, the models in industrial organisation and new trade theory have rarely been used to analyse the interaction of trade and competition policy or the effects of the cross-country harmonisation of competition policies. To find how the adoption of a harmonised standard would affect competition and decisions by competition authorities, it is useful to consider some examples.

Example 1: export cartels

Several countries which are members of APEC exempt export cartels from their competition policies. They include Australia and New Zealand, Canada, the United States, Japan, Korea and Taiwan (Productivity Commission 1996, Table 3.1). Other countries exempt state trading authorities which operate export cartels. These state-owned traders are probably the purest examples of export cartels. They are common in developing and transition economies but there are also important examples in Australia, New Zealand and Canada.

The economic analysis of this case is straightforward. Export cartels increase the price in world markets of the commodities controlled by the cartel. They have, therefore, a terms of trade effect. There is a standard theorem of international economics which shows that an improvement in the terms of trade increases the welfare of the exporting country and lowers that of the importing country. Moreover, the combined world market gains from the removal of the price discrimination in the market. Thus, harmonisation of competition standards which included agreement for all participating countries to remove the exemption from national competition laws for all export cartels will yield world gains.

Export cartels may have further effects on the degree of competition in domestic markets and may distort the allocation of investment funds. It seems likely that strengthening competition laws to eliminate these cartels would yield further benefits if such effects are present.

Example 2: price fixing

Levinsohn (1996, pp. 345–50) provides one of the few examples of the analysis of the harmonisation of competition policies of two countries. It relates to actual or potential cartels operating in the home market of one of two countries. The two countries produce a homogeneous product under constant returns to scale conditions. One country has a lax competition policy permitting a domestic cartel which raises the domestic price and the other has a strict policy outlawing a cartel.

168   *Competition policy in APEC: principles of harmonisation*

In choosing the harmonisation standard, there is a conflict between the interests of producers and consumers within each country. However, both producer interests and consumer interest coincide across countries; what is good for producers in one country is good for producers in the other country, and the same holds for consumers. Essentially, a tolerant competition policy which permits cartelisation in one country has effects which spill over into the other country, benefiting its producers and harming its consumers.

The outcome of harmonisation depends on whether the harmonisation adopts the standards of the lax country or those of the strict country. To assess the change in welfare in each country, the welfare of the producer and consumer groups are weighted equally. Under the adoption of the standards of the strict country, the country with the lax standards may gain or lose and the country with the strict standard gains and the world gains. The possibility that the country with the lax standards may gain contrasts with the result of Example 1, in which there is a clear conflict of interest between the exporting and importing countries. Under the adoption of the standards of the lax country, the country with the strict policy loses, the country with the lax standard gains, and the world loses.

Hence, the choice of standard clearly matters. The main lesson from this example is that harmonisation should be towards the standards of the country which has the more pro-competitive policy. This follows the intuition of basic economics, as Levinsohn noted.

Example 3: mergers

The cross-hauling model of oligopoly can be used to illustrate merger policy. This model is a generalisation of the Levinsohn model. It has been widely used in the analysis of trade with imperfect competition and has been used in discussions of cross-country harmonisation of competition policies (see Bliss 1996; and Richardson 1996). It assumes that there is only one good produced by the industry and there are two (or more) countries. There are a fixed number of producers in each country, and producers of each country sell in each other's markets. There are economies of scale due to fixed costs and constant marginal costs. Competition in the world markets is Cournot. The model is described in Appendix 7.2.

The competition policy of governments is now introduced through merger controls which allow the governments of each country to determine the number of domestic firms.[12] If one country adopts a tougher competition policy which increases the number of domestic firms, the world market price falls. For this country exports increase and imports fall as the share of this country's domestic producers increases in both countries (Bliss 1996). Aggregate country profits fall in the home country and in the foreign country. Thus, as in the Levinsohn model, there is a conflict between the interests of producers and consumers, and producer and consumer interests coincide across countries. Lowering barriers to international trade increases the interpenetration of national markets and increases the importance of competition policies.

To model harmonisation of merger policies, we may suppose that countries differ in terms of the toughness of their merger polices, perhaps because they give a different weighting to producer interests *vis-à-vis* consumer interests. If the country with the less tough merger policy standards adopts those of the other, the number of firms will increase in this country and in the world markets. Consumers will gain and the producers will lose in both countries, as in the Levinsohn model. Both countries gain if we weight the welfare of consumer and producer groups equally. The country which tightens its merger policies and increases the number of its domestic firms actually gains more as the decrease in the profit margins of its firms is partially offset by the addition of profits of the extra firm or firms. The world as a whole gains.

Thus, such harmonisation is beneficial. And, again, the beneficial harmonisation is the one which adopts the standards of the more pro-competitive country. The race is to the top, not to the bottom. One should note, however, that if the welfare functions of the countries are weighted solely or heavily towards the producer interests, the opposite conclusions hold; the countries would harmonise downwards and the world as a whole, including the consumer interests, would lose (see Appendix 7.2).

These results may generalise further to other imperfectly competitive markets, though experience with models of imperfect competition and international trade shows that it may be possible to find combinations of assumptions which yield perverse results in which a more pro-competitive policy is harmful.

WHAT SHOULD BE INCLUDED IN THE CORE?

The examples of minimum standards in the previous section related to horizontal price restraints which are commonly regarded as core problems.

An advantage of the minimum standards approach is that it is flexible. It can begin with a modest coverage and extend the coverage as countries exchange information and experiences.

One problem in achieving effective harmonisation is that elements of competition policy interact. For example, in the oligopoly models considered in the previous section, it was assumed that entry into the industry is blocked. Indeed, the lack of entry into the market is the source of market power of the oligopolists and the fundamental aspect of competition policy in this example. A government might force market access and increase the number of producers. Competition policies require consistency among the elements.

Consistency in turn requires common methods of analysis. If the competition authorities have different views of the nature of competition, harmonisation of other elements will be ineffective. This element seems crucial to effective harmonisation.

Similarly, if the competition authorities have different objectives, harmonisation may be ineffective. Examples 2 and 3 in the previous section showed that different outcomes will arise if countries differ in the weightings they attach to producer and consumer interests. The same problems arise if some countries have competition policies which seek to develop small and medium-sized enterprises or to promote exports.

Another element which might be included in the minimum set is competition policy enforcement. Fox and Ordover (1995) suggest that countries could allow residents of nations which are affected adversely by cartels in other countries to have access to the enforcement procedures of the countries in which the cartels are located, and that the competition authorities of all countries take account of the harm caused by cartels outside the territory of the cartel. In the example above, this would allow the consumers in other countries to take action to terminate the cartel, provided the competition law of the cartel's home country permitted this action. Thus it requires prior harmonisation of the law. If the source of the anticompetitive behaviour is lax enforcement rather than the absence of law, this is the solution.

It may not be desirable to harmonise some elements of competition policies. For example, the thresholds for mergers are in terms of units of the local currencies and they depend in part on the size distribution of firms in the national economy. The lack of harmonisation of these thresholds is, however, consistent with a single view of the competition process and harmonised competition policies.

An important aspect of the desirability of harmonisation is raised by the cases of Hong Kong and Singapore. It was noted in the previous section that these countries have no comprehensive competition policies. The governments of these two countries have contended in APEC debates that they are open economies and that open economies do not require comprehensive competition polices. Openness means 'no tariff, no quantitative restrictions on foreign goods and no capital flow restrictions on foreign investment' (Hong Kong government 1996, p. 9). This applies to markets for services as well as goods.

The removal of barriers to trade in goods and services, together with the application of the GATT principles of most-favoured-nation and national treatment, means that all producers compete on a level playing field. There are no government-imposed barriers to entry or exit. In this environment, the role of the government is to provide legal and regulatory infrastructure that underpins free and fair markets and to encourage enterprise through small government and low and stable taxation. The Hong Kong government recognises that there are circumstances where free competition may not be practicable: they list those where a very high level of investment is required, where there is a need for prudential supervision, and where there is a need to protect the long-term interest of consumers.

In essence, the governments of Hong Kong and Singapore argue that a policy of open markets makes markets contestable (with limited exceptions) and therefore makes a comprehensive competition policy redundant. They have a competition policy; it is to open their economies to all flows of goods and services and capital.

This point has been recognised before at the level of the world economy. Lloyd and Sampson (1995, p. 701) argue that the best policy the WTO might adopt towards competition is not to develop a competition policy within the WTO to complement its trade policies but merely to continue to move towards free international trade in goods and services. This argument applies equally to an individual country with respect to its unilateral trade policy. And it applies to the APEC region as a whole. The best competition policy for the APEC countries may be liberalisation of trade and investment, which makes their markets more contestable.

The same applies to other policies which affect competition in industries such as privatisation and deregulation. Privatisation and deregulation will increase competition in the industries which are privatised and deregulated. Conversely, a government which chooses to maintain a public monopoly in some industry — say, in telecommunications — will not require a competition policy for the industry. Such a policy exempts the industry concerned from normal competition policy rules.

All of these are examples of the interrelationships between competition policies of a country on the one hand and, on the other, the policies towards trade in goods and services and foreign investment that it adopts. They show that the competition policies that are required to make markets contestable for a country depend on policies with respect to the country's trade and foreign investment, privatisation and deregulation and other policies that affect competition in markets.

This conditionality does not, however, rule out harmonisation in the form of minimum standards. Open economies may still have residual competition problems due, for example, to vertical restraints and exclusive dealerships.

Information is lacking about the nature of competition in world markets and how it has been affected by these structural changes in the world economy. This should be an urgent priority for future research.

As regards the political feasibility of harmonisation of competition policies, even if a world view is adopted for the purpose of harmonisation, there is still the difficulty that countries which stand to lose from the adoption of a particular harmonised standard will oppose its adoption. (This applies to the export cartel example above but not to the oligopoly example.) In this respect, international competition policies resemble international negotiations which have reduced trade barriers. Reductions in trade barriers is a positive sum gain in which ordinarily all nations can expect to gain: reducing a country's tariff and non-tariff barriers increases the welfare of the home country as well as that of the exporting countries.[13] However, governments frequently weight producer interests more heavily than consumer interests and see some reductions as 'concessions' which are necessary to achieve gains in other areas. In international competition policies, there is no general proposition or expectation that all nations will gain from the harmonisation of individual competition policy standards and this problem will be exacerbated if governments weigh producer interests more heavily. The development of international competition policies is likely to be more difficult than many other areas of international policy. Nevertheless, as in international trade negotiations, harmonisation across a number of competition standards is likely to bring gain to all countries participating in the harmonisation; what they lose on the swing they would more than gain on the roundabout.

APPENDIX 7.1: BILATERAL AND MULTILATERAL INDICES OF SIMILARITY

In the text of their study, Bollard and Vautier (Chapter 6) construct a bilateral index of the similarity of the competition policies of any pair of countries. This appendix generalises their bilateral index to a multilateral index of the similarity of competition policies among a number of countries.

Suppose that there are m countries whose competition policies we wish to compare and n elements of competition policies in each country. There are $s = {}^mC_2 = m!/2!(m - 2)! = m(m - 1)/2$ pairs of countries; for example, if there are 11 countries (as in sample used by Bollard and Vautier), $s = 11.10/2 = 55$.

Take any pair of countries, say countries h and j. Let E_i^{hj} be the measure of similarity for the ith element of the index. If element i is a binary variable, it will take a value of 0 or 1. If element i is a continuous variable, it can lie anywhere on the closed interval [0,1]. Hence, $E_i^{hj} \in [0, 1]$ for all i. The Bilateral Index of Similarity is simply

$$S^{hj} = 1/n \sum_{i=1}^{n} E_i^{hj} \tag{A1.1}$$

This index can accommodate both binary and non-binary variables. It weights the elements equally. It lies on the unit interval. 1 represents identical policies between the two countries. An increase in this index over time represents convergence of the policies of the two countries.

The Multilateral Index of Similarity averages the value of the index of similarity for any element across all pairs of countries and then calculates the unweighted average across all elements:

$$S = 1/n \sum_{i=1}^{n} E_i \tag{A1.2}$$

where

$$E_i = 1/s \sum_{1}^{s} E_i^{hj}$$

is the average value of E_i^{hj} for all pairs of countries. This index lies on the unit interval. 1 represents identical policies among the m countries. Moreover, changing the order of summation,

$$S = 1/s \sum_1^s S^{hj}$$

That is, the Multilateral Index is also the unweighted average of the bilateral indices for all pairs of countries. An increase in this index represents a convergence of policies among the countries.

If a minimum set of standards is agreed upon by a set of countries, one can calculate an index of the extent to which the countries conform to this standard:

$$C = 1/nm \sum_{i=1}^n \sum_{h=1}^m D_i^h \qquad (A1.3)$$

where D_i^h measures the similarity or degree of conformity of country h to the agreed standard for element i. C lies on the unit interval. An increase in this index represents convergence towards the agreed standards.

APPENDIX 7.2: THE CROSS-HAULING MODEL OF OLIGOPOLY

Suppose there are two countries, indexed by $i=A,B$. In each country there are initially a fixed number of producers, though not necessarily the same number in each country, n^A and n^B. There are $n^T = n^A + n^B$ firms in the world market. The product is homogeneous and there are identical inverse demand functions in each country:

$$p^i = \alpha - \beta x^i \qquad i = A, B \qquad (A2.1)$$

where x^i is the aggregate demand in country I. All firms have identical cost functions:

$$c^f = F + cy^f \qquad f = 1,\dots,n^T \qquad (A2.2)$$

where F is fixed costs and c is the constant marginal cost of producing y^f. Each firm is a Cournot competitor — that is, it maximises profits, given the outputs of all other firms in countries A and B. Suppose that international trade has been freed in this market. Consequently, there is one market price, p. Hence, there is an inverse demand function for the world:

$$p = \alpha - (1/2)\beta(x^A + x^B) \qquad (A2.3)$$

174   *Competition policy in APEC: principles of harmonisation*

The equilibrium is a symmetric one in which all firms are identical. Each of the firms maximises profits by choosing its output, given the outputs of the other firms. The solution for y^f is

$$y^f = [2/(1 + n^T)](\alpha - c)/\beta \qquad f = 1, \dots, n^T \tag{A2.4}$$

For convenient reference, the terms involving n^T are collected in square brackets. Substituting (A2.4) in (A2.3), the price which clears the world market is

$$p = [(\alpha + n^T c)/(1 + n^T)] \tag{A2.5}$$

The profits of the firm are

$$p^f = py^f - (F + cy^f) \quad = [2/(1 + n^T)^2] \cdot (\alpha - c)^2 / \beta - F \tag{A2.6}$$

Each firm sells on both the home and the foreign market — that is, there is cross-hauling.

Total profits of firms in countries A and B are

$$P^i = [2n^i/(1 + n^T)^2] \cdot (\alpha - c)^2 / \beta - n^i F \qquad i = A, B \tag{A2.7}$$

Total profits in both countries combined are

$$P^{A+B} = \{[2n^T/(1 + n^T)^2] \cdot (\alpha - c)^2 / \beta\} - n^T F \tag{A2.8}$$

Thus, the total global profits are divided between the countries in proportion to their share of the total number of firms in the world market.

Consumer surplus in country i is

$$CS^i = (\alpha - p)x^i/2 = [n^{T2}/(1 + n^T)^2] \cdot (\alpha - c)^2 / 2\beta \qquad i = A, B \tag{A2.9}$$

Total consumer surplus in countries A and B combined is

$$CS^{A+B} = [n^{T2}/(1 + n^T)^2] \cdot (\alpha - c)^2 / \beta \tag{A2.10}$$

Because of identical demand conditions, this is double that of either country. Total welfare in each country is the sum of consumer surplus and profits:

$$W^i = \{[(4n^i + n^{T2})/(1 + n^T)^2] \cdot (\alpha - c)^2 / 2\beta\} - n^i F \qquad i = A, B \tag{A2.11}$$

Global welfare is the sum of the total welfare in both countries:

$$W^{A+B} = \{[n^T(2 + n^T)/(1 + n^T)^2] \cdot (\alpha - c)^2 / \beta\} - n^T F \tag{A2.12}$$

To model harmonisation of competition policies, suppose that each country controls the number of domestic firms in the country. One country adopts a more lax merger standard than the other in that it allows a smaller number of firms in relation to the size of the market. It was these merger standards which determined that the initial number of firms be n^A and n^B, respectively.

Now, the two countries decide to harmonise their merger policies. Suppose the country with the lax standards adopts the standards of the other country. It will increase its number of firms (by disallowing some mergers). The total number of firms in the industry worldwide increases and the market price falls (from Equation A2.5). Equations A1.7 and A1.9 are decreasing and increasing in n^T respectively for i = A and B. Hence, consumers gain and producers lose in both countries from the increase in the number of competitors. The expression in the curly bracket in Equation (A2.11) is increasing in n^T and Wi is increasing in n^T too for $(ni/nT) < 3/4$, provided F is not large. That is, this country gains from an increase in the number of firms in the country. The other country loses. If the country which increases the number of firms has $(ni/nT) > 3/4$, this country loses and the other gains, provided the economies of scale are not too large. The world gains from harmonisation, again provided the economies of scale are not too large.

The symmetry of the model can be relaxed, the countries could be of different size, the firms could have different production functions and tariff barriers to trade between countries can be introduced, without changing the qualitative conclusions.

NOTES

I wish to acknowledge the comments and suggestions made on an earlier draft of this chapter by Alan Bollard, Paul Crampton, Kin Kihwan, Martin Richardson and Kerrin Vautier.

1   The international dimensions of competition policy do not constitute an entirely new area. Issues of harmonisation of domestic policies, including what is now called competition policy, were first raised by international trade economists in the early stages of the GATT liberalisation of world trade. See Johnson, Wonnacott and Shibata (1968).
2   See Sauvé (forthcoming) and Zampetti and Sauvé (1996), who discuss contestability in relation to competition policy.
3   Here I overlook the law which is emerging in regional trading arrangements such as the European Union and the Closer Economic Relations (CER) agreement between Australia and New Zealand. This is setting important precedents but the geographic coverage is limited to the members.
4   See Hoekman and Mavroidis (1993) and Lloyd and Sampson (1995) for a review of the powers of the WTO in relation to competition policies.
5   See the Productivity Commission (1996) and the New Zealand government (1996) for some discussion of the application of these principles in the major OECD or Asia Pacific countries respectively.
6   Many options are discussed in OECD (1995).
7   Harry Johnson reached this conclusion in 1968: 'Harmonization in this area however, raises some exceedingly complex issues in both economic theory and legal practice, and consideration of the possible need for it would probably most wisely be deferred until experience of free trade has provided evidence on the question' (Johnson 1968, p.433).

8   Other less detailed surveys of the competition policies in APEC countries have been
    prepared by Waverman and Wu (1995), Green (1996) and the Productivity Commission
    (1996, Table 3.1). Boner and Krueger (1990) review the competition laws of the major
    industrialised countries.
9   The same issues have arisen with regional freeing of trade. For an early treatment of tax
    harmonisation in this context, see Shoup (1967).
10 In the debate as to whether labour standards should be added to the WTO, there has
    been much discussion of a 'core' of especially important labour standards.
11 For a recent survey of this, see Brander (1995).
12 If all firms in one country merge, we have a single seller that operates like the cartel in
    Levinsohn (1996) except for the presence of fixed costs in the cross-hauling model.
13 There are two exceptions to this rule. First, there may be large terms of trade effects in
    countries which have considerable market power. It is generally believed that terms of
    trade effects will not be large for most countries. Second, there may be perverse effects
    when economies of scale and imperfect competition are features of a market. 'New trade
    theory' has produced examples of countries which gain from the imposition of some
    border restrictions, especially export subsidies which shift profits, but even in these cases
    the world as whole gains from trade liberalisation. Moreover, in oligopolistic markets,
    some models predict additional gains following trade liberalisation arising from an
    increase in the degree of competition.

REFERENCES

APEC (1995) *Selected APEC Documents 1995*, Singapore: APEC Secretariat.
Bhagwati, J. N. and R. E. Hudec (eds) (1996) *Fair Trade and Harmonization: Pre-requisites
    for Free Trade?*, Cambridge, Mass.: MIT Press.
Bliss, C. (1996) 'Trade and competition control', in J. N. Bhagwati and R. E. Hudec (eds)
    Fair Trade and Harmonization: Pre-requisites for Free Trade?, Cambridge, Mass.: MIT
    Press.
Boner, R. and R. Krueger (1990) 'The basics of antitrust policy: a review of ten nations and
    the European Communities', Technical Paper 160, Washington DC: World Bank.
Brander, J. A. (1995) 'Strategic trade policy', in G. M. Grossman and K. Rogoff (eds)
    Handbook of International Economics, Amsterdam: North-Holland.
Crampton, P. and C. L. Witterick (1996) 'Trade distorting private restraints and market
    access: learning to walk before we run', Paper presented to the PECC Trade Policy Forum
    IX, Seoul, September.
European Union (1996) *Competition Policy in the New Trade Order: Strengthening
    International Co-operation and Rules*, Report of the Group of Experts, Directorate
    General IV, European Union, Brussels, CM 91-95-124-EN-C.
Fox, E. (1991) 'Harmonization of law and procedures in a globalized world: why, what and
    how?', *Antitrust Law Journal* 60, pp. 593–9.
Fox, E. M. and J. A. Ordover (1995) 'The harmonization of competition and trade law',
    World Competition 119 (December), pp. 5–34.
Graham, E. M. (1995) 'Competition policy and the new trade agenda', in OECD *New
    Dimensions of Market Access in a Globalised World Economy*, Paris: OECD.
Green, C. (1996) 'Competition regulation in the Asia–Pacific region', Paper presented to the
    Asia–Pacific Roundtable Meeting on 'The Global Contestability of National Markets',
    Singapore, 26–28 January.
Hoekman, B. M. and P. Mavroidis (1993) 'Competition, competition policy and the GATT',
    Policy Research Working Paper No. 1228, Finance and Private Sector Division, World
    Bank, Washington DC.

Hong Kong government (1996) 'Open markets as an approach to competition policy', Paper presented to the APEC Workshop on 'Competition Policy and Deregulation', Davao, Philippines, 17–18 August.

Johnson, H. G. (1968) 'The implications of free or freer trade for the harmonisation of other policies' in H. G. Johnson, P. Wonnacott and H. Shibata *Harmonisation of National Economic Policies Under Free Trade*, Toronto: Toronto University Press; reproduced in H. G. Johnson (1971) *Aspects of the Theory of Tariffs*, London: George Allen and Unwin.

Leebron, D. W. (1996) 'Lying down with Procustes: an analysis of harmonisation claims', in J. N. Bhagwati and R. E. Hudec (eds) *Fair Trade and Harmonization: Prerequisites for Free Trade?*, Cambridge, Mass.: MIT Press.

Levinsohn, J. (1996) 'Competition policy and international trade', in J. N. Bhagwati and R. E. Hudec (eds) *Fair Trade and Harmonization: Pre-requisites for Free Trade?*, Cambridge, Mass.: MIT Press.

Lloyd, P. J. (1996) 'A link between international trade and international competition policy', Institute of Applied Economic and Social Research Working Paper No. 4/96, Melbourne.

Lloyd, P. J. and G. Sampson (1995) 'Competition and trade policy after the Uruguay Round', *The World Economy* 18 (September), pp. 681–705

New Zealand government (1995) 'APEC Committee on Trade and Investment: proposal for a work programme on competition policy', Wellington.

Nicolaides, P. (1994) 'Towards multilateral rules on competition — the problems in mutual recognition of national rules', *World Competition* 17, pp. 5–48.

—— (1996) 'For a world competition authority: the role of competition policy in economic integration and the role of regional blocs in internationalizing competition policy', *Journal of World Trade Law* 30 (August), pp. 131–45.

OECD (1995) *New Dimensions of Market Access in a Globalising World Economy*, Paris: OECD.

PECC (1995) *Milestones in APEC Liberalisation: A Map of Market Opening Measures by APEC Economies*, Singapore: PECC.

Pitofsky, R. (1996) 'FTC Chairman says world competition rules currently not feasible', *Inside US Trade* 14, 26 April.

Productivity Commission (1996) *International Cooperation on Competition Policy*, Canberra: Australian Government Publishing Service.

Richardson, M. (1996) 'Trade and competition policies: concordia discors?', mimeo, Department of Economics, Otago University, Dunedin, August.

Sauvé, P. (forthcoming) 'Concept of contestable markets as a framework for multilateral trade negotiations', in H. Corbet (ed.) *The Global Contestability of National Markets: International Regime for Investment, Competition and Anti-dumping Laws.*

Shoup, C. S. (ed.) (1967) *Fiscal Harmonization in Common Markets*, New York: Columbia University Press.

Waverman, L. and Rong-I Wu (1995) 'Trade and competition policy in APEC', Paper presented at the PECC Trade Policy Forum, Taiwan, 20 April.

Willig, R. D. (forthcoming) *Antidumping and Competition.*

Zampetti, A. B. and P. Sauvé (1996) 'Onwards to Singapore: the international contestability of markets and the new trade agenda', *The World Economy* 19 (May), pp. 333–44.

The Asian economic and financial crisis: the effects of market integration and market fragility[1]

Peter J. Lloyd and Kim R. Sawyer[2]

1 Introduction

The foreign exchange market devaluations of July 1997 and the stock market devaluations of October 1997 in a number of East Asian countries are a watershed in the recent economic history of these countries. These devaluations mark the first substantial interruption in the rapid economic growth of the region, a phenomenon which had become known as the Asian Miracle. The devaluations were largely unforeseen and induced significant falls and increased volatility in the stock markets of many industriaized countries, including the USA and Australia.

Although it is still too early to assess properly the causes and the effects of the East Asian asset market devaluations, the following points should be emphasized:

1. The magnitude of the shock has most likely been significantly underappreciated. The equity market shock of 1987, which happened over a shorter time period, was almost immediately measurable. In the 1997 shock, the effect is being amplified by the *contagion* across markets, with successive currency devaluations and equity devaluations. Although the devaluation of a given market over the course of a week has typically been small, the cumulative devaluations have been large and distributed across a large number of markets.
2. When markets devalue successively and volatility increases concomitantly, a significant increase in uncertainty ensues. As a consequence, there is a substantial increase in the risk premia associated with holding equities, and a strong incentive to shift towards safer havens, in this case, US bonds and in general cash balances. Although data on the flow of funds is not available, it is likely that some of this movement in funds has already occurred.
3. The longer the period of uncertainty, the more decisions will be deferred, and the greater the effect on transactions demand and the real economy. The slow devaluation of the Japanese equity market between 1990 and 1992 induced a protracted recession, from which the Japanese economy had still not recovered in 1997.

Market analysts, economists and other commentators are now busy analysing the consequences of these shocks. Most of the attention has focused on the implications for equity markets or for the rate of economic growth and international trade of the East Asian countries and their trading partners. There is particular concern in Australia that reduced growth in East Asia will reduce our exports and our rate of growth because of our export dependence on the markets of these countries.

Important though these effects are, the market crashes signal more fundamental changes in the role of the East Asian countries in the world economy and in world markets themselves. We must understand these changes if we are to understand the reasons for the devaluations and make reliable forecasts of the future path of these economies. In reviewing these events, this paper will focus on the fundamental underlying changes in these economies which are a result of rapid growth sustained over a long period and the changes induced by the market devaluations themselves.

One fundamental change is globalization which has linked the East Asian markets for goods and assets much more closely to the markets of other countries. This linkage resulted from the liberalization of trade in goods and capital in the East Asian countries. The liberalization of trade in goods has increased the size of the tradable goods sector as measured by the trade ratio, the ratio of exports plus imports of goods to gross domestic product (GDP). This increases the exposure of the economy to shocks originating in international trade. The liberalization of trade in capital has similarly increased the stock of foreign-owned capital and of foreign debt such as corporate bonds denominated in foreign currencies. This has increased the exposure of corporations in these economies to shocks in capital markets. However, the financial markets of these Asian countries were less well integrated into the world economy because of restrictions on foreign entry in the financial sector and the lack of development of futures and derivative markets. We shall see that this contributed to the crises and reduces the capacity of the financial sector in these countries to deal with these shocks.

Another fundamental change is the convergence of the real per capita incomes and technologies of these countries to the levels prevailing in the advanced industrialized countries. While this effect is hard to discern, it had begun to affect the rates of growth of these economies in the last decade, that is, well before the financial market crises of 1997, and it will have a profound influence on their rates of growth in future years.

2   The events of 1997

The speculative bubble which has now become the Asian economic and financial crisis had its genesis in the inflow of capital into South East Asia from 1992 to 1996. This capital consisted of investments in major infrastructure projects, particularly in Thailand, Malaysia and Indonesia but also in China. The main implications of this capital flow were:

1.   high current account deficits in some East Asian countries;
2.   high short-term corporate debt, principally to Japanese banks (approximately $30billion), German and US creditors;
3.   high rates of returns on equities;
4.   relatively high and unsustainable exchange rates.

The crisis first appeared in the Thai equities market (see Figure 1). From a high of over 1400 points in January 1996, the Stock Exchange of Thailand index (SET index) has fallen steadily over a period of 22 months to a level of 460 points. The price decline has been offset by minor rallies of the market in response to the International Monetary Fund (IMF) rescue plan, and to the appointment of a new Prime Minister. However, these developments have not been sufficient to arrest the protracted and deep malaise in the Thai equities market. This malaise has had profound implications, leading to the closing of 58 financial institutions, and significantly undermining the corporate and political fabric in Thailand.

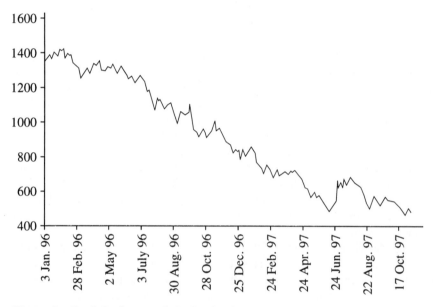

Figure 1   Stock Exchange of Thailand index

The speculative decline which began in the Thai equities market in January 1996, extended to the Thai currency market in June 1997, and induced a large amount of activity by hedging funds, including the well-documented activity of George Soros' fund. These funds became appreciably active in four South East Asian currency markets in June–September 1997, namely in Thailand, Malaysia, Indonesia and the Philippines. It was the activity of such funds which has substantially changed the devaluation of one market, the Thai market, into a set of fund competing devaluations. A feature of these competing devaluations has been the sequencing of the devaluations; the Thai baht first began to decline in June, the Malaysian ringgit, Indonesian rupiah and Philippines peso began devaluing in July, but the Australian dollar and South Korean won did not begin to devalue until October. The equity and currency profiles for 11 Asian countries during 1997, first from the beginning of the year, and secondly from 1 May, are contained in the Appendix (see Figures A.7–A.29). These profiles illustrate that the year can be characterized in terms of the predominant country effect, so that, approximately, the dominant devaluations have been:

January to June:	Thailand
July to September:	Indonesia, Malaysia, Philippines
October:	Hong Kong
October–November:	South Korea, Japan

In the equities markets, country specific effects had considerable impacts. Three effects in particular should be cited. First, the pegging of various currencies to the US dollar accentuated spillovers into the equities markets. No better example of this occurred than in Hong Kong, where the pegging of the Hong Kong dollar initiated a jump in yields, and a commensurate decline in equity prices. Secondly, restrictions in equities markets exaggerated the price declines. In Thailand and Korea, restrictions on foreign investment induced portfolio formation whereby individual stock selection is limited. When markets declined, there was a tendency to reduce the entire country portfolio weighting to zero, rather than a selective approach. Malaysia exacerbated its equity market decline by imposing price limits on the run. Finally, the lack of hedging facilities in many countries meant that investors had no alternative than to reduce their country portfolio weightings to zero. For example, no options or futures market exists in Thailand, so that no adequate hedging facility was available to institutional investors except cross-hedging or synthetic hedging.

Other countries, such as Australia and Singapore, have incurred associated devaluations as a spillover from the principal devaluing countries. The change in equity and currency values for a number of Asian countries is given in Table 1 below.

Table 1   Change of asset prices

Country	1 January 1997 to 13 November 1997 (% change)		1 May 1997 to 13 November 1997 (% change)	
	Equity (Index)	Currency *vis-à-vis* US$	Equity (Index)	Currency *vis-à-vis* US$
Australia	3.8	–12.5	0.7	–11.6
Hong Kong	–26.4	0	–25.4	–0.02
Indonesia	–31.6	–30.2	–32.9	–28.1
Japan	–20.7	–7.7	–20.0	1.3
Korea	–20.6	–14.5	–26.4	–9.5
Malaysia	–45.0	–23.7	–38.4	–24.2
New Zealand	–0.1	–11.9	4.5	–9.7
Philippines	–42.8	–22.6	–30.8	–22.4
Singapore	–24.9	–11.4	–17.2	–8.6
Taiwan	10.4	–11.9	–7.7	–11.4
Thailand	–42.7	–33.1	–30.3	–31.9

The table shows significant depreciations in both equity prices and currencies for the four South East Asian economies – Thailand, Malaysia, Indonesia and Philippines. Hong Kong has suffered a 26 per cent decline in equity prices over the year, and

Korea has suffered a 20 per cent equity deflation and 14 per cent currency devaluation. Australia and New Zealand have been relatively well insulated in terms of equities, but have incurred currency devaluations of the order of 10 per cent. The best insulated market has been the Taiwanese market, which had a substantial run-up in equity prices in early 1997.

The devaluations in equity and currency markets can be better interpreted by considering an investor who invested US$1000 in each country's equity market at the beginning of 1997. This can be regarded as the value in global terms of an investment in local equities markets, thereby providing a measure of the change in wealth of local investors.

The value of this portfolio at successive times during 1997 is shown in Table 2, which represents the combined effect of equity and currency devaluations.

Table 2 shows how significant this East Asian crisis has been in terms of nominal wealth effects. A foreign investor who invested in Thai equities at the beginning of 1997 has seen 62 per cent of their portfolio eroded, most of it by August 1997. For Malaysia, Indonesia and the Philippines, the story is similar. But even South Korea and Singapore have seen one-third of an unhedged portfolio eroded by equity and currency devaluations.

This significant cumulative wealth effect cannot be understated, and it is now a question how this wealth bubble is transmitted through the real economies of East Asia and beyond. It is also important to recognize that the devaluations which began as asynchronous events (Thailand preceding Malaysia and so on) are now increasingly synchronous; that is, many asset markets are moving together.

Table 2   The value of a US$1000 market portfolio over 1997

Country	1 January	1 May	End of June	End of July	End of August	End of September	End of October	13 November
Australia	1000	1020	1064	1064	997	1042	901	909
Hong Kong	1000	985	1149	1238	1069	1139	805	736
Indonesia	1000	989	1103	1026	623	619	512	477
Japan	1000	904	1072	1024	910	879	816	732
Korea	1000	1020	1083	1053	1007	913	630	679
Malaysia	1000	898	876	789	568	515	400	419
New Zealand	1000	933	1011	992	937	975	875	881
Philippines	1000	823	888	754	556	499	428	443
Singapore	1000	879	876	844	752	805	634	666
Taiwan	1000	1189	1304	1409	1376	1223	949	972
Thailand	1000	807	683	668	470	480	353	383

In October and November, we have seen two particularly interesting features in the Asian equity markets. First, there has been increased volatility, sometimes as much as 4–5 times average daily volatility of the past. For such volatility to persist is a concern. In models of experimental asset markets, when a protracted bull market is followed by increased volatility, often a market crash follows. There is now a higher probability than before October of a significant further decline in asset prices. Secondly, intra-day volatility is now quite remarkable. On a given day on the ASX (Australian Stock Exchange), the market may open down 1 per cent, but finish up at the end of the day because of the influence of Hong Kong and Japan. The markets are now seemingly better integrated and synchronized.

The contagion effect across markets has tended to accentuate opening price effects. The best demonstration of this opening price effect was the effect the Hong Kong stock market had on other world stock markets on 24 October. The fall of 12 per cent of the Hang Seng index apparently precipitated global falls across stock exchanges, but most of these falls were captured in the first hour of trading. The opening price effect is one of the most powerful signals of market contagion, and provides some evidence of the extent of the asset pricing bubble which currently exists in world equity markets.

The equity markets are currently characterized by considerable fragility. While volatility encompasses both downside risk and upside potential, fragility refers to downside risk. In the present bubble, the markets have appeared fragile. However, rebounds have also been quite spectacular with the New York equities market in particular rebounding immediately after significant price falls, leading to the general designation of asset price 'bungey jumps'. The upside potential would appear to be limited, and increasingly other effects will begin to dominate. These effects include:

1. The earnings reporting season for Japan begins in November, and the Japanese equities market will be under increased pressure through earnings downgrades. The next earnings reporting season in Australia and the US, which begins in March, will include 2–21/2 months of the Asian markets effect, and this will necessarily reduce stock valuations. It is unlikely that the next set of earnings results will be as favourable as those for the season just reported.

2. Japanese banks and other financial institutions throughout Asia will soon be required to redeem their holdings of US bonds in particular, in order to cover short-term liabilities. This is likely to place some upward pressure on US yields, although this may be offset by a flow of funds to the safe haven of US bonds. In October, there have been some extraordinary increases in overnight yields, most notably associated with Hong Kong which by pegging the exchange rate to the dollar, precipitated an equities and yields bubble. The Brazilian market has also suffered explosive increases in yields. Such changes are again indicative of an asset pricing bubble.

3. There is now considerable emphasis on the likely exposures of Asian financial institutions. Christopher Wood of the Peregrine Group has assessed bad debts of non-Japanese Asian banks to be of the order of US$500 billion, with China and Korea the most exposed. The addition of the non-performing loans of Japanese banks, the most exposed sector of all, cumulates to a significant regional problem. It is unclear that revisions of portfolios, or country by country IMF intervention, will rectify this problem.

There are two final points that should be made when reviewing the Asian equities' and currencies' devaluations of 1997. First, this event was and remains highly unpredictable. The uncertainty of the event is well measured by the small number of economic and financial commentators who predicted the event, but also by the now frequent reassessments of its significance. Secondly, there are already emerging anecdotal signs of the real impacts, such as declines in retail purchases in Japan, and increases in the price of rice in Thailand (from 50 baht to 80 baht in three weeks). If this anecdotal evidence translates into sustained negative real effects, the prospect for further equity price declines will be very real indeed.

3   Macroeconomic imbalance or microeconomic failure

3.1   Macroeconomic imbalance

The crises of 1997 began in the foreign exchange markets of Thailand, Malaysia, Indonesia and Philippines, then spread to the foreign exchange markets of other East Asian countries. These four economies have been most affected by the devaluations in the foreign exchange and equity markets, as shown in Table 2. The first three economies will be called the ' trigger economies'; the Philippines markets are much smaller. When we focus on the sequence of events or the causes of the crises, we shall separate the statistics of these countries from other East Asian countries.

Before the crises, the exchange rate regimes of East Asian countries varied. At one extreme in terms of the fixity of rates the Hong Kong dollar was (and at the time of writing still is) pegged rigidly to the US dollar and the Thai baht was pegged to a weighted basket of currencies. At the other extreme the Philippines peso was independently floating. The currencies of Indonesia, Singapore and Malaysia were managed floats but Malaysia had maintained a stable rate *vis-à-vis* the US dollar, Indonesia had a controlled devaluation *vis-à-vis* the US dollar and the Singapore dollar has been appreciating steadily *vis-à-vis* the US dollar.

Many commentators have observed that the US dollar had appreciated *vis-à-vis* the Japanese yen in 1995 and 1996. Hence the bilateral exchange rates of the East Asian countries against the US dollar and the Japanese yen – the two most heavily traded currencies in East Asia – have moved in opposite directions since mid-1995. One should use for each country an effective exchange rate which is a weighted average of the bilateral rates or, best of all, a real effective exchange rate which is also adjusted for movements in the price index of the country concerned relative to that of its trading partners. Figure 2 graphs the real effective exchange rates for the East Asian currencies. This figure shows that the real effective exchange rates of the Hong Kong and Singapore dollars, the Philippines peso and the Chinese renminbi appreciated significantly from late 1995 until the onset of the crisis but, interestingly, the Thai baht, Indonesian rupiah and Malaysian ringgit rates all remained stable. In the case of the trigger economies, the problem was not an appreciation of the real effective exchange rate but rather the non-depreciation of the real effective rates when exports fell and the balance of payments deficits increased.

Some commentators have attributed the foreign exchange market crises to the pegging of currencies against the US dollar. But this cannot be so since these US dollar rates have been pegged or controlled for years. We need to identify some causal factor which can explain the changes in these effective rates.

The immediate cause was a worsening in the balance of payments deficits of the

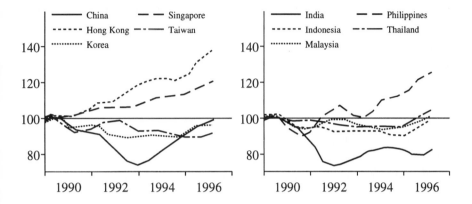

Source: Bank for International Settlements, 1997b, p. 43.

Figure 2 Real effective exchange rates

trigger countries – Thailand, Malaysia and Indonesia. Table 3 reports the deficit in the balance of payment on current account as a percentage of the GDP of the countries concerned. In 1995 and 1996 Thailand and Malaysia had a deficit greater than 5 per cent of GDP and Indonesia around 4 per cent. The figure of 5 per cent is regarded by the IMF as a danger point. Table 4 records the increase in bank external indebtedness in the East Asian countries. Bank external indebtedness increased sharply in 1995 and 1996 in all three trigger economies and in other East Asian economies except Singapore and Taiwan.

The underlying causes of the deterioration in the balance of payments of these countries are more difficult to discern. There was a fall in the rate of growth of exports, in volume terms and an even larger fall in value terms as prices fell too. Especially hard hit by the decline in exports were the electronic industries. Many countries in East Asia had become substantially specialized in electronic products; these products now account for more than one half of total merchandise exports in Singapore and more than one quarter in Hong Kong, Taiwan, Thailand and Malaysia. On the capital account, there was a growth in borrowing, especially corporate debt. The governments of all three countries liberalized restrictions on foreign borrowing and entry of foreign direct investments in some sectors; for example, Thailand introduced special accounts which made it easier for corporations to borrow offshore. Foreign borrowing became more attractive because of the low interest rates in the US and other industrialized countries as a result of low inflation and expansionary monetary policies.

This raises the issue of whether it was the overspending by a booming domestic economy which led to increased foreign borrowing or a policy-induced increase in foreign borrowing which in turn induced greater domestic spending effects through increased liquidity and the easier availability of capital to businesses. Table 3 also reports gross domestic investment (GDI) as a percentage of GNP, the overall surplus/

Table 3   Trends in national income and expenditure

	1991	1992	1993	1994	1995	1996
Thailand						
Balance of payments on the current account (% of GNP)	–7.8	–5.8	–5.2	–5.8	–8.3	–8.1
Gross domestic investment (% of GNP)	43.4	40.8	41.3	42.0	44.2	43.8
Overall budget surplus/deficit of the Central Government (% of GDP)	4.3	2.6	1.9	2.7	3.0	0.9
Growth rate of merchandise exports	23.8	13.7	13.4	22.2	24.7	0.1
Malaysia						
Balance of payments on the current account (% of GNP)	–9.2	–3.9	–4.6	–6.0	–9.0	–6.3
Gross domestic investment (% of GNP)	39.3	37.1	39.8	42.5	45.4	45.1
Overall budget surplus/deficit of the Central Government (% of GDP)	–2.0	–0.8	0.2	2.3	0.9	0.6
Growth rate of merchandise exports	17.0	18.1	16.1	23.1	25.9	4.0
Indonesia						
Balance of payments on the current account (% of GNP)	–3.5	–2.1	–1.4	–1.6	–3.6	–4.1
Gross domestic investment (% of GNP)	33.5	33.9	34.5	33.7	34.8	37.7
Overall budget surplus/deficit of the Central Government (% of GDP)	–0.7	–0.4	–0.4	0.2	–0.2	–
Growth rate of merchandise exports	10.5	14.0	8.3	9.9	13.1	8.8

Source: Asian Development Bank (1997a, Tables A.8, A.11, A.16, A.23).

deficit of the Central Government as a percentage of GDP and the percentage change from year to year in total exports. GDI is a component of national expenditure. The overall surplus/deficit is the difference between government expenditure, which is a component of national expenditure, and government revenue and this balance has a substantial effect on the level of aggregate national expenditure. In 1995 and 1996 export growth was low and the overall balance in the central governments showed no increased deficits but investment spending increased by the trigger economies. Hence, the easing of restrictions on foreign borrowing and low interest rates for offshore borrowing compared to high domestic interest rates, which caused GDI relative to GNP to increase by two or three percentage points and led to an inflow of short-term capital, were the dominant factor in the blow-out in the balance of payments of these economies.

Table 4   External indebtedness (US$ million)

	June 1995	December 1995	June 1996	December 1996
Trigger economies				
Thailand				
Total external bank claims	71,592	92,803	98,307	99,266
Guaranteed claims	2,771	2,928	3,012	2,968
Non-bank credits	6,388	7,442	6,792	6,841
Total	77,980	100,245	105,099	106,107
Malaysia				
Total external bank claims	16,751	18,759	23,578	25,828
Guaranteed claims	1,904	1,792	1,766	1,722
Non-bank credits	2,114	2,674	1,912	1,827
Total	18,865	21,433	25,490	27,655
Indonesia				
Total external bank claims	45,398	48,984	51,541	56,672
Guaranteed claims	6,905	6,985	7,027	7,276
Non-bank credits	10,235	9,118	9,270	8,968
Total	55,633	58,103	60,812	65,640
Other East-Asian economies				
China				
Total external bank claims	61,227	68,050	75,489	80,635
Guaranteed claims	11,770	11,872	12,791	13,023
Non-bank credits	11,387	9,622	9,305	10,064
Total	72,614	77,672	84,794	90,699
Hong Kong				
Total external bank claims	20,744	22,581	24,654	25,964
Guaranteed claims	901	1,061	1,148	1,312
Non-bank credits	2,355	3,411	3,570	3,690
Total	23,099	25,992	28,224	29,654
Korea				
Total external bank claims	75,668	83,260	98,280	108,480
Guaranteed claims	2,060	1,987	1,907	1,909
Non-bank credits	3,567	1,621	1,501	1,286
Total	79,235	84,881	99,781	109,766
Singapore				
Total external bank claims	6,404	5,648	7,675	6,562
Guaranteed claims	210	241	86	84
Non-bank credits	3,374	3,398	3,247	2,541
Total	9,778	9,045	10,922	9,103

Taiwan

Total external bank claims	26,358	22,132	21,511	22,664
Guaranteed claims	268	340	359	329
Non-bank credits	2,754	2,026	1,838	1,723
Total	29,112	24,160	23,349	24,387

Philippines

Total external bank claims	7,565	8,153	11,158	13,431
Guaranteed claims	2,408	2,467	2,493	2,549
Non-bank credits	4,909	4,696	4,317	4,096
Total	12,474	12,850	15,476	17,526

Source: Bank for International Settlements (1997c).

This capital inflow put upward pressure on the exchange rates or, in the case of currencies which were pegged or managed, allowed the authorities to maintain a higher rate. The high level of these exchange rates in turn discouraged exports and encouraged imports. These rates thus prevented any correction of the worsening underlying balance of payments current account and made them vulnerable to capital flights and exchange rate speculation.

3.2   Microeconomic failure

Compounding the failure of macroeconomic management in these three trigger economies was a growing unwillingness to deal with microeconomic problems that were emerging.

More of the capital expenditures were directed to speculative construction of CBD (Central Business District) office space and doubtful public projects which were undertaken for prestige reasons: for example, the twin Petronas Towers and a new airport in Kuala Lumpur. CBD vacancy rates are approaching 20 per cent in Bangkok, Kuala Lumpur and Jakarta. The income risk associated with many investments has increased.

Added to this income risk were increased financial risks. Corporate borrowing increased sharply. Asian corporations and governments had securities to banks, investment banks, pension and mutual funds and other institutions in Japan, the US and Europe. As their exchange rates seemed to be tied firmly to the US dollar and loan rates in the US and other industrialized countries were much lower than domestic rates, a substantial part of these loans were denominated in US dollars, yen or other foreign currencies. Many were not hedged.

These trends have increased the exposure of banks and other lending institutions as well as the corporations themselves. Private bank lending increased absolutely and as a percentage of GDP, as shown in Table 5. Bank lending rose dramatically throughout East Asia between 1980 and 1995, though, with the clear exceptions of Hong Kong and Taiwan, the percentages were not out of line with those in industrialized countries. Default risk for the banks increased. Table 6 reports the non-performing loans as a percentage of total loans in 1996. This shows that the percentages of non-performing loans in East Asia generally is much higher than in industrialized countries (though it is not higher than in many other developing countries in Latin America and South Asia).

Table 5   Bank credit to the private sector (% of GDP)

	1980	1995
Trigger economies		
Thailand	27.5	88.7
Malaysia	33.1	76.9
Indonesia	8.1	49.1
Other East-Asian economies		
China	47.5	83.9
Hong Kong	71.7	321.4
Korea	36.2	55.7
Singapore	62.9	84.9
Taiwan	49.2	143.1
Philippines	37.9	39.3
Industrialized countries		
US	62.1	63.3
Japan	81.0	115.1
Germany	74.2	96.1
UK	39.9	99.7
Other G-10 Europe	61.0	76.2

Source: Bank for International Settlements (1997b, p. 108).

Table 6   Non-performing loans (% of total loans)

	1990	1994	1995	1996
Trigger economies				
Thailand	9.7	7.5	7.7	–
Malaysia	20.4	8.1	5.5	3.9
Indonesia	4.5	12.0	10.4	8.8
Other East-Asian economies				
Hong Kong	–	3.4	2.8	2.7
Korea	2.1	1.0	0.9	0.8
Taiwan	1.2	2.0	3.1	3.8
Industrialized countries				
US	3.3	1.9	1.3	1.1
Japan	–	3.3	3.3	3.4

Source: Bank for International Settlements (1997b, p.107).

These trends have revealed alarming inadequacies in the financial sectors of these economies. Lending criteria and capital backing were inadequate and prudential supervision did not contain risky loans. In Malaysia, the Philippines, Singapore and Thailand commercial banks may engage in underwriting, stockbroking and fund management. In all East Asian countries other than Indonesia and Korea, banks are allowed to hold equity in non-financial and financial institutions, subject to some percentage limitations.

One factor that aggravated these problems was the restriction on entry of foreign banks and financial institutions. Apart from Hong Kong and to a lesser extent Singapore, East Asian countries allow less entry of foreign firms providing financial services than other countries at similar levels of development and they are more highly regulated. Consequently the financial sector is less 'internationalized' in terms of competition from financial service providers based in other countries. In this respect, the financial sector is in marked contrast to the goods trade sector and capital movements which are highly internationalized in all East Asian countries. This segmentation has lowered diversification of financial institutions in these countries and thereby increased the risk of bank failure.

Cross-country empirical evidence compiled by the World Bank suggests this limited internationalization in the financial sector has also led to higher costs of financial services (higher interest margins and lending rates) to borrowers and slower institution development (see Claessens and Glaessner, 1997). This increased the demand for apparently cheap offshore sources of funds.

Another related factor was the absence of futures and derivative markets. It has been already noted in section 2 above that there is no options or futures market in Thailand, and as a consequence, hedging against portfolio declines of the order seen in Table 2 have been more difficult. Derivatives markets also become mechanisms for the dissemination of volatility, so that the shock in equities markets has tended to be amplified.

Western commentators have highlighted the corruption in the award of government contracts, the granting of trading monopolies and other benefits to private groups or corporations through industry assistance and budget outlays. There is a perception that in these trigger economies such practices have become more widespread and blatant in recent years. In East Asia, it seems that one form of corruption is particularly widespread, namely, cronyism. These corrupt practices take the form of government actions which favour some individuals over others rather than the traditional forms of corruption, such as smuggling, which entail the avoidance of government controls. They involve a corruption of political processes rather than administrative processes. They lower the productivity of capital and other resources, provide a disincentive to foreigners to invest by these economies and damage the reputation of the countries for good government.

4 The convergence factor

There is one other factor which has contributed to the present crisis in financial markets but which is little appreciated by market analysts and the public at large. This is the slow-down in the rate of growth of East Asia due to difficulties in sustaining rapid growth when per capita incomes and technology levels rise to those approaching the levels in advanced industrialized countries. Among economic growth theorists this is known as 'convergence'. This process had begun in the 1980s, well before the 1997 crises.

Figures 3 to 5 graph the annual rates of growth of per capita GDP in the Association of South East Asian Nations (ASEAN-4) (Indonesia, Malaysia, Thailand and the Philippines), the three newly industrialized economies (NIEs) (Hong Kong, Korea and Singapore), Japan and China. For comparison, the rates of growth of real GDP in Australia are graphed on the same figures.

Clearly the Asian countries have all grown considerably faster than Australia over the last four decades but there are some differences among the pattern of growth rates of these groups of Asian economies. The NIE-3 have grown faster than ASEAN-4 over the whole period. Their growth rates are 4.75 percentage points higher on average than that of Australia over the same period whereas the ASEAN-4 growth rates have averaged about 2 percentage points faster than those of Australia. Japan has grown by over 3 percentage points faster than Australia and China by 1.4 percentage points faster. However, the Japanese growth rate has slowed dramatically over the period whereas the Chinese rate accelerated during the 1970s, which was after the Cultural Revolution, and again in the post-1979 reform period.

While there are divergent opinions about the reasons for fast growth by East Asia, one factor upon which most analysts agree is the central role of the opening up of these economies. As duty-free ports since the last century, Hong Kong and Singapore have always been open by relation to trading goods with other countries. The other two NIEs, Taiwan and Korea, opened their economies to lowering border barriers to

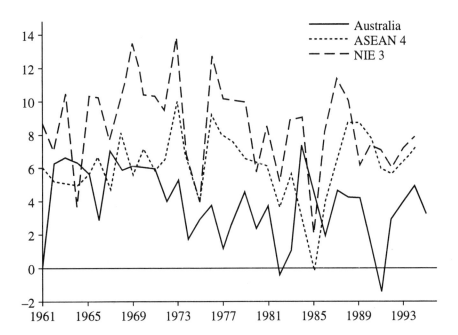

Figure 3   GDP per capita growth rates (per cent)

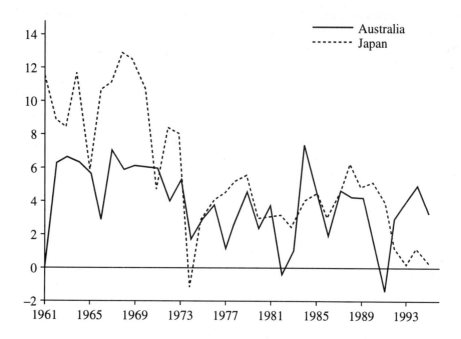

Figure 4   GDP per capita growth rates (per cent)

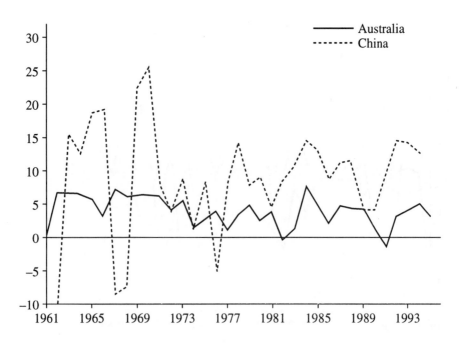

Figure 5   GDP per capita growth rates (per cent)

trade in the mid-1960s, as did Japan. The ASEAN-4 also opened their economies substantially in the 1960s and 1970s. This opening ushered in a period of rapid export-led industrialization and high economic growth which has continued ever since in all of these countries except Japan. This openness and export-led growth distinguished this group of Asian economies from other developing countries which favoured high trade barriers and import replacement strategies until the more recent period of the 1980s and 1990s. Sachs and Warner (1995) document the opening of these economies and the spread of these policies to other developing and transition economies.

These Asian economies have also been relatively open with regard to capital movements and especially foreign direct investments (FDIs). FDI provides an important mechanism for the transfer of technology from the multinational parent company to the affiliates in the host country. In East Asia, FDI has been largely directed towards export-oriented manufacturing. It has been encouraged by the establishment of free trade zones which have offered trading concessions and by FDI incentives (see Lloyd, 1996). Malaysia and Singapore have been particularly generous in terms of FDI incentives.

In the last 10 years or so, growth theorists have emphasized that rapid economic growth cannot be sustained indefinitely. Neoclassical growth models predict a convergence over time in the per capita incomes of countries towards some level because of the operation of diminishing returns to capital. Other things being equal, low-income countries have lower stocks of capital per capita than high-income countries. Because of the law of diminishing returns, the rates of profitability for additional capital investments will be higher in these countries than in capital-abundant countries. If the rates of capital formation are similar across countries, the low-income countries will grow faster than the richer capital-abundant countries. Thus, the rate of growth of a country over a period will be negatively related to its per capita income at the beginning of the period. This process of convergence will be strengthened if the poorer countries have high rates of savings or if technology transfer enables them to improve the productivities of factors (Barro and Sala-i-Martin, 1995).

In order to take account of differences in governments' policies, growth models have been constructed which attempt to control for country-specific factors such as policy variables, human resource endowments, locational and natural resource factors. These models are more realistic and they do not predict absolute convergence in incomes but rather suggest that there will be *conditional* convergence, that is convergence after country-specific factors have been taken into account. This more general formulation of the neoclassical model suggests that growth rates may still converge, but only after other factors have already been taken into account and this convergence will not necessarily be to the same level of income for all countries.

Evidence for convergence has been reported in the literature from empirical studies using data for a wide cross-section of industrial and developing countries. A few recent studies had questioned whether the past rates of high growth in the East Asian economies could be sustained (see Asian Development Bank, 1997b and Institute of Developing Economies, 1997). These studies were published before the October crisis.

A particularly relevant recent example is the work of Sachs and Warner (1995). They examined the growth performance of more than 100 countries for the period 1970–89. For all the countries in their sample, there is no evidence of convergence.

When, however, the sample is confined to those countries which are relatively open, there is clear evidence of convergence. Figure 6 reproduces their scatter diagram for the open economies. Thus, the use of only one conditioning variable, openness to international trade, is sufficient to produce clear conditional convergence. This result strongly suggests that the rate of growth of the fast-growing Asian economies will slow down as their levels of per capita income approach those of the more advanced countries.

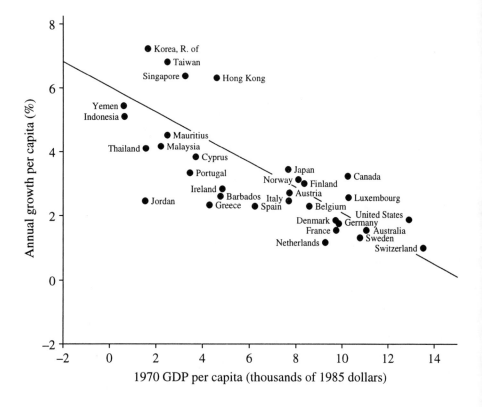

Source: Sachs and Warner (1995, Figure 4)

Figure 6   Growth and initial income, open economies, 1970–89

This figure also sheds light on another aspect of growth in these economies which has been hotly debated in recent years. This is the question of whether there is an 'Asian way' to fast growth. Have the Asian economies really been exceptional in their performance and, if so, are the factors explaining their exceptional growth rates replicable or transferable to other countries? There was an early belief that there are some characteristics of the Asian style of economic management which accounted for their high rates of growth.

In Figure 6, a regression line has been fitted to these observations. (This has been done approximately by hand as the authors do not have the data of the Sachs and

Warner study). Among the Asian countries, it is only the NIEs which have exceptional growth in that their observed rates of growth clearly lie above the average relationship measured by the regression line; their growth rates are two percentage points above that which is predicted by the convergence relationship. By contrast, the growth rates of Indonesia, Thailand and Malaysia actually lie a little below the line. On this evidence there is no Asian way that applies to all of the fast-growing economies. It would take a major study to establish the reasons why the NIEs have done exceptionally well. Perhaps, in the case of Singapore and Hong Kong, it is due to the very high level of openness noted above. One may also note that these four NIEs have been those which specialized on exports of manufactures par excellence. In this regard, they may have been an important element of luck as the period from 1970 has been a period of major global liberalization and rapid and sustained growth of total world trade in manufactures.

Looking again at Figures 3–5, one observes a slowing down in the rate of growth in East Asia. Japan exhibits the clearest case of slowing down. Japan's rate of growth of per capita output has been slowing down steadily since 1970. In the last few years it has been barely positive. While the slow growth in the 1990s has been frequently attributed to a slow recovery from the recession of the early 1990s and other special structural factors, the slow downward trend is evidence of a long-term decline in this rate of growth. The NIEs and the ASEAN-4 exhibit a slow-down from 1988. There is, however, no evidence of a slow-down in the Chinese economy. All of these observations are consistent with the convergence hypothesis as the model predicts that the rate of growth of growth declines with the current level of per capita incomes.

5   Conclusions regarding origin of crisis

5.1   Multiple causes

The events of June to October 1997 can in retrospect be seen to have multiple causes. The immediate trigger was the worsening of the balance of payments current account of the trigger economies which is traceable to the non-devaluation of the real effective exchange rates of these countries. The source of their difficulties was the large capital inflow into these economies which in turn was due to relaxation of capital controls in East Asia, low interest rates in industrial countries and a belief that the rapid growth of the East Asian economies would continue. Underlying these short-term difficulties in Asia, there had been a slow-down in the rate of growth of the high-income, fast-growing East Asian economies but this was not recognized in East Asia which continued to expect very rapid growth. Finally, the globalization of markets for goods, services and capital had increased the rate of transmission of shocks from one economy to another and from one market to another.

5.2   A Crisis of revised expectations

The crises have led to drastically revised expectations concerning the performance of the East Asian region. Where there was great admiration for the East Asian Miracle and much discussion of emulating the policies of these countries (as in the Australian debate about industry policy), there is now a debate about the end of this miracle and a sudden conversion to the belief that these countries are pursing inappropriate policies.

There is no doubt that major changes are required in the macroeconomic and microeconomic policies of these countries in order to restore expectations.

5.3   The lessons of Mexico

Comparisons have been made between the Mexican crisis of December 1994 and the crisis of Thailand or the three trigger economies collectively. There are some notable parallels and some major differences.

In both cases, the crises began in the foreign exchange markets because of widespread belief that the fixed exchange rates could not be maintained in the presence of large balance of payments deficits and increased risk in capital markets. The real effective exchange rate of Mexico appreciated substantially before the crisis as did that of some of the East Asian countries. There was a loss of reserves followed by devaluations and a bursting of the bubble in domestic stock and property markets. The IMF provided an assistance package to Mexico and recently to Thailand, Indonesia and the Philippines. However, the magnitude of the Mexican crisis has been larger than that of Thailand, the worst affected of the East Asian countries. The deficits on the current account of the balance of payments reached 8 per cent of GDP in both the case of Mexico and Thailand at the onset of the crisis.

However, the fall in the Mexican peso was considerably greater than that of the baht, as the peso lost more than half of its value within six months, and the IMF Mexico package was larger (US$50 billion compared to US$40 billion in the case of Indonesia which was larger than the US$17.5 billion package for Thailand).

On the other hand, Mexico had a powerful neighbour who was prepared to back its currency and policies. Moreover, the 1997 East Asian crisis has spread to several currencies and raised issues about the short- and long-term performance of a whole region. These features make the crises more difficult than the Mexican crisis.

The main lesson of the Mexican crisis is that short-term doomsayers should be discounted. The Mexican economy was able to bounce back in a remarkably short time. The Mexican balance of payments deficit was eliminated by the beginning of 1997. Industrial output and aggregate GDP were depressed for less than one year, having recovered by the second half of 1995. The rate of inflation has been reduced from a peak of 53 per cent at the end of 1995 to 25 per cent in early 1997. Exports rose strongly in 1995, reflecting both an upturn in oil prices and a large increase in exports of manufactured goods.

This remarkable turn around stemmed from a combination of floating the exchange rate, the introduction of tight monetary policy through monetary targeting and a tight fiscal policy involving revenue enhancement, cut-backs in public sector employment and welfare benefits. These measures resulted in a real exchange depreciation in 1995 of more than 30 per cent.

Mexico therefore demonstrates the possibility of a quick recovery but only if sufficiently determined measures are taken to address the cause of the crisis and if the world economy remains buoyant.

5.4   Why did so few in Asia or elsewhere forecast these events?

A notable feature of the crises of 1997 is that so few forecast a downturn in asset markets. It is true that the IMF had been warning that the growing current account deficits of the trigger economies were not sustainable but seemed to regard the problems as manageable if corrective monetary and fiscal policies reduced demand. The Bank for International Settlements has become concerned over financial stability in Emerging Market Economies (BIS, 1997b) and, in its last annual report, the BIS noted that

> a fixed exchange rate may lead to potentially dangerous currency mismatches. A common source of trouble in industrial and emerging market economies has been the combination of a fixed exchange rate with relatively high domestic interest rates and inflation, which typically encourages residents (banks and their customers) to borrow foreign currency to finance local currency business or assets. Such mismatches can leave the banking system very exposed if large current account deficits eventually cause a sizable devaluation (BIS, 1997a, pp. 111–12).

The BIS noted the 'fragility' of banks in Asia. In its recent review of *Emerging Asia* the Asian Development Bank identified problems in the financial sectors of Asian economies:

> International capital mobility requires strong, market-based financial institutions. Banks must be well-supervised and well-capitalised; equity and debt markets transparent and well-regulated. Efficient and well-managed financial systems must provide an adequate range of financial instruments, and ensure competition among providers. Many Asian countries are far from fulfilling these requirements (Asian Development Bank, 1997b, p. 37).

Thus, there was an awareness in the major world institutions of growing problems. No one, however, to our knowledge, forecast the major market crises in the region. There were no economist whistleblowers. This is probably attributable in the main to an overconfidence within and outside the region due to two or more decades of rapid and sustained growth in the East Asian trigger economies and other East Asian countries. It may be due in part too to the herd instinct of economists and commentators which caused them to ignore growing signs of macroeconomic imbalance and microeconomic difficulties or to the inability to put together the pieces of a complex picture.

6   Restoring growth – the necessary reforms

A number of reforms are essential if financial market agents outside the region are to be convinced that the East Asian countries offer a stable environment for investments. They must be sufficient in totality to convince outside investors and market operators that these countries recognize the seriousness of the present situation and are determined to address it. They should go beyond the limited commitments of the IMF-managed packages for the Philippines, Thailand and Indonesia, even though there are signs in Thailand and Indonesia of political hesitation in carrying out these packages.

The first area of reform is a change in the foreign exchange regimes of those countries which operated a formal or *de facto* peg. With the exception of the Hong Kong dollar, these pegs have been abandoned as they could not be maintained under the pressure of massive one-way bets; Thailand introduced a managed float of the baht on 2 July, the Philippines announced on 11 July that it had floated the peso and Indonesia announced on 14 August that it had decided to abandon the exchange rate intervention and and allowed the rupiah to float. The regimes needed to be adjusted.

The more important question is what regime will prevail after the foreign exchange market turmoil has subsided?

A number of suggestions have been made. Japan has been urging East Asian countries to peg their rates *vis-à-vis* the Japanese yen rather than the US dollar. Prime Minister Mahathir in particular has made it abundantly clear on several occasions that he prefers a managed float to a free float and he has fulminated against international speculators who dictate the direction of change of the exchange rate. At the annual meeting of the IMF in September, Malaysian Finance Minister Anwar Abrahim called for a new foreign exchange regime under IMF auspices which would monitor market practices, including tougher disclosure requirements for currency fund managers, and these calls were repeated at the G-15 meeting in November. At the IMF meetings Japan proposed an Asian fund to deal with future currency crises. They envisaged a facility with US$100 billion with multiple donors led by Japan. The idea lapsed after opposition by the US, Germany and other G-7 countries. One objection is that the prospect of a regional bail-out would deter governments from taking corrective action and encourage speculators, an example of moral hazard in financial markets.

Western economists on the other hand are generally agreed that the maintenance of pegged rates which lead to a misalignment of the real exchange rates is just another set of examples of the harm of trying to fix the rate in a market in which demand and supply are constantly changing. They would regard a peg in terms of a basket of currencies as preferable to a peg in terms of one currency. This would at least lead to a weighting of the movement of bilateral rates which moved in different directions, such as the US dollar and the yen in the two years preceding the present crises. (Certainly East Asian currencies should reject the Japanese suggestion that they peg to the yen.) But such a basket peg policy did not prevent the Thailand baht from becoming seriously misaligned. A flexible rate allows continuous adjustment to accommodate changes in relative price movements or commodity markets. There is a second argument in favour of exchange rate flexibility. Advocates of flexible exchange rates have argued that a flexible exchange rate provides a clear signal of the effects of government policies. Greater flexibility in exchange rates is both essential and inevitable.

A second set of necessary reforms come under the heading of financial market regulation. The details will vary considerably from economy to economy as the present system of regulation varies among economies. They will include tighter prudential controls and greater regulation in terms of the activities which commercial banks are permitted to engage in. These should follow principles such as those laid down earlier this year by the Basle Committee on Banking Supervision (1997). They will also include a relaxation on the entry of foreign financial banks and other suppliers of financial services as the present restrictions have inhibited the development of a wide range of services at minimum costs and narrowed the diversification of these institutions. The arguments in favour of foreign participation in this sector are essentially the same as those which have proved so successful in the opening up of the goods sectors in these countries to international trade and greater competition. In short, what is required is a different pattern of regulation with tighter controls in some areas and weaker controls in other, rather than deregulation.

A major reform is the introduction and development of derivatives markets, particularly in Thailand, Malaysia and Indonesia. The introduction of options and futures markets will permit better hedging of equities exposures. It is also the case that a number of financial market deregulations should be considered. In particular, the access of foreign investors should be significantly liberalized, the imposition of price limits should be reviewed and finally some consideration should be given to extending trading hours (24-hour trading) in periods of high volatility in order to trade out the shock.

The IMF is calling for macroeconomic restraint including tighter fiscal and monetary policies in the countries subject to IMF bail-outs. The necessity of tighter fiscal policies is not clear. It was noted above that the overall budget deficits had not blown out in the trigger countries. There is a danger that tight fiscal policies would depress the economies and could retard their export recoveries. This does not deny the need for more careful selection of investment projects and other reforms in the public sector.

Thailand and Malaysia have raised tariff rates after the crisis. This is harmful and unnecessary, given the large exchange rate devaluations. Further reforms of trade policies are desirable. The East Asian countries, including all three trigger economies, have an exceptional record of unilateral reductions in tariff and other border restrictions on trade in goods (see PECC, 1995, 1996). Trade liberalization should be continued. In the case of Indonesia, the IMF package requires them to remove the international trading monopolies for some commodities but others remain. These are particularly objectionable because they combine the monopoly powers of single traders (as with the statutory monopolies in Australia) with the transfer of these valuable implicit property rights to the individuals who were granted the monopolies. These countries have been much less active in reducing restrictions on service trade in general. The current WTO negotiations on an Agreement on Financial Services provide an opportunity for them to join the industrialized countries in liberalizing trade in these services.

Another critical area is FDI incentives. East Asian countries have been among the most vigorous in the world in offering incentives to attract FDI. These incentives were a factor in the rapid expansion of FDI and capital formation in the area. Like border interventions in trade policy, these incentives distort the pattern of FDI flows among countries and, because they are not uniformly available to all sectors, distort the patterns within the host economies. Some economists and other groups such as the United Nations Conference on Trade and Development (UNCTAD) (see UNCTAD, 1996, Chapter VI) have sought ways of limiting these incentives but it is difficult to persuade countries to agree individually to limit their policies as they fear FDI will be diverted to other countries which continue to offer incentives. This suggests that multilateral action may succeed better than unilateral action. This matter is under discussion in the APEC draft on Nonbinding Investment Principles and the OECD Multilateral Investment Agreement but the developing Asian countries have opposed limitations on incentives in these fora. There needs to be an appreciation in East Asia of the distorting and the collectively self-defeating nature of these incentives.

Anti-corruption measures are essential to improve the productivity of capital and avoid discouragement of foreign direct investment. The levels of foreign direct investment have risen relative to capital formation in these economies. In China,

Singapore and Malaysia inward FDI was equal to 25, 24 and 16 per cent of gross capital formation respectively in 1994 (UNCTAD, 1996, Annex Table 5) and have probably risen further in the last two years. These are very high levels.

7   The future

We do not attempt forecasts of the main indicators of East Asian countries or Australia for two reasons. First, the crises have not ended. Secondly, the focus for the real economy should be on the medium and long term rather than the short term which dominates the financial sector. Here the main issue is whether the financial market volatility will spill over to the real economies.

Implications for Australia   There is considerable uncertainty associated with this economic event, and that uncertainty extends to the implications for Australia. Already we have seen a number of forecasters downgrade their forecasts of real Australian growth in 1998 by from 0.5 to 1 per cent. We do not attempt to specify our own forecasts. It is clear, however, that the most significant effects for Australian corporations will occur later in 1998, as the full flow on of the Asian markets crisis affects earnings and transactions. The August–September earnings' season of 1998, and the growth rates of the third and fourth quarters in 1998 will reflect diminished valuations of assets and reduced transactions demand. Future growth in Australia will depend on how quickly the Asian economies 'bungee-jump', and how significant are the linkages between the asset markets and the real economy.

We may expect reductions in export of goods and services to East Asia; sectors which were marginally exposed before the 1980s, such as education and tourism, are now rather significantly exposed. The exchange rate effects will be amplified by the wealth effects noted in Table 2. On the other hand, to the extent that our competitors in these markets are countries such as the US and UK whose currencies have strengthened *vis-à-vis* the Australian dollar, we will gain a competitive advantage. Similarly, some Australian exports of materials and intermediate inputs to East Asian producers may gain if the exchange rate devaluations lead to an increase in the quantity of exports, as in the Mexican case. But there will be offsetting pressure on the prices of these goods. It is also the case that imports from East Asian countries may increase substantially in 1998, worsening Australia's balance of payments position. In the foreseeable future, the likely weaker balance of payments position will prevent the Australian dollar appreciating substantially.

It should be re-emphasized that the magnitude of the East Asian bubble is still uncertain, and while excessive volatility persists in asset markets, the possibility of effects on transactions demand remains. As a consequence, there is considerable downside risk in real growth forecasts for Australia in 1998 and 1999.

7.1   A new environment for East Asian countries

Post-1997 the growth environment for East Asia is substantially different than it was pre-1997 in several ways.

East Asian policy-makers will have to be smarter in managing their economies under a regime in which exchange rates are more flexible and capital is more mobile internationally because financial markets are now linked more closely to international financial markets. In addition, there is no longer a widespread acceptance of the East Asian miracle. There will be a closer inspection of their policies and performance by foreign direct investors and investors in equity markets.

7.2 East Asian growth restored in one or two years but at a slower rate

Given the example of Mexico, it should be possible for these countries to resume rapid growth within one or two years of the end of the crisis. This is, however, conditional on the governments of these countries making a convincing response to the present crises by adopting widespread reforms, as noted above. If this is done, there may in fact be long-run benefits to their economies as some reforms which would otherwise have taken years are accelerated.

However, the rates of growth of Asian economies will be lower than the average over the last three decades or so. This seems to be the consensus of opinion around the world. The London-based Consensus Economics is an organization which collates opinions of leading world forecasters. It released in October forecasts of average annual growth rates expected over the next 10 years. While these show a rate for the East Asian countries which is about 1 percentage point lower than the forecasts made six months ago, the average rate of growth expected for the region is more than 6 per cent. The largest reductions are for Thailand which is expected to grow at 4.8 per cent, the lowest rate in the region, compared to the previous forecast of 6.8 per cent. These views are simply an average of different forecasts and most of these are guesses rather than the outcomes of any explicit models of the growth process.

We view this long-run process in terms of the convergence of income levels. This provides a powerful constraint on growth possibilities in the longer term. As an indication of the force of convergence on the rate of growth, one may use the graph and the regression line in Figure 6. For Hong Kong and Singapore, which were the two countries with highest per capita income at the beginning of the period and which had reached income levels equal to those of Australia and other developed countries by the 1990s, one could expect a reduction in the annual growth rate by the end of the period of more than 2 percentage points. If rapid growth resumes in say 1 or 2 years and if the trend is extrapolated to 2000 and beyond, it would mean that the rate of growth in these countries may not exceed about 5 per cent per annum. For the ASEAN countries which had slower average growth and which have currently much lower income levels, the reduction would be less and they should be able to continue to grow at rates in excess of 5 per cent.

In the present environment of a disturbed global market, these forecasts should be taken with more than the usual degree of uncertainty. Indeed the fluctuations are so pronounced that we represent them as given at mid-November 1997. Continued volatility in equity markets and/or political instability in one or more countries would worsen the outlook for East Asia.

Appendix

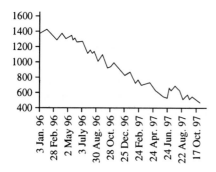

Source: Bloomberg.

Figure A.7   Stock Exchange of Thailand index

Source: Bloomberg.

Figure A.10   Kuala Lumpur Composite index

Source: Bloomberg.

Figure A.8   Jakarta Composite index

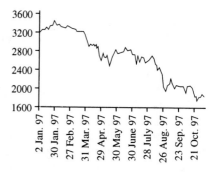

Source: Bloomberg.

Figure A.11   Philippines Composite index

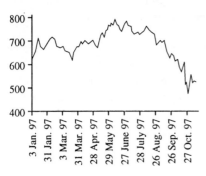

Source: Bloomberg.

Figure A.9   Korea Composite index

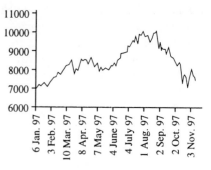

Source: Bloomberg

Figure A.12   Taiwan Stock Exchange index

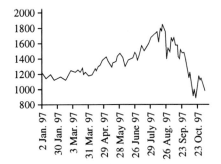

Source: Bloomberg.

Figure A.13   China 40 index

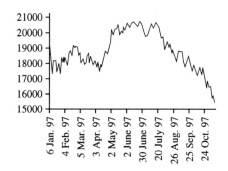

Source: Bloomberg.

Figure A.16   Nikkei 225 (Japan)

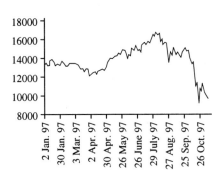

Source: Bloomberg.

Figure A.14   Hang Seng (Hong Kong)

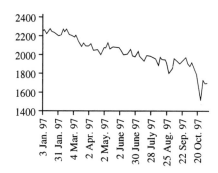

Source: Bloomberg.

Figure A.17   Straits Times index (Singapore)

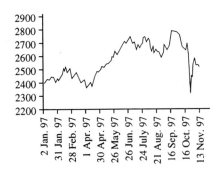

Source: Bloomberg.

Figure A.15   All Ordinaries index (Australia)

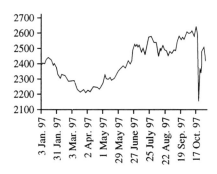

Source: Bloomberg

Figure A.18   NZSE 40 index (New Zealand)

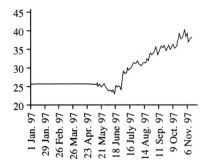

Source: Bloomberg.

Figure A.19   Thai baht per US dollar

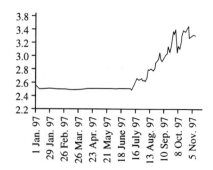

Source: Bloomberg.

Figure A.22   Malaysian ringitt per US dollar

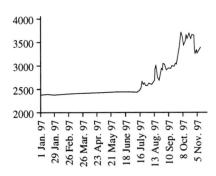

Source: Bloomberg.

Figure A.20   Indonesian rupiah per US dollar

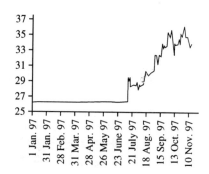

Source: Bloomberg.

Figure A.23   Philippine peso per US dollar

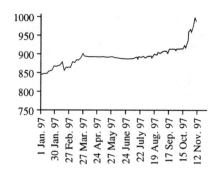

Source: Bloomberg.

Figure A.21   Korean won per US dollar

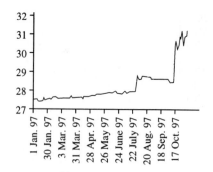

Source: Bloomberg

Figure A.24   Taiwan dollar per US dollar

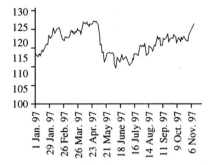

Source: Bloomberg.

Figure A.25   Japanese yen per US dollar

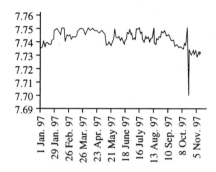

Source: Bloomberg.

Figure A.28   Hong Kong dollar per US dollar

Source: Bloomberg.

Figure A.26   Singapore dollar per US dollar

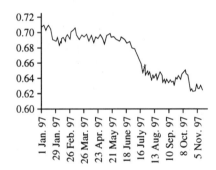

Source: Bloomberg.

Figure A.29   US dollar per New Zealand dollar

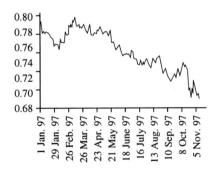

Source: Bloomberg.

Figure A.27   US dollar per Australian dollar

Notes

1. The analysis in this section is conditional on data up to and including 13 November 1997. Kim Sawyer wishes to acknowledge earlier discussions with Kevin Davis and Duncan Ironmonger.
2. We are grateful to the Urban Land Authority for sponsoring some of the research that went into this paper.

References

Asian Development Bank (1997a), *Asian Development Outlook 1997 and 1998*, Asian Development Bank, Manila.

Asian Development Bank (1997b), *Emerging Asia: Changes and Challenges*, Asian Development Bank, Manila.

Bank for International Settlements (1997a), *Financial Stability in Emerging Market Economies: A Strategy for the Formulation, Adoption, and Implementation of Sound Principles and Practices to Strengthen Financial Systems*, Bank for International Settlements, Basle.

Bank for International Settlements (1997b), *67th Annual Report*, Bank for International Settlements, Basle.

Bank for International Settlements (1997c), *Statistics on External Indebtedness*, July 1997, Bank for International Settlements, Basle.

Basle Committee on Banking Supervision (1997), *Core Principles for Effective Banking Supervision*, Bank for International Settlements, Basle.

Barro, R.J. and X. Sala-i-Martin (1995), *Economic Growth*, McGraw-Hill International Editions, New York.

Claessens, S. and T. Glaessner (1997), 'Internationalization of Financial Services in East Asia', paper presented to the Conference on Investment Liberalization and Financial Reform in the Asia-Pacific Region, Sydney, 29–31 August 1997.

Institute of Developing Economies (1997), *Economic Outlook for East Asian Economies over the Next Decade: Is Continuous Growth Possible?*, Institute of Developing Economies, Tokyo.

Lloyd, P.J. (1996), 'The Role of Foreign Investment in the Success of Asian Industrialisation', *Journal of Asian Economics*, **7**, 407–33.

Pacific Economic Co-operation Council (1995), *Perspectives on the Manila Action Plan for APEC*, PECC Secretariat, Singapore.

Pacific Economic Co-operation Council (1996), *Milestones in APEC Liberalisation: A Map of Market Opening Measures of APEC Countries*, PECC Secretariat, Singapore.

Sachs, J.D. and A. Warner (1995), 'Economic Reform and the Process of Global Integration', *Brookings Papers on Economic Activity*, I; 1995, 1–118.

United Nations Conference on Trade and Development (1996), *World Investment Report 1966*, UNCTAD, Geneva.

PART VII

NEW ISSUES IN THE GLOBAL ECONOMY

Introduction

The first two papers in this section deal with two of the three 'new issues' of trade policy which have been recognized in the World Trade Organization (WTO), namely trade and the environment, and the relationships between international trade and competition policies. Both of these issues have emerged rather quickly at the international level and are certain to become more important.

In both papers I argue that the WTO is not the organization which should have primary responsibility for the development of new international rules in these two areas. But the reasons for this conclusion are quite different in the two cases. In the case of trade and the environment, the primary problem is that cross-border spill-overs of environmental effects are not primarily associated with international trade in goods. Rather, they are due to loss of habitat or transmission by common waterways or other factors. The circumstances vary from case to case. In the case of competition policy, the primary reasons are that the development of rules is premature as the issues are unclear and many countries are still concerned over national sovereignty in this area, and the fact that the WTO is a multilateral organization which regulates the actions of national governments, not the private producers who are the subject of actions under competition law.

The next three papers deal with three different aspect of increased interdependence among national economies in the form of increased goods trade. A large part of the increased international trade in goods has taken the form of increased imports of intermediate inputs as they are increasingly sourced from the cheapest global source. Many of these imported intermediates are incorporated in goods subsequently exported. Conversely, some imports incorporate goods which have been exported from the importing country or capital and labour of the residents of the nation which is located abroad.

Such re-export or re-import trade has consequences for tariff policy which are only now being realized. 'Offshore production and import taxation' deals with the case of imports which incorporate goods which have been exported from the importing country or capital and labour of the nation which is located abroad. This local content of imports should be excluded from the value for duty, the base of the taxes on imports. This has long been recognized in an *ad hoc* way in the Offshore Assembly Provisions of the US Tariff and more recently in similar provisions of the tariffs of some other countries, including Australia where they are called the Overseas Assembly Provisions. The non-exclusion of local content of imports discriminates against that part of the national production which occurs overseas. The paper recommends a tax based only on the foreign value added.

A related problem is discussed in the paper on 'A tariff substitute for rules of origin in free trade areas'. With the growth of free trade areas, rules of origin are an increasing problem in the management of the international trading system and they are commonly regarded as a significant source of protection in the North American Free Trade Agreement (NAFTA) and some other free trade areas. The debate focuses on the rule which determines origin. This paper argues instead that the fundamental problem is that all existing rules adopt a binary division of goods, either a good is treated as originating wholly in the region or wholly outside the region. In actuality, a part of the value of an imported good originates inside the region and a part outside. The logical approach to designing rules of origin, it seems to the writer, is, therefore, to substitute for existing rules a new rule which would collect a dollar value in duty payments proportional to the value added in third countries.

The problems in choosing the base of tariffs and in designing rules of origin both arise because of international trade in intermediate inputs. They are both consequences of increased trade in goods and factors. They were written without attention to the relationship between these problems. It is only now in reviewing these papers that the author has come to see more clearly the intimate connections between them. Indeed, they could be regarded as parts of a larger tax problem and they could be combined in a single border tax which only taxed the value added by residents of foreign countries. In a free trade area, the term 'foreign value' would not include the regional partners.

The last paper deals with another consequence of the re-export of imported intermediate inputs. This one deals with the measurement of the commodity terms of trade rather than tariff policies. It turns out that, under these circumstances, the usual definition of the commodity terms of trade may understate the movement of relative prices. This has been recognized for entrepôt trade in Singapore and Hong Kong but the effect applies broadly to all goods which are re-exported in a transformed form, not just to re-exports narrowly defined. Some calculations done for Singapore indicate that the effect may be substantial.

[19]

The problem of optimal environmental policy choice

Peter J. Lloyd

Transfrontier pollution and environmental problems are a particular set of externality or market failure problems, with the added feature of the transmission of the pollutants and environmentally-related products across national borders.

The primary effect of national borders is to limit the instruments available to deal with these problems because the jurisdictions of national governments stop at their borders and there is no international government or law with powers corresponding to those of national governments. Nations which are net losers from international transmission of pollutants have become increasingly concerned about these problems. If international actions fail to address them satisfactorily, there will be increasing agitation to use national measures. Among these in some cases will be trade-based policy measures to achieve national goals. Trade-based measures are also used as a means to ensure compliance with international environmental conventions, as with the regulation of international trade in ivory under the Convention for International Trade in Endangered Species. Conversely, the GATT, the OECD, UNCTAD and other international agencies have become concerned over the potential impact of national and international environmental policy measures on international trade.

The analysis of the policy options for environmental problems is a subset of standard analysis of market failures. As with other externality problems there is, for each environmental problem, a multiplicity of instruments which may be used to seek to correct the market failure. The nature of these problems is such that there is no single instrument or set of instruments which ranks generally above all others. For example, Bohm and Russell (1985) concluded their comparative survey of alternative instruments with the observation that '...no general statements can be made about the relative desirability of alternative policy instruments once we consider such practical complications as that location matters, that monitoring is costly, and that exogenous change occurs in technology, regional economies and natural environment systems'. This result carries over to environmental problems with transnational flows. Transnational environment problems differ in details such as the numbers of polluters or pollutees, the locations of the emission and reception areas, the stock or flow nature of the pollutant, the extent of uncertainty, the form of the damage function and the enforceability of instruments. Each problem must therefore be analysed separately because the ranking of two or more alternative instruments is not robust with respect to variations in these specifications.

Notwithstanding the specificity of each problem, however, there is a common approach. The choice of instrument may be regarded as an optimization problem. One selects an objective function and specifies the structure of the market(s) concerned. An important part of the structure in this class of problem is the transmission mechanism. There is a list of instruments available. The optimization yields an optimal or first-ranked instrument. The other instruments available can then be compared and ranked and, if necessary, a second-best choice can be made. The ranking may not be straightforward. Even the list of available instruments is constantly growing. For example, over almost twenty years the OECD has carried out several studies regarding the principles of selecting instruments in pollution and environment problems. The listing of 'economic' (i.e. price-based) instruments alone in their latest study (OECD, 1989) is considerably longer than earlier lists (OECD, 1976) as it includes newer types of economic instruments such as liability insurance. In some cases, none of the instruments in the existing list may solve the problem or there may be adverse effects on some parties which are not acceptable so that an important part of the analysis may be to try to design a new set of instruments. The analysis of transfrontier pollution problems such as acid rain and waste disposal is of this type.

This paper provides a general survey of the issues involved in selecting instruments to regulate transnational pollution and environmental problems. It begins with a comparison of instruments in terms of the concepts of equivalence and non-equivalence. Then the discussion moves briefly to the jurisdiction of governments which apply instruments of environmental policy. Two archetypal problems which are the source of most conclusions concerning the choice of instruments in a closed economy are outlined. The analysis focuses on the aspects which can be related to the internationalization of pollution. Next the problem of managing environmental policy in a world with nations and the international transmission of pollutants or products is considered, while problems associated with the use of trade-based instruments are discussed in the last section.

3.1   Comparison of instruments

To make the comparison of two (or more) instruments precise, there is one concept which turns out to be particularly instructive, namely, the equivalence of instruments. This concept is useful for all policy problems which must rank multiple instruments. It has been widely used not only in environmental economics but also in tax theory (e.g., the Ricardian equivalence of tax and bond financing) and in international trade theory (e.g., the Lerner 'symmetry' of an export tax and an import tax and the equivalence of a tariff and a quota).

Equivalence or non-equivalence is a relation that holds between a pair of instruments. A three-fold distinction is made. The distinctions are based on the concept of a market solution which was introduced into the comparison of a tariff and a quota in international trade theory by Ohta (1978). A market solution is simply the set of solution values in an optimization problem of all endogenous variables such as the quantities of market production, consumption and imports, the prices to consumers and producers, and the value of revenue collected from the instrument to the government.

Definition 1: One instrument is said to be *identical* to a second alternative instrument if both instruments, when set at appropriate levels, yield the same market solution.

Definition 2: One instrument is said to be *equivalent* to a second alternative instrument if both instruments, when set at appropriate levels, yield the same market solution except for the incomes of the agents. (Otherwise, the instrument is defined as *non-equivalent.*)

Definition 3: One instrument is said to be *quasi-equivalent* to a second alternative instrument if both instruments, when set at appropriate levels, yield the same solution value for one of the endogenous variables.

In Definition 3 it may be that more than one endogenous variable takes on the same values, but the possibility that all variables except the income variables take the same values is ruled out. Thus, Definitions 1, 2 and 3 are mutually exclusive. They are in decreasing order of the set of variables in the market which take the same values. One could define the complements of Definitions 1 and 3, that is *non-identical* and *non-quasi-equivalent* instruments, in the same way if desired.

These definitions are all partial equilibrium but they have general equilibrium analogues. In the general equilibrium version of the policy problems, two equivalent instruments may both be Pareto-efficient, that is, they yield production and consumption allocations which put the economy on the utility possibility frontier, but they will yield different sets of real incomes for the households in the economy. In what follows, for example, equivalence relates to static comparisons, but it should be kept in mind that in a dynamic setting such equivalence may break down. See, for example, Anderson (1988) on the non-equivalence of tariffs and quotas as trade policy instruments in a dynamic setting. It should also be kept in mind that in addition to standard economic policy instruments there are policy options such as publicity campaigns to alter individuals' contributions to micropollution (Opschoor and Pearce, 1991). Economic efficiency rules out the possibility of any slack in the economy in the sense of any possibility of Pareto-improving reallocations.

These distinctions are very helpful. The usefulness of Definition 1 is self-evident. Surprisingly, some pairs of instruments which are identical are not obviously so. An example is the identity of a property rights assignment and the appropriate tax-subsidy together with the rule for the disbursement of the tax revenue or the financing of the funds to pay the subsidy (see below). The usefulness of Definition 2 is that it isolates the efficiency effects of instruments. Definition 3 is useful when one wants to compare the effects on some pre-selected variable.[1] In the environmental literature, the problem is often posed as one of attaining some environmental standard. Thus we are comparing instruments which are quasi-equivalent with respect to the environmental standard. The concern in the GATT and the OECD has recently shifted to the 'trade impact' of environmental policy instruments. These international organizations are concerned with the linkage between environmental policies and trade flows. When examining instruments which impact on the exports or imports of a commodity, it may be useful to fix the environmental standard and then compare the effects of different instruments on other variables, especially the quantities traded between nations.

Two instruments which are equivalent may be compared in terms of their income effects. Thus, economists frequently argue that it is better to auction quota rights to avoid the transfer of rents to quota holders. More generally, a government may be concerned with the distribution of the income effects of instruments among its citizens. One instrument may have an effect which is more progressive or regressive than another or may have a particularly large impact on some households. For example, Harrison (1975) concluded that the costs of controlling air pollution from motor vehicles in the United States have been distributed progressively within cities but have affected the rural poor rather badly because their car ownership is high and they have fewer alternatives, with the overall effect being regressive. The concern over the distribution of the costs and of the benefits may be greater in developing countries. It has been argued that the poor have fewer opportunities to substitute as income-earners or consumers (Eskeland and Jimenez, 1991). A government preference for one instrument over others because of the pattern of income effects implies it is unable or unwilling to compensate losers.

Two non-equivalent instruments may be compared and ranked in terms of their efficiency effects. Frequently, the problem is posed as one of achieving a given improvement in the environment at least cost. Income effects may also be considered.

It is now well understood that any relation between two instruments only holds under certain assumptions. Any modification of one of these critical assumptions will alter the rankings. This non-robustness is the reason why the ranking of policy instruments is so difficult.

3.2   The jurisdiction of the government

Until recently, almost all of the literature on the environment related to problems which were national. That is, all of the agents involved lived within the borders of one nation and were, therefore, subject to the jurisdiction of the one government which could select the instrument of policy. Regulating international transmission of pollutants and/or of commodities whose production or consumption is polluting is complicated by the restriction of the jurisdiction of the policy-imposing governments to the subsets of agents living within their national borders (or to negotiated international agreements in the form of bilateral or multilateral treaties). Initially, the analysis here is restricted to a closed economy. This allows us to consider the choice of policy instrument or the design of new instruments without concern for the limitations on instrument choice which derive from national jurisdictions. The last two sections consider the nature of the second-best problem when the economy is open and the choice of instruments is constrained by national jurisdiction.

The closed economy consists of a given population of people which, in turn, defines the population of agents (polluters, pollutees, consumers, producers). The agents have a fixed geographic location which may or may not be important, depending upon the structure of the market(s) concerned. A sole government has jurisdiction over all agents in the economy.

3.3   Two archetypal environmental problems

In order to develop some principles, the analysis focuses on two archetypes of environmental problems which feature prominently in the literature and which produce some principles of wide applicability. The problem is described as a pollution problem for concreteness. The term 'pollution' can, therefore, be understood to include all environmental problems. The first is the upstream-downstream problem where one or many upstream producers raise costs for a user of water downstream. The second involves not only multiple dischargers but also multiple reception areas for pollution.

54   *Peter J. Lloyd*

3.3.1   *The upstream-downstream problem*

Much of the literature and most of the textbooks – for example, Varian (1984) and Pearce and Turner (1990) – are based on a type of problem involving one upstream producer who produces a pollutant as a by-product and one downstream producer who is adversely affected by the pollutant. We can call them the steel mill and the fishery respectively. This is the simplest form of a unilateral or non-reciprocal producer-on-producer externality with only two agents. This is what is sometimes called the one-on-one problem (see Helm and Pearce, 1990) where the first 'one' refers to the number of polluters or generators and the second 'one' to the number of pollutees or affected parties. Moreover, it is assumed that the pollution problem is a flow problem, the two industries are competitive and there is no uncertainty in the product or factor markets or pollution flows. The pollution is transmitted by water and arrives directly at the fishery without being dissipated and without affecting any other agent in the economy. There is perfect information and no monitoring or enforcement costs. Many authors assume there is no possibility of abatement by means of reducing pollution per unit of output, but this restrictive assumption is easily relaxed.

While this model is over-simplified, it has been the source of most fundamental insights of pollution theory. These include the Pigovian tax (Pigou, 1932), the Coase Theorem (Coase, 1960) and the equivalence of a pollution tax and a pollution abatement subsidy (see, for example, Baumol and Oates, 1975).

The social objective function in this problem is simply the sum of the profits of the two activities since the only two agents involved are competitive producers. If the agent who suffers the damage is a consumer, the problem can be recast in a similar way by taking some monetary measure of the value of the product to the consumer(s) less that of the damage. Let subscripts 1, 2 and 3 denote the outputs of steel, the pollution by-product, and fish respectively. The structure of the problem is given by the technologies of producing the outputs which can be represented by the production functions:

$$y_1 = f_1(x_1)$$
$$y_2 = g_2(y_1, a_1)$$
$$y_3 = f_3(x_3, y_2)$$

$g_2(y_1, a_1)$ is the pollution by-product function. This assumes pollution is some function of the output of steel, y_1, and possibly also of the use of abatement inputs by the steel producer, a_1. The social problem is to find:

$$\max\{[p_1f_1(x_1) - w_1x_1 - w_2a_1] + [p_3f_3(x_3, g_2(y_1, a_1)) - w_3x_3]\}$$
$$\text{such that } (x_1, a_1, x_3) \geqslant 0$$

where (x_1, a_1, x_3) are the vectors of inputs used in steel, abatement and fisheries production and (w_1, w_2, w_3) are the vectors of their prices. (It is useful to note for comparison with the second model below that the social problem can be recast as one of maximising the social profit gain from the pre-intervention situation by reducing pollution.)

The model yields a number of standard results. Steel producers in an unregulated market maximize their own profits, disregarding completely the harmful effect of steel production on fisheries production which results from the river pollution. This yields, under very general restrictions on the functions, a market failure with too much steel output and too little fisheries output. The social maximum solution is achieved by the rule of choosing input levels so that the marginal cost equals the marginal social benefit, taking into account in the benefit function both the value of the sale of steel and the harm imposed by the pollution by-product. The socially-optimal adjusted solution has the property that the optimal quantity of pollution is, in general, not zero.

The social optimum can be achieved by a number of policy choices which include the following: a pollution standard; a pollution charge; a pollution abatement subsidy; an assignment of property rights to (a) the polluter or (b) the pollutee; and the internalizing of the externality through one of the operators taking over the other activity (i.e. unitization).

The pollution standard is fixed in terms of the total emission. The pollution charge is based on the pollution emitted. Examples are taxes on waste discharged, pollutants emitted into the air or water, and the carbon tax proposed to reduce global warming (see OECD, 1991). The pollution charge rate is set at the rate $(p_3 \; \partial f_3 / \partial y_2)$ per unit of emission which measures the social cost of pollution in terms of the value of the loss of fish output at the margin. (Alternatively, it could be set in this example as a tax on steel output if there is a one-to-one correspondence between steel output and emission.)

When there is no possibility of abatement by means of the use of abatement inputs, abatement can only occur through a reduction in the output of the steel mill. When there is a possibility of abatement by the use of abatement inputs, there are two margins of pollution reduction. A tax on pollution (or any of the equivalent instruments) provides the incentive to the polluter to adjust output and/or to use abatement inputs at the margin so as to minimize the private and the social cost of pollution reduction. This solution may call for zero abatement inputs if the abatement technology is expensive. The use of abatement inputs is an example of action the polluting agents might adopt to reduce their tax burden. Other actions might also be possible, such as the relocation of the mill to another site where pollution taxes are lower.

The use of concepts of equivalence sheds further light on the choice. All of these instruments are equivalent to each other, but they are not all identical because the income effects differ between some pairs. An assignment

56   *Peter J. Lloyd*

of property rights to the fisheries is identical to the combination of a tax or charge on the polluter with the proceeds paid lump-sum to the fisheries. This is of interest because many economists have advocated a polluter pays principle but opposed the payment of the proceeds as compensation to the pollutees (see Bohm and Russell, 1985) while others advocate property rights which are equivalent to the charge with compensation. An assignment of property rights to the steel mill is identical to a pollution abatement subsidy in combination with the finance for the subsidy being levied lump-sum on the fisheries. These two sets of instruments are not identical to each other because they affect the profits of the two producers differently. Similarly, a pollution charge and a pollution abatement subsidy are not identical to each other. All equivalent instruments yield the same total pre-tax/subsidy profits of the two producers.

The optimal tax, or an equivalent instrument, is optimal because it has a tax base, namely, the emission itself, which bears directly upon the damage caused and a tax rate which measures exactly the extent of damage associated with a marginal unit of the emission. Other instruments which do not bear directly upon the emission will inflict incidental costs on the economy and will, therefore, be sub-optimal. As the first example, consider a tax on steel output in the circumstance when abatement technology is available. In this case, although an output tax will reduce pollution and pollution damage, there is no longer a one-to-one correspondence between the quantity of pollution and output. Taxing output gives no incentive to the producer to reduce pollution by means of an abatement technology. Similarly, a subsidy based on abatement inputs, as distinct from a subsidy on the abatement of the emission itself, is sub-optimal. It gives no incentive to the producer to reduce abatement by reducing output and therefore raises the cost of abatement reduction through an excessive use of abatement inputs. Such instruments which are based on variables that are themselves related to the level of the damage-causing emissions are sometimes called 'indirect' instruments (see the taxonomy in Eskeland and Jimenez, 1991). These include taxes on the complements of the product with which the pollutant is associated (e.g. taxes on motor vehicles whose consumption of petrol pollutes the atmosphere) and subsidies on substitutes (Sandmo, 1976). All indirect instruments are inefficient and sub-optimal if direct instruments are feasible.

This classification of optimal (or efficient) and sub-optimal (or inefficient) instruments can be refined to give a ranking of more than two instruments. Such a ranking will reflect the rule that an instrument ranks more highly (i.e. is more efficient), the more closely the base is related to the source of the pollution-creating emission.[2] A good example of this principle is the problem of global warming due to carbon dioxide emissions. The optimal (first-best) tax is a tax on carbon emissions. If this is not feasible, taxes on carbon-producing fuels or on the outputs produced by these fuels such as electricity, have been suggested. But each of these produces incidental costs. A tax on fossil fuels does reduce their consumption but each fuel produces different marginal quantities of carbon in different uses. Similarly, a tax on electricity is independent of the source of fuel or power and gives no incentive to substitute carbon-free sources such as water, wind or nuclear energy or to introduce technologies which economise on the use of fuel or produce less carbon per kilowatt. Such instruments do not minimize the social cost of pollution reduction. Some indirect instruments may have such large incidental costs that they lower rather than raise social welfare.[3]

The model may easily be extended to n producer/polluter agents, that is, a many-on-one version of the model. Let the technologies be given by the production functions:

$$y_{1i} = f_{1i}(x_{1i}) \qquad i = 1, \ldots, n$$
$$y_{2i} = g_{2i}(y_{1i}, a_{2i}) \qquad i = 1, \ldots, n.$$
$$y_3 = f_3(x_3, \Sigma_i y_{2i})$$

The subscript i denotes a variable of the ith firm. This specification allows steel firms to be distinct in terms of steel-producing technologies. The pollution damage function may be firm-specific. However, it still assumes that it is the aggregate emission which affects the downstream producer and there is no dissipation of pollutants.

Again in this version a pollution charge or its equivalent is optimal. This should be levied at the rate of $\tau = (p_3 \, \partial f_3 / \partial y_{2i})$ where y_{2i} is the ith firm's contribution to the aggregate emission.

In practice, the extension of the model to many polluters may introduce complications which can change the optimal rule and imply that some equivalences no longer hold. With many polluting agents it may become difficult to identify the contribution of each to the aggregate emission. This has the effect of making all of the instruments less efficient. Some instruments may cease to be feasible as the number of agents increases; for example, unitization is only practicable with one or a very few polluters. This is an example of the non-robustness of instrument rankings with respect to the structure of the model.

The model can also be used to examine the Polluter Pays Principle (PPP), that is, a Pigovian tax. This principle is widely accepted. The OECD Member countries approved this general principle for all Member countries in 1972 and the EC endorsed it in 1975 (OECD, 1991). However, the recommendation is usually made on the realization that such a tax leads to the socially optimal outputs and inputs, that is, it is Pareto-efficient. The existence of other instruments which achieve Pareto-efficiency equally well shows that this is not the only way to approach the problem. In a case involving damage inflicted by a factory owner with a smoking chimney, Coase (1960) recognised that the problem could be equally well addressed by a subsidy paid to the factory owner to induce him to install a smoke-prevention device; that is an abatement subsidy is equivalent to a pollution

58   *Peter J. Lloyd*

charge. The preference for a tax instrument might be based on the view that it is morally wrong for an agent to inflict harm on other agents, but Coase showed that this argument too is false. 'The question is commonly thought of as one in which A inflicts harm on B and what has to be decided is: how should we restrain A? But this is wrong. We are dealing with a problem of a reciprocal nature. To avoid the harm to B would inflict harm on A. The real question that has to be decided is: should A be allowed to harm B or should B be allowed to harm A? The problem is to avoid the greater harm.' (Coase, 1960).

The problem is elucidated by the property rights involved. As has been noted, an assignment of property rights to either the polluter or the pollutee will solve the efficiency problem, at least in the case of one-on-one problems. Now, how are we to decide who should have the rights? In the case of one-on-one problems this is quite unclear. For example, in a one-on-one case of passive smoke inhalation how are we to justify the assumption that the interests of the passive smoker and his/her rights to be free of smoke should prevail over the interests of the active smoker who will be harmed if this is accepted, or vice-versa? The problem cannot be decided on this basis alone.

The extension of the problem to involve more agents gives a clue. In the case of a water pollution problem, such as the steel mill, there are frequently many agents who suffer damage. The riparian view of property rights relating to water applies in most countries and declares that these rights belong to the whole community. The extension of the commons to include air is based on the same view. If the commons belong to all, individuals cannot have the right to use them as they please and to inflict harm on other users. This justifies some intervention but it does not decide the allocation of the scarce resource of the commons. In the steel mill-fisheries example, the uses of the commons by either the fisheries or the steel mill restricts the use by the other agent and both impose a cost on the economy. One may note too that the governments which levy pollution taxes or proxy taxes in defence of the interests of those harmed rarely compensate them by returning the revenue to the agents who have been damaged. The Polluter Pays Principle identifies who should pay but it does not specify who should receive the revenue.

The term Victim Pays Principle is sometimes used to describe the alternative pollution abatement subsidies. This is an unfortunate and unhelpful misnomer as any action produces a victim because of the reciprocity noted above. The term Pollutee Pays Principle would be preferable as it merely identifies the agent who pays.

The choice of instruments is complicated by other considerations. Olson and Zeckhauser (1970) noted that the application of the Polluter Pays Principle gives no incentive to the agents who are damaged by pollution to take evasive action. Sometimes it will be easier for the affected agent(s) to take such action than for the polluting agent(s); for example, by relocation of plants or residences. The earlier example implicitly assumes the possibilities of evasive action were restricted to the polluters. Similarly, in some problems, the enforcement costs of schemes which pay polluters may be less than those which penalize them. Conversely, pollution abatement subsidies may have adverse incentive effects (see for example, Baumol and Oates, 1975).

3.3.2   *The problem of multiple dischargers and multiple reception areas*

In the model above the aggregate of emissions matters but not its location, apart from the fact that the mill is located on the one stream. In many pollution problems the precise location of the source of the pollution matters. This can occur because there are many sources of pollution and the damage occurs at some reception area other than the point of emission. The quantity of many pollutants at the reception area is less than the quantity at the point of emission because the substance or chemical is not entirely conserved. It is chemically changed or physically settled between the source and the reception area and the loss varies from source to source. As well, if there are multiple reception areas, the damage caused by a given quantity of a pollutant measured at the reception area where it arrives may vary from area to area. Indeed, since areas differ in terms of the agents who inhabit them and their preferences and activities, this variation in damage is a universal feature of problems with multiple reception areas.

Numerous pollution problems are of this form; for example, discharge of sewerage or industrial waste into river systems or the sea and air pollution with deposition in many areas. These situations can be modelled by a many-on-many model, that is, a model with 'many' dischargers and 'many' reception areas.

Figure 3.1 illustrates an example in which there are multiple dischargers and three reception areas – A1, A2, and A3. Each cluster of sources has a transmission mechanism such that the waste discharged from all of the sources in a cluster is received at one or two areas. The lines indicate the transmission paths in real space.

Suppose there are $n \geqslant 1$ sources, and $m \geqslant 1$ reception areas. The benefit from reducing pollution is the avoidance of the social damage it would cause if it were not reduced. This benefit is not modelled but it is assumed there is a monetary measure of these damages and the damage function is known. The costs are the costs of reducing pollution at source and the cost function is assumed to be known. Let:

$D_i^0 =$ initial level of pollution discharged at source i.
$\Delta D_i =$ reduction in level of pollution discharged at source i
$A_{ij} =$ pollution discharged at source i arriving at reception area j

60   *Peter J. Lloyd*

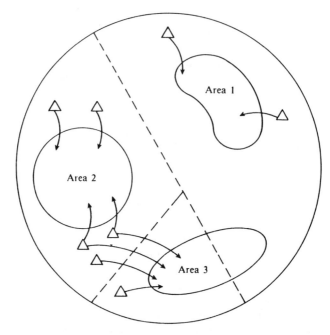

Figure 3.1   A world with multiple polluters and reception areas

$E_j = E_j(\Sigma_i \ A_{ij}) =$ damage function at reception area j
$B_j = -\Delta E_j =$ benefit from reducing pollution at area j
$C_i = C_i(\Delta D_i) =$ cost of reducing pollution at source i

The pollution received in area j from source i is some function of the pollution discharged from this source, $A_{ij}(D_i) = \alpha_i D_i$ where α_i is some fraction. It is assumed that the damage at each reception area depends solely upon the aggregate pollution received at the area. This is the model which underlies the analysis of most of the many-on-many pollution problems.

Formally the problem is to find:

$$\max_{\Delta D_i} \ \{\Sigma_j \ B_j[\Sigma \ A_{ij}(\Delta D_i)] - \Sigma_i \ C_i(\Delta D_i)\} \text{ such that } \Delta D_i \geqslant 0 \text{ for all } i$$

The reductions in discharge below the initial levels are the policy variables. This rule essentially views the problem from the status quo in which there is an excessive level of discharges. The problem, therefore, is to reduce these discharges to the optimal level and in the optimal way, as a given aggregate reduction can be achieved in many ways. This seems to be the way in which policy-makers conceive the problem.

This maximum is achieved by the rule:

$$\frac{\partial C_i}{\partial D_i} = \sum_j \frac{\partial B_j}{\partial A_{ij}} \frac{\partial A_{ij}}{\partial D_i} = \sum_j \frac{\partial B_j}{\partial D_i}$$

assuming the objective function is concave and differentiable. That is, the reductions at each source should be such that the marginal cost of each reduction is equal to the marginal social benefit. The marginal social benefit is the sum of the benefits in each area which receives pollution from this source. (Strictly speaking, this rule holds only if $\Delta D_i > 0$. One should allow for the possibility that there will be a zero reduction at some sources. This will arise when the marginal cost of reduction exceeds the marginal benefit at a source.)

This rule implies that the reductions are not equi-proportionate across sources. The reductions should be greater in those areas where the marginal costs of reductions are less or the marginal benefits of reduction are greater. It also implies that, in general, society should not minimize the cost of achieving a given reduction in pollution. This can be seen readily from the dual problem. The problem of maximizing net social benefit has a dual problem of minimizing the cost of achieving a given level of net social benefit. This minimum problem implies minimizing the cost of pollution reduction if and only if benefits of reducing pollution at source are equal across all sources. This result is intuitively obvious. A rule of minimizing the cost of pollution reduction would forgo possibilities of improving welfare by shifting the pollution reduction from areas with low marginal costs of reduction but little benefit to those with marginal costs which are a little higher but more than offset by gains in benefits.

It is usually supposed that the agent (producer or consumer) producing the discharge or emission acts purely selfishly. Typically the agent is a producer who is assumed to maximize the profits of the firm when activities yield pollutant as a by-product of a production activity but the model also encompasses selfish consumers who smoke cigarettes or consume other products which yield some harmful by-product such as chlorofluorocarbons (CFCs). Thus the initial level is that which maximizes the welfare of the private agents. In this case the social optimum may be achieved by a set of charges on discharge or emission at each source. The charges are location-specific since location matters either because it affects the contribution to the amount of the harmful substance which reaches the reception area or because the damage depends on the reception area. The rate of charge should equal the marginal damage caused, that is, the negative of the marginal benefit, at the optimum point. Any source whose discharge or emission is received at more than one area should pay a charge with components equal to the marginal damage caused to each group of agents.

Under these assumptions the set of discharge taxes is equivalent to a set of discharge abatement subsidies at the same levels. The latter is not usually pursued, apparently because of adherence to the Polluter Pays Principle.

62   *Peter J. Lloyd*

Equally, an administered system is equivalent to both economic instruments, under these assumptions.

Historically, the first model of many dischargers was the model of a river system.[4] This model is important because much of the discussion of charges and trading in emission rights derives from it. The model was one in which there was a single reception area or equivalently an unspecified set of agents who suffer damage from waste disposal. Moreover, the problem was conceived as one of attaining some ambient environmental standard measure at some monitoring point. Much of the literature takes this desideratum either because this standard is believed to be the appropriate goal or in some cases because the damage function is unknown. This is unfortunate in one respect. The way the problem is posed leads to policies which minimize the cost of achieving a reduction in pollution whereas, in a more general model, one should also consider the marginal benefit at each source.

This problem too is solved by a set of effluent charges on the waste load discharged at each source. The charges are source-specific because location affects the contribution of a unit of discharge at source to the standard measured at the monitoring point. This rule equates the marginal cost across sources of reducing the waste at the monitoring point. It takes account of differences in location and of differences in the marginal cost of reduction in each location. It implies percentage reductions at each source which are not uniform. Those sources with lower marginal costs of reduction have larger percentage reductions.

The focus in these river problems has been on emissions trading through marketable permit systems. The difficulty with either an administered system or a charge system is that the controlling government agency must have full information on the locational factors and cost functions of each source (except under very restrictive assumptions which yield a single fixed charge). With a tradeable permit system the government agency fixes the total of the waste or residual at some point, allocates this total in the form of permits among sources and then allows trading of permits among sources. In practice, non-tradeable permits specified in terms of discharge limits or technological specifications are the commonest policy instruments for environmental policy. The novelty lies in permitting the trading of these rights. The advantage is the government need not know the location differences and the costs of reduction at each source. Under certain conditions, the permit trading would ascertain these and produce the desired standard at least cost, provided the rights traded are defined as rights to cause pollution by certain amounts at the monitoring point. Trading of emission permits was first suggested by Dales (1968). Montgomery (1972) provides a proof of efficiency that holds for any initial allocation.

A system of marketable permits is equivalent to a set of optimal charges if the permits are auctioned and certain conditions hold. The difficulty is that these conditions frequently do not hold. There is a growing literature on the comparison of marketable permit systems with a single emission charge or uniform reduction or other systems. When monitoring and enforcement costs are present or the market for permits changes or there is strategic behaviour among permit-holders, the ranking of instruments is not fixed.[5]

3.4   The complication of transnational transmission

Many pollution problems involve the transmission of pollutants or other commodities which embody environmental effects across national borders. Examples include solid wastes discharged into rivers, acid rain, trade in elephant ivory and other animal or bird products which endanger species. Some of these problems are global in nature, chiefly the release of carbon which gives rise to global warming (the 'greenhouse effect') and the release of CFCs which damage the ozone layer of the earth. Problems differ greatly in terms of the location of agents causing the pollution and the location of damage or deposition, the nature of the transmission process and other respects. Problems which are global in nature plainly call for a globally-coordinated solution which involves all nations in joint action. This section concentrates on problems which are transnational in nature but not global, and on the efficacy of international and national instruments to address such problems.

The economy is now the world economy. It consists of a given population of people which defines the population of agents (polluters, pollutees, consumers, producers), each of whom has a fixed geographic location, as before. However, the geographic world is now partitioned into nations, each of which contains the population of agents resident in the area defined by its national borders. The government of each nation has jurisdiction over its own residents only. These nations now trade with each other in the usual sense of exchanging commodities. They also exchange pollutants across their borders, though not every country is necessarily an exporter and an importer. Thus, the economies of nations are open in a dual sense. (It is possible for a nation to have an economy closed in the usual sense of not trading commodities with other countries and still be an exporter or importer of pollutants from other nations, or vice-versa. For example, the East European countries have had little trade with West Europe but have been a major source of pollution in West European countries.)

The many-on-many location-matters model discussed in the previous section captures the essential features of transnational pollution with the addition of the feature that the locations of the sources and reception areas are in different countries. It is further assumed that national governments take account of the cost which pollution from each source in their home country imposes on residents in the reception areas of their own country. They use pollution charges or some equivalent instrument to ensure that

64   *Peter J. Lloyd*

the marginal cost equals the marginal national benefit of pollution reduction. However, the national governments have no concern to regulate activities within their territories for the benefit of residents of another country. Thus, there is, from a global point of view, excessive pollution. This is the model which underlies analyses of many transnational pollution problems (see, for example, Mäler, 1990, and also Newbery, 1990).

Several distinct cases are possible depending on the location of sources and reception areas. As an example, consider the pattern of location shown in Figure 3.1 with the addition of national borders of three nations. The total area can now be considered as a projection of the globe on to two dimensions. The broken lines in this real space mark the borders of nations. They may by-pass completely an area or they may intersect the lines which mark the transmission paths from a source. This generates a number of cases. One case is that of separate clusters of sources and reception areas which fall entirely within the borders of a single nation. This is illustrated in the case of Area 1 and its sources. Obviously no transnational transmission occurs and the previous analysis applies with the national government able to choose instruments which apply to all sources.

The remaining cases involving transnational transmission can be sorted by considering the pairs of countries which are involved when the source area is in one country and at least one reception area is in another. These cases can be cross-classified according to whether the transnational transmission is one-way or two-way (reciprocal) and whether the reception area is in one or two countries. This twofold classification gives four types. Type I is that of one-way transmission with the deposition wholly in the foreign country. Type II is one-way transmission with deposition in both countries. Type III is two-way transmission with the deposition from the sources in each country being wholly in the foreign country. Type IV is two-way transmission with the deposition from the sources of at least one country being partly in the country of source and partly in the foreign country. The latter type is illustrated by the sources that transmit to Areas 2 and 3 in Figure 3.1.

With more than two countries, the pattern of sources and reception areas can be arrayed in a matrix. An illuminating example is the pattern of deposition of sulphur dioxide in the form of gas or particles borne by air currents in the countries of Europe which is reported in Newbery (1990). The data were collected by the European Monitoring and Evaluation Programme set up in 1978 and are measured in thousand tonnes per annum. Fourteen countries or groups of countries are reported. One outstanding feature is that almost all of the entries in the 14×14 matrix are strictly positive. The only group of zero entries relate to sources in the Scandinavian countries which do not deposit to a significant extent on the other countries in Europe with the exception of the Soviet Union because of their location on the north-west fringe of the continent and the prevailing east-to-west wind movements. With this exception, the pattern is one of almost universal reciprocity with the great majority of pairs of countries experiencing two-way or reciprocal flows of the acid rain-producing compounds. A second notable feature is the relatively large numbers in every element of the diagonal. This shows that most of the deposition in fact is within the source country. This is an example of Type IV in the above typology. National policies will not suffice in such cases. The data can also be used to calculate bilateral and multilateral export/import rates or net balances and the ratios of imports/totals received or the import shares.

Previous analyses of the location-matters model showed that the optimal policy response is a set of charges differentiated by source, or an equivalent policy. In terms of the first-best policy response, the global problem does not differ from that of a closed economy. A world of many countries, like a closed economy, contains disparate sources and reception areas and calls for a set of differentiated charges or equivalent instruments. The globally optimal policy produces a non-uniform reduction in pollution by source and, therefore, by country. This takes advantage of the differences across sources (and countries) in the marginal costs and benefits of reduction at each source. One should note that, in the absence of transfers among nations some nations would lose, in the sense that net benefits would be reduced, even when the world as a whole gains from pollution reduction.

The first-best policy could be imposed if there were a global agency with authority to enforce these charges, but there is no such agency. The first consequence, therefore, of introducing nations into the model where each nation has jurisdiction over its own territories only, and the set of instruments is restricted compared to the case of a closed economy, is to make the first-best optimum unattainable. The efficacy of all instruments of national policy is reduced when the enforcement of these instruments stops at the border.[6]

This limitation has spurred economists to seek other ways of agreed action by nations to achieve the first-best policy for the global economy. Early in the debate on transnational pollution the Polluter Pays Principle was extended to instances of transnational pollution. Similarly, the Stockholm Conference of 1972, which resulted in the establishment of the United Nations Environment Programme, stated that 'States have ... responsibility to ensure that activities within their jurisdiction or control do not cause damage to the environment of other states or of areas beyond the limits of national jurisdiction' (quoted in OECD, 1976). This statement can be interpreted as a declaration of the principle. Nevertheless, it was recognised that this principle could not be enforced among nations and that some compensation for nations which are net losers from pollution reduction would be necessary. The Polluter Pays Principle does not indicate to whom the tax proceeds should be paid and the implicit property rights are obscure in these problems. The early emphasis was on burden-sharing schemes (OECD, 1976, 1981).

Mäler (1990) characterizes such international negotiations as a game in which those who gain from multinational cooperation must devise rules so that those who would otherwise lose have an incentive to agree to play the game. He considers situations involving unidirectional externalities and regional reciprocal externalities as well as global externalities. His conclusion is that 'There will be many situations where the victim pays principle, or transfers from the country whose environment has been degraded to the country that causes degradation, will be necessary in order to achieve an efficient solution' (Mäler, 1990). These transfers may take the form of concessions in other areas in which the countries have common interests rather than financial transfers. The reason for the transfers is that the net gains stand to be very unequally distributed among the countries and compensation is necessary to give the losing countries an incentive to cooperate. Adherence to the Polluter Pays Principle would lead to the non-cooperation of these countries and the collapse of the game. The problems are exacerbated if there is incomplete information regarding the costs of abatement or the national damage functions. Countries may seek to understate their net benefits by exaggerating their abatement costs or understating the benefits of pollution reduction. In the case of many countries affected by pollution, there is a free rider problem. Yet, it is still possible to devise rules with side-payments that will lead to participation and the truthful revelation of national costs and benefits. This is an encouraging result.

In practice the difficulties of negotiation seem often to have led to the simple rule that countries agree to uniform percentage reductions. For example, the 1985 Protocol to the Geneva Convention on long-range transport of pollutants called for a uniform 30 per cent reduction in sulphur emissions. The main proposal for reducing carbon emissions in OECD countries is to lower the emissions in all countries to a common percentage, say 80 per cent, of a base level. This is called a Toronto-type rule, after the proposal of the 1988 Toronto Conference on climate change.

In this context a number of authors suggest that internationally tradeable permits are the natural device to achieve efficient social-cost-minimizing reductions (Mäler, 1990; Newbery, 1990; Tietenberg, 1990). These permits could relate to emission reductions. A global market could be established for the trading of (national) emission reduction credits. Suppose, for example, that an international agreement is signed which calls for some reduction in the growth of carbon emissions. Under an offsets policy, countries which reduced their emissions by more than the agreed amount would get a credit which could be traded with a country that had difficulty in achieving its target. Such trading permits the reductions to occur in those locations where there are lower-cost methods of reducing emissions by recycling, treatment, introducing new technologies, etc., or where there are greater marginal benefits. Moreover, it could provide a method of payment to low-income countries who protest that they cannot afford conservation measures. By selling offsets, some third world countries would be in a better position to undertake environmentally sound investments such as protecting forests. Countries such as Brazil may have a new comparative advantage in global emission reduction products.

Negotiation to curb carbon emissions are now taking place under the auspices of the United Nations as part of a convention on global climate change. Burniaux *et al.* (1991) report simulations with the OECD's GREEN model which compare a carbon tax and a carbon tax combined with trade in emission rights as alternative means of achieving a percentage reduction goal for carbon emissions. The latter policy combination distributes the emission cuts optimally to the countries with lower marginal abatement costs. The burden of adjustment shifts from oil and gas to coal as the most efficient way of achieving reductions. China, the USSR and other countries with lower carbon taxes before trading gain by selling their rights. The common carbon tax required to reduce global carbon emissions to 80 per cent of their 1990 level would need to be about US $150 per ton of carbon in the year 2020 with trade in emission rights, compared with about $215 without emission-rights trading. The average fall in real household incomes is only 1 per cent with trading compared with more than 2 per cent for the uniform percentage reduction rule without trade in emission rights. Nevertheless, there is still a problem in persuading all countries to participate, as some countries will not perceive the gains from reduced global warming to justify the loss of real incomes.[7] One possible source of funding is the proceeds of the carbon tax itself. A carbon tax would yield large revenues. For example, a tax of $150 per ton of carbon would add about $18 to the price of a barrel of oil.

In all models of environmental damage with international transmission of the pollutant or emisison, the optimal policy affects international trade in some commodities. A good example is the set of optimal taxes on carbon which would substantially lower the price of fuels to producers, especially that of coal, as well as raising the relative price of these goods to users. The volume and terms of trade of coal-exporting countries, for example, would necessarily deteriorate, but such consequences need to be borne as part of the required change in the competitive general equilibrium. (Second-best arguments for using instruments of environmental policy to correct other market failures are ruled out). There will be pressures on governments to prevent some of the changes in real income, including demands for protection from imports when world prices fall. If governments accede to these demands the costs of pollution reduction will be increased. The next section considers the direct use of trade-based instruments.

3.5   The use of trade-based instruments

Trade-based instruments are the subset of instruments which are based on flows of commodities between nations. They include import tariffs, export

68   *Peter J. Lloyd*

taxes, export and import prohibitions, and quantitative restrictions on trade. These instruments are already used as one means of regulating some environmental problems. Examples are the bans on exports and imports of live birds, animals and reptile species which are considered endangered, or of products made from apparently endangered species such as products made from elephant ivory or the skins of reptiles or fur-bearing animals. Most trade-based instruments are in the form of total prohibitions of export or import trade. A closely related field is the use of barriers at national borders to prohibit the importation of live animals and plants or products made from animals or plants in order to protect domestic animals or plants from contracting diseases which would impose costs on and/or harm the environment of the potentially importing country. This set of transnational environmental and health problems has recently been reviewed by Kozloff and Runge (1991).

While the ranking of trade-based instruments can only be determined specifically for each environmental policy, there is a presumption that trade-based instruments will generally have a low rank and should not, therefore, be used, or at least not as a sole instrument. This conclusion follows as an application of the principle that the optimal instrument for a problem is that instrument among the list of feasible instruments whose base is most closely related to the source of the market failure. In very few, if any, cases is the actual cause of an environmental failure international trade in commodities itself, although some problems will be associated with trade in products.

For most environmental problems involving the transnational transmission of pollutants the transnational transmission occurs via the common property resources of water or air which act as a carrier. There is no direct link to trade in goods and services in such cases and the instrument chosen should be one related to the production or consumption activity or to the use of the inputs (such as fossil fuels) which are the source of the pollutant or emission.

Even for those environmental problems where there is some link with commodity trade in animals or plants, or animal or plant products, there are several aspects of the transmission or the generation of the problem which reduce the efficiency of trade-based instruments. An externality may be transmitted solely by the sale and transport of some product, but sales can occur on domestic markets as well as the markets of foreign countries. An example of this type may be the transmission of diseases among plants or animals. Such cases call for regulation of all sales from infected areas, to both domestic and foreign buyers alike. Export or import taxes or bans are merely a part of the regulation of all sales. If, say, an import ban is used and there is no corresponding restriction on sales of domestically-produced goods, there will be an incidental cost in the form of the distortions due to protection. Moreover, it will generally be more efficient to prevent the sales from the seller whose area is affected. Bans on exports and imports are a second line of defence, as it were, though they are not objectionable in cases where sale bans are appropriate in general, provided the international trade bans are not used for an excessive period or over an excessive range of products as a protective instrument, and they do not discriminate among nations.

The strongest argument for trade-based instruments occurs in cases where the transmission is associated with international commodity trade in all sales, that is, there are no domestic sales of the commodity concerned. A situation close to this may occur in a few instances. For example, almost all of the demand for products made from elephant ivory or certain exotic birds is from buyers resident in foreign countries. But even in such cases export and import bans may have limited efficiency. The reason for the danger to the species concerned may have more to do with the destruction of the habitat than with the killing or the capture of the animal or plant concerned. Primary attention should focus on the preservation of the habitat in such cases.

Another difficulty with trade-based instruments arises from problems of enforcement. A total prohibition on the exports and/or imports from or to the countries concerned gives very strong incentives to smugglers and illegal traders. Enforcement efforts will not always succeed in stopping all trade. If only a proportion of illegal trades is detected, the effect of a ban as distinct from an export tax or quota may be to increase rather than decrease the number of animals or birds traded while at the same time reducing the number of live animals or birds delivered in the importing countries. For birds such as parrots, for example, it is known that many die in transit: in order to achieve each successful trade, many may be attempted. Furthermore, if there is more than one country of supply of an endangered species, the export bans must be enforced equally in all supplying countries, because otherwise production and exports of the product are likely to expand in the countries with less-effective control. In some cases it may be preferable to permit breeding in captivity and to legalize the international trade in the products of a regulated domestic industry.

This paper has mostly ignored a number of features which may be present in particular environmental problems. These include problems of enforcement, uncertainty and dynamic aspects associated with cumulative effects of pollution. The introduction of these features may change the optimal instrument and the ranking of sub-optimal instruments. However, the most basic principles are robust with respect to variations in the specification of the problem. In particular, all instruments should be considered, and the optimal instrument is one whose base is most closely related to the source of the market failure.

70   *Peter J. Lloyd*

Notes

I would like to acknowledge gratefully comments from John Martin.

1. In the comparison of a tariff and a quota, the first statement by Bhagwati (1969) was in terms of the (quasi-) equivalence with respect to the quantity-of-imports variable. But Shibata (1983) observed that quasi-equivalence with respect to the quantity of domestic production was the crucial feature as the policy problem was conceived as one of protecting the domestic producers.

2. This principle was developed by Bhagwati (1971) in international trade theory where the problem was to rank alternative instruments which might be used to achieve a 'non-economic' objective such as employment in an import-competing industry. Generally trade-based instruments such as tariffs and quotas rank lower than instruments such as wage subsidies or output subsidies which bear more directly on the objective.

3. An issue closely related to indirectness is the suggestion sometimes made that the optimal intervention should take into account other distortions in the economy due to taxes, imperfect competition or other market failures. Consider, for example, that the polluter is a monopolist. Buchanan (1969) suggested a Pigovian tax is inappropriate as the monopolist's output is less than optimal. While the monopolist's output is less than the output of a competitive industry, it may be less or greater than the output of a competitive industry which also pays the Pigovian tax. Moreover, the use of pollution control instruments to address monopoly problems would do nothing to control monopolists who happened to be non-polluters. Equally, one could suggest that monopoly controls be used to penalize polluters. This would do nothing to control polluters who happened to be non-monopolists. Given the small intersection of the sets of polluters and monopolists/oligopolists and the very different bases of the instruments required in each case, the linking of pollution control and competition policy is likely to be effective in controlling neither. The two distinct problems require two distinct sets of instruments. Pollution and imperfect competition may be linked in another way. Polluters may prefer administrative controls over taxes and subsidies as the former may inadvertently restrict entry into an industry if the pollution is associated with an essential input or process. This point is emphasized in the chapter by Hoekman and Leidy in this volume.

4. This model is largely due to Kneese (1964). Bohm and Russell (1985) provide a useful discussion and references.

5. Tietenberg (1985) is the standard reference. OECD (1989) and Hahn (1989) survey the extent of such systems and recent experience.

6. In this respect, the problem resembles that of other national externality problems in which the national government is constrained by a constitution to impose charges or grant subsidies which are uniform among agents. The standard reference is Diamond (1973).

7. Little is known of the total benefits from the avoidance of global climate change, nor of the distribution of those benefits across countries, so these benefits are not included in the model. Other empirical studies of policies aimed at reducing greenhouse gas emissions are reviewed in Chapter 5 of this volume, and some new modelling results presented in Chapter 6 include a valuation of benefits from carbon emission reduction.

References

Anderson, J. E. (1988), *The Relative Inefficiency of Quotas*, Cambridge: MIT Press.

Baumol, W. J. and W. E. Oates (1975), *The Theory of Environmental Policy*, Englewood Cliffs: Prentice Hall.

Bhagwati, J. N. (1969), 'On the Equivalence of Tariffs and Quotas', in *Trade, Growth and the Balencce of Payments: Essays in Honor of Gottfried Haberler*, edited by R. E. Baldwin, Amsterdam: North Holland.

Bhagwati, J. N. (1971), 'The Generalized Theory of Distortions and Welfare', in *Trade, Balance of Payments and Growth: Papers in Honor of Charles P. Kindleberger*, edited by J. N. Bhagwati *et al.*, Amsterdam: North Holland.

Bohm, P. and C. S. Russell (1985), 'Comparative Analysis of Alternative Policy Instruments', in *Handbook of Natural Resource and Energy Economics*, edited by A. V. Kneese and J. L. Sweeney, Amsterdam: North Holland.

Buchanan, J. M. (1969), 'External Diseconomies, Corrective Taxes and Market Structure', *American Economic Review* 59: 174–77.

Burniaux, J. M., J. P. Martin, G. Nicoletti and J. Oliveira Martins (1991), 'The Costs of Policies to Reduce Global Emissions of CO_2: Initial Simulation Results with GREEN,' Working Paper No. 103, Department of Economics and Statistics, OECD, Paris, June.

Coase, R. H. (1960), 'The Problem of Social Cost', *Journal of Law and Economics* 3: 1–44.

Dales, J. H. (1968), *Pollution, Property and Prices*, Toronto: Toronto University Press.

Diamond, P. (1973), 'Consumption Externalities and Imperfect Corrective Pricing', *Bell Journal of Economics* 4: 526–38.

Eskeland, G. S. and E. Jimenez (1991), *Choosing Policy Instruments for Pollution Control: A Review*, Working Papers in Public Economics, Washington, D. C.: The World Bank.

Hahn, R. W. (1989), 'Economic Prescriptions for Environmental Problems: How the Patient Followed the Doctor's Order', *Journal of Economic Perspectives* 3: 95–114.

Harrison, D. (1975), *Who Pays for Clean Air: The Cost and Benefit Distribution of Automobile Emission Standards*, Cambridge, Mass: Ballinger.

Helm, R. and D. Pearce (1990), 'Assessment: Economic Policy Towards the Environment', *Oxford Review of Economic Policy* 6: 1–16.

Kneese, A. V. (1964), *The Economics of Regional Water Quality Management*, Baltimore: John Hopkins University Press.

Kozloff, K. and C. F. Runge (1991), 'International Trade in the Food Sector and Environmental Quality, Health and Safety: A Survey of Policy Issues', Staff Paper p. 91–12, Department of Agricultural and Applied Economics, University of Minnesota, St. Paul, May.

Mäler, K. G. (1990), 'International Environmental Problems', *Oxford Review of Economic Policy* 6: 80–108.

Montgomery, D. (1972), 'Markets in Licences and Efficient Pollution Control Programs', *Journal of Economic Theory* 5: 395–418.

Newbery, D. (1990), 'Acid Rain', *Economic Policy* 5, (11), 297–346.

OECD (1976), *Economics of Transnational Pollution*, Paris: OECD.

OECD (1981), *Transfrontier Pollution and the Role of the State*, Paris: OECD.

OECD (1989), *Economic Instruments for Environmental Protection*, Paris: OECD.

OECD (1991), *The State of the Environment*, Paris: OECD.

Ohta, H. (1978), 'On the Ranking of Price and Quantity Controls Under Uncertainty', *Journal of International Economics* **8**: 543–550.

Olson, M. and R. Zeckhauser (1970), 'The Efficient Production of External Economies', *American Economic Review* **60**: 512–517.

Opschoor, J. B. and D. W. Pearce (eds.) (1991), *Persistent Pollutants: Economics and Policy*, Dordrecht: Kluwer Academic Publishers.

Pearce, D. W. and R. K. Turner (1990), *Economics of Natural Resources and the Environment*, London: Harvester Wheatsheaf.

Pigou, A. C. (1932), *The Economics of Welfare*, London: Macmillan.

Sandmo, A. (1976), 'Direct versus Indirect Pigouvian Taxation', *European Economic Review* **7**: 337–49.

Shibata, H. (1983), 'A Note on the Equivalence of Tariffs and Quotas', *American Economic Review* **58**: 137–41.

Tietenberg, T. H. (1985), *Emissions Trading*, Washington, D. C.: Resources for the Future.

Tietenberg, T. H. (1990), 'Using Economic Incentives to Maintain our Environment', *Challenge* **33**: 42–46.

Varian, H. (1984), *Microeconomic Analysis*, New York: Norton.

[20]

Competition and Trade Policy: Identifying the Issues After the Uruguay Round

Peter Lloyd and Gary Sampson

1. INTRODUCTION

OVER the past fifty years, there have been numerous attempts in international organisations to deal with aspects of competition policies that relate to international trade. Anti-competitive business practices, for example, have long been on the agenda of intergovernmental negotiations in organisations dealing with trade issues. Interest in placing trade and competition policy issues on the agenda of international trade negotiations has again surfaced. (See, for example, Brittan, 1992; Jackson, 1992; and Feketekuty, 1993.) Most recently, the Chairman of the Trade Negotiations Committee of the Uruguay Round meeting at Ministerial level in Marrakesh, Morocco (12−15 April, 1994) drew attention to the importance Ministers attached to an examination of, *inter alia*, the relationship between the international trading system and trade and competition policy (GATT, 1994b).

If competition policy is to be addressed through multilateral trade negotiations, the scope of negotiations and the principal issues are not yet clearly defined. The purpose of this article is to identify a number of issues which may be relevant in any future discussion of international trade and competition policy. The approach adopted has been to draw on the experience of past intergovernmental initiatives, including those in the General Agreement on Tariffs and Trade (GATT). This article does not, however, attempt to be comprehensive in the sense of addressing all issues which may be of relevance, nor does it address the experience of customs unions (such as the European Union) or free-trade agreements (such as

PETER LLOYD is Ritchie Professor of Economics, Melbourne University, Australia. GARY SAMPSON is Director, WTO Secretariat, Geneva, Switzerland. They wish to thank Bernard J. Philips of the OECD Secretariat for helpful comments. The views are those of the authors and not the GATT Secretariat.

the North American Free Trade Area) which have elements of competition policies, such as the bilateral competition policy agreements (in the US – EC Agreement on Anti-trust Co-operation).

The article is divided into eight sections. Section 2 examines the reasons why a *multilateral* competition policy may well be needed and the options available to governments for dealing with international competition and trade policy issues. Section 3 describes past initiatives in multilateral discussions; the characteristics of the agreements are presented with a view to providing background to the issues of today. Section 4 briefly describes recent work in the OECD and Section 5 addresses the question of why there are suggestions for initiatives to deal with trade and competition policy considerations at this point in time. It also identifies a number of current issues. Section 6 describes the options available for governments to deal with the issues identified and Section 7 discusses those sections of the World Trade Organisation (WTO) Agreements which have a significant competition policy component. Section 8 examines the reasons why the WTO is the body which should have responsibility for the multilateral regulation of competition policies.

2. NEED FOR INTERNATIONAL ACTION

It seems reasonable to expect that work on the trade policy and competition policy linkages will intensify after the Uruguay Round, as attention will naturally turn to identifying — and liberalising — remaining barriers to trade. Baldwin (1970) drew attention to the fact that after the Kennedy Round tariff reductions were implemented (i.e. 1972), tariffs on dutiable non-agricultural products would average 9.9 per cent in the United States, 8.6 per cent in the EEC, 10.8 per cent in the United Kingdom and 10.7 per cent in Japan. Given these sharp tariff cuts, he noted that it was appropriate to focus more on other impediments to their trade, many of which were either not apparent, or of little consequence, when tariff rates were high. He cites one commentator (Jones, 1968), who observed: 'The lowering of tariffs has, in effect, been like draining a swamp. The lower water level has revealed all the snags and stumps of non-tariff barriers that still have to be cleared away . . .'. Baldwin was drawing attention to governmental non-tariff (and non-border) barriers to trade, many of which were on the agenda of the Tokyo Round.

More than two decades later, the Chairman of the OECD Trade Committee likened the 'process of liberalising trade by removing barriers to market access to the process of peeling an onion' (see Feketekuty, 1993). There are different layers of barriers protecting markets, but each succeeding layer of barriers does not become very visible until the layer above has been peeled away. In his view, trade negotiators in the GATT found that underneath the layer of import restrictions, such as tariffs and quotas imposed at the border, there was a layer of internal non-tariff barriers such as government procurement restrictions, discriminatory standards, restrictive regulatory provisions and preferential sectoral policies.

In short, based on the experience of past history, trade negotiators' attention is likely to be directed increasingly to non-border trade distorting policies and non-governmental barriers to trade. This will presumably provide the vehicle for a number of sensitive areas under bilateral discussion to be brought under the multilateral umbrella. These will include some areas which are traditionally regarded as areas of competition policy; examples include US — Japan talks on the Structural Impediments Initiative and the bilateral Framework Agreement.

Several particular reasons for multilateral action were given in the Draft of an International Anti-Trust Code recently prepared by a Working Group of Experts organised under the Max Planck Institute. The Draft Code was proposed as a plurilateral agreement to be under the auspices of the WTO.[1] The Group of Experts noted that the GATT provisions relating to competition policy deal only with *government* measures and not private actions (apart from dumping actions). There is no GATT regulation of practices of exporters other than the prohibition of export prohibition, quantitative restrictions and export subsidies for manufactured goods from industrialised countries. The Group of Experts noted the problems arising from the co-existence of separate sets of trade and national anti-trust rules relating to the same phenomena; predation, for example, and the Anti-Dumping Agreement of GATT. There is a similar problem due to the overlap, and in some cases conflict, between the rules of competition policies of two or more nations which may apply to the one restraint; for example, the rules of one country may ban a cartel but those of an affected country may not. Such conflicts may be dealt with by means of conflict-of-rules laws, co-operation and harmonisation, convergence and mutual recognition of different domestic competition laws.

More fundamentally, national legislation has a number of practical shortcomings. It is designed to control only those practices which affect the domestic economy. It does not normally address practices of enterprises within its jurisdiction which cause injury or impose costs on the economies of other countries. Further, anti-competitive actions which affect residents in one country may occur in a second country. For example, an enterprise may attempt to eliminate competition facing a subsidiary. The parent company may decide to supply the requirements of its subsidiary at an artificially low price, thus enabling the subsidiary to engage in predatory behaviour in the market for its products.

---

[1] For details, see International Anti-trust Code Working Group (1993). Members of this Working Group worked independently and had no mandate from their Governments.

This problem is under review in the Competition Law and Policy Committee of the OECD. To deal with such practices in an effective fashion may require action to be undertaken simultaneously by trading nations.

Restraints blocking market access are often beyond the reach of national jurisdictions and restraints in a foreign country, such as export cartels, cannot be adequately treated in national jurisdictions. The Group of Experts also draw attention to the costs which arise when the restraints or actions occur simultaneously in more than one country. Both are problems of enforcement; the extent of these difficulties can be appreciated by considering an attempt to apply remedies which are used under domestic laws to deter persons from contravening the law and to compensate injured parties. These include measures such as injunctions, remedies involving prices, pecuniary penalties, damages and divestiture of assets. Obviously, attempts to apply any of these traditional remedies beyond national borders is fraught with legal difficulties.

Another concern is the difficulty of obtaining information from producers located in another country and of enforcing any decision reached by a local legal authority outside its jurisdiction. For example, an enterprise in a particular country may call for tenders internationally. As a result, members of an international cartel may collude and respond accordingly. All the members of the cartel may be located abroad without assets, subsidiaries or affiliates in the country concerned; it may be difficult to prove that the bids are collusive. Transnational corporations have means to avoid providing information; in particular, by keeping information relating to their activities in countries which can prohibit its transmission abroad. At present, the Competition Law and Policy Committee of the OECD is addressing the question of how information can be shared between governments to deal with various practices of 'hard core' cartels.

The problem is, however, larger than enforcement across national barriers. The past attempts at regulation by means of consultation and cooperation are based on an assumed mutuality of the interests of the two or more countries affected by any one anti-competitive act. In many cases, and perhaps typically, there will be a conflict of interests among nations. For example, the Framework discussions between the US and Japan have been intended to improve US access to Japanese markets for automobiles and auto parts, insurance, telecommunications and medical equipment which arise, in the US view, from anti-competitive actions within Japan. In this instance, there is a sharp conflict of interests between the US and Japan, as well as a difference of view as to the source of the lack of penetration of Japanese markets by US producers. In such cases, and in anti-competitive practices which occur simultaneously in more than one country, what is needed is a global or world view which takes account of the interests of citizens of all affected countries.

This view needs to take account of more interests than those dealt with traditionally under national competition laws. The focus of these laws, and of the discussion above concerning options to deal with anti-competitive policies, has been on the conflicting interests of producers competing for market shares and attempts by one or more producers to increase their market share at the expense of other producers. The interests of consumers or buyers must also be considered. An obvious case is the application of anti-dumping measures. World competition laws should be designed to promote efficiency in the world economy, just as national laws should be designed to promote efficiency in national markets; that is, efficiency in production *and* in consumption.

The ultimate cause of the increased attention to the interface between competition policies and trade policies is the greater integration of markets across countries which has come about as a direct result of the multilateral and unilateral reductions in border barriers to trade. There are many facets to this integration of national markets and more producers now sell their products in the markets of other countries, and more consumers now buy products made by producers in other countries in competition with those made by domestic producers. More final products are now manufactured by a sequence of stages distributed across several countries and manufacturers now source inputs at lower stages of production from the cheapest market. Globalisation of production in this sense has enhanced the importance of vertical restraints on trade such as vertical mergers or restrictions on the sales of products to downstream producers if they reduce competition in any of the markets. In such cases, the interests who lose from restraints are those producing the downstream products — and ultimately the consumers or buyers of the final outputs — rather than other competitors in the horizontal markets of the goods concerned.

The integration of markets across countries also involves direct foreign investment and other forms of foreign investment; that is, the linking of production plants and asset holdings as well as the linking of goods markets. Foreign producers may compete in the market of a country by locating their production plants in that country as an alternative to producing at home and shipping to the country concerned. World foreign investment has increased in recent decades considerably faster than the trade in goods and services. This form of competition may be limited by quite different forms of restraint imposed by competing producers; it also involves, in some instances, restraints imposed by the government of the country in which a foreign producer and investor may wish to invest. It enhances the importance of the needs for establishment and achieving national treatment.

A further issue relates to the fact that the ability to compete in foreign markets is increasingly affected by technological developments. This is due to the increasing technology intensity of many processes and the increased global trade in technologies. One clear example is access to telecommunications services — public networks and leased lines. Restraints on this access can eliminate or seriously weaken the competitive position of rivals. An important consideration in the Uruguay Round negotiations on services was the recognition that an offer to provide market access in a specific sector (e.g. financial services) could be nullified by a failure of the member making the offer to provide the access to the public telecommunications network that was necessary to sell the service. To be offered market access in financial services but denied access to leased lines (or use of the telephone as an extreme example) may totally undermine the value of the offer. A Telecommunications Annex to the General Agreement on Trade in Services was negotiated in the Uruguay Round to ensure that 'any other Member is accorded access to and use of public telecommunications transport networks and services on reasonable and non-discriminatory terms and conditions, for the supply of a service' for which it has undertaken a commitment. Similar provisions relate to private leased circuits.

Another major trend in many countries over the last decade is the privatisation of government-owned enterprises. This has often been associated with the breaking up of previous state monopolies by the governments of the countries concerned. It has directly increased the share of world production and of world trade accounted for by private enterprises. In some markets, notably telecommunications, it has greatly increased the degree of competition in many countries and has effectively replaced a number of closed national markets by a global market. Greater market interpenetration due to the integration of national markets has resulted in the need for competition policies to adjust to different circumstances of international competition.

There are reasons of trade policy, as well as competition policy, why some form of international regulation of competition policy is required in the post-Uruguay Round period (see also Petersmann, 1993, pp. 36–37). Examples have been noted above of how the absence of national competition policies or waivers may reduce or nullify the benefits of trade liberalisation. If the rules relating to international competition are inadequate in scope or unenforceable, the new post-Uruguay Round rules-based multilateral trading system may be undermined.

3. EARLIER MULTILATERAL EFFORTS

In the draft Havana Charter for an International Trade Organisation (ITO) which emerged in the late 1940s, an entire chapter (Chapter V) was devoted to restrictive business practices. Subsequently, business practices that affect competition and have trade implications have received attention at the intergovernmental level in the United Nations Conference on Trade and Development (UNCTAD), the Organisation for Economic Co-operation and Development (OECD), the United Nations Commission on Transnational Corporations (UNCTC) and the General Agreement on Tariffs and Trade (GATT).

Article 46 of Chapter V of the Havana Charter (1948) specifically stated that 'appropriate measures' were to be taken to deal with business practices, on the part of private or public commercial enterprises, which restrain competition, limit access to markets or foster monopolistic control. It is noted that such practices might have harmful effects on the expansion of production or trade and interfere with the achievement of other objectives of the Charter. The measures addressed were defined as business practices that restrain competition, limit access to markets or foster monopolistic control. They included, among other things, price fixing, market sharing, production quotas, agreements to prevent the development of technology and certain use of patents, trade marks or copyrights.

The Havana Charter aimed at finding satisfactory remedies to situations due to harmful effects of restrictive business practices. This was to be done by encouraging transparency, consultation and conciliation between the governments concerned. While some provisions of the Havana Charter were incorporated into the text of the GATT, this was not the case for restrictive business practices provisions. The principles drafted for the International Trade Organisation have, however, guided much of the subsequent discussions in international fora.

Certain governments viewed the omission of the provisions relating to restrictive business practices as a deficiency of the GATT system, and in 1954 suggestions were made to deal with matters relating to restrictive business practices in GATT (GATT, 1955, p. 239). In November 1958, GATT contracting parties recognised that the activities of international cartels and trusts might hamper the expansion of world trade and the economic development in individual countries, and thereby interfere with the objectives of GATT (GATT, 1959, p. 29). Subsequently, a group of experts was appointed by the contracting parties to study and make recommendations in this respect. While the experts agreed that business practices may interfere with the objectives of GATT, and that GATT was an appropriate body to deal with such problems, there emerged important differences of opinion concerning the nature of the appropriate GATT action. In the absence of agreement, no substantive provisions relating to restrictive business practices were incorporated into the GATT. An agreement reached in 1960 provided only for *ad hoc* notification and consultation procedures for dealing with conflicts of interest between contracting parties on these practices (GATT, 1961, pp. 170–179). These procedures have never been invoked.

During the 1950s, there were efforts to deal with restrictive business practices at the United Nations Economic and Social Council (ECOSOC). The Ad hoc Committee on Restrictive Business Practices to the ECOSOC proposed an international code largely based on the provisions of Chapter V of the Havana Charter. The proposal did not obtain sufficient support from member countries to

442 International Trade Opening and the Global Economy

688 PETER LLOYD AND GARY SAMPSON

enter into force.

Restrictive business practices have been on the UNCTAD agenda since the second UNCTAD Conference in New Delhi, 1969. At the fourth UNCTAD conference in Nairobi in 1976, it was agreed that restrictive business practices could adversely affect international trade and economic development (particularly that of developing countries), and that action should be taken at the international level. This action included negotiations to formulate a set of principles and rules for the control of restrictive business practices. The subsequent UNCTAD work culminated in the adoption by the United Nations General Assembly of Resolution 35/63 (December 1980), which incorporated the 'Set of Multilaterally Agreed Equitable Principles and Rules for the Control of Restrictive Business Practices' (hereafter referred to as the UN Principles and Rules; UNCTAD, 1985). The UN Principles and Rules explicitly state that they are applicable to all transactions in both goods and services.

The UN Principles and Rules define restrictive business practices as:

> acts or behaviour of enterprises which, through an abuse or acquisition of a dominant position of market power, limit access to markets or otherwise unduly restrain competition, having, or being likely to have, adverse effects on international trade, particularly that of developing countries, and on the economic development of these countries, or which through formal, informal, written or unwritten agreements or arrangements among enterprises have the same impact.

A dominant position of market power is defined to be:

> a situation where an enterprise, either by itself or acting together with a few other enterprises, is in a position to control the relevant market for a particular good or service or group of goods or services (United Nations, 1981, pp. 11–22).

The UN Principles and Rules are not legally binding. They place a moral obligation on governments to introduce and strengthen legislation in the area of restrictive business practices and to ensure that their enterprises, whether private or State owned, abide by the code. They also contain norms of behaviour addressed to firms. The institutional machinery of the UN Principles and Rules is provided by the Intergovernmental Group of Experts on Restrictive Business Practices which meet under the auspices of UNCTAD. The Second United Nations Conference to Review all Aspects of the UN Principles and Rules (26 November–7 December 1990) reviewed matters relating to transparency and the consultation mechanism of the UN Principles and Rules, and paid particular attention to restrictive business practices adversely affecting the interests of developing countries.

A series of recommendations concerning anti-competitive practices affecting international trade were also adopted by the Organisation for Economic Co-operation and Development in 1967, 1973, 1979 and 1986. The recommendations specified notification and consultation procedures to be followed by the OECD member countries in seeking mutually acceptable solutions to problems related to anti-competitive practices. In 1986, the OECD

© Blackwell Publishers Ltd. 1995

COMPETITION AND TRADE POLICY   689

Revised Recommendation to the Council (hereafter referred to as the OECD Recommendations) repealed and superseded previous recommendations, it reiterated the main provisions of the three earlier recommendations and added new guiding principles (OECD, 1987). The recommendations cover trade in both goods and services.

The OECD Guidelines for Multinational Enterprises (hereafter referred to as the OECD Guidelines) provide guidelines for multinational enterprises rather than governments. They are annexed to the Declaration on International Investment and Multilateral Enterprises (OECD, 1976). The OECD Guidlines enjoin enterprises to:

> refrain from actions which adversely affect competition in the relevant market by abusing a dominant position and market power, by means of, for example: (a) anticompetitive acquisitions; (b) predatory behaviour toward competition; (c) unreasonable refusal to deal; (d) anbticompetitive abuse of industrial property rights; (e) discriminatory (i.e. unreasonably differentiated) pricing and using such pricing transactions between affiliated enterprises as a means of affecting adversely competition outside these enterprises.

The OECD Guidelines also call upon enterprises to:

> allow purchasers, distributors and licensees freedom to resell, export, purchase and develop their operations consistent with law, trade conditions, the need for specialization and sound commercial practice.

Enterprises are further asked:

> to refrain from participating in, or otherwise purposely strengthening, the restrictive effects of international or domestic cartels or restrictive agreements which adversely affect or eliminate competition and which are not generally or specifically accepted under applicable national or international legislation.

Observance of the OECD Recommendations and of the OECD Guidelines is voluntary and not legally enforceable (see Baade, 1980). There is no precise legal definition of what constitutes a multinational enterprise in either the Recommendations or Guidelines. The Guidelines only specify that the term 'multinational enterprise' usually comprises 'companies or other entities whose ownership is private, State or mixed, established in different countries and so linked that one or more of them may be able to exercise a significant influence over the activities of others and, in particular, to share knowledge and resources with the others'. The OECD has established consultation and conciliation procedures whereby national governments can meet to reconcile conflicts created by the extra-territorial application of national anti-trust policies.

The UN Commission on Transnational Corporations has attempted to develop a United Nations Code of Conduct on Transnational Corporations which reinforces the UN Principles and Rules for governments, and contains provisions on restrictive business practices. While it has not been possible to reach agreement on a final document, a report by the UNCTC noted that 'many of the concluded provisions of the proposed Code are markedly relevant to trade issues, especially in the area of trade in services' and that 'many of the issues involved in

690   PETER LLOYD AND GARY SAMPSON

the Uruguay Round of multilateral trade negotiations have been for years under negotiation in the Code exercise, and that some degree of consensus has been reached on them' (UNCTC, 1990b, pp. 46–49). The implicit proposal was that the text of the Code where there was a measure of consensus could provide the basis for discussion in some areas of the Uruguay Round; in particular, trade in services. Similarly, an international Code of Conduct on Transfer of Technology has been negotiated for some time under UNCTAD auspices. The proposed Code lists, *inter alia*, the restrictive practices that should be eliminated or controlled with respect to the transfer of technology. Failure to reach agreement on a number of points has prevented the adoption of the Code (UNCTAD, 1985).

In summary, three multilateral instruments have been concluded which contain provisions which apply to restrictive business practices of public and private enterprises for both trade in goods and services. The UN Principles and Rules apply to members of the United Nations, while the OECD Guidelines and OECD Recommendations apply only to OECD countries. All three seek to control only those practices which affect the domestic economy of each nation; they emphasise voluntary action and a non-binding approach, with procedures for transparency, notification and consultation. All are codes of conduct which are not legally enforceable.

The OECD Recommendations and the UN Principles and Rules are directed at actions of governments. The UN Principles and Rules contain norms of behaviour for firms and the OECD Guidelines for Multinational Enterprises complement the Recommendations for governments. The focus of attention today is on the actions of governments which have the responsibility to regulate the activities of corporations, both national and multinational, within their jurisdictions. The remainder of the article is concerned solely with governmental actions.

4. WORK OF THE OECD COMPETITION LAW AND POLICY COMMITTEE

As early as May 1982, OECD Ministers called for work to examine possible longer term approaches to developing an improved international framework to deal with problems arising at the interface of competition and trade policies. As a result of this, the Competition Law and Policy (CLP) Committee has produced a series of monographs and round table papers which develop a comprehensive view of competition policy (OECD, 1994b, and studies cited therein).

Work has proceeded on various aspects of competition policy in the OECD Committees, particularly in the Competition Law and Policy (CLP) Committee, and more recently in conjunction with the OECD Trade Committee. This work lies at the origin of much of the current interest in further discussions of the international effects of anti-competitive business practices. The recent OECD work has been particularly constructive and has, for example, promoted convergence across countries in anti-trust law objectives and substantive rules, as well as transparency, information sharing and co-operation. Much of this relates to the fact that it reflects a rather different view of competition policy than that held by a number of participants in some of the earlier discussions mentioned above.

While the UN Principles and Rules, for example, were negotiated with a suspicious view of transnational corporations, there has been a marked change in the perceptions of transnational corporations and international competition by many government officials. Even the term 'restrictive business practices' has lost favour. The OECD Committee on Restrictive Business Practices was renamed the Competition Law and Policy Committee. Economists now speak less of 'anti-competitive practices' and more positively of 'fostering competitive practices'. They recognise that some (usually vertical) restrictions may well promote competition and trade; for example, a firm attempting to enter a new market might be offered an exclusive territory as an inducement to invest in creating a distribution network in a particular territory. In the same vein, the view of export cartels that has emerged from the CLP Committee discussions is that only 'hard core' cartels should be strictly prohibited. Export co-operation which might be characterised loosely as cartel activity may, in the view of the CLP Committee, be pro-competitive and trade enhancing; for example, when small firms join together to export when they could not do so individually.

The emphasis in the CLP Committee is the promotion of competition rather than the correction or elimination of anti-competitive practices. For example, it considers the concept of predatory pricing, and its harmful effects on the degree of competition, rather than the trade policy concept of dumping with its emphasis on injury to the other competitors. It includes mergers and restraints which give rise to reduced competition as well as market abuses through monopolisation and cartel action, such as market sharing and price fixing. The OECD favours 'adequate' or 'sound' competition rules rather than rigid minimum standards of behaviour. As it is unclear how many individual business practices affect market competition, the OECD favours an examination on a case-by-case basis. The Convergence Project of the CLP Committee has produced a comprehensive statement of what constitutes modern competition policy, and an interim report published in connection with the 1994 OECD Ministerial Meeting (7−8 June) outlines the status of this work in the OECD with respect to the areas of convergence in competition policy and law (OECD, 1994a).

5. INTERACTION BETWEEN TRADE AND COMPETITION POLICIES IN THE POST-URUGUAY ROUND PERIOD

Both competition policy and trade policy deal with public and private restraints that affect competition. It is not surprising, therefore, that there is an area of 'overlap'; for example, anti-competitive business practices can have important effects on the competitive functioning of international markets and therefore concern trade officials; export and import cartels, dumping and 'buy-national' initiatives provide examples. Similarly, trade policy measures that affect international trade have important effects on domestic market structures by changing the nature of competition. Examples include export restraint arrangements negotiated under the Multifibre Arrangement (an Arrangement sanctioned by GATT but to be phased out as a result of the Uruguay Round) and variable levies that have long been a cornerstone of the Common Agricultural Policy of the European Union.

Yet, both competition and trade policies are concepts which are hard to define. A distinction between trade and competition policy was advanced by the OECD Secretariat some time ago (OECD, 1984b). According to this view, *competition policy* is aimed at ensuring the efficient functioning of markets by the removal or control of restrictive business practices; *trade policy* focuses upon the removal of barriers to international trade, both through action to reduce tariff levels and through agreements to limit the effects of non-tariff measures.[2]

While this distinction is useful, it is based on the premise that trade liberalisation measures are those that are taken at the border. Increasingly, however, non-border measures have significant effects on international trade flows. This tendency will continue in the post-Uruguay Round period as tariffs and non-tariff measures will be further reduced. In this environment, *non-border* measures — both public and private — will increasingly affect international trade. Many constitute a grey area that could be classified as trade or competition measures. Conversely, there is the view noted above that the domestic competition policies of indvidual nations are no longer adequate to deal with anti-competition practices involving producers located in other countries.

Work in OECD Committees has for some time reflected the concern expressed at OECD Ministerial level with the overlap between trade liberalisation and competition policy. At the OECD Council meeting at Ministerial level as early as May 1982, Ministers drew attention to the increasing importance of the links between competition and trade policy. They requested the Committee of Experts on Restrictive Business Practices to examine 'possible longer-term approaches to developing an improved international framework for dealing with problems arising at the frontier of competition and trade policies' (OECD, 1984a). To

---

[2] The OECD Committee on Competition Law and Policy defines competition policy as 'the body of laws and regulations governing anti-competitive practices (horizontal or vertical agreements between enterprises and abuses at dominant positions, mergers and acquisitions)' (OECD, 1994, p. 8). This leaves out many areas such as illicit behaviour, corporate control and management, intellectual property and consumer protection law which are regarded as competition policy in some OECD countries. The OECD Convention, which focuses on anti-trust policies, is followed here.

carry out this mandate, the Committee of Experts on Restrictive Business Practices established a Working Party on Competition and International Trade.

The specific terms of reference led the Committee to focus on practices involving both enterprises and governments which raised concern for both competition policy and trade policy, and covered jurisdictional issues such as the participation of competition authorities in trade policy decisions. It was presented as an attempt to alert policy makers and the general public to what was perceived as an important gap in domestic policy formulation and international co-operation. The report suggested an analytical approach to dealing with the interrelated competition and trade policy problems, and set the stage for the consideration of proposals for possible action and policy recommendations in the second phase of the Committee's work on these issues (OECD, 1984a). The basic thrust of the Report that emerged was that the effects of anti-competitive practices (of a trade or competition policy nature) should be evaluated in an economy-wide perspective and that the effects of such practices on both producers and consumers should be considered in the decision-making process.

Since the submission of the report, work on the implications of anti-competitive practices for trade and competition policy has continued in the Competition Law and Policy Committee. As noted above, more recently, work has been carried out in conjunction with the Trade Committee of the OECD. The Communique of the 1992 OECD Ministerial Meeting once again drew attention to the overlap of trade and competition policy: 'Trade and competition policies have a common objective: economic efficiency. But these policies have sometimes impinged on each other. OECD governments will seek to: improve consistency between these policies to enhance competition and market access; provide a foundation for convergence of substantive rules and enforcement practices in competition policy; identify better procedures for the surveillance of trade and competition policies; and enhance the interests of consumers' (OECD, 1994a).

In the post-Uruguay Round era, with tariffs at historically low levels and disciplines on other governmental barriers to trade, public and private enterprises will be subjected to greater international competition. Under such circumstances, some may attempt to insulate themselves from increased competition through engaging in private anti-competitive practices.[3] This process could well contribute to undermining the liberalisation negotiated in the Uruguay Round. The possibility of negotiated trade liberalisation being undermined by restrictive business practices has long been recognised. One of the declared objectives of the UN Principles and Rules, for example, was to ensure that restrictive business

---

[3] A current example is one in which the replacement of country-specific quotas by an EU-wide quota for automobiles in 1993 has been frustrated by relaxation of EU competition policies to maintain the segmentation of national markets (Mattoo and Mavroidis, 1993).

694   PETER LLOYD AND GARY SAMPSON

practices do not impede or negate the realisation of benefits that should arise from the liberalisation of tariff and non-tariff barriers affecting world trade, particularly those affecting the trade and development of developing countries.

Concern over the use of anti-competitive practices to frustrate reductions in barriers to international trade may lead in turn to the use of international trade sanctions. In the current dispute between Japan and the US over access to markets for automobiles and auto parts, the US is threatening to apply trade sanctions against Japan. The US alleges private practices are impeding US access to these markets and seeks action by the Japanese Government to remove the restraints.

Conversely, it is also possible for national governments, acting as agents for domestic producers, to increase trade barriers so as to protect domestic producer interest and thereby to restrict competition in the national market. However, such actions are now more heavily circumscribed by the results of the Uruguay Round; most tariffs are reduced and bound, and a wide range of non-tariff border measures are prohibited or restricted.[4] Indeed, reductions in trade barriers have greatly increased the degree of competition in many domestic markets. Situations in which there were few, or even sole, suppliers on these domestic markets have been converted into competitive markets by the lowering of border barriers to trade and the introduction of new foreign competitors. Indeed, markets for goods and services in the OECD countries and many developing countries are, with a few exceptions, now more competitive than at any time since the establishment of the GATT. At the time of the creation of GATT in 1947, for example, the average tariff on industrial goods imported into OECD countries was over 40 per cent. The post-Uruguay Round average tariff on industrial imports into OECD countries has been estimated to be 3.9 per cent (GATT, 1994a) and 99 per cent of tariff line items are bound against future tariff increases. The reduction and removal of many quantitative import restrictions as a result of the Uruguay Round (e.g. phasing out of the MFA, tariffication of non-tariff barriers in agriculture) will increase competition as quantitative restraints restrict supplies and disconnect the prices between national markets, thereby inhibiting competition.

6. OPTIONS FOR INTERGOVERNMENTAL ACTIONS

a. Consultation and Cooperation Among Governments

As described in Section 3, the focus of attempts at past multilateral action has been the improved application of existing national legislation by national

---

[4] As noted above, industrial imports into OECD countries of industrial goods face average tariffs of 3.9 per cent, 97 per cent of which are bound (GATT, 1994a).

authorities and co-operation among national competition policy authorities. For example, the objective of the UN Principles and Rules is to facilitate the adoption and strengthening of laws and policies in the area of restrictive business practices at the national and regional level. The UN Principles and Rules stipulate that 'States should, at the national level or through regional groupings, adopt, improve and effectively enforce appropriate legislation and implement judicial and administrative procedures for the control of restrictive business practices, including those of transnational corporations'. The UN Principles and Rules note that legislation or regulations applicable to restrictive business practices should be clearly defined and publicly and readily available, and that the treatment of enterprises should be fair, equitable, on the same basis to all enterprises, and in accordance with established procedures of law.

A further example is the OECD Recommendations which require that countries should 'co-operate in developing or applying mutually satisfactory and beneficial measures for dealing with anti-competitive practices in international trade'. In the terms of the OECD Recommendations, the co-operation essentially means exchange of information, consultation and 'sympathetic consideration' as well as conciliation. The UN Principles and Rules additionally mention other forms of mutually reinforcing action on 'national, regional and international level'. This includes work aimed at achieving common approaches in national policies relating to anti-competitive practices.

Hence, the basis of all Agreements discussed to date has been transparency of domestic legislation and the exchange of information, and consultation and co-operation among countries. None of the Guidelines, Recommendations or Principles and Rules create contractual obligations that are legally enforceable across national boundaries. With respect to *transparency*, the provisions in the various arrangements reviewed above refer to: (i) transparency of restrictive business practices, (ii) transparency of restrictive business practices policies and their effects, (iii) transparency of restrictive business practices investigations or legal proceedings of interest to other countries, (iv) transparency of settlements reached through consultations or conciliations, (v) transparency of the observance of multilateral commitments, (vi) exchange, analysis and dissemination of restrictive business practices-related information on international level and, finally, (vii) safeguards confidentiality.

With respect to the *exchange of information*, the OECD Guidelines stipulate that enterprises should provide information to competent authorities of countries whose interests are directly affected in regard to competition issues or investigations; provisions of information should be in accordance with safeguards normally applicable in this field. The OECD Recommendations require that an OECD member country undertaking an investigation of restrictive business practices or legal proceedings will notify any country whose substantial interests are involved. It also recommends that, subject to appropriate safeguards, the competent authorities of one member country should allow the disclosure of information to the competent authorities of member countries by other parties concerned, unless such disclosure would be contrary to significant national interests. The UN Principles and Rules stipulate that the States should institute appropriate procedures for (i) obtaining information from enterprises, including transnational corporations, (ii) promote exchange of relevant information at the regional and sub-regional level and supply the relevant information to other States, particularly developing countries. It also contains a technical assistance provision with respect to systems for the control of restrictive business practices and a confidentiality clause with respect to legitimate business secrets.

These principles are further reinforced through (i) supply by members to the Secretary-General of UNCTAD of appropriate information on steps taken by governments to meet their commitments to the UN Principles and Rules and changes in the domestic restrictive business practices policies, as well as (ii) preparation of an UNCTAD publication, and other relevant studies, documentation and reports. An important role in that respect is assumed by the Intergovernmental Group of Experts on Restrictive Business Practices.

The OECD Guidelines require that enterprises should be ready *to consult and co-operate* with competent authorities of countries whose interests are directly affected in regard to competition issues or investigations. The OECD Recommendations stipulate that if an OECD member country finds that its interests are seriously affected by a restrictive business practice of an enterprise located in another OECD member country, it may enter into consultation with the other country and adopt appropriate remedial action. Moreover, if a country considers that investigations or proceedings conducted by another OECD country substantially affects its interests, it may enter into a new kind of consultation during which the various possibilities for meeting the objectives of the investigation or the requirements of legal proceedings will be examined. The OECD countries engaging in consultations will endeavour to find a mutually acceptable solution. In the event that no such solution can be found, the countries concerned may submit the case to the OECD Competition Law and Policy Committee with a view to conciliation. The Recommendation establishes detailed procedural requirements concerning consultations and conciliation. The conciliation procedures have never been used.

The UN Principles and Rules also rely on consultation as a means of finding mutually acceptable solutions concerning restrictive business practices. UNCTAD may be requested to provide necessary conference facilities for such consultations. The UN Principles and Rules stipulate that enterprises 'should consult and co-operate with competent authorities of countries directly affected in controlling restrictive business practices adversely affecting the interests of those countries'.

b. Other Actions Based on National Laws

More recently, a number of actions have been advanced to deal with cross-nation competition situations. These represent extensions of the forms of co-operation listed above: harmonisation of national rules and procedures, mutual recognition of domestic policies and application of the principle of (negative and positive) comity. Harmonisation of national rules and procedures, or the mutual recognition of domestic policies, would overcome difficulties due to differences between nations, but would not by itself lead to changes in practices or the resolution of disputes. Under negative comity, the traditional concept of international comity, a nation refrains from extending its own legal or administrative activities into the jurisdiction of another nation. Under positive comity, one nation through its courts or the administration of its law assists another to effect the laws and regulations of the latter. Positive comity has become much more important with the spread of bilateral and regional agreements on competition policies.

c. Extraterritoriality

With the growth of transnational corporations and the globalisation of markets, it has become increasingly apparent that to address anti-competitive practices on the basis of national boundaries is inadequate. Some countries have sought to extend national laws beyond national borders by unilateral legislation. Proposed solutions, however, which involve the extraterritorial application of a country's anti-trust laws raise concerns about the loss of national sovereignty in the country or countries in which they are applied. This has led to counter-measures in some instances; for example, the US attempt to enforce its anti-trust legislation extraterritorially has been blocked in Great Britain and France by statutes which limit these applications.

d. An International Code

A code is a voluntary plurilateral agreement. There is a range of possibilities as to how an international code might operate. It might be a stand-alone code such as the UN Principles and Rules. It might be a part of another agreement. They may be a formal vehicle for promoting transparency and the exchange of information and co-operation among governments as discussed under (a) or they may seek to implement trans-border competition policies.

The Group of Experts organised under the Max Planck Institute envisaged an Anti-trust Code as a Plurilateral Agreement to be incorporated into the Final Act of the Uruguay Round; that is, an agreement which is not a part of the 'single undertaking' and signed only by those countries which agreed to it separately. It would, therefore, operate in the manner of the existing UN and OECD codes or the GATT Tokyo Round Codes.

The proposal is quite severely restricted. The proposal relates only to that part of competition policies which is anti-trust policy and then only to restraints that involve cross-border competition; that is, it would not apply to cases that involved only national markets.[5] It would impose minimum standards for the national laws for all signatories. It would be enforced through the remedies of national laws only and proceedings would be initiated by an International Trust Authority.

e. International Treaties

International treaties or agreements signed by member countries and ratified nationally are binding upon the members. The WTO Agreements constitute an international treaty. A treaty relating to international competition law could be a stand-alone treaty, such as the Berne and Paris Conventions, for the protection of intellectual property or a part of the WTO. In the latter case, it would be a multilateral Agreement, have uniform standards and be enforceable under the Dispute Settlement rules of the WTO. It could be covered by a separate article which dealt with all aspects of the competition policy under the agreement, or by several articles which dealt with competition law aspects of other principles or measures.

In listing these options, there is a basic distinction between 'soft law' and 'hard law' provisions. The former are voluntary and non-enforceable whereas the latter are enforceable under international laws. In the foregoing, (*a*) is soft, (*b*) and (*c*) are enforceable (but on the basis of domestic laws), (*d*) may have elements of hard law, while (*e*) is the only truly hard law.

7. COMPETITION POLICIES IN THE WTO AFTER THE URUGUAY ROUND

While the GATT (1947) — or the GATT (1994a) as revised in the Uruguay Round — does not address competition policy *per se*, GATT rules have a number of provisions relating to areas of international competition policies. Article VI dealing with anti-dumping is the only GATT provision intended to counter

---

[5] Not all members of the Working Group agreed, however, that a code was needed. A minority of the Working Group, in fact, proposed a minimalist set of principles which should be applied to 'transactions and conduct with an international dimension'. These principles would extend the coverage of national laws to allow the prohibition of conduct initiated on the domestic territory and causing injury in, or to, another country. Action by the International Anti-trust Authority itself would be limited to the delivery of 'an order of non-interference' in the case of threat against an important national or world interest.

private anti-competitive actions; namely, dumping. This, however, considers only injury to domestic producers, ignoring benefits to domestic buyers.[6] Other Articles of GATT may permit a complaint against government measures which leads to anti-competitive actions in two distinct ways.[7] 'Violation cases' arise when it is alleged that some government measure is inconsistent with a GATT rule. The rules which may be applied here are Article III on National Treatment (e.g. discriminatory distribution or pricing that results from government laws or regulations), Article XVII on State-trading Enterprises (e.g. state import or export monopolies) and Article XI on Quantitative Restrictions (e.g. import quotas that restrict supplies from some sources). All of these possibilities are subject to a number of restrictions. 'Non-violation' cases arise when it is alleged that some government measure nullifies or impairs some condition of market access that has been negotiated under the GATT. These too must satisfy certain requirements, such as that the measures could not have been reasonably anticipated at the time of the negotiation concession and they do not apply to exports.

Hoekman and Mavroidis (1993, p. 27) conclude that: 'Although the scope to use GATT to address competition policy-related concerns is wider than is commonly thought, the foregoing analysis reveals that the reach of the GATT is limited'. Many of these complaints to GATT have arisen because of government subsidies or export subsidies which are measures consistent with the GATT in the first place. For example, most complaints under Article XXIII (Nullification and Impairment) have involved nullification or impairment of a negotiated tariff concession by the introduction of a subsidy.

The results of the Uruguay Round reinforce existing GATT obligations in the area of competition policy and create new ones.[8] The existing obligations and rules relating to competition policy are essentially unchanged. Some of the rules relating to government measures have been strengthened as a result of the Uruguay Round. For example, the Agreement on Subsidies and Countervailing Measures now provides a definition of 'subsidies' and 'specific subsidies' and makes all specific subsidies actionable; that is, action may be taken against them if they cause injury to other members. While the Agreement on Agriculture requires members to undertake specific and binding reduction commitments in areas of export subsidies as well as market access and domestic support, it continues to permit the use of export subsidies in agriculture. None of the changes in these areas amount to a substantial extension of the powers of the GATT in these areas of competition policy.

---

[6] Hoekman and Mavroidis (1993, p. 7) conclude that, in fact, 'Anti-dumping, far from being a pro-competitive practice, is an anti-competitive one' because it facilitates collusion among producers.
[7] These are surveyed by Jackson (1992) and Hoekman and Mavroidis (1993).
[8] See Petersmann (1993) for a discussion of Uruguay Round Agreements that have a competition policy dimension.

700   PETER LLOYD AND GARY SAMPSON

The General Agreement on Trade in Services (GATS), however, provides a good example of new relationships in the WTO between competition policies and trade policies. GATS applies to all measures (governmental and some non-governmental) that affect international trade in services; these include direct investment through commercial presence and the movement of natural persons (entrepreneurs, technicians, managers). The goal of the Agreement is the progressive liberalisation of trade in services. In pursuit of this goal, the Agreement contains provisions that directly address aspects of competition policy business practices. There is a requirement that service suppliers do not abuse their monopoly position (Article VIII) and a recognition that certain business practices of service suppliers may restrain competition and thereby restrict trade in services (Article IX). With respect to business practices, the provisions directly related to competition policies are based on consultation among members and the enforcement is by means of domestic laws and regulations. Each member, at the request of another member, will enter into consultations with a view to eliminating these restrictive practices. When such a member is approached to enter into consultations, it is necessary to accord full and sympathetic consideration to such a request. The member is to co-operate through the supply of publicly available non-confidential information of relevance to the matter in question. The member which has been addressed is also to provide other information available to the member, subject to its domestic law and to the conclusion of satisfactory agreement concerning the safeguarding of its confidentiality of the requesting party.

Many other GATS provisions address traditional areas of concern of competition policy. These include, among others, access to public telecommunications networks, transparency, subsidies, government procurement, and access to the distribution and marketing networks of services. These are important because services are essential inputs into many production activities.

The Agreement on Trade Related Aspects of Intellectual Property Rights (TRIPS) contains two Articles which relate to aspects of competition policies: these concern 'effective protection against certain competition' (Article 39) and control of 'anti-competitive practices' (Article 40). As with the GATS, enforcement of these provisions is by means of civil and administrative procedures and remedies under national laws. More broadly, however, the whole TRIPS Agreement is essentially concerned with fair trade in intellectual property. Much of it concerns issues of pricing for the use of intellectual property which is a classic issue of competition policy. The WTO will oversee trade-related aspects of intellectual property via the Council for Trade-Related Aspects of Intellectual Property Rights as a part of the WTO, and the Dispute Settlement Understanding applies to the Agreement. The Agreement will inject a substantial new element of multilateral regulation and enforcement of intellectual property rights, including

COMPETITION AND TRADE POLICY 701

competition policies. Intellectual property transactions, too, are an increasingly important part of the international trade in technologies and goods.

The Agreement on Trade Related Investment Measures (TRIMS) is intended to discipline trade-related investment measures which had hitherto escaped any international regulation. In particular, it prohibits TRIMS which are inconsistent with National Treatment or the General Elimination of Quantitative Restrictions. The importance of TRIMS in the context of competition policy is that, for the first time, it involves in the regulation of aspects of investment the multilateral body responsible for the management of the world trading system. The Preamble to the Agreement notes that it desires 'to facilitate investment across international frontiers so as to increase the economic growth of all trading partners' as well as to promote the expansion and progressive liberalisation of world trade. More pointedly, Article 9 provides for a review of the Agreement within five years and, 'In the course of this review, the Council for Trade in Goods shall consider whether it should be complemented with provisions on investment policy and competition policy'.

With respect to deciding on the desirable form of multilateral or plurilateral competition policies, there are two primary questions to address. They are the question of how far these policies should go in terms of the coverage of actions and the range of instruments to enforce these policies (that is, voluntary or involuntary enforcement, remedies, etc.), and the question of which body should be responsible for these policies.

Regarding the first question, the emphasis should be on measures which remove barriers to competition. It is important to recall that most markets for goods and services are more competitive now than they have ever been because of the progressive liberalisation of international trade and the opening up of many national markets to foreign competition. This is in large part the result of the eight GATT Rounds of Multilateral Trade Negotiations, as well as the unilateral and regional trade liberalisation arrangements of the past four decades.

It is probable that the greatest service the WTO can render to improve competition in international markets is to maintain an open trading environment. An open and liberal trading system for both goods and services is good competition policy for the trading countries. If liberal international trade were extended to the liberal movement of capital, more national and international competition problems would disappear. In particular, the achievement of commercial establishment for foreign investors and national treatment after establishment would make many markets contestable by firms producing within national markets as well as trading across national borders.

With respect to the range of instruments, the distinction between so-called 'hard' laws and 'soft' laws was noted above. To date, the efforts of the OECD and the UN have all been confined to soft law, whereas the obligations of the GATT and WTO constitute hard law. The enforceability of the WTO trade policies has been increased by the changes in the Dispute Settlement rules which have made the decisions of the Dispute Settlement Body of the WTO final and binding after the report of the Appellate Body.

Regarding the second question, the integration of markets across countries means that both domestic and internationally-traded supplies to the market should be considered together. For example, in a fully integrated world market for some good (or service) in which there is liberal trade and equal market access to all markets for the producers of all countries, such questions as the effects of mergers and acquisitions or of price discrimination should be considered for the one world market, not just in the domestic market of the importing country or countries.

8. WHY THE WTO?

The definition of markets under the competition laws of many countries now transcends national borders, even though national tariffs or non-tariff border or non-border measures still segment some global markets into national markets. This is adequate if the practices affect buyers in only one national market but actions in one country will normally affect prices, outputs and competition in all components of a market as arbitrage occurs across markets which are not segmented. At present, many anti-competitive practices escape all regulation as they are not covered by the WTO and export agreements which have little or no effect on the domestic market are commonly exempted from the scope of application of domestic competition laws. These problems are exacerbated if more than two countries are involved. International markets cannot be regulated adequately by national laws. An independent arbiter is needed to weigh the conflicting interests of producers and consumers in different countries.

Some groups have argued that the WTO is the logical body in which to locate any multilateral or plurilateral organisation dealing with international competition policies and rules. For example, the Report of the Group of Experts (established in GATT in 1958) declared that GATT was the 'appropriate and competent body to initiate action in this field'; after citing an extraordinary body of literature, it states that members of the Group 'were familiar with the lengthy discussions on this subject that have taken place over the past 15 years' (GATT, 1959). The Working Group which recently recommended the establishment of an International Anti-trust Code stated that 'GATT in particular is at the heart of the worldwide trading system. Therefore, it is GATT where anti-monopolistic and pro-competitive rules on international trade and commerce should be integrated' (International Anti-trust Code Working Group, 1993, p. 131).

There are a number of difficulties with expanding the role of the WTO in the area of competition policy. In the first place, the WTO covers private restraints

COMPETITION AND TRADE POLICY   703

only insofar as the change in competition is due to a government measure which affects competition from imports (but not exports). Second, there are severe limits on the remedies available to the WTO. These are confined to government sanctions through trade measures. They do not include the traditional remedies under national legislation such as injunctions and divestiture of assets. Under the WTO, compensation and suspension are intended to be temporary. Private actions are not possible. Third, most nations will no doubt be reluctant to cede authority to an international body in an area which has traditionally been handled exclusively within national jurisdictions.

In their survey of current GATT competition-related policies, Hoekman and Mavroidis (1993, p. 5) conclude that: 'Realistically, the most that can be expected in the multilateral context are further moves towards satisfying the necessary conditions, i.e. attaining the first ideal model described earlier [the maintenance of national sovereignty regarding non-border policies], perhaps with GATT's enforcement dispute settlement mechanism extended to include certain competition policy-related issues'. Similarly, the majority of the International Anti-trust Code Working Group favoured a Code with enforcement by national authorities and a limited coverage of private restraints, and a minority favoured a weaker set of rules based only on minimum standards. However, one may note that members will cede similar powers to WTO in areas such as TRIPS.

The case for the WTO has been strengthened by the Uruguay Round results which have substantially strengthened the rules and procedures in the organisation which deal with competition policies. In particular, they now encompass competition policies relating to trade in intellectual property rights and trade-related aspects of foreign investment, as well as trade in both goods and services. There is no other multilateral or plurilateral body with activities in all of these areas of competition policy. Furthermore, in the area of intellectual property rights, international regulation is currently divided between a number of plurilateral treaty Conventions and the World Intellectual Property Rights Organisation, with all of which the WTO is enjoined to co-operate.

There is an underlying logic to bringing these competition policies under the supervision of one organisation. Historically, international competition policies relating to goods and services, intellectual property and investment income have been regarded as separate. However, they should all be regarded as aspects of trade in goods and services. Both intellectual property rights payments and the returns on all international investments are treated as trade in services in the UN Conventions which lay down the procedures for the compilation of statistics relating to the national income and the balance of payments of countries. There is no reason to distinguish between trade in goods and trade in services in relation to matters of competition policies.

It is this logic which has propelled the GATT and the WTO towards a greater involvement in international competition policies, but the transition, where it is desirable, from laws based on domestic legislation to laws which are enforceable internationally will be long and difficult.

REFERENCES

Baade, H. (1980), 'The Legal Effects of Codes of Conduct for MNEs' in Norbert Horn (ed.), *Studies in Transnational Economic Law: Legal Problems of Codes of Conduct for Multinational Enterprises* (Deventer: Kluwer).
Baldwin, R. (1970), *Non-Tariff Distortions of International Trade* (Washington, DC: The Brookings Institution).
Brittan, L. (1992), *European Competition Policy: Keeping the Playing Field Level* (published for CEPS by Brassey's (UK)).
Feketekuty, G. (1993), 'The New Trade Issues: Competition', OECD, mimeo.
General Agreement on Tariffs and Trade (GATT) (1955), Basic Instruments and Selected Documents, Third Supplement (Geneva, Switzerland).
General Agreement on Tariffs and Trade (GATT) (1959), Basic Instruments and Selected Documents, Seventh Supplement (Geneva, Switzerland).
General Agreement on Tariffs and Trade (GATT) (1961), Basic Instruments and Selected Documents, Ninth Supplement (Geneva, Switzerland).
General Agreement on Tariffs and Trade (GATT) (1994a), *News of the Uruguay Round of Multilateral Trade Negotiations* (Geneva, Switzerland: GATT Secretariat, April).
General Agreement on Tariffs and Trade (GATT) (1994b), Concluding Remarks by the Chairman of the Trade Negotiations Committee at Ministerial Level (Marrakesh, Morocco: 12–15 April 1994, MTN.TNC/MIN(94)16).
Group of Experts on Restrictive Trade Practices (1960), *Report*, adopted by the GATT Council on 2 June, GATT L/105.
Havana Charter (1948), *Final Act of the United Nations Trade and Employment*.
Hoekman, B.M. and P. Mavroidis (1993), 'Competition, Competition Policy and the GATT' (The World Bank, Finance and Private Sector Development Division, Policy Research Working Paper, No. 1228).
International Anti-trust Code Working Group (1993), 'Draft International Antitrust Code — as a GATT–MTO–Plurilateral Trade Agreement', *World Trade Materials*, 5, 126–196.
Jackson, J.H. (1992), 'Competition and Trade Policy', *Journal of World Trade*, 26, 25.
Jones, B.A. (1968), *The New York Times* (New York).
Mattoo, A. and P. Mavroidis (1993), 'The EC–Japan Consensus on Cars: Trade and Competition Policy Trade-offs', mimeo (Geneva: GATT).
Organisation for Economic Cooperation and Development (OECD) (1976), *Declaration on International Investment and Multinational Enterprises* (Paris: OECD, 21 June).
Organisation for Economic Cooperation and Development (OECD) (1984a), *Trade and Competition Policy* (Paris: OECD).
Organisation for Economic Cooperation and Development (OECD) (1984b), *Competition and Trade Policies: Their Interaction* (Paris: OECD).
Organisation for Economic Cooperation and Development (OECD) (1987), *Competition Policy and International Trade: OECD Instruments of Co-operation* (Paris: OECD).
Organisation for Economic Cooperation and Development (OECD) (1994a), *Interim Report on Convergence of Competition Policy* (Paris: OECD, GD(94/64)).
Organisation for Economic Cooperation and Development (OECD) (1994b), *Trade and Competition Policies: Comparing Objectives and Methods*, Trade Policy Issues, 4 (Paris: OECD).
Petersmann, E. (1993), 'International Competition Rules for the GATT–MTO World Trade and Legal System', *Journal of World Trade*, 27, 35–86.

United Nations (UN) (1981), *The Set of Multilaterally Agreed Equitable Principles and Rates for the Control of Restrictive Business Practices* (New York: United Nations).

United Nations Commission on Transnational Corporations (UNCTC) (1990a), *The New Code Environment*, Paper 7, Workshop for GNS Negotiators on the Activities of the Transnational Corporations in Services (Montreux, Switzerland: 11 – 12 November).

United Nations Commission on Transnational Corporations (UNCTC) (1990b), *Key Concepts in International Investment Arrangements and Their Relevance to Negotiations on International Transactions in Services*, UNCTC Current Series, No. 13, Series A (New York: United Nations).

United Nations Conference on Trade and Development (UNCTAD) (1985), *The History of UNCTAD, 1964 – 1984* (New York: United Nations).

[21]

Offshore Production and the Base

of Import Taxation

P.J. Lloyd

1. INTRODUCTION

IN all Western countries a significant part of the national product is produced outside the borders of the nation. This comprises income on capital invested abroad and labour income accruing to citizens temporarily resident in other countries. Much of this income flow is associated with offshore assembly by multinational corporations of goods which are exported to the home country. In such cases the income of domestic factors is embodied in goods which are imported. Imported goods may also embody domestic factors in the form of intermediate goods which have been produced in the home country, exported, and then reimported as part of a product assembled or processed overseas. The conventions of customs valuation, however, do not recognise the existence of domestic content of internationally traded goods. They are based on the anachronistic presumption that all national production takes place within the national borders. The non-exclusion of the domestic content of imports from import taxation amounts to an implicit tax on that part of domestic production which takes place offshore. This is an anomaly which should be corrected.

The implicit tax on the domestic content of imports leads to a distortion in the tax structure which discriminates against that part of the national product which is produced outside the geographic area of the customs territory or reimported. Because offshore assembly and other production activities outside the territory of countries have increased very rapidly in recent years, this distortion is now significant.

Such distortion in the taxation of imports has not previously been noted, as far as the present author is aware. A number of countries have introduced offshore assembly provisions for certain goods which would be covered by the kind of change proposed in this paper, but these have been limited in coverage and they

P.J. LLOYD is from the University of Melbourne, Australia. He wishes to acknowledge the useful comments of the referees and of participants at seminars at the University of Melbourne, and particularly those of Kym Anderson, Duncan Ironmonger and Jonathon Pincus.

720   P.J. LLOYD

were conceived of as a form of tariff concession intended to encourage the use of
domestic materials or components in offshore assembly. Hence, they were
conceived more as a form of assistance to certain domestic producers than as a
recognition of a general principle of equal treatment. Levinsohn and Slemrod
(1993) devise an optimal set of domestic and trade taxes/subsidies for
corporations producing both at home and abroad. They recognise that trade taxes/
subsidies do not apply to goods produced abroad by domestically owned
corporations, but seek to compensate for this restriction on the tax set by varying
income taxes which do apply to foreign source incomes. They do not contemplate
a change in the base of trade taxes.

The problem of the taxation or subsidisation of export goods parallels that of
imported goods and one could, therefore, pose the problem of the choice of tax
base generally in terms of all border taxes. However, subsidies on exports are
prohibited by Article XVI of the GATT with the exception of primary products,
chiefly agricultural commodities, whereas taxes on imports are almost
ubiquitous. This paper focuses on the base of tariffs.

Section 2 of this paper analyses the problems associated with the choice of base
for import taxes. Section 3 proposes a new kind of tariff whose base is the value
added by all factors owned by residents of foreign countries and it considers the
feasibility of such a tax. Section 4 looks at the effects of the proposed change on
the allocation of resources in the economy. In general, this change in taxation
would improve the efficiency of national production in two ways. First, it will
remove the distortion against production outside the customs territory. Second, it
will lower the average nominal and effective rates of assistance and the dispersion
among them and thereby improve the allocation of resources within the territory.
Other applications of the change in the tariff regime to export taxes/subsidies,
domestic labelling and rules of origin are considered in Section 5.

2. THE PROBLEM

Globalisation of production and the sourcing of intermediate inputs from the
cheapest global source yield trade in goods which embodies the services of
factors that are owned by the residents of the importing country.

There are several different ways in which imported goods may have a domestic
content. The most straightforward and common form is intra-firm trade. Intra-
firm trade arises when a good is traded internationally by two units of a
multinational corporation. Intra-firm trade may be between a parent and an
affiliate or two affiliates of the same parent. The parent may be owned by
residents of the importing country or by residents of a foreign country or
countries. When the importing corporation is owned by residents of the importing

country, the intra-firm import is produced substantially by the use of capital, skilled and executive labour and technology owned by residents of the importing country, though it also has a foreign labour content. The domestic content may also include intermediate inputs supplied to the foreign country at an earlier stage by the importing country. In this case, the import contains *indirect* domestic inputs as well as *direct* domestic inputs.

Well-known examples of intra-firm trade are the assembly operations in Mexico on the US border known as maquilas, the US-Canada trade in automobile parts and components, and similar activities by EC global corporations. After the major revaluation of the yen in 1985, Japan relocated many production activities to locations in East Asia which provide low-cost value adding and produce goods which are then shipped back to Japan. In recent years, other Asian Newly-Industrialising Economies such as Taiwan and Korea have been relocating activities to South East Asia. Intra-firm trade is concentrated in manufacturing industries which are intensive in technology and human capital such as machinery, electric/electronic equipment and transportation equipment (Bonturi and Fukasaku, 1993a and 1993b).

Imports of goods with a domestic content by a corporation may be arm's length trade rather than intra-firm trade. If a foreign affiliate of a domestic corporation exports at arm's length to an unrelated corporation in the home country, there is no intra-firm trade but there is some domestic content in the goods imported. Julius (1990, Chapter 4) calls the sum of the intra-firm imports and the imports from affiliates to the home country Foreign Direct Investment (FDI)-related import trade. These are the cross-border transactions between overseas activities of the country's corporations and the home country.

Finally, an economic activity in a foreign country carried out by a foreign corporation may employ labour from the importing country or be part-owned by residents of the country, or use technology or intermediate inputs supplied by producers in the importing country. In these cases, too, the imported good embodies domestic inputs.

A substantial part of the value of imports into all Western countries represents value added by domestic factors. Unfortunately, statistics of the domestic content of imports are not available from standard input−output tables. Nor are there global or comprehensive statistics of the component comprising imports from offshore assembly operations. The US Government records the value of imports under its Offshore Assembly Provision which covers reimports of some US-manufactured products. In 1989, they were $74 billion or 16 per cent of total merchandise imports (US International Trade Commission, 1991).

An indication of the magnitude of international trade in domestic inputs which are embodied in traded goods can be gauged from the extent of intra-firm trade. International trade statistics do not record whether the flow is intra-firm or arm's length, but some data are available for the US and Japan from surveys of firms.

P.J. LLOYD

The US Department of Commerce compiles data for both foreign affiliates of US corporations and US affiliates of foreign corporations. In 1989, imports shipped to US parents by foreign affiliates totalled US$76 billion or 15.4 per cent of total US merchandise imports, and imports shipped to US affiliates by foreign parents were US$128 billion or 26 per cent of merchandise import trade. Both sets together accounted for 41.4 per cent of total US merchandise imports. In the case of Japan, the share of intra-firm trade in total trade cannot be calculated, but the share of intra-firm trade in the total foreign trade involving the corporations covered by the survey was 28.7 per cent of the total trade of the Japanese parent corporations. (The US and Japanese data are from Bonturi and Fukasaku, 1993a and 1993b.) These data indicate that intra-firm trade alone is a substantial part of total world merchandise trade.

When an imported commodity has a domestic content, it is apparent that import taxation should in principle tax only that part of the value of the imported commodity which is value added by foreign factors. In taxing the gross value, tax authorities are imposing an implicit tax on the value added by domestic factors at the time the commodity in which these factors are embodied crosses the national geographic border. This discriminates against that part of national production which takes place outside the geographic area of the customs territory and that part of national production which is exported and reimported.

This logic can be readily appreciated by considering the movement of goods within and between countries. Consider a country which is a federation of states, such as the United States, Canada, Germany or Australia. When goods are imported into one state from another state, they are not subject to an import duty; but when they are imported into a state from another country, they are subject to an import duty, assuming one is applicable to the particular good. In the former case, the value added by domestic factors is not taxed but in the latter it is. When the objective of the tax is to protect or assist domestic production, there is no basis for discriminating against the subset of domestic factors which are located abroad.

Yet GATT defines value for duty in terms of the gross price, not excluding the domestic content of the imported good. Customs valuation procedures in all members of the GATT must accord with Article VII of the GATT. Article VII lays down that:

> The value for customs purposes of imported merchandise should be based on the actual value of the imported merchandise on which duty is assessed, or of like merchandise . . . (GATT, 1986, p. 12).

The Article provides for the exclusion from the value for duty of internal taxes applied within the country of origin or export, but not for the factor content of the merchandise which is domestic content for the importing country. The GATT Valuation Code, which implements this Article, is designed to ensure that all elements of the cost of obtaining the goods for export are included in the customs

OFFSHORE PRODUCTION AND BASE OF IMPORT TAXATION 723

value of goods. Thus, the GATT makes no distinction whatsoever between the content added abroad by foreign factors and that added by domestic factors.

This non-exclusion of the domestic content of imports in customs valuation procedures needs to be contrasted with the treatment of this content as income. The domestic content of imported goods is recognised by the national income conventions as a part of the national income of all countries. And as income it is taxed by the domestic income tax authorities. Very loosely speaking, income taxation in most OECD countries is designed to tax the income of domestic factors, whether they are located at home or offshore.[1] The base of taxes on resident corporations is the global income of the corporation and that of personal income earners resident in the country is also the total global income of the taxpayer.

Similarly, in the theory of tariffs, the distinction between the gross value of output of a good and the value added in its production became appreciated for the first time in the 1960s when the concept of effective protection was constructed. This distinction recognised that it is the protection of the domestic value added, not the gross value of output, which is important in considering the effects of border protection on the production sector of an economy. Many countries now construct series of both nominal and effective rates of protection for some commodities. The recognition here that the (nominal) rate of protection should be adjusted for the domestic content which is embodied in some imports is really the reverse aspect of the separation of stages of production across national borders. It recognises the domestic content of offshore production, whereas effective protection recognises the foreign content of onshore production.

Despite the total lack of recognition of domestic factors in the ordinary valuation of goods for customs purposes, there are instances in which the presence of domestic content in imports has been partially recognised in the calculation of import duties. In the US Tariff, there are two tariff items which are referred to as the Offshore Assembly Provision (OAP). Item 9802.00.60 relates to articles of metal which are manufactured in and exported from the US and then returned to the US for further processing. Item 9802.00.80 relates to articles assembled abroad in whole or in part from components made in the US. The

---

[1] In practice, however, the effective rates of tax are affected by features of the tax system which treat differently foreign-source and domestic-source income and by whether the domestic country allows taxes imposed on foreign-source income by foreign governments as a credit against the tax liability to the domestic country (as in Japan, the US and the UK) or not. In some countries the corporate tax regime discriminates against their moving production offshore; for example, in Australia dividend imputation is designed to avoid double taxation of company income, but it does not apply equally to domestic- and foreign-source income. This is another instance of the need to make neutral the tax treatment of domestic and offshore production. But in other countries, the tax regime discriminates in favour of foreign-source income, whereas the value for duty convention always discriminates against offshore production.

P.J. LLOYD

import duty on products processed or assembled abroad with articles or components that were made in the US is levied on the value of the imports less the value of US-produced products. This lowers the rate of duty on products assembled abroad which contain US components or materials. Most of the products are made in Canada and Mexico. This provision dates back to the 1930 US Tariff. It has been copied in the tariff regime of some other industrialised countries; for example, Australia introduced an Overseas Assembly Provision in 1993.

The US OAP does not establish complete neutrality between US production based in the US and production offshore. It is confined to the exclusion of US-manufactured goods which are assembled or processed abroad. The base of the OAP tariff is still greater than the true foreign value added if there are direct US inputs of labour and capital, or indirect intermediate inputs, as well as US-made components used directly in the foreign assembly. And the provision only applies to imports which contain intermediate inputs produced at an earlier stage in the US.[2] Similarly, as a second example, the Australian Overseas Assembly Provision does not cover the direct inputs of Australian capital and labour overseas, and there are a number of other restrictions on eligibility for the scheme; it is confined to clothing importers and, within this industry, to a firm which is both the exporter of the cut shapes or pieces and the importer of the assembled garment. These features arise chiefly because:

> The Scheme is designed to encourage the maximum use of Australian made fabrics which are cut or knitted to shape in Australia (Textiles, Clothing and Footwear Development Authority, 1993, p. 4).

Evidently, the conventions of customs valuation do not recognise in general the existence of domestic content of internationally traded goods. They are based on the anachronistic presumption that all national production takes place within the national borders. The non-exclusion of the domestic content of imports from import taxation is an anomaly which should be corrected.

3. A VALUE ADDED TAX BASE

The avoidance of discrimination against foreign-located national production can be achieved by redefining the valuation for customs which is the base of all tariffs based on a value for duty. The base should be the value of foreign

---

[2] It could be that the products made in the US and exported and reimported themselves used foreign factors, because the US-located firm was foreign owned or used foreign-produced intermediate inputs. In such cases, the value of the US-made intermediate inputs overstates the US content. In principle, such foreign inputs should be excluded from the adjustment but, like indirect domestic inputs, they could be ignored as an approximation.

production, that is, the foreign value added. This is the transaction value less the value of payments to domestic factors which are embodied in the good. This may be called the *foreign value added* and the tariff might be called a *value added tariff*.

For a traded commodity, commodity i, let v_i and v_i^* denote the proportions of the value added which are added by domestic and foreign factors respectively. Suppose that all tariff rates are *ad valorem*. Let t_i be the schedule tariff rate, which is also the rate levied on foreign value added. Then the tariff rate which is actually levied on a dollar of imports of the commodity by a member country with a value added tariff will be:

$$t_i = v_i^* t_i \qquad v_i + v_i^* = 1 \qquad (1)$$

t_i can be called the *adjusted* tariff rate. This change in the value for duty should be done for all countries by means of a change in Article VII of the GATT, though it could also be applied unilaterally by individual countries.

There are some practical aspects of the determination of the base for a value added tariff which should be addressed before considering the effects of a change in the base of tariffs. First, one should, in principle, allow for the fact that some imports embody indirect domestic inputs because some intermediate inputs used in offshore production processes may themselves have used intermediate inputs which have a domestic content, even though the intermediate inputs were not sourced from the home country. Multi-stage production processes are now common and the domestic content of an imported good should be defined as the sum of the direct and indirect contents over all stages of production.

Such indirect domestic inputs pose a problem for the measurement of the foreign value added. One alternative, at least in the case of intra-firm imports, would be to treat the whole of the value of the import from a foreign affiliate as domestic content. This is a rule of thumb which is preferable to neglecting the domestic content, assuming the domestic content is typically more than 50 per cent, but one should attempt to measure the fraction of domestic content which lies on the continuum from 0 to 1.

As an approximation to the domestic content (or strictly a lower bound to the domestic content and therefore an upper bound to the foreign content which is the base of the tax), the value added could be calculated simply as the value of the import less the *direct* domestic input, that is, the domestic content in the last stage of manufacture before importation. This would exclude the domestic content of inputs used in earlier stages. Domestic inputs used at an earlier stage are of second order importance in most processes and are frequently zero.

As a third alternative, the duty could be levied at the substantive rate and the importer could seek a reduction of duty, at the option of the importer, by demonstrating the amount of the domestic content in the goods subject to the duty payment. This would eliminate the need for statements about the domestic

P.J. LLOYD

content and origin of the goods except where the importer wished to establish a domestic content. The greater the domestic content which is established by the importer, the lower its tax liability. There are few taxes where greater administrative cost borne by the taxpayer results in a lower tax burden.

This optional method is in effect the method used by the US and other countries which operate offshore assembly provisions, though in these cases the provision is limited to the exclusion of intermediate inputs manufactured in the home country. Moreover, this method of an option available to the importer is used extensively in other tariff concessions such as Developing Country preference schemes and concessions for importing certain capital or intermediate inputs used in domestic production at lower rates. Finally, it has the advantage that it could be applied by individual contracting parties of the GATT without a revision of Article VII. It is the method most likely to be used in practice.

The same principles can be applied to tariffs which are not simple *ad valorem* tariffs but based at least in part on a value for duty. The *ad valorem* component can be adjusted in the same way. This applies also to contingent protection resulting from anti-dumping or countervailing duties. In these cases, the duty could be reduced in proportion to the domestic content of the imports concerned.

The second feature of import restrictions is that some imports are subject to non-tariff border restrictions in addition to tariffs. Non-tariff restrictions such as quotas can continue to apply to the goods entering the importing country or they can be waived if the domestic content is 50 per cent or more. A value-based quota might be defined in terms of the foreign value rather than the gross value, thereby exempting the domestic content from the quota. However, a volume-based quota cannot be applied in proportion to the foreign value added. This illustrates yet another advantage of tariffying non-tariff forms of border restriction on trade. Duty remission because of a domestic content would also provide an incentive for importers and producers to pursue the tariffication of quotas.

The tariffication of quotas and other non-tariff barriers such as variable levies as a part of the Uruguay Round has made *ad valorem* tariffs once again the most important instrument of protection. Most of the items which will be tariffied have high barriers and these will remain high despite the cuts of the Uruguay Round. The exclusion of domestic content will be important for some commodity groups such as textiles and clothing which have high barriers and a relatively high proportion of offshore production.

4. THE EFFECTS OF A SWITCH IN THE TAX BASE

The switch to a foreign value added base for tariff duties would result in a significant lowering of tariff rates around the world, especially in countries such as Japan, the US and European countries which have substantial offshore

OFFSHORE PRODUCTION AND BASE OF IMPORT TAXATION 727

investments and production. This would increase world trade but the effects on the efficiency of world production can only be examined by looking at the allocation of resources within the national economies of countries with offshore production.

The primary effect of the switch within countries with offshore production is to remove the distortion in domestic production which stems from the discrimination against that part of national production which is located offshore or reimported. Offshore production by definition provides another margin of production for domestic producers to consider. The removal of this discrimination will allow domestic factors to be employed where their marginal productivity is greatest, given other distortions in the economy, irrespective of whether the production process is located onshore or offshore.

The removal of this implicit tax might be objected to on the grounds that the intention of import taxation is to protect productive factors located within a country, whether they be nationals of the taxing country of foreigners located within its borders; that is, tariffs are designed to protect domestic product rather than national product in the national accounting sense. It seems doubtful to me that legislators chose the tariff base on these grounds. Rather, they followed the standard international convention and the taxation of domestic content arose unintentionally because of the later growth of complex chains of global production. Even if the intention were to protect domestic product, the existing base imposes a tax on this product when the good imported embodies other goods which have been produced domestically, exported and reimported.

A second possible objection is that the value added tariff violates the national treatment principle under Article II of the GATT and is, therefore, discriminatory. For example, if the tariff were applied in Australia, a foreign firm located in Australia which imports intermediates from its parent or an affiliate abroad would pay a higher duty than an Australian-owned firm in Australia which imports the same intermediate inputs from its foreign affiliate. This is true, but it is not discriminatory, because the foreign firm would pay the lower duty if it imported the input from the overseas affiliate of the Australian firm. National treatment requires like treatment under the same circumstances. In all cases the substantive rate of duty is the same.

It might also be objected that offshore producers in many cases have a number of advantages which onshore producers do not have in the form of access to low-cost labour and to materials, components and other intermediate or capital inputs at lower duty rates in many cases than in the domestic economy. The objection concerning labour costs is not tenable as it is just another denial of the principle of comparative advantage. But the objection relating to lower rates of duty raises issues of second-best policy making.

Much offshore production is located in countries with relatively low barriers to trade or in economic processing zones with duty-free access for imports of intermediate and capital inputs. Many developing and semi-industrialised countries have set aside special areas or zones within their customs borders to encourage production of manufactures for export (World Bank, 1992). These are most common in Asia and, in China alone, there are 30 approved economic zones. Much direct foreign investment by US and Japanese corporations and more recently by corporations from Hong Kong, Korea, Taiwan and Singapore has been located in economic zones in China and other Asian countries to take advantage of low labour costs. These zones also provide a number of tax advantages, including almost universally duty-free imports of raw materials and frequently other concessions such as company income tax holidays.

Do these advantages of offshore production due to the concessions of the governments of the countries in which they are located justify on second-best grounds the inclusion in value for duty of domestic content? First, the standard economic argument is that the government of the domestic economy should determine the policies which are in the best interests of the economy, taken as given the policies of other countries. This argument is applicable in the present context, too. Second, the non-exclusion of the domestic content of imports, as under the current customs valuation procedures, does not correct the advantages due to duty-free entry of other imports in the foreign countries. The extent of the duty concessions will vary from product to product within one zone and from zone to zone. In the importing country, the extent of the implicit tax on domestic production offshore from withholding the exclusion of the domestic content of the imports will also vary from product to product: from equation (1), one sees that it is, for any commodity, an increasing function of the two parameters, v_i^* and t_i. The concessions in the offshore location are determined by the governments of the zone countries and the tariffs in the importing country by the government of that country. There is no reason to expect correspondence between these two. Despite its emotive appeal, the second-best argument is not sound economics.

We also need to consider the effects which the change in the tariff regime will have on the allocation of resources *onshore*. Obviously, since $v_i^* \leq 1$, $\bar{t}_i \leq t_i$. That is, the value added tariff cannot be more than the tariff based on the standard value for duty, t_i. If the domestic content of the imported good is strictly positive, the value added duty must be strictly less than the duty based on the standard value for duty for $t_i > 0$.

The substitution of a value added tariff rule would reduce the dispersion in the actual tariff rates paid on all imports entering a country, given the schedule of substantive tariff rates for the country. In particular, there would be fewer imports at the maximum rate ($\bar{t}_i = t_i$) compared to the current value for duty which apply this (maximum) rate to all imports. For each commodity with a single schedule tariff rate (t_i), the adjusted rates ($\bar{t}_i$) levied on imports of the commodity from all sources would vary between a minimum of 0 and a maximum of t_i, depending on the distribution of the foreign components of value added.

OFFSHORE PRODUCTION AND BASE OF IMPORT TAXATION 729

These two effects relate to the nominal rates of protection. The change would also affect the structure of effective rates of protection or, more generally, the effective rates of assistance, as assistance may come from means other than border protection. Under the standard assumptions, the effective rate of assistance for a commodity (or group of commodities), commodity i, is defined as

$$e_i = (t_i - \sum_j a_{ji} t_j)/(1 - \sum_j a_{ji}) \tag{2}$$

where t_i and t_j are the *ad valorem* (or *ad valorem* equivalent) rates of assistance on the ith output and the jth input respectively, and a_{ji} is the proportion of the unit costs of producing commodity i which are accounted for by input j, valuing all commodities at the world prices. The standard assumptions include the assumptions that the country is a price-taker and that the physical input − output coefficients are fixed for all intermediate inputs.[3] This effective rate measures the percentage change in the value added per unit of output and it is the structure of these rates for all commodities which determine the gross levels of output of commodities. With the assumption of fixed intermediate input proportions, the effective rate can also be interpreted as the price of a unit of real value added and it is these prices of real value added which determine the quantities of real value added of all commodities in the general equilibrium of the economy in the standard model.

The standard model also assumes that the base of the value for duty for all tariffs is the gross value, that is, the landed price of the commodity. Now, the effect of switching the base of value for duty from the gross value of the commodity to the foreign value added is to substitute $\bar{t}_i$ and $\bar{t}_j$ for t_i and t_j respectively in the expression for the effective rate for commodity i. This gives an adjusted measure of the effective rate

$$\bar{e}_i = (\bar{t}_i - \sum_j a_{ji} \bar{t}_j)/(1 - \sum_j a_{ji}). \tag{3}$$

If the assistance to the commodity is provided by means of a tariff, the tariff rate is lowered by this adjustment. If, instead, the assistance to a commodity is by means of a quota, the tariff equivalent will be lowered or remain unchanged, depending upon whether the domestic content is more or less than 50 per cent and the quota does or does not apply. The effect of the changes in the calculation of effective rates will be to lower the rates of effective assistance in general, unless the reductions in the t_i and t_j are concentrated in the $\bar{t}_j$ rather than the $\bar{t}_i$. This is not likely to be the case frequently as the goods produced offshore and imported have been processed or assembled abroad and will be mostly final goods. This is true,

---

[3] Hitherto, this model also included the implicit assumption that valuing adding activities are immobile between countries. This has been considered above. In effect, the implicit tax on the traded output yields a negative rate of effective protection for the offshore activities.

for example, of goods assembled offshore under the US Offshore Assembly Provision.

The effect of switching the base of the value for duty on the dispersion of the effective rates in the economy is an empirical issue. Assuming that the effect on the levels is to lower them generally, it is possible that the dispersion in these rates will also be reduced. The opposite may occur if, for example, most of the effective rates which fall are below the average effective rate. This too seems unlikely in general as the industries where offshore production occurs are high cost operations which have moved offshore precisely because of the cheaper value adding in other countries and such industries will, in some cases at least, be those which are relatively heavily protected.

There is a further complication when a final product is produced by more than two stages. The conventional theory of effective protection supposes that there are only two stages of production, the first producing an intermediate product and the second producing the final product by processing the intermediate input produced in the first stage. In some industries three or more stages are involved, two or more of which involve the production of intermediate inputs which go through a sequence of processes.[4] In these cases, the effective rates of protection are not independent of each other. A higher or lower rate of effective protection at a lower stage cascades down the line of processes. This possibility could change the conclusion regarding the dispersion of effective rates in cases where the offshore production yields a good-in-process which is then an input into another domestic stage of production with a relatively high level of assistance. Thus, there is a presumption that the effect of the switch in the base of import taxation will induce a more efficient allocation of resources within the domestic economy.

Offshore assembly has been criticised in the US and other countries on the grounds that it 'exports jobs'. The US OAP has been frequently opposed on the grounds that it results in further job losses. This claim is dubious. The exemption of the domestic content of offshore assembly from customs duty would shift demand to imports of these products away from competing domestic production and foreign-assembled imports with no domestic content. This has both positive and negative effects. The question is whether the positive direct and indirect effects of increased offshore production offset the negative effect on onshore

---

[4] Dixit and Grossman (1982) have constructed a general and elegant model with a continuum of stages. The actual physical sequence of stages can differ from the economic ordering by factor intensities. In this case, a country may produce and export the output of some stage and then reimport more processed goods after they have been processed abroad for more processing in the home country. Furthermore, some of the stages can be carried out simultaneously. For example, automobile assembly is one stage that uses numerous components and parts that have been manufactured previously. The model approximates the production process for manufacturing in industries such as automobiles, textiles and clothing, and chemicals.

assembly production. The OAP was designed to preserve or increase the market share of US produced components and materials. There have been several attempts to establish whether the positive effect of the provision on US value added and employment through the increased foreign use of US components and materials outweighs the loss of value added in the US assembly. (See especially Finger, 1976; and Mendez, 1993.)

In addition, in many cases these activities would have ceased nationally without the establishment of offshore assembly. And there may be other positive effects on exports from onshore production. A recent survey of high value added manufacturing exporters in Australia (McKinsey and Company, 1993, p. 31) concluded:

> When an Australian firm sets up production in South East Asia, it often attracts criticism because it means losing jobs to low-cost labour in the region. However, our study shows that such criticism is not wholly justified. For many firms, offshore production is critical to establishing a long-term position as an insider in the market and therefore is critical to exports from an Australian base.

These effects could be estimated with an empirical version of the model.

One can also consider the effects of a value added tariff regime from the political economy point of view. It might be argued that the change to a value added regime would encourage onshore producers to lobby for higher tariffs to compensate for the increased market access of offshore producers and it would diminish the pressure from national firms producing offshore to lobby for tariff reductions. On the other hand, many of the onshore producers are also offshore producers. As with the employment effects, and for the same reasons, the direction of the incentives to lobby in the aggregate is not clear.

5. OTHER APPLICATIONS

The change in the base of taxation has other applications.

One such application of the principle of using value adding is designating which goods are made in any country for the purposes of domestic labelling laws and regulations. As with the application of quotas, this designation is an all-or-nothing matter and the obvious rule is to designate a product as made in the country if the percentage of value added exceeds a specified percentage, say 50 per cent. Such a rule would obviate the complaints that imported products in some countries circumvent labelling requirements by a small amount of finishing or packaging and it would allow for domestic content in the form of value added offshore and in reimports.

A second application of the tax base developed in this paper is to the problem of choosing the base of taxes or subsidies on export goods. Export taxes and subsidies, like tariffs, are applied to goods at the time they cross a national border.[5] When a tax or subsidy is based on a value, the gross value at the border is used. Again, when a subsidy is paid, this discriminates against national production which takes place offshore. It would discriminate in favour of offshore production if a good subject to an export tax were also produced offshore.

There is a converse side to adjustments of tariffs and export subsidies to allow for value added offshore. In the case of both tariffs and export subsidies, a part of the onshore production is value added by foreign investors and, less frequently, foreign labour. These foreign factors, as well as domestic factors, benefit from border assistance under the standard methods of valuation and eligibility. In the case of goods which receive export subsidies and cross national borders, it would be possible to exclude foreign content from the calculation of the subsidy but, in the case of tariffs, the form of the assistance to domestic producers does not involve a cross-border transaction. It may also be argued that foreign investors bring acccess to foreign technologies and markets. This feature demonstrates once more the inefficiency of border instruments as a means of pursuing the correction of market failures or other goals which are not themselves based on the cross-border flows of commodities.

The third application is to rules of origin. Rules of origin are required whenever the origin of an import affects its treatment for entry or duty purposes. The most common application is to entry in free trade areas, but rules of origin are required for other instances of preferential access, such as the preference schemes for developing countries and for determining MFN entry when some countries are denied MFN status. They also arise in relation to non-tariff restrictions on imports when origin results in differential treatment; for example, when there are quotas specified by country or groups of countries. This section concentrates upon the application of rules of origin in free trade areas, but the same principles can be applied in other applications of rules of origin.[6]

A rule of origin in a free trade area specifies the percentage of the value of a traded commodity which must be added within the member countries and/or its

---

[5] Julius (1990, Chapter 4) suggests a new mode of measuring the value of exports and imports which assigns transactions according to the nationality of ownership rather than the residency. For exports, this would add goods produced abroad by a domestic corporation and subtract goods produced within the territory by a foreign corporation. 'The intent is to create a measure that relates the fact that the firm can choose to supply a foreign market either by exporting to it or by investing in it and selling locally. Such ownership-based measures should be insensitive to shifts in foreign strategy by individual firms' (Julius, 1990, p. 78).

The difficulty with this measurement is that it ignores the foreign content in goods produced abroad by domestic corporations and the domestic content of goods produced at home by a foreign corporation. Similarly, the value of exports produced at home for the purposes of export subsidies should ideally exclude the foreign content, though this is frequently small.

[6] The author's attention was first drawn to the problem of the base of tariffs in this context. This paper grew out of his proposal for an area value added tariff in free trade areas as a substitute for other rules of origin (Lloyd, 1993).

OFFSHORE PRODUCTION AND BASE OF IMPORT TAXATION 733

form before the commodity can qualify for the free or preferential trade provisions of the area. The problem in designing rules of origin is due essentially to intermediate trade in inputs which means that the value added in the production of the traded goods is split between two or more producing countries. The number of free trade areas has increased markedly in recent years. With the signing of the Canada – United States Free Trade Area (CUSTA) in 1988 and the European Economic Accord between the six EFTA countries and the 12 EC countries in 1991 and NAFTA in 1993, a large majority of the member countries of the OECD are members of a free trade area and many developing countries are members of free trade areas in Latin America and the Caribbean, Africa and Asia. And rules of origin are an important and controversial part of the proposed NAFTA (see Krueger, 1992). Rules of origin have become a much more important determinant of the freedom of access to markets within these free trade areas and an important aspect of world trading conditions.

The most common rules of origin are either percentage rules or rules of transformation or changes in tariff headings. Rules of origin have become increasingly diverse and complex. Where percentage rules are applied the percentage varies. The ASEAN Free Trade Area uses 40 per cent. EFTA and the Closer Economic Relations Agreement between Australia and New Zealand use 50 per cent. CUSTA and NAFTA rely predominantly on changes in tariff headings but, for some commodity groups, CUSTA uses a 50 per cent rule and NAFTA uses a rule of 60 per cent where the transaction value method is used or 50 per cent where the net cost method is used. Palmeter (1993, p. 328) concludes:

> Different methods have been used to determine origin, but none has proved totally unsatisfactory, and none is likely to do so.

There have been a number of unsuccessful attempts under the auspices of the OECD, UNCTAD, the Customs Cooperation Council and the GATT to harmonise the rules.

The essential problem is that, with international trade in intermediate inputs, countries produce the value added components but trade the product in which the value added is embodied. The proportions of value added in a single member and in the area collectively can vary all the way from just over zero to 100 per cent.

The difficulties arise because rules of origin try to determine whether the product is *mainly* produced in the area or not. In fact, with value adding in two or more countries, origin should not be conceived as an all-or-nothing concept. The natural way of addressing this problem is to allow the duty payable to vary in proportion to the external value added. This could be done by applying the concept of a value added tariff, as in Section 2, with the difference that the 'domestic' value added is interpreted as *area* value added in place of domestic country value added. This area tariff rate is based on the external value added and exempts from duty any value added within the area. (For details, see Lloyd, 1993.)

A rule of origin based on value added in the area would have effects similar to the value added tariff. The phrase 'within the area' is ambiguous in the context of an area rule of origin if, in addition to intra-area trade in goods, there are foreign-located factors of the type analysed in the previous sections. Value added within the area should, therefore, be interpreted to mean the value added by all factors owned by the area, irrespective of whether the factor is physically located in the area or not.

An area value added tariff rule for free trade areas would have several advantages. It would treat equally all production by factors resident in the area. It would create more and divert less trade than standard rules of origin. (For further discussion of this aspect, see Lloyd, 1993.) It would be simple and not subject to manipulation for hidden protective purposes as with administrative rules. The administration is more complex than most rules of transformation and changes in tariff headings, but percentage rules are already in widespread use.[7] Thus, on national efficiency grounds, the value added tariff would be preferable to standard rules of origin.

Most generally, the analysis can be applied to any problem of government policy affecting output when part of the national production takes place offshore or is reimported. In the presence of growing international mobility of factors, the continuation of government policies which are applied at the border and, therefore, differentiate between onshore and offshore production will impose distortions on the domestic economy which are often unwitting but increasingly significant.

6. CONCLUSIONS

The present definition of the value for duty under Article VII of the GATT discriminates against that part of the national production which takes place offshore and against goods which are produced onshore and exported and then reimported. This distortion has become important with the growth of offshore production and trade in intermediate goods. There has been some relief from this problem in the form of offshore assembly provisions in the tariff of some

---

[7] Palmeter (1993, p. 332) claims that value added percentage rules have other disadvantages because origin may vary with fluctuations in exchange rates and the costs of labour in the exporting country. This is the result of the all-or-nothing nature of the standard criteria, but it is also economically wrong. Values for duty for non-preferential entry vary at all times with exchange rate fluctuations and the costs of manufacture in the countries in which they are produced and so should the values for preferential entry.

OFFSHORE PRODUCTION AND BASE OF IMPORT TAXATION 735

countries, but the coverage of these provisions is small and the general nature of the problem has not been recognised.

This paper proposes a change in the valuation of goods for the duty purposes which addresses the problem directly. A value added tariff would tax only goods produced abroad in the economically relevant sense of the value added by residents of other countries. It would exempt from import taxation the value added by factors owned by residents of the taxing country which is embodied in the goods imported into the country.

This change in the principles of import taxation could be effected by a general change in the definition of value for duty or by a concession for goods which embody national production from offshore operations or the use of domestically-produced intermediate inputs. Such a change in the tax base is feasible and would generally improve the efficiency of onshore production.

REFERENCES

Bonturi, M. and K. Fukasaku (1993a), 'Globalisation and Intra-Firm Trade: An Empirical Note', *OECD Economic Studies*, **20**, 145—159.

Bonturi, M. and K. Fukasaku (1993b), *Intra-Firm Trade* (Paris: OECD).

Dixit, A. and G.M. Grossman (1982), 'Trade and Protection with Multistage Production', *Review of Economic Studies*, **43**, 583—594.

Finger, M. (1976), 'Trade and Domestic Effects of the Offshore Assembly Provision of the US Tariff', *American Economic Review*, **66**, 598—611.

GATT (1986), *The Text of the General Agreement on Tariffs and Trade* (Geneva: GATT).

Julius, D. (1990), *Global Companies and Public Policy: The Growing Challenge of Foreign Direct Investment* (London: The Royal Institute of International Affairs).

Krueger, A.O. (1992), 'Free Trade Agreements as Protectionist Devices: Rules of Origin' (National Bureau of Economic Research Working Paper No. 4352).

Levinsohn, J. and J. Slemrod (1993), 'Taxes, Tariffs and the Global Corporation', *Journal of Public Economics*, **51**, 97—116.

Lloyd, P.J. (1993), 'A Tariff Substitute for Rules of Origin in Free Trade Areas', *The World Economy*, **16**, 6, 699—712.

McKinsey and Company (1993), *Emerging Exporters: Australia's High Value-Added Manufacturing Exporters* (Melbourne: Australian Manufacturing Council).

Mendez, J.A. (1993), 'The Welfare Effects of Repealing the US Offshore Assembly Provision', *Journal of International Economics*, 1—22.

Palmeter, D. (1993), 'Rules of Origin in Customs Unions and Free Trade Areas', in K. Anderson and R. Blackhurst (eds.), *Regional Integration and the Global Trading System* (Hemel Hempstead: Harvester Wheatsheaf).

Textile, Clothing and Footwear Development Authority (Australia) (1993), 'Guidelines and Application Form: Overseas Assembly Provisions Scheme (OAP)' (Melbourne: Textile, Clothing and Footwear Development Authority).

US International Trade Commission (1991), *Production Sharing: US Imports Under Harmonized Tariff Schedule Subheadings 9802.00.60 and 9802.00.80, 1986—89* (Washington, DC: USITC Publication 2349).

World Bank (1992), *Export Processing Zones* (Washington, DC: World Bank Policy and Research Series No. 20, March).

[22]

A Tariff Substitute for Rules of Origin
in Free Trade Areas

P. J. Lloyd

1. INTRODUCTION

█ith the increase in the number of free trade areas in recent years, rules of origin have become a much more important aspect of world trading conditions. They have been the subect of prolonged negotiations between the members of prospective free trade areas and a growing source of friction with outside countries which believe that the rules of origin discriminate against them. In the case of the North American Free Trade Area (NAFTA), for example, there were difficult negotiations between the three prospective members and allegations by Japanese manufacturers of automobiles and other outside producers that some of the rules of origin in NAFTA have been framed deliberately to protect the area producers.

Rules of origin in free trade areas have become increasingly diverse and complex. There has been surprisingly little discussion of them in the literature on international trade. Scant attention has been paid to the problem in texts on customs union theory or economic integration; see, Balassa (1961, pp. 71–72) and Robson (1987, Chapter 2) for some discussion. The seminal paper on the analysis of trade deflection and rules of origin designed to prevent trade deflection is that of Shibata (1967). Shibata (1967) and more recently Krueger (1992) have concluded that rules of origin are a protective device. There is no agreement among international trade economists about the desirable form of rules of origin.

The problem in designing rules of origin is due essentially to intermediate trade in inputs which means that the value added in the production of the traded goods is split between two or more producing countries. It is the conjunction of the rapid growth of world trade in intermediates, especially of manufactures, and the growth of free trade areas which has made the problems of rules of origin much more important in world trade.

P. J. LLOYD is from the University of Melbourne, Australia. He is grateful to Tony Lynch, Richard Snape and an anonymous referee for helpful suggestions on an earlier version of this paper.

Section 2 reviews the nature of the problem of trade deflection and Section 3 dicusses the treatment of the rules of origin in practice in some free trade areas, particularly the European Free Trade Area (EFTA), the North American Free Trade Agreement (NAFTA) and the Closer Economic Relations (CER) Agreement between Australia and New Zealand. The problem is re-examined in Section 4 with the aid of some recent developments in international trade theory. A proposal for a new type of value added tariff which could substitute for all rules of origin is put forward in Section 5. The advantages of the proposed tariff are summarised in Section 6.

2. THE PROBLEM OF TRADE DEFLECTION

In a free trade area, unlike a customs union, the individual member countries agree to free trade between themselves but retain their individual regimes of tariffs and other restrictions on imports from third countries. This means that a commodity exported by third countries may face lower trade barriers into one member country than into another. If no restriction were placed on intra-trade, imports from third countries could enter the markets of both countries by entering the member country with the lowest rate of protection and then being transported to the other member country or countries with no further duty or restriction. Such redirection of trade for the purpose of exploiting the difference in trade restrictions between members is known as trade deflection.[1] Trade deflection has long been recognised as a potential danger in a free trade area; see for example, Meade (1955, p. 529, n. 1).

Since 1948 GATT has defined a free trade area as 'a group of two or more customs territories in which the duties and other restrictive regulations of commerce (except where necessary, those permitted under Articles XI, XII, XIII, XIV, XV and XX) are eliminated on substantially all the trade between the constituent territories in products originating in such territories'. (GATT, 1986, Article XXIV). All free trade areas have rules of origin which are designed to limit the benefits of the free intra-area trade provisions to products produced 'originating in such territories', that is, to products manufactured wholly or principally within the area. Rule of origin specifies the percentage of the value of a traded commodity which must be added within the member countries and/or its form before the commodity can qualify for the free trade provisions of the area. These rules of origin are an integral part of the definition of a free trade area.

If the value in a final product is added solely in the third country, there is no

---

[1] Similar problems arise when there are differences between the member countries of a regional arrangement with respect to indirect taxes/subsidies other than border tariffs/export subsidies. Such differences change and distort trade within the area. (See Georgakopoulos (1992) and references therein). This effect of indirect taxes/subsidies is also called trade deflection.

conceptual difficulty in designing the rule of origin. Goods entering a free trade area pay the duty of the country in which they are consumed or used, whether they enter this country directly or through another member of the area.

If, however, the value is added partly in a third external country and partly in one or more member countries, there is ambiguity as to what is a good produced in a free trade area. The essential issue is what part of the value added should be produced in the area to allow the commodity to be traded freely within the area.

3. THE TREATMENT OF TRADE DEFLECTION IN EXISTING FTAs

The actual provisions vary considerably among contemporary free trade areas. The main type of rule is the percentage rule. For example, Article 4 of the Stockholm convention which established the European Free Trade Area in 1960 deals with the 'Area Tariff Treatment'. The basic rule prescribes that the value of materials imported from outside the EFTA area must not exceed 50 per cent of the export price of the goods enjoying EFTA's preferential access. In the Closer Economic Relations Agreement which established a free trade area between Australia and New Zealand in 1983, Article 3 deals with the 'Rules of Origin'. The basic provision of this article states that not less than one half of the ex-factory costs of production be materials or labour or factory overheads originating in the area. There is a provision for this proportion to be varied if it is considered to be inappropriate by one of the members. These percentage rules prescribe, roughly speaking, that a certain percentage of the value added be added within the area before goods traded between members qualify for area treatment.

There are other rules which may be used to determine area treatment. In EFTA, there are provisions which are more strict for some commodities because they have a requirement that an appropriate process of production should have been carried out in the EFTA area. This is an example of a rule of transformation. On the other hand, there is another provision in EFTA which is less strict because certain raw materials and intermediate inputs on a basic materials list are deemed to have been produced in the area, irrespective of their origin.

Anti-trade deflection measures other than rules of origin may also be used. For example, both the EFTA and the CER Agreement contain provisions relating to what is called the 'intermediate goods problem'. This arises when the commodity that changes the pattern of trade and production is an intermediate input embodied in another produced product which is traded between members of a free trade area rather than a final product which is itself traded between the members. Under the free trade provisions and the rules of origin of the area, such a commodity could be traded freely to another member country but, nevertheless, enjoys a policy-induced advantage over the production of the commodity in the second country because it used some intermediate inputs which enter the first member country at lower rate of duty than they would enter the second member country. Hence, a further provision is introduced to cover such cases. These intermediate goods provisions also apply if the cost advantage is due to a subsidy available to producers in one member country but not the other member country. Like the trade deflection of commodities from outside the area, the intermediate goods problem is due to the differences in the tariff rates between the members of the area.

Such distortions may be eliminated in several ways: adoption of common tariff/subsidy rates for the commodities concerned, the imposition of countervailing duties, or variation of the rules of origin. Intermediate input rules are another reflection of the growing importance of trade in intermediate inputs and the importance of this trade as a determinant of costs of production.

NAFTA has increased the importance and complexity of the rules of origin to a much greater level than in any previous free trade area. The NAFTA rules of content were based on those in the Canada-United States Free Trade Agreement (CUSTA) of 1988. Chapter 4 of the draft NAFTA Agreement contains 193 pages dealing with the rules of origin and interpretation of these rules as they apply to particular products. A variety of rules is employed, as in CUSTA. The main rule is one relating to sufficient transformation. This requires that the product pass through a specified classification change in the Harmonised Tariff Schedule. It is hard to interpret this provision but it will imply that the proportion of value added in the area needed to qualify for reclassification will vary greatly among the products. Some of the transformations specify that particular inputs or proportions of inputs must be from area sources. For some groups of commodities, the rules state that, in addition to the tariff classification requirement, the commodities must include a specified percentage of North American content. Regional value content may be calculated using the 'transaction value' or the 'net cost' method. For automobiles and automobile parts, the percentage is, at the end of the transition period, 62.5 per cent of the net cost. The rules are product-group-specific and complex, though a recent study by Johnson (1992) argues they are simpler than the existing rules in CUSTA.

Overall, the NAFTA rules of origin appear to restrict intra-area trade compared to a simple 50 per cent rule for many commodity groups. Japanese producers are fearful that the rules have been designed to protect US producers of manufactures such as automobiles. A recent study of Japanese affiliates in the US found that 54 per cent felt the percentage rules of the rules of origin would have a major impact on their operations (Fukasaku, Lee and Yamawaki, 1992).

4. A RE-EXAMINATION OF THE PROBLEM

There has been little analysis of rules of origin in the theory of international trade. Consider a single percentage rule applied to all intra-area trade. The higher the percentage the more trade deflection that is prevented but the less intra-area trade and trade creation. Any choice of percentage is clearly arbitrary. In considering this question, Balassa (1961, pp. 71–72) concluded: 'The percentage rule adopted should be the one that maximises the gains from union; this would require the equalization of the marginal advantages of trade creation and the marginal disadvantages of trade and production deflection'. There is no virtue in 50 per cent except as a rough rule when we are in ignorance of the magnitude of the costs and benefits of the changes in trade.

The arbitary nature of a percentage chosen for a rule of origin itself gives rise to incentives to distort the pattern of production. A percentage rule of origin may penalise an increase in the efficiency of production within a free trade area where an increase in intra-area factor productivity which lowered the area content would cause a commodity to cease to be eligible for the free trade provisions. It may also mean that goods which are identical but produced by different firms using different technologies could receive different treatment upon entry to a member country. Rules of origin might, therefore, discourage firms from increasing factor productivity or buying from the cheapest source within an area when they are on the margin of the rule.

In practice the precise form of the rule of origin will also be important. There are also considerable options in framing rules. With a percentage rule, the choice of cost or price as the base of the content and the definition of the components which qualify for area content can make a great deal of difference. These choices and the administration of these rules and the uncertainty arising from definitional ambiguities may be quite considerable. The danger is that the rules of origin may be selected to give protection to area producers over non-area producers. The administrative difficulties will not be considered.

Shibata (1967) analysed the effects of rules of origin as a means of overcoming trade deflection. Shibata's analysis, like almost all of the formal analysis of regional trading arrangements, relates to wholly integrated processes. In this case a rule of origin immediately excludes from free trade within the area any commodity which is imported from outside the area and has 100 per cent value added outside the area. He showed first that trade deflection is not harmful to the area. Indeed, it is generally beneficial in terms of efficient production and consumption as it circumvents high trade barriers. The difficulty is that it is seen as unfair and, if not restricted, as frustrating the ability of the countries to maintain independent national trade restrictions *vis-à-vis* non-members. The absence of any rules of origin would mean that the area became in effect a customs union with the lowest nominal rate of protection for each commodity among the members becoming the effective common external tariff for the whole area.

Moreover, Shibata showed that the use of rules of origin to discourage trade deflection gives rise to Vinerian trade diversion. 'The discouragement of trade deflection by the rules of origin gives rise to trade diversion which benefits protectionist interests,' (Shibata, 1967, p. 174). It is the suppliers in the low-tariff member country who gain from the higher price in the other member country to which trade would otherwise be deflected, compared to the free trade area with no anti-deflection provision. (Compared to the pre-free trade area situation, the producers in the low-tariff country also gain whereas the producers in the high-tariff country do not gain and may lose if the post-free trade area price falls.) The extent of trade diversion with rules of origin depends on the demand and supply functions in the two countries but there must be trade diversion whenever trade deflection is prevented by the rule of origin.

Shibata's analysis did not extend to the intermediate inputs case of trade deflection. Recently, Krueger (1992) has considered trade deflection with international trade in intermediate inputs. When international trade in intermediate inputs is present, Krueger concluded

> Rules of origin agreed upon in forming an FTA in fact extend the protection accorded by each country to producers in other FTA member countries. As such, rules of origin can constitute a source of bias toward economic inefficiency in FTAs in a way they cannot do with customs union (Krueger, 1992, p. 3).

She employs a three-stage production process such as is used with the maufacture of the final product clothing going through the two earlier stages of cotton and then cotton textile production. In the case of NAFTA, clothing producers in Mexico exporting to the US could be encouraged by a rule of origin to source their cloth imports from new or expanded production in Mexico or the US whereas in the pre-free trade area situation Mexico imported the cloth from the least-cost source outside the area. This is a form of trade diversion where the trade diverted is trade in intermediate inputs. The additional production of cloth will be in the US in this example if the effective rate of protection in the US for the cloth is greater than in Mexico and if the rule of origin would not be satisified without such purchases from the US. The percentage of the cloth input which is sourced from the US is endogenous in this model. It is an increasing function of the percentage of value added specified by the percentage rule.

Krueger-type intermediate inputs trade diversion is distinct from the diversion of final goods trade noted by Shibata. Both analyses illustrate protective effects of rules of origin.

Other cases can be constructed. For example, one can consider a Shibata-type diversion of final goods trade with the complication that part of the costs of production are an intermediate input which can be produced in and purchased from outside the area. In this case a free trade area with a rule of origin will divert imports into the high-tariff member from outside the area to the low-tariff member country producing the final good, provided the rule is sufficiently strict to exclude imports of the final good from outside the area.

One needs also to allow for the fact that the intermediate inputs used in some production process may themselves have been produced by a process which used intermediate inputs. The value of this latter intermediate input may itself be partly value added in the area and partly value added in some other country. One should also note that part of the value added in a foreign country may be a payment to capital owners in the home country and, conversely, part of the value added in a country may be payment to foreign owners. Thus the intermediate inputs sourced from within a country may have an import content, and, conversely, the intermediate inputs which are imported may have some area content in the form of lower level intermediate inputs which were exported by an area member country to the foreign manufacturer of the imported intermediate input or an income payment to a primary factor.

To cover these possibilities one needs a more general model of production with itermediate inputs. The most general and elegant model of production processes which involve stages of production is the model of Dixit and Grossman (1982). In their model, there is an industry which produces a final product by a succession of stages, each adding value to an intermediate product to yield goods-in-process ready for the next stage.Every stage may be produced in any country and uses capital and labour inputs as well as a fixed intermediate input. The stages are assumed to have differences in the capital and labour factor intensities which are invariant with respect to the factor prices and they can, therefore, be ordered by their capital intensities. There are assumed to be an infinity of stages which can be ordered on a continuum. Let z denote a stage on the continuum. For convenience, the continuum may be represented as the closed interval $[0,1]$ of the real line. Let the commodities be ordered by decreasing capital intensity so that the initial stage, 0, is the most capital-intensive and the final stage, 1, is the least capital-intensive. (This ordering is arbitrary.) If desired, it can be reversed. This assumption of an infinity of stages is in fact a harmless fiction which greatly simplifies the analysis by allowing the application of calculus to the change in the number of stages of production carried out in one country.

The Dixit-Grossman model is a considerable generalisation of the models usually used to analyse effective proctection in which there are just two stages. It is even more general than it appears. The actual physical sequence of stages can differ from the economic ordering by factor intensities. In this case, a country may produce and export the output of some stage and then reimport more processed goods after they have been processed abroad, for more processing in the home country.[2] Furthermore, some of the stages can be carried out simultaneously. For example, automobile assembly is one stage that uses numerous components and parts that have been manufactured previously. When transport costs are ignored, these components can be ordered on the continuum by their factor intensities. The model

---

[2] This occurs, for example, in Australia with some of the output of wool fibres.

P.J. LLOYD

approximates the production process for manufacturing in industries such as automobiles, textiles and clothing and chemicals.

In the present context it is necessary to extend the Dixit-Grossman model to three countries as this is the minimum needed to analyse the effects of a free trade area. Suppose there is free trade and non-factor price equalisation in the world economy. Suppose that countries 1, 2 and 3 can be ranked in terms of relative capital abundance in the relevant factor price sense; for example, the countries may be in decreasing order of capital abundance. In this case, under free trade, if all three countries produce some of the stages of the continuum industry, there will be two borderline commodities on the continuum which partition the continuum so that all stages immediately below the borderline commodity are produced in one country and all stages immediately above it are produced in the rest of the world, see Figure 1. Let z_{12} be the borderline commodity between production in countries 1 and 2, the two relatively more capital-abundant countries, and z_{23} be the borderline between countries 2 and 3, the two more labour-intensive countries. Then the commodities in the ranges $[0, (z_{12}), (z_{12}, z_{23})$ and $(z_{23}), 1]$ are produced by countries 1, 2 and 3 respectively. The borderline commodities may be produced in one or both countries.

FIGURE 1

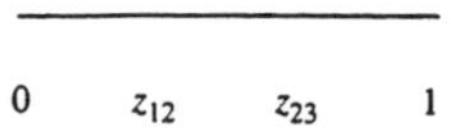

$$0 \qquad z_{12} \qquad z_{23} \qquad 1$$

The ordering of these countries in terms of their location on the continuum corresponds to their ordering by capital abundance. Thus the set of stages produced by each of the three countries are neatly located in adjoining and non-intersecting segments of the line. Each country specialises in stages of production rather than in final commodities as in the usual trade models. No commodity (= stage) is produced by two countries, apart possibly from the borderline commodities. The use of the continuum in this model allows us to analyse the margin in the range of goods produced and to identify these ranges in terms of factor intensities.

Now suppose one of the three countries protects its own producers of stages in the continuum industry by means of a uniform tariff. At the margin between country i and country j, there are now two borderline commodities, z_{ij} and $\bar{z}_{ij}$, the lower and upper borderline commodities which determine the margins of production in country i and country j.[3] The volume of international trade between these two countries contracts as some stages are no longer traded internationally. The commodities in the range $(\bar{z}_{ij} - z_{ij})$ will be produced by both countries and

---

[3] The range of goods produced also increases in the foreign country.

not traded. Total world consumption of the final output of the industry contracts. A uniform tariff reduces the volume of trade in the continuum products at two margins; it reduces the range of commodities traded and it reduces the volume of trade in products that remain traded.

Suppose all three countries protect their industries by means of a uniform tariff on all imports. There are now four borderline commodities, as in Figure 2. Now the commodities in the ranges $[0, (\bar{z}_{12},), (\zeta_{12}, \bar{z}_{23})$ and $(\zeta_{23}), 1]$ are produced by countries 1, 2 and 3 respectively. There is an overlap in the range of commodities produced by countries 1 and 2 and by countries 2 and 3.

FIGURE 2

$$0 \qquad \underline{z}_{12} \qquad z_{12} \qquad \bar{z}_{12} \qquad \underline{z}_{23} \qquad z_{23} \qquad \bar{z}_{23} \qquad 1$$

We can now consider the formation of a free trade area. The rule of origin will be assumed to take the form of a percentage rule. The operation of a rule of origin between two member countries of a free trade area is similar to the effect of a unilateral protective policy in the form of a content plan type of a tariff barrier for imports into one country from the rest of the world in the two-country version of the model. A content plan type of tariff on imports gives protection to the domestic producers of intermediate inputs, (see Grossman, 1981). Similarly, a content rule within a free trade area gives protection to the producers of intermediate inputs within the area. These may in general be the producers of the intermediate inputs in the country exporting to another member of the area or the producers of the intermediate inputs in the importing country itself (or any other member of the area if there are more than two members of the area).

Suppose, first, that countries 1 and 2 are the members of the area and country 3 the outside country. If the ranges of the commodities produced before the formation of the free trade area are as in Figure 2 and if the ordering by factor intensities corresponds to the ordering by the physical sequences of stages, neither country 1 nor country 2 imports any intermediate inputs from country 3 and both produce and export only intermediate inputs. In this case, for this industry, there will be only intermediate inputs trade creation from the formation of the area as the free trade within the area eliminates the overlap in the range of goods produced by countries 1 and 2.

A Krueger-type case can be depicted simply by retaining the ordering of commodities on the continuum and the ordering of countries by relative capital abundance but supposing that it is countries 2 and 3 which form a free trade area. There will again be trade creation as the area eliminates the overlap in goods produced by these two countries. There will be Krueger-type trade diversion with a rule of origin as country 2 increases its range of goods at the lower end which were previously imported from country 1 in order to meet the content requirements of the rule of origin. This is not exactly the Krueger case as the commodity imported into a member of the area from another member is a downstream intermediate input rather than a final commodity. Since there is a clear ordering of costs for all commodities (apart from the unimportant borderline commodities) in this model, the other member country will not increase production of these inputs.

Compared to the Krueger analysis, the use of a continuum of stages allows the formation of a free trade area and the associated rule of origin to increase the range of stages produced in the area as well as the outputs of each stage. It is also possible that such a rule of origin may be anti-protective in terms of the effect on total industry, value added or employment, because of the gross output effect of the rule, as in the two-country version of the model, because the implicit protection increases the relative price of the output of the industry.

Other cases can be constructed. For example, the rules of origin which simply classify some raw materials or components or other intermediate inputs as area production irrespective of the distribution of value added are clearly protective. In this case they protect the activities which use these inputs and divert trade from comptetitive imports of these products. More complex cases are possible when a good is produced in three or more stages.

5. A PROPOSAL

The essential problem is that, with international trade in intermediate inputs and the splitting of the value added in traded goods between two or more independent countries, countries produce the value added components but trade the product in which the value added is embodied. The proportions of value added in a single member and in the area collectively can vary all the way from just over zero to 100 per cent. Rules of origin in such cases try to determine whether the product is *mainly* produced in the area or not. In principle, the free trade provisions of a regional agreement should be applied to the value added component because this is the true production of the country.

This principle could be achieved by introducing a new kind of tariff whose base for the purpose of calculating the value of the duty paid is the value added in the traded commodity. This may be called a *value added tariff*. For a traded commodity, commodity i, let v_{ia} and v_{ie} denote the proportions of the value added which are added in the area and externally respectively. Suppose that all tariff rates are *ad valorem*. Let t_i be the schedule tariff rate, which is now the rate levied on value added outside the area, and t_{ia} be the tariff rate on the value which is added inside the area. Then the tariff rate which is actually levied on imports of the commodity by a member country will be

$$\bar{t}_i = v_{ie}\, t_i + v_{ia}\, t_{ia} \qquad\qquad v_{ie} + v_{ia} = 1,\ t_{ia} \le t_i.$$

Thus the actual tariff rate is the average of the tariff rates on the internal and external value added components. Now, in a free trade area after the transitional period, the intra-area rate will typically be zero. In this case the actual tariff rate is $\bar{t}_i = v_{ie} \, t_i$.

This tariff rate is based on the external value added and exempts from duty any value added within the area. Given the schedule tariff rate, t_i, the actual tariff rate levied will increase with the proportion of the value which has been added outside the area. Such a tariff would automatically overcome the objection of producers within an area to 'screwdriver' type operations which add little value in an activity within the area and otherwise qualify for free trade within the area under some rules of origin.

There is a choice as to the rate of tariff which is levied on a commodity, t_i, under this proposal. In many instances the tariff rates imposed on the goods at different stages will differ. Typically, the tariff rates increase with the degree of processing, that is, with the stage defined in terms of the sequence of manufacturing. The rate of value added tariff could be that of the substantive tariff on the good entering the importing country as classified by a tariff classification schedule or it could be an average of the rates on all of the stages through which the good actually imported has passed and which determine the area value added percentage. There is no reason to prefer one method or the other when the tariff rates on the stages are not uniform. It will be administratively simpler to use the substantive rate which applies to the imported good as defined in the tariff classification.

Compared to the value-added tariff, any rule of origin which classifies a commodity as wholly produced within the area or outside the area will wrongly exclude some output (= value added) of one member from being freely traded with other members. This will occur when the area content is less than that specified by the rule. It will also wrongly admit with no tariff into a member country commodities which satisfy the arbitrary rule of origin but contain significant components and other value added produced in third countries. In many cases, these third country components or intermediate inputs embodied in the traded commodities would not qualify for free entry into the member country concerned if they were traded as separate upstream components or intermediate inputs.

The effect of substituting a set of value added tariffs for a percentage rule of origin would depend on the distribution of the percentages of domestic content in those goods subject to the percentage rule of origin. It could conceivably reduce the volume of trade if a large volume of intra-area trade was exempt from all duty under the present rules of origin because it satisfied the rules of origin but became subject to duty under the value added tariff. It should be noted, however, that such goods would pay duty only in proportion to the non-area content and the goods which are subject to a value added tariff would similarly pay less than the full duty if there is any area content.

The substitution of a value added tariff rule would reduce the dispersion in the actual tariff rates paid on all imports entering a country, given the schedule of substantive tariff rates for the country. For each commodity with a single schedule tariff rate (t_i), the actual rates levied $(\bar{t}_i)$ on imports of the commodity from all sources would vary between a minimum of 0 and a maximum of t_i, depending on the distribution of the external components of value added. In particular, there would be fewer imports at the maximum rate compared to the standard rules of origin which apply this (maximum) rate to all imports which do not satisfy the rule. In those cases where the rule of origin is strict, such as a percentage rule of, say, 62.5 per cent or a strict transformation rule, the value added tariff would lower the average tariff rate without admitting free of duty any imports with a non-area content. For these goods, it will create more and divert less trade than standard rules of origin.

A value added tariff would, moreover, have the right incentive effects. It would encourage area producers to source imports from the lowest-cost source inside or outside the area and it would not discourage them from improving factor productivity. It might in some cases encourage 'screwdriver'-type operations which would have been subject to the full duty under the standard rules of origin but such activities would pay duty in proportion to the non-area content and they would have a continuous incentive to shift production to the duty-free area locations under a value added tariff. Thus, on national efficiency grounds, the value added tariff would generally be preferable to standard rules of origin.

There are some further aspects of the value added tariff which need to be considered. Some imports are subject to non-tariff border restrictions in addition to the tariffs. There is no reason why non-tariff restrictions such as quotas cannot continue to apply to the goods entering the importing country. This is consistent with levying the tariff at the rate laid down for the good imported, even though the base of the duty is adjusted for the area content.

If, for imports entering from another area country, a duty is proportional to the value outside the area, it raises the question of whether imports entering from outside the area should not also be taxed on the same basis. Then value added by the factors owned by the country would be treated equally, irrespective of whether the production process was located in a member of a free trade area or in a third country. This implies that the base of all tariff rates be converted to value added. Such a change in tariffs is radical and is not necessary as the bias against factors employed outside the area occurs under existing rules of origin, although such a tariff regime would have efficiency advantages over the normal tariffs levied on the gross value of imports at the point of entry.[4]

Such a tariff for intra-area imports is practicable. The value added outside the

---

[4] It would lower the average nominal tariff rates and reduce the dispersion among these rates as well as removing the difference in protection for domestically-owned factors which are located in the taxing country or abroad.

area is the value of the commodity per unit at importation less the area content. The value added within the area should in principle include area content in the form of area-produced inputs used in the production of inputs and it should exclude non-area content at each stage.

The precise calculation of the area content would be difficult where there is a domestic input at an earlier stage and generally impracticable in cases where the earlier stages are not carried out by the same corporation. Domestic inputs used at an earlier stage are of a second order or importance, frequently zero. As an approximation to the area content (or strictly a lower bound to the area content and therefore an upper bound to the non-area content which is the base of the tax), the value added could be calculated simply as the value of the import less the direct domestic input, that is, the domestic content in the last stage of manufacture. This would exclude the domestic content of inputs used in earlier stages. Alternatively and more simply, the duty could be levied at the substantive rate and the importer could seek a reduction of duty, if he wished, by demonstrating the amount of the direct area content in the goods subject to the duty payment. This would eliminate the need for statements about the area content and origin of the goods except where the importer wished to establish an area content. The greater the area content which is established by the importer the lower its tax liability. There are few taxes where greater administrative cost borne by the taxpayer results directly in a lower tax burden. These administrative costs borne by producers are largely fixed costs and would diminish for each unit with large or repeated shipments.

The value added tariff would be no more complex than a value added tax unless the importer seeks to trace the area content of inputs used in the production of inputs and, for those countries which operate a value added tax, it would be easily integrated into the administration of this tax.[5] Where a percentage rule applies, the percentage of value added has already to be calculated. The present rules of transformation now used to determine whether a good originates within the area are themselves complex.

6. CONCLUSIONS

Trade deflection does not distort trade but it seen as unfair since, without a rule of origin, imports from outside the area could enter a member of the area with higher import barriers by first entering a member with lower barriers. Rules of origin to counter trade deflection are essentially protective and trade-diverting. There is no percentage rule or rule of transformation which can distinguish between

---

[5] This holds provided the area content at an earlier stage is not claimed. To establish the area content at earlier stages would require that suppliers at each stage declare their own input costs and sources whereas a value added tax requires only that each taxpayer calculate its own value added.

fair and unfair trade because the binary division between goods which 'originate' in the area and those which do not is arbitrary. With international trade in intermediate inputs, production in the area should be defined as value added and there is a range of value added content from 0 to 100 per cent.

The objective of not admitting goods free of duty which are not produced in the area can only be achieved by measuring directly the percentage of the value added which is produced outside the area and using this percentage as the base of the tariff imposed on non-area production. This paper proposes a new type of tariff which is simple and yet achieves the underlying objective. Such a tariff is practicable, even in the presence of chains of production and non-tariff border barriers to trade, and could substitute for all rules of origin.

REFERENCES

Balassa, B. (1961), *The Theory of Economic Integration* (Richard D. Irwin, Homewood, Illinois).

Dixit, A. and G.M. Grossman (1982), Trade and Protection with Multistage Production', *Review of Economic Studies*, **43**, 583–94.

Fukasaku, K., C. Lee and H. Yamasaki (1992), 'EC 1992 and Japanese Direct Investment', *OECD Development Centre Technical Papers* (OECD Development Centre, Paris).

GATT (1986), *The Text of the General Agreement on Tariffs and Trade* (GATT, Geneva).

Georgakopoulos, T. (1992), 'Trade Deflection, Trade Distortions, and Pareto Inefficiencies under the Restricted Origin Principle', *Journal of Public Economics*, **47**, 381–390.

Grossman, G.M. (1981), 'The Theory of Domestic Content Protection and Content Preference', *Quarterly Journal of Economics*, **96**, 583–603.

Johnson, J.R. (1992), *What is a North American Good? The NAFTA Rules of Origin* (C. D. Howe Institute, Toronto).

Krueger, A.O. (1992), 'Free Trade Agreements as Protectionist Devices: Rules of Origin' Paper prepared for the Conference on the Occasion of John Chipman's 65th Birthday, University of Minnesota, September 25–26, 1992

Robson, P. (1987), *The Economics of International Integration*, Third Edition (Allen and Unwin, Boston).

Shibata, H. (1967), 'The Theory of Economic Unions: A Comparative Analysis of Customs Unions, Free Trade Areas, and Tax Unions' in C.S. Shoup (ed.), *Fiscal Harmonization in Common Markets*, (Columbia University Press, New York).

491–99
(85)

[23]

Terms of Trade Indices in the Presence of Re-Export Trade*

P. J. LLOYD   and   R. J. SANDILANDS
University of Melbourne,   *University of Strathclyde,*
Parkville, Victoria 3052   *Glasgow G4 OLN*

This paper shows how the index of the commodity terms of trade as ordinarily constructed should be adjusted to take account of re-exports in the broad sense of the use of intermediate inputs in export activities which had been imported. The neglect of this adjustment produces indices which generally understate the movement of the terms of trade. An empirical study of Singapore suggests that the bias may be substantial.

Most countries define indices of the prices and quantities of traded commodities over the set of traded commodities excluding all 're-export' commodities (that is, commodities which are re-exported in substantially the same form after grading, storing, re-packing or minor processing). Consequently their indices of the terms of trade also exclude the prices of entrepot commodities. This procedure is adequate when trade in re-export commodities is small relative to other trade.

When entrepot trade is relatively large, however, this procedure is clearly inadequate as it ignores completely the earning of income from re-exports as a method of payment for imported commodities. Countries in which entrepot trade is significant usually define the price and quantity indices over the set of all traded commodities including re-exports. While this definition appears to parallel for an entrepot economy the usual definition for economies with zero or little entrepot trade, it raises some serious index problems. Ng (1969) constructed an example in which the usual definition of the commodity terms of trade understates the change in the ability of the economy to purchase imports from entrepot income. His

objection is correct. Morgan and Chua (1970) also note the index number problem.

However, the problem is much wider than Ng, and Morgan and Chua, supposed in two respects. First, the same problem arises when an economy imports intermediate inputs for more substantial processing and then exports the whole or a part of these imported inputs as the import content of its 'domestic exports'. The problem applies to all trading economies to a greater or lesser extent and entrepot trade is only the extreme manifestation of the problem. This note seeks to generalize the index of the terms of trade suggested by Ng to a much wider class of economies. Second, there is a parallel problem for the specification of the indices of the volume of exports and imports.

Section I provides the theoretical derivation of the adjusted indices of prices, quantities and the terms of trade. Section II discusses the direction of bias in the usual unadjusted forms of the indices. In Section III Singapore data are used to examine the magnitude of these biases for one economy with substantial re-export trade.

I Theoretical Derivation

These general problems can be approached by considering the class of trading economies in which all production activities are assumed to have a two-

* We wish to acknowledge the helpful suggestions of two referees.

stage vertical input-output structure. That is, the first or upstream stage produces pure intermediate goods using solely primary inputs while the second or downstream stage produces goods using intermediate inputs and primary inputs.[1] The intermediate inputs may be produced domestically or imported. One intermediate input may be used in the production of more than one final good and one activity producing a final good may use more than one intermediate input. This class is called the class of re-export economies. The term re-export is interpreted in a broader sense than the usual definition used in international trade statistics. Here it is taken to include both imports which are re-exported directly and the import content of 'domestic exports'.

The assumption of pure intermediate goods produced by primary factors alone implies that all intermediate inputs are direct inputs. This assumption appears restrictive. However, if a good is produced by a series of stages these may be integrated vertically into one stage.[1] (This two-stage structure of production processes corresponds to that used in the theory of effective protection (see, for example, Jones, 1975).) For any final good the stages of production may be separated geographically. Thus the model encompasses a variety of forms of international trade including entrepot trade, free trade zones, and offshore production as well as the use of imported intermediate inputs in normal onshore activities.

What is the correct set of price and quantity indices for traded commodities in this class of economies? This can be approached by considering the price indices first. The commodity terms of trade is the ratio of an index of the price of exports to an index of the price of imports. However, there are two difficulties with the choice of import and export price indices. First, there is no agreement on the correct form of the index functions. In this respect the foundation of the indices of international prices is much less developed than in utility theory where the 'true' price index measures exactly

the cost of maintaining a chosen level of utility.[2] Second, international economists have treated the definition of the commodity terms of trade as if there is no re-export trade.

One reason has been suggested for preferring the Laspeyres form of the function for the indices of the prices of exports and imports and of the commodity terms of trade. It has been proven that a small non-re-export country gains when the Laspeyres index of the commodity terms of trade improves and trade is balanced (see Ohyama, 1972).[3] The Laspeyres form of this index is

$$T_L = \frac{\sum\limits_e p_e^t q_e^b / \sum\limits_e p_e^b q_e^b}{\sum\limits_i p_i^t q_i^t / \sum\limits_i p_i^b q_i^b} \qquad e \in E, \quad i \in I \quad (1)$$

p and q denote the border prices and the quantities of the traded commodities. The subscripts e and i denote an export and import commodity respectively. The superscripts t and b denote the current and base period values respectively. E and I are the sets of all export and import commodities respectively. The subscript of the index of the terms of trade, T, indicates the form of the index function (Laspeyres or Paasche). There is also agreement that any satisfactory price index must have the property of homogeneity of degree one in prices and the property of consistency. Consistency is the property that the product of the price and quantity indices should equal the value of the transactions.

In the presence of re-export trade it is necessary to adjust the price and quantity indices. To obtain the desired indices of export prices and quantities one uses the net price or national value added per unit of output

$$p_e^* = p_e - \sum\limits_i a_{ie} p_i. \qquad (2)$$

---

[1] The upstream and downstream stages may be interpreted as two continua of stages in the elegant continuum model of multi-stage production recently constructed by Dixit and Grossman (1982). The proposition below can be extended to cover economies in which the production of exported commodities uses indirectly importable intermediate inputs. This is done by using the direct plus indirect input-output coefficients for each industry.

[2] Recently Lloyd and Schweinberger (1984) have developed true price indices for traded commodities using the concept of a trade expenditure function. This function is analogous for the trade sector of an economy to the expenditure function for the household or the household sector. The true index adjusts, as it were, for the second complications of substitution in production and consumption which is ignored in fixed-weight indices.

[3] This proposition can be reinterpreted as the application to traded commodities of the familiar proposition that the Laspeyres index is an upper bound of the true price index of a consuming household. However, it can also be shown that the Paasche index is a lower bound of the true trade price index when the terms of trade of the trading economy move adversely. These propositions are developed in Lloyd and Schweinberger (1984).

An asterisk is used throughout to denote a variable which has netted out the value or quantity of re-exports. (a_{ie}) is the set of physical input-output coefficients for imported intermediate inputs used in the production of the eth activity and p_e is the market or gross price. If e is an intermediate export $p_e^* = p_e$. If e is a final commodity and has used any imported intermediate inputs $p_e^* < p_e$. The aggregate value of net exports is then defined as

$$x^* = \sum_e p_e q_e - \sum_e \sum_i a_{ie} p_i q_e \qquad (3)$$
$$= \sum_e p_e^* q_e$$

and the index of the aggregate value of net exports is

$$x^* = x^{*t}/x^{*b}. \qquad (4)$$

The adjusted Laspeyres index of export prices and the Paasche index of export quantities are defined as

$$P_{eL}^* = \sum_e p_e^{*t} q_e^b / \sum_e p_e^{*b} q_e^b \qquad e \in E \qquad (5)$$

and

$$Q_{eP}^* = \sum_e q_e^t p_e^{*t} / \sum_e q_e^b p_e^{*t} \qquad (6)$$

respectively. It is clear from equations (4), (5), and (6) that this pair of price and quantity indices is consistent, viz.

$$P_{eL}^* Q_{eP}^* = X^*. \qquad (7)$$

To obtain the desired indices of import prices and quantities one uses the net quantity of imports, or 'retained imports', defined to exclude re-exports in a broad sense.

$$q_i^* = q_i - \sum_e a_{ie} q_e \geqslant 0 \qquad (8)$$

q_i is the total quantity imported of commodity i. In the case of entrepot commodities, all of the quantity is re-exported, viz. $q_i^* = 0$. The adjusted Laspeyres index of import prices and the Paasche index of import quantities are defined as

$$P_{iL}^* = \sum_i p_i^t q_i^{*b} / \sum_i p_i^b q_i^{*b} \qquad i \in H \qquad (9)$$

and

$$Q_{iP}^* = \sum_i q_i^{*t} p_i^t / \sum_i q_i^{*b} p_i^t \qquad i \in H \qquad (10)$$

respectively. These indices are defined over the set of commodities with strictly positive net imports $(q_i^* > 0)$, H. H is a subset of the set of all imported commodities, I. This pair of price and quantity indices is also consistent with the index of the net value of imports, viz.

$$P_{iL}^* Q_{iP}^* = \sum_i p_i^t q_i^{*t} / \sum_i p_i^b q_i^{*b} \qquad i \in H$$
$$= m^{*t} / m^{*b} \qquad (11)$$
$$= M^*$$

where

$$m^* = \sum_i p_i q_i^*$$
$$= \sum_i p_i q_i - \sum_i \sum_e b_{ie} p_i q_e \qquad (12)$$

m^* is the aggregate value of net or retained imports and M^* is the index of this value.

All of these Laspeyres and Paasche indices of prices and quantities are homogeneous of degree one in their arguments and, for appropriate pairs, they are consistent. Thus they are satisfactory indices. If there is zero re-export trade all of the indices revert to the standard expressions.

From equations (5) and (9) the adjusted Laspeyres index of the commodity terms of trade is

$$T_L^* = P_{eL}^* / P_{iL}^*$$
$$= \frac{\sum_e p_e^{*t} q_e^b / \sum_e p_e^{*b} q_e^b}{\sum_i p_i^t q_i^{*b} / \sum_i p_i^b q_i^{*b}}. \qquad (13)$$

In the expression for the commodity terms of trade there is a duality relationship in that the price of the export commodity in the price index is net of its import content whereas the quantity of the import commodity in the quantity index is net of the quantity which has been used as the import content of export commodities. Formally it can be shown that this Laspeyres index of the commodity terms of trade has the same welfare implications for a re-export economy as the standard Laspeyres index has for a trading economy with zero re-export trade. (See Lloyd and Schweinberger, 1984.)[4]

II Comparison of Indices

This section compares the adjusted and unadjusted index forms. We shall consider first the index of the commodity terms of trade because of its welfare implications.

[4] One may also define an adjusted index of the income terms of trade using net prices and quantities. This $I^* = X^*/P_i$. If one uses the Laspeyres index of import prices $I^* = T_L^* Q_{ep}$ (from equation (7)). That is, like the unadjusted series for a non-re-export economy, the income terms of trade is the product of an index of the commodity terms of trade and a quantity index. However, the income terms of trade has no welfare implication, even in the absence of capital flows.

It is evident from equations (1) and (13) that the adjusted and the unadjusted indices of the commodity terms of trade between any two periods will be equal if all export and import prices were to change equi-proportionately and hence relative prices of all tradeables are constant. But this is never the case. As the relative prices of export commodities and/or import commodities change the adjusted index of the terms of trade will differ from the unadjusted index, except for the improbable coincidence that the multiple changes in relative prices happen to exactly cancel each other in the adjustment.

One would like to know the direction of bias between the adjusted and unadjusted indices, that is, the sign of $(T_L - T_L^*)$ if the Laspeyres index is used or $(T_P - T_P^*)$ if the Paasche index is used. For both the adjusted and unadjusted index functions the prices of the export commodities and the quantities of the import commodities will differ for any commodities involving re-export trade. To examine the direction of bias the export and import price indices are re-written as the weighted average of price relatives, viz.

$$T_L = \frac{\sum_{e} (p_e^t / p_e^b) \, w_{eb}}{\sum_{i} (p_i^t / p_i^b) \, w_{ib}} \qquad e \, \epsilon \, E, \, i \, \epsilon \, I \; (14)$$

and

$$T_L^* = \frac{\sum_{e} (p_e^{*t} / p_e^{*b}) \, w_{eb}^*}{\sum_{i} (p_i^t / p_i^b) \, w_{ib}^*} \qquad e \, \epsilon \, E, \, i \, \epsilon \, H. (15)$$

The weights are the appropriate shares of gross or net export and import trade in the base period situation.

The direction of bias can be established by the inspection of equations (14) and (15). First, consider that between the base and current periods only the prices of final import commodities increase, though not necessarily uniformly.[5] In this case both the adjusted and unadjusted indices fall but the bias is always positive, that is, the unadjusted index understates the deterioration in the terms of trade. This is because the final import commodities have larger weights in the adjusted import price index (compare equations (14) and (15)). Conversely, if the prices of final import commodities only decrease, the bias is negative. In both cases, the unadjusted index understates the absolute value of the movement of the terms of

---

[5] This encompasses the example of Ng (1969).

trade index. (A formal proof is given in the Appendix.)

Consider instead that only the prices of exported commodities decrease (increase) though again not necessarily uniformly. Again the unadjusted index understates the movement of the commodity terms of trade if the exported commodities use any imported inputs. In this case the understatement is due to the understatement of the proportionate movement of the net prices. From equations (2), for each export activity, we have

$$\Delta p_e^* / p_e^* = \Delta p_e / p_e \, (p_e / p_e^*)$$
$$> \Delta p_e / p_e \quad \text{if} \; \sum_i a_{ie} p_i > 0.$$

Another case is relevant to the recent historical circumstances of many economies. This is the case in which the price of important imported intermediate inputs increases. This occurred with the sharp rise in the price of petroleum crude after 1973 and in 1978 and 1979. Again one may show that the unadjusted index understates the true movement of the commodity terms of trade if these imported commodities are not re-exported. This is due to the larger weights of these imports in the index of import prices. If the imported intermediate inputs are used in export production, there is a second adverse effect on the adjusted terms of trade due to the fall in net export prices. Since this effect is omitted from the unadjusted index the bias is larger in this event too.

In all three cases the proportionate movement of the index is understated by the adjusted index. The understatement is greater, given the movement of relative prices, the smaller the proportion of domestic value added in the production of the re-export commodities. In this respect the qualitative properties of this index bias resemble the effect of shifting from the measurement of nominal tariffs to the measurement of effective tariffs; for a given tariff structure, the effective tariff diverges from the nominal tariff structure as the value added decreases.

The understatement of the change in the terms of trade does not hold when the prices of exports and of imports change simultaneously. The understatement of, say, the improvement in the terms of trade due to an increase in export prices may be combined with the understatement of a deterioration in the terms of trade due to an increase in import prices. For such changes the net movement of the adjusted terms of trade may be understated or overstated by the unadjusted index. There is one case of a simultaneous increase in export and import prices which is important, namely that in which the prices of a group of imported and exported commodities increase simultaneously. This is a better description for a re-export economy of the oil price shocks in which the price of all traded petroleum products rose sharply relative to other products than that above in which it was assumed that the price of all exports was unaffected by the rise in the price of imported intermediate inputs. Suppose that the prices of an export commodity and an import commodity used in its production rise equiproportionately, viz., $\Delta p_e^*/p_e^* = \Delta p_e/p_e = \Delta p_i/p_i$. It is clear from equations (14) and (15) that the unadjusted index will rise/fall as $w_{eb} \overset{>}{<} w_{ib}$ and the adjusted index will rise/fall as $w_{eb}^* \overset{>}{<} w_{ib}^*$. Now $w_{eb} \overset{>}{<} w_{ib}$ as $w_{eb}^* \overset{>}{<} w_{ib}^*$. Hence the two indices will rise/fall together as the country is a net exporter/importer. The unadjusted index will understate the movement of the adjusted index for major re-export commodities since the movements of gross export and import prices offset each other in the unadjusted index.

The qualitative properties of the bias of the unadjusted Paasche index are identical. The verification is left to the reader.

One may derive the bias for a consistent set of quantity, price and value indices for export or import commodities. Consider the export commmodities. In the case already considered of a change in the prices of export commodities with constant import prices, the index of the value of exports is understated because of the understatement of the movement of the net prices. In the quantity index the quantity relatives are unaffected and the index is affected for non-uniform price movements only by the change in weights for individual commodities. In general, the direction of the bias may be positive or negative for all indices when all prices may change simultaneously.

III Application

Given the qualitative consequences of using the unadjusted form of the index of the commodity terms of trade and other trade indices, it is important to establish the quantitative magnitudes of these errors in those countries which have substantial re-export trade. In Singapore, for example, one may note the extreme stability of the Singaporean commodity terms of trade. (See Table 1, last row). In principle, this index should have included the prices of export and import services

as well as merchandise trade. However, in Singapore, as in other countries, the terms of trade series conventionally omits trade in services and no series of the prices of services traded are available to the authors.

The Singapore series of export and import price indices include 're-exports' and are derived from unit value statistics. We inspected these unit value series for some major imported commodities which are re-exported, and whose price movements therefore appear in both the export and the import price series; for example, petroleum, tin, rubber products and spice. This inspection showed that there was a close correspondence during the 1970s between the unit value series for these commodities in the export and in the import price series. It is, consequently, distinctly possible that the series of the commodity terms of trade for Singapore has been distorted by the importance of re-export trade and the lack of adjustment for this trade in the calculation of the series.

We considered the years from 1972 to 1978. These are the only years for which data are available on a consistent basis. These years include those in which petroleum prices increased sharply in 1973-74 and in 1978 and the prices of other commodities varied considerably on world markets.

In the official series of Singapore, as of other countries, re-exports are defined narrowly as those commodities which are subject to only minor packaging and processing. Thus they are defined much more narrowly than the definition adopted here. It was not possible, unfortunately, to compute an adjusted series. This would require input-output coefficients which are highly disaggregated and based on a classification which can be linked to that of the trade classification. These coefficients are not available. Hence, we use the official series of 're-exports'.

To obtain an indication of the problem due to re-exports, we partitioned the set of commodities reported in the total trade statistics into two subsets, the set of 're-export export commodities' (narrowly defined) and all other commodities. This yields two series for export commodities and two series for import commodities. From these in turn one may calculate a terms of trade for 're-export commodities' and a terms of trade for 'non re-export commodities'. Similarly, one can compare the two export and the two import price series.

In more detail, the procedure was to select the principal 're-export commodities' and non-'re-export commodities', according to the value of export and import trade in 1976, the mid-year of

TABLE 1

Trade Price Indices for Export and Import Groups, Singapore, 1972 to 1978

Commodity Group	1972	1975	1976	1977	1978
Principal 're-export' exports	54.1	84.2	100.0	116.5	115.0
Principal 're-exported' imports	63.9	93.2	100.0	109.1	112.6
Terms of trade for 're-exports'	84.7	90.3	100.0	106.8	102.1
Principal 'non-re-export' exports	37.9	93.5	100.0	104.5	103.4
Principal 'non-re-exported' imports	38.1	93.6	100.0	105.2	102.2
Terms of trade for 'non-re-exports'	99.5	99.9	100.0	99.3	101.1
All principal exports	44.0	90.0	100.0	109.0	109.7
All principal imports	56.8	93.3	100.0	108.0	109.7
Terms of trade for all principal commodities	77.4	96.5	100.0	100.9	98.2
Official series of terms of trade (with base 1976 = 100)	96.7	98.5	100.0	100.3	100.7

the sample period.[4] The selection accounts for over 70 per cent of both export and import trade in all years. These commodities were defined at the six-digit levels of the export and import classifications and the unit values for these commodities were computed from the official trade statistics. There is an added complication in that the years from 1972 to 1974 were based on an earlier classification which was changed in 1975. The later classification was again changed in 1979. For the years before 1975 the data are published separately for West Malaysia and Other trade. Since the aggregation of Singaporean trade within these two areas and the recalculation of all unit values was very time-consuming it was decided to exclude the years 1973 and 1974. Despite the changes in classification and the use of unit values rather than price series the series for the commodities selected seem reliable. There are few substantial year-to-year variations in the series such as are usually exhibited by unit value series, and those which do occur exhibit a similar pattern across closely related six-digit commodity groups, reflecting genuine price movements on world markets. This is no doubt due to selection of the commodities in the regimen of the

[4] Because of the restriction of the sample of selected export and import commodities to export and import commodities in each case, there are some principal 're-export commodities' which do not appear among the sample of principal 're-exported import commodities', and vice versa. This also applies to 'non-re-export commodities'. This makes the stability of these series all the more remarkable.

official series by the Department of Statistics which has weeded out commodities which are not homogeneous. The indices are of Laspeyres form rather than the Paasche used in the official Department of Statistics series.

Table 1 reports the resultant series for the two sub-groups of commodities, the 're-export commodities' and the 'non-re-export commodities'. The 'terms of trade' for these groups are the ratio of the appropriate export and import price series for the commodities in a group. The series reported in the final three rows are the indices of export prices, import prices and the terms of trade, as conventionally defined, for the sample of 'principal' traded commodities, including both the 're-export commodities' and the non-re-export commodities'. The Laspeyres index of the price of all principal exports (imports) is the weighted sum of the indices for the two subsets of commodities, the weights being the respective shares in total export (import) trade in the base (1976) year. The terms of trade for all principal commodities show a remarkable stability of the commodity terms of trade for all commodity groups similar to that of the offical series for these years.

The series for the 're-export commodities' separately shows considerable stability. This is what one would expect for a terms of trade series which includes in both the numerator and the denominator series for individual commodities which are subject to only minor processing. However, the series for 'non-re-export commodities' is also stable. The stability of this series is also due to the fact that the movements of the prices of imported inputs and the prices of corresponding processed export outputs offset each other in the calculation of the terms of trade series. We noted in Section (II) that the movements of the terms of trade index of a re-export economy are understated when the prices of major exports and their imported inputs move together. We can conclude that the unadjusted series understates the movement of the adjusted index. The adjusted index for all traded commodities would show greater year-to-year variation and perhaps a different trend than the unadjusted official series.

One feature of the Singapore results is of interest to economists in all trading economies. Despite the well-recognized importance of entrepot trade in Singapore, it is the re-exports in the broad sense which enter the indices for 'non-re-export commodities' which mainly accounts for the stability of the terms of trade for all commodities. For example, the conversion of crude petroleum into cracked petroleum products and the making up of textile fabrics into garments and other products and the manufacture of electronic goods from components all entail the uses of important imported inputs. The export sectors of all trading economies today use significant imported inputs. These results indicate the desirability of further attempts to adjust for the presence of re-export commodities in the international trade indices of national economies.

Appendix

Proposition

The unadjusted Laspeyres index understates the movement of the commodity terms of trade index when there is a change in any single export or import price.

Proof

The unadjusted Laspeyres index of the terms of trade is

$$T_L = \frac{\sum_e p_e^t q_e^b / \sum_e p_e^b q_e^b}{\sum_i p_i^t q_i^b / \sum_i p_i^t q_i^b} \tag{A.1}$$

Hence,

$$\frac{p_e^t}{T_L}\frac{\partial T_L}{\partial p_e^t} = \frac{p_e^t q_e^b}{\sum_e p_e^t q_e^b} \tag{A.2}$$

and

$$\frac{p_i^t}{T_L}\frac{\partial T_L}{\partial p_i^b} = \frac{p_i^t q_i^b}{\sum_i p_i^t q_i^b} \tag{A.3}$$

The adjusted index can be rewritten in terms of gross prices using equation (3):

$$T_L^* = \frac{(\sum_e p_e^t q_e^b - R^t)/(\sum_e p_e^b q_e^b - R^b)}{(\sum_i p_i^t q_i^b - R^t)/(\sum_i p_i^b q_i^b - R^b)} \tag{A.4}$$

where $R^S = \sum_e \sum_i a_{ie}\, p_i^t q_e^b$ for $S = t, b$ is the value of re-exports in the base period valued in terms of prices of period S. Hence,

$$\frac{p_e^t}{T_L^*}\frac{\partial T_L^*}{\partial p_e^t} = \frac{p_e^t q_e^b}{\sum_e p_e^{*t} q_e^b} \tag{A.5}$$

and

$$\frac{p_i^t}{T_L^*}\frac{\partial T_L^*}{\partial p_i^t} = -\left(\frac{p_i^t q_i^b}{\sum_i p_i^t q_i^{*b}}\right) + \frac{p_i^t[\sum_e a_{ie} q_e^b]}{\sum_e p_e^{*t} q_e^b} \tag{A.6}$$

It follows immediately from equations (A.2), (A.5) and (A.6) that, for any price change, dp_a with $a = i$ or e,

$$\left|\frac{p_a^t}{T_L}\frac{\partial T_L}{\partial p_i^t}\right| < \left|\frac{p_a^t}{T_L^*}\frac{\partial T_L^*}{\partial p_a^t}\right| \tag{A.7}$$

As this inequality holds for all local changes in any one price, it holds for the cumulative movement of the price from its base level, and for multiple changes in export (or import) prices such that all export (or import) prices change in the same direction.

Q.E.D.

REFERENCES

Dixit, A. and Grossman, G. M. (1982), 'Trade and Protection with Multi-Stage Production', *Review of Economic Studies*, **43**, 583-94.

Jones, R. W. (1985), 'Income distribution and effective protection in a multi-commodity trade model', *Journal of Economic Theory*, **11**, 1-15.

Lloyd, P. J. and Schweinberger, A. G. (1984), 'Trade Expenditure Functions and Applications', mimeo.

Morgan, T. and Chua Joon Eng (1970), 'The Terms of Trade for Singapore's Entrepot Economy', *The Malayan Economic Review*, **XV**, 64-78.

Ng, S. H. (1969), 'The Terms of Trade in the Case of Entrepot Trade', *Economic Record*, **45**, 288-99.

Ohyama, M. (1972), 'Trade and Welfare in General Equilibrium', *Keio Economic Studies*, **9**, 37-73.

PART VIII

THE THEORY AND MEASUREMENT OF INTRA-INDUSTRY TRADE

Introduction

Increased intra-industry trade is another important and widespread consequence of the greater integration of national economies. It first came to the attention of international economists as a consequence of integration through regional trading arrangements and in particular the formation of European Economic Community (EEC) in 1957. Increased intra-industry trade is, however, also the product of unilateral and multilateral liberalization of goods trade and, though this is less well recognized, of the liberalization of trade in capital.

The first paper on 'The empirical measurement of intra-industry trade' is a part of a larger collaboration with my friend and former colleague at the Australian National University, Herbert Grubel (Grubel and Lloyd, 1974). It is the location in which we first advanced the measure of intra-industry trade which has become standard in the literature and known as the Grubel–Lloyd Index of intra-industry trade.

The second paper records reflections almost 20 years later on the intense debate over the nature of intra-industry trade and utilizes developments in continuum models of international trade to explain this trade.

The third paper on 'Aggregation by industry in high-dimensional models' is a sequel to the second. Despite its off-putting title, it deals with intra-industry trade. It shows how one may construct a very complicated model with many goods and many factors and analyse it by splitting trade into intra- and inter-industry trade. There may be different causes of intra-industry trade in the one model, say vertical intra-industry trade in one industry and horizontal intra-industry trade in another. The appropriate measure of the degree of intra-industry trade is the Grubel–Lloyd Index. Formally, the construction of the model involves the formation of aggregate industry-wide production and consumption indices. This paper won the Silver Award for the best essay in the *Review of International Economics* in 1994.

Reference

Grubel, H.G. and P.J. Lloyd (1974), *Intra-Industry Trade: Theory and Measurement of International Trade in Differentiated Products*, Macmillan, London.

The empirical measurement of intra-industry trade[*]

H.G. Grubel and P.J. Lloyd

Empirical research in international economics is beset by the problem that available statistics on output, prices and trade by industries show countries importing and exporting simultaneously products of many important industries. This phenomenon, known as 'intra-industry trade', is inconsistent with the standard pure theories of international trade derived from Ricardo, Heckscher and Ohlin. Normally, it is attributed to statistical aggregation and most studies employ net imports or exports as the relevant magnitude in the empirical calculations.[1]

Clearly, the phenomenon is a product of aggregation because a country will not import and export simultaneously *identical* commodities. All measured intra-industry trade must be due to the fact that the products recorded in the same statistical class are differentiated by location or time, appearance, or some functional characteristic. In principle, one should be able to find, at a sufficiently disaggregated level of statistical recording, that no country ever simultaneously exports and imports the same commodity. This raises the practically important and theoretically difficult problems of obtaining an operational definition which corresponds to the concept of an industry or a commodity as used in pure theory. Some types of analysis, such as the measurement of price and income elasticities of demand, seem logically defensible for industries in which intra-industry trade exists. However, for other analyses, such as the testing of models of comparative advantage, it seems logically inadmissible to use aggregated data on individual industries' trade which show both exports and imports. Cost or production functions of an industry can explain in principle why a country has a comparative advantage or disadvantage, but not why it can have both.

The literature in international economics does not contain a discussion of the theoretical questions raised by the existence of simultaneous exports and imports by industry nor does it contain any comprehensive empirical study of the magnitude of the problem. The first purpose of the present paper is to examine empirically the importance of intra-industry trade under the Standard International Trade Classification (SITC) used by the majority of countries today. In Part II, we examine first Australia's trade, analysing the magnitude of intra-industry trade as a function of different levels of aggregation from 7-digit to 1-digit SITC classes, and consider whether intra-industry trade is a real phenomenon or an accident of statistical aggregation. Second, we measure the magnitude of intra-industry trade for the major industrial countries of the OECD at the most widely used 3-digit level of aggregation.

The second major objective of this paper is to present some evidence on the causes of the phenomenon of intra-industry trade. This evidence is useful for choosing the level of aggregation for empirical studies and for assessing the significance of intra-industry trade. The phenomenon of intra-industry trade calls for a re-examination of the traditional Heckscher–Ohlin models of international trade. In one way the phenomenon resembles the Leontief paradox, which gave new directions to empirical and theoretical work in international economics without, however, changing the validity of the basic principles of comparative advantage as derived in the Heckscher–Ohlin model. In other papers we have indicated how product differentiation by style, model, and quality can give rise to intra-industry trade (Grubel, 1967, 1970; Grubel and Lloyd, 1970) but unfortunately the series needed to test these hypotheses are not available. In Part III we discuss cases of intra-industry trade which occur because of economies of scale due to the length of production runs, joint production and border trade in high transportation cost industries.

Part I
For the present purposes of analysis we consider the commodities grouped together in each SITC class at all levels of aggregation as being the output of an 'industry'. Thus, 'aviation gasoline' (SITC class 332.10.02) is considered to be produced by the 'aviation gasoline industry', which in our terminology is a part of the 'motor spirit industry' (SITC class 332.10), which itself is part of the 'petroleum products industry' (SITC class 332), and so on.

Under this pragmatic definition of an industry, intra-industry trade for industry i, at any given level of aggregation, is defined as the value of exports of an 'industry' which is exactly matched by the imports of the same industry. That is,

$$R_i = (X_i + M_i) - |X_i - M_i| \tag{1}$$

where X_i and M_i are the value of the exports and imports in the same industry, valued in the home country's currency.[2] R_i can be calculated for the home country's trade with one, or a subset, or all foreign countries. Inter-industry trade is defined as

$$S_i = |X_i - M_i|. \tag{2}$$

It is clear that intra-industry trade is the value of total trade $(X_i + M_i)$ remaining after subtraction of net exports or imports of the industry $|X_i + M_i|$.

To facilitate comparisons of these measures for different industries and countries, it is useful to express them as a percentage of each industry's combined exports and imports. The resultant measures of inter- and intra-industry trade are:

$$A_i = [|X_i - M_i| / (X_i + M_i)] . 100 \tag{3}$$

and $$B_i = [(X_i + M_i) - |X_i - M_i|] \ 100 / (X_i + M_i). \tag{4}$$

Both measures vary between 0 and 100. Since the level of inter-industry trade is always given by 100 minus the measured level of intra-industry trade, all further discussion is in terms of intra-industry trade.[3] When the exports are exactly equal to the imports of an industry the measure of intra-industry trade, B_i, is 100, and when there are exports but no imports or vice versa the measure is 0, which is desirable.

When the measures of intra-industry trade are calculated for all individual industries at all levels of aggregation, the analysis of these measures proceeds in two directions. First, at a given level of aggregation, we examine the distribution of these measures among some or all individual industries; and second, for a particular set of traded goods, we examine the measures of intra-industry trade computed at different levels of aggregation.

Concerning the first direction of analysis, the most useful statistic for summarizing the distribution of a set of individual measures is the mean, using as weights the relative size of exports plus imports of each industry in the total value of exports plus imports of the set of n industries:

$$\bar{B}_i = \sum_i^n B_i (X_i + M_i) / \sum_i^n (X_i + M_i). \ 100$$

$$= \frac{\sum_i^n (X_i - M_i) - \sum_i^n |X_i - M_i|}{\sum_i^n (X_i + M_i)} . 100. \tag{5}$$

$\bar{B}_i$ measures average intra-industry trade as a percentage of the export plus import trade. It is also equal to the sum of the intra-industry trade for the industries as a percentage of the total export plus import trade of the n industries.

$$\bar{B}_i = \frac{\sum_i^n [(X_i + M_i) - |X_i - M_i|]}{\sum_i^n (X_i + M_i)} . 100. \tag{6}$$

The mean is a biased downward measure of intra-industry trade if the country's total commodity trade is imbalanced or if the mean is an average of some subset of all industries. With an imbalance between exports and imports, the mean must be less than 100 no matter what the pattern of exports and imports because exports cannot match imports in every industry. This is an undesirable feature of a measure of average intra-industry trade which is due to the fact that it captures both the trade imbalance and the strength of the intra-industry trade.

When considering all commodity trade, an adjustment is made for the aggregate trade imbalance by expressing intra-industry trade as a proportion of total commodity export plus import trade less the trade imbalance. This gives the adjusted measure

$$\bar{C}_i = \frac{\sum_i^n (X_i + M_i) - \sum_i^n |X_i - M_i|}{\sum_i^n (X_i + M_i) - |\sum_i^n X_i - \sum_i^n M_i|} . 100 \tag{7}$$

where n is the total number of industries at the chosen level of aggregation. When the measures relate to trade with individual countries, this adjustment makes a substantial difference if the bilateral trade imbalances are large relative to the combined total export and import trade. For example, if the trade deficit (surplus) is equal to one-tenth or one-fifth of the value of export plus import trade, the adjustment increases the measure by one-ninth or one-quarter respectively. For trade with a given country or with all countries, this adjustment increases the average measures by the same proportion at all levels of aggregation. The adjusted measures lie in the closed interval [0,100].

The second direction of analysis involves the comparison of the B_i's at different levels of aggregation. For the ith industry, at a particular level of aggregation, X_i and M_i are each made up of the exports and imports of industries defined at a more disaggregated level (that is, a higher level of the SITC), called X_{ij} and M_{ij} respectively. The percentage of intra-industry trade for the ith industry is calculated by using the sums $\sum_j X_{ij}$ and $\sum_j M_{ij}$. From equation (4)

$$B_i = \frac{\sum_j (X_{ij} + M_{ij}) - \left| \sum_j X_{ij} - \sum_j M_{ij} \right|}{\sum_j (X_{ij} + M_{ij})} . 100. \tag{8}$$

It is important to note the following result of this aggregation. Since[4]

$$\sum_i (X_{ij} - M_{ij}) - \left| \sum_j X_{ij} - \sum_j M_{ij} \right| \geq \sum_j (X_{ij} + M_{ij}) - \sum_j \left| (X_{ij} - M_{ij}) \right| \tag{9}$$

and since the denominator of B_i is unaffected by aggregation, it follows that the measure of intra-industry trade at a more aggregative level is greater than, or at least no less than, the measured intra-industry trade with a finer commodity breakdown. Aggregation increases the measure of intra-industry trade by a greater amount the greater the extent to which the terms $(X_{ij} - M_{ij})$ at the less aggregated level are of opposite sign. Indeed in the extreme case it is possible that an aggregated measure is 100 when at the disaggregated level of j measures are zero.

This effect of aggregation also applies to aggregation across countries, at a given SITC digit level. Therefore, the weighted average of the measures for bilateral trade with individual countries, with each country's weights determined by its share of the total export plus import trade, is usually less than the measure for intra-industry trade between the country and all other countries combined.

Part II

The statistics in Parts II and III below are based on Australian trade data for the year 1968–69. We have chosen Australia for this study because of the availability of the data in convenient form on an electronic tape.[5] The disadvantages associated with a study of Australia are that it is a semi-industrialized country and that its manufacturing industry is highly protected by transportation costs and tariffs. Consequently, Australia's intra-industry trade at the 3-digit level of the SITC is 17 per cent of its total commodity trade whereas the average for 10 major industrial countries examined is 50 per cent. In some ways, therefore, the results of the analysis are not representative. On the other hand, the high levels of intra-industry trade for some Australian industries indicate that the phenomenon of intra-industry trade is not restricted to trade among highly industrialized countries, but exists even in the trade of nations which are more specialized in the production and export of agricultural and mining products and which have high levels of protection for their manufacturing industries. The data on Australia's trade therefore supplement the evidence on intra-industry trade among the countries of the European Economic Community (EEC) presented by Verdoorn (1960), Balassa (1965, 1966) and Grubel (1967).

Table 1 gives the averages of Australia's intra-industry trade adjusted and unadjusted (in parentheses) for bilateral imbalances, for all industries, broken down by trading partners. As can be seen (last row), at the most detailed, 7-digit level of classification, intra-industry trade represents an average of 6.2 per cent of total trade.

Table 1   Australian intra-industry trade with major trading partners at different levels
of aggregation, 1968–69

Country or country group	Digit level of aggregation				
	7	5	3	2	1
USA	3.2	10.0	14.6	25.0	39.7
	(2.3)	(7.0)	(10.3)	(17.5)	(27.8)
UK	1.3	4.2	7.7	12.5	31.5
	(1.0)	(3.1)	(5.7)	(9.3)	(23.5)
Japan	0.2	2.2	4.8	10.6	18.0
	(0.2)	(1.5)	(3.3)	(7.2)	(12.2)
EEC	1.0	3.2	4.9	6.3	15.3
	(1.0)	(3.2)	(4.9)	(6.3)	(15.3)
Canada	0.8	7.2	17.6	27.5	38.6
	(0.4)	(4.1)	(10.0)	(15.7)	(22.0)
New Zealand	4.4	19.5	30.5	47.5	79.8
	(2.8)	(12.3)	(19.3)	(30.1)	(50.5)
Hong Kong	1.4	6.5	13.3	17.3	50.5
	(1.1)	(5.0)	(10.3)	(13.4)	(39.1)
India	0.2	1.8	5.5	9.5	49.5
	(0.2)	(17.8)	(5.5)	(9.5)	(49.5)
South Africa	0.7	7.3	16.3	30.3	65.4
	(0.4)	(4.5)	(10.0)	(18.7)	(40.3)
South East Asia	1.5	4.4	8.7	9.8	17.4
	(1.0)	(3.0)	(5.9)	(6.6)	(11.7)
Rest of World	3.1	10.6	18.9	27.0	52.0
	(3.0)	(10.3)	(18.3)	(26.1)	(50.3)
All countries	6.2	14.9	20.2	25.9	42.9
	(6.1)	(14.6)	(19.7)	(25.3)	(42.0)

Notes:
(1) The statistics are global averages for all SITC sections. The unbracketed figures are adjusted for global bilateral trade imbalances, the bracketed figures are unadjusted.
(2) Countries are ranked in decreasing order of the value of exports to Australia in 1968–69, except for the remainder groups of South East Asia and the rest of the world. South East Asia consists of Brunei, Cambodia, Laos, Malaysia, Indonesia, Philippines, Singapore, Thailand and the Republic of Vietnam.

It is difficult to judge whether this percentage of intra-industry trade is important since there is no ready standard of comparison. However, it is important to note that the SITC classification is not sufficiently sensitive, even at the 7-digit level, to discriminate among the forms of differentiation which give rise to the simultaneous import and export of the 'industry's' output.

It is not surprising to find that measured intra-industry trade rises rapidly as the degree of aggregation increases, reaching 20 per cent at the most widely used 3-digit and 43 per cent at the 1-digit levels. As noted above, this increase in the measure depends on the extent to which the differences between exports and imports of the sub-industries are of different sign.[6] It is quite possible for a low level of intra-commodity trade among several 'industries', reflecting the fact that the country exports and does not import the products of some of these industries while it imports and does not export the others, to become a high level of intra-industry trade when these industries are aggregate. We examined the data to assess the significance of these changes by calculating the averages of the 3-digit measures within each of the 2-digit items and the averages of the 5-digit measures within each of the 3-digit items. The simple correlation coefficients between the 2-digit measures and the corresponding 3-digit averages and between the 3-digit measures and the corresponding 5-digit averages are 0.905 and 0.705 respectively. This demonstrates that over the 2-, 3- and 5-digit levels of aggregation the patterns of intra-commodity trade are essentially preserved when the data are aggregated from 5-digit to 3-digit and to 2-digit items. This result implies that industries preserve their relative strength of intra-industry trade through these levels of aggregation and studies of differences among industries would be insensitive to the level of aggregation chosen.

Returning to the data presented in Table 1, it is noteworthy that there are significant differences in the levels of intra-industry trade among Australia's trading partners at all levels of aggregation. Most remarkable is the fact that the level is the highest for trade with New Zealand and South Africa, which are countries with resource endowments and levels of development similar to those of Australia. It is surprising that intra-industry trade with the EEC and South East Asia are at almost identical levels. As indicated earlier, the adjusted averages are generally higher than the unadjusted figures and more so for bilateral than total trade. However, the general conclusions about differences in the measure at different levels of aggregation and among countries are the same for the adjusted and unadjusted measure.

One important aspect of the distribution of these measures that is worth considering separately is the number and nature of the industries which have high measured intra-industry trade. Appendix Table 1 lists the industries, and a brief description of each, which had averages for Australian trade with all countries of over 75 per cent in 1968–69 at the 3-, 5- and 7-digit levels of aggregation. This tabulation supports our conclusion above that high levels of intra-industry trade persist at all levels of aggregation of the same 'industry'. It also reveals that although the *average* measure increases with aggregation, the *number* of individual industries with very high levels decreases with aggregation. There are 13 industries above 75 per cent at the 3-digit level, 74 at the 5-digit level and 135 at the 7-digit level. The last figure is perhaps the most surprising since the large number of non-matching numbers in the export and import classifications at this level must have seriously biased these measures downwards (see note 5).

A careful study of the SITC classification, and the results of the calculations already presented, has convinced us that the 3-digit SITC statistics separate commodities into groups most closely corresponding to the concept of an 'industry' conventionally used in economic analysis. (One exception is the iron and steel industry for which the 2-digit level (67) appears to be more appropriate.) We have calculated the percentage of intra-industry trade at the 3-digit level or nine member countries of the Organization for Economic Cooperation and Development (OECD) in the same manner as above for Australia.[7] (The table giving these results for all 10 countries – including Australia – is available on request from the authors.)

By coincidence, the unweighted mean across the sample countries of the adjusted global averages for all industries was 50 per cent. That is, one-half of the total trade of all OECD countries plus Australia consisted of trade within the 3-digit SITC categories. While Verdoorn (1960), Balassa (1965, 1966), and Grubel (1967) have drawn attention to the increase in trade within industries after the formation of the EEC, the average intra-industry trade as a percentage of total commodity trade has not previously been measured. The percentage is greater than 40 for all individual countries in the sample except Australia and Japan which have much lower averages of 17 per cent and 22 per cent respectively. There is a considerable variance among the mean measures for intra-industry trade in individual industries of all 10 countries, but again it is remarkable that there is significant intra-industry trade in every industry. Indeed, only two industries – 071 (coffee) and 271 (crude fertilizers) – had averages below 10 per cent. While the averages across all countries are highest for Section 7 industries (machinery and transport equipment) and Section 5 industries (chemicals), the averages for all 1-digit section groups of industries are 30 per cent or more. The prevalence of quite significant measured intra-industry trade in all industries, primary goods and manufactures, raw materials and semi-processed and processed goods alike, clearly is a phenomenon worthy of further analysis.

Part III
The calculations presented in the preceding section could be used as data input to the testing of hypotheses about the differences in intra-industry trade among individual industries of the same country or among countries for the same industry. Such hypotheses require theoretical models and series of data for industry and country characteristics which can serve as explanatory variables. We have developed theoretical models for this purpose (Grubel, 1967, 1970 and Grubel and Lloyd, 1970), but have been unable to produce data series relevant for the testing. The problems encountered with the data were, first, that it is very time-consuming to collect and process national trade data by 3-digit industries for more than the 10 countries, and hence regressions are limited by the small number of degrees of freedom; second, that the incompatibility of SITC and production census data makes it extremely difficult to generate industry measures of research intensity, strength of quality and style differentiation, costs of transportation and other properties of output and industrial organization, which our theorizing had predicted as determinants of intra-industry trade levels.

Because of these data limitations we first present a preliminary, impressionistic analysis of the pattern of intra-industry trade through the study of a few selected industries in Australia. Second, we use a matrix of international trade in products of the 'stone, sand and gravel' industry to illustrate another cause of intra-industry trade.

Using the 3-digit industries shown in Appendix Table 1, which have over 75 per cent intra-industry trade in Australia, there are a few instances for which the causes of the simultaneous exports and imports require little theorizing once the precise nature of the goods in the subclasses is realized. Thus, trade in Group 941, which consists principally of zoo animals and pet dogs and cats, is based on absolute national advantage or purely historical factors. Similarly, in Group 212 (fur skins, undressed) Australia exports rabbit skins worth a little over $0.5m and imports mink worth $0.8m.[8] This is an example of different products in the one aggregate.

Different causes are responsible for the two observed high levels of intra-industry trade in important Australian industries, iron and steel goods (SITC 67) and petroleum products (SITC 332). Appendix Table 2 shows the absolute levels of exports and imports and intra- industry measures for the 3-digit and the important 5-digit industries of the iron and steel industry. As can be seen, intra-industry trade is high for all of the 3-digit industries, except 671 and 672, and for most of the 5-digit industries. The results for industry 671 should be disregarded since, for reasons of confidentiality, most exports in the group were deleted from the records.

A study of the descriptions of the 5-digit industries reveals that they leave much room for the inclusion of very similar products differentiated in apparently minor ways. But it must be these minor product differences which give rise to the trade. The basic explanation for this pattern of exports and imports of iron and steel products is that Australia is an efficient producer of some, but not all, of the finely differentiated products of this industry. Australian producers of iron and steel goods have ready access to abundant supplies of high-grade iron ore deposits and coal, conveniently located near tide water (and both of which are now exported on a substantial scale). Thus, Australia's source of comparative advantage or disadvantage must be found in costs specific to individual, narrow product lines. There is evidence suggesting that these cost differences may be related to plant capacity and product mix which determine the length of runs and which, through the optimum level of specialization of labour and machines appropriate for these runs, determine average cost of production.[9] While we have not been able to document the importance of these sources of scale economies in the case of Australia's iron and steel industry, the existence of scale economies in narrow product lines is sufficient to explain the observed intra-industry trade. They are also consistent with the findings of the Australian Tariff Board which studied part of the industry: 'Comparisons which could be made of British and local unit costs suggest that local manufacturers are at an advantage in producing some types of tube but that in other cases they have significant cost disadvantages' (1965, p. 10). Quantitatively these scale economies must be significant because of the high levels of transportation costs faced by Australian exporters and importers and the high levels of tariff protection on some Australian imports.[10]

Appendix Table 3 provides the statistics of exports, imports and intra-industry trade for petroleum and petroleum products (Groups 331 and 332 of the SITC) at the 3-, 5- and 7-digit levels in classes accounting for most of the production and trade in refined petroleum products. As in the case of the iron and steel industry, we find that the intra-industry trade percentages are very large even down to the 7-digit level of aggregation in nearly all products except crude petroleum. The explanation of Australia's simultaneous export and import of aviation kerosene (332.20.02) and marine diesel fuels (332.30.05) is simply that fuel purchases by foreign carriers in Australia are considered to be exports and by Australian carriers abroad are considered to be imports. However, the intra-industry trade in the other products is due to a different cause that has not previously been discussed, namely the economics of joint production resulting from the following technical and legal conditions. Since 1964 indigenous crude has been used by Australian refineries, first from the Moonie field in Queensland and later in 1967 from Barrow Island in Western Australia and in 1970 from Gippsland. Until 1970 production and trade were determined essentially by government import policy according to which a price of $3.14 per barrel of indigenous crude was established, based on an 'import parity' formula. This price was substantially in excess of the landed price of imported crudes even when adjustment is made for the superior quality of the light sulphur-free local crudes.[11] To ensure that all Australian crude oil was absorbed in Australian refineries, crude oil of Australian origin was allocated to companies supplying or marketing refined products in proportion to their imports of refinery feedstock and/or refined petroleum products. Heavy contingency duties were levied on imports of these products by importers who failed to take up their allocations of Australian crude.

As a result of these events Australian demand for light refined products, especially motor spirt, in relation to the demand for middle distillate and heavy oils was greater than the proportions of these oils in total refinery output. Hence additional imports of these products were required at the same time as surplus production of fuel and lubricating oils was exported. This pattern persisted after the refinery companies increased the percentage of light oils produced by means of secondary processing equipment and after some light Australian crude was used by refineries. In sum, the petroleum products industry illustrates a case where joint production, with a limited range of products from a plant once installed, which is not matched by complementarity in demand for these products, leads to significant levels of intra-industry trade in functionally very homogeneous products. Additional secondary intra-industry trade arose because the northern ports import all their petroleum product supplies to avoid the transport costs around the long Australian coastline.

Our approach to the intra-industry trade in 'stone, gravel and sand' is different. The trade among all countries, or a group of countries, in the products of one industry can be arranged in a square matrix of order m, where m is the number of trading countries. Every model of international trade makes some predictions concerning the form of the industry trade matrices. For example, both the standard Classical and Heckscher–Ohlin models in which each industry produces only one product, predict that in one country the product of an industry may be exported or imported but not both. That is, there is no intra-industry trade. The matrix for any industry in these models can be arranged by re-ordering the countries so that there is one off-diagonal sub-matrix containing positive elements with all other elements zero. This sub-matrix is of order $k \times (m - k)$, where k is the number of countries which export the product and $(m - k)$ is the number of importing countries. This matrix can be partitioned further into sub-matrices with positive elements and zero elements elsewhere, if trade takes place within distinct trading blocs with no trade between countries which are members of different blocs. Our consideration of actual matrices for OECD trade in the products of some industries showed that the class of industries in which the matrices can be arranged to conform basically with this pattern is made up of primary goods such as oil, wheat and iron ore, in which natural endowments with raw materials or climate provide countries with an absolute advantage. However, even in these industries there are positive entries outside the main blocs though these tend to be small, and there is a little intra-industry trade.

There is one class of industries which give rise to a distinctive form of the industry matrices involving intra-industry trade. These are industries in which there are high transportation costs relative to the economies of scale, if any, at the points of production. They give rise to what may be called border trade. An outstanding and analytically almost pure case is the industry 'stone, sand and gravel' (SITC 273) which has an average level of intra-industry trade of 76 per cent for the 10 countries. Appendix Table 4 shows the results of arranging actual trade data for 14 OECD countries such that countries with contiguous borders are next to each other. It is not possible to do this uniquely as several of the Continental European nations border a number of countries. The particular ordering was decided upon after a little experimentation, although the basic pattern of ranking was easily decided as countries fell into one of several groups – the two North American countries, the Continental European countries, the Scandinavian countries and Japan and the UK. It is apparent that most of the trade in the 'stone, sand and gravel' products among these 14 countries occurs within three or four groups of countries. These are the North American countries, the Continental European countries, the Scandinavian countries. Austria, Switzerland and Germany could be included in the group of seven Continental European countries. They may also be treated as a subgroup of three, as Austria and Switzerland do not export to or import from any other country in significant amounts. Germany trades extensively both with Austria and Switzerland on the one hand and with the other members of the EEC on the other.

Ninety-seven per cent of the trade in 'stone, sand and gravel' within the OECD falls within the two groups, the North American countries or the European countries which have been marked in Appendix Table 4 with a heavy border. Within Europe there are discernible blocs, namely the EEC countries plus Norway and the smaller group of Austria, Switzerland and West Germany. Looking across the rows we see that Italy in particular exports more than $100,000 to all the countries listed except Norway. Italy's exports consist to a large extent of Carrara marble, which is more properly considered a Heckscher–Ohlin rather than a border trade good.[12]

In the real world intra-industry trade explained by border trade is probably restricted to perishable foods, some building materials and electricity.

Experimentation with other partitioned forms of industry trade matrices is one method that may help to explain the causes of intra-industry trade in other industries. However, this will have to wait for the development of models of international trade which carefully specify the conditions which may give rise to this trade.

Part IV

In this paper we have presented evidence on the magnitude of intra-industry trade at different levels of aggregation in Australia's trade and at the widely used 3-digit SITC level for nine industrialized countries of the OECD (together with Australia). The data suggest that nations' simultaneous export and import of goods produced by the same industry are quantitatively important and merit further attention by researchers employing international trade data in empirical studies and by international trade economists generally to explain the phenomenon.

We have shown that in the case of some industries the phenomenon is due to simple statistical procedures which make its explanation within traditional theory obvious and easy. Even in these cases trade data on net exports or imports do not correspond to the concept of trade derived from pure theory, and empirical work may require disaggregation which is not available in published statistics. However, the examination of Australian data showed that most intra- industry trade persists below the 3-digit level of the SITC. It is a real phenomenon. The fact that significant intra-industry trade was present in Australia, which is an isolated semi-industrialized country, and that it is prevalent in almost all industries in the OECD countries making primary goods or semi-processed or processed manufactures alike, may have important implications for commercial policy in developing countries as well as in developed countries. Different actual cases called for diverse explanations in terms of advantages of specialization in narrow product ranges, joint production unmatched by complementarity in demand, and trade across borders in high transportation cost industries. The explanation of other intra-industry trade flows may require consideration of product differentiation strategies in oligopolistic markets which have also been neglected by most international trade theorists.[13]

Table A.1 *Intra-industry trade above 75 per cent from 5-, 3-, and 2-digit industries with SITC Statistics of Australian Trade, 1968–69*

	Digit level of aggregation	
5	3	2
Section 0 Food and live animals		
03202 Prepared or preserved crustaceans and molluscs		03 Fish and fish preparation
04812 Prepared foods obtained by swelling or roasting cereal grains		
04830 Macaroni, spaghetti, noodles, vermicelli and similar products		
05350 Fruit and vegetable juices, unfermented		
	054 Vegetables, fresh frozen or simply preserved	
05551 Vegetable and fruit preserved with vinegar		
06202 Flavoured or coloured sugars, syrups and molasses		
07130 Coffee extracts, essences, concentrates	073 Chocolate and other cocoa food preparations	
07300 Chocolate and other cocoa food preparations		
	081 Feeding-stuff for animals	08 Feeding-stuff for animals
08140 Flours and meals of meat or fish	099 Food preparations, n.e.s.	09 Miscellaneous preparations chiefly for food
09907 Vinegar and substitutes for vinegar		
Section 2 Crude materials, inedible (except fuels)		
21200 Fur skins, undressed	212 Fur skins, undressed	
22150 Linseed		
22190 Flour and meal of oil-seeds		
26320 Cotton linters		
26640 Synthetic and man-made fibres, waste	273 Stone, sand and gravel	29 Crude animal and vegetable materials, n.e.s. (not elsewhere stated)

513

Table A.1 *(continued)*

5	3	2
Section 3 Mineral fuels, lubricants and related materials		
33220 Kerosene, jet fuel, white spirit and other refined burning oils		
33230 Distillate fuels		
33240 Residual fuel oils		
33292 Pitch from coal tar		
33295 Bitumen and other petroleum residues	332 Petroleum products	
Section 4 Animal and vegetable oils and fats		
41110 Oils and fats of fish and marine mammals		
43131 Fatty acids		
Section 5 Chemicals		
53331 Prepared pigments, enamels, glazes	533 Pigments, paints, varnishes and related materials	51 Chemical elements and compounds
54163 Bacterial products, anti-sera, vaccines		
55430 Polishes, pastes, powder and similar preparations		
57121 Mining, blasting and safety fuses		
58191 Hardened proteins (for example, casein and gelatin)		
59955 Gelatin and gelatin derivatives		
59994 Preparations for soldering, brazing or welding		
Section 6 Manufactured goods classified chiefly by materials		
61220 Saddlery and other harness-makers' goods	611 Leather	61 Leather, n.e.s. and dressed fur skins
63240 Builders' woodwork and prefabricated wood buildings		
64211 Paper boxes, bags and other packing containers		
64220 Writing blocks, envelopes		

Table A.1 (continued)

5		3		2	
				67	Iron and steel
66110	Quicklime, slaked lime and hydraulic lime				
66320	Natural or artificial abrasive powder or grain				
67312	Wire rod of high carbon steel				
67343	Angles, shapes and sections				
67421	Untinned plates and sheets	674	Universals, plates and sheets of iron or steel		
67342	Uncoated plates and sheets				
67701	Iron and steel wire of solid section	677	Iron and steel wire (except wire rod)		
67702	Wire of high carbon steel				
68213	Copper master alloys, n.e.s.				
68410	Unworked aluminium and aluminium alloys	684	Aluminium and aluminium alloys		
68422	Aluminium plates, sheets and strip				
68425	Aluminium tubes, pipes, blanks				
68524	Lead tubes, pipes and blanks				
68950	Cadmium and other base metals and their alloys, n.e.s.	689	Miscellaneous non-ferrous base metals and their alloys		
69212	Copper tanks, vats and reservoirs				
69232	Aluminium compressed gas cylinders and containers				
69312	Copper stranded wire, cables and the like				
69313	Aluminium stranded wire, cables and the like				
69331	Iron and steel gauze, cloth, netting				
69422	Copper nuts, bolts, screws and the like				
69711	Iron and steel household non-electric cooking and heating appliances				
69894	Articles of aluminium, n.e.s.				

Section 7 Machinery and transport equipment

71523	Gas-operated welding, brazing and cutting appliances
71839	Other non-domestic food-processing machines, non-electric

515

Table A.1   (continued)

5	3	2
71915 Refrigerators and equipment non-domestic and non-electric		
72505 Electric water and immersion heaters		
72912 Electric batteries		
73220 Public service passenger vehicles (motor-buses, coaches, and so on)		
Section 8 Miscellaneous manufactured goods		
81220 Ceramic sinks, wash basins and other sanitary fixtures		
85105 Gaiters, leggings, cricket pads and similar articles		
86121 Frames and mountings for spectacles and the like		
86161 Projectors, enlargers and reducers (except cinematographic)		
86198 Instruments and apparatus for physical or chemical analysis		
89410 Baby and invalid carriages and parts		
89424 Equipment for table and fun-fair games		
89595 Sealing wax – copying paste		
89601 Works of art – paintings, drawings and pastels		
89932 Matches		
89933 Combustible materials and preparations, n.e.s.		
89996 Fans and hand screens, non-mechanical		
Section 9 Other merchandise		
94100 Animals, n.e.s. (including zoo animals, dogs and cats)	941 Animals, n.e.s. (including zoo animals, dogs and cats)	94 Animals, n.e.s. (including zoo animals, dogs and cats)

Source: Data used for calculations of these measure were on Commonwealth Bureau of Census and Statistics tapes.
The brief descriptions of SITC numbers were taken from the *Australian Import Commodity Classification, 1968–69*, which is based on the SITC (Revised) classification.

Table A.2   Intra-industry trade in iron and steel goods (Division 67), 1968–69

SITC item	Brief description	Exports ($'000)	Imports ($'000)	5-digit measure and average‡	3-digit measure
671	Pig iron, spiegeleisen, sponge iron and ferro-alloys	151*†	6,339†	3.5	4.6
672	Ingots and other primary forms of iron and steel	31,656†	1,116†	0.2	6.8
67311	Wire rod of iron or steel (except high carbon or alloy steel)	8,136	363	8.0	
67312	Wire rod of high carbon steel	20	15	86.0	
67313	Wire rod of alloy steel	11	1,038	2.0	
67321	Bars and rods (except wire rod)	5,074	1,575	47.4	
67322	Bars and rods (except wire rod) of high carbon steel	269	627	60.1	
67323	Bars and rods (except wire rod) of alloy steel	398	5,286	14.0	
67341	Angles, shapes and sections, 80 mm or more (except of high carbon or alloy steel)	5,064	1,751	51.4	
67342	Angles, shapes and sections, 80 mm or more of high carbon steel	17	5	44.9	
67343	Angles, shapes and sections, 80 mm or more of alloy steel	69	88	88.1	
67351	Angles, shapes and sections, less than 80 mm (except of high carbon or alloy steel)	2,051	403	32.9	
67352	Angles, shapes and sections, less than 80 mm of high carbon steel	33	20	74.1	
67353	Angles, shapes and sections, less than 80 mm of alloy steel	33	59	71.8	
673	Iron and steel bars, rods, angles, shapes and sections	21,797	11,230	29.7	68.0
67411	Untinned plates and sheets more than 4.75 mm thick (except of high carbon or alloy steel)	4,548	1,281	43.9	
67412	Universals, plates and sheets, more than 4.75 mm thick, of high carbon steel	24	57	59.6	
67413	Universals, plates and sheets, more than 4.75 mm thick, of alloy steel	72	2,391	5.9	
67414	Universals (except of high carbon or alloy steel)	73	7	18.0	
67421	Untinned plates and sheets, 3 to 4.75 mm thick (except of high carbon or alloy steel)	8,001	6,859	92.3	
67422	Plates and sheets, 3 to 4.75 mm thick, of high carbon steel	1	24	8.9	
67423	Plates and sheets, 3 to 4.75 mm thick, of alloy steel	71	726	17.7	

Table A.2 (continued)

SITC item	Brief description	Exports ($'000)	5-digit Imports ($'000)	measure and average‡	3-digit measure
67431	Uncoated plates and sheets less than 3 mm thick (except of high carbon or alloy steel)	2,064	10,986	31.6	
67432	Uncoated plates and sheets less than 3 mm thick of high carbon steel	37	50	85.4	
67433	Uncoated plates and sheets less than 3 mm thick of alloy steel	82	5,156	3.1	
67470	Tinned plates and sheets (except of high carbon or alloy steel)	5,424	546	18.3	
67481	Coated plates and sheets less than 3 mm thick (except of high carbon or alloy steel)	15,784	1,941	21.9	
67482	Coated plates and sheets less than 3 mm thick of high carbon steel	1	0	0.0	
67483	Coated plates and sheets less than 3 mm thick of alloy steel	3	2,573	0.3	
674	Universals, plates and sheets of iron and steel	28,984	26,424	24.6	95.4
675	Hoop and strip of iron or steel	1,952	7,163	42.8	42.8
676	Railway and tramway track construction material	653	286	23.5	60.8
677	Iron and steel wire (except wire rod)	3,070	3,948	69.7	87.5
678	Tubes, pipes and fittings of iron or steel	8,041	39,114	32.8	34.1
679	Iron and steel castings and forgings, unworked, n.e.s.	992	227	37.3	37.3

Notes:
* Exports of spiegeleisen (671.10.00) and pig iron and cast iron (671.20.00) have been excluded as they are confidential.
† Some of the 50 digits in 671 and 672 do not match because of differences in the Australian export and import commodity classifications at this level.
‡ The averages in column 5 are the weighted averages of all 5-digit items in the respective 3-digit commodities.

Table A.3 Intra-industry trade in petroleum and petroleum products, 1968–9

SITC item	Brief description	Exports ($'000)	Imports ($'000)	Measure
Group 331	**Petroleum, crude and partly refined (excluding natural gasoline)**	11	214,244	0.0
331.01	Crude petroleum	0	174,791	0.0
331.02	Petroleum, partly refined	11	39,453	0.1
Group 332	**Petroleum products**	26,414	36,941	83.4
332.10	Motor spirit (automotive and aviation)	6,919	13,457	67.9
332.10.01	Automotive spirit	6,469	8,173	88.4
332.10.02	Aviation gasoline	47	20,070	4.5
332.10.09	Other petroleum spirits	402	3,214	22.3
332.20	Kerosene, jet fuel, white spirit and refined burning oils	2,893	3,310	93.3
332.20.01	White spirit	522	193	54.1
332.20.02	Aviation kerosene (aviation turbine fuel)	2,146	1,791	91.0
332.20.03	Power kerosene	10	283	6.9
332.20.09	Lighting kerosene and other light, heating and burning oils, n.e.i.	216	1,042	34.3
332.30	Distillate fuels	4,234	4,336	98.8
332.30.02	Automotive distillate (diesel oils)	3,750	3,757	99.9
332.30.05	Industrial and marine diesel fuel	433	579	85.6
332.30.09	Heavy distillates, n.e.i.	51	0	0.0
332.40	Residual fuel oils	4,012	5,668	82.9
332.40.01	Furnace fuel (including ships' bunker fuel)	} 4,012	} 5,668	82.9
332.40.09	Other		0	
332.51	Lubricating preparations (at least 70% by weight petroleum products)	} 7,811	} 3,668	76.1
332.52	Lubricating preparations (less than 70% by weight petroleum products)		1,133	
332.61	Petroleum jelly	12	184	11.9
332.62	Mineral waxes	84	1,592	10.0
332.91	Non-lubricating oils	71	1,264	10.6
332.92	Pitch from coal or other mineral tars	52	51	98.5
332.93	Pitch coke	0	0	0.0
332.94	Petroleum coke	0	2,025	0.0
332.95	Petroleum bitumen and other shale oil residuals	86	124	82.3
332.96	Asphalt mastic and other bituminous mixtures	239	129	70.1
Group 341	**Petroleum gases and other gaseous hydrocarbons**	112	31	43.6

Table A.4   International trade in 'stone, sand and gravel', 1967–68

From \ To	USA	Canada	Australia	Switzerland	West Germany	Belgium	Netherlands	France	Italy	Norway	Sweden	Denmark	UK	Japan
USA	–	125			2	1	1	1	3	1			1	2
Canada	105	–												
Austria			–	3	18			1	1					
Switzerland			1	–	12	1	1	1	1					
West Germany			13	24	–	55	187	6	7	1	4	4	1	
Belgium–Luxembourg			1	3	28	–	100	76	27	3	4	2	8	1
Netherlands					8	82	–	–			5	4	1	
France	4		8	19	72	54	16	–	34	1	2		4	
Italy	22	5		17	63	21	8	45	–	11	5	2	22	4
Norway	2	2		1	24	4	14	14	11	–	5	7	7	
Sweden	1			1	31	3	1	3	5	2	–	11	5	
Denmark					31		4	3		1	11	–	2	
UK	1	1			3		4	3		1	1	2	–	1
Japan													1	–

Note: Numbers have been rounded. The empty cells indicate the value of trade was less than $50,000.

Source: OECD, Commodity Trade, Exports and Imports, 1967.

Notes

*   We wish to acknowledge gratefully the assistance given by the Programming Unit of the Joint Schools of Social Science and Pacific Studies at the Australian National University and the tapes of Australian exports and imports supplied by the Commonwealth Bureau of Census and Statistics. The paper has also benefited from comments from Harry Johnson and from members of seminars at the Australian National University, University of Pennsylvania, and Simon Fraser University.

1.   See, for example, the studies by Balassa (1966), MacDougall (1951), Stern (1964), and Vaccara (1960). (Figures in square brackets relate to references listed at the end of the article.)

     The first attempts to measure intra-industry trade were those of Verdoorn (1960), Balassa (1965, 1966) and Grubel (1967), all of whom showed that trade liberalization in Western Europe resulted more in increased intra-industry than in inter-industry trade. There is a long list of antecedent studies of the commodity pattern of trade which have noted that the exchange of manufactures for manufactures among the industrialized countries of Western Europe and North America has increased steadily in this century. Of these, those by Hirschman (1945) and Kojima (1961) are the most relevant to our study. Hirschman's procedure of dividing total export plus import trade into the trade imbalance, the exchange of manufactures for manufactures and non-manufactures for non-manufactures is equivalent, for a two-commodity division, to our unadjusted measure.

2.   Exports and imports should both be measured f.o.b. or c.i.f. F.o.b. valuations are preferable because they exclude the value added by international transporters either of the home country or typically of some foreign country. C.i.f. values would give the same measures as f.o.b. values only if the margins for costs of insurance were the same for exports and imports of the same commodities. For countries that value exports f.o.b. and imports c.i.f., the measure may be biased upwards or downwards depending on whether exports of commodities are greater or less than imports.

3.   The measure we employ was developed after a careful consideration of alternative measures which have been used in the past or could be used. Verdoorn (1960) measured the strength of intra-industry specialization by computing the ratio of exports to imports of a commodity, whereas Kojima (1964) used the ratio of the smaller of the values of exports and imports of a commodity to the larger, and Grubel (1967) the ratio of the larger to the smaller. The principal disadvantage of all these measures is that they do not provide a direct measure of average intra-industry trade. Actually, there are one-to-one correspondences between both measures previously used by Kojima and Grubel and our own measure. If the lesser of the values of exports and imports is expressed as a percentage of the greater, u_i, then the function relating these measures is $B_i = 2u_i/1 + u_i$. Balassa (1966) used the average $1/n \sum_i |X_i - M_i| / (X_i + M_i)$. This really measures inter-industry trade as previously defined. It has the two drawbacks that as an unweighted average it gives equal weight to all industries, irrespective of their size, and there is no correction for the aggregate trade imbalance.

4.   The inequality follows from the generalized Triangle Inequality $|\sum_i a_i| \leqslant \sum_i |a_i|$, where a_i are real numbers.

5.   In addition to the enormous computational advantages, the tape has the advantage over official printed statistics in that all flows under \$500 are lumped together under item number 999.99.99 in the printed statistics whereas they are recorded under the proper numbers on the tape. It should be noted that the Australian export figures employed include re-exports. Australian commodity trade statistics are based on the SITC. Both exports and imports for 1968–69 recorded the values of trade in commodities at the 7-digit level.

     There are two sources of error with these data, although fortunately both are minor. First, there are differences between the Australian import commodity classification and the Australian export commodity classification at the 7-digit and the 5-digit levels. At the 7-digit and 5-digit levels there are some import items with no corresponding item in the export classification. The larger number of import items will tend to bias downward the measures of intra-commodity trade at this level of aggregation, but since those SITC items which are not listed in the export classification are those for which there are no significant Australian exports the bias is small. The second problem is that the records of some 46 out of approximately 2,000 7-digit export items and some 32 out of an even larger number of import items have been deleted because they are confidential. The total value of trade deleted is \$89m., which is 1.3 per cent of total export plus import trade. Fortunately, these exclusions are spread fairly widely throughout the sections of the import and export classifications, and as exclusion may bias a measure either downwards or upwards the effect of these exclusions on the global averages for trade with individual countries or with all countries combined is negligible. These exclusions may have biased slightly some of the individual commodity measures at the 5-digit level and in a very few cases at the 3-digit level.

6.   It is worth noting that the variance of the components of an aggregate does not determine the effects of aggregation. The components may have a wide variance and yet aggregating these components

will not change the average level of intra-commodity trade if exports exceed imports in all components, or vice versa. This sometimes occurs in the Australian statistics.

7. The principal reason for restricting the country coverage to these countries was the ready availability of trade statistics, all classified according to the SITC at the 3-digit level, for these countries in the OECD *Commodity Trade, Exports and Imports*. No other publication systematically presents comparable trade statistics at this level of disaggregation for a number of countries. Although this sample is restricted to so-called developed countries, it does contain countries that are quite variant in terms of their participation in regional trading arrangements, the proportion of manufactures in total trade, their principal trading partners, and other trade characteristics.

8. But it should be noted that Australia also exports mink worth $1.2m.

9. See especially Daly et al. (1968), and Wonnacott and Wonnacott (1967).

10. The structure of tariffs within Chapter 73 of the Brussels Tariff Nomenclature (iron and steel and articles thereof) is complex. Many steels and steel products outside the range of Australian production enter duty-free. Other duties tend to increase with the degree of fabrication, reflecting the greater relative costs in Australia of products requiring more sophisticated methods and fewer basic materials. Duty collected on all imports of goods classified within Chapter 73 was 13 per cent of the value of these imports in 1968–69.

11. Dr Hunter has estimated that the former price for Australian indigenous crude was roughly equivalent to a 43 per cent *ad valorem* tariff, or $US1.00 per barrel in 1965, rising to 57 per cent in 1968 because of greater discounts from posted f.o.b. prices for foreign crude (Hunter, 1969, pp. 11, 26). However, the trend has reversed in the last two years with increases in the posted prices and international freight charges.

12. It is interesting to note that intra-industry trade between Australia and the rest of the world in this industry was 87 per cent in 1968–69, despite Australia's geographic isolation and the high freight costs. It consisted largely of Australia exporting one group of commodities to one group of countries (mainly gypsum to New Zealand, Taiwan and the Philippines) in exchange for another group of commodities imported from a different group of countries (marble from Italy, and limestone flux and stone used for the manufacture of lime and cement from Japan).

13. See Johnson (1967).

References

Balassa, B. (1965), 'Trade Liberalisation and "Revealed" Comparative Advantage', *Manchester School of Economic and Social Studies*, **XXXIII**, May, pp. 99–123.

Balassa, B. (1966), 'Tariff Reductions and Trade in Manufactures among the Industrial Countries', *American Economic Review*, **LVI**, June, pp. 466–73.

Daly, D.J., B.A. Keys and E.J. Spence (1968), *Scale and Specialization in Canadian Manufacturing*, Staff Study No. 21, Economic Council of Canada, Ottawa.

Grubel, H.G. (1967), 'Intra-Industry Specialization and the Pattern of Trade', *Canadian Journal of Economics and Political Science*, **XXXIII**, August, pp. 374–88.

Grubel, H.G. (1970), 'The Theory of Intra-Industry Trade', in I.A. McDougall and R.H. Snape (eds), *Studies in International Economics*, North-Holland, Amsterdam.

Grubel, H.G. and P.J. Lloyd (1970), 'Intra-Industry Trade', manuscript.

Hirschman, A.O. (1945), *National Power and the Structure of Foreign Trade*, University of California Press, Berkeley and Los Angeles.

Hunter, A. (1969), *Petroleum Prices in Australia: A Report to the Australian Automobile Association*, Canberra.

Johnson, H.G. (1967), 'International Trade Theory and Monopolistic Competition Theory', in R.E. Kuenne (ed.), *Monopolistic Competition Theory: Essays in Honor of Edward H. Chamberlin*, Wiley, New York.

Kojima, K. (1964), 'The Pattern of International Trade among Advanced Countries', *Hitotsubashi Journal of Economics*, **5**, June, pp. 16–36.

MacDougall, G.D.A. (1951), 'British and American Exports: A Study Suggested by the Theory of Comparative Costs. Part I', *Economic Journal*, **LXI**, December, pp. 697–724.

Stern, R.M. (1964), 'The U.S. Tariff and the Efficiency of the U.S. Economy', *American Economic Review*, **LIV**, May, pp. 459–70.

Tariff Board (1965), *Tariff Revisions. Tariff Board's Report on Hollow Bars, Tubes and Pipes of Iron and Steel*, Canberra.

Vaccara, B.N. (1960), *Employment and Output in Protected Manufacturing Industries*, Brookings Institution, Washington, DC.

Verdoorn, P.J. (1960), 'The Intra-Bloc Trade of Benelux', in E.A.G. Robinson (ed.), *Economic Consequences of the Size of Nations*, Macmillan, London.

Wonnacott, R.J. and G.P. Wonnacott (1967), *Free Trade between the United States and Canada*, Harvard University Press, Cambridge, Mass.

523-41

[89]

4210
9413

D 57 F11

R15

[25]

Reflections on Intra-Industry Trade Theory and Factor Proportions

P. J. Lloyd

This chapter offers some reflections on the recent evolution of intra-industry trade theory. These are selective and mainly relate to the interpretations of intra-industry trade in factor proportions models including some recent continuum models.

2.1 IS INTRA-INDUSTRY TRADE REAL?

From the time that intra-industry trade was first observed using data classified by the SITC in the period immediately after the Second World War a number of sceptics have regarded these observations as a spurious phenomenon (see Finger (1975), Lipsey (1976), Rayment (1976, 1983) and Chipman (1986)).[1] For example, in his review of the book by Grubel and Lloyd (1975), Lipsey (1976, pp. 313–14) concluded that 'much, although not all, of intra-industry trade is a statistical phenomenon'. In order to distinguish between theoretical predictions and empirical observations, Finger (1975) insisted upon calling the former 'intra-industry trade' and the latter 'trade overlap'. Similarly, Rayment (1983, p. 5) 'placed inverted commas around the industry of intra-"industry" trade as a reminder that this is a statistical construct'.

The common concern of these sceptics is that the trade data have been grouped within categories of products which are heterogeneous. Product heterogeneity has been interpreted by the authors as differences in factor intensities. Rayment (1976) observed that intra-industry variation among factor intensities in UK manufacturing industries was almost as large as inter-industry variation. In his opinion, this fact alone was sufficient to make the trade classification

16   *Intra-Industry Trade and Factor Proportions*

invalid. Similarly, for US manufacturing industries, Finger (1975) found that the intra-industry variation among measures of both physical-capital intensity and human-capital intensity accounted for 39 per cent of the total variation.

Finger then related his observations to trade theory by adapting the two-factor many-commodity model of Jones (1956). He developed a particular version of this factor proportions model in which each industry produces a number of different varieties of one product. Making the further assumption that the capital–labour intensities vary only slightly among varieties of a product, the factor intensities could be ordered so that:

$$r_{1a} > r_{1b} > \ldots > r_{2a} > r_{2b} > \ldots r_{na} > r_{nb} > \ldots > r_{nx}$$

where r_{1a} is the capital-intensity ratio in the production by industry 1 of the variety a, and so on. r_{nx} is the least capital-intensive variety of the least-capital intensive industry, n. (This ordering is independent of factor price ratios only if there is no factor intensity reversal for any of the commodities.) In the country which is labour-abundant in the sense that it has the lower wage-capital rental price ratio, the pre-trade output cost ratios will have the same ordering, i.e.:

$$c_{1a} > c_{1b} > \ldots > c_{2a} > c_{2b} > \ldots c_{na} > c_{nb} > \ldots > c_{nx}$$

If trade is free and does not equalise factor prices there will be a cost ratio for some variety such that all varieties to the left of this location in the ordering will be imported and all varieties to the right will be exported. 'The only product of which some varieties might be exported and others imported is the one product at the margin between a country's exports and its imports' (Finger, 1975, p. 582). With this solitary exception, intra-industry trade is inconsistent with this model. Since the observed level of intra-industry trade for the US manufacturing industries in 1962 (42 per cent) was roughly the same as the intra-industry variation in factor intensities, he concluded – rather immoderately – that his results 'will cause readers to be shocked by the liberties which have been taken with the scientific method' and he described intra-industry trade literature as 'valueless' (Finger, 1975, p. 581).

There are a number of problems with this reasoning. First, his ranking requires the strong additional assumption that technologies are identical across countries. Second, when there are more than two factors, there is no ordering of industries on the basis of a single measure of factor intensity unless very strong restrictions are imposed on the technologies (see, for example, Kemp, 1976, Part I). Third, even if the assumption of only two factors is retained, there is no single ordering of commodities by comparative costs when there are more than two countries in the world economy. Countries may be ordered by their factor price ratios but each country will be capital-abundant with respect to one subset of trading partners and capital-scarce with respect to other partners (apart from the two countries at the extremes of this ordering). What was needed was a many-commodity, many-country, extension of the Heckscher–Ohlin model. We know now that the association of the exports (imports) with low (high) autarchy prices only holds as a tendency or average (see Deardorff, 1980).

Chipman (1986) developed a factor proportions model expressly to evaluate observed intra-industry trade. First, in a similar vein to the earlier work of Finger and Rayment, Chipman (1986, p. 1) argues 'there is nothing in the empirical observations of international trade statistics that cannot be explained perfectly easily by the "Heckscher–Ohlin theory"'. He fits curves to the percentages of intra-industry trade between Australia and its major trading partners which Grubel and Lloyd (1975) had calculated separately at the 1-, 2-, 3-, 5-, and 7-digit levels. Supposing that these curves would hold for still higher digit classifications which correspond to increased disaggregation of the trade data, Chipman (1986, p. 6) finds 'for all of the individual countries and groups, the curves predict that intra-industry trade will cease to be observed if the SITC is refined to the ninth level of disaggregation'. Similar results hold for other observations of intra-industry trade.

The interesting part of Chipman's paper, in my opinion, relates to his version of the Heckscher–Ohlin factor proportions model in which there are three factors, three commodities and three countries. The Heckscher–Ohlin theorem predicts only the direction of trade, not its amount. Taking all production and utility functions as identical across countries and Cobb-Douglas in form, Chipman (1986) shows that if two of the three countries have similar endowments (as defined by the Euclidean distance between them) and export commodities with similar factor proportions, they will trade more with each other than with the third country. This dominance of trade between countries with similar endowments and factor contents is accentuated if the commodities these countries trade have a higher

18   *Intra-Industry Trade and Factor Proportions*

share in consumer budgets or if these countries have a greater productivity in the Hicks-neutral sense.

However, we do not know how robust this amount-of-trade result is with respect to the dimensions or structure of the model. Qualitative propositions in trade theory are notoriously sensitive to dimensional variation and more examples are shown below. The structure of the matrix of factor-intensity coefficients which Chipman (1986, p. 41) uses to obtain his results is highly restrictive. Industries 1, 2, and 3 are unambiguously intensive in factors 1, 2, and 3 respectively in the sense that the proportion of costs accounted for by factor 1 is higher relative to both factor 2 and factor 3 than the proportions in industry 2 and 3, and similarly for industry and factor 2, and industry and factor 3. Furthermore, countries 1, 2, and 3 are well endowed with factors 1, 2 and 3 respectively. Consequently countries 1, 2, and 3 export commodities 1, 2 and 3 respectively and import the other two commodities. This is a very special symmetric pattern of factor intensities and endowments and trade. Nevertheless, at the least the model provides a counter-example to the widespread belief that higher levels of trade between countries which are similar are inconsistent with a Heckscher–Ohlin model and require a Linder-type hypothesis or some other alternative to explain them (see Greenaway and Milner, 1986, chap. 7.3 for the empirical studies linking per capita incomes and intra-industry trade). This is a valuable result.

One other feature of these criticisms of observed intra-industry trade requires comment. Three sceptics – Finger, Rayment, and Chipman – view the world as a Heckscher–Ohlin world and argue that intra-'industry' trade may be explained away by differences in factor proportions among commodities. It may be, but it is important to recognise that it may not. All depends on one's view of the world. Rayment (1983, p. 5) errs in making the statement that 'Intra-"industry" trade does not exist in trade theory.' By the time of his writing a number of models had generated genuine intra-industry trade. Lipsey (1976) in particular and also Finger (1975) allowed the possibility of such models but were sceptical of their ability to explain observed intra-industry trade. This is not surprising given that at the time of their writing there were no fully articulated intra-industry trade models. To construct such models one must first define an industry in a meaningful way.

2.2 THE CONCEPT OF INDUSTRY REVISITED

Given the dependence of their measurements and explanations upon the concept of industry the early authors on intra-industry trade were remarkably casual in the definition of 'an industry'. Indeed, the concept of an industry is still defined only implicitly in some more recent work and the general problem of defining industries in an economy has received sparse attention in the total intra-industry literature.

Many definitions have been used. We have noted Finger's view of an industry as a group of products which use (primary) factors in similar proportions. Such a group is not in general independent of the vector of factor prices and is well-defined only for restricted technologies, and, furthermore, such an industry plays no role in a model with freely mobile factors. Falvey (1981, p. 496) introduced factor specificity and argued that 'for the purpose of this paper, an industry is best defined by the range of products a certain type of capital equipment can produce'. These groups are well defined if all producers have the same technology and the product sets do not intersect. Lancaster (1980, p. 153) defined the industry differently. 'A "group" . . . is a product class in which all products, actual and potential, possess the same characteristics, different products within the group being defined as products having these characteristics in different proportions.' This is precise for a two-characteristic model but is a highly specialised definition as it derives from a specialised model of consumer product differentiation. By contrast, Krugman (1979) defines an industry producing differentiated consumer products by a group of commodities which are arguments of a (symmetric) sub-utility function, $u(x_1, \ldots, x_n)$ where n is the finite number of such products in the group. Such an industry is well-defined only if all consumers in the world economy have the same preferences at least with respect to groupings of commodities. Other definitions have been used.

The problem of defining industries is the problem of partitioning all production and consumption activities in an economy into proper subsets which are mutually exclusive and exhaustive. For internationally trading economies the appropriate economy is the world economy. There are two alternative bases for such a partition, one based on demand relationships and one on supply relationships.

Some intra-industry trade theorists have opted for a demand-based definition. Within the class of theories that yield intra-industry trade in groups of consumer products, there is a further division. Lancaster

20   *Intra-Industry Trade and Factor Proportions*

(1979) distinguished between 'horizontal differentiation' and 'vertical differentiation' of consumer products. The former occurs when there are a number of varieties of a product. In some models consumers choose many varieties. Helpman and Krugman (1985, chap. 6) call this the 'love of variety approach'. A number of models have followed this approach. In Lancaster's own model each consumer consumes only one variety, his/her most-preferred variety. Helpman and Krugman (1985, chap. 6) call this the 'ideal variety approach'. Helpman (1981) and Eaton and Kierzkowski (1984) have produced variants of this type of model. Vertical differentiation occurs when there is a ranking of varieties according to 'quality'. Each consumer in each period consumes only one variety, his/her most-preferred variety. All consumers have identical tastes but because quality preferences change with household incomes which differ among consumers, they prefer different varieties. Falvey (1981), Gabszewicz, *et al.* (1981) and Shaked and Sutton (1984) followed this approach. In terms of their parenthood, these models are descended from the older but incomplete intra-industry model of Linder (1961).

Since products can be differentiated in terms of many characteristics or dimensions, each of these models is rather specialised in terms of the characterisation of the preferences of consumers but considerable specialisation is necessary to make the models tractable, especially if other complications such as economies of scale or entry barriers due to sunk costs are introduced at the same time.

To obtain a grouping of consumer commodities into an industry one also needs to use some measure of substitutability among commodities to define the boundaries of the group. This difficulty has plagued the theory of industrial organisation since the invention of the Chamberlinian group. The solution in intra-industry trade theory has followed the device introduced by Dixit and Stiglitz (1977), namely, it has been assumed that the product group enters the utility function as the arguments of a weakly separable sub-utility function. This defines the product group unambiguously. Sometimes the utility function has also been restricted to be homogeneous. These joint restrictions of separability and homogeneity of the utility function have two implications.[2] First, and most usefully, it can be shown that the Allen partial elasticities of substitution between any commodity in a separable group and one commodity outside the group are equal for all commodities within the group. This equality applies everywhere in commodity space, that is, for all prices and incomes. For any functional form one can then choose parameter values such that all commodities within a separable group are more substitutable for each other in terms of these partial elasticities than they are for all commodities outside the group.[3] This defines a 'close substitute group' unambiguously. Second, the demand for all commodities/ varieties can be derived by a two-stage budgeting process (see, for example, Helpman and Krugman, 1985, pp. 122–3).

As an historical aside, I note that the first use of the device of separability in intra-industry trade theory is usually attributed to Krugman (1979). It was the Krugman paper which largely began the avalanche of intra-industry trade models. However, one very important precedent has been overlooked – Armington (1969). In the Armington model products are differentiated by location (country of origin) as well as by type. Armington then assumed that the utility function was separable in groups of commodities which consisted of one variety from each country, and that the sub-functions were linearly homogeneous. This implied homogeneous separability.[4]

The second basis for defining industry groups is in terms of supply relationships. On this basis there are a number of distinct criteria which can and have been used. Falvey (1981) favoured a grouping in terms of the set of commodities which can be produced using mobile labour and industry-specific capital. The use of a common resource in the industry introduces a type of jointness even though production functions exist for each commodity. (Falvey also links his commodities on the demand side by associating higher capital intensity with a higher quality of output.)

Another possible basis is to group together products which use the same material inputs, such as the textile industry which weaves or knits fabrics from common fibres, or the clothing industry which makes up diverse clothing articles from common fabrics. This appears to be the basis of many activities referred to popularly as the 'clothing', 'textile', 'rubber', 'iron and steel' industries, etc. However, it does have the effect, as Lipsey (1976) observed, of grouping together some products which use different production techniques and sell in entirely separable markets. This is not necessarily a disadvantage. Dixit and Grossman (1982) linked products in the vertical chain of inter-industry flows. With fixed intermediate input–output coefficients all products in such a grouping are perfect complements for each other in the sense that more (or less) of all products together must be produced somewhere in the world. However, the relevant definition of substitutes or complements in production for any pair of commodities is in terms of the partial elasticity of output of one commodity in the *national* economy with respect to the (national) price of the other. By itself the grouping of continuum commodities in the Falvey or Dixit and Grossman model does not imply that commodities in the group are closer substitutes in production nationally for each other than for commodities outside the group but it is reasonable to assume they are so since the commodities in the group can substitute two common factors whereas only labour is mobile between groups.

Any industry or set of industries defined in one of these ways may be embedded in a multi-country general equilibrium model to yield meaningful intra-industry trade. It should be noted that some 'industries' may produce only a single commodity. All that is required for intra-industry trade is that there be at least one suitably defined multi-product industry.

2.3 CONTINUUM MODELS OF INTRA-INDUSTRY TRADE

There is now a large number of general equilibrium intra-industry trade models. Each is distinct and may explain some part of observed intra-industry trade. There is little point in contrasting all of them. However, a number of them do have a similar structure because they were expressed in terms of some appropriately defined continuum. These include the models of Lancaster (1980) and its extensions, Helpman (1981), Falvey (1981), and Dixit and Grossman (1982). There are interesting parallels and differences among these models.

Lancaster introduced a continuum of commodities in order to model diversity of tastes among consumers with respect to commodities within his separable product group. There are assumed to be only two relevant characteristics for the commodities in the group (see, especially, Lancaster, 1984, p. 138). The characteristics specification of commodities can then be defined in terms of the ratios of these two characteristics embodied in them. All specifications lie on a one-dimensional spectrum which is assumed to be continuous, that is, a continuum. Lancaster (1979) represented these differentiated products as a segment of the real line. Any consumer can choose any available product within the group. Each consumer has a most-preferred product. All consumers have identical preferences except for their most-preferred product. The population of consumers is assumed to be distributed continuously and uniformly over the commodity spectrum. Hence there is a continuum of consumers as well as commodities.

Helpman (1981) modifies the Lancaster model by locating the most-preferred product of each consumer on a circle. This approach avoids having to make special assumptions about the supply of the markets at the ends of the spectrum.[5]

Falvey (1981) constructed a continuum of commodities in a quite different way. As noted, his industry group is the group of commodities which can be produced given the industry's stock of industry-specific capital. The industry can produce an infinite number of commodities which are differentiated vertically by quality. This enables the author to construct a continuum of products, indexed by α over an interval of the real line, $\underline{\alpha} < \alpha < \bar{\alpha}$. Moreover, the capital intensity of the production process increases with the quality of output. 'Units are chosen so that production of a unit of quality α requires the services of α units at this industry's capital stock, and one unit of its (hired) labor force' (Falvey, 1981, p. 498). This continuum indexes both the quality of output and the capital intensity of the inputs.

Dixit and Grossman (1982) also base their continuum on supply relationships and define the 'manufacturing sector' in terms of commodities that use sector-specific capital. In contrast to Falvey, they consider that the final product of the manufacturing sector goes through a succession of stages, each stage adding value to an intermediate product to yield a 'good in process' ready for the next stage. This is 'vertical differentiation' among inputs and the output of one final product in the sense of Grubel and Lloyd (1975, p. 101). They allow a continuum of stages on the interval [0, 1] of the real line with the final product indexed by 1. All stages in the half-open interval [0, 1) produce pure intermediates. The intermediate good at stage $i + di$ is produced from one unit of stage i output. The stages are assumed to differ in factor intensities and they can, therefore, be ordered on the continuum by their labour intensities. This is an elegant and appealing model in view of the fact that more than one-half of the intra-industry commodity trade of developed countries consists of trade in intermediate or semi-fabricated goods rather than trade in final consumer goods or investment goods (Culem and Lundberg, 1986, Table 3).

Thus we have models in which the continuum is defined in terms of the variety of a pure consumer good, the quality of a pure consumer good, and the stage of a pure intermediate good. In each case there is an infinity of commodities. (In the Dixit–Grossman model there are only two final products whereas in the other three models there is an infinity of final consumer commodities.) The commodity index defined on the continuum is a continuous and differentiable function. This is what makes analysis of the number of commodities produced and consumed easier than in a discrete model with a finite number of commodities.

In all these models a continuum of commodities is an expression of a situation in which there are 'many' commodities. It is a natural device for industries where a complex pattern of trade in related commodities is observed. Each author selected a different feature to order commodities but in all cases the group defined by the continuum is a proper subset of commodities which are related to each other in some way that is not shared by commodities not in the set. It is this relatedness which gives rise to genuine intra-industry trade.[6] All the continua can be defined to be of unit length but because the structures of the models differ they yield different patterns of production and trade.

One basic aspect is whether all the commodities in the continuum will be produced. In the Dixit–Grossman model, in order for the final good to emerge it must pass once through each stage in one or other of the two countries. (This also permits goods in process to cross the international border more than once.) By contrast, in the Lancaster and Helpman models the continuum relates to potentially available commodities. With economies of scale in their differentiated products industry, the number of products actually produced is finite. In equilibrium the consumer chooses that product in the continuum which is closest to his/her most-preferred product. In the Falvey model the demand for commodities is specified only in terms of being a function of the relative price of all commodities including all qualities of the quality-differentiated product. Consequently, some qualities will not in general be demanded and will, therefore, not be produced in either country.

The pattern of intra- and inter-industry trade also varies sharply between models. In the Falvey and Dixit–Grossman models the structure of production and trade is delineated by the existence of a 'borderline' commodity in the continuum.[7] Products produced and exported in the continuum are either all above or all below this borderline commodity, and products imported are all below or all above it. The borderline commodity itself may be produced and exported, or produced and imported. In the Falvey model, the country whose exports are below the borderline commodity is the relatively labour-abundant country in terms of the relative price of labour because the capital intensity increases with commodity index. In the Dixit–Grossman model, the country whose exports are below the borderline commodity is the capital-abundant country because capital intensity decreases with the commodity index. But in both cases the labour-abundant country specialises incompletely in and exports the relatively labour-intensive commodities. (The order of indexing commodities is arbitrary and can be reversed in one of these models.) This borderline feature is a carry-over from the Dornbusch, Fischer and Samuelson (1980) model in which there are two countries, two factors and a continuum of capital–labour intensities for *all* commodities produced in the economy. In the Dixit–Grossman model there is a single commodity produced by the non-continuum sector. It will be convenient to call this the outside commodity. Dixit and Grossman called it 'agriculture'. Falvey does not specify the outside sector. In both models only labour is mobile throughout the economy.[8] One country will produce and export the outside commodity and one will import it. Thus, despite their very different interpretations, these two models yield a similar pattern of intra-industry and inter-industry trade.[9]

In the models with differentiation of consumer products, the patterns are very different. The model of Lancaster (1980, 1984) has a complex structure due primarily to the combination of a continuum of commodities and the differences among consumers with respect to their most-preferred products. To make the model tractable, Lancaster assumes that consumers have identical compensation functions (which define in terms of spectral distance the utility of varieties which are not their most-preferred) and they are distributed uniformly over the spectrum, and the cost functions for all varieties are identical. Within the continuum industry the equilibrium is a symmetric Nash equilibrium. The finite number of commodities produced are spaced at equal distance on the continuum, produced in the same quantities by a single producer and sold for the same price. To complete the model, there is an outside commodity called the 'agricultural sector'.

International trade in the Lancaster model takes place between two identical economies. With such a complex model structure any of the possible patterns of intra-industry trade is permissible. Trade may consist entirely of intra-industry trade or of inter-industry trade or a mixture. The 'normal' case is that of all intra-industry trade in manufactures and no exchange of agricultural for manufacturing output. In the continuum group each of the two countries will produce exactly half the number of these goods produced in the world economy and export one-half of this output. However, the composition of a country's production and exports and imports is indeterminate. This occurs because, unlike the factor proportions models of Falvey and Dixit–Grossman, there are no different endowments or other differences such as technologies (as in the Armington models) to give rise to cost differences. The demonstration of gains from trade between two identical economies in the presence of strict economies of scale everywhere in the continuum sector was a remarkable *tour de force* but it was achieved at a considerable cost in terms of unreal symmetry and indeterminateness.

Lancaster (1980) produced an extension of the model in which there are two non-specific factors, labour and capital, and one country is relatively well endowed with labour and one industry ('sector') – 'manufacturing' – is relatively labour-intensive. He also assumes that all varieties of manufactured commodities on the continuum are equally capital-intensive. (This is the opposite assumption to that of Falvey.) Helpman (1981) and Helpman and Krugman (1985, chaps 7 and 8) make the same assumptions regarding supply conditions and derive the same pattern of inter-industry specialisation.

Indeed, we may consider all four continuum intra-industry trade models as extensions of the Heckscher–Ohlin model. In effect all four continuum models have been constructed by taking the $2 \times 2 \times 2$ Heckscher–Ohlin model and then disaggregating one of the two industries into a horizontal or vertical continuum. Falvey (1981) and Dixit and Grossman (1982) also simultaneously introduce some factor specificity, thereby giving three factors. Plainly one could use the same device in a Heckscher–Ohlin model of any dimensions; that is, m commodities, n factors and p countries. One simply takes a set of industries and disaggregates each horizontally or vertically.

This interpretation of the continuum models helps to integrate continuum models which appear very different and to integrate them with standard non-continuum models. Using the method of Deardorff (1980, 1982), one can assert that the general law of comparative advantage and the general Heckscher–Ohlin theorem apply to any continuum models which yield intra-industry trade and which satisfy his restrictions. The law of comparative advantage holds in the sense that the exports of a country are on average those commodities which had relatively low prices before trade. The Heckscher–Ohlin theorem holds in the sense that the exports are on average those commodities which use intensively the factor with which the country is well endowed. These theorems hold with or without factor price equalisation and with or without specific factors and with or without free trade. However, the restrictions on supply conditions rule out economies of scale. Hence, these general theorems apply to continuum models of Falvey (1981) and Dixit and Grossman only. In the Helpman and Lancaster models with two factors, the law of comparative advantage does not apply because economies of scale may give rise to what Lancaster (1980, p. 167) called a 'false comparative advantage' and because identical countries with identical pre-trade prices may specialise and gain from trade. However, Helpman and Krugman showed that the Heckscher–Ohlin theorem continues to apply to *net* (= inter-industry) trade, utilising factor price equalisation and the symmetry of the production equilibrium. This result shows that there is no inconsistency between intra-industry trade, and the factor proportions theory of comparative advantage. It also shows that the early empirical studies which sought to explain net trade may be meaningful, although they leave a large part of trade unexplained. Hence we require a full specification of a model including the intra-industry component of trade.

In the light of the earlier criticisms of intra-industry trade by Finger and Chipman, a further interesting result is that Lancaster and Helpman models yield international trade in manufactured commodities that have the same factor intensity ratio. This arises because the constant returns to scale assumption of the Jones (1956) multi-commodity model, and the continuum version of it due to Dornbusch, Fischer and Samuelson (1980), has been relaxed. In this context, Helpman and Krugman (1985, p. 131) note 'If we were to aggregate groups of products into sectors defined by similarity of factor proportions, we would expect to find substantial amounts of two-way intrasectoral trade.'

We are also interested in the proportion of intra-industry trade in total trade. In the Lancaster–Helpman models in which there are only non-specific factors one strong proposition emerges. In free trade situations this share increases as factor endowments become more similar (Helpman and Krugman, 1985). However, this result does not carry over to the Falvey and Dixit and Grossman models which have specific factors.

Do these continuum models predict that the share of intra-industry trade increases as trade barriers are reduced in a distorted-trade situation? This is a most interesting question since it was the sharp increases in these shares in the EEC countries after the formation of the Benelux Union and the EEC which stimulated the original interest in intra-industry trade. It is also a difficult question since comparative statics are complex in these models. With an infinity of commodities the quantities of commodities produced adjust at three margins. For the continuum commodities there are the extensive margin on the continuum itself of which commodities to produce, and the intensive margin of how much to produce of each commodity, and there is the margin of production between the continuum group and the outside commodity. For the quantities consumed in each country, there is an extensive and intensive margin.

Consider the introduction of a uniform tariff on all continuum commodities imported in the models of Falvey and of Dixit and Grossman.[10] Because these models are close analogues they have similar comparative statics properties. Such a tariff reduces trade in continuum products in two ways. It reduces the volume of trade in products that remain traded and it creates a range of non-traded commodities. There are now two borderline commodities, one for each country. The commodities between these borderlines are the set of non-traded commodities. This set includes the single free-trade borderline commodity. Consequently the set of continuum commodities which are traded internationally is reduced for both countries. This led Falvey to a conclusion:

> given that the imposition of the tariff creates a range of non-traded qualities, a tariff reduction will have the effect of increasing intra-industry trade by reversing this process. Our framework therefore predicts that the formation of a preferential trading area, such as the EEC, will lead to an expansion of intra-industry trade among its members. In particular, this model predicts an increase in the range of imported and exported qualities for each trading partner, even if only one reduces its tariffs (Falvey, 1981, p. 505).

The reduction in tariffs will also increase the volume of intra-industry trade as the prices of the protected commodities in each country fall relative to the prices of other commodities.

Thus the volume of intra-industry trade must increase. This result is highly significant for the debate on intra-industry trade. However, it does not imply and increase in the *share* of intra-industry trade. This share will depend in addition on the change in inter-industry trade. Lowering trade restrictions will increase inter-industry trade as well as intra-industry trade, even when the commodities can be grouped into industries consisting of commodities which are close substitutes in consumption or production. There are too many margins of production to predict the shares. Moreover, in a free trade area the trade barriers which restrict inter-industry trade will also be lowered.

Much will depend on the structure of initial trade restrictions. These are highly non-uniform in most countries. Suppose the initial levels of restrictions on trade in the products of industries with a high level of intra-industry trade in a free trade situation are higher than the national average. In this situation one can expect that an across-the-board reduction in trade restrictions by one or all countries will increase the share of intra-industry trade. Alternatively the increase in the share of intra-industry trade will be greater if the depth of cut is greater in 'manufactures' or other commodities with high potential intra-industry trade than in industries with low potential intra-industry trade. This seems to have been the case in the the formation of the EEC.

2.4 SOME FINAL OBSERVATIONS

The models of intra-industry trade that are already extant provide a very rich variety. Indeed, the rate of growth of general equilibrium trade models in the short time since 1979 has been astounding and without precedent in the history of trade theory. In my opinion, the intra-industry trade models and the expansion of the dimensionality of Heckscher–Ohlin-type models have been the two outstanding areas of development of trade theory in the last decade. These two developments have been linked in the continuum intra-industry trade models. The effect of the introduction of continua in trade models is to allow for the first time the analysis of the extensive margin of production. This is central to intra-industry trade theory. Some of the methods of analysis used by builders of intra-industry trade theories reflected methods developed by economic model-builders at large; for example, the use of commodity continua. However, other methods are more closely linked to the concept of an industry. For example, economies of scale might be introduced into any trade model but it seems natural as well as tractable to group such commodities into industries.

But, as in all areas of decision-making, variety poses a problem of choice. There are now alternative models to explain an observed trade phenomenon. For example, the two-way trade in commodities using similar or even identical factor intensities has been explained by Chipman (1986) by a factor proportions model with no intra-industry trade and by Helpman and Krugman (1985) by a factor proportions model with intra-industry trade.

A second difficulty is that the criteria used to group commodities into 'industries' differ between models and, therefore, the resultant groupings may conflict. Any two partitions of production and/or consumption activities into 'industries' may yield subsets that have a non-zero intersection across partitions. If one believes that in reality two (or more) sources of comparative advantage, such as those in a Lancaster-type or a Falvey-type or a Dixit–Grossman-type model, may both be significant in explaining observed intra-industry trade, the problem of industry classification may be insoluble, even in principle. There may be no single partition which can be used to test a multiplicity of intra-industry trade hypotheses.

The empirical attribution of observed trade flows to sources of comparative advantage is likely to continue to prove difficult and contentious. Yet, the production of these new varieties of trade models has surely increased our understanding of trade flows and mutual gains from international trade.

Notes

1. When Herbert Grubel and I first presented our analysis of intra-industry trade patterns in the Australian manufacturing sector at seminars in Australia in 1969 we encountered this view almost immediately from our colleagues. We thought we had dealt with it adequately in our book (Grubel and Lloyd, 1975), principally by developing various models of industry behaviour which yielded meaningful intra-industry trade. In retrospect, I concede that we left the question open by the imprecision of our definition of industries and by the lack at that time of general equilibrium models with intra-industry trade.

2. Homogeneity and separability can be weakened to the assumption of separability and homogeneity of the *sub*function(s), that is, homogeneous separability. This is a weaker restriction because homogeneity and separability of the utility function imply homogeneous separability of the subfunction but the converse is not true. Homogeneity and separability of the subfunction is the necessary and sufficient condition for both the relationship among partial elasticities of substitution and two-stage budgeting to hold (see Blackorby, Primont and Russsell (1978, pp. 264–6)). The economic implication of homogeneous separability of the subfunction only for intra-industry trade models is that it can encompass a change in the budget share devoted to the separable quality good in a Falvey-type model whereas the assumption that the utility function is homogeneous imposes unitary income elasticities of demand everywhere.

3. The members of such a group are also more substitutable for each other than for commodities outside the group in terms of the partial cross-price compensated-demand elasticities. That is, the members are a group of close net substitutes. It is not necessary to assume as Krugman (1979) did that the subfunction is symmetric. Symmetry imposes the additional and undesirable restriction that all commodities in the group are equally good substitutes for each other in that the partial cross-price elasticities *within* the group are all equal.

4. A large number of computable multi-country models have followed Armington in making these assumptions. The earliest of these were Dixon, Parmenter, Ryland and Sutton (1977), Deardorff, Stern and Baum (1977), Boadway and Treddinick (1978), Lloyd (1979) and Brown and Whalley (1980). These models have the disadvantage that product differentiation is merely a national characteristic and is unexplained, but Armington deserves an honourable place in intra-industry trade history.

5. It is debatable whether this property of the circle is preferable to the disconnectedness of the ends of the line. The assumption certainly affects the division of the market among suppliers. The line form seems more appropriate in those cases in which a characteristic ranges from one extreme to another; for example, differentiation by colour or sweetness.

6. Continuum trade models do not necessarily give rise to intra-industry trade; see, for example, the model of Dornbusch, Fischer and Samuelson (1980). This is an extension to infinitely many commodities of the finitely many-commodity two-factor Jones model. The first economic model with a continuum of commodities was that of Hotelling (1929). This clearly was the inspiration for Lancaster who himself described his model as 'neo-Hotelling' (Lancaster, 1984, p. 138).

7. This assumes that factor prices are not equalised by trade.

8. If the second sector used the same two factors as the first, its output becomes just another commodity in the capital-intensity continuum. Thus it is the presence of three inputs which distinguishes these models from that of Dornbusch, Fischer and Samuelson (1980).

9. The two models are not isomorphic because Dixit and Grossman require all commodities in the continuum to be produced in fixed proportions and because Falvey indexes quality as well as capital-intensity on his continuum.

10. Lancaster (1980, 1984) considers a number of cases in terms of the initial structures of trade and of trade restrictions. His results must be considered as tentative. In particular, the indeterminateness of production on the continuum makes the patterns of specialisation which Lancaster assumes to be arbitrary. Helpman and Krugman (1985) considered that in Lancaster-type models 'To carry out policy analysis will require a further development of analytical tools.' Using numerical simulation in an Armington-type model, Lloyd (1979) found that the intra-industry trade share was little affected by changes in trade restrictions. However, this model has a specialised structure. In particular, there can be no adjustment in the number of commodities produced or consumed in any country.

References

ARMINGTON, P. S. (1969) 'A Theory of Demand for Products Distinguished by Place of Production', *IMF Staff Papers*, vol. 16, pp. 159–76.

BLACKORBY, C., PRIMONT, D. and RUSSELL, R. R. (1978) *Duality, Separability and Functional Structure* (Amsterdam: North Holland Publishing Co.).

BOADWAY, R. and TREDDINICK, J. (1978) 'A General Equilibrium Computation of the Effects of the Canadian Tariff Structure', *Canadian Journal of Economics*, vol. 11, pp. 424–46.

BROWN, F. and WHALLEY, J. (1980) 'General Equilibrium Evaluations of Tariff-Cutting Proposals in the Tokyo Round and Comparisons with more Extensive Liberalization of World Trade', *Economic Journal*, vol. 90, pp. 838–66.

CHIPMAN, J. S. (1986) *Intra-Industry Trade, Factor Proportions and Aggregation* (Sonderforschungsbericht 178, Internationalisierung der Wirtschaft, University of Constance).

CULEM, C. and LUNDBERG, L. (1986) 'The Product Pattern of Intra-Industry Trade: Stability among Countries and over Time', *Weltwirtschaftliches Archiv*, vol. 122, no 1, pp. 113–30.

DEARDORFF, A. V. (1980) 'The General Validity of the Law of Comparative Advantage', *Journal of Political Economy*, vol. 88, October, pp. 941–57.

DEARDORFF, A. V. (1982) 'The General Validity of the Heckscher–Ohlin Theorem', *American Economic Review*, vol. 72, September, pp. 683–94.

DEARDORFF, A. V.; STERN, R. and BAUM, C. F. (1977) 'A Multi-Country Simulation at the Employment and Exchange Rate Effects of Post-Kennedy Round Tariff Reductions' in N. Akrasanee *et al.* (eds) (1977) *Trade and Employment in Asia and the Pacific* (Honolulu: University of Hawaii Press).

DIXIT, A. K. and GROSSMAN, G. M. (1982) 'Trade and Protection with Multistage Production', *Review of Economic Studies*, 49, pp. 583–94.

DIXIT, A. K. and STIGLITZ, J. E. (1977) 'Monopolistic Competition and Optimum Product Diversity', *American Economic Review*, vol. 67, pp. 297–308.

DIXON, P. B.; PARMENTER, B. R.; RYLAND, G. J. and SUTTON, M. J. (1977) *A Model of the Australian Economy* (Canberra: Australian Government Publishing Service).

DORNBUSCH, R.; FISCHER, S. and SAMUELSON, P. A. (1980) 'Heckscher–Ohlin Trade Theory with a Continuum of Goods', *Quarterly Journal of Economics*, vol. 95, pp. 203–24.

EATON, J. and KIERZKOWSKI, H. (1984) 'Oligopolistic Competition Product Variety and International Trade', in H. Kierzkowski (ed.), *Monopolistic Competition and International Trade* (Oxford: Oxford University Press), pp. 69–83.

FALVEY, R. E. (1981) 'Commercial Policy and Intra-Industry Trade', *Journal of International Economics*, vol. 11, pp. 495–511.

FINGER, J. M. (1975) 'Trade Overlap and Intra-Industry Trade', *Economic Inquiry*, vol. XIII, no 4, pp. 581–9.

GABSZEWICZ, J.; SHAKED, A.; SUTTON, J. and THISSE, J. F. (1981) 'International Trade in Differentiated Products', *International Economic Review*, vol. 22, pp. 527–35.

GREENAWAY, D. and MILNER, C. R. (1986) *The Economics of Intra-Industry Trade* (Oxford: Basil Blackwell).

GRUBEL, H. G. and LLOYD, P. J. (1975) *Intra-Industry Trade: The Theory and Measurement of International Trade in Differentiated Products* (London: Macmillan).

HELPMAN, E. (1981) 'International Trade in the Presence of Product Differentiation, Economies of Scale and Monopolistic Competition', *Journal of International Economics*, vol. 11, pp. 305–40.

HELPMAN, E. and KRUGMAN, P. R. (1985) *Market Structure and Foreign Trade: Increasing Returns, Imperfect Competition and the International Economy* (Brighton: Wheatsheaf, and Cambridge, Mass: MIT Press).

HOTELLING, H. (1929) 'Stability in Competition', *Economic Journal*, vol. 34, pp. 41–57.

JONES, R. W. (1956) 'Factor Proportions and the Heckscher–Ohlin Theorem', *Review of Economic Studies*, vol. 24, pp. 1–10.

KEMP, M. C. (1976) *Three Topics in the Theory of International Trade: Distribution, Welfare and Uncertainty* (Amsterdam: North Holland).

KRUGMAN, P. (1979) 'Increasing Returns, Monopolistic Competition and International Trade', *Journal of International Economics*, vol. 9, pp. 469–79.

LANCASTER, K. (1979) *Variety, Equity and Efficiency* (Oxford: Basil Blackwell, and New York: Columbia University Press).

LANCASTER, K. (1980) 'Intra-Industry Trade under Perfect Monopolistic Competition', *Journal of International Economics*, vol. 10, pp. 151–75.

LANCASTER, K. (1984) 'Protection and Product Differentiation', in H. Kierzkowski (ed.), *Monopolistic Competition and International Trade* (Oxford: Oxford University Press), pp. 137–56.

LINDER, S. B. (1961) *An Essay on Trade and Transformation* (New York: John Wiley).

LIPSEY, R. E. (1976) 'Review of Grubel, H. G. and Lloyd, P. J., 'Intra-Industry Trade (1975)'', *Journal of International Economics*, vol. 6, pp. 312–14.

LLOYD, P. J. (1979) 'Intra-Industry Trade, Lowering Trade Barriers and Gains from Trade', in H. Giersch (ed.) (1979) pp. 19–41.

RAYMENT, P. B. W. (1976) 'The Homogeneity of Manufacturing Industries with Respect to Factor Intensity: the Case of the UK', *Oxford Bulletin of Economics and Statistics*, vol. 38, pp. 203–9.

RAYMENT, P. B. W. (1983) 'Intra-"Industry" Specialization and the Foreign Trade of Industrial Countries', in S. F. Frowen (ed.), *Controlling Industrial Economics: Essays in Honour of C. T. Saunders* (London: Macmillan), pp. 1–28.

SHAKED, A. and SUTTON, J. (1984) 'Natural Oligopolies and International Trade', in H. Kierzkowski (ed.), *Monopolistic Competition and International Trade* (Oxford: Oxford University Press), pp. 34–50.

542-56

(94)

F19

[26]

Review of International Economics 2(2), 97–111, 1994

Aggregation by Industry
in High-Dimensional Models*

D24

D58

Peter J. Lloyd

The University of Melbourne, Parkville, Victoria 3052, Australia

Abstract

Models of trading economies have become very large in dimensions and complex in structure. Conditions which are sufficient for aggregation in production and/or consumption are derived. They require the existence of linearly homogeneous indices of production and/or consumption in the industries or sufficient similarity among agents. These methods are applied to the Armington model and to a group of models in which the commodities in an industry are defined on a continuum. The results are applied to the method of constructing general-equilibrium models with many commodities, tests of comparative advantage, and the measurement of effective protection in multicommodity industries.

1. Introduction

Beginning with the pioneering paper of Krugman (1979), a number of models which feature industries with multicommodity production and consumption and intra-industry trade between countries have now been constructed. The introduction of more detail has increased the realism of trade models, but it has produced models which are large in dimensions and complex in structure. The main properties of trade models are not robust with respect to dimensions. For example, in models with international trade, the most basic feature is the explanation of the pattern of trade. When the dimensions of the model are extended beyond two commodities and two factors, the Heckscher-Ohlin theorem ceases to hold generally when either the physical or the factor-price definition of factor abundance are used.[1] This paper seeks to derive properties of such models by means of an explicit process of aggregation of commodity groups within well-defined industries.

The basic question this paper pursues is whether and under what conditions it is possible in high-dimensional models to aggregate the production and/or consumption of the groups of commodities in industries. The most extreme form of aggregation is the aggregation of the same commodities simultaneously, using the same aggregator functions, on both the production and consumption sides of the model. This may be called "complete aggregation," as it applies to all parts of the model. If this can be done one can reduce the commodity dimensions of a model drastically, perhaps to two or a few. In such cases, one can reverse the traditional procedure and regard such an industry as producing a single "commodity." As this form involves the same groupings on both the demand and supply sides, it is unlikely to occur.

In other cases it may be possible to aggregate commodities only on the production side or the consumption side. If meaningful aggregation is possible on the production side, this may suffice to resurrect those properties which involve only production. These include many of the main propositions of trade theory, such as the Stolper-

---

* I would like to acknowledge helpful comments from Eric Bond, Avinash Dixit, Jurgen Eichberger, Dominique van der Mensbrugghe, Ian McDonald and a referee. Some of the work was done while the author was working at the OECD Development Centre in Paris.

Samuelson theorem, univalence, and the factor-price equalization theorem. This form of aggregation is quite reasonable for some industries.

The first model of international trade in which explicit aggregation is made is that of Armington (1969). On the demand side, Armington assumed that there is only one consumer in each country whose utility function allows commodities to be nested into groups called "industries." This permits aggregation in demand.

Many large-dimensional models have used a continuum in some way to represent the many commodities produced by an "industry." The first model of multicommodity production in industries and international trade which featured a continuum of commodities was that of Lancaster (1980, 1984). He wished to model diversity of tastes among consumers with respect to commodities within a group. Lancaster (1980, p. 153) identified the group with the "manufacturing sector": "A 'group' . . . is a product class in which all products, actual and potential, possess the same characteristics, different products within the group being defined as products having these characteristics in different proportions." There are assumed to be only two relevant characteristics for the commodities in the group. The characteristics specification of commodities can then be defined in terms of one variable, the ratios of these two characteristics embodied in them. All specifications lie on a one-dimensional spectrum which is assumed to be continuous, that is, a continuum. Lancaster's model also introduces economies of scale within the continuum industry. This model was extended by Helpman (1981) and Helpman and Krugman (1985). It is an illustration of the growing family of models with imperfect competition.

Falvey (1981) constructed a continuum of commodities in a quite different way.[2] An industry, called "manufacturing," can produce an infinite number of commodities, using a fixed stock of industry-specific capital and homogeneous labor. Falvey (1981, p. 496) defined the industry in terms of supply characteristics: "For the purpose of this paper, an industry is best defined by the range of products a certain type of capital equipment can produce." The products are differentiated by quality. There is assumed to be a continuum of commodities defined over an interval of the real line. The capital intensity of the production process increases with the quality of output for all factor price ratios.

Dixit and Grossman (1982) also base their continuum on supply relationships and define their "manufacturing sector" in terms of commodities that use sector-specific capital. In contrast to Falvey, they consider that the final product of the manufacturing sector goes through a succession of stages, each adding value to an intermediate product to yield goods-in-process ready for the next stage. They allow a continuum of stages on the closed interval [0, 1] of the real line with the raw material indexed by 0 and the single final product indexed by 1. All stages in the half-open interval [0, 1) produce pure intermediates. This model captures the main feature of globalization of production.

Thus we have, in this sample, models in which the continuum is defined in terms of the variety of a pure consumer good, the quality of a pure consumer good, and the stage of a pure intermediate good. The continuity of the commodity index makes the analysis of the number of commodities produced easier than a discrete model with a large finite number of commodities. These continuum models will be used to illustrate aggregation in general equilibrium models, though the methods can be applied to models with a large finite number of commodities.

In section 2 the aggregation is presented formally and conditions sufficient for consistent aggregation are derived. One example of demand side aggregation and two examples of complete aggregation are given in section 3. The Lancaster-

Helpman model with increasing returns violates the linear homogeneity condition used in the other models. It turns out that the Heckscher-Ohlin and other theorems relating to production still hold in the Lancaster-Helpman model, as Helpman (1981, propositions 2 and 3) observed, because of the large amount of symmetry. We can regard all of these results as an application of consistent aggregation. The Falvey model is an example of a model in which consistent aggregation is not possible. Section 4 discusses three applications of aggregation by industry. These applications are to the methods of constructing general equilibrium models with many commodities and with empirical tests of comparative advantage, and to the measurement of the average effective rate of protection for multicommodity industries.

2. Sufficient conditions for Aggregation

Formally, one needs to define a function which aggregates the commodities in a model and to show that this process of aggregation is consistent. Consistency is the property that the aggregation produces the same value of all unaggregated variables as the original model, and that the sums of the unaggregated variables are equal to the appropriately defined aggregated variables. This aggregation procedure is used in other areas of economic theory; for example, the aggregation of commodities in a separable subfunction of the utility function of a household, and the construction of value-added functions in the theory of production. Before the discussion in section 4 trade is assumed to be free.

Aggregation in Consumption

Aggregation in demand is a direct application of the aggregation procedures in the theory of the consumer. Let the utility function of a consumer agent be homogeneously separable. A function, $U(x)$, is homogeneously separable if it is weakly separable, viz.,

$$U(x) = V[v^1(\bar{x}_1), \ldots, v^j(\bar{x}_j), \ldots, v^m(\bar{x}_m)], \tag{1}$$

where $\bar{x}_j$ is the commodity group and the subfunctions, $v^j(\bar{x}_j)$, are linearly homogeneous. If there is a finite number of commodities, $\bar{x}_j = (x_{j1}, \ldots, x_{jk}, \ldots, x_{jnj})$ for $j = 1$, $m < n$, and $\Sigma_{j=1}^m n_j = n$. This is a general form of separability in which there are m groups of the n elementary commodities.

The functions $v^j(\bar{x}_j)$ may be regarded as quantity indices for the groups. Because of the property of linear homogeneity, each of these functions has a dual price index,

$$p^j = \phi^j(\bar{p}_j), \quad \bar{p}_j = (p_{j1}, \ldots, p_{jk}, \ldots, p_{jnj}), \tag{2}$$

which minimizes the cost of a unit of the quantity, v^j, and is a function of group prices only. It is well known that, under these conditions, the consumer can treat these groups as consistent aggregates and maximize utility in two stages (Blackorby, Primont, and Russell, 1977).

In a general-equilibrium model with many consumers, we must also assume that all consumers in one country have identical preferences. Otherwise, each consumer would have a different set of quantity- and price-aggregator functions, and there would not be a unique set of national prices for the groups in the competitive equilibrium. Under these assumptions of identical homogeneously separable utility functions, there exist quantity and price indices for each commodity group in each country. Utility maximization in each country may be regarded as a consistent two-stage process.

There are other possible methods of aggregation in consumption, such as the Hicks assumption of price proportionality or the Leontief assumption of quantity proportionality.

Aggregation in Production

Aggregation on the supply side is possible under similar conditions. Suppose the technology for each commodity is nonjoint and can be represented by a linearly homogeneous production function

$$g_i = f^i(v_i, \hat{g}_i), \quad \forall i, \tag{3}$$

where $v_i = (v_{i1}, \ldots, v_{is})$ and $\hat{g}_i$ are the vectors of primary and intermediate inputs respectively which are used in the production of commodity i. The primary inputs may be mobile or specific. With intermediate input usage, g_i is the gross output of commodity i. The net output of this commodity is

$$y_i = g_i - \sum_{i=1}^{n} a_{ij} g_j, \tag{4}$$

where a_{ij} is the intermediate input requirement of input i into output j.

This model is sufficiently general to encompass the particular multiple-output industry models of Dixit and Grossman and of Falvey which are considered in the next section, but not the Lancaster–Helpman model with increasing returns to scale. Even when there is a continuum of commodities, finitely many may be produced, as in the Falvey model. In the Dixit–Grossman model, infinitely many are produced in each country, but each of the continuum commodities which is produced is used as an input in only one other commodity.

The competitive-equilibrium conditions for the production sector are given by

$$p_i - c^i(w, p) \leq 0,$$

$$[p_i - c^i(w, p)]g_i = 0, \quad \forall i; \quad \text{and}$$

$$g_i \geq 0, \tag{5}$$

$$\sum_{i=1}^{n} a_{ji}(w, p)g_i - v_j \leq 0,$$

$$\left[\sum_{i=1}^{n} a_{ji}(w, p)g_i - v_j \right] w_j = 0, \quad \forall j.$$

$$w_j \geq 0.$$

The term $c^i(w, p)$ is the unit cost function for commodity i, which is the dual to the production function, $f^i(v_i, \hat{g}_i)$. The variable $w = (w_1, \ldots, w_s)$ is the vector of market prices of the primary inputs, and $p = (p_1, \ldots, p_n)$ is the vector of prices of produced outputs, which is taken as given. The first set of equations and inequalities are the familiar zero-profit conditions. The second set of equations and inequalities are the factor-market equilibrium conditions.

The joint solution to these sets of equations yields $w = w(p, v)$ and $g = g(p, v)$. In most low-dimensional models it is assumed that the competitive equilibrium is such that all gross outputs and factor prices are strictly positive, thereby reducing the system to two sets of equations. This is the case with the models below at the aggregated level, although there is specialization at the disaggregated level.

There is one condition which is sufficient for consistent aggregation on the supply side and analogous to the previous condition on the demand side. This condition is that, for a group of commodities, group k, there exists a linearly homogeneous production function,

$$q_k = H^k(v_k), \quad v_k = (v_{k1}, \ldots, v_{ks}), \tag{6}$$

where

$$q_k = J^k(\bar{y}_k) \tag{7}$$

defines the index of the output of the group as an aggregate of the outputs of the commodities in the group, $\bar{y}_k$, and is itself linearly homogeneous. The industry inputs are merely the sum of the inputs used in the production of the commodities in the industry. Thus J^k is the aggregator function which defines units of the output of the group, and H^k is the aggregate production function which maps from input space to output space. This form of aggregation is possible only if the marginal rates of transformation between outputs are independent of the factor proportions. This condition is satisfied if the factor proportions are identical (which requires identical technologies), or if the factors are combined in strictly fixed proportions for all output levels.[3] A group of commodities which has such functions will be called "industry" k. There is a finite number M of such groups.

PROPOSITION 1. *Commodities may be aggregated into groups which yield values that are consistent with those in the unaggregated competitive equilibrium if there exists a set of industries each of which has a linearly homogeneous output aggregator function and a linearly homogeneous aggregate production function that represents the technology of the group.*

Proof (Sketch). One chooses J^k as the index of the quantity produced of the group. This quantity has a dual cost function:

$$\begin{aligned} C^k(w, p, q_k) &= \min v_k\{wv_k : H^k(v_k) \geq q_k\} \\ &= c^k(w, p)q_k, \end{aligned} \tag{8}$$

where $c^k(w, p)$ is the unit-cost function. The variable c^k is itself linearly homogeneous in (w, p). The zero-profit condition implies that there is a price for the industry's output, q_k, assuming the output is produced. Moreover, this price is equal to the unit-cost index for the group. The production conditions for the competitive equilibrium are defined in terms of these aggregate quantity and price variables. The linear homogeneity of the indices of quantity and price ensures that the consistency requirement is satisfied. This can be verified by showing that the aggregated version of the competitive equilibrium yields the same values of the sums of the values for the elementary commodities.

Complete Aggregation

The third type of aggregation is complete aggregation. This is an aggregation which applies to the same group of commodities everywhere in the model, that is, to both the production and consumption relationships and to all countries. One may identify the group *j* of the consumer problem with the group *k* of the producer problem above.

The central requirement is that the utility *and* production functions for the industries be homogeneously separable. In this event the industry is a device which allows us to view the world economy at two levels, the industry level and the commodity or intra-industry level. At the top level the dimensions have been reduced from the number of elementary commodities to the number of aggregated commodities. These requirements are very strict and unlikely to occur.

3. Examples of Aggregation

Example 1: The Armington Model

On the demand side Armington assumed that in each country there is one consumer whose utility function is homogeneously separable, precisely as in equation (1) above. For each group there is a group aggregator function, $v^j(\bar{x}_j)$. Each of these quantity indices has a dual price index, $p^j = \phi^j(p_{j1}, \ldots, p, \ldots, p_{jnj})$, which minimizes the cost of producing a unit of the quantity, v^j. This price index is itself linearly homogeneous. Moreover, $p^j v^j = \bar{p}_j \bar{x}_j$, that is, expenditure on the aggregated product equals the sum of the expenditures on the commodities in the group. Utility maximization is a two-stage process, and one may examine the demand at the top level, which greatly simplifies the demand functions.

Armington (1969) did not specify the supply side of the model. Subsequent general-equilibrium models with the Armington demand assumption have usually assumed that each country produces only one product in each group and have followed the Heckscher–Ohlin model in having two mobile primary factors of production. The Armington demand assumption can, however, be combined with any set of assumptions on supply which may or not permit aggregation in production. The following models consider aggregation in production.

Example 2: The Dixit and Grossman Model

In the continuum industry, let *z* index the stage (= commodity). (To emphasize the comparability of results from these models, the symbol *z* is used throughout to denote a commodity on a continuum.) The intermediate good at stage $z + dz$ is produced using one unit of stage *z* output. There is a dual unit-cost function $c(w, r, z)dz$ for each commodity, *z*, where *w* and *r* are the price of the factors labor and capital respectively. The strong Samuelson factor-intensity assumption is made for each commodity with respect to all other commodities. With the further assumption that there are identical technologies in the two countries, the commodities on the continuum can be ordered by decreasing capital intensity, with the most capital-intensive on the extreme left. Factor prices are not equalized because of the presence of specific factors.

A commodity *z* on the continuum will be produced in the home country if the condition

$$c(w, r, z) \leqslant c(w^*, r^*, z) \tag{9}$$

is satisfied. The asterisks indicate variables which are those of the foreign country. The price of commodity *z* in the home country relative to that in the foreign country is a continuously increasing (decreasing) function of z, depending on whether $(w/r) > (<) (w^*/r^*)$. For a given competitive equilibrium, there will be a single commodity, $\bar{z}$, for which the unit costs are equal across the two countries:

$$c(w, r, \bar{z}) = c(w^*, r^*, \bar{z}). \tag{10}$$

This is the borderline commodity. The borderline commodity falls within the continuum industry.[4] It partitions the continuum.

Assume that the home country is abundant in the capital used in the continuum industry, in the sense of having the higher wage rate/capital rental ratio. The subset $[0, \bar{z})$ is produced and exported by the home country, which is more capital-abundant, and the subset $(\bar{z}, 1]$ is produced and exported by the other country. The borderline commodity may be produced in one or both countries, depending on the demand. All of the commodities on the continuum will be produced and each country produces infinitely many commodities on a subset of the continuum. The exchange of manufactured products is intra-industry trade, and there is inter-industry trade with one country exporting the other commodity, agriculture.

Before aggregation, one can regard the commodities produced on the lower end of the continuum by the home country and those produced on the upper end of the continuum by the foreign country as vertically integrated commodities. These commodities and the outside commodity are denoted commodities 1, 2, and 3 respectively. In this model it is useful to write out the production conditions for the competitive equilibrium as given by equation (5) above. These are:

Home Country	Foreign Country

$$c_1(w, r, \bar{z}) = \int_0^{\bar{z}} c(w, r, z)\,dz = p_1, \quad c_2(w^*, r^*, \bar{z}) = \int_{\bar{z}}^1 c(w^*, r^*, z)\,dz = p_2,$$

$$c_3(w, v) = p_3, \qquad\qquad\qquad c_3(w^*, v^*) = p_3,$$

$$c_{1w}(w, r, \bar{z})y_1 + c_{3w}(w, v, \bar{z})y_3 = L, \qquad c_{2w^*}(w^*, r^*)y_2^* + c_{3w^*}(w^*, v^*)y_3^* = L^*,$$

$$c_{1r}(w, r)y_1 = K, \qquad\qquad c_{2r^*}(w^*, r^*)y_2^* = K^*,$$

$$c_{3v}(w, v)y_3 = V, \qquad\qquad c_{3v^*}(w^*, v^*)y_3^* = V^*, \tag{11}$$

plus equation (10). The input–output relation $y_1 = y_2^*$ holds, and the condition that the price of the final commodity which is the end-product of the continuum is given by

$$\int_0^{\bar{z}} c(w, r, z)\,dz + \int_{\bar{z}}^1 c(w^*, r^*, z)\,dz = p_1 + p_2. \tag{12}$$

The variables c_{iw}, c_{ir}, and c_{3v} are the requirements of the inputs of labor, capital, and land per unit of output of the appropriate industry, and v is the price of a unit of land. For one country, the first three equations in (10) are the standard cost-minimizing conditions and the next three are the full employment conditions. The remaining three equation applies across the two countries.

When the commodity prices are known from the equilibrium, we can define $p_1/(p_1 + p_2) = \alpha$ and $p_2/(p_1 + p_2) = \beta$, which are the proportions of the cost of producing the final product of the continuum industry in the foreign and the home countries respectively. Using α and β as price weights, we can now aggregate commodities 1 and 2 to form the manufacturing industry.

Denote the continuum industry as industry I, and relabel the outside industry as industry II. Now $p_I = p_1 + p_2$. The output of the industry, y_I, is the output of the end product of the continuum which, by assumption, uses an input of each prior stage of production in fixed proportions. These quantity indices are linearly homogeneous in their quantity arguments, which include the inputs from both countries because all stages of production are involved. The unit cost of production is $c_I = \int_0^{\bar{z}} c(w, r, z)\,dz + \int_{\bar{z}}^1 c(w^*, r^*, z)\,dz = c_I(w, r, w^*, r^*)$. This is the dual of the production function of the industry and it is linearly homogeneous. Consistent aggregation of the set of commodities produced on the continuum requires that $p_1 y_1 = p_1 y_1$ in the home country and $p_1 y_1^* = p_2 y_2^*$ in the foreign country. To satisfy these equalities, the aggregate quantity of the outputs of the industry I in the home country and the foreign country are defined as $y_I = \alpha y_1$ and $y_I^* = \beta y_2^*$. That is, each country is considered to produce a part of the final output, y_I, in proportion to the share of the value added in industry I.

The production conditions for competitive equilibrium in terms of the two industries are now given by:

$$
\begin{array}{cc}
\textit{Home Country} & \textit{Foreign Country} \\[4pt]
c_I(w, r, w^*, r^*) = p_I, & c_I(w, r, w^*, r^*) = p_I, \\[4pt]
c_{II}(w, v) = p_{II}, & c_{II}(w^*, v^*) = p_{II}, \\[4pt]
\begin{aligned} c_{Iw}(w, r, w^*, r^*)y_I \\ + c_{IIw}(w, v)y_{II} = L, \end{aligned} & \begin{aligned} c_{Iw^*}(w, r, w^*, r^*)y_I^* \\ + c_{IIw^*}(w^*, v^*)y_{II}^* = L^*, \end{aligned} \\[10pt]
c_{Ir}(w, r, w^*, r^*)y_I = K, & c_{Ir^*}(w, r, w^*, r^*)y_I^* = K^*, \\[4pt]
c_{IIv}(w, v)y_{II} = V, & c_{IIv^*}(w^*, v^*)y_{II}^* = V^*.
\end{array} \tag{13}
$$

The aggregation on the supply side enables us to treat the production conditions in all respects as if only two commodities are produced.

On the demand side the aggregation is simpler because only one final product is produced by the vertically integrated industry. Hence, $x_I = x_2$ and $x_I^* = x_2^*$. The quantities consumed enter the utility function of all agents as a single argument, viz., $U^h = U^h(x_I, x_{II})$ for all h. The final output of industry I is a single consumable commodity. It is not necessary in this model to assume all agents have identical utility functions within or across countries.

The aggregate value of the net imports of the continuum industry are now, in the home country,

$$
\begin{aligned}
M_1 + M_2 &= -y_1 p_1 + x_2(p_1 + p_2) = -\alpha y_1 p_1 + x_2 p_1 \\
&= [(x_2) - (\alpha y_1)]p_1 = (x_I - y_I)p_I = m_I p_I = M_I;
\end{aligned} \tag{14}
$$

and, in the foreign country,

$$
\begin{aligned}
M_1^* + M_2^* &= y_2 p_1 + (x_2^* - y_2^*)(p_1 + p_2) = \alpha y_2 p_1 + (x_2^* - y_2^*)p_1 \\
&= [(x_2^*) - (\beta y_2^*)]p_1 = (x_I^* - y_I^*)p_1 = m_I^* p_I = M_I^* \\
&= -M_I \neq 0,
\end{aligned} \tag{15}
$$

where the variables x and y denote consumption/use and production of the commodities respectively. Equations (14) and (15) state that the value of net imports and exports of industry I in the two countries, defined as the sums of the imports and exports of the components and final products of the industry are equal to the value of the net imports and exports of the aggregated commodities. That is, this aggregation of the quantities traded is consistent. These results use the equalities $y_1 = y_2^*$, which follows from the fact that the production of one unit of commodity 1 requires one unit of commodity 2 because of the fixed assumption in the continuum industry, and $x_2 + x_2^* = y_2$.

This consistent aggregation is possible because of the assumptions of constant returns to scale and fixed proportions of all stages in the production of the continuum commodity. These enable us to use the quantity of the final output as the quantity index.

Example 3: The Falvey Model

In the Falvey model there are also two industries, the continuum industry and the outside industry. The Falvey model produces a pattern of production and industry trade similar to that of the Dixit–Grossman model when the Falvey model is extended to a full general-equilibrium model. Again there is a borderline commodity, partial specialization, and intra-industry and inter-industry trade. However, the explanation of the intra-industry trade is quite different. In this model the commodities on the continuum below the borderline commodity which are produced and exported by the relatively capital-abundant home country are the higher qualities of the final consumer good.[5] Some qualities will not be demanded and will not be produced in either country.

To aggregate these commodities, one must be able to form an index of the aggregate output of the industry and a production function for the industry. The quality of a product, a, is measured on a continuum. The ranking on the continuum is common to both countries, as they are assumed to have the same technology. One can, therefore, measure the quantities produced by the industry in terms of one product, say, the maximum-quality product. Let the continuum be $[0, 1]$, as in the Dixit–Grossman model, and the quality of the ith product be a_i. Then the aggregate output of the continuum industry is $y_I = \Sigma_i a_i y_i$. Falvey (1980, p. 498) defined the technology of production such that "units are chosen so that production of a unit of quality a requires the services of a units of this industry's capital stock, and one unit of its (hired) labor force." That is, each product has a different production function. One cannot, under these assumptions, obtain an aggregate production function for the industry, since a given set of inputs (K, L) will produce a different aggregate output for each distribution of the outputs among the different products. There is no reason to restrict this distribution, which will be determined by the competitive equilibrium.

Example 4: The Lancaster–Helpman Model

International trade in the Lancaster model takes place between identical economies. Lancaster (1979, p. 25) imposed the conditions that all consumers have identical preferences except for their most-preferred product, and that the utility function is separable in the continuum group. With such a complex model structure, almost any of the possible patterns of production and intra-industry and inter-industry trade is permissible. In the continuum group, each of the two identical countries will produce exactly half the number of these goods produced in the world economy and export one-half of its output. However, the composition of a country's production and exports and imports is indeterminate, because there are no differences in factor endowments or technologies to give rise to cost differences.

The Lancaster and Helpman models do not enable aggregation in the same way, because the commodity production functions are not linearly homogeneous. Nevertheless, Lancaster (1980, p. 171) postulated that the *inter*-industry pattern of trade would follow Heckscher–Ohlin lines. There are two homogeneous factors, labor and capital, in the neoclassical version of the Lancaster model. "If country 1 is relatively capital-abundant in its endowments, the trade equilibrium will be such that country 1 produces a higher ratio of manufacturing output to agriculture than does country 2. If the countries are similar enough in other respects to give approximately the same ratio of manufactures to agriculture in consumption, country 1 will be a net exporter of manufactured goods and a net importer of agricultural products." This is the Heckscher–Ohlin theorem in the stronger form of physical abundance in a standard 2 × 2 Heckscher–Ohlin model.

Helpman (1981) provided the proof of the Lancaster proposition. He modified the Lancaster model by locating the most-preferred product of each consumer on a circle instead of a line. He assumed that consumers in each country have identical incomes, and that there is a continuum of consumers distributed uniformly over the circle in terms of their most-preferred product. On the supply side the production of all varieties in both countries have the same technology but countries may differ in factor endowments. Under these assumptions the equilibrium in the continuum industry is a symmetric Nash equilibrium. The finite number of commodities produced are spaced at equal distances on the continuum, produced in the same quantities by a single producer, and sold for the same price.

The continuum industry and the outside industry can be denoted by I and II again. Let n and n^* denote the number of commodities produced by the continuum industry in the home country and the foreign country. The aggregate outputs of the continuum industry are $y_I = yn$ and $y_I^* = y^*n^*$, where y and y^* are the outputs of the individual commodities in the industry which are indistinguishable in terms of production. The price of these outputs is $p_I = p$, where p is the common price of the individual commodities. The production conditions are given by:

Home Country	*Foreign Country*
$C_I(w, r, y_I) = p_I y_I,$	$C_I(w, r, y_I^*) = p_I y_I^*,$
$c_{II}(w, r) = p_{II},$	$c_{II}(w, r) = p_{II},$
$R(p_I, p_{II}, n) = q(w, r, y_I),$	$R^*(p_I, p_{II}, n^*) = q(w, r, y_I^*),$
$C_{Iw}(w, r, y_I)n + c_{IIw}(w, r)y_{II} = L,$	$C_{Iw}(w, r, y_I^*)n^* + c_{IIw}(w, r)y_{II}^* = L^*,$
$C_{Ir}(w, r, y_I)n + c_{IIr}(w, r)y_{II} = K,$	$C_{Ir}(w, r, y_I^*)n^* + c_{IIr}(w, r)y_{II}^* = K^*.$ (16)

These equations can be compared with those of the Dixit–Grossman competitive equilibrium before aggregation in equations (13). As in equations (13), these equations separate into two subsets of equations, the first three describing the zero-profit conditions and the last two describing the full employment in the factor markets. In the zero-profit conditions there is an extra pair of equations to determine the number of commodities produced in the manufacturing sectors. These equations state that the Lerner degree of monopoly in the continuum industry, R, is equal to the degree of elasticity of the cost function, q, which is a measure of the degree of economies of scale. This is a feature of the equilibrium. In the full-employment conditions, the factor prices are equal across countries because of factor-price equalization in the model. It then follows, from the properties of factor price equalization and the output levels of all firms being the same, that the country with the higher capital-labor ratio produces more manufacturing varieties and less food per capita than the other. Finally, given identical preferences across countries, and assuming manufacturing products are relatively capital-intensive, the country which has the higher capital-labor ratio is the *net* exporter of manufactures and the *net* importer of food, though both countries export and import manufacturing varieties. Helpman (1980, p. 324) concluded that "we use Heckscher–Ohlin to explain inter-sectoral trade while intra-industry trade is explained by the existence of economies of scale and differentiated products."

On the demand side, the aggregate demand for the industry output is $x_I = xL$ and $x_I^* = x^*L$ in the two countries. The variables x and x^* denote the demands for each variety, which are identical. The aggregate value of the net imports of the continuum industry are, in the home country,

$$xLp - ynp = (x_I - y_I)p = m_1p_1 = M_I; \tag{17}$$

and, in the foreign country,

$$xL^*p - yn^*p = (x_I^* - y_I^*)p = m_1p_1 = M_I. \tag{18}$$

Thus, in this model, as in the Dixit–Grossman model, the aggregation of commodities is consistent.

An industry in this model is like a perfectly competitive industry. There are many producers, each of whom is indistinguishable from the others. As they have the same commodity-production function for a commodity, this function can be used as the industry-production function. Similarly, consumers have the same utility functions except for the choice of the most-preferred product and the same incomes. The resulting symmetrical solution allows aggregation in both production and consumption, and it is enough to show that the properties of univalence and factor-price equalization, provided the production functions are homothetic, and the Rybczynski theorem (and, by the reciprocity relation, the Stolper–Samuelson theorem) also holds. This result follows from the identity of the output levels of all firms and, unlike the Heckscher–Ohlin model, does not require an assumption about the cone of diversification. Unfortunately, these results will not continue to hold when the symmetry is relaxed because of non-homothetic technologies or differences among consumers. In the former case production in the model is still given by equation (16), but the output levels of firms will differ, depending upon the demand and technologies.

The methods of aggregation in the Dixit–Grossman and the Lancaster–Helpman models parallel those in consumer theory. It is well known that demand functions can be aggregated across households if the consumer goods are consumed in fixed proportions or the consumers have identical homothetic preferences or, as an alternative, if the consumers are identical in all respects (preferences and incomes). The analysis of the Dixit–Grossman model has followed the first method and that of Lancaster–Helpman the second. In the Lancaster–Helpman model the assumption of identity in all respects is relaxed to allow differences in respect of the most-preferred product. Aggregation is still permissible.

4. Applications

When consistent aggregation is possible, these aggregation results have a number of applications. First, the aggregation may help greatly in understanding the nature of the competitive equilibrium and its comparative static properties. For example, Dixit and Grossman do not consider the inter-industry trade in their models. Nor do they consider the qualitative properties of the model such as the effect of changes in commodity prices on the real incomes of factors. Having aggregated the variables in the commodity group and thereby reduced the commodity dimensions of the model, one may now use the much lower dimensional version of the model with the aggregated commodities to derive some propositions.

The production conditions of the aggregated version of the Dixit–Grossman model in equation (13) resemble those of the standard Jones specific-factor model of the minimum dimensions, that is, there are two "commodities" and three factors. The only difference is that the unit cost of the output of the continuum industry depends in each country on the factor prices in both countries, because these determine the location of the borderline commodity. This linkage across countries produces an element which is not present in the Jones model. Once the borderline is located, the pattern of trade in the two products will follow the pattern in the three-factor two-commodity Jones specific-factor model. Each country will specialize incompletely in one of the two industries. Other properties follow.

For example, consider the pattern of the sign change of real incomes when the (aggregated) commodity prices change. We know the sign pattern for the Jones model (Ruffin and Jones, 1974): if the price of one commodity rises, the real income of the specific factor used in the production of this commodity must rise and the real income of the specific factor used in the production of the other commodity must fall, and the sign of the change of real income of the mobile factor is ambiguous. In the Dixit–Grossman model, there are, from equation (13), six equations which determine the six factor prices, as in the Jones model, but they do not separate into two country subsystems because of the countries' interdependence. The sign pattern of the Jones model for one country is not altered by the presence of an extensive margin within the aggregated commodity if one holds constant the factor prices in the other country. However, the changes in factor prices in the two countries will cause the extensive margin to shift and consequently the outputs of the two industries will change. It is possible now for the real income of the specific factor used in the production of the commodity whose price has increased to fall and that of the other specific factor to rise in one country but not in both countries. By the reciprocity relation, an extension of the Rybczynski theorem holds. These propositions are not evident from the higher-dimensional unaggregated version of the model with infinitely many commodities.

The second application of the aggregations is to the methods of constructing applied general-equilibrium models, extensions of the Heckscher–Ohlin type model. All the multicommodity trade models above have been constructed by taking the Heckscher–Ohlin or Jones specific-factor model of the world economy with two commodities and then disaggregating one of the two industries into a horizontal or vertical group or continuum. Plainly one could use the same device in a Heckscher–Ohlin or Jones model of any dimensions. One simply takes a set of industries and disaggregates each horizontally or vertically. Moreover, the method of disaggregation can and should vary among the industries. Some industries are obviously of the sequential Dixit and Grossman type, some involve instead jointness in production, and some have differentiated consumer products.[6]

This two-level view of the high-dimensional models leads to the construction of theoretically sound empirical tests of comparative advantage when there is intra-industry trade. For the explanation of inter-industry trade, the appropriate dependent variable in all the models is the net or inter-industry trade flows, because exports and imports of the aggregate industry are defined as the net industry flows (see, for example, equations [14] and [15] or [17] and [18]). Many early and recent studies of comparative advantage have intuitively used net trade flows, but until now the justification for this choice has been absent. For the intra-industry trade the appropriate dependent variable is the Grubel-Lloyd index of intra-industry trade.

The explanatory variables for intra-industry trade will generally vary among industries. In the Dixit and Grossman model, factor proportions determine the patterns of inter-industry and intra-industry trade. This is also true of other models involving jointness due to a common industry input. However, in the models with increasing returns to scale and imperfect competition, factor proportions cannot explain intra-industry trade precisely because all of the products of the industry are produced in a competitive equilibrium with identical factor proportions. Instead, the aggregate country size determines intra-industry trade in the model. Even in this model, however, the absolute and relative amounts of intra-industry trade still depend on factor proportions. The more similar the endowment ratios of the countries and the smaller the size of the capital-abundant country, the larger the share of intra-industry trade in total trade; see Helpman (1980, Proposition 4), and Helpman and Krugman (1985, ch. 8). Thus factor proportions and other variables must be used simultaneously in all models to test the determinants of inter- and intra-industry comparative advantage. In a general-equilibrium model neither inter-industry nor intra-industry trade is independent of the other.

Finally, the indices of prices and quantities may themselves be useful. For example, international economists frequently measure the effective rates of assistance going to different industries by a procedure which is equivalent to taking some arbitrary average of the effective rates of assistance given to the individual commodities in the industry group. Typically these measures are weighted by the value-added shares in the industry. These weights should properly be derived from a model of the industry. In the models above, the aggregate industry price index provides immediately the correct measure of the percentage change in the value added due to assistance measures for the industry. The effective assistance to the industry is correctly measured as the increase in the value added per unit of the industry output, treating this output as a single (aggregated) commodity, that is, $E = (p_1^d - p_1^f)/p_1^f$, where p_1^d and p_1^f are the distorted and free trade prices respectively.

The Dixit–Grossman model is especially instructive in this context as it is designed to capture complex intra-industry input-output relations. Dixit and Grossman (1982) noted that a uniform tariff is unambiguously protective in terms of increasing the range of products produced in the tariff-imposing country, but it may be antiprotective in terms of the aggregate labor employed and value added in the protected industry. We can obtain further results using the aggregate price measures. In this model p_1 measures the value added in the country per unit of output. Consider the capital-abundant home country. Let t be the uniform tariff imposed by this country. The measure of effective assistance to the industry is

$$E = \left\{ \int_0^{z_1} c(w^d, r^d, z)\, dz - \int_0^z c(w^f, r^f, z)\, dz \right\} \Big/ \int_0^z c(w^f, r^f, z)\, dz$$

$$= \left\{ \int_0^z [c(w^d, r^d, z) - c(w^f, r^f, z)]\, dz + \int_z^{z_1} c(w^d, r^d, z)\, dz \right\} \Big/$$

$$\int_0^z c(w^f, r^f, z)\, dz, \qquad (19)$$

where the borderline commodity of the home country $\bar{z}_1$, is now given by the condition

$$c(w', r', \bar{z}_1) = c(w^{*'}, r^{*'}, \bar{z}_1)(1 + t). \tag{20}$$

A number of results follow. There are two components of the rate of effective assistance for the industry, the first measuring the increase in the value added for those commodities which would be produced under free trade, and the second measuring the increase in value added due to the increase in the number of stages produced in the protected situation. The first component is the simple sum of the increases in the value added (at domestic prices), which is equivalent to equal weighting of the individual commodities protected. This equal weighting holds because of the assumption that a unit of the previous stage is required at each stage of production. However, the margin of the increase in the value added at each stage which is weighted in this way is not the tariff imposed on the stage, as in the usual formula. In this model, some of the protection for all commodities below the borderline is redundant, as the margin by which the domestic price exceeds the foreign price will be less than the tariff. If the rate of assistance is uniform among all commodities in the industry, the effective rate of assistance does not reduce to t. For other models with consistent aggregation, the appropriate measure can be derived in the same way using the aggregate function.

Notes

1. Attempts have been made to generalize the theorem in terms of bilateral comparisons, factor-content propositions, and relationships that hold on average. Excellent surveys are provided by Ethier (1984), Chipman (1987), and Jones (1987).
2. Falvey uses partial-equilibrium analysis and does not specify the nature of the other sector or sectors. However, his model can be embedded in a general-equilibrium model with one other sector or industry to make it comparable with the other continuum models.
3. If there is jointness in production, this aggregation is possible for a group of commodities for which the technology is joint and input-output separable.
4. The possibility that the competitive equilibrium is such that the borderline commodity is at the end of the continuum, that is, that all of the continuum commodities are produced in one country and there is only inter-industry trade between the countries, is ruled out by imposing the Inada condition on the derivatives of the production functions.
5. This reverses the ordering convention used by Falvey in order to be consistent with the model of Dixit and Grossman.
6. Unfortunately, most of the many-industry, applied general-equilibrium models that have been constructed are either ones in which all of the industries are standard constant-returns-to-scale single-product industries or industries with, say, economies of scale and the same strategic behavior. (Richardson [1989] surveys the second class of models.)

References

Armington, Paul, "A Theory of Demand for Products Differentiated by Place of Production," *IMF Staff Papers* 16 (1969):159–78.

Blackorby, Charles, Daniel Primont, and R. Robert Russell, *Duality, Separability and Functional Structure: Theory and Applications*, New York: North Holland, 1977.

Chipman, John, "International Trade," in John Eatwell, Murray Milgate, and Peter Newman (eds.), *The New Palgrave: A Dictionary of Economics*, vol. 2, London: Macmillan, 1987, pp. 922–55.

Dixit, Avinash, and Gene M. Grossman, "Trade and Protection with Multistage Production," *Review of Economic Studies* 43 (1982):583–94.

Dornbusch, Rudiger, Stanley Fischer, and Paul A. Samuelson, "Heckscher-Ohlin Trade Theory with a Continuum of Goods," *The Quarterly Journal of Economics* 95 (1980):203–24.

Ethier, Wilfred J., "Higher Dimensional Issues in Trade Theory," in Ronald W. Jones and Peter B. Kenen (eds.), *A Handbook of International Economics*, vol. 1, Amsterdam: North Holland, 1984, pp. 131–84.

Falvey, Rod E., "Commercial Policy and Intra-industry Trade," *Journal of International Economics* 11 (1981):495–512.

Helpman, Elhanan, "International Trade in the Presence of Product Differentiation, Economies of Scale and Monopolistic Competition: A Chamberlin-Heckscher-Ohlin Approach," *Journal of International Economics* 11 (1981):305–40.

Helpman, Elhanan, and Paul R. Krugman, *Market Structure and Foreign Trade: Increasing Returns, Imperfect Competition and the International Economy*, Cambridge, Mass.: MIT Press, 1985.

Jones, Ronald W., "Heckscher-Ohlin Trade Theory" in John Eatwell, Murray Milgate, and Peter Newman (eds.), *The New Palgrave: A Dictionary of Economics*, vol. 2, London: Macmillan, 1987, pp. 620–27.

Krugman, Paul R., "Increasing Returns, Monopolistic Competition and International Trade," *Journal of International Economics* 9 (1979):469–79.

Lancaster, Kelvin, "Intra-Industry Trade under Perfect Monopolistic Competition," *Journal of International Economics* 10 (1980):151–75.

———, "Protection and Product Differentiation," in Henryk Kierzkowski (ed.), *Monopolistic Competition and International Trade*, Oxford: Oxford University Press, 1984, pp. 137–55.

Richardson, J. David, "Empirical Research on Trade Liberalisation with Imperfect Competition," *OECD Economic Studies* (1989):7–50.

Ruffin, Roy J., and Ronald W. Jones, "Protection and Real Wages: the Neoclassical Ambiguity," *Journal of Economic Theory* 14 (1974):337–48.

Index

Economists of the Twentieth Century

Monetarism and Macroeconomic
Policy
Thomas Mayer

Studies in Fiscal Federalism
Wallace E. Oates

The World Economy in Perspective
Essays in International Trade and European
Integration
Herbert Giersch

Towards a New Economics
Critical Essays on Ecology, Distribution and
Other Themes
Kenneth E. Boulding

Studies in Positive and Normative
Economics
Martin J. Bailey

The Collected Essays of Richard E.
Quandt (2 volumes)
Richard E. Quandt

International Trade Theory and Policy
Selected Essays of W. Max Corden
W. Max Corden

Organization and Technology in Capitalist
Development
William Lazonick

Studies in Human Capital
Collected Essays of Jacob Mincer, Volume 1
Jacob Mincer

Studies in Labor Supply
Collected Essays of Jacob Mincer, Volume 2
Jacob Mincer

Macroeconomics and Economic Policy
The Selected Essays of Assar Lindbeck
Volume I
Assar Lindbeck

The Welfare State
The Selected Essays of Assar Lindbeck
Volume II
Assar Lindbeck

Classical Economics, Public Expenditure
and Growth
Walter Eltis

Money, Interest Rates and Inflation
Frederic S. Mishkin

The Public Choice Approach to Politics
Dennis C. Mueller

The Liberal Economic Order
Volume I Essays on International Economics
Volume II Money, Cycles and Related Themes
Gottfried Haberler
Edited by Anthony Y.C. Koo

Economic Growth and Business Cycles
Prices and the Process of Cyclical Development
Paolo Sylos Labini

International Adjustment, Money and
Trade
Theory and Measurement for Economic Policy
Volume I
Herbert G. Grubel

International Capital and Service Flows
Theory and Measurement for Economic Policy
Volume II
Herbert G. Grubel

Unintended Effects of Government
Policies
Theory and Measurement for Economic Policy
Volume III
Herbert G. Grubel

The Economics of Competitive Enterprise
Selected Essays of P.W.S. Andrews
Edited by Frederic S. Lee
and Peter E. Earl

The Repressed Economy
Causes, Consequences, Reform
Deepak Lal

Economic Theory and Market Socialism
Selected Essays of Oskar Lange
Edited by Tadeusz Kowalik

Trade, Development and Political
Economy
Selected Essays of Ronald Findlay
Ronald Findlay

General Equilibrium Theory
The Collected Essays of Takashi Negishi
Volume I
Takashi Negishi

The History of Economics
The Collected Essays of Takashi Negishi
Volume II
Takashi Negishi

Studies in Econometric Theory
The Collected Essays of Takeshi Amemiya
Takeshi Amemiya

Economics and Social Justice
Essays on Power, Labor and Institutional
Change
David M. Gordon
*Edited by Thomas E. Weisskopf and
Samuel Bowles*

Practicing Econometrics
Essays in Method and Application
Zvi Griliches

Economics Against the Grain
Volume One
Microeconomics, Industrial Organization and
Related Themes
Julian L. Simon

Economics Against the Grain
Volume Two
Population Economics, Natural Resources and
Related Themes
Julian L. Simon

Advances in Econometric Theory
The Selected Works of Halbert White
Halbert White

The Economics of Imperfect Knowledge
Collected Papers of G.B. Richardson
G.B. Richardson

Economic Performance and the Theory of
the Firm
The Selected Papers of David J. Teece
Volume One
David J. Teece

Strategy, Technology and Public Policy
The Selected Papers of David J. Teece
Volume Two
David J. Teece

The Keynesian Revolution, Then and Now
The Selected Essays of Robert Eisner
Volume One
Robert Eisner

Investment, National Income and
Economic Policy
The Selected Essays of Robert Eisner
Volume Two
Robert Eisner

International Trade Opening and the
Formation of the Global Economy
Selected Essays of P. J. Lloyd
P. J. Lloyd

Production, Stability and Dynamic Symmetry
The Selected Essays of Ryuzo Sato
Volume Two
Ryuzo Sato

Variants in Economic Theory
Selected Works of Hal R. Varian
Hal R. Varian